MANAGEMENT BY ETHICS

Innovative Discoveries for
Corporate Ethical and Market Moral Reform

VOLUME I

Richard H. Guerrette

University Press of America,® Inc.
Lanham · Boulder · New York · Toronto · Plymouth, UK

Copyright © 2015 by
University Press of America,® Inc.
4501 Forbes Boulevard
Suite 200
Lanham, Maryland 20706
UPA Acquisitions Department (301) 459-3366

Unit A, Whitacre Mews, 26-34 Stannery Street,
London SE11 4AB, United Kingdom

Library of Congress Control Number: 2014952572
ISBN: 978-0-7618-6484-4 (clothbound : alk. paper)
eISBN: 978-0-7618-6485-1

Excerpts reprinted in chapter 1 by permission from
The Ford Pinto Case: A Study in Applied Ethics, Business, and Technology
edited by Douglas Birsch and John Fielder, the State University of
New York Press © 1994, State University of New York.
All rights reserved.

This Career-Long Study is dedicated to the

Yale University Faculties and Students

of the

Divinity School,

School of Organization Management

School of Forestry and Environmental Studies

for

Internship Programs toward Consulting and Teaching Careers

in applied

Corporate Ethical and Global Ecological Studies.

VOLUME I

MANAGEMENT BY ETHICS

INNOVATIVE DISCOVERIES FOR CORPORATE ETHICAL
AND
MARKET MORAL REFORM

Table of Contents

Preface: *Innovative Discoveries for Corporate Ethical and Market Moral Reform: Management Reformations and Aesthetic Transformations*   ix

Acknowledgements   xi

Case Studies and Reference Examples   xv

Introduction: *The Reformation of Management by Objectives (MBO)*   1

    MBE Delivery of Corporate Moral Consistency   2
    Chapter Previews and MBE Themes   13

Chapter 1   *The Implementation of the MBE Paradigm*   22

    The Cost-Benefit Analysis of the Ford Pinto Trial   25
    Ethical Principles and Social Processes   31
    Organizational Morality in Collectivities and Bureaucracies   34
    Conclusion   36

Chapter 2   *The Dynamic Corporate Conscience*   41

               The Organizational Location of the Corporate Conscience   42
               The Interactional Activation of the Corporate Conscience   46
               Managerial Leadership and Critical Ethical Consistency   48
               Management Processes and Value-System-Building:
               The Assertive Corporate "We" and the Reflexive Corporate "Us" 50
               Impression Management Theory and Ethical Image Projection   52

Chapter 3   *The MBE Paradigm: A Delivery System for Corporate Moral Reform*   56

               Moral Development Theory   57
               Moral Development Application for Corporate Moral Reform   63
               Moral Development Education in the Workplace   67
               Moral Development Scaling in the Workplace   73
               Authority Styles and Moral Development   84
               Moral Reasoning in the Workplace   88
               Moral Leadership in the Workplace   93
               Contemporary Moral Problems and Intervention Methodologies   96
               Moral Atmosphere in the Workplace   100
               Democracy in the Workplace   104
               Moral Reformer Profiles and Gender Authority Types   105
               Gender in the Workplace   109

Chapter 4   *MBE Moral Performance Evaluation in the Workplace*   114

               Moral Performance Evaluation Instruments   114
               Moral Reconstruction and Organization Change   116
               Learning Methods for Organization Change   117
               MBE and Performance Progression Planning   119
               The Organizational Levels of Corporate Responsibility   127
               Performance Evaluation and Moral Reconstruction   132
               Organization Defensive Routines and MBE Reconstructive Themes 134
               MBE Leadership in the Church   136
               Vitalistic Renewal Ideas for the Reformation of the Church   138
               Managerial Placement Scanning of Priest Assignments   140
               Environmental Gender Scanning and Reconstructive
               Apocalyptic Planning   142

Chapter 5   *Moral Incentive Building in Workplace Associations
                   and Academic Education*   147

               Moral Incentive Building through Cooperative Learning   147
               Coaching Interventions for Advanced Moral Performance   149
               Associative Cooperation in the Workplace   151
               The Unethical Cultural Problem of Executive Compensation   155
               Moral Development Measuring and Principle Ethical Learning   159

Moral Incentive Building through Academic Learning 163
Graduate School Business and Organization Management Education 165
MBE Re-Orientations to the New Curricular Perspectives 168
Orientation to Management 169
MBE Organizational Perspectives 170
MBE Integrated Leadership Perspectives 179

Chapter 6 *Socio-Economic Organization Structures for*
Moral Incentive Inducement Building 182

Moral Leadership and Economic Incentive Models 182
MBE Socio-Economics and Caring Reciprocities 187
Evolutionary Management and Moralities of Scaling 189
MBE Economics and Post-Conventional Moral Management 190
MBE Caring Reciprocity and Human Resource Economy 191
Caring Associations and Workplace Teams 195
Conclusion: MBO Political Economic Strategies of Scale and
MBE Socio-Moral Economies of Scale 197

Chapter 7 *MBE Organization Governance and Resistance to Change* 200

Cultural Hegemony in Moral Development
"This is the Way MBO *Operates* Around Here" 200
Established Realities and Innovative Possibilities
"This is the Way MBE *Generates* Around Here" 201
MBE Renovations of Established Realities 207
Ethical Reliability and MBE Corporate Personhood 209
Planning for Change in Complex Organizations 209
MBE Practical Solutions:
Realities and Possibilities for Corporate Ethical Discourse 211
Passing into the Future: From Corporate Ethics to Global Ethics 214
The Global Ethic Foundation 215
The MBE Moral Framework and Collectivity Structures of the
Global Conscience 218

Chapter 8 *Social System Problems and Global Moral Reform* 225

Moral Development Problems and Faith Development Solutions 225
Analytical Theories 226
Faith Development Solutions 231
MBE Innovations for Social Faith and Public Trust 237
The Faith Development Scale 245
Faith Development and the Safeguarding of Public Trust 252
Global Networks of Public Trust 253

Chapter 9   *The Corporate Conscience and Involved Moral Leadership*   263

             MBE Strategies of Managing Involvement   264
             Comparative Organization Leadership Styles   265
             Comparative Interactional Examples of CEO Leadership Styles 267
             Post Conventional Moral Development Conclusions   272
             Post Conventional Faith Development Conclusions   273

Chapter 10   *The Personal Conscience and Integrated Moral Leadership*   274

             Ethical Integrity in Leadership   275
             MBE as Associative Integration in Moral Leadership   276
             The Leadership Model of Management by Ethics   277
             The Inspirational Power of Integrity   279
             Moral Leadership and Corporate Integrity   279
             An Innovative Search for Integrity   281
             Graduate Internship Learning   285
             Executive Retreat Living   287
             Executive Retreat Options   288

Appendix   *Managing Moral Development in Sexual Ethics*   291

References   302

Innovative Author and Theme Index   329

Significant Author and Subject Index   343

PREFACE

Innovative Discoveries for Corporate Ethical and Market Moral Reform:
Management Reformations and Aesthetic Transformations

The innovative discovery themes of this book have been composed as a sociological and ethical study of corporate culture. As the author of the study, I invite the readers to explore with me the social, ethical and ecological pathways through the organizational domains of corporations to open the minds of corporate executives toward reaching deeply into their value-system-planning and Board Room deliberations about the priorities of their ethical thinking and moral managing of their businesses.

The traditional academic studies and the customary practical experience of these executives and their management staffs have been driven by the expedient operational strategies of structural functional leadership planning toward attaining the *profit maximization* goals of their businesses through the unifocal disciplinary management paradigm of MBO, Management by Objectives. These focalized business studies have been motivated by the sociological theories of structural planning and functional production, which in corporate bargaining language denotes an *instrumental management insight* impaired by a pre-conventional moral development stage of "instrumental relativity" within business transactions. In clear simple business language, this structural functional value-system planning is motivated by the MBO paradigm of managing for profit maximization goals.

The innovative discoveries of this book, as Volume I open a new paradigm with a multi-disciplinary vision of managing businesses by ethics, MBE, toward attaining the *moral maximization* goals of their companies focused on contemporary apocalyptic demands of global population poverties and environmental planetary catastrophes for ecological survival. These multi-focal studies are *rooted* in the social psychological theories of "symbolic interactional sociology" which open applied (*praxis*) research tracks toward exploring contemporary socio-economic problems with corporate ethical answers and globally ecological solutions. These innovative discoveries flow through the book with moral incentive-*inducement* building for readers with *practical* language explaining these complicated social scientific theories by indicating ethical themes and moral applications through a *coherent* innovative design of a *Case Study and Reference Example* listing. In addition to this design, two final innovations have been placed at the end of the book to replace the traditional incoherent alphabetically static charting index of names and numbers:

An Innovative Author and Theme Index
and
A Significant Author and Subject Index

In conclusion, I urge readers to reflect and enjoy Volume II of this study as an innovative aesthetic *Passion Play* of the MBO forest upheaval and a narrative poetic *Memorial Stay* of the
MBE Forest Primeval. . .

Ethical Theories and Moral Narratives in Art:

An Aesthetic Gallery Tour through the Corporate Moral Forest.

Finally, I graciously invite my readers to make a pilgrimage to the

EquiPax Gallery and Corporate Retreat Center

to marvel at the wonder of the Ecological Forest

and to ponder on the mysteries of

its "symbolically interactional" Trees. . .

in the

Environmental Green Mountains of Vermont and

The International Canadian Lake Waters of Quebec. . .

With the Pride

Of Newport's Astrological Touring Boat of

The Northern Star

Richard H. Guerrette, Ph.D

ACKNOWLEDGEMENTS

This historical career long study began with my search for a *New Identity for the Priest: Toward an Ecumenical Ministry* (Paulist Press, 1969). This search launched an experimental ministerial career with the innovative formation of a "floating parish" community in Watertown and Bethlehem, Connecticut. This pastoral innovation expanded the organizational boundaries of parochial appointments toward liturgical discoveries for open system ministries; and for this grace, I wish to thank all the devoted members of the Emmanuel Servant Community and the Regina Laudis Abbey of Bethlehem, CT. Subsequently, these devout believers inspired my first case study of organizational behavior with a Doctoral Dissertation from the University of Connecticut, whose illustrious Professors, William D'Antonio, Bill Newman and Ray Elling served as my advisors. I am grateful to this learning institution of my home state for subsequently appointing me to Lectureships at the UConn Hartford and Stamford Extensions.

Moving on to the ecumenical boundaries of Yale Divinity School, I was greeted by Associate Dean Harry Adams and Dean Collin Williams whom I thank for writing the Preface of the above-mentioned book. In turn, I was the first to greet the arrival at Yale of the ever "early" and *Late* Henri Nouwen who helped to heal the "wounds" opened, in the organization management of the Church, from our liberal innovations. During these exploratory years, I continued to "consult" with him *With Open Hands* about our common "innovative discoveries" for *Creative Ministries*. Finally, upon leaving Yale after my two Research Fellowships, I am particularly grateful, to Associate Divinity Dean, Christopher Reaske, as Director of Corporate and Foundation Relations at Yale, who described my academic studies as being at "the real *cutting edge* of helping the scholarly community redefine and understand a number of important issues in the area of corporate ethics."

I especially wish to thank Amitai Etzioni for his own critical sociological work on the applied studies of "deontological of ethics" and for his personal support of my work by inviting me to present papers at the Conventions of SASE, the Society for the Advancement of Socio-Economics at George Washington

University and for its dual Convention with IAREP, the International Association for Research in Economic Psychology at the Stockholm School of Economics in Sweden. His support has opened my own discoveries of MBE socio-economics, as presented in Chapter 6 of this book, segments of which were first presented in "Management by Ethics: A New Paradigm and Model for Corporate Ethics," as a leading Chapter in *Ethics and Economic Affairs*, eds. Alan Lewis and Karl-Erik Warneryd (Routledge, London, 1994).

For the most supportive references and recommendations relative to my *practical* applied research studies, I extend my personal expressions of gratitude to Robert Dilenschneider, who, as CEO of Hill and Knowlton, International Public Relations Counsel in New York and subsequently of his own Public Relations Group in the Met-Life Building, had learned of my corporate ethical consulting work at the SASE convention in Washington. After reviewing the portfolio of my *Forestry Art Collection*, he related to me that he would personally inform Dr. Klaus Schwab at the World Economic Forum about my corporate art collection, stating that "On your letter on corporate art, I would very much like to send a note to Dr. Klaus Schwab at your convenience. . . He is big into corporate art, and I think he would benefit from knowing what you are doing."

As a participating member and subsequent Chairman of the Business Round Table Institute for Corporate Ethics, Robert's supportive interest encouraged me to explore their memberships' interest in corporate ethics where I discovered the works of Patricia Werhane, an early scholar in Business Ethics. Her works led me to her colleagues at the Darden School of Business at the University of Virginia whose contributions to "Business Ethics" established a research reference resource for me to explore my innovative moral development tracks in "Corporate Ethics." I especially appreciate her exemplary work on the *Philosophical Issues in Art* and thank her especially for introducing me to the renowned works of Wassily Kandinsky on "Concerning the Spiritual in Art." I have since acquired an Apocalyptic *expressionistic* painting of his "White Horse" racing him toward the Celestial global horizons of Planet Earth placed at the bottom of the wrought-iron spiral staircase of the EquiPax Gallery's artistic impressions of Heaven.

I also extend my gratitude to all the research colleagues of "Moral and Faith Development" whose works at Harvard University with Lawrence Kohlberg and especially, James Fowler, who's "Faith Development Studies" have significantly contributed to Chapter 8 of this book. In addition, I especially thank the scholars, at the University of Minnesota's Center for the Study of Ethical Development, James Rest, Darcia Narvaez, Muriel J. Bebeau, and Stephen J. Thoma whose *Post-Conventional Moral Thinking* has applied "A Neo-Kohlbergian Approach" to moral development studies. Their works have significantly helped me to expand my *praxis* research studies as more extensive "practical applications" of their contributions for "Management Ethical Education and Corporate Culture Reformation.

In addition, I thank Tony Blair and his Faith Foundation for allowing the use of the Conclusion of his Speech, on its inauguration and its association with the Yale Divinity School and the School of Organization Management, as a case study analysis of Faith Development Education in Chapter 8.

Finally, and most importantly for the future caring of the EquiPax Gallery and Corporate Retreat Center, I thank God for *providing a sacramental* visitation with the scholarly couple, Dr. Barbara Mabbs Robinson and Daniel Robinson, both of whom bear complementary intellectual and faith credentials, to serve as Co-Curators of the Gallery. I am also grateful to His Divine Providence for guiding Professor Joseph Healy, Chair of the Philosophy Department at Immaculata University, to EquiPax and for his promoting my work at St. Michael's College among his colleagues at the Pontifical Institute of the University of Toronto. They are graciously committed toward fulfilling the EquiPax ecumenical mission of offering *private retreats* to Chief Executive Officers of Corporations and *corporate retreats* to their respective Vice President Executives of Human Resources and their associated trainers.

Barbara's doctoral transformational studies in the Arts and Sciences and Daniel's ecological architectural innovations of their own Homestead Gallery in the White Mountains' forest of neighboring New Hampshire expand further multi-disciplinary options for applied practical learning with added seasonal retreat accommodations for the corporate retreat programs. While their own scholarly *praxis* works have graciously prepared them to conduct the Retreat and Leadership Programs designed in Chapters 9 and 10 of Volume I, Barbara's management experience and aesthetic vision and Daniel's architectural experience and artistic composing have efficaciously prepared them to serve as Curators of the Gallery and Research Corporate Art Consultants for Volume II.

In conclusion, I gratefully express my thanksgiving to Father Thomas Berberich, Heroic Chaplain Brigadier General of the Army in the Gulf War, and Pastor of the Sacred Heart Parish in Kent, Connecticut, whose fraternal friendship has supported me through ascetic fears and aesthetic tears. I also thank all of my Seminary classmates who surrounded me with concerned support, even when they failed to hear from me.

The Reverend Fathers:
Henry Cody
Joseph DeCarolis
Al Cushing
Frank Johnson
George Burnett
Herby Clarkin
Henry Frascadore
Francis McNary
John Montgomery
William Field
Neil Parado
James Fanelli
Stanislaus Kozakiewitz

✝

Ecce quam bonum et quam jucundum, habitare in unum,
Fratres, Fratres
Cum EquiPax in Deum.   .   .

✝

Ultimately, and at End-of-Life-Care, I thank God for the privilege of caring for:

My Father and Mother
Hector and Leona Guerrette
Blessed with Eighty Years of Marriage
And Each in Providential Time
with Their Last Breath in My Arms
Sanctifying Every Moment
of My Sacramental Care
for Them at Their Death.

Requiescant in Pace
Amen.

✴

CASE STUDIES AND REFERENCE EXAMPLES

This *innovative* reference model is presented to guide the reader toward comprehending many of the numerous interdisciplinary theories of this study by referring to "mini-cases" and reference examples as narrative illustrations of the theories and how they are applied as practical (praxis) managerial strategies for changing organizational systems to meet the moral needs of societies.

The following format is designed as a practical coherent indicator of the Table of Contents at the beginning of the book for guiding the reader through the chapters and promoting integrative understanding of the complex organization theories and their applied reconstructive discoveries. It is far more effective for *praxis* learning of these theories and discoveries with a coherent flow of practical cases and reference examples than an incoherent *static* listing of names and subjects structured by the alphabet at the end of the book.

This literary innovation follows the pedagogy of Peter Drucker's use of "mini-cases" and "examples" in his own studies of Innovation and Entrepreneurship (1985 p. ix).

CHAPTER	CASE STUDY OR REFERENCE EXAMPLE	PAGE
1	*The Implementation of the MBE Paradigm*	
1	Examples of paradigm changes: on-line investing and models of electronic trading	24
1	Ford Motor Pinto case study and the judicial recognition of the corporate conscience	24-30
1	United States Securities and Exchange Commission (SEC): A *closed system* review	34-37
1	MBO-MBE analysis of Newtown, CT school shootings: An *open system* review	36-37
2	*The Dynamic Corporate Conscience*	
2	Boeing Corporation and the Pentagon: insider dealing for a lucrative contract	42
2	Enron Corporation: dominating MBO deals with dormant ethical reflexivities	44
2	Evaluating WorldCom and MCI moral performance comparisons	46
2	Antioch New England University: defining Collective Operational Reflexivity	46-47
2	Enron: evasive defensive posturing and MCI: value-system-building incapacity	48
2	Philip Morris (Altria Group): product in-validity and conscience in-authenticity	48-50
2	Ameritech Corporation: principled value-system-building as an "ethic of care"	50-51

2 The Dilenschneider Group and the power of symbolic leadership   51-52
2 Alcoa MBO fiscal problems & MBE value system solutions   52
2 Ben & Jerry's: symbolic ethical image projection & market profitability   53
2 Cantor Fitzgerald and 9/11: *authenticity* as the voice of the corporate conscience   54-55

3   *The MBE Paradigm: A Delivery System for Corporate Moral Reform*

3 "Occupying Wall Street" and the "Halls of Congress"   56
3 Federal Emergency Management Agency (FEMA) & moral performance ineptitude   64
3 Gulf oil-rig disaster: power & wealth effects on moral consciousness and public trust 65-66
3 The collapse of Bear Stearns and the overnight dismissal of a work force   66-67
3 Workplace intervention strategies & workforce moral transformation (Watergate)   70-71
3 The moral under-development of Congress on health and gun safety care at stages 1&2 71
3 Managerial role-taking moral sensitivity and worker family illness issues   72
3 Managerial "coaching" tips on moral development upgrading   73
3 Comparing examples of ethical reasoning in U.S. & Canadian Accounting Firms   75-76
3 Case Study and Reference Examples of moral development scaling   81-84
3 Ford Pinto 1st and 2nd stage MBO moral management   81
3 J P Morgan Chase 3rd stage moral buyout of Bear Stearns   82
3 Ford, GM, Chrysler and UAW 4th stage Congressional Hearing   82-83
3 State of New York & Berkshire Hathaway 5th stage stock buyout of AIG   83
3 PIMCO 6th stage *gratis* offer to direct TARP for the Treasury Department   83-84
3 Moral reason-action discrepancy in personal & collective roles: Kenneth Lay - Enron 85
3 Environmental "power domain" collaboration on the Kohlberg scale at "Love Canal"   87
3 Authority style reference to the Vatican bureaucracy and the Catholic Church   88
3 Moral reasoning-performance inconsistency: BP a "morally split corporate personality" 88
3 "Ego strength"-"moral virtue" exposing moral corruption at Enron-Sherron Watkins 90-92
3 A family business: upgrading through MBE and moral development training   94-95
3 Scandals: Union Carbide - ethical image projection vs. moral learning protection   95
3 Pentagon's MBO strategies of dealing with Contractor corporate ethical scandals   95-96
3 Examples of Contemporary Moral Problems and Intervention Methodologies   96-100
3 Health Care Agency: 1st stage instrumental utility vs. 6th stage moral sensitivity 97
3 Moral Development scaling and abortion debate evaluating   97-98
3 Cloning & stem-cell research: Jewish Biblical theology & moral development affinity: 99
   The moral reciprocities of the "cells of one *caring* for the cells of others"   99-100
3 Examples of Moral Atmosphere in the Workplace   100-112
3 Congressional polarizing of gun-control lobbying and sequestration caucusing   101
3 Workplace democracies and moral reciprocities: CNN Heroes Program   101
3 Resistance to change & *parallel structural strategies*: Proctor and Gamble in Egypt 103
3 Workplace democracy & workforce teams: IBM Global Crisis Response Team   104
3 Profile examples of moral type reformers   105-108
3 Ameritech Corporation gender specific caring ethic in the workplace   109
3 Reconstructing prison life moral climate: CT State Farm for Women: end note 9   112

4   *MBE Moral Performance Evaluation in the Workplace*

4 Integrating MBE performance evaluation into a Refrigeration Company Manual   115
4 MBO 9/11 Investigatory Commission: an exemplary MBE *resurgency plan* need   116-117
4 Case study *reflexivity* "write-ups" as useful for Pedophile scandals in the Church 120
4 Management evaluation of Captain Phillips and the Somali pirate episode   120-121
4 Hill and Knowlton's ethic: "turn(ing) away big business in the name of integrity" 125-126
4 The Morgan Stanley sexual harassment scandal (moral aspects of the case)   126-127
4 Anita Hill - Clarence Thomas sexual harassment case: consistency vs. responsibility 127

4 Medicaid Waiver Program- organizational consistency and corporate responsibility 128-131
4 Pentagon and Abu Ghraib- organizational consistency vs. operational discrepancy 131-132
4 "Organization defensive routines" and the Priests' sexual child abuse scandal 134-137
4 "Vitalistic Renew Ideas" for the MBE management of the Catholic Church 138-140
4 Management planning and environmental scanning of Priest Assignments 140-141
4 MBO Vatican policies & MBE caring moralities 142-144

5   *Moral Incentive Building in Workplace Associations and Academic Education*

5 Lane Refrigeration Contractors and workplace collectivities 149
5 The moral character of Pope Francis breaking structural traditions & Papal roles 150
5 Examples of moral character and principled thinking in the workplace on Kohlberg scale 151
5 Goldman Sachs' 2006 Christmas bonus distributions: pre-conventional moral greed 151-155
5 Examples of bonus giving at Christmas and Hanukah and altruistic philanthropy 156
5 Goldman Sachs' 2006 "corporate personality split" of executive compensation 156-157
5 Goldman Sachs' 2010 "corporate impersonality split" settlement fine by the SEC: 157-159
5 Applying examples of DIT scores in Accounting Firms and Educational Schools 162-164
5 Undergraduate curricular moral learning interventions: Bethel College 164-165
5 Graduate core curricular moral reform learning: Yale School of Management 165-181

6   *Socio-Economic Organization Structures for Moral Incentive Inducement Building*

6 The economy as a social sub-system shield against poverty 187
6 Global Poverty and "Moralities of Scale" 189
6 European/American quaking economies and Asian/African quaking poverties 190
6 Associative 6[th]stage moral development management & *Ocean Blue Fish-Farming* 190-191
6 Kiel Institute of World Economics and "global poverty" 191
6 "Food for the Poor" & "Doctors without Borders" with m*ulti-cultural moralities* 191
6 Moral reciprocity building & the "power of ethical thinking": The TARP bailout 192
6 Motivation-incentive building: in worker-owned companies with a "caring" climate 192
6 National survey: reciprocity trust, ethical integrity and commitment reliability 193-194
6 Workplace cooperation, caring reciprocities & imaginative role playing examples 194
6 Taj Mahal terrorized victims: 6th stage moral imagination & caring reciprocity 194-195
6 Workplace teams and the TONY Awards 195-196
6 Team working climates: Military Heroes, CNN Poverty Heroes 196
6 Analogical and Horticultural Team Working Climates: "Bumble Bees"! 196-198
6 Inducement work incentives & economies of moral purpose: High Tech Professionals 198-9

7   *MBE Organization Governance and Resistance to Change*

7 Morgan Stanley sexual harassment scandal: hegemonic aspects of the case 201
7 NY Stock Exchange CEO salary (value incongruence & moral inconsistency issues) 201-202
7 Niagara & Love Canal systematic electric development power 202
7 Love Canal: Electric or Hegemonic Power in a *Death Canal!* 203
7 Moral development economic policies of Myanmar in the Far East military zones 204
7 Environmental Falls of Niagara and the Gulf regions 207
7 BP America, Transocean, Ltd. Halliburton blame-shifting in Gulf rigging explosion 207-208
7 Morgan Stanley sexual harassment scandal (economic & sexist determinant factors) 208
7 UN (Oil for Food Program) MBO operational distributions at lowest moral stages 208
7 Problems of established realities & organization inconsistencies: WorldCom and Enron 208
7 Solutions of "moral organization *consistencies*": Somalia Sudan Relief Aid Delivery 210-211
7 The Global Ethic Foundation and the Practice of Ethical Principles 215-219
7 United Nations *collectivity infrastructures* for a "Global Conscience" 219-220

7 CNN global conscience network: Haiti Hurricane Disaster & Sandy Hook Massacre 220-221
7 The Clinton Foundation and its global conscience networks   221
7 The Clinton Global Initiatives and its Global Moral Collectivities   221-223

8   *Social System Problems and Global Moral Reform*

8 The *problem of time* with unbalanced investing: EuroZone, Greece and Cyprus   225
8 Market immoral investing: *the problem of evil* and the insecurities of "ponzie" schemes 226
8 Obama election celebration: *shared symbols* of racial & social *reconstruction*   227
8 Ben & Jerry's symbols of an ethically & environmentally sensitive company culture   228
8 British Petroleum - a causation analysis of its broken corporate ethical image   228-229
8 Congressional hearings on corporate fraud and deceitful scheming   229
8 Enron Corporation's moral spin down - how to observe moral *under*-development   229
8 A refrigeration family co. - how to observe the operational moral aptitude of workers 230
8 Dilenschneider Group: on the importance of a "globally uniform standard of values"   231
8 Hurricane Katrina: moral development & end of life meaning: "Would I die for stage 6?" 232
8 Executive compensation & 3rd world starvation: "Would I contribute for stage 6?"   232
8 Business Roundtable &A.W. Page Society -"Restoring the Public Trust in Markets" 233-234
8 World Economic Forum: "Discussion Highlights on Faith and Business"   235-236
8 Mark Johnson's innovative action with "Music for Social Change   237
8 Kiel Institute of World Economics: critical analysis of its ethical theories agenda   237-238
8 Liquidity collapse & public trust market breakdown of Bear Stearns Brokerage Firm   238
8 Economists'' graphs and executives' greed: as marginalizing the poor   239
8 EuroZones and the depleting "economies of scale" in Greece, Italy and Spain   240
8 The bankruptcy collapse of Bear Stearns   240-242
8 Kiel Institute Forum: "short-sighted" on deontological ethics   243
8 Alan Greenspan on the MBO credit problems lacking social faith and public trust   243-244
8 Faith Development Scale: stage 1-6 descriptions   245-246
8 Faith Development profiles: (see note 5 on Bono's cause to' end extreme poverty') 247-248
8 The 5th & 6th stage social religious faith and the martyrdom of the Iranian "Neda" 248-249
8 Tony Blair Faith Foundation: rebuilding religious & global social faith networks: 249-251
8 Yale Divinity School -Yale School of Management "Faith & Globalization" course   250
8 Malaria Mission with UN's Millenium Development Goals   250
8 Social unrest: *Occupiers of Wall St* & Time Magazine *Corporate Persons* of the Year 252-253
8 The Clinton Global Initiative and developing systems of moral accountabilities   253-255
8 Multinational corporations as mediating institutions: UN Global Compact Initiative 255-256
8 African famines and causation politics   255-256
8 Mediating moral complexities: Bank of America & Merrill Lynch merger   256-257
8 Eco-system cosmic trust: Re-building corporate trust in British Petroleum: 258-259

9   *The Corporate Conscience and Involved Moral Leadership*

9 Dilenschneider Group CEO "ritual delegation" or *personal involvement leadership*   263
9 CEO leadership differential between health care facility and steel industry company 264
9 MBO "Corporate Leadership Development Programs" a base for MBE moral upgrading 264
9 MCI Corporation impersonally delegating leadership   265-266
9 Berkshire Hathaway *Corporation paternal style* leadership involvement   266
9 Apple Corporation: Steve Jobs' MBO leadership style   269-267
9 Amazon Corporation: Jeff Bezos' MBE leadership style   267
9 Cantor Fitzgerald Investment Services: Howard Lutnick 6th stage *caring* leader   267-270
9 Executive leadership comparisons: MCI, Apple, Amazon and Cantor Fitzgerald   270-273
9 The "Elder-Wise Model of Transformational Leadership": Barbara Robinson   273

10 *The Personal Conscience and Integrative Moral Leadership*

10 Symbolic Memorial of the 9/11World Trade Center: Ethical inter-relationship need
of the Personal Conscience 274
10 Yale School of Management—A Critical Reconstructive Segment Analysis of the
New Core Curriculum on "Integrated Leadership Perspectives" 275
10 Yale SOM Dean's critical leadership role description in MBO cultures as:
"dissociation of self from professional behavior" 276
10 Evaluating MBO "leadership splits" as *dis-integrative* within personal moral profiles:
Kenneth Lay: A corporate moral disintegration of a personally moral upright man 276-277
10 Evaluating leadership profiles as *integrative* with personal moral profiles
Warren Buffet and Bill Gates and their *generative power* of "integrity" 279
10 Evaluating the personal leadership of Steve Jobs: his aesthetic life & ascetic moral integrity 280
10 EquiPax Corporate Retreats and Internships: *The Search for Integrity* 281-289

INTRODUCTION

THE REFORMATION OF MANAGEMENT BY OBJECTIVES (MBO)

As corporate executives, treasury and federal reserve officers, senators and congressional representatives desperately tried to "bail out" Wall Street in 2008 to avoid an "economic tsunami" on Main Street from the undertow of collapsing brokerage firms and insurance companies, CEOs were walking away from their rip-tide failures with multi-million dollar salaries and gratuitous bonus compensations. These catastrophic events, which caused widespread mortgage meltdowns and credit crises in a recessionary economy, morally awakened the ethical consciousness of the public and were critically reported in the media with CNN's coverage of "The Ten Most Wanted Culprits of the Collapse" and National Public Radio's stories of "Bankers, Brokers and Bandits." Corporate culture had lost its moral compass in the ethical slumber of its MBO Conscience.

The Dormant Corporate Conscience. Just a few years earlier, at the beginning of the twenty-first century, *corporate* America was burned by a moral meltdown of criminally convicted CEOs from WorldCom to Tyco to Enron which was graphically covered by the media whose commentators and guests were reciting litanies calling for the incarceration of executives engaged in corporate fraud. TV cameras focused on the handcuffed marches of senior level executives escorted by police into courthouses. Clean corporate executives and learned scholars from academic chairs began the chant for ethically rectifying corporate governance. The major business channels gave prime time coverage of congressional hearings on corporate fraud and followed-up with interviews of experienced consultants and knowledgeable professors, searching for directions toward corporate responsibility. Very few, if any, provided a blueprint for corporate moral reconstruction. Hardly anyone seemed to acknowledge the primal direct connection between corporate responsibility and the corporate conscience. The corporate conscience was asleep—and so was a snoring management.

Corporate Conscience and Management Ethics. The corporate conscience is an operational delivery system for corporate responsibility. It achieves delivery by the application of universal ethical principles to corporate moral behavior in the workplace and in the marketplace. The top line of this delivery system is that the corporate conscience delivers an ethical feed into management decision making processes with moral responsibility awareness for corporate governance. The bottom line is superlative moral performance of the workforce with morally authentic leadership and operational managerial integrity by ethics. That the mass public and especially its future generations understand the need for a promotive ethical principle feed into management decision making processes is evident from a recent Marist Poll on Shaping a Generation as reported on CNBC January 22, 2010. The survey of respondents from 18-29 was chosen in this poll at this time to represent the "generation of the future" as a "millenarian" age group inasmuch as they are going to surpass the size of the "Baby Boomer" generation which up to now was constituted as the largest segment of the economy. The poll found that this new millenarian group, as compared to the overall makeup of the country, surprisingly remained "consistent with the general attitudes of the society" as its respondents were "optimistic" as "hard-working" people for achieving a high standard of living. They also reflected a general moral consistency manifesting concern for their neighbor and expressing a commitment to help those in need. But in comparisons of this national optimistic make-up, they complained against "greed in business" and called for the delivery of "ethical decision-making in business." In conclusion, they were focused on their "ability to achieve a higher standard of living, if they can get into a business that is operated ethically" (Anderson, 2010).

MBE DELIVERY OF CORPORATE MORAL CONSISTENCY

Part of the blame for the lack of a "blueprint" for corporate responsibility delivery in corporate culture with its structured "economies of scale" and the evidence of "greed in business" subcultures rests in the fact that ethics are embedded in the academic domain of philosophy and its studies, focused within the un-applied abstract methodologies of the inductive natural sciences (see Goulet, 1974). As a result of this disciplinary claim, few interdisciplinary scholars have followed the lead of Patricia Werhane (1999) toward addressing the reconstructive challenges of applying ethical studies to management systems and organization structures with empirical methodologies. Whereas Werhane's work applied philosophical ethics to the grounding of moral incentives in management decision processes, this book shifts the theoretical methodologies of corporate ethical studies from the abstract language and terminological constructs of philosophy to the more clarifying, *practical* terminologies of social scientific and organizational psychologies toward the moral developmental upgrading of individual occupational behavior and corporate organizational performance.

The Social Psychological Activation of the Corporate Conscience. The study attempts to make that application by empirically demonstrating how the personal and corporate conscience operate in the interactional arrangements and departmental structures of corporate organizational behavior, in the internal hierarchies of managing workforces and the external environments within the bargaining encounters of business transactions. To focus on these interdisciplinary viewpoints, the book opens a projection theoretical study of the corporate conscience as analogically compared to the personal conscience of individuals and describes its practical operations through the symbolic interaction theories of social psychology. Inasmuch as social psychology identifies the personal conscience in the inner zones of the objective self as the individual reflexive "ME" in the "looking-glass mirror" of the subjective self as the individual assertive "I," it is scientifically plausible to posit the corporate conscience in the collective organizational reviewing entities of the objective corporate self as the reflexive corporate "ME." It thus rediscovers the corporate conscience in an applied scientific process that allows ethical analysis of value systems in corporate culture and moral performance *measuring* of corporate responsibility in the workplace and throughout the marketplace. Through these projective insights of an applied inter-theoretical analysis, this study has discovered a new paradigm, Management by Ethics (MBE), as a dialectical counterpart to Management by Objectives (MBO), a widely taught paradigm in management science from the work of the renowned Peter Drucker (1954).

While Professor Drucker has passed over to his rewards, his MBO legacy must not be forgotten. Remembering him in a recent (June 2010) Guest Edition of the Harvard Business Review, Frances Hesselbein described the moral and ethical legacy of Peter Drucker in these terms:

> Peter strived to make business leaders see community as the responsibility of the corporation. He called on leaders to embody "the Spirit of Performance" by exhibiting high levels of integrity in their moral and ethical conduct; focusing on the results; building on strengths; and leading beyond borders to meet the requirements of stakeholders, ultimately serving the common good.

As President and CEO of the Leader to Leader Institute, formerly the Peter F. Drucker Foundation, Dr. Hesselbein concluded: "It is my personal belief that leadership is a matter of how to *be*, not how to *do*."

With respect for his existential leadership and functional scholarship, the following study of this book is to re-formulate business ethics in terms of "how to *be*" *ethical* by incorporating universal principles into the souls of executive leaders that they may transmit the meaning of these philosophical principles toward applying them to the managerial operations of their companies so that managers and workers may *do* their jobs with honesty and integrity. Though it has indeed been forgotten by many managers and especially high level executives and CEOs in ways that would be embarrassing to him, Professor Drucker did live to see how they interpreted his structural and functional objectives for organizational stability and production profitability. What he did not see were some contaminated MBO sets with investment marketing bets, such as, "naked short selling" and unbacked mortgage security transactions and AIG's mismanaging its objectives, all of which have caused a global economic crisis by a morally crippled managing paradigm. His MBO legacy, however, can still be critically functional in helping MBE to "put all the 'President's' men (*and women*) together again." But its own function must be limited to *morally responsible* economic production calculations; and for those objectives, MBO needs a complementary innovative paradigm with an over-arching organizational caring integrity of *holistic management by ethics* with the MBE paradigm. Whereas MBO emerged out of the structural-functional themes of management operations and shaped the pragmatic ego-centric consciousness of executives for decades in corporate culture (see Sonnenfeld, 1988), MBE is focused on the humanistic themes of management interaction processes and is designed to shape ethical consciousness in corporate culture and moral leadership in management operations. MBE thus identifies the corporate conscience in organization structures and shows how it deliberates with ethical reflexivity through social, organizational and moral psychology. With the scholarly advantages of these interdisciplinary sciences, it further locates the corporate conscience within the "organization self" in its reflexive entities, such as, the board of directors, the executive hierarchy, production-reviewing teams, governance committees along with workforce collective-ities. Within these collaborative organizational spheres of supervisory ethical insight and moral behavioral oversight, MBE critically defines ethical reflexivity in accordance with the moral development theories of Lawrence Kohlberg, the cooperative behavioral moral measuring methodologies of James Rest and the interactional caring reciprocities of Carol Gilligan. With these self-reflexive organizational entities, corporations and companies of all sizes can utilize these moral developmental scaling methodologies for reliably evaluating individual and corporate moral performance. As a reconstructive moral orientation in management science, MBE is not only practical for pedagogical programming toward corporate moral reform but also is prophetic for discovering a socio-economic moral incentive model generating ethically focused inducement building toward achieving individual and corporate responsibility delivery. This orientation is based on the value system priorities of the Eli Lilly Foundation which have guided the research of this two volume study of caring for people and for their ecological environment.

The Essential Operation of the Corporate Conscience. Why the need to become so theoretically profound about the conscience, which everyone has, as a simple mental evaluating instrument to judge what is right and wrong? Simply, because this book analyzes the corporate conscience as a relatively new term about what is right and wrong in the workplace, in the marketplace and in all of corporate culture. And if this need is not convincing enough, consider the words of Michael Capellas, the CEO of MCI, highly regarded for his integrity, whose redeeming charge was to direct the moral reconstruction of his company out of the financial and moral bankruptcy ruins of its merger with WorldCom. In all of his moral reconstruction planning, he made not one single reference to the corporate conscience, while stressing implementation of an ethics education program on company values, guiding principles and a code of ethics. In summary of his entire moral reconstruction plan on the company website, he stated, "By clearly defining the ethics road maps we should all follow, we have established a common culture committed to upholding the highest standards."

But road maps do not deliver transportation. Nor do ethical principles deliver moral performance. Ethical principles need *morally evaluative reflection* about judgments and behavior as cognitive and affective *starters to generate motivation* for moral performance. This is *the essential activity of the corporate conscience,* as it reflects and learns about aligning company policy planning and operational behavior with the moral developmental stages of socially responsible performance. Within this reflexive realm of inner organization self-evaluating activity, the corporate conscience generates incentives which induce the moral motivation within departmental entities and among individual personnel, often with the stimulation of nurturing socialization processes, to comply with company policies, ethical codes and guiding principles.

As a new experience in learning about the fascinating re-discovery of the corporate conscience and how it can work in any corporation or company, the book presents a comprehensive understanding about its simplicities and its complexities for multiple audiences and market domains. The study will show how a corporate conscience can operate in every corporation or company of any size as a "blueprint" for planning the moral reconstruction of a specific corporate ethical culture and for achieving moral integrity in the particular organizational unit sectors of its operational business domains.

Readership Audiences and Market Domains. Relative to these morally reconstructive goals, the book is composed for CEO's and chairpersons of boards and other directors, senior level executives and especially for vice-presidents of human resources and their corporate trainers. Its interdisciplinary theories and reconstructive models are also for management consulting firms, particularly those which have an interest in or an assignment for corporate ethics education. In addition to the ethical interests of these corporate executives and their consultants, it is also written for shareholders who have been demoralized by the lack of moral leadership in the companies and by the grave losses in 401k retirement funds in which they have invested. They too have a vested interest in corporate moral reform, as delivered by the corporate conscience. Thus, they have a need to know where to find the corporate conscience and to understand how it should work. By comprehending the operations of a company conscience as the delivery system for corporate moral reform, shareholders could become active in some ethically overviewing role as independent external morally informed collectivities in their companies, not just to demand moral performance but to *participate* in its delivery.

With this specialized corporate readership in mind, the book does get fairly heavy with theory and somewhat complicated with multiple inter-theory linkages. But this interdisciplinary grounding is intended to create a legacy for corporate moral development and corporate cultural enlightenment. The targeted readership, though, from corporate culture and its ever widening organization spheres, includes highly educated professionals ranging from all the business sectors of the economy encompassing law firms, politicians, elected officials, government regulatory bodies, the courts, and now, even officials of criminal justice systems. It is critical, therefore, that all these professional leaders, who constitute the "power elite" in society, not just to be informed about the corporate conscience but to be *formative leaders* of its constitution and *reformative framers* of its application in their respective companies and operational domains. They need to study this treatise in order to apply the theories of moral development in the workplace and fulfill their leadership roles in the marketplace directing its reactivation in all of the organization spheres of the economy toward achieving multinational corporate moral reform and even global market moral reform.

Finally, the most important strategic readership of all is conjoined among the students and faculties of business and management schools in universities and colleges throughout the international domain of higher education. Since it is within this expansive global domain where the future leaders of multinational corporate cultures and international market economies are in training, it is essential for curricular reform that an interdisciplinary work of this kind be adopted to generate *a new orientation to management education.* That this need exists is highlighted in a previous issue of *The Chronicle of Higher Education* which identifies *leadership, ethics, global thinking, and management skills* as formulating a new curricular agenda for the training of future business leaders:

> Business-school deans must remove the departmental silos into which business school faculty members segregate themselves, and reward cross-disciplinary research and teaching projects. . . . The responsibility of

business schools for the effective training of future leaders for these enterprises is enormous. (Quelch, Dec. 2, 2005, B 19)

As a "cross-disciplinary research and teaching project," MBE delivers this new curricular agenda for studying the *moral enterprises of the corporate conscience.* Taking the lead for promoting new curricular studies in business ethics education on the international scene are the studies of Susan Phillips, Dean of the School of Business and Public Management at George Washington University and Chair of the Ethics Education Task Force of the International Association to Advance Collegiate Schools of Business. In her Foreword to a Report by the Association's Task Force Committee on Ethics Education in Business Schools, Dean Phillips states:

> The Ethics Education Task Force was established by the AACSB board of directors on the premise that the crisis in business ethics is not only a challenge for companies but also an opportunity to strengthen management education. At issue is no less than the future of the free market system, which depends on honest and open enterprise to survive and flourish. While financial markets have seen the beginnings of a recovery in the past year, the threat of corporate malfeasance similar to Enron or Parmalat continues to weigh on investors' trust of the marketplace. The main purpose of this document is to urge and encourage administrators and faculty in business education to contemplate their current approaches to ethics education and to explore methods to strengthen this vital part of the curriculum. The ideas, examples, and other information put forth here and in AACSB's Web-based Ethics Education Resource Center are intended to stimulate interest in alternative approaches and models for developing the design, delivery, and evaluation of business ethics education. All of us in management education need to ponder more deeply and creatively on how to advance the awareness, reasoning skills, and core principles of ethical behavior that will help to guide business leaders as they deal with a changing legal and compliance environment. We must ground students in the duties and rewards of stewardship, including the concerns of multiple stakeholders and the responsible use of power. (2004, p. 7)

The time for grounding students in the ethical development of their management education is most strategic in this period for corporate moral reform and constitutes a critical intervention need for curricular moral reform. Professor Muriel Bebeau, Executive Director of the Center for the Study of Ethical Development at the University of Minnesota, has alluded to the timing dimension of intervening inasmuch as she cites studies which examine the effects of professional education on ethical development. In an article for the Journal of Moral Education (2002), she reports that most studies have observed that the moral judgment of students "plateaus" during the time period of their professional schooling, unless an ethical intervention is present. Thus, it is incumbent upon the faculties of business and management schools in the global college and university environment to begin the planning for the intervention of ethical education in the core curricular development of their graduate level programs. Such intervention planning is not just to address the moral judgment suspension gap of their students but especially to advance their moral sensitivity, to activate their moral motivation and to form their moral character.

Other ethical education scholars calling for alternative approaches and models for business ethics education in the accounting and auditing professions have confirmed this need for curricular reform:

> Effective pedagogical interventions at both the university and the firm level may foster the moral development of individual accountants and auditors. . . . As a starting point, perhaps accounting educators in the United States should seriously consider the effectiveness of traditional ethics interventions in accounting and, when necessary, replace these with formal courses and programs that are designed to foster the highest order of ethical reasoning.   (Ponemon and Gabhart, 1994, pp. 116-117)

As a new paradigm for management stewardship, MBE develops new approaches and models for the design of business ethics in education at "the highest order of ethical reasoning" precisely for the delivery of moral performance learning in academic as well as in corporate cultures.

Judy Olian, Dean of the Anderson School of Management at UCLA, has prepared a critical analytical report as Chairperson of the Task Force in Management Education (2002) for the International Association to Advance Collegiate Schools of Business (AACSB) on the reconstructive need for curricular change in business schools in association with continuing executive education and corporate non-degree learning. This AACSB study describes that a turbulent marketplace in the global spheres of business education has developed to the extent of demanding a globalized reformative response to the divisive turbulence through industry-wide management education leadership encompassing continuing innovation, curricular design and coordinated structural change in the delivery systems of corporate learning. The report reveals that a scarcity of doctoral educational resources in business and management education has also developed along with problems of enrollment erosion and educational fragmentation. To address these curricular and structural fragmentation problems in the globalization and reformation of international management education, the Task Force recommends the following conclusions on pp.16-18:

> (1) the pedagogical introduction of interdisciplinary doctorate level resources;
> (2) curricular redevelopment planning inducing business and management learning through multidisciplinary levels of research and teaching;

(3) the convergence of degree and non-degree programming; and, the stimulation of ongoing innovation in the management education industry.
(4) the stimulation of ongoing innovation in the management education industry.

In a more recent (2010) Task Force Report on the "Innovation Mission" of business school education, Andrew Policano, Chairman of the AACSB Board of Directors and Dean of the Graduate School of Business at the University of California, Irvine, stresses the theoretical need for universities "to motivate business school leaders to elevate the concept of innovation to be a defining characteristic of the mission of their schools." In the Foreword of the Report, he outlines "how managers can impact innovation" toward exploring "ways that management education can make a difference" by introducing "a new conceptual framework to show how any business school can be a catalyst for innovation." This is precisely the practical purpose of this book—to open an innovation paradigm for business and management education toward motivating managers to advance lower moral instrumental priorities of the MBO paradigm toward higher ethical *conceptual* priorities with pedagogical strategies for moral development by the MBE paradigm.

As a multidisciplinary study in management education, this book on MBE is a timely and well overdue response to all of the above recommendations of the two AACSB Task Forces. It's timely and forward looking paradigm bridges the disciplines of philosophical ethics, social psychology, socio-economic psychology, social organization behavior, complex organizational structures, moral development socialization in these structures, and expands an interdisciplinary exposure to liberal and fine art resources as a linkage to corporate conscience ethical awareness and corporate culture development programing. Most importantly, this innovative study operationalizes the elemental philosophical zones of the corporate conscience allowing the empirical tracking of corporate moral performance on the stages of moral development not just in the internal departmental workplace divisions of corporations but also in the external marketing domains of complex organizational environments. Accordingly, through this latter social scientific tracking methodology, the book offers a morally critical and an innovative aesthetic study of the integrative relationship between corporate art and corporate culture and its consequent effects on corporate ethical consciousness and global environmental conscientiousness.

For those readers, however, who are not all that interested in university academic theories or in executive education curricular reform planning, multiple relevant contemporary examples of corporate corruption and moral development reformation, are listed in "*Case Studies and Reference Examples*" to engage and expand one's critical practical interest. (See this listing immediately after the Table of Contents, which serves as an

innovative improvement of a functionally insignificant alphabetical Index.):
All of these examples and studies are presented for the purpose of illustrating
the interdisciplinary theories toward clarifying many of the complex research
citations upon which these theories are based. Most perceivably critical,
though, is that every reader should keep in mind that these complex
reconstructive theories explained throughout the book can restore hope and
"*Planning for Change*" with Mark Johnson (see ch.8) through practical
learning by exploring the answers to these following questions and applying
these answers to the Case Studies and References Examples traced in the
book:

1.   what is the corporate conscience and how does it operate?
2.   what are the organizational structures for locating the corporate conscience?
3.   what are the social psychological operations of the corporate conscience?
4.   how does one (re)activate a dormant and or an uninformed corporate conscience?
5.   how does the corporate conscience deliver moral reform?
6.   what is MBE (Management by Ethics)?
7.   what are the corporate ethical benefits from "moral development studies?"
8.   how does one evaluate the level of moral awareness in workers and managers?
9.   how does a manager advance a worker to a higher stage of moral performance?
10. what is the relationship between moral development and social faith development?
11. what is the relationship between social faith development and public trust?
12. how does moral development promote involved and integrative moral leadership?
13. how does moral development increase production quality and company integrity?
14. what is the relationship between corporate ethics and environmental ethics?
15. what is the relationship between corporate art and corporate culture?
16. what is the relationship among the scientific bridges of social psychology, religion, culture and the arts?

From the simplicity of this outline, it is evident that there is an
operationalizing scale for moral awareness and moral performance. Get to
know that scale, as well as you know the ages of your children. It is much
easier to learn the scaling evaluations from the one word simplicities of
Exhibit 3:5 in Chapter 3 than from the more complicated exhibits which
explain the theories of moral development. You will easily recognize the
moral awareness progression in that scale, especially since you have more
than likely reached the highest level of moral performance in most sectors of

your private life, if not in your company employment—which might be the result of your employer's need to read and study this book! Another relatively simple exhibit to consult is Exhibit 4:1 in Chapter 4. The design here is to demonstrate how to coach your employee subordinate, friend or colleague and even your son or daughter, to advance to the higher more attractive stages of moral development by entering their respective worlds through imaginative role taking processes (see note 7 ch.1), watching their moral performance in the context of their agenda interests, attitudes and dispositions and plotting these items on the scale. Then, as supervisor or parent, you should have ample opportunity to describe the moral self-dissatisfaction they are likely to experience when they compare any dissatisfaction of their own moral underperformance with the projected moral performance attractiveness of the next higher stage. Using this awareness advancement as an inducement incentive for the higher stage performance, you may be in a position to help re-set your employee's work environment from a competitive to a cooperative performance climate or to revolve your teen(s') social spheres around charitable and community service activities, thus improving their moral motivation and their personal attitudes. Consider also opening a discussion with your teen(s), about the moral propriety of rap music, encouraging them to rate its lyrics and dancing motions on the moral development scale. They may have heard or even know that some major corporate media outlets are promoting the dancing motions and lyrical references with overt pornographic impressions and covert profit-making intentions and may very well be prepared and even anxious to talk with you about these troubling immorally undercurrent "raptide" productions. What a satisfying experience for you to become an activating part of the ethical awareness sensitivities and the moral development progression of your subordinates or colleagues and especially of your own son or daughter.

Rather than getting discouraged with parts of the more complicated theories and multiple citations in the book, skip these parts and go directly to these two above-mentioned exhibits. To activate your interests in moral development, you might try the experiment of using the scale described in these simple exhibits with your younger children and you will be amazed at their willingness to listen to you as a parent in motivating them to strive for their own higher moral performance in the family, or in the school or even on their sports team. One small tip for its practical use in a family environment is to apply it to evaluate the moral performance of subjects in the evening news or in other forms of the media, especially in competitive sports and in the entertainment arts in which the children and teens have an acute interest. Open discourse with them about the social behavior of these newsworthy people, government officials, politicians, religious leaders, athletes, actors, entertainers, etc., both in their character roles and personal lives, as reported in the news, and invite them to suggest where the moral awareness and/or performance of these subjects might be plotted on the scale.

The recent exposure of the "Stop Snitching" scare regarding the code of silence about witnessing murders in the underworld of rap music imposed by producers and performers is an alarming example of a grave social moral problem about which your own teen(s) may need to talk. Remind them that they must not judge the person but only his/her moral performance. Within a few weeks, you will be fascinated by your own knowledge of moral development and prepared to do the very same experiment in your place of employment and/or home. And again, most importantly, don't miss another practical tip on the implantation of your children's moral development learning in their own individual conscience. Ask them, or for that matter, even any adult colleague or friend in your workplace, what their conscience is; how it operates; and where it is located. Your family or friendship respondents would likely know what the conscience is in the common terms of alerting one's self about matters of "right and wrong." But, it is highly unlikely that anyone you ask could define its cognitive and morally reflexive operations, let alone its location in their inner selves. If you still have a conversation left, suggest that they might be surprised if they tried a simple experiment of their own as a self-revealing base for demonstrating how they can discover for themselves the exact location of their personal conscience. By whatever technological means they may have, ask them to record a day's or even an hour's conversation with anyone or with a multiplicity of ongoing conversations and then count and compare how many times they referred to their personal pronouns of the "I" and the "ME" in their discourse. Though the references to these personal pronouns obviously would not all be related to moral matters or conscientious deliberations in their discourse, and thus not intended to be a scientific experiment, their general tabulations would at least demonstrate the frequency differential between the "I" and the "ME." In turn, the frequency difference, therefore, would, at least, demonstrate the usually overwhelming volume of the assertive "I" side of the self over against its less voluminous but much more luminous reflexive "ME" side of the deeper, inner morally conscientious self. Then, they can be coached to notice that the comparative infrequency of the "ME" is indicative of the silence of the inner reflecting self. With that engaging experiment as a lure for further discourse with you, as a parental or friendly moral mentor, you are likely to have the revealing opportunity to illustrate that their assertive "I" dominates their personal life and self-satisfying preferences while their reflexive "ME" evaluates the moral propriety of their decisive choices. They will likely grasp the logic of discovering the location of their individual conscience in the objective case of their personal pronoun and begin to befriend their innermost morally reliable "ME." This engaging experiment is a practical way to awaken one's personal conscience. And once that conscience is aroused, moral reform is possible on all fronts: personal, family, corporate, and market, etc. Awakening stimulates awareness and awareness activates incentive-producing knowledge for performance. That is the tracking equation for moral reform. One cannot participate in corporate moral reform, if one's own personal conscience is not yet awakened.

CHAPTER PREVIEWS AND MBE THEMES

The *first two chapters* of the book are about managing corporate ethics through the operational delivery system of the corporate conscience. *Chapter one* introduces MBE as a new paradigmatic orientation for management studies and outlines the humanistic value benefits of *managing by ethics* in a morally hierarchic comparison to the instrumental objectives of the functional cost benefits of the MBO paradigm. The chapter demonstrates the need to extrapolate ethics from the domain of philosophy and to apply its principles of universal values and social psychological theories to the behavioral and organizational sciences. It thus explores the interdisciplinary linkages of ethics to the academic domains of social and organization psychology and management studies as a more *practically applied* and multidisciplinary scientific way to study corporate ethics. Accordingly, it opens the focus of corporate ethical studies beyond the individual executive, manager and worker to the collective body of the corporation as the organizational entity for corporate responsibility. By so establishing a scientific grounding for the analysis of and applied research in corporate ethics, the chapter sets the stage for the structural organizational location of the corporate conscience in the *Corporate "Me"* and the socialization of its ethical formation through the moral development of human resource education.

Chapter two identifies the corporate conscience as its corporate *objective* "self" through theories in social psychology, enabling researchers and readers to locate its *reflexive* operations in various *collective* units of the organization structures in corporations. It describes these operations as a *reflexive organizational mirror of a company's value system and corporate ethical imagery*. It demonstrates how this *morally reflexive* organizational mirror of the corporate conscience can remind corporate executives to insure that its imagery projection is *ethically consistent* with its cultural value system and operational moral performance.

Chapters three, four, five and six are about Management by Ethics (MBE) as a social scientific *operational* delivery system of the corporate conscience for building a morally responsible company or for re-building a company image and value-system from the effects of ethical scandals through corporate moral reform. These four chapters are grounded in theories from organization management science, the educational psychology of moral development and the measuring methods of moral stage awareness and the socio-economic psychology of incentive inducement building for moral stage advancement. These chapters provide an inter-theoretical base for the legacy of corporate conscience research studies and applied *praxis* strategies for corporate moral reform. They are thus more theoretically complex with important interconnecting references and "case study" citations which are necessary for establishing an interdisciplinary learning linkage between policy theory and business practice. Multiple contemporary examples from recent corporate scandals and current events are cited in this section and throughout the book to help the reader grasp the ethical theories and evaluate the business practice.

Chapter three presents the moral development theories and selected ancillary studies which demonstrate how to apply these theories in the workplace for the purpose of advancing workers through the incremental stages of the moral understanding of ethical issues. It further applies moral understanding to the *internal domain of workplace ethics*, relative to authority styles of managers and compliance patterns of workers and to personal and organizational moral consistency behavior of workers and management. In this chapter, exhibits are offered to explain the moral development stages and how they can be measured in the interactional workspace of authority and subordinate relations. The chapter then introduces an ethical governance planning framework for executives and managers to reconstruct the internal moral climate of the company through moral education and the socialization processes of moral advancement coaching.

Chapter four addresses the need for periodic moral performance evaluation of the stage development of workers and even managers and collectivities, including company executives and board directors. It further applies moral performance understanding to *the external domain of the company's complex interorganizational sectors* within which transactions of commerce can be a critical variable to the company's own moral performance advancement or impairment. Company evaluation themes, such as, "moral consistency in the workplace," "organizational consistency and corporate responsibility" in the marketplace are analyzed by performance evaluation instruments of the MBE paradigm. Two examples of sexual harassment scandals in the workplace are cited in this section to explain the correlational ethical issues between *personal moral consistency and interpersonal moral responsibility*. Likewise, one case study of an actual sex abuse scandal within the organizational structure of a military prison is cited to demonstrate the correlational *organizational inconsistencies* of the military's role to defend the prescriptions of the American Constitution regarding fundamental human rights and the *collective irresponsibility* of military prison guards sexually abusing and torturing inmate prisoners of war. A final case study cited in this chapter is a management performance evaluation analysis of organizational inconsistencies and *hierarchical irresponsibility* on the part of the bishops of the Roman Catholic Church relative to the widespread multinational priest pedophile sex abuse scandal. In addition, this MBE performance evaluation instrument is used to critically evaluate the pedophile case study of the "management by clerics" aberration model rather than the *management by ethics* reparation model which could have spared the Church the cost of its integrity, let alone the purity of its corporate conscience dignity. Finally, executive policymaking formulation and strategic management planning skills are offered to help the Pope and Bishops draw on contemporary scientific management literature toward the "*reformulation*" of pastoral policymaking and the *reformation* of organizational recovery strategies.

Chapter five clarifies methods of integrating moral performance measuring with performance evaluation processes and presents a relatively simple and practical way of measuring moral development and evaluating moral performance through interactional *conceptions of cooperation* in the workforce. The discussion also opens some "critical practical" and sociologically imaginative ways to measure personal moral development and collective and corporate moral performance in the workplace. It demonstrates how dialectic conceptions of cooperative versus un-cooperative decision-making and work performing arrangements can significantly alter ethical awareness and moral performance outcomes. The Goldman Sachs Christmas bonus distribution of 2006 is used as a case study to illustrate the dialectical moral issues of cooperative corporate social generosity and uncooperative executive compensation greed. The chapter also opens further discussions on measuring morally defined issues relative to principled moral reasoning and thinking in selected groups of the applied professions. Among the average to lower level moral awareness and reasoning scores in these groups were graduate students in business schools, an alarming outcome of which critically moves the discussion to the need for *radical ethical core curricular reform*. The Yale University School of Management curricular reform program is presented as a case study to evaluate the defining issues of an ethical core to business and management education and curricular reform programing. By intense content analysis of the "new core" curricular design, there is no "room in the inner" core of the curriculum for an ethical course of studies which could feed directly into any and every course of the graduate students coherent learning and integrative knowledge application for applied business managing or consulting careers. The chapter, thus, offers an innovative core curricular design to demonstrate a pedagogically integrative learning course of studies for students to graduate from any business school with a reassuring knowledge of how to apply MBE management and consulting skills for their professional careers.

Chapter six introduces innovation themes with the following quote from a past CNN interview of Niall Ferguson, Harvard Professor of Economics, conducted by Fareed Zakaria, anchor of the GPS program on the *Global Public Square*: "The core, the heartbeat of economic growth, is innovation —technological innovation, managerial innovation, and financial innovation"

(Ferguson and Zakaria, 2008; see also Ferguson, 2008). This quotation serves as an introduction to the innovative MBE socio-economic moral incentive model which compares worker incentive models from traditional organizational economics and more recent models from political science, economic psychology and evolutionary economics. The comparison indicates that the MBE socioeconomic moral incentive model confirms the plausibility of inducing higher stage worker incentives through *moral leadership* in organizational hierarchies, workplace democracies and market economies. A more recent and comprehensive nationwide study of worker incentive attitudes is critically reviewed to support a primary contention of this book that workers are much more capable of *advanced moral performance* at stages 5 and 6, than was documented in earlier moral development research. The chapter demonstrates that this contending advanced moral performance is most plausible with the awakening of the corporate conscience throughout an integrated and collaborative management hierarchy and the implementation of MBE moral education throughout workforce populations and corporate marketing economies. The innovative theoretical economic insight of this chapter suggests that the MBO plausibility structures of "economies of scaling" should warrant the ethically corresponding marketing "heartbeat" response of MBE parametric "moralities of scaling." This innovative scaling insight on the economic parametric *moralities of scaling* is based on the ethical principle of reciprocity and is traced through this chapter with reference examples of *caring* for others in crisis situations of economic poverty, catastrophic emergencies and workplace contingencies.

Chapters seven and *eight* discuss research complications with established realities and resistance to change along with practical applications of the MBE model, providing re-*creative* possibilities for a climactic conjunction of the evolution of the corporate conscience with the multinational organizational development of a global conscience. By so expanding the corporate conscience reflexive framework to focus on global moral problems, such as, the breakdown of global social faith from the fears of international terrorism and the collapse of global market economies by the loss of public trust, this section prepares the reader for critical practical resolution planning toward the rebuilding of the intercultural theologies of social faith and the restoring of the integrity of international markets through the mutualities of public trust.

Chapter seven opens a critical sociological analysis of why moral development research could not deliver consistently significant higher stage ethical awareness and moral performance findings among its respondent populations. In response to these unimpressive results, the chapter offers critically reconstructive sets of questions provoked by social system blockages of established realities against moral development *practical* possibilities formulated to design *value-oriented research to invoke social change enhancement and moral development advancement.* With historical and contemporary reference examples, such as the Love Canal environmental disaster in 1978 and the more recent examples of the Morgan Stanley sex scandal and the United Nations Oil for Food scandal, the chapter discusses the interpersonal and organizational power relationships that influence the *underdeveloped* moral reasoning and *inconsistent* moral performance outcomes in corporate and organization cultures. Finally, the chapter presents a practical inducement incentive for CEO's and other executives to initiate corporate moral reform. It describes how to induce ethical discourse in a company even when no one in the hierarchy is listening or interested by starting with one's own *inner executive self.* It discusses ways to personally develop the inner self-reflexive "reliable ME" for honestly evaluating the functionally operating *realities* of MBO while dealing with its tendencies to moral reasoning underdevelopment and moral performance inconsistencies. It concludes by offering executives, as the "reliable US" of the corporation, a variety of *possibilities* for preparing themselves through reflexive pondering, aesthetic wondering and proactive learning through corporate retreats toward directing the moral reconstruction of their companies with a *moral plan of action* for *passing into the future with* MBE.

Chapter eight defines the social system problems associated with the reconstructive task of social change and global moral reform. It outlines a moral plan of action by demonstrating how to change a morally inept organization culture into a morally responsible corporate culture by means of *reality construction analysis* and *reality reconstruction planning.* From this abstract theoretical mandate to change "realities," the chapter clarifies the practical *praxis* methodologies of symbolic reconstruction for effecting change in social and organization realities by citing the example of a relatively unknown musical composer whose re-creative goal is to change the global social system realities and international political rivalries of discord into multinational social system *harmonies* of con-"chord" by *Playing for Change.* His musically aesthetic work arranged players and singers from the global complex organizational environment of nations collating the musical score of "Stand by Me" with the composition of singing voices from the continental divides into the unities of sharing peace and harmonies of multinational *caring* voices. The chapter follows through from this highest stage example of post-conventional moral performance to respond to the alarming report on the *Dynamics of Public Trust in Business* by the Business Roundtable Institute of Corporate Ethics (2009) on the breakdown of international public trust in global markets and investing economies. Responding to this report, the chapter opens an extensive description of how to rebuild the ethical foundations of market economies and to restore the *moral constructs of social faith and public trust.*

Chapters nine and ten present theoretical insights and practical suggestions for CEO's and executives to develop their authority styles and personality traits for effective moral leadership.

Chapter nine encourages CEO's to become *involved moral leaders* in their companies by personally directing the implementation of MBE socialization within their respective workforces and disavowing the traditional procedures of delegating ethical education to internal human resource trainers and/or external corporate ethical consultants. The analogical model of the parent as the primary socialization agent of his or her child is presented as one who would never think of delegating the nurturing of the child's conscience to others. The chapter dramatizes an exemplary model of executive moral leadership involvement with a descriptive account of a grief-stricken CEO, who lost 658 members of his workforce in the 9/11 World Trade Center disaster. His moral performance reflected an *involved* parental moral leader who designed a financial plan to take overall care of the families and children of his lost workforce for ten years. This CEO intuitively and instantly activated a morally responsible corporate conscience for his company, expressing its value-system and *managing* its workforce *by ethics*. Finally, the leadership styles of Amazon's Jeff Bezos, with his ethic sensitivity, and of Apple's Steve Jobs, with his sister's dramatic eulogy, are evaluated with bereaving sensitivity in mourning memory of the latter's death.

Chapter ten analyses the moral dualism encountered among many CEO's and executives who display exemplary moral virtues in their private, personal lives but manifest low levels of moral accountability and ethical integrity in their business dealings and professional behavior. The case study of Kenneth Lay, (the late CEO of the Enron Corporation, a religiously faithful man but a morally divided executive by a succession of un-integrative leadership positions and morally contaminated corporate business decisions,) is presented to trace the internal latent tribulations and ultimate moral downfall of this helpless corporate unethical victim. The analysis attributes this dualism to the blind MBO instincts of executives committed to a functional leadership role with a focal fixation on profit maximization for their companies and on the proximate calculations of the immediacy of urgent business decision-making processes. The discussion demonstrates how a refocusing projection, (beyond the imminent calculative now, with a MBE holistic moral commitment to the enduring integrative history of the moral value system of the company) demands an integrative moral leadership not just for the integrity of their own personal conscience but especially for the integrative corporate leadership of the company entrusted to their ethical care for the "*sequence of generations*" (Erikson 1968). By so drawing from the classical work of Erik Erikson, on human development, the chapter cultivates the virtue of *integrity* in executives directing them to integrate their personal moral traits with their professional business roles toward opening an ethical vision for successive leadership planning and enduring moral performance. Corporate retreat centers are suggested as resource sites for their continuing management education and their personal moral redevelopment. A critique is offered on these centers to guide executives to select one which offers the authentic human and ethical resources *to develop the personal conscience of the executive and to deliver an integrative moral leadership for nurturing the corporate conscience of the organization.*

Finally, as a climactic innovative visual study of the relationship between corporate art and corporate culture, the EquiPax Gallery invites its corporate retreatants and academic graduate internship guests to take "An Aesthetic Gallery Tour through the Corporate Moral Forest"—a permanent exhibition on *Ethical Theories and Moral Narratives in Art* in the EquiPax Gallery within the Corporate Retreat Center and its Environmental Gardens in Northern Vermont (see Guerrette, 2014, Vol. II). The exposition serves as a critically *reconstructive* response to an earlier contemporary work bearing on the "powerful" and "dramatic" relationship between the corporation and corporate culture in terms of its "capitalistic" policies and an enterprising ethos (see Lipartito and Sicilia, 2004). Through a *dramatic* multi-media presentation of paintings, sculpture, prosaic and poetic literary forms, and architectural ecological designs, the aesthetic themes of the exposition represent an innovative methodology to reshape corporate culture through the *inspirational power* of corporate art and to realign the moral focus of the corporation on the *cultural ethos* of *ethical priorities* and *humanistic ecologies.* (See Geertz, 1973, ch. 5 on "The Analysis of Sacred Symbols.")

Conclusion. This exhibition is presented by the Gallery's international roster of artists from the United States, Canada, France, Switzerland, Germany, and Romania and visually portrays the corporate ethical struggle between the primeval "Forest Mythos" and the industrial corporate ethos. Variations on the correlational conflicts of these dialectical themes define the moral purpose of humanistic production and demonstrate the ethical relationship between corporate art and corporate culture. The narrative unfolding of these correlational themes is presented in the form of an epic poetic "Passion Play" describing the corporate ethical struggle in aesthetic imageries of the paintings, sculptures and architectural designs in the visual, literary and musical arts. Pertinent allegorical citations from the literary and performing arts are presented for the viewers to contemplate the scenic impressions and thematic variations in the Mystical Forest, the Biblical Forest, the Liturgical Forest, the Commercial Forest and the Ecological Forest.

An Epilogue Seminar. With corporate ethical reflection and critical *environmental* projection opened from this aesthetic tour and its consequent affective impressions within the personal conscience of viewers, a final Epilogue in seminar reflections for retreatants and interns discusses the scientific rational legitimacy and the multidisciplinary emotive efficacy of an *aesthetic dimension* in corporate ethical studies. While it's pedagogical implications are intended to inspire personal and corporate moral purpose, the seminars' applied research reflections are guided to expose latent and expand salient themes for generating inducement incentives toward interpersonal involvement in corporate moral action. In terms of its scientific validity and its purposeful reflexive efficacy, these critical epilogical reflections are drawn from the support of the late Paul Pruyser, as the founding President of *The Society for the Scientific Study of Religion*:

> I have discovered that exposure to great art, as in a museum or concert hall, often leads one, with or without the artist's or composer's intention to recognize corporate and historical associations between religion and art. These associations shape the idea of culture as an enormously old and large matrix preceding the individual and his family, which legitimizes and reinforces the personal associations by its dense network of corporate associations which have all become a matter of public record (1976, p. 2).

Reinforcing this implanted purpose from *associative* public records, *The Aesthetic Dimension* of Herbert Marcuse (1978), as a social theorist, the scientific revolutionary theories of Thomas Kuhn (1970), as an historian of science, and the philosophical works of Charles Taylor (1991, 2007), as a philosopher and political economics, and of Patricia Werhane (1984), as a management science and art scholar, are cited through the seminars to support responsive attitudinal and behavioral evidence that exposure to the arts is generative of personal engagement in social change. Accordingly, this tour through the "Corporate Moral Forest" was composed and is presented to open viewers' "*moral imagination*" with compassionate care for fallen "tortured" forests to a critically reactive passionate concern for corporate ethical hope and for the survival of our planet to *the full cycle of its life.*

At the conclusion of his chapter on "The Life Cycle: Epigenesis of Identity," in *Identity, Youth and Crisis*, Erik Erikson wrote:

> . . . a civilization can be measured by the meaning which it gives to the full cycle of life, for such meaning, or the lack of it, cannot fail to reach into the beginnings of the next generation, and thus into the chances of others to meet ultimate questions with some clarity and strength (1968, pp. 140-141).

These volumes have been composed precisely for the related purpose that corporations, government bureaucracies and educational institutions may be able to measure the moral meanings they give to the "full cycle of life" for populations, nations and the environments in which they operate and for whom they serve. In accordance with this epigenetic purpose, the MBE paradigm is now presented that executives of these corporations and officers of federal bureaucracies and especially the professors and graduate students of management, forestry and environmental studies and business schools around the world may identify and develop moral meanings in their roles as management leaders and professional educators that their successors in forthcoming generations may meet the "ultimate"—*ethical*—"questions with clarity and strength."

In the above-cited scholarly studies of the history of the American Corporation, Lipartito and Sicilia describe the need to reconfigure the "periodization" of the powerful growth of this remarkably productive paradigm of the American corporate institution. They conclude:

> The era from the Civil War to the First World War has long been the defining moment in the historiography of the American corporation. . . Much of how we think about what happened before and after the Age of Giant Enterprise is defined by the dramatic transformations of that period . . . In this way, business history has largely been an exercise in the backward and forward projection of the fin de siècle paradigm (p. 334).

Through the applied studies of these two volumes, business history will be re-configured from the MBO paradigm by "forward projections" through the *arts and sciences* with dramatic MBE transformations toward reconstructing the ethical foundations of both corporation cultures and market economies.

Richard H. Guerrette, Ph.D.
EquiPax Gallery and Corporate Retreat Center
Newport, Vermont USA

CHAPTER 1

THE IMPLEMENTATION OF THE MBE PARADIGM

When reputable business firms and conscientious executives see their companies exposed in ethical scandals, they soon discover the costly consequences to the corporate image and often pay the heavy price of moral bankruptcy. They then realize that corporate ethics cannot be left to uninformed individual consciences nor to corrective strategies with public relations face-saving imageries. When the verdicts are in and culprits are out, they face the retributionary mandate that management ethics must convert fallen executives and *reconstruct* their wayward companies with a morally resonant corporate conscience that *operationalizes* corporate moral behavior, reflective of a management "evolutionary" ethical image (Van Der Erve,[1] 1994; see also Berger and Luckmann, 1967).

The Corporate Conscience: The Operationalizing Instrument of MBE. It is thus time that these hard lessons from the business "scandalgates" and the judicial "bailout rates" of this era be critically and analytically operationalized into an evolutionary management study of corporate ethics through the social psychological instrumentation of the corporate conscience. Such a paradigm needs to identify and locate the *corporate conscience* in organization structures and federal agencies and explain its operations as a reflexive ethical delivery system for moral learning development in the workforce and moral performance behavior in corporations and government programs. Operationalizing the corporate conscience involves personal and collective organizational reflexivity, with focus on the ethical principles, first and foremost on the part of executives and managers, as accountable moral leaders and exemplars for the workforce toward building and insuring a corporate ethical image for the company and its moral performance in the complex organizational environments of business operations. As a socio-ethical operational system this MBE paradigm and its corresponding model for management practice offers an innovative design through an integral evolutionary management program for executives and managers in moral education and corporate ethical socialization. As a reconstructive paradigm,

MBE is drawn from the social and behavioral sciences with interdisciplinary linkage to philosophy, economics and ecological studies. Accordingly, it is grounded in social psychological theory within which the corporate conscience can be traced through social interactional processes, such as the specific communication lines in companies responsible for decision-making policies and practices. It is also anchored in sociology and organization behavioral studies from which value-system-building can be planned through management operational policy decisions, such as determining that the prioritizing formulations of these decisions reflect a hierarchy of ethical principles and moral values, over and above profit multiples and production priorities. Finally, upon this inter-theoretical base, MBE opens an applied management model of an "integral meta-theoretical" program with corporate conscience formation at executive levels of management leadership, moral consciousness organization development through the workforce, moral incentive building for optimal performance efficiency in the workplace, morally sensitive accountability in the marketplace and ethical sustainability awareness in the global space (Edwards 2011).

In summary, the MBE paradigm is instrumental for *locating* the "sources of the moral self" (Taylor, 1989) relative to the corporate conscience in the "corporate mind" of its "organization self" (Guerrette, 1994); and the model is practical for *applying* its social psychological components and its behavioral operational functions for the scientific value-driven purpose of measuring its corporate moral performance.[2] Without actually defining the social structural compass of the "organization self," Charles Taylor helps to locate a social organizational sphere for the corporate conscience and to "trace" the "moral topography" of its inward organizational focus to clarify its ethically reflexive perspectives:

> What we are constantly losing from sight here is that being a self is inseparable from existing in a space of moral issues, to do with identity and how one ought to be. It is being able to find one's standpoint in this space, being able to occupy, to *be* a perspective in it.   (1989, p. 112)

It is through the MBE paradigm that the organization self of a corporation can *find its authentic moral standpoint* within the reflexive ethical perspectives of its corporate conscience so as to determine how its management *ought to perform*. The innovative MBE paradigm shall define the ethical principles of this moral standpoint and open the leadership perspectives for corporations and nations to responsibly "*occupy*" Wall Street and Main Street. (Moore, 2012)

Reintegrating "models" for the MBE *Paradigm.* MBE is a new paradigm because its views "provide models from which spring particular coherent traditions of scientific research" (Kuhn, 1970, p.10) and practical change. A paradigm is a design about a new way of looking at things, whereas models are procedures for implementing the new changes according to the design. An example of such a new *paradigm* in the business world of economic marketing would be "on-line" investing e.g. Charles Schwab from which multiple *models* of electronic investing have sprung forth along with competitive forms of electronic investment procedures in stock market exchanges, such as ETFs (Exchange Traded Funds) offered in brokerage firms. Accordingly, new models of conducting management policies by MBE amount to practical change from the old way of managing companies according to the MBO way as the dominant paradigm for well-over half a century.

The Cost-Benefit Analysis Model. Through this time period of MBO, corporate responsibility was assumed to be part of the consciousness of executives and managers and the notion of the "corporate conscience" was hardly or likely never heard of. What was heard of, in the aftermath of any scandal in a company was criticism of the particular manager or executive who may have been responsible for the scandal. In such cases, the focus of the criticism was either explicitly or implicitly on the individual conscience of the involved manager or executive. This focus began to change radically, however, in 1980 with the outcome of the Ford Motor Company's corporate responsibility in its compact automobile "Pinto" case trial.[3] When the court held *the company* accountable for its deliberate decision for the continued production of the unsafe cars with foreknowledge of engineering reports of the model's serious explosion-prone safety risks (Redman, 1980), the corporate conscience was conceptually acknowledged in corporate culture as well as in the judicial system.

At the trial, Ford was charged with reckless homicide for the violent burning death of three teen age girls in 1978 when the Pinto vehicle in which they were riding was struck in the rear by a van. This charge was provoked by the company's deliberate continuance of the Pinto's production *objectives* after the dangers of the faulty placement of the gas tank were exposed in the early seventies. The company's persistence with ongoing production continued even after the earliest manifestation of the homicidal recklessness in 1972. At this time, a stalled Pinto vehicle was slammed in the rear and burst into flames, resulting in the death of the owner and the disfigurement of a passenger. The disfigured victim sued the company and was awarded $6.5 million. In the following years, numerous other law suits were filed while the company raced on with the Pinto production schedule. In accordance with "cost-benefit analysis," the company rationalized its production purpose in MBO pursuit of *company objectives*.

THE COST-BENEFIT ANALYSIS OF THE FORD PINTO TRIAL

Applying the New Paradigm Shift. The following narrative analyses of the Ford Pinto trial by the SUNY scholar Douglas Birsch from the State University of New York trace the significantly important details of the Ford Motor Company's deliberate MBO ironclad objectives of calculating profiting priorities at the expense of MBE caring reciprocities:

> The discussion of these issues and the Pinto case will be framed by a set of questions about product safety and one question of cost-benefit analysis: (1) Is it wrong for manufacturers to market any product that could be made safer using current technology? If a safer product can be made, should companies be required to give the public the option of purchasing the safer product? Is it wrong for businesses to market products that are not safe as competing products on the market? Should manufacturers be forbidden to market products that do not meet the reasonable safety expectations of consumers? (2) Is it unethical for a company to use a cost-benefit analysis that places a monetary value on human life? My conclusion is that, with respect to product safety, manufacturers should be required to obey the law, follow industry standards, and meet the reasonable safety-related expectations of consumers. In the Pinto case, Ford failed to do the latter and hence produced an unsafe vehicle. In regard to the ethical evaluation of cost-benefit analysis that places a monetary value on human life, both human rights advocates and utilitarians might make a case that Ford acted unethically by performing such an analysis and using it as the justification for not making the car safer. Of course, in the Pinto case, there is uncertainty about whether or not Ford actually used a cost-benefit analysis as the basis for the decision not to upgrade the integrity of the fuel system. Even if the company did not, I believe that their money-saving decision was foolish and unethical. (Birsch, 1994: p.148)

It is impossible to make a completely safe automobile. The use of automobiles always involves some risk, and for many people, a safe car is one that allows the person to drive with an acceptable degree of risk. In the Pinto case, it seems that both the supporters and critics of Ford agreed that, in general, automobile fuel systems were hazardous in 50-mph crashes. People should have expected serious injury or death if they were involved in rear-end collisions at that speed. While this situation presented a risk of death or serious injury, it was an acceptable risk. The National Highway traffic Admin-istration (NHTSA) and most people involved in the case also seemed to have agreed that drivers and passengers should sustain only minor injuries in crashes at or below 30 mph. Driving a car that might burst into flames in a 25-mph crash would have been an unacceptable risk. I am unclear about what people believed about the range from 31- to 49- mph crashes. Therefore, I will simply consider whether the belief that they would sustain only minor injuries in 30-mph or slower crash was a reasonable safety expectation with respect to the Ford Pinto.

Consumers would have expected to survive low-speed, rear-end collisions, and in connection with the Pinto, it would have been a reasonable safety expectation since it was technologically feasible without changing the basic characteristics of the product.

Assuming that consumers did expect to survive low speed crashes, the Pinto did not meet the reasonable safety expectations of consumers, and therefore with respect to product safety, Ford engineers and executives produced an inadequate vehicle (pp. 152-153).

The Pinto Controversies and Placement of the Fuel Tank.

Another dispute concerns the placement of the fuel tank. Ford had two options to choose from: an over-the-axle tank, which had been used on the Ford Capri, and a behind-the-axle tank. (See Figures 1 and 2) Placing the tank behind the axle was standard for the industry in regular sized cars and was also the standard for the Japanese subcompacts. Crash tests on the Ford Capri, however, had shown that over-the-axle tank performed very well in rear-end collisions.   There were some drawbacks to the design, though, since it required a circuitous filler pipe, which was more likely to be dislodged in an accident. The tank was also closer to the passenger compartment and therefore might increase the threat of fire to the passengers. In addition, the higher placement of the tank raised the center of gravity of the car and might have adversely affected handling. Finally, the design led to reduced trunk space and could not be used on a hatchback or station wagon model. The behind-the-axle model was not as safe in rear-end collisions, but it did provide more trunk space and could be utilized in a hatchback or wagon. Ford decided to build the Pinto with the behind-the-axle gas tank. One claim is that the over-the-axle tank was rejected because of undesirable luggage space. Ford representatives later argued that this claim over-simplified the issue. There were also safety considerations in favor of the behind-the-axle model, and it was the industry standard.
(Birsch from the Introduction pp. 7-8)

The following Figures of the Pinto Crash Tests demonstrate the structural dangers of MBO *care*-less profit prioritizing and the need for interpersonal MBE awareness of *care*-full priority planning.

Above shows gas tank in a safer position for passengers.

Above shows gas tank in a more vulnerable collision location.

Images by Mabbs Robinson llc

To further consider the inadequacy of the vehicle, it is critical to identify the philosophical scope of the SUNY studies, which cite the "ethical reasons" for advancing a morally *utilitarian ethic* for analyzing the Ford Pinto case.

> Ethical reasons could also be advanced for satisfying consumers' safety expectations. A case could be made that doing this would be consistent with an act utilitarian approach to ethics since it usually maximizes net benefits to the greatest number of people. In the Pinto case, upgrading the integrity of the fuel system would allow to have the car meet the reasonable safety expectation of the consumers: that they survive low-speed crashes. This outcome would have produced satisfied customers and repeat business for Ford, while promoting safety and therefore minimizing danger to consumers. It also would have allowed Ford to avoid many of the liability suits and much of the bad publicity. It seems that all those involved would benefit (p.153).

> An argument could be also advanced supporting the view that meeting the reasonable safety expectations of consumers would be in accord with a human rights approach to ethics. Doing so would respect the rights to life and well-being of consumers by helping to protect them from death or injury. It also respects the right to liberty of consumers by not deceiving them about the product they are buying since they are getting a product that meets their expectations.
> Unless there are human rights being violated by meeting these reasonable safety expectations, it also would be ethical to meet them on human rights grounds. While this human rights analysis is only a first approximation, it reaches the same conclusion as the utilitarian view: that if companies want to act ethically, they should attempt to satisfy the reasonable safety expectations of consumers, Proponents of the human rights approach to ethics would also want a more substantial analysis of the issue than the short discussion offered here (p.154).

To respond to the human rights approach to ethics requires the MBE vision of *Managing by Ethics*. This new paradigm offers the social psychological sensitivity awareness of morally developed managing interaction with role-taking ethical sensitivities of interpersonal caring for others, especially for employees of workforces and customers of injured passengers. The philosophical theories of traditional "utilitarian" business ethics studies, such as this SUNY "Study in Applied Ethics of Business and Technology," do not even begin to provide the *caring* ethos for ethical *sensitivity awareness* learning for academic students and especially for the morally sensitive helpless injured among the "Wholly Innocent" victims of MBO cost-benefit calculations.

See also the following updated and contemporary studies of automaker companies, who would *carefully benefit* their automotive productions with MBE calculations. (See the pertinent YouTube and Reuter links):
   1978 Ford Pinto Case: https://www.youtube.com/watch?v=PAI5T8UecEY

2014 Toyota Case: https://www.youtube.com/watch?v=R1x4RDntOU4
2014 General Motors Recall: https://www.youtube.com/watch?v=N30ajtwQCig
http://www.reuters.com/article/2014/04/11/us-gm-recall-accidents-idUSBREA3A0AQ20140411

This critical practical analysis of symbolic interactional theories in sociology is not to inflict blame on this otherwise concise structural functional study of Birsch in corporate ethics. There is plenty of blame to go around and about in the scholarly world of traditional corporate ethical studies. See, for example, Chapter 8 below in this study by Horst Siebert (ed.), *The Ethical Foundations of the Market Economy, International Workshop*, Kiel Institute of World Economics, University of Kiel, Tubingen. Like this SUNY scholarly study, this International Forum did not have *one paper* delivered on Deontological Ethics which foster "respect for persons" and *caring altruism.* [4]

As concluded in the above exhibit, Ford executives defensively persisted in traditional business philosophies of unconscionable calculative pursuit of company objectives by "cost-benefit analysis" and were clearly driven by a MBO mind-set without any reference to, let alone any comprehension of, an ethical value-benefit analysis. What a difference in the outcome of lives and the financial and morally responsible benefits that the company could have accrued, had its president and its executives *managed* this historical crisis by MBE with an *informed corporate conscience.* (See Chapter 2)

The Value-Benefit Analysis Model. The difference between cost and value-benefit analyses can be clearly projected at the onset of this study through a brief comparative analysis of the functional MBO *production driven* paradigm as traced in Exhibit 1:1 and the humanistic value benefits of MBE analysis as an *ethically motivated* paradigm described through this book. In general, the operational priorities of MBO functional production objectives determine the value system of a company as a *closed system* of profit-producing operations methodically insensitive to humanistic values and systematically un-open to ethical reflection and immoral prevention (see Graves, 2007). As a result, MBO priorities are focused on *objects as products* and seldom on *subjects as persons.* Furthermore, these priorities are fixed on the *systemic or operational maintenance* of production lines with little or no attention to *ethical principles* for management lines and with little or no concern for the *moral development* of workforce personnel. In these kinds of organizational environments, governance almost always operates with *authoritarian* bearing and hardly ever with *participatory* sharing.

Finally, as seen in the above-described Ford Pinto MBO production driven system, hardline authoritarian governance is morally static and sometimes very prone to severe and *costly dysfunctional vulnerabilities*, often beyond what an instrumental cost-benefit analysis can calculate. What a difference an interpersonal value-benefit analysis can make through a MBE *ethically reflexive corporate conscience system* in terms of developing *internal reconstructive moralities* definitively beyond what a MBO *hierarchically assertive system* can generate with a static fixation on profit maximization (See Exhibit 1:2).

Exhibit 1:2 MBO – MBE Comparative Value-Benefit Analysis

MBO Values	MBE Values
Product driven system	Ethically motivated system
Functionally closed system	Humanistically open system
Product priorities	Person priorities
System maintenance	Moral development
Authoritarian governance	Participatory governance
Statically assertive	Ethically flexible
Costly dysfunctional vulnerabilities	Beneficially reconstructive moralities

As the notion of corporate conscience began to be recognized in corporate culture, other paradigmatic changes in organization science were also taking place during the period. Organization scientists were beginning to develop research methods to study the complexities of the organizational environment, such as the overarching involvement of a company, not just with its workforce and clientele, but with its organizational sectors and interorganizational networks of operations. From this multi-level spectrum of comparative interorganizational relationships, new methodological directions have opened research perspectives to *the organization itself as the unit of analysis* (see Brinkerhoff and Kunz, 1972; Brinkerhoff, 1984; Perrow, 1972; Levine and White, 1972; Etzioni, 1960). It is thus critical to note that having expanded the focus of analysis to the corporate entity itself, the interdisciplinary context of analyzing and evaluating corporate moral performance was *scientifically ready for the notion of the corporate conscience.* In effect, this change of focus has set the interdisciplinary stage not only for the philosophical and social psychological analysis of the corporate conscience but also for the moral responsibility and legal accountability of corporate behavior (see Goodpaster and Matthews, 1982; see also Goodpaster, 1983 on conceptualizing corporate responsibility and Redekop, 2010, especially for the ecologically long term *sustainability* of the planet; and see also Edwards, 2011 on transforming organizations for sustainability). As a new research paradigm focusing on the corporate entity itself, MBE is thus effectively compatible with Kuhn's paradigmatic criteria for providing "models from which spring particular coherent traditions of scientific research."

ETHICAL PRINCIPLES AND SOCIAL PROCESSES

Since corporate ethics arise out of the social organizational context of corporate culture and management interaction processes, the practical application of their philosophical principles in the day-to-day business operations of a company requires more *strategically coherent clarification* for executives and managers in *organization scientific terms*. More attention is due to the "critical practical understanding"[5] of corporate ethics as *social psychological processes emanating from the complex organization environment of a company*. It is in these domains that corporate ethical behavior is managed as a complexity of a company's interrelationships both in its internal departmental structures, including individual and collective units of production, and in its external environmental structures encompassing interorganizational networks of co-operation. The MBE paradigm thus attempts to trace the social psychological dimensions of the corporate conscience in and through these structures and networks, exploring its interactional operations within these wider organizational units of analysis. With these new directions, it offers an innovative "critical practical" model for the ethical management of corporate behavior through the organization reconstruction of a moral climate. As such, MBE is a *praxis* paradigm formulating change, not only in the way moral performance is analyzed in a company but in the way it is measured in research. Social scientific studies need to analyze a company's culture, its value-system and its moral performance in the interorganizational environment of its investors, suppliers and clientele. Studies of this kind could not only help to clarify the organizational processes for applying abstract ethical principles to concrete corporate practices but would also specify the data-gathering methods for reviewing corporate moral performance (see Blasi, 1980). Etzioni (1988) affirms this need to move the study of corporate ethics beyond the inductive margins of philosophical categories to the deductive methods of socio-economic organizational realities and networking complexities. This more objective scientific approach to corporate ethics could open more socialization and training benefits to companies for moral performance development and more effective management planning for moral performance consistency (Blasi, 1980). It could also open more ethically reconstructive discourse among organization analysts, economists, and moral educators along with business and political leaders beyond philosophical ethics to moral economics (Hausman and McPherson, (1993) and even to global ethics (Kung, 1991, 1998, 2004; Kung and Schmidt,1998). "What's needed... is a moral framework that is both 'interdependent and interactive' with the economic functioning of markets, governments, civil society and multinational organizations" (Kung, 2004, p. 8).[6] In this period of the interdisciplinary studies of Hans Kung, moral frameworks were still structured in the fixed paradigm of philosophical ethics. (See chapter 6 below toward breaking beyond this paradigmatic fixation through MBE economics). The contemporary need for this paradigm is convincingly stressed at the Boston University School of Management whose pedagogical curriculum is expanded with MBE priorities: "What we are trying to do is provide undergraduate and graduate students with ethical frameworks they can use in decision-making—the tools needed to recognize and consider the ethical dimensions of decisions—just as we provide them with the tools for doing strategy or finance." (Bloomberg Businessweek Business Schools, 2013/12/18)

Philosophical Ethics—A Fixed Paradigm. Whereas ethics has been traditionally studied in the domain of philosophy, moral behavior among individuals and moral performance in corporations are actually in the interdisciplinary domains of social psychology. Philosophers reason about principles that guide behavior. Their philosophical thought patterns have been shaped by methods of inductive reasoning and have produced important normative theories, such as, utilitarian, contractarian and deontological theories[5] (see Beauchamp, 1988), that have for so long constituted the paradigm for business ethics. But it is people who act and corporations who perform and their behavior and direction do not always reflect ethical principles. One reason for this is that human behavior and corporate performance are outcomes of social processes.

Social Psychology—An Open Paradigm. It is therefore plausible to expect that the practical improvement of ethics in the workplace should arise out of a social psychology of ethics (Baum, 1974; Doris, 2010). Researchers and managers must begin to pay attention to the socio-economic context of ethics and to the complex organization environment within which corporate performance is conducted. The new studies need to go beyond the philosophical analysis of what happens in Washington terms and Wall Street firms. The new paradigm needs to *open* a view to the social reconstruction of ethics beyond the corporate ruins of "account-cooking" and fraudulent booking. Philosophical theories and ethical principles will not stop conspiring executives, shredding auditors nor insider traders; but the moral development of the corporate conscience and the strategies of value-system-building by corporate executives will change fraudulent calculation into ethical inspiration.

The Social Psychology of the Corporate Conscience. The innovative MBE paradigm here being proposed for the social psychology of corporate ethics is based on symbolic interaction and role theory in sociology (Cooley, 1902; Mead, 1934; Blumer, 1969) open system theory in the social psychology of structural organizations (Allport, 1962; Katz and Kahn, 1972) and the moral development theories in educational psychology (Kohlberg, 1981, 1984 and Rest, 1994). These theories will be explained in greater detail with Case Studies and Reference Examples, as they are applied through the text in the construction of the paradigm.[6] Out of this inter-theory linkage, one can begin to understand the social psychology of the corporate conscience; and, therefore, how it might be cultivated in the organizational context of management interaction and corporate culture. A similar interdisciplinary approach linking psycho-social role theory to moral development studies has already been opened by William Kurtines (1984) with wider research perspectives for analyzing the social contextual variables that influence moral decision-making and moral behavior. This approach likewise draws on open system theory in organization studies (Katz and Kahn, 1978) and views human behavior as governed by rules in situation-specific activity within larger social systems. As in complex organization research methodologies, it expands the units of analyses in moral development studies to rules, roles and systems. These perspectives led Kurtines to suggest the importance of considering particular situational factors and social system contingencies as influencing moral conduct. Kurtines' psycho-social approach, however, appears to be laden with structuralist influence from sociology. He follows Talcott Parsons' (1956) functional imperatives and views morality in terms of "system maintenance and integration" (idem, 1984, p. 305).[7] In the end, his focus is less projective than his own approach, as he continues to maintain the individual as the immediate focus of analysis and the ultimate agent of responsibility.

ORGANIZATIONAL MORALITY IN COLLECTIVITIES AND BUREAUCRACIES

Socio-Cultural Moralities in Collectivities. In contrast, the MBE social psychological paradigm opens a vision to explore moral responsibility *beyond* the individual person and the isolated situation to wider interactive levels of the complex organization environment where moral reasoning and socio-cultural meanings shape the understanding of morality in collectivities as well as the individual (Weinreich-Haste, 1984). Accordingly, its focus expands the unit of analysis, broadening the scope of corporate ethics to internal organizational collectivities, such as, departmental divisions and work-teams and their situation-specific vulnerabilities; and to the corporation itself with its open system complex organization environments, such as, culturally specific industry domains and rule-governing agencies.

Closed System Moralities and MBO Bureaucracies. The importance of open system environments in establishing a social psychological paradigm for corporate ethics can be understood more clearly when one analyzes the contradictory problems often provoked especially by conventional rule-governing agencies which often operate as closed systems organizations by MBO regulatory policies. The author had the personal experience of contacting the Securities and Exchange Commission (SEC) in Washington for the purpose of alerting this high level government regulatory agency about MBE as an organization scientific work on the corporate conscience and corporate moral reform. At the time of the contact, when the SEC was actively pursuing corporate moral offenders, it was thought that the agency might be timely interested in encouraging their target offenders to upgrade their moral vision toward eliminating corporate fraud in management structures and exchange markets by exposure to ethical consulting.

This morally applied thinking about MBE appeared rather plausible inasmuch as the courts and their associated law enforcement agencies as the conventional government organization brethren of the SEC do not hesitate to refer offenders to rehabilitative counseling, even though these law and order agencies generally operate as closed system organizations. While the SEC's response was sensitive to the MBE paradigm, the hierarchy was clearly caught by a closed system statutory mandate not to allow the imposition of ethics requirements on corporations (see Exhibit 1:3).

Exhibit 1:3 Open System Theory Analysis

UNITED STATES
SECURITIES AND EXCHANGE COMMISSION
WASHINGTON, D C 20549

DIVISION OF
CORPORATION FINANCE

April 13, 2004

Richard H. Guerrette, Ph.D.
EquiPax
Center for Human and Ethical Resources
96 School Street
Newport, VT 05855

Dear Dr. Guerrette:

Thank you for your March 30th letter to Chairman Donaldson. In your letter, you express concerns about the current paradigm for managing corporations and suggest that corporate responsibility can only be achieved through a paradigm shift creating an ethically informed corporate conscience.

Although our statutory mandate generally does not allow us to impose ethics requirements on corporations, pursuant to the Sarbanes-Oxley Act of 2002, we received the authority to require companies to disclose whether they have adopted a code of ethics that applies to their CEOs and senior financial officers. We also defined the term "code of ethics" for purposes of this requirement.

We appreciate your taking the time to write to inform us about your work to achieve corporate moral reform and we wish you great success in your efforts to reinforce moral commitment and corporate responsibility.

Sincerely,

Shelley K. Parratt
Deputy Director

While this exhibited letter reveals an open system ethic of a MBE caring sensitivity, it is bureaucratically laden with a closed system ethos of a MBO calculative complexity. The implausibility of promotional thinking about opening moral development opportunities to "CEOs and senior financial officers" as offenders, notwithstanding, Daniel Katz and Robert L. Kahn emphasize the critical importance of a *social interactional imperative* for human organizations to be *open and responsive to the needs of people* served by these organizations emanating from external events associated with the forces of social change:

> System theory is basically concerned with problems of relationships, of structure, and of interdependence rather than with constant attributes of objects. . . . Older formulations of system constructs dealt with the closed systems of the physical sciences, in which relatively self-contained structures could be treated successfully as if they were independent of external forces. But living systems, whether biological organisms or social organizations, are acutely dependent upon their external environment and so must be conceived of as open systems. . . . Open systems import some form of energy from the external environment. . . . In other words, the functioning personality is heavily dependent upon the continuous inflow of stimulation from the external environment. Similarly, social organizations must also draw renewed supplies of energy from other institutions, or people, or the material environment. No social structure is self-sufficient or self-contained. . . . The structure is to be found in an interrelated set of events which return upon themselves to complete and renew a cycle of activities. It is events rather than things which are structured, so that social structure is a dynamic rather than a static concept. (Katz and Kahn, 1972, pp. 37-39)

CONCLUSION

In the context of open system theory, corporate morality, in the MBE paradigm, is not conceived as system-maintenance or even integration but as *dynamic interactional development* for "the preservation of the character of the system" (Katz and Kahn, 1972, p. 42). This simply means that inasmuch as corporate morality is about corporate behavior and since corporate behavior is manifested in the context of *operational events* in business enterprises, corporate moral behavior needs to be directed by the *open dynamism* of the company's ethical character of caring reciprocity (MBE) and not by any static vested-interest objectives of system maintenance pre-conventional morality (MBO). (See Chapter 3, Exhibit 3:1).

A current example of such a *closed* "statically vested-interest system" is blatantly evident in the political and corporate complex organization environments within the sub-cultural manufacturing industrial compounds of the MBO corporate power structures among the National Rifle Association (NRA) gun culture establishment and the Congressional Party advocates of the "right wing" lobbying cultures. In these turbulent times of corporate unethical scandals and immoral operational events in complex organizational markets and fraudulent investing schemes, even reaching into the safe sanctuaries of shopping markets, theatrical environments and innocent elementary schools with the most recent trauma of the Newtown, Connecticut Sandy Hook School, the American Nation is finally awakening to *the need of a new management paradigm* for the moral integrity of its democracy and the securing safety of its society. Since the tragic events of this Sandy Hook massacre of the "Holy Innocent" children, with flashing biblical memories of the despotic massacres of Herod, the MBO gun culture continues to spread throughout the nation *armed* with the pre-conventional moral policies of the NRA. These morally inept policies have blind-folded the post-conventional sense of political party politics with the outdated amendment of the MBO functional right to bear arms at the expense of the MBE moral right to share the constitutional safety of the nation. It is only through the MBE dynamism of an *active* corporate conscience that the children of our nation can be safe and secure in their schools.

Finally, in brief systemic focus of this introductory chapter, it is critical to remember that as the *social psychological structure of corporate morality* is framed in the complex organizational environment of its external operational events and in the complex interdepartmental social interactional roles of internal workforce collaboration (Cushman, Young and Greene, 2010), its moral integrity is formed and its company character is preserved by a *dynamic corporate conscience*.

END NOTES

1. Van Der Erve describes "evolutionary management" in terms of a "complexity-resonance continuum" through which the "motion or dynamics of strategies" and their "related processes" cause managerial evolution "to advance from stage to stage" (1994, p.10-11). Chapters 3 and 4 of this book will define the organizational management strategies of this continuum in terms of the dynamic interactional coaching of executive, and line and staff managers toward advancing workplace performance through the ethically resonating processes of *moral development stages*. This process methodology in human resource management coaching will blend with a *caring* complexity-resonating continuum in Chapter 6 in "evolutionary economic" terms toward developing a socio-economic moral incentive model for human resource training.

2. It is historically significant for this study of the corporate conscience and the organization self to note that while the "self" concept is derived from the literature of social psychology and applied in the interdisciplinary domains of complex organization studies, historical studies of the corporation and its business and management disciplines have traced the terminological development of this "self" concept, since the earliest appearances of its significance, with the nomenclature of "corporate personhood." (Lipartito 2004): "The personhood doctrine evolved slowly and unevenly. . . . But the general drift was from the corporation as a state-created "artificial" person, to the corporation as the aggregation of individuals who owned it, to the corporation as a "natural" person by the late nineteenth century" (p.117). See also Hagar (1985).

3. For reviews of the events, perspectives and controversies associated with this landmark trial, see Birsch and Fielder (1994).

4. Deontological ethics are studies of *Being and Becoming* responding to the rights to live granted from the Deity and the duties to respect persons with dignity as human beings. The studies in Kantian ethics are promotive of incentives for ongoing life and ethically preventive for dying in a crash. These brief philosophical premises are innate to being and inspire morally developed virtues of an *elan vital* as a "vital force" of every being to live with dignity and not to die from the ignominy of a marketing induced crash. (See *Ethical Theory and Business*, Beauchamp and Bowie, pp. 33-40).

5. This phrase from the literature of critical philosophy and reflexive sociology implies *planning for change* in an established order through practical *(praxis)* strategies activated for the social reconstruction of a new order. (On "critical theory" in philosophy, see Bernstein, 1971, and McCarthy, 1978; on reflexive sociology and its affinity to the practical reconstructive aspects of critical thought, see Gouldner, 1970; see also the section on "Critical sociology and human potential" in the *Berkeley Journal of Sociology*, vol. XV, 1970.) A most helpful study in blending critical philosophical thought with practical scientific planning in organization systems and corporate cultures can be found in *The Planning of Change*, eds. Bennis, Benne and Chin (1969). This work also presents the "Dynamics of Planned Change" based on the "force-field" action theories of Kurt Lewin (1951) dealing with organizational environmental and social interaction dependencies, the moral developmental

dynamics of which can be most effectively applied by MBE organization development training. Accordingly, this task of applied change demonstrates how to change the strategies of MBO decision-making priorities based on such functional goals of profit maximization to the innovative MBE decision-making priorities anchored in the ethical principles of the moral development theories of Lawrence Kohlberg (1981), as presented in Chapter 3.

6. The work of Hans Kung, President of the Global Ethic Foundation at the University of Tubingen in Germany, has expanded a global scope to the complex organization environment, thus opening the need to explore plausible structures for a global corporate conscience. He has called on all religions of the world to unite with "universal ethical norms" to resolve the "problems of global terrorism, international crime, ecology, nuclear technology, and genetic engineering (which) threaten to overwhelm the world" (2004, pp.8-9; see also chapter 7 on the international scope of Kung's "principles for a global ethic" and his "moral frameworks" for the "collectivity structures of the global conscience"). Though the work of Hans Kung was monumental at the end of the last century, it did not contain the social scientific parameters for empirical studies, let alone the innovative structures for a new paradigm in corporate ethics, as described by Thomas Kuhn in his own innovative work, *The Structure of Scientific Revolutions* (1970).

7. *Utilitarian theory* is a teleological theory which explains morality in terms of function and consequences. It thus focuses on the moral propriety of behavior measured by the overall goodness of actions accomplishing the greatest possible benefits and the least consequential harm. Its linguistic significance is from the Greek word *teleos* specifying *end* or *purpose*. *Deontological theory*, from the Greek root *ontos* which means *being*, explains moral behavior as based on a respect for the nature of being. In the business transactions of corporate behavior, this translates into doing things right essentially because of what things *are* in themselves (Buber, 1958) and functionally for what and how they can be useful. This theory is a value theory, a humanistic one which *morally* induces one to consider the priorities of being, especially human beings in corporate responsibility decisions. *Contractarian theory* defines morality as emanating from social contracts at least formulated by ethical principles of justice and reciprocity and activated by the intuitive and innate sense of "systems of social cooperation" (Velasquez and Rostankowski, 1984, pp. 122-149).

8. Symbolic interaction theory "focuses on how the symbolic processes of role-taking, (i.e. taking the role of another), imaginative rehearsal, and self-evaluation by individuals attempting to adjust to one another lay the basis for the understanding of how social structure is constructed, maintained, and changed" (Turner,1978, p. 324). A contemporary "reference example" of how symbolic interaction can be used with "imaginative rehearsal" to change global social realities, in accordance with Turner's explanation, by "role-taking" and role-playing is in the musical production of Mark Johnson's (2008) *Playing for Change: Peace through Music*; see Chapter 8.

9. Parsons identifies four functional imperatives: *adaptation, goal attainment, integration* and *latency* (AGIL) as requisites which promote the survival of a system. In this context, Turner describes Parsons' functional analysis as involving "understanding how specific processes and structures operate to meet system requisites, and in turn, how varying degrees of meeting requisites fosters equilibrium (or disequilibrium) of the social whole" (p. 100).

CHAPTER 2

THE DYNAMIC CORPORATE CONSCIENCE

The dynamism of the corporate conscience is not a figure of speech but an interactional symbol of the etymological essence of language and historical presence of culture. *Dynamis,* in Greek, signifies "power," "force" and "resources." In contemporary corporate culture, these terms are usually associated with "money" and the "human resources" of an employed workforce. In ancient historical Greek cultures, these terms were commonly associated with military resources of power. In ancient religious and Biblical Greek cultures, *Dynamis* was associated with the Divine inspirational resources of truth. This kind of dynamic power thus meant more than just money and military force; it meant the *illumination of truth enlightening the human resources of the conscience.*

> Only by this can we be certain that we are children of the truth and be able to quieten our conscience in his presence, whatever accusations it may raise against us, because God is greater than our conscience and he knows everything. My dear people, if we cannot be condemned by our own conscience, we need not be afraid in God's presence...
> (1 John 3:19-21, *The Jerusalem Bible,* Jones, ed., 1966).[1]

The corporate conscience is thus *dynamic* as an internal organ of truth in a company's value system to illuminate an external corporate cultural identity of social responsibility through its management operational reflexivity. Its collective illuminating voice, therefore, should reflect this dynamism of *integrity and truth* through every channel of corporate communications, such as, the official pronouncements of: the Board of Directors, the Chief Executive Officer of the Corporation, the Offices of Corporate Responsibility, the Departments of Human Resources, and the Annual and Auditing Reports of the Corporation. Within these infrastructural channels, other company executives, managers and workers may more readily and informally reflect their impressions of the corporate conscience through their work performance commitment more quickly and pertinently than in the customary deliberations of these company internalities.[2]

In short, the corporate conscience has an ancient historical corporate cultural root system which generates the power of credibility from the communication of the truth among its internalized human resources. In the corporate training of these human resources, all company personnel should be encouraged and, at times even rewarded, to reveal their "heartfelt" reflections freely and openly in collectivity discourse toward building and nurturing a corporate conscientious *ethos*, as the *ethical spirit* of a company value system, in the corporation. Such an inspirational ethos creates a productive rationale for the critical importance of each individual and every collectivity in a company to contribute to the *integrity of truth* and thus strengthening the reliability of the total corporate conscience (Dilenschneider, 1990, ch. 5). When one smaller entity violates this conscientious pact, the entire corporation can be vulnerable to grave scandals of corporate fraud and lose its credibility. Take, for example, the historical collapse of the hierarchical integrity of the Boeing Corporation, several decades ago, when a senior financial officer of the corporation collaborated with a senior Pentagon weapons buyer in Boeing's complex organization environment on an inside deal which allowed the company to gain a lucrative airline tanker contract. The Pentagon official was subsequently hired in 2002 as a Senior Vice President at Boeing, with an annual salary of $250,000. During her trial, in the fall of 2004, she was forced to admit that she had awarded Boeing other billion dollar contracts with special consideration and that her daughter and her future son-in-law had also been given jobs at the company (Phinney, 2005). It should be alarmingly clear from this example that while the cited individual and corporate consciences of the Boeing Corporation and the Pentagon were dormant, the corruptive dynamic in this case was energized not by truth but by money and weaponry of the fraudulent few. Boeing not only lost its credibility and its renowned CEO, but more critically, the *corporate character* of its gracefully symbolic "high-flying" imagery.

THE ORGANIZATIONAL LOCATION OF THE CORPORATE CONSCIENCE

Corporate Operational Dimensions. To locate the organizational constructs of the corporate conscience and to understand how they operate, it may be helpful to compare its social processes and organizational dimensions with the individual conscience and its corporate operational dimensions. If the individual mind and the self-develop out of the social context of self-other role interaction processes, it can be postulated that the development of the "corporate mind" and the "corporate self" would follow the same social psychological processes. Locating the *individual processes of reflexivity* projects the complex organizational understanding of the collective interactional and operational dimensions within the corporate conscience.

Individual Reflexivity:

Self-Imagery Processes and the Identification of the Individual Conscience.
George Herbert Mead (1934) demonstrated that the individual mind and the self-develop out of what others say about that individual. He explained these processes through role theory: The self-interacts with others, hearing and noticing how others are perceiving him/her. Taking their roles, the self begins to reflect on itself in the mirror of these perceptions. The individual's self-image thus forms in the processes of reflexivity out of the feedback from the perceived impressions of others. "Reflexiveness, then, is the essential condition, within the social process, for the development of the mind" (p.134). William James (1892), had located these kinds of psycho-social interactive operations of the inner self in the simplest analogical way through the grammatical constructs of the personal pronouns, the "I" and the "ME." Later, Mead moved this analytical discourse more graphically, tracing an interactional dialectic between the I and the ME. His graphic descriptions identify the I as the *assertive* side of the self and the ME as the *reflexive* side. *This reflexive side* is not only where the self-image forms but also *is where the individual conscience resides.* This conclusion is self-evident inasmuch as the conscience is defined in moral philosophy as an instrument of moral reflexivity, which, of course, is nothing more than reflexive thinking (Bittle, 1950, p. 140). In practice, therefore, when the "ME" applies knowledge to what the "I" has done, it is attempting to render objective judgment on the moral propriety of the "I's" subjective behavior. In theory, this conscientious "application of knowledge" is consonant with the grammatical case typification in the English language which appropriates subjectivity to the "I" and objectivity to the "ME." In the reality of strategic decision-making practice, though, especially in the subjective lanes of vested-interest corporate enterprising, "conscience has the last word, and passion and will the last deed" (Gouldner, 1969, p. 616). But in the integrity of philosophic truth, the corporate conscience formulates the last transactional deeds with ethically *intensive* vision and morally *reflexive* passion.

Organizational Reflexivity:

Self-Imagery Processes and the Location of the Corporate Conscience.
Charles Horton Cooley (1902) typified these identity-making attributes as the "looking-glass self." Projecting his analogy from the individual to the collective unit of analysis helps to trace the social psychological processes of corporate conscience formation. Thus, when the "corporate mind" sees its collective self in the internal organizational mirror of its own workforce and hears about its management behavior from its employees, it knows in truth how it looks. When it sees itself in the "looking-glass" reflectors of its complex organizational environment and hears about "the moral issues" of its own corporate behavior from its suppliers, clients and the public, the company begins to face the *ethical "sources"* of its "organization self"

within the inner reflexive zones of its corporate conscience (see Taylor, 1989, p. 112).

Complex Organization Activity:

Organization-Self Reflection and Corporate Conscience Activation. Facing one's inner conscience, though, is not an automatic process. Reflexivity, both individual and corporate, can never be taken for granted. This is so because the "looking-glass self" analogy does not provide a total comprehensive view of inner-self-reality or infra structural morality. Mirrors reflect the outside, not the inside. The Enron case, for example, demonstrates the inner organization self-reality that its "Corporate US" was asleep. The assertive Corporate "WE" was dominating the deals, without any moral reflexivity. This kind of a corporation, which is not in touch with its conscience, is not only lacking in moral leadership but is one that breeds immorality throughout the system. The latest evidence of this systemic corruption has been revealed with the releasing of the audio tapes which trace the judgments of an assertive collective "I" even at lower levels of the Enron Corporation hierarchy, in conspiracy to rig prices for the purpose of capitalizing with profit-maximization on the 1996 energy crisis in California. Total organizational reflexivity within the executive chambers of a company and throughout its infrastructure, thus, constitutes a comprehensive model for the complete formation of the corporate conscience and *its activation within the reflexive operations of the "Corporate US"*(see Exhibit 2:1; see also King & McCarthy 2005).

Exhibit 2:1   Operational Deliberations of the Corporate Conscience:
The Reflexive Operations of The Corporate "US"

THEORETICAL AND INTERACTIONAL ACTIVATION
OF THE
CORPORATE CONSCIENCE

Conceptual Theory: *Descriptions*   Applied Theory: *Formulations*

Reflexivity Processes: Operational Applications:

identifying corporate conscience 43   locating the corporate conscience 43

The "Corporate US" 44

Evaluating

Corporate Operational Deliberations 42-55

Defining: Reconstructing:

organization reflexivity 43   organization imagery 43-44

complex organization reflexivity 44   complex organization activity 44, 47

critical ethical consistency 48-49   value-system-building 50-52

impression management theory 52-53   ethical-image-projection 52-55

THE INTERACTIONAL ACTIVATION OF THE CORPORATE CONSCIENCE

Organizational Moral Reflexivity and Corporate Ethical Imagery. Having located the corporate conscience in the social psychological zone of the "Corporate ME," the moral imperative of total organizational reflexivity is therefore a truth-facing mandate to integrate the business mission of a company's operational performance to reflect the integrity of its corporate ethical imagery. Executives seeking to create such an ethical image for their companies must keep this imperative vision in focus in all of their *operational deliberations.* Inasmuch as the corporate conscience is a relatively new term in management science, most executives are not familiar with the social psychological operations of moral organizational reflexivity especially in the complex interorganizational environment. This does not mean that they are not striving for that ethical image. Many of these officials have sought consultants to formulate ethical policies by composing codes, outlining rules and regulations for value-system-building and ethical-image-projecting. But it is clear from the scandals that have erupted and continue to spread in and through some of the most reputable companies in the business world, that such formulations are not enough. From the bankruptcy rubble of the WorldCom scandal, the new MCI executive directed an extensive restructuring of the company value system for the purpose of "proving its commitment to good corporate governance, ethics and integrity." In the complete text of the company website statements on its "Guiding Principles," its "Code of Ethics and Business Conduct," its "Ethics Brochure," and its "Actions and Reforms," there was not one statement about or reference to the corporate conscience, let alone to its collective identity or to its reflexive operations. In contrast, here are some statements by Mitchell Thomashow (1995), Co-chair of Environmental Studies at Antioch New England Graduate School, about *personal and collective operational reflexivity.* These statements clearly define reflexivity in terms of professional and moral leadership operations which can be applied to the corporate conscience as a prelude to the social psychological explanations of how this conscience works:

> Reflection involves mindfulness, introspection, and deliberation–thinking carefully about the personal meaning of knowledge, considering the wider ramifications of personal and collective action, and using information and relationship to attend to the moment, the direct experience of the here-and-now.... (p. 173).

> The goal of reflective practice is to understand the consequences of professional action, to assess how one is perceived as a practitioner, to use professional activities as an educational laboratory to learn about the issues of the profession, and to connect those activities to one's value system and personal growth. Hence "reflective practitioners" always consider the broad context of their work, placing particular emphasis on the learning process

of professional activity. They construct and integrate a professional and personal vision, stepping out of their work to consider whether their actions conform to that vision (p. 164).

When people face challenging decisions, do they have the reflective capacity to look deeply at the ramifications of their choices? This is an educational imperative, to provide people with the orientation and experience to confront moments of risk, ambiguity, moral conflicts and controversy. When practitioners are willing to confront these matters, both publicly and privately, then they take seriously their role as healing practitioners. This is the kind of leadership that the environmental profession requires (p. 166).

What needs to be more clearly and specifically defined for this moral leadership role, however, is the "critical practical" depths of this "reflexive capacity." A moral leader needs to probe the reflexive depth within the corporate conscience towards policy-planning change and decision-making reform based on ethically sensitive perception and morally specific coordination. What this means for the activating mandate of corporate conscientious decision-making is that a company needs to conduct its business mission with honesty, integrity and universalized justice and fairness, without selective favoring for vested interest pursuits. This reflexive depth-perception involves moral reasoning consistency which is prepared to coordinate basic operational considerations, even those emanating from non-moral sources, such as, legal, economic or political ones. So if a company is faced with a choice of relocating its plant operations in a foreign country as an outsourcing plan to decrease labor costs, it needs to coordinate these economic demands with the moral considerations of retaining the plant in its local based community whose population largely depends on continued operations for job security and economic survival. The socio-economic and moral complexities of these kinds of ethical depth-reflections can break the integrity of a company's character, if "corner cutting" and "trade-off" practices are recognized as compromising tactics disjunctive of reputational honesty and company loyalty.

The "Corporate US" and the Complex Organizational "Mirrors" of the "Company Organizational Self." In the contemporary realities of corporate culture and the good faith struggling efforts of CEO's like Michael Capellas, to create an ethical image for their companies, the search becomes an internal struggle for the corporate mind to achieve unity between its assertive organizational "self WE" and its reflexive organizational "self US." The social psychological operations of these two inner organizational domains of the corporate conscience are the same. That is, both self-images derive from the perceived impressions of others; the difference between the formations, however, arises from the respective culturally specific meanings (Weinreich-Haste, 1984) in the corporate mind as it perceives itself in the different organizational "mirrors" of its complex organization environment. Thus, when former Enron highest level executives dramatize their trust in the company's stock, encouraging 401K investing personnel to continue to buy additional shares, while silently selling their own, their asserted executive self-images become dependent on their perceived impressions of admiring colleagues and compliant subordinates. These images can be quite different from how their reflexive self-images appear when they perceive the responses of the investigating media, complaining investors, punitive courts and a distrustful nation. Rediscovering a company's ethical image then is a matter of exposing executives and managers to knowledge of the reflexive processes of self-image formation and how these are dependent upon organizational reference group perception. Executives and directors have to pay attention to the differences in how and why the company is being perceived by its networking reference groups. It is through these comparisons that organizational reflexivity becomes plausible and ethical image reconstruction, possible. Enron did not learn this lesson with its double-talk, Fifth Amendment pleas and evasive defense posturing. Neither did MCI, with its best efforts to reconstruct its own corporate identity, as divorced from its WorldCom merger, but failing to retrieve its ethical image through value-system-building and moral development reformation of its corporate conscience (see Exhibit 2:1 above and pp. 51-52 below). Such reconstructive work demands the application of reality construction theory (Berger and Luckman, 1967) to the ethos of corporate culture and to the ethics of management process (Guerrette, 1988).

MANAGERIAL LEADERSHIP AND CRITICAL ETHICAL CONSISTENCY

Reality Reconstruction and Ethical Consistency. Inasmuch as this theory explains reality as shaped by the social interactional symbols of an organization as constituted on the values of its culture, executives can change an established organization by rebuilding the interactional value symbols of its business enterprises and managerial operations. Not only can they so change the reality of its organization culture and reorder its value-system; but with MBE *leadership planning*, they can also manage its corporate ethical image to preserve the "character" of the system. And because every organizational image needs flexibility for adjusting to the various reference groups in its interorganizational environment, executives have to direct the reflexive processes of the company conscience in order to coordinate necessary corporate image variations in its multiple organizational self-images. Notice the ways that the Altria Group (formerly Philip Morris Corporation) has had to struggle in its defensive efforts to rebuild its ethical image in its complex interorganizational environment, encompassing the litigation organizations of law firms and the courts. Through decades of law suits and trials in the aftermath of the complicit "smoke-screening" testimony of the tobacco industry CEO's in Congress, the company, still striving to recover an ethical image, now has assumed a different name and a more complex corporate identity with mergers and acquisitions. It has even gone as far as producing a website (*http://philipmorrisusa.com*) expressing concerned public health awareness. The site warns smokers of the serious health risks of its tobacco products and strongly discourages under-age-smoking, thus manifesting interorganizational flexibility and an appreciable degree of corporate ethical reflexivity. There is clearly here some critical depth-reflection in Philip Morris's quest for corporate responsibility. Yet, the company persists in the production of cigarettes and is still facing, in a current "landmark trial," the litigation mirrors of its "complicit" organization environment which are continuing to reflect industry-wide fraud to mislead the public about cigarette safety (Watkins, 2004). The ultimate reflexive question, in any complex organizational attempts to recover a corporate ethical image needs to be *philosophically posed* in terms of ethically principled priorities and *scientifically graded* in terms of behavioral operational activities in genuine attempts to project an overall *interorganizational ethical consistency.* These complex ethical needs are posed by the eminent scholarship of William Carlo with this simple question: "How can ethics be taught without a thorough grounding in notions of essence and nature?" (1967 p. 70). Such complex ethical reflexivity needs to consider even production validity and purpose in order to achieve this critical ethical consistency in the overall corporate image, the praxis reconstruction of which need to be ethically grounded in the philosophical components of "*rationality and respect*" (see Goodpaster, 1983). These two components offer a connective social psychological structure for conducting the operations of ethical reflexivity in the corporate conscience and achieving ethical consistency in the corporate imagery. Rationality is the *self-directed* moral component in any business whereby a company defines its goals and works toward their attainment by carefully calculated operational choices designed to minimize risks and maximize opportunities. Respect is the *other-directed* moral component through which a company relates to the perspectives and needs of others within the interorganizational ambit of its operational order.

Rationality represents the value system of a company containing the rationale for corporate existence in terms of goal-setting organizational arrangements and the priorities for marketing behavior in terms of goal-attainment operational procedures. It induces a company to assume a business identity with an organizational purpose for *product validity* and to acquire a marketing image with an operational practice for *product reliability*. It is that value component in a company that establishes its commercial enterprise with corporate authenticity. Clearly, the Altria Group continues to miss the mark of *rationality* here both in its marketing behavior and promotional practices. At least, it admits that the cigarette product is not safe nor reliable.

Respect represents the moral system of a company through which an organizational disposition manifests itself in terms of the social psychological processes of role-taking reciprocity. It induces a company to assume a reciprocal business posture toward its clients with an awareness of consumer roles and needs in its advertising promotions and marketing transactions. It is that moral component in a company that establishes its business reputation with corporate integrity. Overtly, the Altria Group continues to strive to re-establish the respect of its clients by taking the roles of their addicted victims and their families. But their corporate integrity is suspect simply and possibly covertly because of intentionally insufficient depth-reflexive perception which fails or decides not to comprehend the critical connective issues of *product invalidity* and *conscience inauthenticity*. In conclusion, it is only through the authentic and ethically reflexive processes of rationality and respect that a company can earn and recover the trust of its clientele, the markets and the public. This kind of comprehensive depth-reflexivity is anchored in the corporate conscience of a company and creates the "looking glass mirror" of the corporate inner self. This kind of corporate mirror reflects the inside of company values as well as the outside of corporate ethical imagery and establishes the social psychological groundwork in a company for ethical plausibility in its corporate governance and value-system-building in its management processes.

MANAGEMENT PROCESSES AND VALUE-SYSTEM-BUILDING:

THE ASSERTIVE CORPORATE "WE"
AND
THE REFLEXIVE CORPORATE "US"

Building values in a company is a basic reflexive social organization process that more often than not happens intuitively in any business enterprise or economic venture. Since values are defined in sociology as really nothing more than priorities, any company which sets policy goals and designs a strategy for attaining these goals, obviously has its priorities in place and thus can be said to have values. The *reflexive* questions are, however: are these values good, honorable and ethical? Are they based on universal principles? Only with these kinds of values and the moral performance they would generate in a company can a corporate ethical image be created. The task in value-system-building is to synchronize company priorities with values grounded in the universal ethical principles of *justice and reciprocity* (Kohlberg et al., 1990) and the human resource concerns of interactional *caring and sensitivity* (Gilligan, 1982).

Justice and reciprocity. William Weiss, former Chairman and CEO of the Ameritech Corporation, has demonstrated a facility for synchronizing these reflexive management processes with principled value-system-building. Perceiving his leadership role as the principal architect for establishing the corporate culture and for defining the character of its business, he anchored his value-system-building in *three basic operational principles* that signify universal morality: first, *moral consistency* with the corporate conscience; second, *moral efficiency* with ambiguous reality; and third, *moral governance* with interdependent benefits (1986). In observance of these principles, he built the company's value-system on *seven fundamental value cornerstones* that established the corporate culture of the company in a *value*-service reciprocity: (1) *the dignity of the individual*, by which he meant "leading people to self-realization and giving them the freedom to achieve it;" (2) *openness to people and to ideas* – to "allow us to do the job, not just well, but better" (3) *optimum standards of service* in preservation of the company's historical tradition of contractual excellence; (4) *entrepreneurship* for attitudinal creativity and latitudinal responsibility; (5) *synergism* as a corporate motivating force for shaping a social and global environment; (6) *leadership through competence*, analogizing from academic freedom to managerial freedom to promote initiative; (7) *behavior based on values* to preserve organization consistency. On these value cornerstones, Weiss shaped a social character for Ameritech with his own morally stimulating mandate:

> I want everyone in Ameritech to have respect for one another, respect for their co-workers and for their ideas and aspirations respect for our customers and their needs and expectations. Respect for others, in my book, is an essential characteristic. Without it, you cannot have self-respect. . . Finally, I want us to trust ourselves and to trust one another, so that together we can achieve more than we ever thought possible (247).

Accordingly, he set this conscientious mandate as the moral charter of the company value-system. As moral leader, he made it expressively clear that his executive mission was to expect no less from his workforce than moral consistency with this value-system:

> Our task is to discuss and crystallize issues of a corporate value-system-values that have meaning and are useful in reality, as well as in the forum that created them. In short, we should be able not just to *define* a value system – "we must be able to *live* by it" (p. 243).

Living by a value-system empowers not just a CEO but everyone in the "Corporate WE" to reflect conscientiously through the MBE paradigm. Robert Dilenschneider, former CEO of Hill and Knowlton, an international public relations firm, and now Chairman and CEO of his own firm, the Dilenschneider Group, expressed the "Corporate US" in this reflexive way: "One of the best ways to stand out in any organization is to understand its values and then show how you embody them. You don't have to be the CEO to be a symbol. And the CEO, if he is worth his salt, is delighted to showcase other symbolic leaders within the company." (1990, p. 85)

By discussing and crystallizing issues of the company value-system, executives enable management to be in touch with the corporate conscience. It is through these discussions that executives can direct organizational reflexivity and assess ethical image consistency in the company in accordance with its value-system and its own operational versions of universal ethical principles.[3] With this reflexive awareness in place, management can pay attention to corporate ethical image-projection, keeping the company on a moral course by managing the appropriate symbolic imagery for achieving this critical ethical consistency.

Interactional caring and sensitivity. Advancing value-system building to a higher moral awareness stage, Carol Gilligan opens the attention of executives and managers to a wider universal version of 6th stage leadership and moral advancement sensitivity with her focus on *caring* sensitivity. Applying her ethic of care to MBE managing interaction in the workplace can effectively be traced by the following brief case study analysis of Paul O'Neill, the former United States Secretary of the Treasury during his tenure of CEO at the Alcoa Corporation. Prior to his leadership appointment at this firm, the company's workforce had been struggling with multiple fiscal problems of production. Notwithstanding, this primary functional management concern, Mr. O'Neill directed his staff to conduct an internal organizational report on "industrial safety" in the workplace. His MBO management staff were "baffled" at this request, quite puzzled by his immediate focus on what turned out to be his investigation of human resource attitudes and performance as revealing indicators of a need for MBE enhancement (Zakaria, 2012).

IMPRESSION MANAGEMENT THEORY AND ETHICAL IMAGE PROJECTION

Processes of Impression Management Theory. Erving Goffman demonstrated how one can take charge of one's own self-image formation through his applied theory on the "techniques of impression management" (1959). He showed that individuals deliberately select an array of symbols in the orders of dress, fashion, style, etc., to manage a distinct impression on others. Analogously, corporate planners need to select the appropriate ethical symbols of policy formulations and company operations that render corporate ethical behavior and the organizational image plausible (Guerrette, 1988). This can be accomplished by dramatizing, *with reflexive authenticity*, such symbols as: ethical policy and value statements; ethical guidelines for business practice and management operations; interactive "face-work" (Goffman, 1955) which pays attention to company history, seniority and service, performance management and employee development planning, employee assistance programming, organization ritual and ceremony, *art and architecture in the workplace* (see Guerrette, 2014, vol. II),[4] occupational health and safety for the workforce; etc. In this symbolic corporate cultural context, the dramatization of interactional encounters among personnel in companies can be creatively managed for intentional and planned outcomes through organizational rituals. These kinds of ritualized impression management techniques can thus serve as an embodiment of social order (Goffman, 1973, 1971) and function as symbolic representations of a corporate value-system.

Projections of Ethical Management Imagery. Per-Olof Berg of the Copenhagen School of Economy and Business Administration identifies such impression management techniques as "framing the context" for company-image-building (1986). In such a frame, the corporate planner fashions the kind of organizational image he or she wants projected and presents the company through, what he calls, "symbolic fields of action" or "shared frames of meanings" (p. 559). A successful company, which has engaged in ethical image projection through authentic dramatization of symbolic management impression strategies and which has framed a local context for the interactional caring of its workforce, clients and even the community, has been Ben and Jerry's Ice Cream. In the years before its acquisition by Unilever, Ben Cohen, CEO, and Jerry Greenfield, president of the corporation, had consistently fashioned a socially conscious and corporate ethical image for their company through shared frames of socio-cultural meanings in the workplace and had projected this image to the entire Vermont community through symbolic festival activities in the marketplace. By means of these organizational ethical strategies and interactional festival rituals, they demonstrated how a corporate conscience is an effective managerial instrument for economic planning and development and market profitability (see Lawson, 1988).

According to Berg, framing the corporate image through such shared interactive symbols and organization rituals provides symbolic constructs for the priorities of the company, generates a common purpose for its workforce and opens direction for its business mission. A symbolic field of reference creates a common reality perspective in an organization and a value orientation for its members to follow. Berg further contends that this kind of strategic planning of corporate image projection not only creates the desired company identity but its reflection in the reference group "mirrors" of its interorganizational environment feeds back into the company and impels the workforce to live up to the projected image. In this way, the reflexive feedback induces incentives for worker pride and performance, thus creating among the workforce a cyclical process of corporate self-image affirmation.

A corporate ethical image, framed to manage an impression may be the product of planned social psychological and organization management processes; but it is imperative that the "symbolic fields of action" and "shared frames of meanings" be reflexive of an authentic reality. This is simply to say that a corporate ethical image demands validity. Impression management and contextual framing may project a desired corporate face; but such strategies do not automatically deliver the corporate ethical image, especially when there may be covert flaws in the image (see Lutz, 1983; Olasky, 1985).[5] These very phrases have a hollow sound. An image needs more than an impression, more than a frame. It needs, above all, *authenticity*. The image needs an identity; and its representation, a reality. Occasionally, a dramatic unplanned reality creates and shapes an authentic identity. Take, for example, the catastrophic reality of 9/11 and the instantly authentic shaping of the heroic corporate ethical image of Cantor Fitzgerald, a World Trade Center broker house firm. This international company lost 658 member workers of its staff. The CEO of Cantor Fitzgerald International, Lee Amaitis, described the instant "voice" of the company's corporate conscience:

> Everybody who was in the building was lost, so . . . to remember it as vividly as we do on September 11, that happens every day for me. . . . This is a family firm, we lost brothers, family members, fathers and daughters. I mean there was a tremendous loss of life in this firm that was so connected. (CEO) Howard (Lutnick) lost his brother and his best friend, I lost my best friend. I mean I can't tell you how that affects people. . . .The emotions are really tough to go through because you're bleeding at the same time you know you're grieving, bleeding, going through this whole process, yet at the same time you are tremendously proud of the people that did the job to keep the firm going. (Muriel, 2002)

Howard Lutnick provided the moral leadership not only to keep the firm going but to keep the families of the firm securely "connected" Pledging to give them a quarter share of the firm's profits for five years, he raised $147 million to provide for their health care needs for ten years. This performance prompted Lee Amaitis to confirm the authentic reality of the company's corporate ethical identity: "That 25 percent needed to mean something. I mean you can't say you're going to give 25 percent and then say you have no profits, so you're motivated to say, 'OK, that's real money'" (Muriel, 2002). A corporate ethical image needs the reality of a corporate ethical identity. Planned or unplanned, it is the corporate conscience that frames this identity and establishes its ethical reality. Not only must corporate planners understand this but also corporate advertisers as well. The public knows a fraud when it sees one and the "organizational other" can see through any hollow frame. In the end, if ethics are a constitutive part of that framed context (and this means *constituted in the symbolic constructs and organizational operations of a corporate conscience*, as described above,) the company value-system will be in place and its ethical image secured.

If ethics, however, are not that constitutive in a company, i.e., a company which is not informed by an operative corporate conscience, a value-system may be in place but its ethical image may very well be insecure. Case after case of corporate fraud and executive malfeasance demonstrates this conclusion. And the reasons why many of the most reputable corporations and companies in corporate culture today are being investigated by the SEC or other law enforcement bodies are precisely because of ethical image insecurity and, more fundamentally, because of *corporate conscience dormancy*.

END NOTES

1. It is not just interesting to note but more revealing to comprehend that in the Revised Standard Version of the interlinear Greek-English translation of this text, the Greek word for the operational center of reflexive activity in the conscience is "cardia" with the literal meaning of "heart" (Marshall, 1970, p. 940). The direct connection between the analogical location of the *resources of one's inner truth* and the biological identification of the heart is universally common among all cultures and religions of the world and revealed in multiple sources of biblical, liturgical and lyrical literature as well as in music through time.

2. For a more intensively focused study of corporate social responsibility in the global spheres of multi-cultural externalities and organizational networks of corporate social responsibility, see Amaeshi and Nnodim (2012).

3. For empirical evidence on the importance of consistency in value-system-building in the workplace, see Posner *et al.*, (1985). This study demonstrates that value articulation in the workplace and value congruence in the workforce, regarding personal and organization values, make a significant positive difference in individual and organizational performance. It also suggests programs and measures for human resource managers to facilitate ongoing value-consistency-building between the company and its workers through training, reward systems and counseling support. On value-system-measuring and training, see Payne (1988). On value-system-building and ecology, see also Teilhard de Chardin (1964, p. 40).

4. The second volume of this study is critically important to this chapter, particularly in memory of the eminent Jewish philosopher and Marxist scholar, Herbert Marcuse, whose work on *The Aesthetic Dimension* (1978) reflects the corporate ethical significance of art in corporate culture and value-system building in the workplace in the words of his publisher: "The result of his exploration of this important new direction is the evolution of a dialectical aesthetic in which art functions as the conscience of society." (see v.II for his own words on pp. 64-67)

5. On the individual's use of impression management techniques to project a favorable work image as a means for escaping moral accountability in performance flaws, see Goffman (1971), Wood and Mitchell (1981) and Payne and Giacalone (1990). This kind of accountability escaping was blatantly noticeable in the Congressional testimony of a former Enron CEO.

CHAPTER 3

THE MBE PARADIGM:
A DELIVERY SYSTEM FOR CORPORATE MORAL REFORM

The alarm clock has sounded.... It is still ringing.... Ringing throughout corporate culture and beyond.... In the markets of Wall Street, the Halls of Congress, and the homes of America, still calling for the arousal of ethically dormant corporations to face themselves in the complex organizational "mirrors" of their environments. *Main Street culture* has begun to "*Occupy* Wall Street" culture demanding that corporations and companies of all sizes, market organizations and investment firms in all exchanges and even government bureaucracies throughout all their agencies *trace the reflections of their corporate consciences* to face all the demoralizing projections of their performance profiles toward a global organizational search for *corporate ethical and market moral reform.*

Corporate Conscience Formation and Moral Development Socialization. The process of facing the reflections of corporate inner truth and discovering a need for the moral reformation of one's company is in itself an arousal of the corporate conscience. This process of arousal happens more often than not in the experience of a company's scandal exposure, as seen in this prevailing period of punitive parades to courthouses and prisons for convictions of corporate fraud. And thus, moral reform is a costly and shameful price a company or a bureaucracy has to pay for corporate conscience dormancy. As most everyone knows, it takes a very long time to regain market credibility or agency reliability, let alone moral integrity, after the damage has been done. Re-formation is much harder than formation. The practical, preventive challenge, therefore, is the *formation* of the corporate conscience rather than its reformation.

The formation of the corporate conscience is actually a socialization process of "in-formation" in the sense of cultivating the development of moral awareness in the entire workforce of a company and especially its reflexive entities. Corporate executives can meet the challenge of cultivating the corporate conscience by recognizing their roles as company socialization agents charged with ethical leadership responsibilities to reconstruct a conducive moral climate for organization and governance change (Guerrette, 1994). The literature of social psychology characterizes parents and teachers as *"caretakers"* (Lindesmith, *et al.,* 1975, p., 300 – emphasis added) and "socialization agents" (Sewell, 1970) for the cultivation of the individual conscience in the child. In this sense, senior management and especially CEOs can fulfill this role as involved moral leaders for the cultivation of the corporate conscience, as sensitively expressed by Howard Lutnick, CEO of Cantor Fitzgerald in the aftermath of 9/11 who literally and compassionately *took care* of the bereaving families of his workforce (see Chapter 9). Executive development seminars and management training workshops can provide an effective communication forum for enacting these socialization roles. These seminars and workshops can demonstrate how moral develop-ment theory and its practical application in company operations can shape worker attitudes and contribute to their moral performance (Guerrette, 1986, 1988).

The shaping of worker attitudes in company operations as a socialization effect of the interactional authority styles of management has been a subject of analysis with some moral significance in critical sociology (see Mills, 1948, 1970; Rioux, 1970). Mills defined how the "power factor" in authority systems conditions the response levels of workers and thus shapes workforce morale. His critical thought challenged earlier attempts in applied industrial sociology and humanistic management models (Mayo, 1945; Roethlisberger and Dickson, 1946) to adopt a more practical, political approach to morale-building and the social reconstruction of industrial relations. Blumer (1947) also promoted the need for the *moral* and political critique of industrial relations. Based on his development of G. H. Mead's theories into symbolic interactionism in sociology (Blumer, 1969), MBE represents a "critical practical" model designed to reconstruct a post-conventional morality of workplace integrity and to reshape workforce morality through the application of moral development theory and the interactional reformation of authority.

MORAL DEVELOPMENT THEORY

Moral development theory was constructed by Lawrence Kohlberg (1976) to explain how moral reasoning functions within the cognitive structures of individuals and how it progresses through time to higher stages of moral judgments and responsibility awareness. The theory is grounded in developmental learning through informal life experiences and formal education which gradually opens a moral cognition toward formulating moral judgments and inducing one's motivation to moral behavior. This theory of Kohlberg was derived from a series of longitudinal and cross-cultural research studies of "the child as a moral philosopher" in the middle of the 20th century. The studies were designed to trace the moral reasoning of his subjects, in a sample of ten to sixteen-year-old boys, from their responses to hypothetical moral dilemmas (1984).

Historical Overview of the Research. In the first period of his research, Kohlberg observed that these responses revealed six stages of moral reasoning which his subjects invoked to support their moral judgments: (1) a fear of punishment stage; (2) an instrumental exchange stage; (3) an interpersonal conformity stage; (4) a social system stage; (5) a social contract stage; and (6) a universal ethical principle stage. He also noticed that these stages were divided into three larger categories of moral reasoning, reflecting developing levels of socio-cultural conventions: I, pre-conventional; II, conventional; and III, post-conventional (1976, see Exhibit 3:1).

By repeating the studies every four years with his original sample, Kohlberg noticed that his subjects progressed through the sequence of these stages without skipping a stage, though not all reached the higher stages. He subsequently introduced these studies into other cultures in addition to the United States, including Mexico, Taiwan, Israel and Turkey. In this work, not only did he discover these same sample patterns and progressions; but he also learned that they manifested no significant variance with reference to social class, religious or non-religious affiliation, or cultural conditions. Eventually, Kohlberg found that progression through these stages reflected learning patterns of cognitive organization with increasing differentiation of stage meaning and incremental integration of stage reasoning.

In later periods of his research, Kohlberg initiated experiments in moral education in schools and in prisons, studying pedagogical methods and organizational climates that were conducive to the moral development of his subjects through these stages, Kohlberg, 1972, 1975, 1986). By developing measurement instruments for assessing populations, he subsequently found that very few reach stage 6; that only about 15 per cent reach stage 5; and that most attain a 3rd and 4th stage conventional level (Kohlberg, 1990). He also found that, in the American study, increased role-taking opportunities for middle-class children allowed experiences of societal integration and thus facilitated social system reasoning. In this study, he likewise noticed that formal education was a facilitating factor in development to higher stages. These critical findings challenged Kohlberg to redefine his stages and to reformulate his descriptions of their sequences, as applied in the studies of this Chapter and especially along with the practical innovations as traced in both volumes of this study. It is also to be noted that the following Exhibit scale has been most effectively applied beyond the MBE academic domains of moral development research toward

Lickona's (1976) *praxis* application of *sexual ethics in family management studies* traced in the Appendix below.

Exhibit 3:1

The six stages of moral judgment (The Kohlberg Scale)

Content of Stage

Level and Stage	What is right	Reasons for doing right	Social perspective of stage
Level I. Pre-conventional **Stage 1: Heteronomous morality**	Avoiding breaking rules backed by punishment, and obedience for its own sake, to avoid physical damage to persons and property.	Avoidance of punishment, and the superior power of authorities.	*Egocentric point of view.* Doesn't consider the interests of others or recognize that they differ from the actor's, doesn't relate two points of view. Actions are considered physically rather than in terms of psychological interests of others. Confusion of authority's perspective with one's own.
Stage 2: Individualism, instrumental purpose and exchange	Following rules only when it is to someone's immediate interest; acting to meet your own interests and needs and letting others do the same. Right is also what's fair, an equal exchange, a deal, an agreement.	To serve your own needs or interests in a world where you have to recognize that other people have their interests too.	*Concrete individualistic perspective.* Aware that everybody has his own interest to pursue and these conflicts, so that right is relative (in the concrete individualistic sense).
Level II. Conventional **Stage 3: Mutual interpersonal expectations, relationships and interpersonal conformity**	Living up to what is expected by people close to you or what people generally expect of people in your role as son, brother, friend, etc. 'Being good' is important and means having good motives, showing concern about others. It also means keeping mutual relationships, such as trust, loyalty, respect and gratitude.	The need to be a good person in your own eyes and those of others. Your caring for others. Belief in the Golden Rule. Desire to maintain rules and authority which support stereotypically good behaviour.	*Perspective of the individual in relationships with other individuals.* Aware of shared expectations which take primacy over individual interests. Relates points of view through the concrete Golden Rule, putting yourself in the other guy's shoes. Does not yet consider generalized system perspective.

Stage	What is right	Reasons for doing right	Social perspective of stage
Stage 4: Social system and conscience	Fulfilling the actual duties to which you have agreed. Laws are to be upheld except in extreme cases where they conflict with other fixed social duties. Right is also contributing to society, the group or institution.	To keep the institution going as a whole, to avoid the breakdown in the system 'if everyone did it', or the imperative of conscience to meet your defined obligations (easily confused with Stage 3 belief in rules and authority).	*Differentiation of societal points of view from interpersonal agreement or motives.* Takes the point of view of the system that defines roles and rules. Considers individual relations in terms of place in the system.
Level III. Post-conventional or principled			
Stage 5: Social contract or utility and individual rights	Being aware that people hold a variety of values and opinions, that most values and rules are relative to your group. These relative rules should usually be upheld, however, in the interest of impartiality and because they are the social contract. Some non-relative values and rights like *life* and *liberty*, however, must be upheld in any society and regardless of majority opinion.	A sense of obligation to law because of your social contract to make and abide by laws for the welfare of all and for the protection of all people's rights. A feeling of contractual commitment, freely entered upon, to family, friendship, trust and work obligation. Concern that laws and duties be based on rational calculation of overall utility, 'the greatest good for the greatest number'.	*Prior-to-society perspective.* Perspective of a rational individual aware of values and rights prior to social attachments and contracts. Integrates perspectives by formal mechanisms of agreements, contract, objective impartiality and due process. Considers moral and legal points of view; recognizes that they sometimes conflict and finds it difficult to integrate them.
Stage 6: Universal ethical principles	Follow self-chosen ethical principles. Particular laws or social agreements are usually valid because they rest on such principles. When laws violate these principles, one acts in accordance with the principle. Principles are universal principles of justice: the equality of human rights and respect for the dignity of human beings as individual persons.	The belief as a rational person in the validity of universal moral principles, and a sense of personal commitment to them.	*Perspective of a moral point of view from which social arrangements derive.* Perspective is that of any rational individual recognizing the nature of morality or the fact that persons are ends in themselves and must be treated as such.

Source Kohlberg (1976)
Reprinted with permission by Thomas Lickona

In this work, he addressed the problems of subjectivity and relativity in the conscience decisions of some stage 6 adolescents. In turn, these practical complications forced him to redefine this stage in terms of the psychological components and philosophical principles which, open a consistent "moral point of view" (Kohlberg *et al*, 1990). By this he meant a "moral method" for arriving at moral judgments. Reviewing former research, he saw this method as a way of reasoning to right judgments that are *prescriptive,* i.e. duty-bound; *reversible,* i.e. applicable equally to one as well as to another in all situations; and *universal,* i.e. consistent "to any life and to anyone's point of view" (Kohlberg, 1973; Kohlberg and Candee, 1984, p.61). Responding to the lack of evidence from his empirical findings regarding the plausibility of such an ideal development of moral reasoning at this level, Kohlberg concluded that "stage 6 may perhaps be viewed as part of a broader level of 'ethical and religious philosophy' supporting moral action" (1984, p.35).

More recent and ongoing studies of Kohlberg's work have been highlighted by one of his faithful colleagues, James Rest, Director of the Center for Ethical Development at the University of Minnesota. For this writer, the late Professor Rest has "laid to rest" not only the usual array of academic critics but has especially resurrected practical and *praxis* innovations of applied moral development theory which is presented in this book. Memory of his mentor and the scholarly eminence of his historic contribution to the literature of moral development. Stressing that the legacy of Kohlberg's work is "still fruitful," Rest critically spent his last years by opening moral development studies with multidisciplinary perspectives expanding his own research into the domains of educational psychology, encompassing the sister disciplines of social and organizational psychology as well as philosophy and moral epistemology (1994, 1999). From these wider research perspectives, Rest concluded that the moral development process was more complex than a compressed six stage incremental progression at any given period of one's life. His research demonstrates that stage analysis is limited to time points and must be understood in the larger temporal framework of life span moral development which was the ultimate historical focus of Kohlberg. His multidisciplinary overview allows him to identify four critical psychological components which *generate the formulation of moral judgments and activate the operation of moral performance.* As an educational psychologist, Rest defines the four psychological components with this multidisciplinary analytical comprehension:

> In addition to being a framework for viewing disparate literatures, the Four Component Model is presented here as a theory of what determines moral behavior. Rather than dividing morality into cognition, affect, and behavior—as many contemporary accounts of moral development do (as if

these were the basic psychological elements)—the Four Component Model starts with the question, "What must we suppose happens psychologically in order for moral behavior to take place?" We wind up with at least four distinct processes.

Component I: Moral Sensitivity. Moral sensitivity is the awareness of how our actions affect other people. It involves being aware of different possible lines of action and how each line of action could affect the parties concerned. It involves imaginatively constructing possible scenarios, and knowing cause-consequence chains of events in the real world. It involves empathy and role-taking skills.

Component II: Moral Judgment. Once the person is aware of possible lines of action and how people would be affected by each line of action. . . , (he/she) judges which line of action is more morally justifiable (which alternative is just or right). . . . Deficiency in Component II comes from overly simplistic ways of justifying choices for moral action. For instance, acts of terrorism justified in terms of revenge for previous wrongs may be shortsighted, counterproductive, and targeted at innocent people.

Component III: Moral Motivation. Component III has to do with the importance given to moral values in competition with other values. Deficiencies in Component III occur when a person is not sufficiently motivated to put moral values higher than other values—when other values such as self-actualization or protecting one's organization replace concern for doing what is right. (For *critical practical* philosophical approaches and more recent scientific findings on moral motivation, see Schroeder et al. 2010, pp. 72-110. See also chapter 6 in this book for the integration of interdisciplinary theories into the discourse of these four components. The reader should note how the MBE paradigm integrates moral development theory with social and economic psychology demonstrating how a socio-economic moral incentive model in corporate ethical socialization training programs can induce moral motivation in managerial hierarchies and throughout a workforce with post-conventional moral performance consistency toward the moral transformation of the corporate culture.)

Component IV: Moral Character . . . involves ego strength, perseverance, backbone, toughness, strength of conviction, and courage. A person may be morally sensitive, may make good moral judgments, and may place high priority on moral values, but if the person wilts under pressure, is easily distracted or discouraged, is a wimp and weak-willed, then moral failure occurs because of deficiency in Component IV (weak character). Psychological toughness and strong character do not guarantee adequacy in any of the other components, but a certain amount of each is necessary to carry out a line of action.

In summary, moral failure can occur because of deficiency in any component. All four components are determinants of moral action. In fact, there are complex interactions among the four components, and it is not supposed that the four represent a temporal order such that a person performs one, then two, then three, then four—rather the four components comprise a *logical* analysis of what it takes to behave morally. (1994, pp. 23-24)

Inasmuch as this book is most complementary to Rest's work, it identifies these four components throughout the text within the reflexive zones of the corporate conscience. Within these zones of reflexivity about corporate behavior in business enterprises and transactions, these four moral components constitute the starting points for building a corporate ethic through the social psychology of morality. (See Cushman, Young and Greene 2010 who explore "a larger constellation of psychological systems that enable the human capacity for moral judgment" p.49). Rest's work provides an interdisciplinary holistic overview for this mission:

> Furthermore, one must recognize that there is much more to the psychology of morality than moral judgment or Kohlbergian moral reasoning. For example, we refer to moral sensitivity, judgment, motivation, and character as four components in producing moral behavior. Different components are the starting points for different approaches to morality (psychoanalytic, social learning, various social psychology approaches; Rest, 1983).

> Although most researchers would agree that there is much diversity of constructs, processes, phenomena, and starting points for the psychology of morality, the greater challenge is to formulate how all these parts fit together.　　(1999, p. 6)

As a social organization psychologist, the author of this book views, with interdisciplinary integrative vision, the emotive, cognitive, deliberative and determinative skills associated with the four components "to formulate how all these different parts fit together." Accordingly, it is the focal purpose of this vision to open a critical practical *(praxis)* "moral point of view" *toward* reconstructive planning for corporate moral reform.

MORAL DEVELOPMENT APPLICATION FOR CORPORATE MORAL REFORM

Opening Moral Educational Theory. Inasmuch as MBE is a social psychological model to support and improve moral action in the workplace, the application of Kohlberg's moral development theory and its redefined scale, with the six stages, will be utilized to advance the workforce through the scale, even to the higher stages. Retaining stage 6 in this use of the scale is not a matter of an idealistic value bias, either in religion or philosophy. It is rather supported by a certain "psychological attractiveness" that bears "empirical significance" from "a verified line of development" (Kung, 1985), which would suggest stage 6 projection as the culmination of empirical progression. The retention of stage 6, moreover, is grounded in a critical sociological perspective from symbolic interaction theory and dialectical conflict theory (Guerrette, 1981), suggesting that the lack of empirical verification of stage 6 may be attributable to social system problems and hegemonic organization contradictions impairing its performance and promoting leadership ineptitude (Heydebrand, 1977; see Chapter 6 below where these problems are discussed in terms of political and hegemonic factors). This means that when organization systems break down and contradict the very purpose of their missions by the moral development ineptitude of their directors or leaders, the organizational and/or social conflicts which ensue often demand not only the replacement of leadership but also anti-structural social movement behavior toward ultimate moral organization development and social reconstruction outcomes (Turner, 1969; Guerrette, 1981). An example of the leadership replacement outcome was seen in the horrendous breakdown of public administration services among federal and local government offices and agencies and some private corporate health care enterprises in the aftermath of the Gulf region hurricanes. Such morally irresponsive ineptitude provoked the dismissal of the Director of FEMA with surging demands for its organizational reconstruction.

Relative to the retention of stage 6, the fact that few can be documented in Kohlberg's research as having attained sixth-stage moral consciousness is not a reflection on the validity of the stage but is likely evidence of the futility of such hegemonic, conventional hierarchical systems in social structures to allow and support fuller moral development of people.[1] Etzioni (1988) alludes to the "Moral Implications" of socio-economic hegemony as a determinant to moral behavioral outcomes: "Preferences are to a significant extent socially formed and hence reflect the society's values, culture, and power structure" (pp. 246 – 247). He also recognizes the natural moral development capacity of people for making right moral choices:

> In short, it seems quite clear that neo-classical economics, and its 'consumer sovereignty' assumptions, in effect reflect a value system and a social, economic, and political structure—that of mature capitalism [Hirsch, 1976] —rather than *human nature* [emphasis added]. To maintain otherwise, leads those who internalize such theory to assume that their buying preferences reveal normatively correct choices, because they made them, presumably on their own, while in effect they are largely culturally bound and conformist (p. 247).

Alvin Gouldner explains the latent sociological forces of power and wealth which bear upon a population's preferences relative to an established moral code conformity in this way:

> Essentially, then, the stability of a moral code within a society having a significant measure of class stratification will depend on the society's

ability to mobilize *approval* or prestige for conformity with its pre-scriptions. This means that approval must be given for things other than wealth or power themselves, and yet things defined as being of great importance. Without this, the poor and the powerless would have only the slimmest chance to achieve the gratifications.

To the extent that a moral code stresses spiritual values and defines them as superior to materialistic values, it therefore reduces the pressure on established wealth and power hierarchies. It diminishes motivation to reform or change by enabling the poor and powerless to achieve gratifications through approval or a sense of rectitude. It thus commits them to value elements they may share with the more fortunate, and thereby contributes to *the maintenance of the given social system* [emphasis added]. (1970, pp. 329-330)

Susan Phillips, Dean of the George Washington University School of Business, complains that business education must address these kinds of deficient moral codes and promote corporate ethical leadership committed to the responsible use of power:

It is essential for business in general—and management education students in particular—to understand the symbiotic relationship between business and society, especially in terms of the moral dimensions of the power placed in the hands of owners and managers. The actions of business leaders affect not only themselves, but customers, employees, investors, suppliers, governments, citizens, and communities. Moreover, abuse of dependence by corporations undermines trust in business and in the markets needed to ensure commercial success. A society where those holding power are neither moral nor accountable creates a state where the strong do what they will and the weak what they must. In short, the power of business must be exercised so that it does not punish or exploit those who are dependent on its largesse or vulnerable to its demands. Business must faithfully exercise its responsibility in the use of power. (2004, p.10)

MBE, as a management education model, awakens students in business schools in particular and employees in the workforce in general, especially in terms of recognizing MBO uses of power and its consequential dependency effects along with its demoralization of trust results, as seen in the aftermath of the Gulf of Mexico oil rigging disaster. The "holding power" of the strong oil companies, who have been operating in the depths of the sea, where the "weak" cannot see or the Congress does not oversee or even the Coast Guard does not under-see, has gripped the nation and especially the working people and small business owners in morally bewildering 1st stage fear. Such socio-economic pulverizing power clearly explains the hegemonic grip that big business and corporate wealth hold on the moral consciousness of the intra-dependent working classes.

Thus, it seems quite evident, from a socio-economic perspective and the latent philosophical assumptions in moral development theory, that this "abuse of dependence by corporations" has undermined the public trust in business and has hegemonically pulverized the ethical consciousness of closed government systems and the moral development capacities of legislators. If hegemony has this kind of a moral under-development grip on the federal government, is it any wonder why the people of the Gulf have lost the virtue of their innocent trust. . . . It would also seem that if few of these law abiding citizens can reach stage 6 in hegemonic conventional systems, moral development capacity might be more fully realized in *reformed* moral structures and *open* organization systems.

Opening Systems for Moral Structural Reform. What is needed to open workplace systems to a fuller realization of moral development capacity are reformed morally interactive structures which foster a clear communication ethic and attitudinal moral cooperation between and among workers and managers (see Chapter 5). The ethos of this open system reform must be grounded in a *communication ethic which prioritizes the treatment of workers by management as persons rather than objects* (Stewart, 1982; Stewart and D'Angelo, 1980). Richard Johannesen describes the social contrast of these two dialectical ways of treating people:

> Persons—each are unique biologically and psychologically, are actors capable of choice among means and ends, are beings whose feelings and emotions are not readily measurable or quantifiable, are of value simply because they are human, and are *reflective* [emphasis added] in the sense of being aware of life's meaning and time-flow. In contrast, when we communicate with others primarily as objects, we see them as essentially similar and interchangeable, as of value only as used to achieve ends, as responding without choice to external stimuli, as measurable and quantifiable in all important respects, and as *unreflective* [emphasis added] and unaware of their "self" or their "place" in human existence (1983, p.54).

How poignantly this analysis describes the corporate contrast of these dialectical ways of treating workers in the closed system structures of MBO as opposed to the open system structures of MBE. Pondering this analysis provokes the disturbing question of how many workers and even line and staff managers are impersonally *used as objects* to achieve the ends of the corporation and even the wealth of MBO-minded executives.

When the collapse of Bear Stearns occurred, it was pathetic to see the thousands of demoralized employees filing out of corporate headquarters *dismissed overnight as objects*, marching toward oblivion with anxieties and fears of a stage 1 future for their careers while the executives were clutching their bonuses safely in the stage 2 privileged purses of their protected accounts. The prudential John Stewart (1980), who originally described these contrasting dichotomies of interpersonal communication, concluded:

> The ethic which emerges from this perspective on persons is grounded in response-ability. Since each communication contact has person-building potential, ethical communication is communication which promotes realization of that potential. Such communication is responsive, attentive to and concretely guided by as much as possible of one's own and the other's humanness, that is, uniqueness, choice-making, more-than-spatiotemporal aspects, and reflexivity.

Finally, inasmuch as opening systems for moral structural reform is radically dependent on such a communication ethic, MBE application of moral development theory is consistent with the approach of the works of Jurgen Habermas (1979, 1984, 1990a, b; see also Forester, 1985 and Johannesen, 1983). Sharing the critical reconstructive perspectives of this approach, the applied MBE model represents an attempt to build the social psychological constructs in organization planning and reform that can facilitate a reflexive humanistic communication ethic in workplace structures and lead to both an individual and a corporate *moral point of view*.

What is so critically important in opening and maintaining this "moral point of view" in the MBO "power elite" interactional associations of the corporate hierarchy is an institutionalized reluctance and an interpersonal resistance to hierarchical imagery and organizational change (see Klein, 1969). An *individual* and *corporate* "moral point of view", however, can be effectively opened and morally perceived through the culture changing strategies of Kurt Lewin's force-field *praxis* theories (1948, 1951) through which a morally developed hierarchical atmosphere of MBE can be reconstructed throughout the interactional social and organizational communication networks of any company with the following programs of moral education in the workplace.

MORAL DEVELOPMENT EDUCATION IN THE WORKPLACE

MBE as a Moral Education Model and a Moral Socialization Reform Plan. MBE, therefore, presents a moral education *model* for corporate executives and managers with a six-step *socialization plan* to recreate a moral climate in the company and to open its systems to organization and governance change. As such, the model is a reconstructive intervention plan to cultivate the corporate conscience and to morally educate the workforce. Although it relies on Kohlberg's development theories and teaching methods for moral education advancement, its *model* is, moreover, a critical practical socialization plan to *activate* a company-wide corporate conscience by developing techniques and skills to advance moral awareness and moral performance throughout the workforce. Accordingly, its overall purpose is to raise an ethical consciousness in the workforce that develops moral reasoning skills towards a "moral point of view" in work performance. In effect, the moral education program aims at motivating moral responsibility and inducing advanced moral performance. The six step *praxis* plan applies actual interactional strategies for *measuring* moral awareness among workers and line management; for *coaching* these groupings to awareness advancement; for *restructuring* organizational climate conduciveness toward moral incentive inducement building; and for *evaluating* personal and organizational moral performance consistency.

The pedagogical dynamic for such moral education intervention is *ethical communication*. Adopting an interactional medium for communicative ethics (Habermas, 1990b), the MBE plan offers an informing socialization design for managers to ethically communicate with workers within the infrastructural moral performance evaluation procedures of work assignments and job performance. This design demonstrates how senior executives, corporate trainers and supervisors are to proceed with the measuring, coaching, restructuring and evaluating interventions toward upgrading moral awareness and performance through the workforce. (It is suggested that the reader consult the graphic design of "Moral Development Socialization" in Exhibit 3:2 to be guided through these intervention paths of the moral education program. This graphic design was constructed to facilitate the coordination and understanding of the intervention sequences as they pertain to different intervening and specific intermediary processes cited in other related workplace research studies. It is also particularly helpful in the *socialization process for tracing the transitional and transformative sequences of moral awareness advancement* among individual workers and collectivity groupings in any company. Without this graphic design, it is relatively easy to lose one's holistic grasp of the program and the simplicity of incremental moral advancement from one stage to the other. With indicators of the graphic learning sequences within the design, it is holistically functional to grasp how other workplace studies, cited therein, and may *generate the operational flow between moral judgments and moral performance* encouraging managers to inspire more progressive, post-conventional advancement through the stages.)

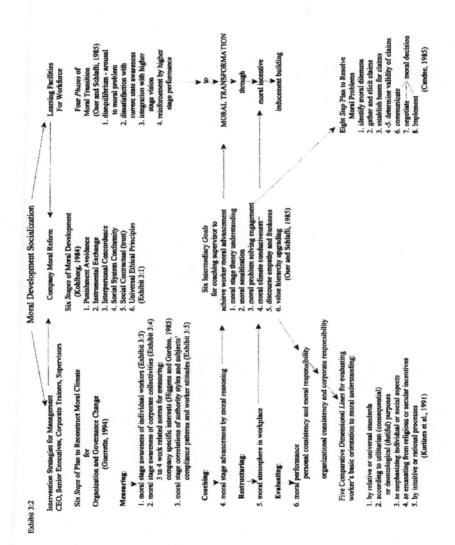

Exhibit 3:2 — Moral Development Socialization

Applying the Graphic Design for Moral Development Socialization. By means of this ethical communication medium and its practical coherent viewing of the Kohlberg scale, the design can help all socialization agents to reconstruct a forum for managers toward their own higher post-conventional performance and "care-taking" roles as moral leaders (Baxter and Rarick, 1987; Harding and Snyder, 1991). In such a reconstructed moral climate, designed to gradually open a "moral point of view" among executives, managers and workers, it is reasonable to conclude that moral performance outcomes will reflect these higher post-conventional stages in more significant numbers at stage 5 and even *beyond* Kohlberg's reluctantly "bonded" hopes of a limited "few," at stage 6.

Similar conclusions were reached by Oser and Schlafli (1985) whose moral education interventions with banking apprentices in Switzerland were posited on the higher expectations of the moral development capacity:

> And it is especially apprentices, whose training is above all geared to production, who should have a right to acquire a higher socio-moral competence and thereby a greater social identity.... What we have striven for, and achieved, must however be judged by the general human goal of education toward social autonomy and competence. This means that higher socio-moral development enables an individual who has the requisite thinking ability to attain the highest universal principles of justice and of society with which he can understand and tackle what he encounters in his dealings with others in his work.
> (p.294)

Moral Education and Moral Transition. The six-step MBE plan for raising moral consciousness in the workforce can be facilitated by applying the intervention strategies of the Oser and Schlafli experiment. Their study stressed that moral learning stimulation by the socializing supervisors requires *defined intervention paths to higher-level development.* These paths need to follow *four phases* of a *subject's moral transition* towards higher development: first, the phase of *disequilibrium,* through which a worker is stimulated to realize that there is a moral problem or conflict; second, the phase of *dissatisfaction* which emanates from the worker's disturbance that his or her solutions are inconsistent or inadequate; third, the phase of *integration* that evolves out of discourse with others, directing previous insights towards new visions for better or more just solutions; and fourth, the *reinforcement* phase, during which the integrated vision is confirmed by practice or performance (see Exhibit 3:2 again). These transitional phases were clearly evident in the aftermath of the Watergate political moral scandal of the Nixon administration when several of President Nixon's White House staff changed their value systems, upgraded the stages of their moral awareness with integrative ethical vision, and pursued more honorable careers in political consulting engagements and even reinforcing their moral transitional paths to higher levels of performance development with religious ministry engagements, such as, John Dean, John Erlichman and Charles Colson.

Moral Education and Intermediary Goals. Along these moral transitional paths to higher development, it is imperative, according to Oser and Schlafli, that the supervising leaders understand the social and interactional processes of moral development transformation in terms of *six intermediary goals*: (1) moral stage theory understanding; (2) moral sensitization; (3) moral problem-solving engagement; (4) moral climate conduciveness; (5) discourse empathy and frankness; and (6) value hierarchy upgrading. To more fully comprehend the understanding of moral stage theory and the intermediary goals of moral transition to higher moral performance, it is helpful to view the wider social and cultural framework of the stages including especially the interactional processes of political power and economic value hierarchies in terms of social class and partisan rivalries. Such value hierarchies have dramatically clashed in the Halls of Congress at the pre-conventional levels of the moral development scale with un-ending debates on health care and gun policy formulations for universal health and safety care coverage for the elderly and children with failure to grasp the ethical significance of the above inter-mediary moral goals of caring for the health of the nation. These morally political and socio-cultural ethical perspectives can open "critical practical" breakthroughs of how individuals and organizational collectivities can (re)develop moral awareness vision with *role-taking* "discourse and empathy" and "moral sensitization" shaped by interactional communication and social behavior at the conventional and post-conventional levels of the Kohlberg scale. With such *reciprocally caring* reconstructive moral vision, legislators and policymakers can be guided by these intermediary goals toward resolving partisan ethically insensitive gridlocks and delivering the ultimate goals of morally responsible legislation for the nation at these highest levels of moral development in these desperate economic and terrifying times.

Some other practical examples of intermediate goal attainment strategies in workplace cultures, which can (re)shape moral awareness framing and moral reasoning staging, occur when higher level conventional and even post conventional workers encounter a hard line authoritarian boss. In the organizational context of these encounters, these higher level workers may become prone to moral reasoning scheming and calculating compliant behavior from fear of reproach. Social organizational contexts such as these demonstrate that workers can and often must adjust their moral reasoning schemes moving in and out of stage differentiation to survive in their respective organization cultures and departmental subcultures. In morally reverse roles where a higher level supervisor is dealing with lower stage level workers, it is helpful in his/her socialization role for advancing worker moral performance to remember that while moral reasoning can be constructed simply and relatively by ethical theories and principles, moral behavior and workplace performance can be significantly obstructed by the social mores of a main line culture and particularly by the respective subcultures in the complicated mix of values in their wider social organization environments.   Thus, in the most challenging role of supervising company moral socialization strategy planning at any level of this complex environment, the intervening executive, manager, supervisor or trainer must be prepared to *role-take* the individual worker or the organizational collectivity. This means that he/she must take the role of the worker, sensitively passing over into the internal and external roles of the worker to learn what he/she is going through and consequently what one may be internally dealing with in the multiple levels of his/her complex personal, social and organizational environment. To put it simply, it is not enough to understand the moral theory of the stages in the internal occupational domain of the workplace; it is equally important to understand the social reality of the worker in the external operational domains of his/her interpersonal world and affiliated transitional organization domains. This kind of managerial role-taking is what delivers moral sensitization to the subordinate worker inducing reciprocal incentives to care for his/her job and to perform for the company. If, for example, a supervisor learns that one of his/her worker's spouse has been diagnosed with cancer and needs time-off to accompany the spouse for radiation treatments, a morally sensitive outreach to this subordinate worker, encouraging him/her to take whatever time is needed, would likely engender the intermediary goal of inducing a higher stage moral incentive to perform more responsibly for the company. Such an outreach needs to be clearly focused on the moral issues involved in any given situation or specific request and not on a social, religious or political menu within the situation or request. If, for instance, the request contained such a menu of controversial moral issues, such as right to life or free choice motives for time-off purposes, the problem-solving engagement requires strict moral focus on the worker's right to time-off according to his/her moral choice. The moral resilience of an understanding and compassionate caring supervisor creates a climate of moral development conduciveness with discourse empathy and frankness for value hierarchy upgrading. The moral developmental purpose of these examples is not to become the worker's analyst or counselor but to be an intermediary coaching guide toward his/her higher stage goal attainment of moral understanding and performance improvement on the job and in the workplace. By clearly understanding their supervisory roles in the moral education process through these intermediary goals, managers enjoy a framework and a direction for their interventions, allowing them to coach workers through their transitional phases towards the ultimate goals of higher moral development transformation. The intervention paths through these transitional phases and the socialization processes of their intermediary goals will open more practically *(praxis)* and reconstructively through the unfolding of the six-step MBE plan.

MORAL DEVELOPMENT SCALING IN THE WORKPLACE

(Learning to implement the scale in the workplace, it is most important for the reader to recognize the editing note between the STEPS and *stages.* The steps refer to managerial implementation planning in Exhibit 3:2, while the stages refer to developmental advancement grading.)

Upgrading Moral Performance. The first STEP of the MBE plan to implement higher workforce moral performance is to demonstrate how a worker's moral awareness can be measured on the Kohlberg scale. (See Exhibit 3:3—aligning the moral stages with worker occupational perspectives in terms of work, work performance and work relationships.) The importance of measuring individual workers' moral awareness is demanded by the research findings of Kohlberg himself that the moral development process is incremental with gradual ethical focus toward the wider expanding moral issues of life. Accordingly, if the purpose of moral development socialization is to advance the moral awareness of the workforce, it is imperative that management educators and corporate trainers, including the CEO, senior executives and line and staff supervisors, learn how to judge the actual stage of a given worker's moral reasoning and performance in order to identify the next incremental stage(s) for moral advancement. To this point, however, it is encouraging to note that this incremental step may be relatively easy for *coaching* most adult workers in the moral advancement process, inasmuch as most adults, as law abiding citizens and socially responsible parents, manifest degrees of higher stage moral awareness and performance in the multiple social interactive contexts of their lives. (For added learning in the area of plotting worker moral awareness, see the work of Stephen Payne [1988, 1991] to review a variety of measuring instruments which can be used for instructional purposes and for planning "critical practical" strategies toward workforce moral advancement and company moral reform.) (See Payne and Pettingill, 1986-87).

Measuring Individuals. In becoming familiar with the Kohlberg scale, executives and managers should recall that the measurement findings Kohlberg and his associates report, namely, that most subjects' scores were at the conventional levels of stages 3 and 4, and that only about 15 percent reached stage 5, with very few reaching stage 6. They should also know that, as this research found its way into corporate culture and management studies, early findings did tend to confirm these averages.

Exhibit 3:3   **Measuring Moral Stage Awareness of Individual Workers**

Stages	Workers occupational perspectives
1. Punishment avoidance	*Egocentric point of view* Considers work as imperative for personal goals and engages in work performance with purely functional efforts to complete orders. Considers authority relations to be avoided for fear of punishment.
2. Instrumental exchange	*Individual expediency perspective* Considers work as instrumental for personal goals and engages in work performance for functionally expedient self-interest gain. Considers work relationships as relative to vested-interest and need exchange.
3. Interpersonal conformity	*Interpersonal concordance perspective* Considers work as expressive for personal accomplishments and engages in work performance with self-affir dependability incentives. Considers work relationships as opportunities for interpersonal caring reciprocities.
4. Social system	*Generalized system perspective* Considers work as good for the company and as functional for the system and engages in work performance as a moral obligation to the company and to society. Considers work relationships with caring reciprocity as integral to operations and as profitable for the company.
5. Social contractual	*Individual rational perspective* (Utilitarian perspective with a social justice point of view) Considers work as beneficial for the company and the overall good of society and engages in work performance with moral consistency as a legal obligation to the company and society. Considers work relationships as egalitarian with a contractual commitment to fairness, according to the principle of social justice for all
6. Universal ethical principles	*Individual universal perspective* (Deontological perspective with a 'moral point of view') Considers work in its own integrity, i.e., in an overall ecology and engages in performance with an ideal valu latency in positive or negative conditions(e.g., working in a company with congruent or contrary values). Considers work relationships in terms of ideal role-taking and caring reciprocities according to the universal ethical principles of justice, equality of human rights and respect for the dignity of persons. Source: Kohlberg

Higgins and Gordon (1985), for example, found that in two worker-owned companies, in Northern and Southern regions of the United States, both management and worker averages in the Northern company were at stage 4. With ownership restructuring and increased democracy, the new president, one board member and two other executives, who stayed on, used stage 4/5 reasoning. All other board members and two executives from the past were at stage 4 and another at stage 3. In the Southern company, they found that the moral reasoning of managers was at stages 3 and 3/4, and the workers were at stages 2/3 to 3/4.

In another more representative sample of seventy-four managers from different sized corporations with thirty-seven interviewed respondents, Weber (1990) found that 86.4 percent were at the conventional level of the scale, with 45.9 percent at stage 3 and 40.5 percent at stage 4. As these scores tended to reflect averages among adults (Blasi, 1980) and other business professionals (Wood *et al.,* 1988), it should also be remembered that, at the time of these studies, the research had only just begun to be applied in the corporate domain. It is quite plausible to expect, however, that newer interdisciplinary theoretical paradigms and management models, such as MBE, may significantly influence future measurements and their methodologies (see below and also Payne and Giacalone, 1990).

Measuring Groups. The work of Rest and Narvarez (1999), to this point, has expanded moral development research in the professional sectors of corporate culture. Rest himself introduced new quantitative instrumentation for measuring moral thinking with the Defining Issues Test (DIT) which can be group-administered and computer scored. The test is designed to evaluate the most important considerations in moral dilemmas and to identify "principled moral thinking" (P-score) in stages 5 and 6 of the Kohlberg scale. This quantitative test has provided more validity and reliability to the research processes of moral development in terms of operationalizing scores for *moral educational advancement interventions* (see ch. 3, p. 46). To its empirical efficacy, when used to measure the moral scoring of different groups, the DIT found that graduate students in business were significantly lower in their P-scores of principled moral thinking than other graduate students whose majors did not specialize in emphasizing moral thinking (see Rest's findings in Exhibit 5:3 of Chapter 5 for the comparative ratings of these P-scores and for some plausible explanation of the business students' lower levels). Furthermore, when used to study accountants in public accounting firms and accounting students in educational institutions, the DIT found that partners in U.S. firms tended to score at the conventional level of moral reasoning (see these findings in Exhibit 5:4 of Chapter 5; for more of the latest research studies on the DIT, see Thoma, 1999, 2006 and 2007). In discussing the research implications of these findings on accounting practitioners and students, accounting scholars Ponemon and Gabhart found that practitioners in Canadian firms have a higher post-conventional reasoning range in serving their clients than those in American firms. They attribute this higher range to the tendency of partners in U.S. firms to be primarily influenced by peer and/or referent group affiliations and thus bear a corresponding tendency to impairment of post-conventional principled moral reasoning. They therefore offer this critical analysis:

> Assuming that the referent group is the accounting firm, adherence to the rules of the profession will result as long as such rules are consistent with the norms of the firm. If, on the other hand, rules of the profession are not consistent with the norms of the firm, then the norms of the firm will take precedence. By virtue of higher DIT *p* scores, partners in Canadian CPA firms may be better able to independently frame ethical judgments in a manner separate and apart from the values and needs of clients, colleagues within the firm, or the accounting firm as a whole. In addition, in comparison to U.S. partners, these individuals may have a greater sensitivity to ethical conflict not well defined by the firm or the profession. . . . Although those at higher ethical reasoning levels would be expected to be better able to resolve difficult ethical conflicts, this research, as well as earlier studies by Ponemon (1990, 1992a) and Shaub (1993), suggest that relatively few of these individuals rise to upper management positions in U.S. firms. If this is true, then CPAs making it to the top of the auditing firm hierarchy may be ill-equipped to deal with and resolve ethical conflicts that require postconventional reasoning. (1994, p. 115)

With a critically speculative and reconstructive viewpoint, Ponemon and Gabhart conclude:

> Thus, as long as firms in the United States are profitable, ethical standards must be acceptable to the public at large. However, this justification is inappropriate. . . . First, if selection-socialization in U.S. firms effectively weeds out those individuals with high ethical reasoning, it will be difficult to attract and retain such employees. That is, many of the best and brightest accounting students will choose alternative career paths. The lack of diversity among those progressing to partnerships will cause the ethical culture or moral atmosphere of U.S. public accounting firms to become stagnant. Perhaps stagnation and an inability to adapt to new cultures will cause accounting firms in the United States to find it increasingly difficult to compete and survive in the global business community. This may not be the case for Canadian firms, where the ethical reasoning of public accounting professionals may not diminish at higher position levels. . .
>
> Furthermore, and perhaps more importantly, the trend of decreasing DIT *p* scores brought about by firm socialization may not extend to audit firms operating in other countries. Hence, the management of U.S. public accounting firms should look to practice offices in other countries (such as

Canada) to model a firm wide moral atmosphere that permits an individual's development to the highest levels of ethical reasoning. (1994, pp.117-118)

These findings are especially important for establishing the introductory claim in this work that the most important target readership for this book is the international consortium of business and management and accounting and auditing schools around the world. Inasmuch as these ethical development scholars have introduced the science of psychology and applied ethics to the business professions of corporate culture, their studies provide an invaluable research base and an interdisciplinary reference resource for these schools of higher education and for companies which already have instituted ethical education in their human resource programing. But for most companies and their CEOs who grasp the "critical practical" connection between corporate responsibility and the corporate conscience and the imminent need for corporate moral reform, *it is imperative to understand that such responsibility and reform must come from within each company's own socialization programming to awaken, educate and activate the corporate conscience.* This corporate ethical mission is one of *internal collective in-search* which can be guided by external consultative research. Companywide socialization thus must be kept simple in the measuring of moral awareness and the nurturing of moral performance. These measuring and nurturing processes in this book are not framed in research methodologies for moral development literature but are focused on practical (*praxis*) pedagogies for corporate moral reform in business, market and government cultures around the world. This is not to dismiss the exemplary references in the literature of moral development, just cited, but actually to draw from Professor Rest's own recommendation of *simplicity* for the *applied* study of the stages:

> I think that the best short description of the six stages is to view them in terms of six conceptions of how to organize cooperation. Accordingly, the key conception that develops over time is people's understanding of how it is possible to organize cooperation. (1994, p. 5)

Incentive Inducement Building and Organizing Co-operation. What better way to measure individual and collective moral awareness and performance in the workplace than by focusing on the key concept of *cooperation* and using inducing incentives for organizing cooperation. For the greater number of companies which do not have an advanced corporate ethical education program, it is thus recommended that the following graphic summation of Rest's description of the six moral development stages in terms of the "concept of cooperation" be reviewed.

These descriptions of the moral stages should help all company socialization agents from CEO to supervisors in daily workplace interaction at all levels of the workforce *to begin over time a "critical practical" understanding of how to organize cooperation to induce personal and collective incentives for moral performance advancement.*

Rest's Table on the Six Stages in the Concept of Cooperation:

Stage 1	The morality of obedience: do what you're told.
Stage 2	The morality of instrumental egoism and simple exchange: Let's make a deal.
Stage 3	The morality of interpersonal concordance: Be considerate, nice, and kind: you'll make friends.
Stage 4	The morality of law and duty to the social order: everyone in society is obligated to and protected by the law.
Stage 5	The morality of consensus-building procedures: You are obligated by the arrangements that are agreed to by due process procedures.
Stage 6	The morality of nonarbitrary social cooperation: Morality is defined by how rational and impartial people would ideally organize cooperation. (1994, p.5)

While this table offers executives, managers and supervisors a morally developmental starting point to construct the conceptual framework for the measuring processes of cooperation in their specific companies, it must be understood that organizing cooperation requires an external modular framework, not just an internal conceptual one. This external framework needs to serve as an organizational bedding for the interactional building processes of cooperation in terms of the construction of workplace democracies and the reconstruction of management hierarchies. Such a reconstructive organizational framework would go a long way in creating a moral atmosphere for the incentive inducement building of collectivity workplace co-operation and the moral development of the workforce (see Chapters 4, 5 and 6).

Organizing Cooperation. A relatively simple way to organize cooperation for the moral development agenda of measuring its awareness and performance in the workplace is to have line managers and supervisors initiate the silent interactional processes of unobtrusively observing and evaluating manifest attitudinal demeanor and behavioral performance of their respective individual subordinates and collectivities in accordance with these six stages of cooperation. This experiment should be kept as simple as possible by focusing the observations and evaluations on *two of the most important moral developmental elements of cooperation,* namely, *worker collaboration and interpersonal role-taking.* In due turn and over a relatively short specified time, records of these observations and evaluations can be particularly helpful in the processes of moral performance evaluation reviewing, the processes of which are more "critically" presented for *praxis* change in Chapters 4 and 5. While external worker collaboration is very easy to determine, internal role-taking interaction among workers is a more latent and rather complicated social psychological process which may be manifest in multiple behavioral symbolic ways, for example, by attitude, demeanor, language, action, etc.). Moreover, and more specifically important to accurately identify the stage development level of role-taking, the observer must determine whether the role-taker in any collaborative work engagement is motivated by his/her *functional* agenda, such as, helping another worker for one's own benefit or self-esteem, which is expressive of third stage moral intentions to look good in the presence of others especially the boss or motivated by his/her *interactional* purpose of *caring* for another worker with a moral sensitivity for his/her performance and for the company good. Role-taking of the latter kind is principled moral performance at the level of stages five and six. This second kind of collaboration is one which can project managers as well as workers very fast to these higher levels of post-conventional moral performance, even without work democracies.

Measuring Collectivities. Inasmuch as collectivities in a company are already constituted as an organizational framework for measuring cooperation, it is important to single out the interdisciplinary approach and methodological advancement of the Higgins and Gordon study which included the *measuring of caring and cooperation* (1985). This work has not only opened new interlinking tracks between moral psychology and sociology, but has created new measuring instruments, similar to those used in complex organization studies, shifting the unit of analysis in corporate ethics from the individual to the organization (see Chapter 1). By measuring, for example, work-related norms in their two sample organizations, in terms of (1) their legitimacy of origin, i.e., authority imposed or collectively decided; (2) their regulative power, i.e., their commitment efficacy and institutional holding power; and (3) their "moral stage" of articulation, i.e., the reasoning level of their social understanding, individual or collective, the study has introduced a method to begin ways of measuring the collective dimensions of the corporate conscience. "The stage of representation of a truly collective norm, therefore, is the shared meaning a norm has for the functioning of the group and not the average stage of the individuals within it" (p. 250). The following Exhibit 3:4 thus traces the "corporate operational perspectives" of companies noting the morally developmental comparisons between the operational norms of production, as grounded in the functional imperatives of Talcott Parsons (1956) and the interactional norms of production, as generated by the ethical imperatives of moral development reasoning.

Exhibit 3:4　　Measuring Moral Stage Awareness of Corporations and Collectivities

Corporate operational perspective

Stages

1. Punishment avoidance

Corporate-centric point of view
Doesn't consider the interests or well-being of workers or consumers or other corporations in its organization-set or domain. Considers production in exacting operational terms for optimal efficiency and in functional economics terms for profit maximization. Stay out of court.

2. Instrumental exchange

Corporate expediency perspective
Considers the interests of workers and others in its organization-set or domain in exchange for the company good or for operational advantages. Considers production in expedient instrumental terms relative to Company goals and purposes and in exchange-economic terms by bargain-dealing calculations.

3. Interpersonal conformity

Corporate relations perspective
Considers the interests of workers and others in its organization-set or domain for company-affirming corporate responsibility. Considers production in conventional operational terms and conforming to normative interorganizational expectations and government regulations and in traditional economic terms of what's profitable for the company is good for workers.

4. Social system

Corporate system perspective
Considers the interests of others in its organization-set relative to the functional social and economic good. Considers corporate relations in terms of the company's place in the socio-economic system. Considers production from functional imperatives of integration and latency of values in terms of 'pattern maintenance' and 'system management'.

5. Social contractual

Corporate rational perspective
Considers the interests of others relative to individual and corporate rights through social justice and legal contractual processes. Considers production contractually with organization consistency in the workforce and corporate responsibility in the marketplace according to the overall good of society from a corporate rational point of view.

6. Universal ethical principles

Corporate universal perspective
Considers the interests of others with respect for the dignity of all persons and beings and especially with care for its human and natural resources. Considers production from the interactional imperatives of integrity and Caring role-taking reciprocity from a corporate and cooperative 'moral point of view'.

These comparisons would suggest the hypothesis that functional imperatives in the hierarchical structures of an authoritarian work climate, especially as operationally managed by the MBO model, would not generate attitudinal dispositions of cooperation in the workforce nor encourage collaborative associations in work performance, leaving workers to fend for themselves in interpersonal instrumental exchange behavior and even impersonal competitive performance behavior at the 2nd stage of the scale. They would, however, suggest that the ethical imperatives in the cooperative associations of an interactional caring and role taking work climate, especially as ethically managed by the MBE model, and would motivate the workforce to the highest levels of moral performance in the 5th and 6th stages of the scale. It is with this comparative hypothesis that executives should approach the *second step* of MBE ethical consciousness development by plotting *their company's moral reasoning and ethical norms on the Kohlberg scale.*

Examples of Moral Stage Awareness. In studying the scale of this Exhibit, notice, in the following descriptions of case studies and reference examples, the gradual moral development of "corporate operational perspectives" of companies as organizational collectivities as driven by the "functional economic imperatives" of the MBO paradigm in the first two stages of the scale. Notice also the *morally advancing descriptions* of companies gradually reconstructing their "dominant operational imperatives" with developing moral awareness toward ethically motivating collaborative associations in accordance with the MBE paradigm and morally reflecting corporate moral performance at the highest stages of the scale.

The Ford Pinto case studied in Chapter one is dramatically indicative of the first two stages. In the *first stage*, the company's moral compass is clearly indicative of a MBO system. In the *second stage*, the company's moral profile develops from a unifocal centric value system to an expediency perspective focused on instrumental operational exchanges as calculated toward achieving the best deals for the "bottom line," in accordance with the computations of cost-benefit analysis. These two stages are clearly indicative of the lowest dealing pre-conventional stages of corporate moral performance a company can bear without distinctly and deliberatively falling into immoral and even criminal behavior.

The *third stage* on the scale defines a pivotal developmental corporate moral relations perspective from which companies begin to turn toward more conventional and pivotal moral considerations of the interests of others in the management of its personnel and in its business and commercial operations within its organization-set as long as these relations are "profitable for the company good." (The organization-set is the interacting network of a company's co-operational organizations within its wider interorganizational business environment (Evan, 1972). A clear example of this stage is in the banking and broker corporate relations industries when executives of the J P Morgan Chase firm worked indefatigably through late night and weekend overtime deliberations with officials of the New York Federal Reserve Board to prevent the imminent bankruptcy of the Bear Stearns Brokerage firm. Jamie Dimon, CEO of J P Morgan Chase, responded with "company-affirming corporate responsibility" sparing the Bear Stearns bankruptcy and a predicted consequent and severe downturn ripple effect on the multinational economy. With moral pivotal turning from a 4th and 5th stage open system climate and a social contractual mixed motivation leniency to a closed system expediency to avoid overnight bankruptcy and to secure promising vested-interest returns, Mr. Dimon bought the company with a stage 2 bargaining calculation for $2 a share "in traditional economic terms of what's profitable for the company is good for the workers." As a consequence of this reverse moral development vested-interest turn from an open system personal climate to a closed system instrumental posture, thousands of Bear Stearns workforce   personnel were factored as dispensable "objects" and lost their jobs and career benefits from these strategic calculations.

The *fourth stage* on the scale is defined by a "corporate system perspective" A critical example of this stage is in the auto industry involving the Ford Motor Company again, along with its competitive rivals and its cooperative partners of the industry's larger complex organization set, namely, the General Motors Corporation, the Chrysler Corporation, the United Auto Workers and the Automotive Industries of their organization sets. With some evidence of CEO humility in their appearance before Congress, the "Big Three" were forced by the fearful events of the economic "bailout" failures to actually plead in hearings before Senate and House committees for their own "bailout" because of their concerns over their own bankruptcy and its widespread unemployment effects through its automotive organization set with a consequent catastrophic collapse throughout the entire national socio-economic system. While some ethical analysts might conclude that the CEOs of these corporations do not warrant this high rating because of their usual 2nd stage expediency performance record and the strong moral repudiation they encountered during the Congressional Hearings for flying into Washington in their private jets and walking into Congress with "tin cups" for a magnanimous "bailout," it must be pointed out that this evaluation is focused on their performance in this critically recessionary period. Their combined testimony at the precipice of a catastrophic economic depression and their emotive sincerity and moral sensitivity for their own workforces and the international populations of their interconnected complex organization sets of all the automobile dealers and automotive parts industries clearly revealed moral judgments at this social system 4th stage rendered in good faith. In conclusion of this analysis, it must be pointed out that in learning to use the moral development scale in the workplace, the evaluator needs to be aware that workers and managers themselves live in multiple sectors of their own private, domestic and interpersonal units of their specific cultural organization sets and are often observed as behaving at different levels and stages of moral performance in accord with the ethnic value systems of these sets. Being aware of these complex factors, the important consideration which the evaluator should focus on is to look for the dominant and morally consistent behavioral stage of the worker. This is the reason for the importance of the corporate evaluator to be open to the learning about the worker's and/or the executive's as well as the collectivities' wider interactional ambits and respective behavioral attitudes and moral performance in these social and corporate spheres (see Exhibit 4:1 in ch. 4). Workers, managers and even CEOs often experience conflicting moral stage inconsistencies in their private, personal lives and in their occupational or professional careers. (These moral inconsistencies are critically examined and reconstructively evaluated in Chapter 10 of this book on the integrative virtues and the degenerative failures of corporate executive leadership.)

The *fifth stage* on the scale deals with a "corporate rational perspective." Morally exemplary rational responses to the AIG "bailout" emergency developments in the global financial and insurance markets were illustrated by the socially responsible and concerned interventions of David Patterson, Governor of the State of New York and Warren Buffet, CEO of the Berkshire Hathaway Corporation. While these interventions were stock buyouts of this largest international insurance provider for global financial markets, they were motivated by MBE socially concerned and corporate responsibility investment incentives both of which significantly helped to induce global public and corporate investor confidence in the AIG Corporation.

Finally, *the sixth stage* of "corporate universal perspectives" is admirably exemplified by the post-conventional moral leadership of Bill Gross, the founder of PIMCO and Co-Chief Investment officer of its firm, the Pacific Investment Management Company. At the beginning of the economic meltdown crisis and the composition of the $700 billion "bailout" plan by Henry Paulson, the Secretary of the Treasury, Mr. Gross offered to direct the Troubled Assets Relief Program (TARP) in order to prevent an international market collapse and to stabilize the economy. His intervention offer was to devote his company's expertise to uncover the "toxic assets" and analyze the subprime mortgages with the expertise of his company's staff: "We have a large and brilliant staff that can analyze and has analyzed subprime mortgages that can help the Treasury out. . . . And I'd even be willing to say that if the Treasury wanted to use our help, it would come, you know, free and clear" (Wyatt, 2008). This offer reflects the interactional ethical imperatives of integrity and the collaborative *caring role-taking generosity* from a MBE "corporate moral point of view."

AUTHORITY STYLES AND MORAL DEVELOPMENT

Individual Management Domain and Workforce Morality. The 3rd STEP of MBE ethical consciousness development is *to communicate to managers how their authority styles might be influencing the compliance postures and attitudinal dispositions of their subjects* (see Exhibit 3:5). This is to suggest that if we conceptualize workplace relationships as rule-governed (Kurtines, 1984), it is plausible to expect the authority-subordinate correlations as aligned in the exhibit. According to Kurtines, this rule-governing approach based on psycho-social role theory:

> ...views moral development as the outcome of an interaction between the individual rule user, follower, or maker and the network of rules that constitutes the essence of morality [Piaget, 1965] and focuses on the attitudes, affects, and cognitions of the individual toward those rules" (p. 306). (According to a simpler read, in common functional workplace settings, "how the boss uses rules to govern the worker.")

The interactional correlations, therefore, between the individual employee and the rule-governing manager can be assessed on this scale according to their respective levels of reasoning about the rules, their authority style enforcement, and their compliant postures and attitudinal effects. For these assessments, it should be noted that the correlations in the exhibit are plausible when one recalls the research of Hertzberg (1968) who found that 60-75 per cent of workers reported that their immediate supervisor was the most stressful aspect of their job. Moreover, it should be remembered that socialization and selection processes for leadership in corporations are not known to have moral criteria as significant for hierarchical promotion, in spite of widespread public opinion among employees that honesty and ethics are very important qualities for management (Emler and Hogan, 1991). The functional rationale for this discrepancy clearly emanates from the dysfunctional management rationale of MBO which prioritizes industrial production efficacy over personnel interaction integrity driven by product output rapidity rather than MBE employee input sensitivity. With such discrepancy between leadership selection significance and employee preference insignificance, it is no small wonder that Emler and Hogan conclude: "Almost all employed adults report that they had to spend some considerable time during the course of their career working for an *intolerable* boss" (p. 86). Neither is it any wonder that Hogan *et al.*, (1988) report exactly the same results of 60%-75% as a base-rate for "flawed leadership" in corporate America, further suggesting the plausibility of the correlations in Exhibit 3:5 (p. 86). Furthermore, it should be noted that the correlations in the exhibit are supported, in part, by Etzioni's (1961/1975) studies of authority-subordinate relations in terms of authority styles and compliance patterns. These studies found that coercive authority types provoke alienative compliance among their subjects; that remunerative (exchange) types evoke calculative compliance; and that normative types receive moral compliance (i.e. customary or obligatory, in accordance with company social mores). While these findings represent correlations through the first three stages of the scale, they would suggest that similar correlations, as those presented in the exhibit, are likely to be found at the remaining stages, along with the worker attitudes plotted for these corresponding stages.

Finally, it should be also noted that the authority styles, compliance patterns and worker attitudes noted for stages 5 and 6 could also be found at stages 3 and 4, respectively. The differences between these categories are that, at the post-conventional levels of 5 and 6, the reasoning prompting the attitudes and behavior would be emanating from principles with universal application, beyond an individual company or manager.

Corporate Power Domains and Organization Morality. The reason why it is so important for executives and managers to pay attention to their authority styles is not just because they may be influencing compliance patterns and attitudinal dispositions among workers but even more critically because the overall authority culture in a company and its organization-set may be actually controlling the way its executives and managers think and the way its workers perform relative to moral issues (Emler and Hogan, 1991). This "critical practical" matter recognizes the complex power domains and cross-cultural influences that bear upon moral reasoning and moral action discrepancy both at individual personal and collective organizational levels (Turiel and Smetana, 1984). For instance, at the individual level, workers, managers and even some executives, like the late Kenneth Lay of Enron, may reflect high-stage moral reasoning and behavior in other cultural domains of personal life and moral activity, but display serious inconsistent discrepancies in lower moral performance in the workplace because of persistent hierarchical conflicts between higher personal performance goals and lower organization production goals of other senior company executives and policy makers (see Gellerman, 1986; see also Chapter 10 below for a case study of the tragic outcome of Kenneth Lay).

Exhibit 3:5　　　**Measuring Correlation of Authority Styles and Subordinate Interaction**

<u>Stages</u>	<u>Authority style</u>	<u>Compliance</u>	<u>Worker attitude</u>
1. Punishment avoidance	Coercive	Alienative	Avoidant
2. Instrumental exchange	Remunerative	Calculative	Vested-interest
3. Interpersonal conformity	Normative	Moral(customary norms)	Conforming
4. Social system	Systemic	Social	Conscientious
5. Social contractual	Rational	Committed	Trustworthy
6. Universal ethical principles	Collegial	Cooperative	Caring

Source: (Etzioni,1961/1975):
　　　　Stages 1,2,3

Source: (Guerrette,1994):
　　　　Stages 4,5,6

Again, at the collective level, a company may be striving to live up to the corporate responsibility norms in production and marketing in its industrial sector; but because of unyielding competition forces and less responsible normative policies or operational strategies among other *power domain* collectivities within this sector, its corporate performance may fall well short of its ethical codes and environmental goals. (See Thomashow, 1995: pp. 118-135 on "Power Flow and Political Identity;" see also Chapter 7 below, where the actual case study of the Love Canal toxic waste disaster in Niagara Falls, NY is critically analyzed to demonstrate how corporate and municipal power domains *morally contaminated* not only the "compliance patterns and attitudinal dispositions" of municipal authorities and corporate executives but also the entire environmental land sites and water-ways of the proposed canal).

Inasmuch as these multidimensional influences can factor into moral performance consistency problems in the workplace, it may help to identify the power domains in the company's organization-set. In organization studies, this interacting network set locates the "organizational domain" of companies (Levine and White, 1972) in the "task environment" of their production sectors, e.g., suppliers, competitors, customers, regulatory groups, etc.(Dill, 1958). Since companies cannot arbitrarily set their own domain, an exchange agreement among their co-operative organizations is generally reached within the organization-set (Thompson, 1967). This agreement is referred to as the "domain consensus" and is critical for the power relationships that form between an organization and its task environment (Braito *et al.*, (1972). These structural organization terms open multiple-level interorganizational units of analysis to "critical practical" understanding of moral development studies in the workplace (see note 2 Chapter 2) in terms of "who is *dominating* whom" (stage 1); "who is *using* whom" with under the table deals (stage 2); "who is *conforming* to whom" in order to look good (stage 3); "who is *cooperating* with whom" to maintain operational patterns and manage system collaboration (stage 4); "who is *reasoning* with whom" to insure corporate responsibility (stage 5); and "who is opening with whom" global perspectives with a "moral point of view" toward universal corporate operational concerns for ethical, environmental and human resources (stage 6). Such analyses would observe the interactional authority style profiles of executives and line managers throughout companies and even within the structural authority lines of their organization-sets. Reconstructively critical observations of these kinds would allow the morally responsible hierarchical power domains to identify lower stage morally unproductive authority styles toward coordinating critical practical approaches to change the "authoritarian bosses" to meet the "humanitarian authority" needs of the system. Such reconstructive organization morality analyses would address moral reasoning and moral performance inconsistency problems for "critical practical" *praxis* change to operationalize moral atmospheric reconstruction of the organization-sets and the moral coordination of their organizational domains (see Turiel and Smetana, 1984; see also ch. 4 where the studies of Argyris, 1993 are critically applied to deal with the structural authority lines of the Church and the organization sets of the Vatican bureaucracy relative to the priest pedophile scandals). More practically, these terms can be useful to executives and managers inasmuch as they identify and open wider interorganizational areas for knowing where to look when they assess authority-style stages and for knowing what to target to convert power relationships into moral collectivities. In sum, this "critical practical understanding" suggests that authority-style adjustments at the lower pre-conventional levels of the scale may not be enough to reconcile moral reasoning and performance inconsistencies in a company, but that the political and economic power structures of its corporate culture and its organization domain may themselves require extensive MBE reform to reach the higher levels of the scale to achieve corporate moral reform. If improved moral performance is to be an attainable and permanent goal for any company, executives must be prepared to identify performance inconsistencies throughout its corporate cultural power domains and use MBE socialization strategies and moral development programing to coordinate moral reasoning among all levels of its organization-set. One of the most tragic examples of moral reasoning and moral performance inconsistencies in the modern history of corporate culture power domains lies within the deep recess "wells" of the corporate conscience of British Petroleum. The dysfunctional split of its historical and irrational operational immoral performance as BP will be more critically and morally analyzed in Chapters 4 and 8. At this preliminary analytical point, it is depressively sufficient to conclude that the company's moral reasoning in the workplace was deeply submerged within the immoral "riggings" of its "split corporate personality" in the marketplace.

MORAL REASONING IN THE WORKPLACE

The *fourth* STEP *of* MBE moral consciousness development is to train managers how to use the Kohlberg scale for advancing a worker's moral performance through *moral reasoning.* While advanced moral consciousness does not necessarily translate into higher moral action, it can serve as a reasonable predictor of this desired outcome and help managers to attain the attractive goals of superior moral performance.

Moral Reasoning and Moral Action. Kohlberg himself recognized the relationship between moral awareness and moral behavior through the teaching of virtue. His understanding of virtue was immune to the cultural problems of moral relativism. He appears to have understood virtue as the *courage* (from the Latin, *virtus)* emanating *from a knowledge conviction* which engenders effective incentives for action. He simply explained the reasoning-action morality linkage this way: "... true knowledge, knowledge of principles of justice does predict virtuous action" (1971, p. 305). In later empirical studies, he confirmed his predictive understanding by testing for ego control factors, analyzing IQ and attention variables as moral reasoning determinants which resist cheating. He suggested that "... *ego strength* (emphasis added) helps to carry out whatever decisions are derived from one's moral outlook, whether it is high or low" (see also Blasi, 1980, p. 25). This finding would appear to relate the moral reason-moral action linkage to the associated virtues of moral consistency and personal integrity, which generate the strength "... to act in ways that are consistent with one's normal insights" (Blasi, 1980, pp. 40-41). As seen above (p. 61), his associate, James Rest, identified this personal strength as "moral character" and as a principal component of moral action, defining its associated virtues in more descriptive terms: "(Moral character) involves ego strength, perseverance, backbone, toughness, strength of conviction, and courage" (1994, p. 24).

It is relevant to note that these associated virtues are particularly efficacious for moral character formation and stamina in workplace environments and in executive and management deliberations, particularly within stressfully demanding occupational and professional situations. Finally, Kohlberg found that moral reasoning and moral action consistency can be cognitively traced through knowledge of what is right to knowledge of what is responsible. His testing here revealed that moral consistency increased not only at the higher stages of moral reasoning but even at lower stages with subjects who tended to have an aptitude for autonomous judgments. This finding led him to "... give credibility to the notion that moral action is responsible choice guided by intuitions of moral values not dependent on stage sophistication." (Kohlberg and Candee, 1984, p. 63)

In later case-study work, Haste (1990) not only gives credibility to this notion but confirms its plausibility through a wider level of developmental analysis. She expands insight into the moral reasoning-moral action continuum by tracing an affective linkage through moral responsibility and moral commitment. She identifies three paths to moral commitment: *cognitive, affective* and *associative*, the latter two of which converge into generating an experiential response to moral engagement. The *cognitive* path opens a commitment consciousness through the understanding of moral issues in a social justice reference; the *affective* path leads to a commitment disposition from experiencing these issues in a political context; and the *associative* path derives from an historical background of exposure associations with other committed role models in a politically aware environment. Haste suggests that moral commitment can open from any of these three paths. Her explanations thus allow for responsibility as emanating *from an affective conviction* integrated with some degree of moral issue awareness, either suddenly by a conversional experience or gradually *by associative exposure*, compelling a moral agent to a moral action.

These moral commitment pathways from gradual cognitive moral awareness to sudden moral responsibility compulsion to political moral action were affectively demonstrated by the *courageous* Sherron Watkins, as she testified before Congress about her *historical associative* discovery of the Enron hierarchical corruption. It is revealing to trace her moral commitment pathways to moral engagement whistle-blowing, according to Haste's analysis, in the following account of her associative exposure to the "rogue models" of the Enron hierarchy which appeared in The Guardian (2003). This kind of associative exposure often generates a morally repelling disposition against corporate immoral behavior inspiring the *virtuous* ethical executive with "moral courage" and *ego strength* for *conversional* moral action (see Kidder, 2005):

> The Guardian:
> The woman who made global headlines for telling her boss, Ken Lay, that Enron was mired in accounting fraud is now, after more than a year in the media spotlight, happy to talk about her life at the firm. 'The money was good, the bonuses and the stock options. And the trips were always top notch,' she says.
>
> *(Gradual associative exposure):*
> Her company, the world's biggest energy trader, often won awards for innovation. Gradually it became clear that some of its accounting practices were more than innovative.
>
> In December 2001, Enron filed the biggest US bankruptcy case to date. Thousands of workers lost their jobs and their pensions invested in its shares, and other investors lost billions of dollars.
>
> Back in 1996, Watkins was working with Andrew Fastow, the chief financial officer now charged with fraud, when she began to witness aggressive accounting. "I was starting to see Andy Fastow cross the line," she says, claiming he asked her to lie to one of Enron's partners about an investment. "It should have been a huge warning flag," she admits. It merely prompted her to move to a different part of the empire, Enron International, where she later became a vice-president.
>
> All this time, Harvard graduate Jeffrey Skilling had been growing in influence at Enron, reinventing what it did for a living to include power trading, selling retail electricity and even the provision of broadband internet services. In 2001, he became chief executive officer. "Jeff Skilling was incredibly charismatic," she explains, "but very, very

intimidating. He can really cut people off at the knees. You were certain he was just the brightest guy around, but in hindsight I really feel we were somewhat like cult followers."

By mid-2001, Watkins was working with Fastow again. This time she stumbled across evidence of massive fraud.

(Cognitive understanding of moral issues):
She was looking at an Excel spreadsheet listing 200 assets which Enron wanted to sell to raise cash. Against half a dozen, she saw the name Raptor. These were complex, off the books partnerships used to hedge assets. "I was seeing hundreds of millions of dollars in the loss column," she recalls. "I mean you couldn't do the math, it didn't work."

(Experiencing the moral issues):
She questioned other staff, was shown stupefyingly complex charts of boxes and arrows, and at last the penny dropped. She realized these Raptor structures were empty, shell companies capitalized with nothing but a promise of Enron stock. They were hiding debt.

(With an affective conviction):
"When I saw that I just knew this was accounting fraud. It's outrageous. I thought, I have got to get out of here. I can't work for a company that is doing this. I'm gonna work up the guts, if I can, to confront Jeffrey Skilling on my last day." But soon after, Skilling resigned unexpectedly, for what he said were personal reasons. "He beat me out the door," she now says.

(For compelling moral action):
So Watkins sent an anonymous memo to the man who'd taken the helm, the founder and chairman, Kenneth Lay. Touchingly, she showed it to her mother first, who corrected it. The memo details her eerily prescient fears that Enron might "implode in a wave of accounting scandals." Soon after, she met Lay to convey her fears face to face. She showed him comments from a colleague close to the Raptor transactions, who'd said: "I know it would be devastating for all of us, but sometimes I wish we would get caught, we're such a crooked company." Watkins pauses. "When Ken Lay read that, he actually winced, you know, a crooked company, how could that possibly be?"

Enron began an inquiry, but it failed to use independent investigators and her claims were largely dismissed. Months later, it revealed the black hole in its earnings, and confidence in the company evaporated. "My warnings came too little, too late to save Enron."

Some former colleagues take a dim view of her actions, arguing she raised concerns only when the ship was going down, and they point out that she sold Enron's stock options worth $17,000 shortly after talking to Ken Lay. That's minimal compared to sell-offs by other executives. Others claim that what she did doesn't even qualify as true whistle blowing, because

she never took her concerns outside the company, to the financial
regulator or a third party.

Why not? She clears her throat at what's obviously a recurring question.
"When a company cooks the books, it rarely has a chance of surviving, but
to do that it has to come clean itself, to admit its problems and re-state its
financials. I felt here was Enron's chance to come clean."

Soon after Enron's bankruptcy, her part in its drama suddenly came to
light. In January 2002, a Congressional committee published her memo to
Ken Lay. Overnight, massed ranks of TV and press reporters beat a path to
her door in Houston. "It was mind-boggling," she recalls, "but in some
respects it was vindication that I had been right." . . . (Curwen, 2003,
adapted).

Socialization Training and Experiential Leadership. From the lessons
learned in this Enron case study testimony of the authority structure moral
implosion in the company, the *fifth* STEP of the MBE socialization plan
needs to address the mandate of moral leadership managing as a symbolic
interactional ethical imperative incumbent on corporate executive
hierarchies to serve in their respective companies as ethically committed
role models for their workforces to experience 5th and 6th stage post
conventional moral leadership. The moral reasoning training challenge,
therefore, is not only open to communication structures with workers about
understanding the corporation's value-system and normative policies, but
also to create an organization climate that allows workers *to experience the
moral commitment of its managers to company values and norms.* In this
case study, the managerial communication structures with workers was not
open nor was there an understanding about the company's value system and
normative policies among senior level managers themselves. As a result of
this gravely systemic moral inconsistency problem, the workers certainly
did not experience the moral commitment of management and were
devastated in whatever career advancement aspirations they held and in
whatever retirement plans they lost through the company bankruptcy.
Workers need to *experience* the moral commitment of its managers to
company values and norms. They need to perceive *leadership socialization*
as a pedagogical imperative in the moral reasoning training challenge.
Ethical training, therefore, must start at the highest levels of *morally
involved* executives and managers and not simply be delegated to external
ethics advisors or internal line managers (see Chapter 9). Morally involved
executives and managers open the interactional pathways of supervising
responsibility to authentic moral commitment toward insuring not only the
learning linkage between moral reasoning and moral action but the moral
performance consistency of the company ethic. In sum, interactional
(*associative*) exposure to morally thinking (*cognitive*) executives and
managers creates an experiential (*affective*) and convincing "practical

understanding" inducement to higher stage moral action. (On inducement-incentive-building, see Chapter 6).

Moral Reasoning and Learning Structure. Inasmuch as Kohlberg left a body of research on the communication structures of moral reasoning, it might be helpful for executives and managers to draw from this legacy to plan an efficient learning structure conducive for moral development in the workplace. The value of this legacy is that it demonstrates how to provide a structured learning context for interactive ethical discourse as a forum for moral reasoning. The studies show that moral development awareness occurs over relatively long periods of time in the interactional processes of *role-taking*[2] and *within communal structures* of *shared learning* through moral dilemma resolution. Kohlberg found that when his subjects were exposed to one another in meetings, classrooms or learning groups, they engaged in open discussions, learned the viewpoints of others by taking their roles and were stimulated to higher moral reasoning manifested by others. By using the participatory structures of Socratic discourse in such peer groupings, he evoked reasoning differentiation through discussions of hypothetical moral dilemmas, allowing participants' comparisons of moral judgments between two adjacent stages. He found that when students perceived the differences of moral judgment at one stage higher than their own, they became dissatisfied with their own perceptions, integrated their learning into their own moral reasoning and tended to advance to that next higher stage. He summed up his findings this way:

> Knowledge of the good is always within but needs to be drawn out... we have found that children and adolescents prefer the highest level of thought they can comprehend. Children comprehend all lower stages than their own, often comprehend the stage one higher, and occasionally two stages higher, although they cannot actively express these higher stages of thought. If they comprehend the stage one higher than their own, they tend to prefer it to their own. This is basic to moral leadership in our society (1971, p. 307).

From these findings it would indeed be expedient to explore incentive inducing methods in the workplace which engage the comprehension of adult workers who, like children, can easily be inspired by moral actions of managers and executives at stages higher than their own.

MORAL LEADERSHIP IN THE WORKPLACE

Management Training, Executive Learning and Moral Leadership Advancement. This research on moral reasoning offers executives and managers a structured method for moral leadership in their companies. Through executive development and management-training seminars at different hierarchical levels of a company, MBE programing can be initiated with an introduction to moral development theory and practice. In the initial stages of the programing, management trainers may need more consultation resources for planning and implementing these moral reasoning learning methods, as explained here. But, subsequently, by their familiarity with the scale and their facility with Kohlberg's Socratic methods of discourse, they could easily disseminate the learning through the company, even to the levels of engaging workers in peer groups with their line managers, discussing ethical workplace dilemmas and moral performance problems (Payne, 1991).[3]

This kind of programing was utilized by a refrigeration contractors company in the Northeast for whom the author served as management consultant. Through periodic executive development seminars, this small family-owned business firm with a management hierarchy of three brothers became familiar with moral development theory in a practical experimental manner by their personal readings of the Kohlberg scale, as illustrated in Exhibit 3:3, and their company level assessments from Exhibit 3:4. Their interests grew rapidly by their authority-style reflections in Exhibit 3:5, as they faced the actual organizational moral dilemmas of internal executive peer rivalry, which was demoralizing the workforce. They discussed their interpersonal rivalries with frankness and admitted that their 2nd stage instrumental authority posturing, relative to family ownership and fraternal seniority, was causing significant degrees of calculative compliance and scheming behavior among the workforce and even with their line managers. They also agreed that their own divisive and vested-interest exchanges were causing inter-departmental allegiance rivalries and promoting self-interested shirking behavior on the part of service crew individuals. Continuing these seminars, weekly over several months, the brothers argued through these organization moral dilemmas, analyzing and comparing both management and workforce performance levels according to the Kohlberg scale. Ultimately, through this short period of executive moral learning, they perceived that their individual assertive "I"'s were impairing their company's performance at the pre-conventional levels of instrumental morality. Confronted with the reflexivity of their shared interest in the corporate reflexive "Us" of their family company, the executive brothers began to perceive the higher stage attractions of rational and collegial authority styles and pulled together as a team, inviting their line managers into the seminars. Like the children cited above who tended to be morally inspired by the next higher stages of their own behavior, these family brothers were inspired to advance the higher stage performance as a family team. The sharing of a basic and simple theoretical orientation to moral development theory with them in the collegiality of team interactional learning engaged the team's reasoning on the relevant workforce problems at actual job sites, including abuse of company privileges and the labor cost of unapplied time. Assessing their own authority styles and matching these with the compliance patterns and attitudes of their workers in their respective departments, the line managers and the executive brothers themselves reasoned to their own management performance dissatisfaction. As a result, the line managers reflected a certain motivation responsibility for having been invited into collective authority deliberations with the fraternal ownership, which, in turn, appeared to motivate the executive brothers to assume their own collegial authority-style adjustments while inducing their incentives for the fraternal moral leadership advancement of their family owned company.

By so utilizing Kohlberg's scale and integrating his moral reasoning methods with their actual experiences, the executives *cognitively awakened* to "courageous convictions" for personal change and to an *affective engagement* for restructuring the moral atmosphere of their small company. From their *associative exposure* to the moral commitment of their family owner superiors, the line managers, in turn, *affectively assumed* their own individual moral responsibility for changing their departmental climates and resolving the divisive allegiances and abuses of their subordinates. In conclusion, this case study demonstrates the operational strategies and moral pedagogies for advancing workers and even executives to the next higher stages by helping them to recognize the moral attraction of these stages in comparison with the disparaging dissatisfaction of their current moral stage.[4]

Ethical Image Projection vs. Moral Learning Protection. Upgrading moral leadership reasoning of this kind which engages executives, line managers and workers in ongoing participatory learning structures can be much more effective in raising ethical consciousness and moral commitment than costly episodic consulting programs. These latter programs are usually framed to address ethical problems, especially those that are exposed in the aftermath of public, media-ridden scandals. The company motivation, in these crises-driven eruptions, is often forced into frantic corporate face-saving tactics to restore an already ruined company image. Recall, for example, how the Union Carbide Corporation responded to the Bhopal environmental disaster in India in 1984 with a pre-conventional moral development attempt to project a corporate ethical image (see Guerrette, 1986). While media conferences of these MBO types are responsively apologetic, their media projections are usually irresponsively short on compensatory needs for a reconstructive corporate ethic. Such approaches are limited, hollow and quite ineffective in forming an enduring and morally sensitive ethical consciousness. Compare, for example, the long-term MBE multiple step and morally structured learning plan in this chapter to the short term scandal-solving approach of a Pentagon defense contractor, whose moral reasoning conclusion, after costly workshop consultations with a prestigious ethical institute, was to establish an ethical ombudsman office within the company to investigate unethical production complaints. The comparison reveals a significant difference in the ways that corporate and even government cultures deal with ethical scandals. A common trend in these cultures is to approach these scandals with defensively prescriptive strategies by engaging third party consulting and public relations firms to investigate the problems and to protect the company image. The failure here is simple to describe:

> Ethics do not happen by edicts. They are not prescriptions of authorities imposed on subordinates. Neither are they commodities that can be supplied on demand. With competitive strategies for contract procurements, some defense companies have speedily adopted the demanded regulations of their trade association by programing ethics into management training. In accordant consumer fashion, they have acquired curricular packages in business ethics from corporate vendors as an expedient tactic toward compliance, while conveniently continuing business as usual. But ethics cannot be bought. They are learned and the learning is radically dependent upon long term socialization and moral development process. (Guerrette, 1988: pp. 373-374)

MBE is such an internally managed socialization program for learning and moral development process to upgrade an externally managed ethical *praxis* performance. Its paradigmatic corporate cultural ethos is not just to prevent scandals and protect images but to raise ethical consciousness through moral reasoning development and to foster *moral commitment through courageous and affective convictions.* In short, it is a program that is designed to create moral education for preventing immoral action and promoting moral responsibility, not an ethical office for unethical liability.

CONTEMPORARY MORAL PROBLEMS AND INTERVENTION METHODOLOGIES

Moral Education and Moral Problems. While preventive moral education may be an attractive reason for avoiding unethical scandals, its ethical consciousness-raising benefits are not always sufficient to deal with moral problems in the workplace. These actual problems can develop in any company or industry over complicated moral issues that require practical procedures for analysis and resolution. Candee (1985) has developed systematic intervention methodologies for addressing and resolving these kinds of company internal moral problems. Though his work was conducted in the healthcare sector and addressed moral problems in medical ethics confronted by practicing professionals, his analytical methods and measuring instruments can be applied to moral problems in any workplace situation. (Note that the final 6th STEP of the *Socialization Plan* is presented in the next Chapter on "Moral Performance Evaluation" methodologies. Also note that the following 8 step intervention plan has been developed by Daniel Candee as a practical specific methodology for health care workers, not to be confused with Kohlberg's socialization plan.)

Candee's *intervention methodologies* offer an eight-step plan that guides health care workers through a moral reasoning process for analyzing a workplace problem and clarifying the choices for its moral resolution (see graphic design above on Moral Development Socialization, Exhibit 3:2). The *first step* is to identify the moral dilemma. Since not every workplace problem is a moral one in the strict sense of justice and rights and of fairness and integrity (honesty, consistency, equality, reciprocity, etc.) and since moral problems in this strict sense have multiple non-moral dimensions within their dilemmas, it is necessary to screen problems for their moral issues. For example, in a case study of a private Health Care Agency, a management order for a non-ambulatory patient transfer to a commode strictly insisted that the transfer be conducted by means of a mechanical lift. After several mechanical transfers, the patient developed topical skin bruises from the straps of the mechanical lift which were worsening with continued usage. When the primary family care giver insisted on terminating the mechanical transfer procedure for his mother, an ensuing disagreement discourse with the assigned home health care providers clearly revealed that the rigidity of the Agency regulations, which they were explaining, was emanating from fears of being sued for malpractice injury, if regulations were not followed. As the son persisted with requests that the Agency providers respect the *moral issues* of his complaints, it became apparent that the Agency itself manifested a "litigation paranoia" emanating from their policy restraints. But when the son identified the possibility of such a legal problem as covert and caused by latent paranoid fears emanating from the task environment of the Agency's organization-set, he managed to encourage the Nursing Supervisor from the Agency to reach a *moral* compromise by utilizing *caring* manual transfer procedures with the interpersonal nursing assignment of two personal care lifting assistants. This *praxis* plan identified the moral dilemma with practical humanistic strategy of a manual humanistic transfer and avoided a mechanistic safety program which was impractical for the particular needs of the bruised patient.

The *second step* is to gather and elicit claims. This is done by defining a moral claim in terms of what a claimant wants or feels entitled to. This step was clearly defined by the family care-giver in the above cited example.

The *third step* is to establish *bases* for the claims. This is accomplished by evaluating the rights or entitlements in terms of the moral language that establishes a moral argument. An example of this comparative evaluative process in medical ethics and corporate health care delivery is in the moral choice entitlements of the abortion rights and right to life groups as they are framed in political and economic terms and multi-cultural persuasions rather than "moral language" *based* on "moral arguments" addressing universal ethical principles. These universal principles constitute the *bases* for moral argumentation, as presented and defined in all the measuring scales of this chapter. Nearly all of the controversy and language of these groups is perceived and expressed in the political and legal terminology of social movement sub-cultures and civil and even Supreme Court main-line cultures. While the right to life groups have a strong moral case because of their moral *ontological* language, as it relates to the *being* of the unborn, they fail to perceive the morally theological *base* of the argument that God is "pro-choice" by the convincing evidence from philosophical theodicy[5] that human beings were created by Him with *free will*. Pro-choice is now, however, *hard-core* political language and whatever is left of the moral language signifies the indiscriminate elimination of *being*, even if its supporters do not accept the "being" as yet *human.* . . While the free choice implementation may not be actually immoral, if it is simply being, the moral judgment to proceed with the actual abortion would have to be reconciled with the particular circumstances of the woman's life, for example, as to whether this moral judgment is an *instrumental decision* at the second stage of the moral development scale relative to her career goals or whether the judgment is a *principled altruistic decision* at the fifth and sixth stages of the scale based on her total health care needs to remain as a mentally and physically effective maternal provider for the child. The ethical argument evoking this moral conclusion is specifically addressed to the moral problems encountered by a *mother* who has been a victim of an unwanted and enforced pregnancy from rape. "Free will" in cases of this kind is always moral language and it signifies the inalienable right to one's own life from the ethical principle of self-determination, as it relates to the already born of *her* wanted family and the totality of *their* needs. This ethical conclusion is supported by the principles of the Second Vatican Council of the Roman Catholic Church and its ecumenical "Declaration on Religious Freedom." (Murray, 1966).

The *fourth and fifth steps* are to determine the *validity* of the claim. The criteria for these assessments are either to determine utilities or overall consequences of the claims (utilitarianism) or to determine entities as *beings*, i.e., people, collectivities, natural and environmental resources in their overall ecologies for *becoming* (deontological-see Guerrette, 1988; see also Chapter 8 for a discussion of the "commonwealth of beings" and the "ecologies of becoming"). Examples of *validity claim* determination are the arguments of the stem cell research and the human cloning advocates.[6]

It might be helpful to these advocates to evaluate the philosophical differences between the utilitarian "moral point of view" and the deontological "moral point of view." Extrapolating from political, cultural and even theological argumentation, the plotting difference on the Kohlberg scale clearly demonstrates that the deontological argument represents the higher "moral point of view" with its *value orientation* focused on (1) universal ethical principles, (2) respect for being and human life and (3) devotion to caring reciprocities. These moral points of views open analytical affinity with the studies of William Galston where "believers" can begin to compare language of moral claims based on these principles. For example, notice the affinity of Galston's use of propositional bases to defend Jewish theological and philosophical positions of cloning and stem cell research:

> The three propositions I have discussed—human agency as the image of divine creation, the imperatives of curing disease and of saving life, and the moral status of the pre-embryo as less than fully human—lead Jewish Orthodoxy to endorse a range of stem-cell research that involves therapeutic cloning. As Rabbi Tendler puts it, "In stem-cell research and therapy, the moral obligation to save human life [is] the paramount ethical principle in biblical law," one that "supersedes" concerns for the pre-embryo. And even when materials intended for life-saving therapy are drawn from acts that Jewish law forbids, including many abortions, the Jewish tradition does not forbid their use: "An illicit act does not necessarily result in a prohibition to use the product of that act" (2005 p. 16).

This moral argumentation for cloning is based on the maximization of the "common utilitarian good." While this post-conventional moral development base constitutes valid philosophical thinking for critical therapeutic medical practice, the following steps are morally reconstructive for positing a post-conventional maximization of the *personal ontological good,* which has been a primary focus of the Catholic tradition. These resolution steps, as critically analyzed here from the persuasive insights of Jewish Biblical theology and *moral development affinity*, can open wider morally reconstructive frameworks for moral education in the corporate domains of health delivery workplaces.

The *Sixth, Seventh and Eighth Steps* are the problem resolution steps, involving *communicating, negotiating* and *implementing* the moral decision. These systematic steps provide an inter-religious and interdisciplinary framework within which executives, managers and even religious scholars along with professionals in medical, legal, technological and scientific workplaces, can open a *deliberative, ecumenical and ethical forum* for communicative ethics and collaborative moral reasoning and moral problem resolution (see Bowen and Power, 1993). Continuing with the stem cell research example, problem resolution is quite plausible were the advocates of this position to argue, in a collaborative moral reasoning climate, that though their utilitarian moral point of view is focused on the greatest therapeutic benefits for the common good of humankind, the focus is at the same time impressively deontological motivated by the 6th stage *moral reciprocities* of the cells of one "caring" for the cells of others precisely because of one's *respect for being and human life*. (On these morally sensitive issues, see "why Christians should support stem-cell research:" Peters, Lebacqz and Bennett, 2010; see also O'Brien 2010 and more convincingly, in Meredith Vieira's *A Leap of Faith*, NBC TV 6/27/2014,   and her narrative report on MBE surgical innovation with *praxis* stem cell research in health *caring* regenerative medicine).[7] This is not to simplify intricately complex moral problems within pluralistic cultures but to *ratify the call for a "global ethic"* (Kung, 1991) and to identify "universal ethical norms" (Kung, 2004, p. 8; see also note 3 in Chapter 1) through a deontological moral vision focused on a respect for "*being* and *becoming*."

MORAL ATMOSPHERE IN THE WORKPLACE

Reconstructive change in moral atmosphere does not always follow so easily from moral reasoning and its structured learning methods. Moral reasoning, with *courageous and affective* convictions, may induce *moral commitment to moral action*; but these paths to organization change do not in themselves create moral atmosphere. What is needed to create a moral atmosphere in the workplace, therefore, is first and foremost a moral climate in the interactional associations of the organization. As developed in this chapter, the fundamental sociological architecture for the organizational reconstruction of this climate is to implement MBE and its moral development socialization program throughout the workforce, as designed in Exhibit 3:2 above. Such MBE interactional associations constitute the operational delivery system for the creation of a morally conducive atmosphere in the workplace.

Moral Climate and School-Place Democracies. Again, Kohlberg's research has so much to offer executives and managers for such a reconstructive mandate. He realized that for individual moral development to be an attainable goal in education, a conducive moral atmosphere would be required in schools which encompassed systematic organization change and governance reconstruction. With his colleagues, he thus developed the "just community" model as a cluster design in participatory democracy (Power, 1988). Through this democratic approach to organization management, he created a conducive moral atmosphere in selected secondary school environments which engaged students with equal voice in organization deliberations and rule-making regulations. Accordingly, his experiments allowed students to experience meaningful justice in communal structures which naturally evoked their emotional sensitivities to role-taking interaction (Levine, 1976). Through active participation in assemblies and meetings and classroom discussions, students were led to take the role of the other, feeling the anxieties of another classmate and understanding the dilemmas of the principal or teacher. As these communal experiences awakened their consciousness to moral reasoning in group life situations, moral responsibility opened into *collective awareness*, establishing an organizational climate for individual and *collective reciprocity.*[8] As one of Kohlberg's colleagues described: "This shared consciousness represents the authority of the group and is the real agency of moralization" (Power, 1988, p. 203). Thus, a "just community" approach to MBE moral consciousness development, as a participatory democratic model for *sharing moral responsibilities* as well as moral meanings, can open a more comprehensive, interactional strategy for conducing organizational reframing in companies and moral atmosphere reforming in the workplace.

Moral Climate in Workplace Democracies. A similar democratic approach to moral atmosphere reform from the Kohlberg research legacy can be derived from the workplace democracy studies of his colleagues (see Higgins and Gordon, 1985). This research has opened a socio-moral perspective on the workplace and has developed methods to measure the moral levels of a work climate. By analyzing the normative culture of a company and comparing its work-related norms to the individual values of its workers, these studies can assess the various role-taking opportunities of the workers in the organization and within its subgroups. They can also determine the motivational dispositions of workers by comparing their moral judgment stages to the moral reasoning stages of the norms. *Opening these analytical dimensions into workplace operations, the studies can predict organizational efficiency and corporate stability.* In two worker-owned companies studied, Higgins and Gordon found that when the norm stages of the companies were lower than or congruent to the worker stages, the work climate was not conducive to the moral development of the workers. They therefore concluded:

> Theoretically, a company and workforce that are able to create norms understood at a stage higher than the mean individual stage should create a work climate that is seen as challenging and exciting and, thus, would lead to the moral development of individuals within it [p. 265].

They also found that when organizational diversity became manifest through value-subgrouping exclusivities, role-taking opportunities among workers diminished and polarized the organizational climate. They suggest that role-taking impairment is a sign of a low moral climate and a predictor of organization instability. These studies suggest that organizational diversities of pre-conventional moralities, such as, the sequestration policies and gun-control lobbies encumbering the political parties and Congressional caucuses in Washington are polarizing the "body politic" of the nation and diminishing the democratic hopes of its citizens all of whom would be better served with MBE political governance.

More positively, the above studies of Higgins and Gordon conclude that caring and helping norms, democratically formulated by collaborative sub-groupings in a company, enjoy more workforce legitimacy than authority-imposed norms. As such, these democratic norms create a deliberative learning climate in the company, facilitate role-taking reciprocity and strengthen organization stability. The companies and collectivities described annually in the "CNN Heroes" programming are exemplary models of care-grouping organizations and their "collaborative sub-groupings" as inspired by 6th stage moral reciprocities.

Although these early studies of moral climate were conducted in two democratically organized work sites, they have particular relevance for MBE implementation and significance for contemporary corporate re-organization planning of executives. *First*, regarding MBE implementation, it needs to be acknowledged that studies like those of Higgins and Gordon are moral development research approaches. They are conducted to advance the theory and/or to intervene in organization development strategies designed to reconstruct a moral climate. Their legacy represents a resource wealth in the theory and its application in different organization settings which can guide parents, teachers, prison officials,[9] and now executives and managers towards implementing moral development programing. While MBE implementation does require some working knowledge of the theories, it does not require formal research studies of these kinds, unless particular re-organization problems are encountered that demand scientifically reliable data for their resolution.

Second, to the extent that corporate re-organization planning may develop in a company where democratizing strategies are being seriously considered, pursuance of these research and consulting interventions, as described in Higgins and Gordon (1985), is strongly recommended:

> The ability to recognize the fragility of organizations and whether they represent environments conducive to socio-moral development is a critical aspect of our work climate research.... The use of the research to identify organizational stress and environments of manageable diversity is only one way that research can aid the democratization process. It can also explain the ways that workers understand democracy and the democratization process....Knowing this is critical for determining how to intervene, (p.266)

In democratizing deliberations, such interventions can spare executives the stressful concerns about organization instabilities and hierarchical defenses (see Argyris, 1990).

Organization Hierarchies and Parallel Structure Strategies. While this research legacy from Kohlberg offers executives and managers several approaches to moral atmosphere reconstruction in the workplace, the participatory democratic forms discussed here and in the research may not offer them impelling incentives for engaging in reconstructive organizational change. Corporations are obviously not schools or prisons. For the most part, they are organizations in the private sector and are thus governed by private ownership structures. Most of these structures are hierarchically arranged in established corporate cultures which may not be readily receptive to "work democracy" and "just community" governance. However, in deciding what structures might be appropriate for their companies, it may help executives in their planning to recall Kohlberg's own critique of organizational hierarchies: "For various reasons, 'cooperative structures go with democracy; competitive ones with autocracy. In an authoritarian system, all members are competing for rewards from an authority, in a democratic system they are exchanging rewards with each other." (Kohlberg *et al.,* 1975, p. 60) It might also be helpful for executives to recall that research on workplace democracy has consistently demonstrated *positive results* regarding job satisfaction and work productivity measures (Blumberg, 1973) and social reasoning development about work (Hamilton *et al.,* 1985).

If, however, corporate governance is firmly established in an authoritarian system, executives may be able to assess the structural plausibility for MBE programing and moral atmosphere reforming within their own organizational realities. In many traditional hierarchies, for example, it is strategically plausible to integrate MBE programing through *parallel structures*, on a micro-organization scale, into existing corporate structures and organiza-tional divisions. Simply setting up corporate ethical discussion groups within such units could begin to generate *collaborative* seminal reform proposals toward expanding collective moral awareness at executive and managerial levels of hierarchy. "Vanguard companies tend to emphasize this skill because it facilitates the interaction, attraction, collaboration, and integration that the new way of working requires" (Kanter 2009, p.191). Recognizing new ways of looking at things, Professor Kanter cites the example of how Egyptian students at Harvard Business School facilitated the introduction of health care benefits from the "vanguard Trans-national Corporation of Proctor and Gamble in Egypt through their "parallel" *interactional* Report on "The Development of Human Capital in Egypt."

In accordance with these collaborative strategies, Stephen Payne stresses the dialogical efficacy of such these kinds of parallel interactional structures: ". . . Through this dialogue ethical sensitivities and creative visions should occur that otherwise would not be recognized" (1991, p.75).

Following Habermas (1984, 1990b) on communication ethics in organizations, Payne also outlines actual content issues and process recommendations for starting such groups and for directing their influence to decision-making power centers in corporations (see pp. 75-77); see also Deetz, 1983; Trevino, 1986; Rusk, 1993).

DEMOCRACY IN THE WORKPLACE

Workplace Democracies and Workforce Teams. From such seminal reform proposals, more organization development strategies could plan for the wider macro-organizational introduction of MBE with the gradual implementation of its moral atmosphere reform program. In hierarchical cultures that are not so resistant to governance change, newer innovative management models, that are more conducive to collegial forms of work performance and company production, can serve as re-organization compromises towards wider MBE horizontal implementation. The early wave of work-team structures within traditional organization hierarchies (Orsburn *et al.*, 1990; Stewart, 1991; Miller, 1990; Miller, 1992; Walker and Hanson, 1992; Schweiger *et al.*, 1992), for example, can open a conveniently conducive path for introducing "just community" and "work democracy" strategies to the workplace. Later studies, as traced in Rosabeth Kanter's work, report on significant international developments in teamwork assignments, such as IBM's global "Crisis Response Team" tracking missing persons in natural disasters. These workplace structures and collaborative humanitarian role assignments are ready-made organizational units for MBE workplace democracies. As collaborative work-management formations in a company, such teams offer an ongoing structured learning context for moral reasoning responsibilities and a social interactional reciprocities for interactive role-taking and for collective social and corporate responsibility building (Baker and Hunt, 2003).

As Alvin Gouldner pointed out above, reciprocity, as a moral behavioral response of role-taking processes between individuals and among groups, "generates...higher-stage generalized system perspectives" and thus strengthens organization system collectivities. If this is the case, *role-taking* workplace teams are bound to strengthen workplace collectivities, hierarchical as well as democratic. And furthermore, such organizational strengthening effects are not just limited to "social system stability" but extended to *moral development agility* through "higher-stage... perspectives." Thus *the growing trend in workforce-team-building and coverage of its research is germane for MBE programing.* For example, the cited work of Baker and Hunt has explored the importance of teams relative to gender composition and ethical decision-making processes in workforce organizations. Their lead study is important because it stands out as one of the first studies which has "simultaneously investigated the role of gender and teams on ethics and moral development in the firm." While their study found that "gender plays little or no role in the moral orientation of teams," they did note that teams composed entirely of all females' revealed significantly higher moral orientation than those composed exclusively of males. Baker and Hunt concluded:

> Although exploratory, this study has potential significance for both practitioners and researchers. For managers, our results indicate that one would expect the same level of moral decisions to be made by groups regardless of gender make-up or the gender majority within the group. The implication is that managers should be able to form groups without regard to the impact of the gender composition of the groups on the moral nature of the decisions being made. Given that females are expected to increasingly move into middle-and upper-management, this should help to allay any fears managers have regarding the impact of increasing gender diversity on the ability of the firm, via groups, to act in a moral manner (2003, pp. 106 (14).

While Baker and Hunt do not explain the significant difference in the higher moral orientation of the exclusive female team composition, the critical moral development works of Helen Haste, cited above, and those of Carol Gilligan, cited below, offer plausible explanations of the higher moral orientation of women *in terms of the psychosocial affective and caring domains of female moral development.*

MORAL REFORMER PROFILES AND GENDER AUTHORITY TYPES

Moral Climate Reform and Moral Type Reformer. Whatever form of corporate restructuring is pursued to reform the moral atmosphere of a company, particularly in workforce selections of team compositions, executives would be wise to carefully consider the strategic implications that are significant from other findings in Kohlberg's research on heteronomous and autonomous moral reasoning (Kohlberg, 1987). These studies indicate that moral reasoning, at its different incremental levels, reflects two development types: "A," the *heteronomous* type, whose authority judgments tend to be dependent on others, like superiors; and "B," the *autonomous* type, whose authority judgments tend to be independent, as self-formulated. (See Exhibit 3.6 for a comparative descriptive analysis of the types according to personal, social and organizational criteria, which have operational relevance to moral management and authority types in corporations).

Exhibit: 3:6   Organizational Climate Reform and Moral Authority Types

Criteria upon which heteronomous-autonomy distinction is based:

Freedom: Autonomous judgments are made without reference to external parameters, such as authority, traditional or law, for justification or validation. Heteronomous judgments fall under the constraint of external parameters for justification and validation.

Mutual respect: Autonomous judgments reflect an awareness of the importance of cooperation among equals in coming to just and fair moral decisions. Mutual respect also entails treating others as one would like to be treated. Heteronomous judgments exhibit unilateral respect towards authority, law, tradition or power— whether in the form of persons or institutions.

Reversibility: Autonomous judgments are reversible or equilibrated because they explicitly involve some form of (at least rudimentary) mutual and reciprocal role taking. Thus all the actors in a particular situation are understood to consider each other's interests, claims and points of view before a just or fair solution to the problem can be reached. Heteronomous judgments do not involve explicit role taking to this degree, and tend to focus on a particular moral problem from only one perspective.

Constructivism: Autonomous judgments reflect an awareness that rules and laws used to guide and frame moral decisions are actively formulated by the human mind, in the context of a social group ideally based in cooperation among equals. Thus rules and laws are understood to be flexible and able to adapt to special situations and circumstances. Heteronomous judgments reflect a sacred, rigid and inflexible view of rules and laws.

Hierarchy: Autonomous judgments reflect a clear hierarchy of values that places moral values and prescriptive duties above pragmatic, descriptive, consequentialist or aesthetic considerations in the resolution of a moral dilemma. Heteronomous judgments do not reflect a clear moral hierarchy. Instead non-moral and pragmatic considerations are weighed heavily in the resolution of a moral dilemma.

Intrinsicalness: Autonomous judgments are based on a fundamental valuing of persons as ends in themselves, tied to a basic respect for moral personality, personal autonomy and human dignity. Heteronomous judgments are based on a much more pragmatic and instrumental view of persons. Consequently, heteronomous judgments are much more likely to advocate treating persons as means to another end than are autonomous judgments.

Prescriptively: Autonomous judgments reflect a view of moral duty that prescribes a certain set of moral obligations and actions regardless of the inclination of the actor, or various pragmatic considerations. Moral duty is based on inner compulsion, moral necessity or conscience. Heteronomous judgments reflect an instrumental or hypothetical view of moral duty.

Universality: Autonomous judgments reflect the willingness to generalize and universalize moral judgments in order that they apply to anyone and everyone in the same or relevantly similar circumstances. Heteronomous judgments are not explicitly universalized or generalized. Instead, heteronomous moral judgments or values are either uncritically assumed to be held by everyone, or understood to be relative to instrumental self-interest.

Choice: In response to a particular moral dilemma, the individual who makes autonomous moral judgments is much more likely to choose and justify the solution to the dilemma that is generally seen as *just* and *fair* from the standpoint of the post-conventional stages of moral judgment than is the individual who makes heteronomous judgments.

Source: Colby and Kohlberg (1987, p. 349) Cambridge University Press publication. Reprinted with permission.

Colby and Kohlberg explain that while these types are found at most stages, a stage 1 person could not logically make type "B" judgments and a stage 5 person would not very likely render type "A" judgments. They found that these types are age-related and developmental. In this regard, they explain that subjects who initially rely on heteronomous judgments tend to shift at some particular developmental awareness point to autonomous judgments; and that reversals to heteronomous judgments are not likely. As an effect of this awareness growth, they claim that autonomous-type individuals are more likely to translate their judgments into moral action than the heteronomous type. They also stress that both developmental types are related to socio- cultural environments and social relations. The relevance of these findings and analyses for executives, who may be deliberating on organization restructuring plans for moral climate reform, is salient from the predictions of Colby and Kohlberg themselves:

We expect socio-cultural environments and social relations that stress democracy, equality, cooperation, and mutuality of relationships to be likely to exert a positive influence on the development of autonomous moral judgment. In contrast, we expect environments that are authoritarian, where a strict traditional social hierarchy is followed, and where obedience and generational respect are stressed, to be less likely to facilitate the development of autonomy (p. 351).

While this second hypothesis was only partially supported in their samples, which included strongly established cultural variables in Turkish and Taiwanese gerontocratic societies, it still warrants the consideration of executives in corporations where strict social hierarchies and ranking seniority status arrangements persist.

Inasmuch as there is likely to be in any given company, hierarchical or democratic, a significant number of both moral types at different stage levels among its management staff and within its workforce, the following practical considerations become relevant matters for executives in their deliberations and planning for change: (1) calculating what receptivity levels are viable in their respective corporations for introducing type "B" managers; (2) balancing efficient manager-worker combinations and integrations of types "A" and "B"; and (3) assessing what effect these introductions and balancing strategies would have on the organization and on individual managers and also on workforce teams. For example, what would be the effects of introducing stage 5 type "B" autonomous manager(s) into the company at large or into any particular department or team in its current hierarchical alignments and moral type postures and attitudes? And, what would be the effects of such an introduction on the manager him/herself? The admonishing predictions of Colby and Kohlberg might influence these assessments:

we expect that a change in social environment from one that is supportive of moral autonomy to one that is not may cause an individual to change from making autonomous to making heteronomous moral judgments (p. 350).

A more encouraging prediction for guiding these assessments, however, in terms of reform planning and reformer action, is the following conclusion from Kohlberg and Candee (1984):

if we are going to look for a relationship between moral thought and moral action, we should look to those persons who judge that it is right to perform the more moral behavior either by virtue of their Stage 5 reasoning or the type B intuitions (p. 64).

Because of actual moral dilemmas that these kinds of assessments may generate for executives in their deliberations, one last consideration would seem to be in place, namely, that they consider engaging other colleagues from their senior and junior level staffs in the deliberations. This kind of consultatory climate could itself serve as a barometer of what moral reasoning stages and types prevail in the company and what appropriate governance structures are plausible for reforming its moral atmosphere.

GENDER IN THE WORKPLACE

Moral Reasoning and Gender Issues. Any deliberations about moral atmosphere reform and hierarchical governance arrangements need to include gender issues relative to moral reasoning in the workplace. Inasmuch as the Colby and Kohlberg (1987) research did not find moral-type differences to be gender specific, the relevant issues about this subject should focus on the interactional arrangements and organization structures of a *corporate caring ethic.* This ethically specific focus is not intended to ignore the controversies in the moral development field regarding Gilligan's (1982) contention that an "ethic of care" is gender related (see Tronto, 1987). It is rather intended to explore what her theories imply for executive deliberations over moral atmosphere reform and caring in the workplace. Gilligan's findings suggest that men and women generally develop along different cultural tracks which tend to shape their identity impressions and reasoning perspectives with alternate views of social realities and moral priorities. For example, women are usually acculturated into stronger and more enduring intimacy attachments than men, especially in early adolescence, whereas men, in this same period, tend to be socially and culturally encouraged to separation and independence. Their developmental life experiences thus lead them to different moral awareness and moral value viewpoints, with women more focused on responsibilities and caring relationships, and men on reciprocities and just partnerships. These different viewpoints do not reflect on the moral character or moral type of men or women but they do reflect on the cultural mores of society and on the economic and organizational arrangements of the workplace. What is at issue is that if executive deliberations are really as serious about a respect and caring ethic for their companies, as was CEO William Weiss for Ameritech, they need to address the problems of organizational moral consistency not just in "glass ceiling" boardrooms but in sexually harassing cloakrooms (Davidson, 1992; Morrison, 1992). Critical, reflexive ethical discourse is needed in executive deliberations to confront the moral inconsistencies of gender discrimination in the workplace in areas of economic opportunities and occupational and managerial equalities (see Martin, 1989).

A corporate ethic of care must not be gender biased, lest the alarming words of Gilligan for the research patriarchy come to haunt the corporate hierarchy:

> But while women have thus taken care of men, men have, in their theories of psychological development, as in their economic arrangements, tended to assume or devalue that care (1982 p. 17).

Conclusion. MBE is a reconstructive plan to re-create a moral atmosphere in companies with an interactional climate that engenders and integrates caring reciprocities and just partnerships of equal opportunities with sixth stage principled purpose-reasoning to insure "critical moral consistency" in the workplace, as evaluated in Chapter 2. This new management paradigm can make a *difference* in clearing the "corporate voice" and proclaiming the values of morally developed psychological attitudes and ethically economic balances which value *equal care.* To complete the proclamation of such needed values of morally equal care in corporate workplace environments, one last step of the MBE reconstructive learning plan is strategically needed to evaluate not just the inequalities of gender care but the associated inequalities of moral care. MBE pursues its innovative methodologies of these evaluations in the following Chapter 4.

END NOTES

1. In critical sociological and socio-economic literature, hegemony is described as culturally bound preferences which reflect the prevailing value system of the social institutions of family, religion, government, education and the economy and their respective power structures (see Gouldner, 1970 and Etzioni, 1988). For more updated documented evidence on the moral development *capability* of workers to prefer a higher level of moral motivation and caring relations in their work performance arrangements with their managers at stage 6, see the research studies of Minkler, 2002 analyzed above in Chapter 7 of this book).

2. Role-taking is a social psychological concept synthesized by Mead from the works of James, Cooley and Dewey. It involves an internalized self-other interaction process whereby individuals "imaginatively rehearse" the anticipated action lines of others, allowing them to coordinate their own responses towards socially organized and cooperative behavior (Turner, 1978).

3. For some relevant literary resources on ethical issues in the workplace, see Richardson (2004). His *Annual Editions* offers articles on business ethics and management dilemmas collated from public press sources for study and discussion purposes.

4. More specific directions on the moral advancement coaching of both subordinate supervisors in line management authority roles and employed workers in departmental workplace settings are discussed in Chapter 4 on performance evaluation processes and moral leadership roles (see especially pp. 123-125).

5. Theodicy encompasses the natural theological studies of creation anchored in the philosophical sciences of nature and being as a co-disciplinary counterpart of the physical sciences. Its research methods are inductive as its disciplines examine principles with application to particulars. In collaborative contrast, the research methods of the physical sciences are deductive as their disciplines examine particulars of data to arrive at principles for scientific learning and research exploration. (See Bittle, 1953. Chapter 1.)

6. A most informative and incisive critical analysis of the complex moral arguments presented here on "validity claim determination" is, for the most part, philosophically and theologically consonant with the work of William A. Galston, Director of the Institute for Philosophy and Public Policy at the University of Maryland School of Public Affairs. See his study on "Catholics Jews and Stem Cells: When Believers Beg to Differ" in *Commonweal* (May, 2005). When reading his following quotation of Rabbi Moshe David Tendler, it becomes apparent how much Christians can begin to think in common with "classical Jewish. . . biblical moral theology":

> The Judeo-biblical tradition does not grant moral status to an embryo before forty days of gestation. Such an embryo has the same moral status as male and female gametes, and its destruction prior to implantation is of the same moral import as the "wasting of human seed". . . . The

proposition that human hood begins at zygote formation, even in vitro, is without basis in [Jewish] biblical moral theology.... In stem-cell research and therapy, the moral obligation to save human life [is] the paramount ethical principle in biblical law (2005 p.16).

7. Extrapolating from the conventional complex moral issues of "stem-cell research" in the religious, political and legal cultures of Church and State, O'Brien opens the scientific plausibility structures of post-conventional moral insights into the personal, ethical decision-making discourse of un-wanted pregnancies: "Art, science, religion, and morality rest on differing basic assumptions that cannot be fused. It may be immoral to pursue stem-cell research, but it may be very good science" (p. 133). His 6th stage morally careful reconstructive analysis is reflected in his concluding *Afterword:* "Abortion goes to the core of a woman's sense of self, the mystery of the human heart. Those who would speak about the mystery of God and his care for the human heart should speak with care and compassion, not ready censure and condemnation" (p. 153). For one who speaks about the "mystery of God", see the works of Robert Lanza, at Advanced Cell Technology, particularly on "Essential Stem Cell Methods" (2008) and "Human Embryonic Stem Cell Lines Generated *Without Embryonic Destruction*" with (Klimanskaya, et. al., 2008). The research sources of these "stem cell methods and lines" have been derived from the work of Dr. Shinya Yamanaka, who has been awarded the Nobel Prize for Medicine on October 8, 2012 for his discovery of creating stem cells "with all the same properties as those derived from embryos without killing—or even using—embryos at all." (Anderson, 2012.).

8. On reciprocity and its relationship to moral development and social system process, see Gouldner(1970). Gouldner claims that reciprocity generates interactional inducements within individuals that awaken their consciousness to higher-stage generalized system perspectives. Reciprocity thus strengthens organizational system collectivity and promotes social system stability. "For reciprocity, unlike complementarity, actually mobilizes egoistic motivations and channels them into the maintenance of the social system" (p. 242).

9. In 1971, the Connecticut Department of Corrections participated in two of these Kohlberg research studies attempting to reconstruct the moral climate of prison life through moral development programing. The site of one of these studies was the Niantic State Farm for Women where the customary moral climate of punishment (stage 1) was already set in structures of small cottage work units of 20-30 women. After presenting the moral development model in a series of training session to prison officials and inmates, the research team seized the opportunity to restructure one model unit into a work democracy cottage toward achieving stage 4 rule observing and stage 5 trusting relationships among inmates and their prison staff supervisors.

This experimental pilot cottage was formed with the selection of twenty-two women, one parole agent, six line and staff managers and the supervisor trained in moral development theory, all of whom served as counselors and small group discussion leaders for the moral development intervention. The "critical practical" purpose of the intervention was to open a 4th and 5th stage awareness in the moral consciousness of the offenders that this new modality of rehabilitation treatment was *reframed as moral justice education* rather than penal correction incarceration. The inmates participated in the self-governing process of the unit, enjoying equal voting privileges with the selected prison officials. Early results of the experiment facilitated the moral advancement of the selected inmates with half of the original inmates earning placement in parole and work release programs (Kohlberg *et al.,* 1972).

CHAPTER 4

MBE MORAL PERFORMANCE EVALUATION IN THE WORKPLACE

If MBE interactional learning in a morally conducive atmosphere is so critical to moral reasoning advancement with equal gender opportunities and caring role-taking reciprocities toward ultimate moral performance improvement in the workplace, then it would seem ethically productive as well as practically strategic in management leadership coaching that the concluding *sixth final step* of the Kohlberg moral development socialization plan, would have to include some form of interactional *moral performance evaluation.* Since many companies already have their particular manual forms of performance evaluation instruments in place, this step should not be that difficult to implement, especially if the forms and procedures are based on customary long-standing recommendations in the organization management literature (Boyett and Conn, 1988; Vroom *et al.,* 1990), Orsburn *et al.,* 1990; Willis and Dubin, 1990; see especially Vroom, 1995, Part IV).

MORAL PERFORMANCE EVALUATION INSTRUMENTS

Inasmuch as most of these traditional instruments do not contain effective moral evaluation components in their systems relative to ethical gender issues and morally caring stages, it may be necessary to revise or adapt their forms and procedures to coordinate evaluation instruments with MBE organizational development programs. Any revisions or adaptations to these instruments should be composed not just to reflect value-system symbolization in the company, as discussed earlier in Chapter 2, but to detect value-system inconsistencies in its operations. Revisions would also be needed to incorporate MBE governance strategies, socialization and learning pedagogies, and open system organization processes toward building a company ethic. The easiest and most comprehensive method for revising performance evaluation instruments for these MBE purposes is to implement the cited versions of the Kohlberg scale on worker occupational perspectives in Exhibit 3:3, on corporate operational perspectives in Exhibit 3:4 and on authority styles, compliance patterns and worker attitudes in Exhibit 3:5 from Chapter 3 toward upgrading traditional evaluation manuals. It would also be especially helpful to utilize Rest's conceptual cooperation model of the scale (as presented in Chapter 3 and as developed further in Chapter 5) in the evaluation processes. This cooperative form of the scale can be inserted into the manual or its appendix with industry-specific language that respects the particularities of a company's mission, and the cooperative specifications of its professions and/or occupations. In the Refrigeration Company case analysis, described in Chapter 3, similar versions of the Kohlberg scale and references to Rest's conceptual cooperation model were integrated into the company's Performance Evaluation Manual of the Employee Handbook with language appropriate for its industrial sector, its organization-set, and for its service and contracting divisions.

In any case, this revised instrument should be careful to focus integrally on morally productive reasoning and work performance. The Kohlberg scale was not designed to be utilized as an instrument of moral inquisition. It is a reconstructive and an ethically useful instrument for moral education and stage performance evaluation advancement in any domain, including corporations, banking and investment firms and government bureaucracies. It contains, moreover, an untapped assessment and critically reconstructive review potential for restoring the credibility of many traditional performance evaluation systems. Kurtines *et al.* (and associates -1991), for instance, have utilized the basic Kohlberg development categories to construct their own socio-moral performance instruments for measuring a respondent's social orientation to moral understanding. Following their instruments, MBE can allow preliminary assessments of how workers view morality along five comparative dimensional lines of application: (1) "by *relative or universal standards*" i.e., are the moral standards specific to our company or to every company?; (2) "according to *utilitarian or deontological* purposes" i.e. are the products designed for useful functional convenience or for the *environmental integrity* of their use? e.g."do you want paper or plastic?" (3) "as emphasizing *individual, social or gender aspects*" i.e., are the moral standards of executive compensation reflecting stage 2 vested interest in personal preferences for private gain or stage 6 *invested* interest in social references and *gender equality preferences* for the public good? (4) "as emanating from *religious or secular* incentives;" i.e., from spiritual faith *motivation* or social faith purposes to gain the trust of a customer clientele and the dependability of a market commercial base with the securities of product reliability;[1] and (5) "by *intuitive or rational* processes;" i.e., are the working assignments and communication standards so *ethically* authentic in company *policy* and managing *practice* that workers don't have to figure out the moral stage advancement of what their employer expects? While this simple commentary on these contrived categories allows the performance reviewer preliminary evaluative knowledge for probing how one can apply these multi-dimensional lines to moral development coaching and performance upgrading, the moral examples and applied references offered above allow more simple, comprehensive and even *intuitive motivational understanding* on the part of the worker of what the evaluation manager expects from his/her moral understanding associated with work performance.

MORAL RECONSTRUCTION AND ORGANIZATION CHANGE

In further work, Pollard *et al.* (1991) moved beyond traditional moral learning categories in the evaluation process to the critically reconstructive review potential of organization change which MBE programing conducts to upgrade moral performance. In this regard, their evaluation instruments are readily compatible for the social and organization reconstruction of performance evaluation systems and methodological processes. They have developed moral-issue or moral-dilemma competence scales for facilitating the use of critical deliberative thinking and the social evolutionary development of co-constructive performance planning. Their studies stress the importance of these kinds of moral evaluation instruments as institutionalizing the democratic and participatory processes of competency development through critical reconstructive performance education. An admirable example of this kind of intensive democratic and participatory performance evaluation process was recently conducted by the 9/11 Investigatory Commission. Composed of delegates of both political parties and an array of highly trained experts from the Intelligence organizations, this commission finally recommended to the President the need for a complete reconstruction of the Intelligence operations of the government with the appointment of an Intelligence Czar. While this participatory democratic performance evaluation process was "admirable" in terms of the "critical practical" reconstructive purposes of evaluating the complex organization environment of Intelligence operations, it does not appear very intelligent to suggest the appointment of a "Czar". Imperial symbolic language does not reflect nor share the meanings of democratic reconstructive processes, let alone the moral leadership for bureaucratic reformative purposes. Though the moral issue and moral dilemma competence scales seem practically relevant to deal with the needs of Intelligence reconstruction in the maze of the multiple agencies and rivalries of their allegiances, the MBE use of the Kohlberg scale still has critical *praxis* relevance for the reconstruction of the Intelligence complex organization environment.

First, and foremost, Intelligence operations in all the agencies need a MBE ethics consultant as well as a managing coordinator to advise the President and Congress. There does not seem to be much moral awareness of a developing grave and fundamental ethical global problem in the CIA, FBI and their international counterparts with the increasing use of deception, and the lack of truth-telling in necessary security undercover and secret operations. When allies, such as the United States and Israel are discovered as spying on each other, the international ethical climate of truth and trust has clearly degenerated into a socially pathological climate of distrusting political paranoia, if not somewhat symbolic of counter insurgency behavior. This generalized ethical problem is far more serious and imminently more critical for activating a morally developed counter *resurgency* plan to rebuild international and global social trust between and among nations. A MBE moral development *resurgency plan* is what is needed among nations not just to define particular unethical issues and evaluate moral policy making dilemmas but more gravely to deal with immorally terrifying eruptions which radically and rapidly undermine the global social trust among nations and terror-stricken populations. These latter terrorizing effects were exactly the imminent immoral consequences of the devastating plight of the Bombay Mumbai terrorist attacks which broke the bonds of social trust in adjacent nations of the Far East and provoked global alarming anxieties of multinational populations around the world. In the aftermath, of these horrifying events, Clint Van Zandt, former FBI Hostage Negotiator, remarked that in dealing with terrorists one has to engage them in distracting discourse at any cost to stop the killing massacres, even if it means *not telling the truth* to get them to talk (MSNBC news interview 11/27/08). This is a morally basic and questionable elementary flaw in ethically uninformed deliberative discourse bargaining in Intelligence operations which compounds the moral problem breakdown of social trust and perpetuates global social anxieties among populations and international distrust among nations. Intelligence operations need to abide by the universal ethical principles of truth, honesty, justice and reciprocity. Without concern for these principles, the performance evaluation of their operations often deserve, at best, first and second stage moral development ratings and, at worst, un-ranking, immoral degrading ratings. *Second,* the "Czar," as the managing coordinator of all the Intelligence agencies, would be well-advised to rebuild the Intelligence community with a globally sensitive government *federal conscience.* No Intelligence "Czar" will coordinate the Intelligence community, advise the President and Congress and uphold the traditional integrity of Intelligence operations without the *intelligent* moral re-development of its own internal bureaucratic divisional *conscience.*

LEARNING METHODS FOR ORGANIZATION CHANGE

MBE *and Case Study Appraisal Systems.* Inasmuch as the procedures of traditional performance appraisal systems are so often conducted perfunctorily for regulated compensation ends and calculated promotion purposes (Hackman, 1986), the evaluation usually suffers from a lack of learning and has become symbolic of pre-conventional moral reasoning processes. Argyris (1991) claims that these processes are counter-productive and "locked in defensive reasoning." He proposes that workers can be taught how to reason productively and to identify performance inconsistencies by reflecting on the discrepancies "between their espoused and actual theories of action" (p. 106). While he offers no social psychological formulas for individual or corporate conscience arousal about these discrepancies nor moral climate restructuring plans for reasoning development and organization change, he does suggest an important self-evaluation learning method through the composition of "situational case-study write-ups" by executives and managers. He illustrates a *reflexive* format for these case studies, through which the individual executive can reflect on his or her own leadership reasoning skills utilized in communicating an actual company business problem to the management staff. He suggests how the case-study write-up should have a simulated meeting column, describing the imaginary authority-subordinate communication flow; and a corresponding self-reflexive column, describing predictive suppressions of self-generated thoughts and feelings provoked by the imagined responses of subordinates. He cites this private, self-reflexive, role playing case-study:

> The case became the catalyst for a discussion in which the CEO learned several things about the way he acted with his management team.
>
> He discovered...his conversations as counter-productive. In the guise of being "diplomatic," he would pretend that a consensus about the problem existed, when in fact none existed. The unintended result: instead of feeling reassured, his subordinates felt wary and tried to figure out "what is he *really* getting at?"
>
> The CEO also realized that the way he dealt with the competitiveness among department heads was completely contradictory. On the one hand, he kept urging them to "think of the organization as a whole." On the other, he kept calling for actions—department budget cuts, for example—that placed them directly in competition with each other.   (p. 107)

Argyris concludes that by so role-playing the case study privately, and subsequently sharing its unmasked write-up with the staff, comparative role-taking reasoning is evoked and authentic performance evaluation occurs:

> In effect, the case study exercise legitimizes talking about issues that people have never been able to address before. Such a discussion can be emotional—even painful. But for managers with the courage to persist, the payoff is great: management teams and entire organizations work more openly and more effectively and have greater options for behaving flexibly and adapting to particular situations (1991, p. 107).

By so utilizing the revised performance evaluation instrument in concert with such reflexive models of case-study simulations, MBE performance evaluation can create the intermediary goal of an empathic and frank moral evaluation climate (Oser and Schlafli, 1985) and engage participants in *cooperative* moral learning "loops" (Argyris, 1991; see also 1990). It is exactly here where the *cooperative concepts* of Rest's moral development stage model, seen above in Chapter 3, can be utilized as a moral performance evaluation instrument.

> Conceptions of cooperation help the person sift among the many details to identify the most important aspects. They provide a way to link the relationships of the parties to each other and an integrating strategy for deciding which are the most important considerations that lead to advocating some course of action as morally right. Conceptions of cooperation help a person manage all the bits and pieces of dilemma information, and help guide what an individual ought to do. . . (Rest, 1994, p. 8).

And it is precisely this guidance that an interactive cooperative performance evaluation is meant to deliver. As Argyris' model offers a self-evaluation learning method through the *imaginary* composition of situational case-study write-ups by executives and managers, his specific expertise on performance evaluation, as described above, is aimed at developing leadership reasoning skills utilized in communicating an actual company business problem to the management staff. What is impressive about his model is that he has regenerated the concept of "reflexivity" which, as seen in the MBE model, is *the social psychological activator of the corporate conscience*. As such, Argyris' work is most compatible with the MBE model and is indeed functionally reconstructive for improving the MBO model of performance evaluation. Moreover, his creative use of "role playing simulation" in his reflexive case study write-ups for training managers to improve performance evaluation methodology is analogically used in Volume II of this study, as an innovative critical practical study of the forest industry's moral performance evaluation in the "Corporate Moral Forest."

MBE AND PERFORMANCE PROGRESSION PLANNING

To expand Argyris' business performance evaluations and methodologies into the moral performance domain, this MBE study offers the social psychological formulas for advancing the worker's moral reasoning in the workplace and a reconstructive plan for its moral climate reform. Its plan invokes the human resource socialization medium by coaching the workforce toward the postconventional stages of moral performance through role taking *collaboration* and task performing *cooperation* on the work floor. Accordingly, whatever forms or procedures that may be designed or selected as appropriate for such moral performance evaluation in a company, their instruments should be applied as consistent with the implementation of the first four steps of the MBE program in such a way as to maintain a moral organizational unity and a managerial ethical integration. This admonition is imperative because the first four steps of the MBE program (1. measuring worker moral awareness; 2. measuring company moral awareness; 3.

measuring authority styles; 4. inducing moral reasoning advancement coaching) are designed to measure and advance the moral consciousness of workers and collectivities to achieve a unified moral vision for the company and to correlate the authority styles of the executives and managers to promote a morally integrated workforce and an ethically sensitive company. Were such case study instruments of performance evaluation reviews applied throughout all of the organizational ecclesiastical structures of the Roman Catholic Church from Rome to Germany, to Ireland, to Canada and to the United States, etc., the Corporate Body of the Universal Ethical Catholic Church might have been spared of the greatest immoral priesthood pedophile scandal against its *pastoral responsibility* and its *sacramental integrity*. (See pp.134-144 on the need for upgrading moral performance management in the church).

Performance Evaluation and Moral Organization Unity. Achieving a unified moral vision throughout a workforce is one of the most important benefits which the scaling instruments of moral development performance evaluation can render to a company and to its organization-set. These instruments, as described in the exhibits of the previous chapter, provide the same unified moral learning framework for all personnel including management and executive hierarchies to expand moral awareness understanding and *moral reasoning principle-learning* toward advancing moral performance delivery. This consistent and unified scaling framework, as integrated into a company's performance evaluation manual, should insure continuing and applied moral learning with role specific descriptions and *ethical principle-thinking prescriptions*.

With regard to moral organizational unity, it is also imperative that performance evaluation be conducted in an open system moral atmosphere. This social psychological mandate is based on the interactional dynamics of open system theory described in Chapter 1. Accordingly, it stresses the importance of achieving a cyclical flow of activities and events in an organization which feed back into its system, strengthening its processes and structures (Allport, 1962) thus opening the system to a moral reconstruction flow. The performance evaluation, as a periodic activity and a cyclical timing event, can be an effective developmental experience that not only opens performance morality to individuals and collectivities in a company but also feeds ethical principles and moral reasoning back into its system.

A serious and dangerous contemporary example of broken organizational unity in a small closed system of intra-departmental disunity between management and subordinates has recently been exposed in the drama driven case study event of Captain Phillips and his crew of the Maersk Alabama during the episodic captivity of the ship off the coast of Somalia. While this relatively small organizational unit of the shipping industry exposed a closed system example of management and subordinate interaction, it demonstrated the counterproductive polarities between moral authoritarian performance and moral collectivity attitudes in terms of moral stage differentiation. While the details of this example, as exposed in the media (Griffin and Fitzpatrick, 2010), reveal different versions of the captain's heroic captivity, the moral behavior of the crew and the captain was surely exemplary in terms of interpersonal 6th stage caring for one another during the terrorizing incident. The one constant interactional variable in this case study analysis is that the organizational climate of the episode was firmly structured by a military-like ranking hierarchy, which can account for interactional discrepancy evaluation in terms of moral performance scaling. The captain was described as being aloof, as is often the interactional pattern in closed systems of authoritarian hierarchies. The main practical conclusion of this event, though, is that Captain Phillips did risk his life as a hostage for the safety of the crew and the veracity of his office as a morally responsible and caring 6th stage leader. Accordingly, this divided outcome confirms the conclusions of the above analysis that moral reconstruction cyclical flow is significantly more plausible in open system structures with morally consistent interactional dynamics than in closed system structures. "One thing that any investigator's data show us . . . is his formulation of a type of person. . . . He must try to provide explicit rules for allowing us to see how he has assembled what he knows." (Phillips, 1971, p. 174) It is clear from this brief assembly of data that Captain Phillips is a stage six morally caring leader.

Managerial Evaluating: An Interpersonal Ethical Intervention. With regard to managerial ethical integration, it is humanistically sensitive that executives, managers and even supervisors entrusted with the performance evaluation process, understand that *moral evaluation is an interpersonal ethical intervention* and not just a ritual organizational convention. They should, therefore, keep in mind the organizational unity of the whole MBE program, as they intervene with these added moral evaluation instruments and procedures. With this unified focus, encompassing an understanding of their own hierarchical place as moral leaders on these intervention paths, they will be prepared to use these instruments and procedures as integrated into the MBE system. This implies moral leadership by the evaluator at all levels of the managerial hierarchy, especially at the level of the supervisory evaluator. In many companies, supervisory evaluators can be most effective in stimulating the moral consciousness raising processes of their intra-departmental domains inasmuch as they often enjoy more personal and even friendly relationships with their subordinates. Dean Susan Phillips describes the role of evaluators in this way:

> Executives become moral managers by recognizing and accepting their responsibility for acting as ethical role models. They must also "manage ethics" by communicating about ethics and values on a regular basis and by

holding organizational members accountable for ethical conduct. Most students will not be executives early in their careers; but they need to understand that, even as supervisors, they will play a key ethical role in the organization by influencing their daily conduct in their direct reports. Supervisors demonstrate ethical leadership through being open, fair, trustworthy and caring with employees; by communicating about ethics and values; by role modeling ethical conduct; by focusing on means as well as ends in reward systems; and by disciplining unethical conduct when it occurs.   (2004, p. 11)

Accordingly, as management evaluators assess and review worker performance measures, they need to monitor the *four phases of moral transition by getting* "inside" the reasoning and consistency tracks that lead to moral performance upgrading (Oser and Schlafli, 1985, p. 276; review Exhibit 3:2 above again to retain an ongoing holistic understanding of the socialization intervention strategies of the MBE reconstructive plan). As moral evaluators, they need to watch for "*disequilibrium*" in the workforce relative to any moral problem arousal incidents of lower moral stage attitudes of cooperation among workers in their particularized intra-departmental climates. Furthermore, they need to be prepared to coach any such un-cooperative workers to responsibility arousal toward addressing whatever moral problems are exposed. In these ethically sensitive supervising roles, they can often coach workers to specifically define their own moral "*dissatisfaction*" in the company, or at least within their respective departments, and encourage them toward recognizing the practical need for holistic attitudinal "*integration,*" especially in the department, and with a higher stage morally cooperative vision for the whole company. And finally, these more accessible on-site supervisory evaluators need to affirm worker attitudinal "*reinforcement*" awakening in the moral transitional processes toward the ultimate goal of moral transformation through moral incentive inducement building in their coaching supervision roles. (See Chapter 5 for more on moral incentive inducement building.)

As the evaluators assess these four phases of transition to higher moral performance among individual workers and their collectivities, they also need to critically reassess the moral climate conditions in the company or in their respective divisions, re-evaluating the "six intermediary goals", cited again in Exhibit 3:2, as the conduciveness factors for moral problem resolution and performance growth toward the ultimate goal of moral transformation. Most importantly, they need to understand this ethically integrating role of moral leadership as one that takes time and patience and that moral performance growth is not always visible even with the evaluating instruments. If, however, they persist in their moral leadership and coaching roles, they will achieve the ultimate goal of the *moral transformation* of the company and the workforce:

For these six measurements are movements without which there can be no transformation in stage. It could, therefore, be said that achieving positive changes in these six fields does actually signify development, provided that the basis is a stimulation of moral conflict. For this reason, we can make the assumption that development also takes place if prerequisites are first stimulated by *pushing them along* (emphasis added).   (Oser and Schlafli, 1985, p. 277)

It should thus be clear that the administration of performance evaluation encourages executives, managers and supervisors to perceive their socialization coaching roles in terms of moral stimulation as a "pushing" of their subordinate colleagues along (see Exhibit 4:1 for a detailed performance evaluation plan for moral progression).

Exhibit 4:1

Manager's Employee Evaluation Chart

Moral Development Progression Plan
for
Personal or Collectivity Interactive Performance Evaluation

Present Stage	Employee's Interpersonal and Social Realities	Employee's Work Performance
	Manager's assessment of employee's attitudes on: Cooperative meanings and moral learning	Manager's evaluation of employee's work performance
	re:	re:
Actual	personal values	motivation incentives
	family relations	job commitment
	friendship circles	cooperative behavior
	political views	team-work skills
	recreational habits	reliability
Moral development stage	cultural activities	productivity

Desired Stage	Plausible Context	Actual Outcome
	Manager's conclusions/plans for resetting attitudinal and situational context in employee's work environment	Manager's evaluation of employee's performance progression
	re:	re:
Upgrade to	attitudinal context	situational context	motivation incentives
	moral character	departmental climate	job commitment
	moral sensitivity	cooperative atmosphere	cooperative behavior
	role-taking empathy	team-work promotion	team-work skills
	value hierarchy upgrade	authority relations	reliability
next higher stage	self-appraisal evaluation	collective evaluation	productivity

This "pushing along" strategy can be done privately with the worker in a hierarchical setting; or collectively in both collegial work-team and participatory democratic settings. Whatever setting seems appropriate, the executive or manager needs to integrate analysis of role-taking interaction in his or her evaluation assessments along with other hierarchical and peer reciprocity evaluation, especially if the setting is a work-team or a collective unit. This implies the need to integrate the evaluation process into a non-threatening organizational climate within the moral atmosphere of the company that allows frank and interactive constructive feedback. Executives and managers need to be open to such feedback and cooperate themselves in resetting any necessary moral climate conditions in the workplace to stimulate or "push" the moral progression. By so integrating performance evaluation into a morally conferential learning forum, workers should feel safe to discuss their performance with their superiors and their peers from the job-role standpoint of their position, the departmental needs of the collectivity, the managerial overview of the hierarchy and the organization responsibilities of the company (see Turner, 1956). Through this integrating role, as sensitive moral leaders, executives, managers and supervisors should be ready for inviting workers and/or teams to engage in self-appraisal strategies, for drawing out and coordinating *their own* moral reasoning to higher moral performance outcomes (Kohlberg, 1971).[2] This performance evaluation model of managerial ethical integration analysis needs to be open to include the evaluation of the executive branch of the company, including the moral performance evaluation of the CEO and its Board of Directors. This holistic degree of critical ethical consistency in performance evaluation processes is an authentic efficacious symbol of corporate moral transformation and corporate executive ethical integrity.

Moral Consistency in the Workplace. If moral reasoning, moral atmosphere and moral performance are integratively linked within the organizational complex and the hierarchical constructs of the corporation through the ethically reflexive deliberations of the corporate conscience, it can be concluded that the product of this morally efficacious ethical delivery system is *integrity.* With a practical leadership knowledge of symbolic interaction theory, Robert Dilenschneider manifests a reversible *praxis* understanding of how executives and managers can effectively create moral consistency in the workplace:

> Give employees clear ideas and symbols for what ethical behavior means. . . .
>
> The manager had better be a symbol of integrity in the company. Managers should always have in mind two or three examples when their personal ethics were tested and they triumphed. A manager should find occasions to relate these episodes, not for notoriety but because employees need symbolic behavior toward which they can aspire. They need tough, real-

world situations where it would have been easy to concede and where they must not. At Hill and Knowlton, we always publicize inside the firm any business that we turn away because it doesn't meet our ethical standards or might represent a conflict. Last year, that kind of business totaled roughly $10 million. Our employees feel good about our company and its character when they know we turn away big business in the name of integrity (1990, pp. 37-38).

Clearly this kind of moral leadership, motivated by ethical integrity, represents a consistent coordination of moral reasoning and moral action demonstrating the leading role of management in setting a workplace operational climate for achieving personal and organizational ethical consistency and corporate moral responsibility.

Personal Consistency and Organization Responsibility. Since the coordination of moral reasoning and moral action is ultimately a matter of self-consistency for both manager and employee through the personal domain of one's moral identity (Blasi, 1984), it would be appropriate that this phase of performance evaluation be self-conducted. And since self-evaluation in the workplace is a complex process overlapping personal and intra-organizational domains, these self-appraisal strategies may need to be redesigned to respect the internal private zones of moral conscience and the external collective norms of moral performance. Moreover, these strategies need to reflect interactive self-appraisal processes that achieve a balance between the subjective personal judgments of the worker and the objective company norms of work performance. These interaction appraisals are the reflexive processes of conscience, as described earlier in Chapter 2, and should take place in the two noted domains. First, in the *personal domain*, the individual worker will usually take care of the reflexive processes regarding personal consistency and moral responsibility over work performance within his or her own conscience. Second, in the *intra-organizational domain*, the individual worker needs to present his or her self-appraisal judgments to the superior and/or collectivity in professional occupational ethical discourse covering moral-norm and moral-performance consistencies. In some cases of moral inconsistency problems, especially those dealing with serious unethical performance complications that might be over spilling into individual compensation responsibilities, the worker may be disposed, or might even need counseling, to open ethical communication with the superior or the collective leadership about personal consistency and moral responsibility redevelopment strategies.

The Morgan Stanley sexual harassment scandal is a morally sensitive dialectical example in the intra-organizational domain of moral inconsistency problems, among individuals in the workplace, over spilling into individual, departmental and even corporate compensation responsibilities. In such a corporate wide scandal, workers may be indisposed to reveal sexual harassment behavior in the performance self-evaluation forum, either as a male aggressor or as a female victim or vice versa. In reviews of this kind, *inner-depth-reflexivity* is the only morally conscientious "mirror" that can *reflect* the truth. Beyond this private zone of the personal conscience of the accused aggressor or the abused victim, however, there could, at times, possibly be a small cluster of organization or departmental witnesses representing a morally consistent and reliable sub-entity of the corporate conscience whose *collective inner-depth-reflexivities* could *reveal* the truth. But since collective inner-depth-reflexivities hardly ever surface in these kinds of sexual harassment cases in the organizational structures of the workplace, more often than not the inner truth of these kinds of scandals remains in the internal forum of sin over which the transcendental Judge presides. Though this Judge has not intervened in the external forum of crime in post-historical biblical times,[3] the individual aggressor as well as the victim may give evidence of his/her conscientious reflections of the inner truth relative to the charged scandals in the external forum of the courts or in the public domain of governments.

The Anita Hill and Clarence Thomas case of sexual harassment accusations in the judicial workplace of government serves as a pertinent example of the limitations of the external forum searches for the inner truth of the accusations. During the wide media coverage of the Congressional hearings for the Supreme Court confirmation of Judge Thomas, Professor Hill gave ample evidence of her inner truth searches, leaving long-lasting impressions of her innocent victimhood to this day. While Judge Thomas appeared to be anxiously indisposed to face the accusations from the mirroring postures of his own inner-depth-reflexivity and his reluctance to conduct his performance self-evaluation beyond the personal zones of his own individual conscience in the internal forum, the ultimate verdict of his innocence or guilt had to be left to the Supreme Judge of the Highest Court.

THE ORGANIZATIONAL LEVELS OF CORPORATE RESPONSIBILITY

The performance evaluation challenge here is to implement the same interactive self-appraisal processes, just described, at the collective and corporate levels of the company. Coordination at these levels can become much more complex, particularly when the evaluation focus relates to other interorganizational units or entities within the company's organization-set. Whatever the scene, these interactive appraisals need to trace the same reflexive processes within the *collective spheres* of the corporate conscience, as described earlier in Chapter 2, and should take place both in the corporate and interorganizational domains of the respective complex organizations. First, in the *corporate domain*, the company and/or its internal lower-level intra-organizational collectivities need to reflect over organizational consistency and collective or corporate responsibility matters regarding its moral norms and its corporate performance. Second, in the *inter-organizational domain*, the company needs to evaluate organizational consistency and corporate performance in the wider sectors of its organization-set. These two domain evaluations may require extensive revisions of the performance evaluation instruments so that effective communication feedback can be drawn from within the company and from other organization-set units, such as from its suppliers, clientele and industry-sector organizations. If the company has redesigned appropriate governance structures in its reconstructed moral climate, it should have competent review boards representing higher-stage and autonomous type "B" moral leadership from every level of management, workforce and its organization-set in open critical ethical discourse of this feedback (see Exhibit 3:6, ch.3). These boards need to deal with company policy, corporate ethical responsibility and corporate moral performance consistency at all levels of both domains (see Hausman and McPherson, 1993, on policy evaluations and the moral appraisals of economic arrangements). They need to review from the evaluation feedback data whether company business and operational decisions reflect moral consistency in performance behavior throughout the organization-set.

A conflicting participatory observation example of business policy and operational decision discrepancy reflecting a grave organizational moral inconsistency occurred in a personal study of an end-of-life care arrangement of a son engaged as the primary care-giver of his parents in his home. This son has provided exclusive home caring of his father and mother for four years, the last two of which he and his parents have qualified for the Medicaid Waiver program in the State of Vermont. In this program, he has received regulated compensation from the State for the daily hours of personal care rendered and even for a 6th stage role-taking consideration on the part of the State for 720 yearly hours of companionship time for each of his parents. As such, this program reflects an exemplary principled planning governmental ethic manifesting the State's moral sensitivity for the family care-giver and its moral commitment to an ethical business policy. The mission statement of the program clearly manifests role-taking and caring reciprocity as it stresses "Person-centered" care as "the *core* of all plans and services" (emphasis added) and "respect" for "providers" as care-giver in conformance with the "State Plan on Aging" (see Exhibit 4:2).

Exhibit 4:2   VERMONT STATE PLAN ON AGING

MISSION STATEMENT

The Department of Disabilities, Aging and Independent Living's mission is to make Vermont the best state in which to grow old or to live with a disability—with dignity, respect and independence.

To achieve this goal, the Department is committed to fostering the development of a comprehensive and coordinated approach to the provision of community-based systems of services for older adults and people with disabilities. Our goal is to enhance the ability of these Vermonters to live as independently as possible, actively participating in and contributing to their communities. As we approach this work, we are guided by the following core principles:

➤ *Person-centered:* the individual is at the core of all plans and services.

➤ *Respect:* individuals, families, providers and staff are treated with respect.

➤ *Independence:* the individual's personal and economic independence are promoted.

➤ *Choice:* individuals will have options for services and supports.

➤ *Self-determination:* individuals direct their own lives.

➤ *Living well:* the individual's services and supports promote health and well-being.

➤ *Contributing to the community:* individuals are able to work, volunteer and participate in local communities.

➤ *Flexibility:* individual needs guide our actions.

➤ *Effective and efficient:* individuals' needs are met in a timely and cost effective way.

➤ *Collaboration:* individuals benefit from our partnership with families, communities, providers, and other federal, state and local organizations.

We are proud of Vermont's history of constantly re-evaluating the system of aging and long-term services and supports and in developing innovative approaches to using our limited resources to respond to the needs and preferences of Vermont's aging population. . . .

Our mission must include the work of the Area Agencies on Aging (AAAs) and other community partners to provide services which prevent poverty, isolation, poor health and institutionalization. We are committed to assisting communities in identifying prevention models and in working with other state agencies and our community partners to explore new approaches to managing chronic conditions and promoting healthy aging. We will assist in planning for, supporting and implementing community-based programs, services and initiatives which offer front line support to assist older adults in retaining their maximum level of independence, because we recognize this is an essential component for successful aging and independent living. We also recognize and strive to support the contributions of family caregivers, since without them many Vermonters would be at great risk of losing independence and the key social connections that result in a high quality of life.

(Source, Vermont State Department of Aging)

In accordance with this plan, the policy reflects the 6th stage universal ethical principle of caring reciprocity in recognition of the son's having saved the State two years of Medicaid nursing home costs for two persons. The nursing home costs to the State through this two year period for his parents would have been $297,024. The total compensation which the State awarded the son for his personal care services of his 100 year old father and his 95 year old mother in the family home through this period was $104,521. Thus, the actual cost savings for the State was $192,503. Though the State has been morally responsible in its business policy of reciprocating these benefits to the son for his personal care services to his parents, an operational decision by the Long Term Clinical Coordinator of the Department of Disabilities, Aging and Independent Living, assigned to this case at the local level of the State's reviewing process, reduced the total of one hundred hours biweekly care for his mother to seventy eight hours amounting to more than a $600 payment loss for the son, even though his care of services for his mother had doubled with her end-of-life caring needs. This decision cost him grave anxiety, inasmuch as the yearly home heating costs have tripled. Clearly, this operational 2nd stage non-personal bureaucratic decision was morally inconsistent with the State's 6th stage role-taking sensitive ethical business policy. The coordinator, notwithstanding her professional medical role as a nurse, could not find the time to conduct a personal bedside evaluation of the mother. She was thus placed in an impersonal contradictory role of rendering her decision from a structured evaluation worksheet submitted by the case manager of the area Home Health Agency, who had requested an additional three hours of biweekly personal care. This injudicious second hand decision-making was flawed by a lack of a critical practical (*praxis*) bed-side understanding of the mother's daily deteriorating end-of-life caring needs. This organization flaw was primarily due to an operational moral inconsistency problem at the local operational levels of the State's Medicaid line and staff ethical training program which failed to provide applied moral development awareness training relative to 6th stage personal care priorities in the State's exemplary focus on person centered health care delivery. When this account of operational decision discrepancy was brought to the attention of the Deputy Commissioner of the Vermont Agency for Aging and Independent Living in a Fair Hearing by the son, she intervened with her own performance evaluation review of the case with assistance from legal counsel of the State. In this forum, she compared the prevailing conventional reviewing process judgments of the nursing coordinator (at moral stage 3) and her fixed administrative role-functioning assignments with the complaints of the care-giving son protesting the absence of an affective caring and (6th stage) person-centered bedside review. With 6th stage principled ethical leadership in her own decisive moral judgments and with moral sensitivity for the bed-ridden mother and the bureaucratic role constraints of a system belabored caring nurse, she directed this Clinical Coordinator to reassess her own review at *bedside* along with the Home

Health Case Manager. In the home structure of this review, the nurse emotionally grasped the end-of-life caring context and was compassionately motivated to relieve the anxieties of the care-giving son. Upon her final report, the Deputy Commissioner rendered an objectively fair compromise to the son and his mother, restoring sixteen hours of biweekly care, and re-generating their appreciative confidence in the caring ethic of the State and in its Fair Hearing forum for insuring *moral organizational consistency.* (Relative to this kind of professional moral performance and affective caring in health delivery systems, see Rule and Bebeau, 2005).

Bowen and Power (1993) emphasize the importance of these kinds of Fair Hearing reviewing of ethical forums for corporate performance evaluation processes and moral interorganizational consistencies. Drawing from contemporary decision theorists regarding uncertainty contingencies in decision-making processes, such as those that were encountered in the Exxon Valdez disaster, they offer a set of decision criteria that adds to the organizational consistency moral imperative. They suggest that in addition to consistency monitoring, decision-makers should explore different situational perceptions and resource availabilities for implementing solutions to all expected and assessed possible outcomes (see also Trevino, 1986 and Kurtines, 1984).

Organizational Consistency and Operational Discrepancy. Applying Bowen's and Power's suggestions to a more recent institutional and penal military organization "environment" disaster in 2004 during the Iraq war, the top Pentagon decision-makers clearly did not have any kind of review board coordination in the situational aspects of perception consistency and operational discrepancy on the sex scandal in the *Abu Ghraib* Iraqi prison. Neither did the military authority line of command demonstrate any competency, let alone consistency, in providing resource availabilities in terms of training military prison personnel to abide by the latent ethical principles on the dignity of fundamental human rights toward upholding the Constitution of the United States which the military is charged to defend. In the general run of organizational inconsistencies, Bowen and Power stress the need for corporate decision-makers faced with the uncertainties of unexpected outcomes to at least strive in a co-responsible forum for the possible realities of reasonable judgments rather than the "impossible dream" of infallible strategies:

> Our approach to moral management is thus grounded in, and builds upon, this approach to making *reasonable* decisions; an approach that emphasizes dialogical decision making procedures. It follows then that the requirements for managing ethically are consistent with those for managing effectively, and we suggest . . . that a sensible approach to evaluating the performance of managers facing dilemmas (moral and other) must deal directly with the uncertainty that exists at the level of policy making (p. 104).

While this conclusion of Bowen and Power would seem to be "reasonable" and "sensible" and consistent with the way the Pentagon and Congress dealt with the scandal, these latter two "intra organization-sets" of the United States government did not seem to strive enough in a "co-responsible forum" to face the compelling need for the moral reconstruction of the corporate conscience of the federal government. This example is one of the worst cases of corporate organizational inconsistency performance on record and has given evidence of not just the lowest stage of moral development but more disgracefully the lowest "stage" of corporate immorality. It also is a critically important example of how complicated a complex organization environment can become in the different domains of multiple bureaucratic organization-sets and how difficult it is to maintain, let alone to achieve, consistency on all fronts. And finally, to analyze the least, this corporate military scandal of organizational inconsistencies has not brought forth many type "B" moral leaders (as described in ch. 3), especially when the revelations of "accepted" forms of torture were discussed in the Congressional hearings. This prison scandal was and still remains a nightmare of immoral strategies and remains a blatant call for corporate moral reform of the Pentagon and the military to awaken the corporate conscience of at least these two divisions of the government. Conversely, therefore, to the moral management approach of Bowen and Power, it dialectically follows that the requirements for managing *effectively* are consistent with those for managing *ethically*. The moral performance evaluation of the military leadership in this grave organizational and constitutional inconsistency demands ethical certainty at the level of policy-making at the Pentagon and suggests a critical need of moral development education for military prison management (Pfeifer and Owens, 2002). Ethical certainty at the policy level must be the driving force for management efficacy throughout the operational lines of moral reconstruction and organizational change.

PERFORMANCE EVALUATION AND MORAL RECONSTRUCTION

Moral Reconstruction and Organizational Change. All MBE integrated forms of performance evaluation instruments, including supervisory, self-appraisal, collective, interactive and collaborative review boards can become critical symbolic mechanisms for *moral reconstruction and organization change*. An overall review of these forms, as presented in this chapter, along with Rest's *theoretical* cooperative and *practical* reconstructive models, as covered in the last Chapter 3 and to be applied in the next Chapter 5, offers a precise focalized methodology on how to generate actual and operational planning for moral reconstruction and organizational change. First and foremost, these evaluation processes should be used as *learning instruments*. Second and utmost, these learning instruments should *reveal* and *produce* two critical openings for moral development reconstruction and organization development change.

The first *revelation* to look for through the stages of moral development reconstruction in the performance evaluation process is the discovery of actual or potential type "B" moral leaders. While this should be a relatively easy search in the overall picture of evaluating a worker, the discovery may take some time in terms of how the worker presents his/her moral profile. As the executive, manager or supervisor conducts the evaluation in the framework of Rest's moral stages of cooperation, he/she should look for the worker's critical insights and creative abilities relative to work performance and job satisfaction. Does the worker, for example, manifest constructive critical insights for improving performance or is he/she a complainer? One who bears a constructive outlook may very well be a potential type "B" leader for moral reconstruction and an innovative planner for organization change.

The second *revelation* to look for in terms of organization development change is the leadership capacity for overcoming resistance to change. From the pool of type "B" leaders emerging from the performance evaluation process, the supervising evaluator should find promising "critical practical" leadership within the workforce to participate in the developmental coaching for moral reconstruction and organization change. This leadership pool could easily be formed as an interdepartmental collective for planning organization change and especially for addressing the practical departmental problems associated with systemic organizational resistance. Meanwhile, the more theoretical and policy problems associated with such resistance could be studied and addressed by the MBE socialization management team, as guided by the eminent practical and scholarly work of Chris Argyris. In his study, *Knowledge for Action* (1993), Argyris presents a guide to overcoming barriers to organizational change. This work is an excellent analysis of why and how workers and even management and executives resist change. He identifies symptoms of "organizational defensive routines" which evolve in the infrastructure of organizational interaction impelling defensive postures and self-protective behavior on the part of individuals and even collectivities to by-pass or cover-up interactional immoral matters which may cause them embarrassment or threat. His account reads like symptoms of an organizational disease which pervade institutions of government and education as well as of business and markets which can and often do promote irrational persistence of error and unethical consequences of behavior (see Shiller, 2005). His explanation is quite graphic and pervasive as his description traces this behavior to early life experiences among these individuals and collectivities which promote self-defensive action to avoid embarrassment and threat. Argyris' analysis is, moreover, verifying and convincing as his graphic account further traces an infectious vicious circle of the seeds of corruption between a morally undeveloped individual and a morally unaware organization which now helps to explain the origins of the widespread corporate cultural and global immoral cover-up epidemics of this contemporary era.

The use of defensive routines learned early in life is reinforced by the organizational cultures created by individuals implementing strategies of by-pass and cover-up. These strategies persist because organizational norms sanction and protect them. Once this occurs, individuals find it rational to hold the organization responsible for the defensive routines. Thus, there is a circular self-reinforcing process, from the individual to the larger unit and back to the individual.   (Argyris, 1993, pp.20-21)

Type "A" executives, managers and workers are prone to this "disease." Type "B" tend to be immune from it. The MBE corporate moral reform mandate thus is to change type "A" personnel into type "B" persons by the infrastructural *continuous learning* of moral development training and performance evaluation reviewing.

Learning occurs when we detect and correct error. Error is any mismatch between what we intend an action to produce and what actually happens when we implement that action. It is a mismatch between intentions and results. Learning also occurs when we produce a match between intentions and results for the first time.

. . . Learning is also an action concept. Learning is not simply having a new insight or a new idea. Learning occurs when we take effective action, when we detect *and* correct error. How do you know when you know something? When you can produce what it is you claim to know.   (1993, p.3)

ORGANIZATION DEFENSIVE ROUTINES AND MBE RECONSTRUCTIVE THEMES

MBE " *can produce what it claims to know* " namely, that moral development *praxis* training, supplemented by the personal and collective opportunities for continuous learning engagements with corporate trainers and performance evaluation reviewers, *induces moral reconstruction and delivers organizational change.* Continuous learning discourse with these trainers and reviewers will strengthen the ethical purpose of the company and empower its management with type "B" leadership for developing moral reconstruction and directing organizational change. It will, moreover, *disinfect* its culture from any organizational defensive routines and immunize its workforce from moral inconsistencies and immoral cover-ups and scandals.

Upgrading moral performance management in the Catholic Church. A rather demoralizing example of immoral cover-ups and scandals uncovered by the work of Timothy Lytton (2008) in the Catholic Church's problems with pedophile priests demonstrates the case study theories of Argyris and his analyses of "organizational defensive routines." Lytton's work is a comprehensive historical litigation study of these priests' scandals and the helpless and inefficacious management policies of the Church with its 1st and 2nd stage morally irresponsible abdication practices of a type "A" hierarchical leadership in a bureaucratic religious organization. While his work is honest, thorough and conclusively helpful to comprehend what is needed to help the church recover from these scandals in terms of organizational reform, it is not intended to be a treatise on how to morally reform the church and its managerial hierarchy. Out of the litigation complexity of his work, he simply states:

> I do not mean to suggest that the frame of institutional failure originated in litigation. It is probably impossible to determine where it first arose and, for our purposes, it does not matter. My point is that a number of competing frames have been offered to characterize the problem of clergy sexual abuse and that tort litigation made the frame of institutional failure more persuasive and pervasive than it would otherwise have been. It is because of litigation that clergy sexual abuse is so widely considered a problem of institutional failure requiring institutional reform. (2008. p. 107)

Within the *reformation* complexity of this work, MBE planning simply suggests that the management policies of scholars like Chris Argyris and the "Planning for Change" theories of Warren Bennis (1969a) be adhered to and that, most practically, the following *praxis* strategies for "*organizational management interventions*" with type "B" leadership practices in the diocesan and pastoral domains of the church be implemented with these fourfold remedial steps:

> As a religious organization, whose social ethical mission is to be an institutional model for corporate ethical authenticity at the highest levels of the moral development scale, the papacy and episcopacy of the Roman Catholic Church need to open new directions on how to reconstruct its organization re-development policies toward formulating pastoral management strategies for *organizational caring interventions* at the highest levels of the Kohlberg scale:
>
> 1. To admit personnel problems of immorality as soon as they are discovered and verified.
> 2. To submit first time sex offender priests to immediate moral development rehabilitation in private retreat centers and to dismiss repeat offenders from the priesthood permanently.
> 3. To prohibit any and all "organization defensive routines" of hiding or relocating priest offenders within the ecclesiastical re-assignments of parochial and diocesan transfers.
> 4. To exhibit authentic episcopal and pastoral caring interventions for the victims and families of the abused.
> 5. To commit to the moral education of future priests by introducing moral development education in seminary curricular studies. (There is virtually no attention given to the moral education of seminarians in their training for the priesthood. It is simply assumed that candidates of the priesthood are morally advanced and sensitively caring individuals. A repeating sexual predator is not a sixth stage caring

individual but a first stage careless criminal who should be prosecuted and should not be admitted into the priesthood; and if already ordained, *wholly* defrocked from his "holy orders.")

This latter remedial curricular step needs to acknowledge that the moral theology curriculum in the seminary training of priests has been exclusively focused on the impersonal teaching of the immorality of sin and not at all on the personal development of morality from ethics. Roman Catholic scholar, George Dennis O'Brien, identifies the latent confusion between morality and sin which may be the rational cause for the curricular lacuna in seminary moral development studies:

> The Catholic Church seems confused on the relation of morality and sin. There is a valuable tradition of Catholic moral argument based in natural law. What is not clear is how natural law morality relates to the theological notion of sin. Sometimes natural law gets an extra endorsement from the fact that God created "nature," but the basic presumption of standard natural law theorists is that considering nature alone would be enough to prove the moral point.   (O'Brien, 2007, p. 151)

The moral point to be proved by natural law studies is the relationship between personal moral development through the social and behavioral psychological learning of "rationality and respect" for other human beings, especially for children (see pp. 50-51 in Chapter 2). Moral development studies in these natural law interdisciplinary tracks are based on the ethical principles of universal justice and caring reciprocity which *must not be presumed* in the curricular moral education of seminarians and their ministerial formation as priests. These kinds of morally compassionate and management remedial interventions implanted in a 6th stage caring ethic and a curricular reform program in moral development studies for candidates in the priesthood would prevent these morally inconsistent scandals from disgracing the church and degrading the ministerial workforce of its faithful priests and devoted missionaries. Such a type of *caring* corporate managerial leadership on the part of the bishops is needed to *upgrade* ministerial pastoral reform particularly because of the theological profession that the church is the *"Corporate Body of Christ."*

MBE LEADERSHIP IN THE CHURCH

Executive Laity Management. In the aftermath of this traumatic Vatican breakdown of an inbred clerical organizational hierarchy, the Church needs to morally reflect on the pastoral authenticity of its bureaucratic managerial inefficacy in the contemporary arrangements of its complex organizational and multinational environments, as compared to the *original simplicity* of the apostolic structures of the Early Church in its pristine organizational pastoral development. Clearly, the organizational management of priestly "shuffleboard" transfers of its pedophile offenders from parish to parish, diocese to diocese and even from country to country reflects a morally shameful and ethically degrading incompetence at the lowest levels of managerial moral *under*-development on the part of the episcopacy and the papacy.

It is quite evident that the church is in need of radical organizational management reform in the aftermath of these scandals. It is moreover imperative that its hierarchy needs to retreat into the reflexive zones of reforming its ministerial authenticity of pastoral caring with the moral integrity of hierarchical managing. Toward these practical reformation goals, the Vatican needs to consider re-assigning the managerial leadership of the church's complex organizational environments and its priestly personnel placements to the human resources of academically trained and professionally experienced managerial laity.

The church is a huge religious multinational corporate institution and cannot be morally managed, as contrived by any "organizational defensive routines." The management of such a global multi-ethnic institution would be more efficaciously served in this religious age of cultural pluralism by an *executive* body of the Vatican hierarchy appointed by the Pope as a pluralistically cultural Board of Directors responsible for the *organization management* of the temporal affairs and public relations of this Universal Church.

Whatever form a restructured organization management of the church assumes, its leadership would benefit from the moral efficacy of MBE as a *reformational* management paradigm toward rebuilding the ethical image of the church and the morally upgraded identity of its priesthood with a re-creative caring ecumenical ministry (Guerrette, 1973 and 1974).

The papacy itself needs some restoration of its own efficacious apostolic re-identity as an ethically caring Holy Father and as a 6th stage morally sensitive religious leader open to the managerial caring reformation of the Vatican bureaucracy. As an authentic fulfillment of the pastoral dominical order of its Lord to "feed (His) lambs and (His) sheep," the papacy needs to rediscover its corporate ecumenical identity with a fatherly compassionate voice, as Pope Benedict himself manifested during the audiences he gave to numbers of the sexually abused and their families in his first papal visit to the United States.

The Holy Fatherhood of the papacy was conceived as an apostolic office of the church for the liturgical and pastoral leadership of its faithful that its believers may proclaim *their own authentic voice in the church* (O'Brien, 2007) and demand retributive justice for its "holy innocent" victims. Listening to this voice with *Pope Francis*[4] will generate "*vitalistic renewal ideas*" toward reconstructing a *collegial management* of the church with analogical imaginative planning and ecumenical pastoral reform:

> Vitalistic renewal ideas in the widest sense of the term are founded upon analogies with the reproduction and growth of human life and of life in general. Such (is) the idea of Renaissance. . . .
> The most characteristic trait of the Renaissance idea is at any rate the assumption of rebirth or renewed growth or return of vital values in an individual, community or institution, in a nation or in humanity as a whole. (Ladner, 1959, pp.16-17)

VITALISTIC RENEWAL IDEAS FOR THE REFORMATION OF THE CHURCH

From these vitalistic ideas of reform by a Patristic Age scholar of the early church, it will become clear in a more expanded ethical sense that the scandals of the complex religious organization of the contemporary church need the remedial expertise of a competent MBE managerial leader who knows the difference between degrading moral inconsistency and upgrading moral reliability.

"Vitalistic Renewal Ideas" and Management Reformation Strategies. Strategic managerial planning and performance evaluation reviewing, as proposed above, in such a universally grave organizational scandal facing the Catholic Church, requires the expertise of contemporary managerial executive policy making and reformative strategic organizational planning.

Executive policy making and strategic planning operations of any corporate institutional organization, including especially a universal church, need executives and managers who have studied and applied the basic knowledge and skills of attaining the fundamental managerial goals of the organization. This knowledge and experience are dependent on the strategic planning of executives toward formulating management decisions to attain the corporate goals of the organization through appropriate ongoing structural and functional adaptation (Parsons, 1956) and *interactional praxis* integration in the ministerial management of the Church (Guerrette,1981). Professor Thomas McNichols of the Graduate School of Management at Northwestern University affirms the *strategic importance of corporate integration* in this way: "Despite a comprehensive knowledge of the operations of the multiple functions of the modern corporation, policymakers must make judgments about the whole organization, and their decision-making efforts must be directed toward the attainment of objectives which attempt to maximize the efforts of the enterprise as an integrated unit which is greater than the sum of its parts." (1977, p. 4)

While strategic management studies in the business world are primarily focused on securing a competitive advantage in marketing operations, it is especially helpful to explore the importance of their relevance in "reformulation planning" toward the development of *recovery strategies* in the complex organization structures of the church for its authentic pastoral governance in the aftermath of the priest pedophile sex scandals around the world. As an urgent case study matter, it would be strategically reformative to let the Pope take care of the policy making for pastoral ministries and re-assign the reformulation of organizational methodologies and the strategic planning of the church's ministerial goals to the collegial bodies of the bishops, priests and the laity at local diocesan levels. This reformulation plan would significantly help to de-bureaucratize the church in the stagnating inefficacious bondage of a MBO Vatican Curial organization culture. This historically outdated clerical "organization-set"[5] has evolved into a dysfunctional hierarchy of *dis*-graceful managerial performance which has "disfigured . . . the face of the Church" (Pope Benedict XVI's own words in https://www.youtube.com/watch?v=rviYNeMNJLI, emirates247.com3/3/13) and contaminated its sanctity (Tuckman, 2010).

Not only does the Pope need to support this strategic managerial reformation, he also needs to reformulate a globally symbolic renewal of the church with a new ecumenical identity—morally consistent with the etymological significance of its authentic claim as a *universal* church. Pope Benedict's resignation may allow an opportune *practical* change for Pope Francis to consider the implementation of a symbolic interactional reformulation strategy of re-organizational renewal to "*re*-configure" the titular face of the Church as the Ecumenical Catholic Church. Such a re-identifying imaging projection, *beyond* Rome, may symbolize a re-*vitalistic* renewal pledge that the Catholic Church is serious about critical *praxis* change and its multinational global ministry to the world.

The innovative discoveries of this plan would help to restore the universal pastoral role of the Pope and protect the integrity of the Papacy more efficaciously than the bureaucracy of a "Roman" Curia. This re-imagery projection of its universal identity has already been established by Pope John Paul, Pope Benedict and now Pope Francis themselves with their distinct 6th stage moral caring profiles of their multi-continental visitations around the world. Such ecumenical pastoral leadership continues to inspire the laity and the clergy to collaborate in the mission of corporate ecclesiastical reform for the moral imagery of the Church itself and especially for the sexual integrity and the moral re-development of its priesthood. The theological doctrine of the Mystical Body of the Church would be far more authentic and morally trustworthy with a universal commitment to these kinds of recovery strategies and managerial planning directed by a collegially appointed hierarchy of laity and clergy committed to these "vitalistic renewal ideas" and trained by MBE leaders.

MANAGERIAL PLACEMENT SCANNING OF PRIEST ASSIGNMENTS

Leadership Planning and Environmental Scanning. Authentic *practical* pastoral recovery for the priesthood and for the integrity of managing priestly appointments, Bishops should consider the organizational "reformulation" strategies of *managerial placement scanning used in corporations.* With the organizational managing experience of executive *laity* assignments to needed parishes through the strategic planning of "environmental scanning" within *dioceses,* such scientific MBE managing methodologies would significantly help to assign the morally developed right priest to heal the pediatric caring needs of the violated "holy innocent" victims of the Church.

> Reformulation is at the base of the strategic planning system; it is in this stage of the policymaking process that management assesses its position, progress, and market (or *ministerial)* posture vis-a-vis its stated objectives and the environment in which it operates. This ongoing monitoring of the control system is a major function of management at all levels. The interpretation of the information supplied by the system is a *vital* (emphasis added) responsibility of the top management group who must determine when and if reformulation should take place and to what extent the policymaking process should be recycled.

> Environmental scanning must also be incorporated into the reformulation process by management to aid in detecting threats to the well-being and survival of the firm (or *church*), to determine opportunities which would be compatible with its skills and resources, and hold out the potential for profitable growth (or *pastoral* efficacy). . . . The control system may indicate weakness in the root strategy and thus signal the need for the development of a recovery strategy, a complete recycling of the policymaking process, and a redesign of the overall strategic plan, with its consequent effects on the operating, organizational, and control strategies. (McNichols, 1977, pp. 129-130)

Such scanning focusing on the analysis of relationships within the church's "complex organizational-sets" internal and external environments would alert managers to make decisions about social, moral and organizational solutions toward achieving pastoral efficacy (see managementstudy-guide.com and Brinkerhoff and Kunz, 1972).

Implementing such managerial recovery strategies in the universal Catholic Church would clearly take the expertise of professionally trained and experienced savvy and seasoned executives, especially those who have managed multinational corporations. If the Pope is reluctant to make such a radical change in the organization management of the church, he might be willing to consider appointing an exploratory Board of Directors composed of carefully selected CEOs and senior executives from these multinational corporations. Such professional directors and executives from the laity would know how to conduct scientific environmental scanning[6] throughout the universal church and accurately define any "weaknesses" in the organizational root systems of the church which may be causing a membership exodus of devout believers, as in the nation of Germany because of the traditional ecclesiastical tax burdens on the laity in the aftermath of the widespread scandals in the parishes of that country (search Google on "German Church Taxation"; see also Ayed, (2010) on the extensive proportions of the priest scandals in Germany). These kinds of problems require the reformulation of organizational "root strategies" specific to the nations and cultures of a universal church to achieve policymaking processes toward the development of *recovery strategies* for the Catholic Church in these troublesome times for priests and especially for the devout and faithful believers of its communion.

Ecclesiastical Management Planning and Diocesan Environmental Scanning. Reformulation and recovery strategies with this organizational depth and international scope will deliver moral performance evaluation results for the Pope and Bishops that will insure universal policymaking stability and postconventional ethical leadership consistency in the Church. Stuart Nagel, scholar in political science and policy analysis studies, describes methodological procedures on how to improve policy-making deliberations in strategic management planning relative to "environmental monitoring." His work traces the development of reformational "values" with "sensitivity analysis" to allow "variation" in "policy recommendations." These tracks can be *scanned* by skilled CEOs from the laity toward the strategic management of ministerial assignments as recovery strategies to *restore parochial faith and personal trust* in priestly appointments, especially in the recent scandalous aftermath of the "hide and seek" revolving appointments of pedophile priests in the Philadelphia Archdiocese (Turlish, 2012). Such value sensitive monitoring by ecclesiastical authorities must be transparent with honesty about a priest's moral profile and with the history of his integrity in pastoral ministry to restore parochial faith for people and personal trust in their priests. The most serious strategic managerial problem in the pastoral domain of *moral transparency*, however, that bears significant causal effects on widespread scandalous outcomes of pedophile behavior in the priesthood is "the seal of confession." It would behoove the Pope and Bishops of the church to reevaluate this sacramental privilege, which has no biblical nor theological foundation, to change the canonical practice of this confessional system to meet the transparency needs of the ecclesiastical moral environment. Since this guarded seal was innocently intended for the private protection of sincere penitential remorse of the sinner and should therefore be *honored and preserved for the sake of seal-amendment authenticity*, "repeat pedophiliac offenders" *must not be granted* this privilege at the expense of *sacramental dignity* under the confessional curtains of criminal indignity. With this reformulated mandate, the papacy and the episcopacy can regain the proper efficacious power to terminate the sinful pathological disease of child abuse and allow the CEO laity managerial legacy to conduct moral development scanning without ecclesiastical canonical blinders. (Note how such a legacy could provide a critical *practical* managing team of *experienced* devout Christians toward implementing the MBE paradigm of organization management for the Universal Church in *The Pope and the CEO*, Widmer, 2011; see, especially, his interview with Doug Keck on EWTN 3/10/1). These recovery and reformulated strategies could then proceed to include variation in the monitoring processes of management planning to respect differentiation circumstances that would be specific to congregational cultures and to corresponding personality traits of the appropriately assigned priest. As a policy analyst of social science research methodologies, Stuart Nagel states: "Policy analysts can also attempt to justify the values they are seeking to achieve by showing how they relate to higher, widely-accepted values. They can especially vary the normative and factual inputs into their models (parishes) to see how that variation or sensitivity analysis affects the policy recommendations" (1980, p. 9). Policymaking stability with variation flexibility can significantly improve performance evaluation in the strategic organization management of the Church toward restoring personal and corporate moral consistency in the priesthood.

ENVIRONMENTAL GENDER SCANNING
AND RECONSTRUCTIVE APOCALYPTIC PLANNING

Applying an innovative version of environmental scanning to the wider global changes in the cross-cultural spheres of *ecclesiastical management policies* and clerical *human resource moralities* reveals the need for the Church to re-evaluate its sacramental pedagogies in addressing the revolutionary domains of human sexual relations in terms of the *sanctity* of sex, the *dignity* of gender and the *integrity* of marriage.

In these apocalyptic times of global warming, planetary surviving, gender transforming and marital union evolving, the Church needs to open its MBO Curial tracks to review its international management of pedophile and sexual cover-up scandals with MBE Christological scanning. Such innovative scanning analyses can open the MBO moral containment window by addressing these apocalyptic indicators of planetary survival with cosmological scanning and *re-evolutionary indicating* among earth scientists—toward opening the MBE cosmic windows for *evolutionary redeeming*. Such multi-disciplinary vision needs the cooperating voices from the Ecumenical Churches of the World toward opening *ethical appointment planning* with *morally re-formative* defining of sexual ethics and erotic aesthetics (see Appendices A and D in Guerrette's *Ethical Theories and Moral Narratives in Art* (2014, vol. II) with other recognized scholars, such as, Eminent Sociologist of Religion, Max Weber (1920);[7] Sister Margaret Farley (2006), Professor Emerita of Yale Divinity School and Past President of the National Association of Ethical Studies; and Joseph Blenkinsopp (1969) Emeritus Professor of Biblical Studies and Sexual Ethics Scholar at the University of Notre Dame.

These innovative versions of MBE sexual, marital and celibate scanning definitions need to trace the sacramental relationships of marriage with a *morally developed pedagogy* of Eros as a 6th stage interpersonal *caring* love toward recognizing the social interactional and symbolic imaginative expressions of *aesthetic* love-making which, in *praxis, sanctifies* sex. This sanctifying focus is critically important for scholars of the *social science of sexuality* and especially for theologians and philosophers of the natural science of its existential beauty, because such *interdisciplinary depth perception* clarifies that the *actual* area of the sacramentality of the marital union is psychosocially embedded in the sacramental *aesthetics of Love*[8] and that the interactional and social relationships of the lovers are functionally guarded by the legal structures and liturgical rites of "marriage." If the Church authorities could explore the apocalyptic warnings from the Bible's book of *Revelation* that the salvation of the Planet could be imminent with *nations rising against nations* (Mt.24:7) and *cosmic storms pounding on its populations*, it becomes plausible that the *prophetic* works of the saintly Divinity School Nun on "same sex marriage" might awaken the "Caring" Curial "managers" of the Church toward exploring MBE "scanning" methodologies for population control.

Aesthetic sacramental sexual activity should *not* be indissolubly bonded to the liturgical sacramental structure of marriage, inasmuch as millions of "*Holy Innocent*" persons, unable or incapable of being married, such as, the lonely, invalid, blind, retarded and impaired populations, could be counseled about the *sanctity* of sex as a "sacramental encounter" with *God* (Schillebeeckx, 1963). Every human being is born with the genetics of sexuality[9] and should deserve the re-*creativity* and the "nobly *pure* emotions" of sacramental graces through its *aesthetic celebration*. Authentic liturgical theology teaches that sacraments are meant to celebrate as a spiritual form of worship not to regulate as a ritual form of governance. It must always be remembered that the sacraments are liturgical acts of grace (Roguet, 1962) not merely structural "states of grace." Accordingly, marriage is a structural state to secure the fidelities of committed pledging lovers *vitally bonded* in the sacramental *"elan vital"* of Love (Bergson, 1935 and Marcel, 1982: p.133, as an *open* "novel application" of the sacrament); see also Appendix A in Guerrette, 2014 vol. II, for an *aesthetic* archetypal erotic "Passion Play" of love and the *Sanctity of Eros*; and, finally, review Blenkinsopp, 1969: ch. 1 "Eros and the Christian" pp. 3-15).

The pedophile scandal, *in the church,* is a sociologically symptomatic outbreak of MBO systematic in-breaking of organization subcultures within parochial ministries in the Church; and even, *beyond the Church,* more widespread of out-breaking trafficking of children in global third world cultures. It is incumbent on the Papacy and the College of Cardinals to *lead* all global cultures of the world with MBE organization management policies and post-conventional moral development sexual moralities as *sacramental aesthetic encounters* with God.

Conclusion: The Critical Importance of Organizational Moral Consistency. Organizational moral inconsistencies not only reflect lower-stage performance in a company, let alone in a church, but even more seriously, de-moralize its workforce and impair its own corporate ethical integrity. The Kohlberg research legacy clearly shows the critical importance of moral consistency in moral development progression. Every phase of performance evaluation and all of its instrumental forms should not only be monitoring for the individual and organizational manifestation of *moral consistency* in the workplace, but for its open-system ethical promotion in company structures. It can thus be concluded that organizational consistency and corporate responsibility, as its moral development link, are the ethical keystones for MBE programing. Without such ethically related transparency, the moral atmosphere of any company or church will remain a vulnerable organizational climate and environmentally open to the wounding scandals of corruption within the corporate body of its workforce and to the disgrace of its management. The "Management of the Church by Ethics" can heal the "wounds" of its Sacred Corporate Body and renew the purity of its Christological Identity, as *The Wounded Healer,* Nouwen (1979) and as *"The Aesthetic Leader"* of sacramental love, as prosaically and poetically presented in Volume II of this study: *Ethical Theories and Moral Narratives in Art: A Gallery Tour through the Corporate Moral Forest.*

END NOTES

1. For a critically important discussion on the increasing relevance of social faith among workers and public trust among investors, see Chapter 8 on the ethics of social faith and the "dynamics of public trust."

2. For assessing the kinds of organizational conditions and operational skills that would guide the executive or manager in the implementation of self-appraisal systems toward achieving individual and collective responsibility, see Hackman (1986).

3. In the Greek and Latin versions of the Hebrew Bible, there is one such case of divine judicial intervention in a sexual harassment trial involving two elderly judges who had conspired to lure the beautiful God-fearing wife (Susanna) of a wealthy noble and well-respected man (Joakim) in Babylon. After a reception at the couple's

home, when all other guests had departed, the two judges made sexual advances on Susanna while she was bathing in her private garden. When Susanna resisted by crying for help, the judges falsely accused her of being with another man and brought her to public trial to have her stoned to death. Susanna pleaded for her innocence before God. "The Lord heard her cry and, as she was being led away to die, he roused the Holy Spirit residing in a young boy named Daniel who began to shout, 'I am innocent of this woman's death!' " (Daniel 13:44-46). The Prophet Daniel argued her case and convicted the judges of false evidence. He saved Susanna's life and spared her honor. Upon this divine intervention, the assembly of the Jewish people sentenced the same punishment on the judges as they had planned to inflict on Susanna. The virtue of personal moral consistency prevailed over the corruption of collective immoral inconsistency through the incisive power of prophetic Wisdom.

4. Pope Francis is gracefully introducing "vitalistic renewal ideas" in his charismatic assumption of his papal role relationships in the global ecumenical environment of ecclesiastical management of religious organizations. Review his recent visits to Jerusalem and to Bethlehem inviting the Abrahamic Religions of Judaism, Islam and Christian Orthodoxy to pray with the respective government hierarchies and to worship with him in the geographic areas of Palestine and Israel. See the media coverage of these events on www.ewtn.com/holyland.

5. The organization-set is the interacting network of a company's co-operational organizations within its wider interorganizational business environment (Evan, 1972; see Chapter 3 above for a review of managerial net-working in complex organizational environments.)

6. "Environmental scanning" is a technical term relating to the measuring and evaluating of social organization trends and cultural directional changes occurring within national boundaries and/or global spheres with specific reference to their impact on social, political, business and religious, etc. organizations. It is especially utilized in business enterprising to predict marketing expectations and economic planning for industrial growth and corporate development. Its importance for executive policy-making decisions and strategic managerial planning is defined by McNichols and included herein with appropriate relevance for MBE application in the international spheres of ecclesiastical management needs, "to predict" pastoral "expectations" and *to reformulate strategic ministerial clergy appointment planning*, especially in Germany, in Ireland and in the United States: "The policymaker must have an awareness of the potential impact on the organization of economic, political, social, and technological changes in order to formulate the strategic decisions which will determine its future course. To facilitate the creation of this awareness, environmental monitoring should be incorporated into the strategic planning process of the company (or the *church*) as part of the control and information system" (1977, p. 189). The *praxis* role of the lay management team would be to assess the specific organizational needs of parishes, especially those which have endured scandal by tracing the socio-economic status of parishioners and the clerical moral developmental profiles of priests. The applied *practical* purpose of such organizational environmental scanning is to prevent scandalous interpersonal damaging from impersonal systematic appointing and especially from deliberately hiding pedophile offenders with stage 1 fears of punishment avoiding "hide and seek"

strategies, at the "pre-conventional levels" of the Kohlberg scale. (see Chapter 3, Exhibit 3:1, pp. 59-60)

7. With interdisciplinary vision of sexual ethics, and erotic aesthetics, Max Weber, in the 19th Century, traced the sociological history of morally under-developed sexual mores with his own critical practical conclusion of the *aesthetic dignity of sexuality* in these morally spiritual terms: "The decisive development from the point of view of the sociological problems which concern us, is the *sublimation of sexual expression* into an eroticism that becomes the basis of idiosyncratic sensations and generates its own unique values of an extraordinary kind." (emphasis added; see *Sociology of Religion* (1993);" see also Guerrette, 2014 vol. II Appendix D and end note 25.)

8. This liturgical sacramental description of Eros, as a celebration of the aesthetics of love, is significantly and theologically different from the psychology of "eros", as described in the work of Erich Fromm in *The Art of Loving* (1956) as an "enquiry into the nature of love." His work is strictly framed in the interpersonal dimensions of sexual love and reflects a morally under-developed perception of Eros unreflective of ontological beauty and sacramental integrity, in contrast to the musically composed *Eighth Symphony* of Gustave Mahler and the romantic poetry of love-making in the *Faust* by Wolfgang Goethe, setting the scene for the reverent paintings of Francoise Hauben of Canada and Rene Durocher of France in the "Holy Sanctuary of Love," as presented in the EquiPax Gallery Collection (Guerrette 2014 vol. II in Appendix D).

9. See the studies of O'Neil and Donovan (1968 ch. v) who have opened the works the works of Schillebeecxk through a critical practical review of cultivating a psycho-sexual moral ethos of caring love as an authentic treatise of sexual development addressing the "Magic Years" of child development and the "tragic years" of guilt development as a pathological outcome of sexual masturbation. Their work has drawn the MBO "confessional curtains" of sexual liberation as a moral theology for MBE *caring sexual celebration*. It is with incomprehension that even they did not critically analyze the literary term "masturbation" with the "content analysis" of social scientific "symbolic interaction theory" identifying the Latin term "turbatio" as a moral psychological *"turbulence"* to the ethical sacredness of *loving sexuality*. The word in itself is "disturbing" to the *aesthetics* of the sexuality of moral development, the noble emotions of which inspire the *ideal impressions of sexual ethos* toward the sacred induction of *sacramental ecstasy*. (See vol. II, pp. 21-23 and especially the "Escalated Mystical Ecstasy" of St. Teresa of Avila, pp. 87-88.") To conclude this critical practical analysis of the pedagogy of sexual development, it would make more morally theological sense to re-identify this innocent sexual activity as a *natural sexual "elevation."* It is morally certain that the Divine Father of sexuality, Who designed the nocturnal seminal emission process of natural sexual development, would approve this conclusion of sexual innocence toward emitting peace of conscience to youth in the most important years of their sexual moral development.

CHAPTER 5

MORAL INCENTIVE BUILDING IN WORKPLACE ASSOCIATIONS AND
ACADEMIC EDUCATION

Moral Incentive Building and Operational Moral Upgrading. This is a
"critically" strategic chapter in applied *"praxis"* terms of making the whole
process of moral performance evaluation *operative* to effect *interpersonal
change* in the attitudinal incentives of workers, managers and executives
along with *organizational change* in the departments, divisions and
boardrooms of corporations. In order to direct attitudinal moral upgrading in
the organizational alignments of a company's operational mandates from
hierarchical boardrooms and corporate executive offices through departmental divisions to work floor associations, it is critical to reconstruct an
interactional value system of authority and subject relations through the
medium of *cooperation*, as traced by the six steps of "moral stage
development learning in the previous two chapters. The operational need in
this chapter is, thus, to include the critical *praxis* methodology of inducement
incentive building strategies through companywide *caring cooperative
associations* that will *operationalize the highest stages* of workplace moral
performance throughout the entire workforce. In addition, the academic need
in collegial management education is to develop moral incentive building
with MBE curricular learning reform, especially in graduate schools of
business, economics and management, as advocated by AACSB
International: The Association to Advance Collegiate Schools of Business.

MORAL INCENTIVE BUILDING THROUGH COOPERATIVE LEARNING

Cooperative Associations and Moral Upgrading. To begin, it is helpful to
clarify the specific theoretical importance of James Rest's work *in*
identifying the "concept of cooperation" as an *operational* research first step
to use the term to organize work performance in accordance with the six
stages of Kohlberg's moral development scale. It is therefore necessary to
review this organization of the six developmental concepts of cooperation on
the Kohlberg scale, as presented earlier in Chapter 3:

Moral Development Table on the Six Stages in the Concept of Cooperation
(Rest: 1994, p. 5)

Stage 1 The morality of obedience: do what you're told.

Stage 2 The morality of instrumental egoism and simple exchange:
Let's make a deal.

Stage 3 The morality of interpersonal concordance: Be considerate,
nice, and kind: you'll make friends.

Stage 4 The morality of law and duty to the social order: everyone
in society is obligated to and protected by the law.

Stage 5 The morality of consensus-building procedures: You are
obligated by the arrangements that are agreed to by due
process procedures.

Stage 6 The morality of nonarbitrary social cooperation: Morality is
defined by how rational and impartial people would ideally
organize cooperation.

Moral Conceptions of Work Associations. The above moral conceptions
presented in this Table are cited to offer executives, managers and corporate
trainers a graphic understanding of how to *measure* the stage level of worker
interactional associations in terms of how they conceive their work
performing roles in accordance with their cooperative motives. Their
cooperative motives, in turn and over time, should manifest a larger portrait
of their moral profile as traced by their role-taking sensitivity range, their
moral reasoning depth and their ethical character strength. Rest explains his
conceptions in this way:

> How does an underlying conception of cooperation lead to a moral
> judgment of right or wrong action in a particular situation? As the stages
> are described here, you may have some intuitions about this process. We
> assume that the conceptions of cooperation are *deep structures* (that they
> are among the individual's fundamental categories for interpreting the
> social world). Now imagine that a person faces some sort of dilemma. . .
> The story material contains a multitude of stimuli and events. Conceptions
> of cooperation help the person sift among many details to identify the most
> important aspects. They provide a way to link relationships of the parties to
> each other and an integrating strategy for deciding which are the most
> important considerations that lead to advocating some course of action as
> morally right.
>
> Conceptions of cooperation help a person manage all the bits and pieces of
> dilemma information, and help guide what an individual ought to do (in
> order to sustain a particular kind of cooperation).   (1994, p. 8)

While the use of the concept of cooperation and its explanation according to
the developmental stages of moral upgrading do apply specifically to the

measuring of worker attitudes about the moral meanings of cooperation in workplace assignments, Rest's *un-applied* moral scaling explanations and theoretical *un-tried* conceptualizations render the measuring of cooperation concepts unproductive for *operationalizing* realistic practical change to actively upgrade moral performance. His explanations in the above table are more theoretically related to an ideal moral development on stages of the Kohlberg scale.

A more *applied explanation* of cooperation in workplace interaction is described by social psychologist, Michael O'Malley, who graphically tracks the social psychological development of worker compliant trust in terms of an obedient operational judgment of cooperation which is more consistent with the Kohlberg scale at the pre-conventional stages of 1 and 2. Following this tracking of the social interactional processes of cooperation in terms of moral development upgrading, O'Malley describes its *social* development advancement to the 3rd and 4th stage conventional levels of the scale as actively building a "trust dependability" in worker performance and ultimately advancing workers to the higher 5th and 6th stages of post-conventional *trust reliability* (2001: p.130). Accordingly, therefore, there is an applied strategic managerial need for the MBE plan of socialization *learning interventions to* achieve the goals of moral performance upgrading with *workplace praxis collectivities* of associative cooperation, as experienced among the management and collaborative workforce of the Lane Refrigeration Contractors in ch. 4.

Learning Interventions and Social Cooperation. With periodic reviewing of these associative job assignments and with the help of case studies presented through this chapter, one should more clearly understand when interactional *working interventions* are needed to upgrade workers to *socially cooperate* in the workplace in accordance with the "Moral Development Progression Plan" in Exhibit 4:1 of the previous chapter and "social faith and public trust" development to be discussed in Chapter 8. Such timely strategic coaching intervening will help to produce clarified *learning* for the worker(s) of the *practical* moral meanings of *caring cooperation on the job* and thus *induce* incentive interpersonal upgrading of the desired moral performance goals in working engagements.

COACHING INTERVENTIONS FOR ADVANCED MORAL PERFORMANCE

Rest himself has been promotive of attaining these desired learning goals and describes their "critical" *praxis* learning importance in terms of the following coaching interventions toward *inducing*:

    1. Moral sensitivity (Interpreting the situation);
    2. Moral judgment (Judging which action is morally right/wrong);

3. Moral motivation (Prioritizing moral values relative to other values*)*;
4. Moral character (Having courage, persisting, overcoming distractions, implementing skills). (1994, p. 23)

These interventions constitute a "practical" starting guide for *leadership coaching* of workers toward advanced moral behavior and participatory cooperation in the workplace (see Sherman, 2010-2011). With his "Four Component Model" in place, as described in Chapter 3, within the individual's and/or the collectivity's inner moral conceptual framework, the MBE evaluating supervisor has the external *educational and interventional framework* for coaching the worker to:

1. take the role of others for whom and/or with whom he/she is co-operating (role-taking others is the most effective interactional way to interpret a need for a *sensitive and caring response* in a cooperative situation);
2. reflect on what the right moral response is called for in a cooperative situation with an *inner conscientious judgment*;
3. reflect on what inner deliberative inducement incentives might be activated in a cooperative situation from moral and/or faith development personal resources to *motivate* the most effective response to moral action toward achieving a sensitive caring response. (on "Faith Development," see Exhibit 8.1 Chapter 8.)
4. Implement this morally active response with altruistic purpose, principled reasoning and cooperative virtue, as manifested in the *moral character* of the newly elected Pope Francis, having the *courage* to break structural traditions for the ultimate purpose of *living with the poor* and *washing their feet.*

Attitude Building and Moral Performance Advancement. To clarify Rest's own explanatory conceptions of cooperation, one needs *to probe into the depth structures of motivating incentives which induce cooperation* and actually activate the interactional cooperative processes. For example, in workplace situations, human resource evaluators and especially supervisors in actual evaluating roles within the interactional structures of departmental workflow sites, need to assess attitudinal demeanor, along with cooperative and even possibilities of uncooperative reaction, to more precisely determine whether or not there *actively is* cooperative engaging beyond the conceptions. To clarify the cooperative process even more simply, this social psychological explanation means that *attitudes are the windows of cooperation* as a practical in-depth reality check for identifying its interactional existence and its moral stage performance between and among workers. Probing this deeply does not require the analysis of a social psychologist; it only requires a developed moral awareness of the evaluator with "principled thinking" at the higher post-conventional levels of the Kohlberg scale and his or her moral acumen to examine any manifest attitudinal signals of why a given worker may actually be cooperating.

Again, for more simply clarifying the example: at stage 1, is this worker cooperating for fear of losing his/her job?; at stage 2, for vested-interest benefits?; at stage 3, to look good in view of the boss?; at stage 4, because it's the unwritten rule of the company?; at stage 5, to keep his/her word of honor and reputation of trust?; at stage 6, because he or she believes in the "Golden Rule" and to help others in their needs? These kinds of attitudinal manifestations will open clarifying perceptions of cooperation and supply experiential motivating evidence for reliably determining the moral stage of the worker in the performance evaluation process.

ASSOCIATIVE COOPERATION IN THE WORKPLACE

Goldman Sachs: A Moral Evaluation Case Study of Associative Cooperation. To use Professor Rest's explanation of the concept of cooperation in a company in this in-depth way, it would be critically reconstructive to evaluate the moral stage awareness level of Goldman Sachs' 2006 Christmas bonus distribution payouts to its CEO, executives and brokers. This case study is most relevant, at this point, to evaluate the practical importance of the concept of cooperation, especially in this critical *praxis* analysis of 2nd stage vested interest benefits, as morally inept. Pertinently, the release of information to the media about the company's Christmas bonus scaling clearly reflected someone's mismanagement of "all the bits and pieces" of the bonus payouts rendering *moral dilemma* impressions of *inoperative* cooperation in the company's *dissociative* corporate communication hierarchy. To make this evaluation fairly without direct internal knowledge of all the procedural and organizational facts of these payouts, it is, at least, imperative to critically evaluate why such morally scandalous corporate executive greed is so widespread in executive compensation benefits, especially in a company that has created an exemplary model of corporate ethical policies with *praxis* execution of innovative global programs and internships for Third World Nations. (See the company's Global Reporting Initiatives G3 Guidelines: *www.globalreporting.org*; and also the Global Conference on Sustainability and Reporting for Amsterdam, May 22-24, 2013).

The actual description of these bonuses as "Christmas" payouts turned out to be a *linguistic fuse* which sizzled through the business media channels, the international market exchanges and the world-wide audiences of the evening news during the most sacred winter festivals of Christians and Jews. The imbalanced problems of the maldistribution of wealth and the social class divisions of the rich from the poor manifested by these bonuses provoked social unrest far beyond these faith believing traditions. Instantly, the announcement created flaring symbolic impressions of inordinate wealth and discrediting greed. These assessed lowest stages of moral depressions and pre-conventional impressions were attributed to the vested interest benefits of "power elite" behavior (Mills, 1954). This kind of perceived 2nd stage pre-conventional moral performance aroused the latent intuitions of the wider and mid-to-lower social classes of the un-invested population that this "Christmas bonus" "course of action" was morally inept and ethically insensitive for interpreting the needs of the social world. Evidence of the socio-economic forces and the class conflict divisions flowing to the wider public appeared in the following editorial published the day after Christmas on the Opinion page of USA TODAY (Snider, 2006). See Exhibit 5:1.

Exhibit 5:1 "The Nations Growing Disparities in Wealth"

USA TODAY
WALL STREET'S BIG HOLIDAY GIFTS HINT AT NATION'S WEALTH GAP
Posted 12/25/2006 5:25PM ET

For workers lucky to get a turkey as a Christmas bonus, the year-end payouts to top Wall Street executives must seem unimaginable.

Earlier this month, Morgan Stanley CEO John Mack took home $40 million, a record bonus for a single year's performance. Days later, his record was smashed by the $53.4 million payout to Goldman Sach's Lloyd Blankfein.

If executive pay as a whole has reached insane levels, at major securities firms it is insanity on steroids. The payouts to Mack and Blankfein are part of $24 billion in bonuses New York's comptroller expects will be paid by securities firms this year, thanks to surging 2006 profits.

Some might see it as Scrooge-like to begrudge big bonuses in such a bountiful year. But the whopping payouts underscore something of greater social importance: the nation's growing disparities in wealth. The top 10% of income earners in the USA own 70% of the wealth, according to a Federal Reserve study. And while hourly wages are forecast to increase about 3.5% this year, Wall Street bonuses are expected to jump 15% from last year. These trends are a recipe for resentment and class conflict.

To be sure, senior Wall Street executives are highly skilled workers and deserve hefty pay. Yet the surge in profits on Wall Street is the result of global economic forces—rising markets and a wave of corporate mergers—that these fortunate executives did not create and can't claim credit for.

If the rationale is their expertise, do they deserve to profit from events beyond their control any more than unskilled workers? And should they be able to do this at the expense of, and with little input from, shareholders in their companies?

These payouts are also hard to justify on the basis of retaining top talent. At Goldman Sachs, they might actually be driving people away. After all, when you're fabulously wealthy, why stay? Blankfein's two immediate predecessors, Treasury Secretary Henry Paulson and New Jersey Gov. Jon Corzine, left and took the enormous pay cuts associated with public service.

At Mack's company, some of the biggest paychecks have been to get rid of people. His predecessor was paid $113 million to leave after fomenting a state of near insurrection in the ranks.

Defenders of Wall Street's pay packages say they are actually quite reasonable in the context of the fortunes made by hedge fund managers, Silicon Valley entrepreneurs, entertainers and athletes. That argument illustrates the problem. Advancing technology and mass media have created an environment in which vast fortunes can be made in a virtual blink of an eye. So be it. That is to be expected, perhaps even encouraged, in the name of capitalism.

But the Wall Streeters don't put their own capital at risk. They haven't devised hugely innovative products such as Google or YouTube. People don't buy tickets to see them perform. Yet they look to the people who do these things as benchmarks.
For those on Wall Street who feel envious or left behind, we offer this advice: Go start your own company, or else take up acting.   (Source: *USA TODAY*)

Critical Praxis Analysis of the "Disparities in Wealth." The morally fundamental fault of these astronomic bonuses is that they were antithetically off the "course of action" *relative to the meaning of the Christmas "story material"* and consequently *divisive* of the rich from the poor, the greedy from the hungry, and the corporate "operatives" from the "unfortunate" cooperatives (see Krugman, 2009 on "corporate boards," p.144 and "corporate profits," p. 201). As a case study example of the anomaly of this kind of *inoperative* cooperation, the Goldman Sach's executive bonus payouts, as critically analyzed in the above Exhibit in the USA Editorial Opinion, reflect double-standard policies of pre-conventional moralities from the ethical impressions of their otherwise exemplary high level virtues of a socio-moral responsibility ethic reflective in website statements on the company culture.

An intensive critical review of these statements generates a *dissociative bureaucracy*, if not a *latent* hypocrisy, in identifying the bonuses with Christmas. The message immediately generated to the markets and conveyed to the public an analogical contradiction between the traditional historical spirit of the Christmas story and the *ethical policy spirit* of the sixth stage post-conventional corporate moral reasoning of the Goldman Sachs cultural ethos, as was historically described on its own website.

The Ethical Policy Spirit of the Goldman Sachs Corporation. The *historical essence* of the Company's Ethos from its origin in 1869 by its Founder Marcus Goldman, stresses the "core values" of conducting its business with an entrepreneurial spirit as focused on the ethical values of professional excellence. These values were to be guided by the following operational principles of Meritocracy, Excellence, Entrepreneurial Spirit and Collegial Teamwork in service of its clientele. The following descriptions trace the exemplary spirit of the company's ethical value-system, as originally proposed on the company website:

An incentive inducement statement to the workforce based on an interactional value system of inclusive unity and inclusive cooperative performance focused on value-expectations of the company's clientele.

An operational value-system motivated by the ethical virtues of the highest stage corporate interactional responsibility to the social order of their civic clients and the communal needs of their clientele with an operational philanthropic commitment to their global organizational working environments.

A conclusive and morally impressive incentive inducement statement (for their internal workforce and their individual and collective clientele) on the company's historical value system based on the history of the company's global performance.

With its active presence in established international locations in "23 countries and 40 cities" throughout the world, the company operates with an interpersonal commitment not just to business clients but to partnerships encompassing non-profit organizations toward *interpersonally* assisting international citizenries with morally 6th stage motivation in the "public arena."

Its ethical value-system of corporate *citizenship* reflects a commitment to socio-economic and environmental policies and ecological values which includes programs for global market operations, international finance facilities for immunization. Along with this record of sixth stage moral motivation, the company has established *The Global Sachs Foundation* endowed with $200 million toward the educational needs of secondary schools around the world toward supporting learning programs in the arts and culture.

In addition to this global servicing programming, the Foundation has instituted *practical* operational affiliating groups to support and collaborate with global charitable institutions and with employees matching selected giving programs along with *praxis* community team-working groups:

> A public servicing program: a unique fellowship model offering the best performing candidates to serve as leaders for the development of innovative capability initiatives and capacity relieving programs to serve communities in the aftermath of natural disasters and social funding needs.

Finally, this Global Sachs Foundation value system has structured these humanitarian services for volunteers to devote an annual humanitarian service of one day per year to participate in relief projects around the world toward serving the needs of the elder populations, the mentoring of youth servicing needs and the restoration of natural environmental domains.

After multiple attempts toward seeking copyright permission to credit the company with its own exemplary descriptions of their 6th stage corporate ethical policies and moral development services to the global universe of humanitarian needs, it is important to examine how such double-standard exemplary profiles can impair the highest standards of this corporation's historical record of ethical policies and moral practice. The following critical practical analysis defines how the best of corporations can be compromised in their values-system deliberations without the moral compass of MBE principles.

In a more recent subsequent interview of Lloyd Blankfein by Charlie Rose (2014), it is apparent that morally exemplary companies like Goldman Sachs are often trapped within the customary protocols of MBO rituals and morally pre-conventional regulations of paranoid managerial communications. Throughout this interview, Mr. Blankfein excelled with *charismatic* descriptions of Goldman Sachs operational principles as an honest CEO guided by a 5th and 6th stage post-conventional profile of moral development policies and organizational development sensitivities. What he needs to develop in the company value-system-building mission is to create a MBE *organization ethos* toward integrating a morally developed awareness from the bureaucratic chambers of his Executive Office and Board Room Tables throughout the operational structures of the highest management divisions, including also the lower ancillary divisions of copyright grantings. Morally effective MBE managing in complex organization environments require operational integrative structures from internal company communications to external copyrighting contractors.

THE UNETHICAL CULTURAL PROBLEM OF EXECUTIVE COMPENSATION

Critical Praxis Reflections. It is incomprehensible why the Goldman Sachs' Office of Corporate Communications or the company's Public Relations Counsel did not respond to the mass public criticism by citing the company's corporate ethic and its culture of corporate social responsibility with its 90 million dollars of worldwide charitable services specified on their own website through recent past years. It goes without saying that the *conceptions of cooperation* (described in the above exhibits of this chapter, let alone the organization reality of the corporation's moral consistency in the various team operations of 90 million-dollar bonus payouts to worldwide charitable institutions) *is visibly at work* within the company itself, as stated above in the Community Team Works agenda: "Since 1997, CTW has offered innovative volunteering opportunities worldwide that make a tangible difference in our communities and that foster inter-and intra-divisional camaraderie within the firm." Moreover, this material of the company's own story of abundant bonus giving, as recounted in these philanthropic programs, could have been translated in multiple creative associative ways to connect with the Christian "story material" of bonus gift-giving in the Christmas season and the Hanukah "Festival of Lights" with bonus "gelt"-giving (Yiddish for money). Furthermore, such reference connections could have generated additional authentic symbolic impressions of post-conventional moral interaction, genuinely cooperating with the story materials of other philanthropic leaders and their programs in similar post-conventional moral action altruistic programming outreaches, such as: President Clinton and his Global Initiatives (see Exhibits in Chapter 7); Oprah Winfrey and her educational foundation in South Africa; Bill and Melinda Gates and Warren Buffett and their recent foundation announcements creating the largest innovation charity in the world for "health and learning in the global community."

The Corporate Personality "Split" of Executive Compensation. The ethically fundamental fault of these astronomic bonuses is that they were antithetically off the "course of action" relative to the meaning of the company's own ethic. All of the Goldman Sachs' website exhibits reflect post-conventional moral planning based on principled moral thinking. However one divides and distributes the bonus sharing, as described in the *USA TODAY* exhibit, the appropriated astronomical amounts to executives were individually inordinate and disproportionate with the rest of the workforce collectivity with *no trace of cooperative planning* nor space for favorative sharing. The ethical problem with these bonuses is symptomatic of social psycho-pathological problems of a corporate ethical "personality split" between the contradictory and conflicting domains of a captivated corporate culture and a free market capitalism. Within this sick "hierarchical" subculture of the workforce collectivity, the organizational climate of the company is contained in an antiquated caste dialectic of superiority versus inferiority, equality versus inequality as inconsistent organizational contaminants, reflecting pre-conventional moral planning and *unprincipled moral thinking*. As long as the corporate culture hierarchy of Goldman Sachs divides itself from its otherwise cleanly cooperative and morally sensitive organizational profile, as outlined in the statements of its cultural ethos, it renders itself ethically inconsistent with the company's own corporate ethical image and finding itself encumbered with its own "organizational defensive routines" (see Argyris, 1993). These routines are clearly symptomatic of rationalizing the capitalistic astronomy of its morally under-developed second stage Christmas bonus payouts framed by the vested-interest greed of a pre-conventional morality in the sub-cultural organizational traps of this "corporate personality split."

The MBE *Moral Resolution of Executive Compensation.* What, in fact, is needed to effectively address this prevailing contradictory problem of disproportionate compensation is a moral resolution of all compensation policy salaries and bonuses through a fifth stage moral observance of socio-economic policies formulated by "moralities of scale" based on the ethical principle of proportionality (see Chapter 6). When corporate culture illuminates the "festivities of light" from the MBE paradigm, executives, directors, shareholders and workforce or union delegates will *cooperatively and reflexively* examine the corporate conscience in the moralities of principled moral thinking and post-conventional salary planning in proportion to the social justice issues of compensation fairness among the entire workforce levels of their respective companies. Only then will the moral clarity of corporate ethics reflect corporate moral behavior of bonus and dividend distributions as ethically balanced and socially sensitive executive compensation. These critical reflections of the company are not considered with unscientific speculation. They are rather practically presented by the ethically principled reflections with a "sociological imagination" of post-conventional morality:

> The release of imagination can sometimes be achieved by deliberately inverting your sense of proportion. If something seems very minute, imagine it to be simply enormous, and ask yourself: What difference might that make? And vice versa, for gigantic phenomena. What would pre-literate villages look like with populations of 30 millions? Nowadays at least, I should never think of actually counting or measuring anything, before I had played with each of its elements and conditions and consequences in an imagined world in which I control the scale of everything (Mills, 1959, p. 215).

In the real world of investing research, it is not *psychologically possible* to control the scale of a company's divesting "insearch" (Hillman, 1978). But in the real world of morality and ethics, it is *re-constructively plausible* to control the scale of *principled moral thinking.* This control can be realized by honest, sensitive and virtuously involved and integrative corporate leaders with *moral character*, who are prepared to examine the historical elements, the complex organization environment conditions and the social class consequences of their business and investing transactions. Nearly a half century ago, C. Wright Mills had some further "sociologically imaginative" conceptions about these matters, as follows:

> Whatever the problem with which you are concerned, you will find it helpful to try to get a comparative grip on the materials. The search for comparable cases, either in one civilization and historical period or in several, gives you leads. You would never think of describing an institution in twentieth-century America without trying to bear in mind similar institutions in other types of structures and periods. That is so even if you

do not make explicit comparisons. In time you will come almost automatically to orient your reflection *historically* (emphasis added). One reason for doing so is that often what you are examining is limited in number: to get a comparative grip on it, you have to place it in an historical frame. To put it another way, the contrasting-type approach often requires the examination of historical materials. This sometimes results in points useful for a trend analysis, or it leads to a typology of phases. You will use historical materials, then, because of the desire for a fuller range, or for a more convenient range of some phenomenon—by which I mean a range that includes the variations along some known set of dimensions. Some knowledge of world history is indispensable to the sociologist; without such knowledge, no matter what else he knows, he is simply crippled. (1959, p. 215)

Had the CEO and the bonus distribution executive planners enjoyed such an historical orientation, at least of the very company they are directing, their historical reflections of the Goldman Sachs post-conventional ethic would have aroused their incentives to induce the firm to integrate a distribution strategy which reflected the higher levels of principled ethical proportionality and moral organizational consistency with the company's corporate ethos. The historical excellence of this firm deserves and demands this kind of measuring of its *cooperative ethical image* and its *corporate moral profile*.

The fact that this kind of measuring is not a part of the current ethical management record of its corporate moral profile is evident from a later scandal that the company faced in its response to the Securities and Exchange Commission (SEC) of charges that the company was complicit in conflict of interest business dealings with clients regarding "mortgage-backed securities." This alleged behavior was even more serious than the Christmas bonus packages described above because of traces of actual and deliberate immoral behavior on the part of the company by the scandalous fact that it marketed and sold mortgage bonds as a good investment to clients without revealing that it had knowledge from another client that the bonds would fail. The company reached a record settlement fine of $550 million with the SEC only to appear with *blame* from a *corporate impersonality split of its moral profile* at the same pre-conventional stages of 1 and 2 on the Kohlberg scale. This historically renowned company with its otherwise morally anchored culture, as reviewed above at the highest stages of the scale, desperately needs the critical moral reflexive *in-viewing* of the "operational dynamics" of the *corporate conscience* toward rebuilding its value-system priorities with "critical ethical consistency," as graphically designed in Chapter 2 and economically defined in Chapter 6 with "moralities of scale."

MORAL DEVELOPMENT MEASURING AND PRINCIPLE ETHICAL LEARNING

Measuring CEO *Principle Moral Profiles.* Another and more complex measuring instrument developed by Professor Rest which can be used in academic learning for the Performance Evaluation of professionals and executives in corporations, government agencies, and in institutions of higher learning and health delivery systems is the Defining Issues Test (DIT). Described earlier in Chapter 3, this test can be used for review of prospective CEO and Board Director candidates of corporations to obtain a reliable measurement of their moral profiles in terms of "principled moral thinking" as an updated ethical assurance search from their previous performance evaluation reports. This suggestion would likely have provoked cynical laughter among most CEOs steeped in the functional cultures of MBO traditions and among Directors in the elite friendship subcultures of 2nd stage exchange morality of Board appointment reciprocity networks. But in the "changing of the *ethical* guard" to the 6th stage principled leadership and moral reciprocities of MBE prescriptions, moral profiles of executives are now being *illuminated* by the continuous learning exposures to executive education programs as promoted by the International Association for the Advancement of Collegiate Schools of Business (AACSB). On the importance of continuing business education as an ongoing resource for upgrading the moral performance of executives, Rest offers this report of a ten year longitudinal study of the DIT:

> There were the usual findings of gains in moral judgment with age, but it was also found that education is a far more powerful predictor of moral judgment development than merely chronological age, per se. The general trend is that as long as subjects continue in formal education, their DIT scores tend to gain; when subjects stop their formal education, then their DIT scores plateau.   (1994, p. 15)

In view of these findings by Professor Rest, it would be especially important for corporations to utilize this DIT measuring instrument on younger business executives who may be just beginning their first executive career search, especially in view of the more recent testing of graduate students in business compared to other professions and different groups on their DIT (P) - Scores of (principled moral thinking). In this test, the P-Scores of graduate students in business were significantly lower than other graduate students whose groups did not specialize in moral thinking, as indicated in Rest's table of these groups (1994, p. 14). Notice the discrepancy in the following Exhibit 5:2.

Exhibit 5:2 Defining Issues Test (DIT) on Principle Moral Thinking (P)	
Different Groups on the DIT *P* Score (Rest, 1994)	
P – Score	*Group*
65.2	Moral philosophy and political science graduate student
59.8	Liberal protestant seminarians
52.2	Law students
50.2	Medical students
49.2	Practicing physicians
47.6	Dental students
46.3	Staff nurses
42.8	Graduate students in business
42.3	College students in general
41.6	Navy enlisted men
40.0	Adults in general
31.8	Senior high school students
23.5	Prison inmates
21.9	Junior high school students
18.9	Institutionalized delinquents

This discrepancy is alarming and needs to be probed for causal discovery of this disturbing dormant moral awareness. One of the discernible causes which helps to explain this lower level educational trend of the graduate students in business is noteworthy from the specific work assignment differences inherent in the various professions measured in the groups themselves. Notice that all of the groups which scored higher, as listed in the table, are already *cooperatively* engaged in or at least are preparing for the direct interactional service of people in the helping and health professions. Graduate business students, however, are generally not all that focused on cooperative relationships in the workforce or direct interactional service with any particular clientele as they begin their graduate education. Their educational focus, for the most part, is aligned with the discovery of a business career which is self-satisfying for personal enrichment and with learning business and management skills which are financially gratifying for professional goal attainment. Thus, the only clarified goal for this group tends to be instrumentally focused on pre-conventional and, at best, conventional morality. Moreover, inasmuch as graduate students in business tend to experience a noticeable "plateau" in their moral judgment level during their professional education, as observed by Muriel Bebeau (2002) and since they generally do not experience any exposure to moral education during their academic learning in their respective schools, their DIT scores on principled moral reasoning would likely reflect significant impairment.

Similar DIT (P) scoring studies of accounting students and even of accounting practitioners by Ponemon and Gabhart (1994, p. 116) also reflect significant impairment. (See their table in the following Exhibit 5:3)

Exhibit 5:3

DIT P Score	Accountant Group Studied	Location	Author(s)
	Panel A: Accountants in Public Accounting Firms		
49.6	Senior-level female accountants	Midwest	Shaub (1993)
47.7	Accountants with liberarts education	Northeast	Ponemon&Glazer (1990)
46.8	Supervisory-level accountant	Nationwide	Ponemon (1992a)
44.7	Accountants at the staff level	Nationwide	Ponemon (1992a)
44.2	Canadian auditors	Ontario	Ponemon&Gabhart(1993)
43.6	Third-year staff accountants	Midwest	Shaub (1993)
43.0	Second-year staff accountants	Midwest	Shaub (1993)
42.4	Accounting seniors	Nationwide	Ponemon (1992a)
41.9	Accouning managers	Midwest	Shaub (1993)
41.4	Accounting seniors	Midwest	Shaub (1993)
41.4	Senior-level male accountants	Midwest	Shaub (1993)
41.0	First-year staff accountants	Midwest	Shaub (1993)
40.0	American auditors	Northeast	Ponemon&Gabhart(1993)
39.8	Accountants at staff level	Southwest	Lamp & Finn (1992)
38.6	Internal and governmental auditors	Northeast	Arnold & Ponemon(1991)
38.5	Manager-level accountants	Midwest	Shaub (1993)
38.1	Accountants (general sample)	West	Armstrong (1987)
38.1	Accountants with business education	Northeast	Ponemon&Glazer(1990)
38.1	Senior manager-level accountants	Midwest	Shaub (1993)
37.1	Partner-level accountants	Midwest	Shaub (1993)
35.7	Manager-level accountants	Nationwide	Ponemon (1992a)
35.6	Senior-level male accountants	Midwest	Shaub (1993)
32.2	Partner-level accountants	Nationwide	Ponemon (1992a)

Panel B: Students in Educational Institutions

47.4	Liberal arts accounting seniors	Northeast	Ponemon & Glazer (1990)
45.8	Female accounting majors	Midwest	Shuab (1993)
45.1	Accounting majors in ethics course	West	Armstrong (1993)
41.8	Graduate-level accounting majors	Southeast	Icerman (1991)
38.6	Graduate-level accounting majors	Northeast	Ponemon (1993)
37.4	Business school accounting seniors	Northeast	Ponemon & Glazer (1990)
37.1	Business school accounting majors	Midwest	Jeffrey (1993)
36.3	Male accounting majors	Midwest	Shuab (1993)
35.5	Business school accounting majors	Southeast	Icerman (1991)
34.5	Undergraduate accounting majors	Southeast	Lamp & Finn (1992)

Notice that the scoring impairment among the graduate students in accounting is similar with those of the above-cited graduate students in business and thus can be explained by the comparable analysis of these business students and their moral judgment professional education "plateau" phenomenon. It is therefore critical to acknowledge that these low P-score levels among graduate students in business and accounting schools and the relative low scores of accounting practitioners affirm the *critical need for direct MBE moral educational interventions* and *ethical core curricular reforming* of business and management education in colleges and universities and auditing and accounting schools around the world. These educational interventions and curricular reforming needs have been called for relentlessly by the International Association for the Advancement of Collegiate Schools of Business since the publication of its Task Forces' Reports on *Management Education at Risk* (Olian, 2002), *Ethics Education in Business Schools* (Phillips, 2004), and *Business Schools on an Innovation Mission* (Policano, 2010), as reviewed in the Introduction to this MBE book.

MORAL INCENTIVE BUILDING THROUGH ACADEMIC LEARNING

Innovative MBE Moral Education and Ethical Core Curricular Reform. This need for direct moral education for business school students and faculty curricular designers has long been recognized in the literature of moral development studies, especially as a result of the research by Rest (1986) and Penn, W.Y. (1990). Most importantly, Penn stressed the need to address the "plateau" phenomena in moral awareness 23 years ago and yet *the need still prevails*, as more earlier identified in 2002 by Bebeau and more recently in the cited AASCSB studies just above. As long as these phenomena prevail in business and accounting school education, moral performance evaluation measuring in corporations where these graduate students serve will continue to be impaired.

Not at all satisfied by the pedagogical use of real and imaginary moral dilemma problems in ethical education interventions as a curricular stimulant for moral reasoning learning, Penn is a strong advocate of the need for more direct course intervention. He describes a course for teaching moral judgment skills citing data that this kind of learning intervention has a very powerful effect. Commenting on his advocacy to a colleague in personal communication about dilemma learning interventions as providing opportunities for students to discover higher stage moral reasoning from their peers for deeper moral perception awakening higher moral conception, he argued:

> There is a more effective and powerful way to enhance moral judgment than by requiring people to discover completely for themselves the power of principled moral thinking. We don't require people to discover calculus for

themselves . . . instead we teach them the concepts. Why wouldn't it also be more effective and efficient to directly teach the component skills of moral judgment, for example, skills of logic, role-taking, and justice operations?   (Penn, 1990, pp. 124-138)

During this historical period, Steven McNeel studied the pedagogy of moral development as an advocate of direct moral learning in college education. Utilizing Penn's methodologies, he designed a general education course for senior students at Bethel College, addressing the integration of psychology and philosophy in the teaching of ethics. By so replicating Penn's direct intervention approach, he taught these component skills for awakening critical reasoning and stimulating principled moral thinking. To ultimately test the generality of Penn's theories on direct learning efficacy, he administered the DIT instrument on the first and last days of the two semesters during which he taught the course. McNeel reported the following results:

> The results from 28 students showed that there was a strong growth in principled reasoning from (41.7-50.6; d=0.65). This modest effect size is very impressive since it is about 80% of the average effect size associated with 4 years of liberal arts college and because it took place in just 3½ months. Two additional points are important. First, the course appeared to be powerful only for a portion of the students. About one third of the students showed sharp gains in moral judgment, whereas the remainder showed only modest average gains at best. In a personal communication, (1991) Penn had reported a similar pattern among his students. Second, the gains were much sharper among business and education students taking the course than among the remaining students. Average growth among the former was 12.4 points (d = 0.98) compared to only 5.9 points among the latter (d = 0.39), even though both groups started at the same level of principled reasoning. This is important because, as reported earlier, business and education students were precisely the type of students who did not otherwise grow strongly in moral judgment during college. There remain important questions (e.g., is the result partly a testing effect?), but it seems that Penn's direct approach to teaching principled thinking can work well when used by other teachers and with other populations. And it works well with students who have tended not to grow as sharply during college.   (1994, pp. 41-42)

While these noble efforts of Professors Penn and McNeel do have "powerful" merit in undergraduate ethical education at the college level, the greater challenge is to broaden this "power" of ethical thinking at the graduate level of business and management schools and its potential related moral learning benefits on the moral performance evaluation levels of principled moral thinking throughout the future careers of these graduates. This greater moral educational challenge would demand *radical* (as in the Latin term *radix* signifying the root system of) *core curricular reform* in these business and management schools.

GRADUATE SCHOOL BUSINESS AND ORGANIZATION MANAGEMENT EDUCATION

One such school currently implementing core curricular reform in business and management education is the Yale School of Management. Dean Joel Podolny described the reform in these terms:

> The SOM faculty unanimously approved a sweeping MBA curriculum reform plan. . . .
>
> A new core curriculum for first year students will be implemented in the 2006-2007 academic year. While the management profession has changed profoundly in recent decades, management education has not. This interdisciplinary curriculum will provide Yale MBAs with the skills to work effectively and lead in today's private, public and non-profit organizations.
>
> As news of the reform has spread, SOM has seen a substantial increase in the percentage of admitted applicants who chose Yale over other schools. (2006a, p. 85)

Upon reviewing the school's curricular reform efforts on its tab of the Yale University website, one notices that there are three impressively reconstructive references to its early implementation status: first, an *open system* corresponding outreach to alumni for critical feedback and co-curricular input; second, its own internal moral profile symbolized by the exemplary *cooperative* planning designs of the entire faculty and mentoring programs of upper level students; and third, its own external moral profile symbolized by the *organizational moral consistency* of sharing its exploratory curricular planning and development programing with the wider academic community.

This news release from Dean Podolny on September 5, 2006 presented the new curriculum in these terms:

> The Yale SOM faculty unanimously approved the framework for the new curriculum in March, 2006. Since then, teams of senior faculty have worked to design all new courses and original materials. Courses in the new first year curriculum are taught in three segments: Orientation to Management, Organizational Perspectives, and the Integrated Leadership Perspective. (See Exhibit 5:4a.)

Exhibit 5:4a   The New Yale SOM Curriculum

ORIENTATION TO MANAGEMENT

Introduces basic language, concepts, tools, and problem-framing methodologies
that will be drawn on broadly throughout the curriculum but are not easily
introduced in subsequent courses;
develops techniques for interpersonal effectiveness in
critical relationships and teams;
and begins the process of focusing career aspirations.

ORGANIZATIONAL PERSPECTIVES

Presents each course from the viewpoint of a key internal or external role,
rather than a discrete function.
Contextually grounded, each course frames the managerial questions
necessary for engagement of that role,
brings insights from the functional management disciplines
(Finance, Marketing, etc.)
to provide answers to those questions, and
affords the opportunity for
focused consideration of values-based and ethical issues,
creating a coherent view of
problem-solving, engagement, and leadership.

INTEGRATED LEADERSHIP PERSPECTIVE

Merges perspectives in a series of interdisciplinary cases
structured to describe challenges faced by leaders of organizations
of differing size, scope, and sector.

Exhibit 5:4b The New Yale SOM Curriculum (Circular Integrative Design)

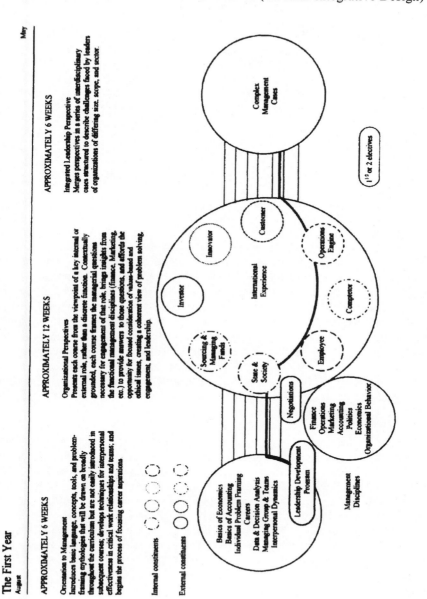

Source: With copyright permission from the Yale Alumni Magazine

The news release source description continues:

> The *heart* (emphasis added) of the new first year curriculum is a series of
> eight multidisciplinary courses, called Organizational Perspectives,
> structured around the organizational roles a manager must engage,
> motivate, and lead in order to solve problems – or make progress – within
> organizations. These roles are both internal—the Innovator, the Operations
> Engine, the Employee, and Sourcing and Managing Funds (or CFO)—and
> external—the Investor, the Customer, the Competitor, and State and
> Society. Each course draws on topics and insights from a variety of
> *functional* (emphasis added) management disciplines to study the
> managerial challenges each role presents.

MBE RE-ORIENTATIONS TO THE NEW CURRICULAR PERSPECTIVES

If this description is the "heart" of the new curriculum, a corporate ethics
analyst wonders where is its soul? This analyst discovers the *radical* problem
of its absence as evident in the fact that the above description of the new
curriculum reveals that its managerial focus is still fixed on the MBO
paradigm and its *functional* imperatives. Since the faculty's work on this
curriculum is exemplary in the multidisciplinary range of its courses of study
encompassing the complex organization environment and networks of
business operations and management negotiations in the multiple spheres of
global international commerce, this innovative curricular design would be
even more impressive if its *ethical soul* were located in the radical core of
MBE paradigm "Orientation to Management" studies. This re-constructively
critical judgment is based on the innovation studies of Professor Sharon
Oster whose descriptions of the favorable factors of introducing innovation
in organization structures are more conducive if the *diffusion* rate is slow and
without technological complexities (1999, see Table 16:1, p. 315). A more
strategically interactional "diffusion" of the MBE innovation would place the
new curricular design at the very beginning of the graduate students'
orientation to management careers in this diffused age of critically needed
corporate ethical and market moral reform. Accordingly, the *radical* MBE
core curricular design would deeply *implant* "*ethics*" as an interdisciplinary
course within the "soul" of the first segment of the new curriculum with its
innovative rediscovery of the *corporate conscience*. This kind of *in-depth*
implantation of ethics at the very beginning of one's academic graduate study
track to professional managing careers would cultivate *gradual* ongoing
interest in management ethical learning and moral performance commitment
to leadership integrity.

To satisfy graduate student interest in this degree of ethical depth dimension
in core curricular reform, one needs to remember Dean Podolny's brief
description of the impressive "substantial increase in the percentage of
admitted applicants who chose Yale over other schools" (2006, p. 85). His

report manifests growing latent evidence of students' interest in corporate moral reform.

An Adapted Revision of the Core Curriculum. The following revision of the descriptions in the "First Year" segments of courses in Exhibit 5:4 offers these ethical depth dimensions with reconstructive *ethical adaptation perspectives* for the new core curriculum. It is submitted as a critical *praxis* review toward changing management ethics teaching from the immobile categories of philosophical ethics to the mobilization activities of applied ethical learning in organizational scientific management ethics for motivating morally developed work performance through the personal workers' and the company's corporate conscience. The MBE paradigm, as *the soul* of this revision, would offer a more emphatic corporate ethical integrative impression *within the core* of the three divisional segments of the curricular reform design. As such, this is how the design would read, if *this ethically* "Integrative Leadership Perspective" were *adapted into the core* of each segment of the MBA curricular reform plan. In effect, this ethical management paradigm shift at the initial orientation of management learning to the First Year, would feed into all courses of the new curriculum, including its "electives" and "leadership development" programing of the Second Year with the interactional caring ethic of MBE (The following suggested textual changes are noted in italics.)

ORIENTATION TO MANAGEMENT

Introduces *MBE (Management by Ethics) as an innovative orientation to management studies and practice to inform the* basic language, concepts, tools, and problem-framing methodologies *with ethically integrative language, morally conscious concepts and corporate responsibility roots socio-psychologically implanted in the corporate conscience. From these managerial ethical perspectives, problem-resolution methodologies* will be drawn on broadly throughout the curriculum *to easily introduce* in subsequent courses *more ethically sensitive reflection and morally developed responses with* techniques for interpersonal effectiveness in critical work relationships and teams and *for beginning* the process of focusing *on* career aspirations.

(Critical *Adaptive* Commentary of the above italic inserts):
This ethically substantive *root system* grounded in a morally intrinsic revision of the Orientation to Management segment is *integratively* significant as it defines an ethical direction to the curricular orientation and *coherently* locates the core of the reform in all subsequent courses throughout the two year MBA program. Other introductory related and even traditional courses can be designed or revised accordingly to critically configure to the new ethical orientation through the initial 6 weeks. This reconfiguration of

courses prepares the students to more practically apply their ethical learning and their own moral awareness advancement to the "Organizational Perspectives" of all the other management disciplines in the original concentric designs to be studied through the following 12 weeks.

MBE ORGANIZATIONAL PERSPECTIVES

Presents each course from the *ethical* viewpoint of a "key" internal or external role rather than a discrete function. Contextually grounded *in principled moral thinking*, each course frames the managerial questions necessary for *the interactional* engagement *and moral enactment* of that role, brings *ethically sensitive and morally practical* insights from the functional management disciplines (Finance, Marketing, Accounting, Economics, etc.) to provide *ethically informed multi-disciplinary* answers to those questions, and affords the opportunity for focused consideration of *morally based values and ethically grounded principles*, creating a coherent view of problem solving, engagement, and leadership.

(Critical *Adaptive* Commentary of the above italic inserts): These organizational perspectives are well-focused on traditional MBO perspectives which would be more effectively and *integratively adapted* to the wider MBE *praxis perspectives* toward moral organization development learning and ethical leadership training.

The following critical analysis of a sample syllabus course on "The Competitor's Perspective," which was presented on the Yale SOM website in 2006, is offered to demonstrate the need for a *core curricular ethical viewpoint* in contemporary management education. Such a core curricular viewpoint should open a focus to integrate ethical principles with morally developed vision into organization management studies and functional disciplinary courses toward deepening internal *reflexive* ethical learning and expanding external *cooperative* moral action (see Bernstein 1971). Such critical "*praxis*" ethical learning in management studies is what motivates leaders to change functional systems to meet the needs of moral environments as well as competitive *moral* practice, which was *not* "implanted" in this sample syllabus. Notice in the following Exhibit 5:5 how such *core ethical grounding* is an essential need for MBE critical moral action planning as an "external" course on "The Competitor's Perspective" by Professor Oster.

Competition in the business world and marketing economies is, more often than not, conducted in the aggressive instrumental relativity stage of Kohlberg's "pre-conventional morality" with structural-functional marketing strategies and profit maximization morally imbalanced economies of scale and sometimes scaring smaller business enterprises with immoral threats of retribution consequences. A core-curricular grounding in moral development learning with a "primer" in competitive ethical managing would significantly add to applied practical planning at the post-conventional learning levels of MBE co-operative marketing strategies. It would be strategically reconstructive to focus on a business evaluation of a "competitor's ethical intelligence" and moral development awareness toward responding with higher moral stage planning and ethical performance.

Exhibit 5:5 A Sample Syllabus of an Organizational Perspectives Course

Yale School of Management   Professor Sharon M. Oster
MGT 410   Fall (2) 2006

THE COMPETITOR'S PERSPECTIVE

This course enables students to be better managers by equipping them to:

- Identify key players in the environment both from a competitive and a cooperative perspective
- Identify the objectives and constraints of those players given the environment in which a manager's own organization and competing organizations are embedded
- Anticipate the likely actions that competitors will take given their objectives and constraints
- Recognize and deal with the feedback between their own actions and the actions of other agents

The course explicitly recognizes that relevant players in the environment include government and nonprofit organizations as well as corporations and that these players act both cooperatively and competitively. Thus, an important premise of this course is that the environment within which organizations compete is multi-layered, encompassing not only the market but political, cultural and legal dimensions. Finally, the course explicitly draws attention to the fact that objectives and constraints arise not only from the external faces of the environment but from internal features of the organization.

Over the twelve sessions, the course will draw from the disciplines of economics, marketing, organizational behavior and politics.

COURSE REQUIREMENTS:

Course grades will be based on class performance (50%) and written work (50%). All written work must be handed in before class begins; since the material will then be used in class, there are no exceptions to this rule. Students may discuss assignments in groups if they wish, but all written assignments are to be done independently. If there are data to be gathered, this must also be done independently to ensure that each of you has the benefit of the requisite practice.

Day 1: Monday, October 30

Introduction to the Perspective: The Sony-Toshiba Case (New SOM case) (Oster)

Readings:
1. Oster, Modern Competitive Analysis, Chapter 3: Review from Economics Foundations.
2. Oster and Podolny, "A Framework for thinking about the Competitor," memo, August 2006.
3. Varian, "Competition and Market Power," in Varian, Farrell and Shapiro, The Economics of Information Technology, 2004.

This set of readings will set you up for the perspective in terms of background. The last reading is relatively dense, and you should plan to look back on it again as we proceed through the class.

Case: **Sony and Toshiba in the HD-DVD Market**
Case Questions: In reading this case, you should think about the following two issues. The case begins with a break-down in talks between Sony and Toshiba over standards. Why did the talks break down and what industry structure do you predict will ensue? Sony and Toshiba seem to be following different strategies in this market. Characterize the differences in their strategies and think about why they are different.

Day 2: Wednesday, November 1

Competitor Intelligence (Oster and Garstka)

This class focuses on identifying the kinds and sources of data available to a firm in trying to understand its competitors' strategies and positions. In your review session you will be introduced to the major SEC filings and how to access them on-line, industry data from Computstat and Bloomberg, as well as the major data source for nonprofits, the Form 990's. In class we will also introduce you to some of the proprietary data sources that firms purchase to learn about product sales and prices in various industries.

***Assignment:** We will be looking at data from the airline industry. Choose one of the following four firms: Southwest Airlines, Jet Blue, American Airlines or United Airlines. Download the most recent 10 K for your firm. You will be focusing on the financial data contained in these reports. Using either Bloomberg or Compustat, provide yourself with benchmark financial data for the industry that you can use to analyze your own firm. Prepare a brief memo that uses the financial data to describe the ways in which your firm differs from the "average" firm in the industry and how those differences fit together and might be connected to an overall strategy that the firm is pursuing. If there are data that surprises you in the sense that it does not fit into the overall pattern you should also present this.*

Day 3: Monday, November 6

Wal-Mart Reprised: Is Competitive Advantage Sustainable and/or Extensible? (Oster)

Readings: Review Wal-Mart Stores, Inc (HBS 9-794-024) from the Foundations of Economics course. After reminding yourself of the competitive advantages of Wal-Mart in this earlier stage of its corporate life, consider one of the following two issues:

Issue 1: **(For anyone with last names alpha A-K; trading permissible)**
There is in your packet a 2005 10-K for Target, one of the current competitors to Wal-Mart, along with one for Wal-Mart. Based on this material and a visit to Target (there is one in North Haven), what you can say about how Target is trying to compete against Wal-Mart? How successful is this attempt likely to be? What can and should Wal-Mart do in response?
Or:
Issue 2: **(For anyone with last name alpha L-Z; trading permissible)**
Wal-Mart has been growing to locations outside the US. Your packet contains a recent 10-K from Wal-Mart describing this expansion. Considering the material in your packet and any other material (including personal reflections) you wish to bring into the class, think about how extensible the several different sources of competitive advantage you see in the early Wal-Mart case are to non-US sites.

DAY 4: WEDNESDAY, NOVEMBER 8

Competitive Strategies and Rules: **(Oster)**

Readings:
1. Oster, "A primer on Antitrust laws"
2. Saloner, Shepard and Podolny, Strategic Management, 231-238.
3. Besanko, et al, Economics of Strategy, 310-320.

In the last class, we looked at how Target tries to compete against Wal-Mart. This class focuses us back on the position of Wal-Mart. As a general matter are there things that a strong initial entrant like Wal-Mart can do to reduce either the likelihood of a Target entering or affect its success from doing so? We will consider pricing, product proliferation and vertical contracts as entry deterrents. This class also explicitly introduces the state in terms of antitrust rules that govern the behavior of an incumbent firm in trying to affect entry.

DAY 5: MONDAY, NOVEMBER 13

Slaying the Giant **(Oster and Podolny)**

Readings:
1. Christensen and Raynor, The Innovators Solution, Chapter 2.
2. Nalebuff, Co-opetition, pp. 237-245.
3. Baron et al, "Organizational Identities and the Hazard of Change," May 2006
4. Siklos, "Sony's Road Warrior," NY Times 5/28/06.

In a number of markets, we see ways in which early entrants have an advantage. In this class, we will explore some of the reasons that early powerful firms sometimes end up losing the competitive battle.

All three of these readings explore ways in which established firms can be challenged, sometimes by smaller, nimbler upstarts other times by firms within the same or adjacent industries. In this class we will explore each of these perspectives, with applications to the contrast between Sony and Apple described in the Times article.

DAY 6: WEDNESDAY, NOVEMBER 15

***Reputation and Identity as Advantage and Constraint* (Podolny)**

Readings: *Podolny, "Investment Banks"*
***Case*: Prudential Securities**

DAY 7: MONDAY, NOVEMBER 20

***Motivations* (Podolny and Oster)**

Readings:
1.   Podolny and Scott-Morton: "Love or Money: The effects of motivation in the California Wine Industry."
2.   Glaeser, pp. 1-6 in The Governance of Not-For-Profit Organizations
3.   Chevalier and Ellison, "Risk Taking and Mutual Funds Managers," University Chicago Paper #77.

Clearly, as we learned in some detail in Professor Polak's session in the Problem Framing course, the motivations of your rivals are important in determining their actions. A common assumption in the economics literature is that firms try to profit maximize, albeit with some imperfections in the implementation, and as a first approximation profit maximization often turns out to work very well. In this segment we go beyond this first approximation, to look explicitly at the motivations of organizations of varying structures and he managers within those organizations. The readings cover three industry types: the nonprofit, the for-profit but closely held wine industry and the mutual funds industry. We will reflect on both what motivations different organizations might have but how those differences in motivation affect an organization's ability to compete against them.

*For class discussion: Reflect on an organization you have been part of, either as work or in a board or volunteer capacity. Look at one decision that organization has made and use it to make inferences about the underlying motivations of the decision makers in that organization.

DAY 8: MONDAY, NOVEMBER 27: Competing and Cooperating

Readings*: Nalebuff, Co-opetition,* Chs. 1, 2

In preparation for class discussion, please answer the following questions:
•   You are a manager for the Chicago Tribune, the largest daily paper in Chicagoland. USA Today has just entered your market. How can you best respond?

Turning to cooperation:

- How can banks (e.g., Chase and Citibank, ANZ and Westpac) do a better job of cooperating with each other while competing? Where do they cooperate today and what opportunities are they missing?

- How can Mastercard and Visa do a better job cooperating?

- How about Shell and Exxon, Microsoft and Oracle, Barnes and Noble and Amazon? Similarly for Yale-New Haven and St. Raphael, The Met and MOMA, and HBS and SOM?

- How do you draw a bright line betyween legitimate cooperation and collusion?

- What types of cooperation do you think will be easy and what types will be hard?

Thinking beyond the value chain:

Memorial Sloan Kettering Hospital is a leading oncology center in the world. Its mission statement contains the following:

> "The staff at Memorial Sloan-Kettering Cancer Center endeavors to care for the person -- not just the illness -- from the moment that someone arrives at the hospital until long after he or she has gone home.... Special services designed to ensure that patients get through their illness whole in mind and spirit are an integral part of Memorial Sloan-Kettering."

What are some of the implications of that statement? Take the specific case of a high school kid who comes in from Ohio for 4 weeks of chemotherapy.

Write a similar statement for GM. Does GM appear to be living up to that statement?

DAY 9: WEDNESDAY, NOVEMBER 29

***The Complexities of Forming Alliances: Legal Rules and Organizational Issues* (Oster and Podolny)**

Readings:
1. Toby Stuart, "Mastering Financial Strategy," Financial Times
2. Podolny, "Network Firms of Organizations."
3. Three caselets on alliances

**Assignment for in class discussion: Based on the material in the readings, consider how each of the alliance characteristics contributes to the likely success or failure of the alliance.
The next few lectures explore some creative ways for organizations to differentiate themselves from their competitors...

DAY 10: MONDAY, DECEMBER 4

Using Consumer Insights to Gain Differentiation Advantage (Dhar)

Readings TBA

From packaged goods to high tech products and financial services, firms face the problem of trying to differentiate their products and services when the underlying assets and activities are seemingly easy to replicate. In many markets, customer insights can help to identify features that create competitive advantage. For example, as you have seen in a case from the Customer Perspective Oral-B added a patented blue strip to its toothbrush that provided users with a benefit based on the insight that most brushers are uncertain as to when to replace their brushes. A framework is provided to identify features based on differentiation by looking at the entire consumption process—from need recognition to how a product is disposed (Evian example in recycling). This segment also highlights the role of brands as differentiation.

DAY 11: WEDNESDAY, DECEMBER 6

Social Responsibility as a Competitive Advantage (Oster and Rae)

Readings:
1. Oster, "The Strategic Use of Regulatory Investment by Industry Sub-Group"
2. BP Annual Report material.

Case: Global Climate Change and BP Amoco (HBS 9-700-106). Read this case quickly as background material.

In this class we explore the possibilities of using corporate social responsibility as a competitive advantage, focusing on environmental issues. As the material indicates, BP has made a decision to embrace stronger rules on global warming than is legally required. As you read the various company documents, think about whether and how this stance will affect BP's competitive advantage and its overall profit potential. You should consider long and short run issues, and pay attention to the expected behavior of other agents.

* *Group Assignment:*
- *Groups A-E: Put together a collection of documents in the public domain that BP uses to address its customers, its employees—potential and actual—and regulatory bodies.*
- *Groups F-H: Do the same collection for Exxon*
- *Groups I- K: Do the same collection for Shell*

One of the groups from each company will be asked to present their material to the class and summarize their impressions of the themes pursued by each firm.

DAY 12: MONDAY, DECEMBER 11

Re-thinking the Game (Nalebuff)

The discussion of social responsibility highlights one way a firm can re-configure a game to make it more likely that it will succeed. In this last class, Professor Nalebuff will work with you to think more broadly about how to change the competitive game.

Readings:
1.   Paul Klemperer, "The Flaws of a Dutch Auction," Financial Times.
Case: Bitter Competition: Holland Sweetener Company versus NutraSweet

Case Questions for Bittersweet: (Not to be turned in)

1.   Why is HSC trying to get into the aspartame business?
2.   What is HSC's added-value?
3.   How, as HSC, do you expect NutraSweet to respond to your entering the European and Canadian markets?
4.   What should you do as HSC to make money?

Questions to go Along with the Klemperer reading: Strategies for Versatel: (Please turn in your list of strategies for Versatel)

In the Netherlands G3 spectrum auction there were six bidders and five licenses. The way the auction worked is that as soon as one bidder dropped out the auction would be over. The six bidders in the auction were

- KPN is the incumbent telephone provider, like the AT&T of the Netherlands. It formed a partnership with Hutchison for this auction.
- Libertel is owned by Vodafone/Airtouch.
- Telfort is an arm of British Telecom.
- Dutchtone is an arm of France Telecom.
- Ben is a consortium comprised of Belgacom, TeleDenmark, and T-Mobile. SBC is a large stakeholder in some of these companies.
- And Versatel. Versatel was the only player in the auction who did not have a 2G license.
- Moreover Versatel's market capitalization ranged from 3 to 6 billion and was at least an order of magnitude lower than that of all the other bidders. In short, everyone (Versatel included) thought that Versatel would lose the auction.

Make a list of all the possible strategies that Versatel might employ. There are at least five options worthy of consideration. Rank them.

(Critical *Adaptation* Commentary on Professor Oster's Course)

This course not only studies the functionally market driven business processes of competition but also its dialectical counterpart in the interactional collaborative processes of *cooperation*. Remembering that cooperation was conceived by Rest, at the beginning of this Chapter, as a concept model for measuring moral development, projects a suggested *adaptive ethical focus* for Professor Oster and her students to expand this course as an excellent interdisciplinary study for evaluating moral behavior and introducing ethical principles in management supervision and business transactions. This added expansion would project and "integrate" a critical *praxis* focus on applied studies with corporate social and environmental responsibility themes as "competitive advantages" in analyzing such case studies as British Petroleum, Transocean, and Ltd. Halliburton and the unethical blame-shifting of the rigging explosion in the Gulf of Mexico and their moral accountability awareness of Global Climate Change, as ecologically analyzed in Chapter 8).

How much closer can a student get to learn about management, business and environmental ethics than this! And, yet, on the second page of the syllabus, the student reads:

> The course explicitly recognizes that relevant players in the environment include government and nonprofit organizations as well as corporations and that these players act both cooperatively and competitively. Thus, an important premise of this course is that the environment within which organizations compete is multi-layered, encompassing not only the market but political, cultural and legal dimensions. Finally, the course explicitly draws attention to the fact that objectives and constraints arise not only from the external faces of the environment but from internal features of the organization. Over the twelve sessions, the course will draw from the disciplines of economics, marketing, organizational behavior and politics.

With such an incisive view of the "Competitor's Perspective" and the explicit attention drawn to the objectives and constraints arising from the complex organization environment and from the internal interactive domains of the organization, the MBE paradigm would significantly add promotional *ethical dimensions* to competition processes and marketing forces with "post-conventional morally developed" *caring dimensions* of collaborative interaction and *cooperative* inter-organizational behavior. Accordingly, it is precisely within this core that the social psychological elements of the corporate conscience, along with the cognitive psychological reflexive cooperative components of *moral sensitivity*, *moral judgment*, *moral motivation* and *moral character* (review pp. 150-151 in this chapter), would clearly open "competitor's perspectives" with integrity for ethical reflection toward conducting business and re-formulating organization management with *cooperative* unity at the highest levels of MBE corporate moral performance. To her credit, Professor Oster did stress the moral priorities of *caring ethics for persons* over competing options for profits in conducting business transactions.

These social psychological elements and cognitive psychological components are morally imperative for constructing a corporate ethic in any company or business venture and they need to be critically addressed as *core analytical inputs* throughout the curricular reform program. Without these core analytical references in this course by Professor Oster, the bottom line of learning about competition and cooperation will be, in effect, strategic management facts and calculative legal maneuvers and not ethical operational principles; nor will this line of learning reveal where the principal management players should perform on the moral development scale.

As a core curricular component for the 12 week Organizational Perspectives courses, the MBE orientation would activate references to the corporate conscience and would evaluate corporate moral behavior of the companies and the personal moral behavior of the managers studied in this sample course. Moreover, beyond this course, MBE is designed to open critical *praxis* organizational perspectives in all the "management disciplines" of the new SOM curriculum and to apply a *"Socio-Economic Moral Incentive Model"* for the purpose of inducing "planning for change" and re-evaluating contemporary global social problems of hunger with MBE "moralities of scale:" (see the explanation of this model in the following Chapter 6 of this book). These organization development perspectives, generated from the MBE paradigm, are charged with moral development incentive building toward *activating* post-conventional moral behavior in organizational workplaces in its ethical mission for corporate moral reform.

MBE INTEGRATED LEADERSHIP PERSPECTIVES

> Merges *involved and integrated leadership* perspectives in a series of interdisciplinary cases *and morally problematic events* structured to describe challenges *of the personal conscience and the corporate conscience* faced by leaders of organizations of differing size, scope and sector *to care for their workers with personal integrity, to serve their companies with a corporate ethical sense of its history, and to integrate their personal ethic with the corporate ethic.*   *(2006, p.86)*

(Critical Commentary of the above italic inserts)

This interpolation of the Integrated Leadership Perspective is only to reinforce the efficacious strategic importance of the personal engaging *incentives* of CEOs as morally sensitive integrative leaders. A stellar exemplar of CEO performance in the phenomenological context of the catastrophic events of 9/11 is "described" in Chapter 10 of this book to demonstrate the "challenges" of how the *personal engaging involvement* of the CEO made the difference in the efficacious delivery of integrative *moral leadership.* The chapter recounts how the Cantor Fitzgerald CEO, Howard Lutnick, *made the morally right things happen* by assuming a *cooperative caring* role in rebuilding the company morale from ground zero of the terrorist catastrophe, after having suffered the loss of 658 members of his workforce. Compassionately facing the survival needs of their bereaving families, he extended the scope of his caring involvement by "integrating his personal ethic with the corporate ethic" making *interpersonal* home visitations and promising long-term-funding for family-benefit-planning.

These ethically informed and morally developed adaptations to the First Year Curriculum, as presented above, would significantly prepare students for the exemplary curricular reforms, as presented in the Second Year Curriculum. (See: *http://mba.yale.edu/mba/curriculum/pdf/diagram.pdf*.)

MBE *Conclusions for Critical Praxis Curricular Reform.* These suggested inter theoretical revisions of the Yale SOM curricular reform design are based on the need to integrate the ethical orientation of MBE into the wider perspectives of graduate academic learning and continuing executive education curricular programs. The revisions have been composed for the *praxis* purpose of *practically* preparing graduate level students of business and organization management schools with the highest grading levels of DIT aptitudes for "Principle Moral Thinking" (see pp. 157-161) and especially with post-conventional ethical aptitudes and morally sensitive caring attitudes for *leadership* careers in complex organization environments. The second year curricular reform programing of multi-disciplinary *electives and leadership development studies* offers multiple opportunities for integrating MBE graduate learning toward launching career opportunities for its multi-national body of matriculating students.

Subsequently, through an intensive content analysis research method (Selltiz, Wrightsman, and Cook, 1976) of reviewing the Courses of Study offerings in the 2012-13 SOM Curriculum, it is to be noted that over 20 coherent courses were added to the original curriculum, within which this innovative MBE corporate ethical paradigm, described through this book along with its second volume on "Corporate Art and Ecological Studies," could be offered toward significantly improving applied graduate learning with careers waiting for them in corporate consulting opportunities.[1]

Furthermore, with the latest co-curricular planning of Dean Edward Snyder in 2014, the Yale SOM program has meritoriously expanded to include collaborative post-graduate studies with global *praxis innovation programs* among intercollegiate associations of international business education schools for *practical learning* toward corporate ethical consulting careers in the Global Network for Advanced Management. See the following website: (http://advancedmanagement.net)

Dean Snyder has also promoted the interdisciplinary curricular development of graduate management studies exploring innovative problem solutions with environmental partnership programs with the Yale School of Forestry and the Environment and the World Business Council for Sustainable Development. See (http://cbeyale.wordpress.com/2014/04/07/wbcsd-partnership)

END NOTES

1. Consider this "offline" timely advice on "Executive Pursuits" from the Personal Business page of the *New York Times*:

> The best career advice you may be able to offer someone entering the workforce today is: "Become a corporate ethics officer and compliance officer, my son (or daughter)." "In the wake of high-profile accounting scandals, investigation into stock option backdating practices and passage of the Sarbanes-Oxley Act, many companies are hiring more ethics and compliance officers in higher-level positions." HR Magazine reports, adding that the salaries are booming as a result. The median compensation package for top global ethics and compliance executives is $623,900; for top domestic executives it is $464,500. If the trends continue, there is going to be no shortage of work. Membership in the Ethics and Compliance Officer Association has more than doubled in the last three years. (Brown, 2006)

The Ethics and Compliance Association is an international association for corporate ethical learning in the areas of social and corporate responsibility. It is composed of an international news network with literary resources and a professional net forum for studies and collegial discourse with a classified directory and search net communication with articles in five languages, as a "Project of the Corporate Responsibility Foundation." Its impressive Global Website and Navigation service contains its Top 500 membership Corporations and Institutes along with Organization listings of Businesses and Consultants, Business Councils, NGO's, Cities, Academic Networks, Research Institutes, Foundations and Journals.

CHAPTER 6

SOCIO-ECONOMIC ORGANIZATION STRUCTURES
FOR
MORAL INCENTIVE INDUCEMENT BUILDING

Economic Associations for Interactional Ethical Integration. With this six-step moral education program presented in Chapters 3 and 4 as the *ethical archway* of a company's "architectural" moral climate, it is promising to note that MBE also represents an organizational psychological planning system for addressing the perennial moral problems of under-developed worker incentive inconsistencies and persistent organizational workplace inefficiencies. As a morally innovative socio-economic incentive inducement building model, MBE can offer long-term *moral education economies* for developing personal *consistency*, individual *responsibility* and managerial *accountability* in the workforce along with *organizational* consistency, *corporate* responsibility and *cooperative* accountability in the company, (see Part A in Exhibit 6:1).

As a managerial innovation, MBE ethical management strategies and moral socialization processes can also create economic benefits for the company by *inducing* the moral incentive "character" linkage in the interactional and collaborative process terms of "cooperative virtue" traced in the previous chapter with Rest and Narvaez (1994) among workers and managers as the strategic "heartbeat" of moral performance reliability for persistent *organizational consistencies and enduring economic efficiencies.* "The core, the heartbeat of economic growth, is innovation—technological innovation, *managerial innovation*, and *financial innovation*" (emphasis added; see Ferguson and Zakaria, 2008, and Ferguson, 2008).

MORAL LEADERSHIP AND ECONOMIC INCENTIVE MODELS

MBE *Incentive Inducement Building and Moral Leadership Efficiencies.* The traditional problems of "persistent organization inefficiencies" in corporate

Exhibit 6:1 MBE Architectural Moral Climate

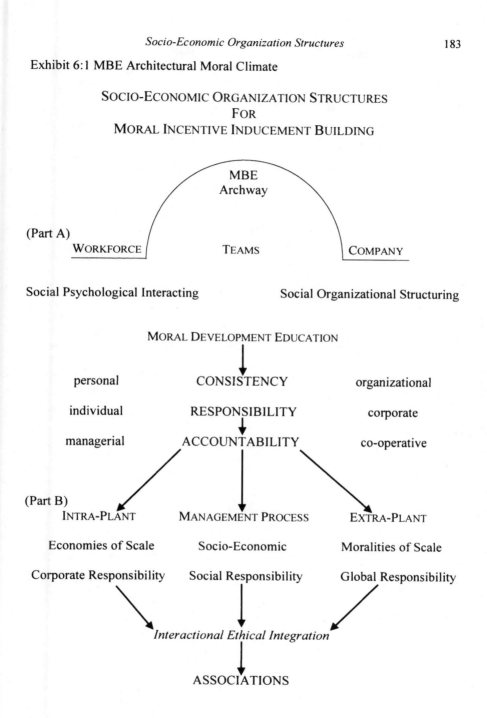

SOCIO-ECONOMIC ORGANIZATION STRUCTURES
FOR
MORAL INCENTIVE INDUCEMENT BUILDING

MBE
Archway

(Part A)

WORKFORCE   TEAMS   COMPANY

Social Psychological Interacting   Social Organizational Structuring

MORAL DEVELOPMENT EDUCATION

personal   CONSISTENCY   organizational

individual   RESPONSIBILITY   corporate

managerial   ACCOUNTABILITY   co-operative

(Part B)

INTRA-PLANT   MANAGEMENT PROCESS   EXTRA-PLANT

Economies of Scale   Socio-Economic   Moralities of Scale

Corporate Responsibility   Social Responsibility   Global Responsibility

Interactional Ethical Integration

ASSOCIATIONS

culture remains controversial for numbers of organization behaviorists and some organization economists (see Bengt Holmstrom, 1979 and Gary Miller, 1992). Much of the controversy centers on the role of leadership. While the literature in the field of organizational economics tends to de-emphasize the role of leadership in incentive system models, other schools of thought from political science and organization psychology stress the role of leadership for inducing workplace incentives. Briefly, the debate follows this argument: Traditional economists propose that no matter what incentive system models are used in the workplace, there remains a latent self-interest drive within individuals that determines a certain "moral hazard" towards "shirking behavior," causing performance inefficiency Holmstrom, p.74). Acknow-ledging this hazard, Miller presents arguments from political science and organization psychology, contending that incentive-building leadership in the workplace can efficaciously make an inspirational difference: "Those organizations whose managers can inspire members to transcend short-term self-interest will always have a competitive advantage" (p. 3).

With some linkage to classical organizational economics, Miller stakes his position in modern game theory and provides a theoretical structure for building an incentive system by achieving work-team cooperation through political leadership in organizational hierarchies. In contrast, with inter-theory linkage to economic psychology and socio-economics, MBE provides a moral development *incentive building structure* for *inducing* more enduring individual and collective work performance through *moral leadership* in workplace democracies as well as organizational hierarchies.

A Moral Critique of the Political Economic Incentive Model. Whereas Miller's rational economic and behavioral incentive system attempts to address the problems of persistent organizational inefficiency, his design focuses on organization and human resource development strategies. He attempts to resolve the complicated managerial dilemmas between authoritarian hierarchy and incentive system inadequacy by proposing rational behavioral models for intra-firm cooperation. His analyses describe the inverse complexity of self-interest preference problems as potentially dysfunctional in all traditional economic incentive systems. Consistently enough, he starts his incentive building premise by acknowledging the "moral hazard" problem: "While a great many contractual forms and incentive systems have been proposed, the best economic analysis argues that in every such system there must remain incentives for at least one individual to persist in behavior that leads to organizational inefficiency" (p. 12).

Accordingly, the best inter-theoretical explanation from philosophical ethics for addressing this traditional economic rationale in Miller's incentive-system-rebuilding is "psychological egoism" (see Beauchamp, 1983). While this theory may realistically explain why people behave the way they do in workplace environments in terms of ulterior vested self-interest motivation drives, it tends to fix some executives and economists into low expectation postures regarding the persistence of organizational efficiency. And, what is worse, it shapes their reasoning negatively and defensively into low expectation attitudes regarding moral development potential (Argyris, 1991, review above in Chapter 5 p. 157). The theory of psychological egoism does not deny this potential but it certainly is not heuristically encouraging nor effectively promotive of any moral pedagogies for its attainment.

Miller's attempt, however, is courageous. He offers organization hierarchies as an inspirational management model for building worker trust, job commitment, company loyalty, social reciprocity and self-responsibility that form the irreducible elements of intra-firm cooperation. His model projects a rational behavioral incentive track beyond the managerial dilemmas of efficiency losses and personal preference gains by structuring work-team designs for intra-firm cooperation. His approach is surprisingly close to that of Piaget (1965) who studied the moral judgments of children in games and to that of Kohlberg *et al.* (1975) who traced their moral development paths through hypothetical dilemma activation. Miller suggests the use of "repeated game theory" to indicate how adults arrive at cooperative behavior through cyclical game conventions in social interaction (the so-called "games that people play"). He thus demonstrates how workers can rationally "play" their way to "cooperative solutions to social dilemmas" in long-term work-group structures (p. 180). But inasmuch as Miller's behavioral incentive track is only rationally grounded in the organizational realities of corporate culture and vested interests, he himself admits that his work-team designs and cooperation equilibriums are flawed with fragile endurance span:.

> However, individuals in social settings constrained by social norms still have important choices to make. The choices they make help to determine the expectations that others have about how the game is to be played and help to shape and alter the conventions that govern the outcome of coordination games . . .
>
> The folk (game) theorem suggests that the beliefs of the various players about the likely responses of other players are all-important: It is this psychological network of mutually reinforcing expectations that makes one perfectly feasible outcome (e.g., cooperation) occur instead of another perfectly feasible outcome (e.g., noncooperation). This suggests a certain fragility in cooperative equilibriums. While it is rational for an employee to cooperate under the perception that others are cooperating and that one's own noncooperation would be sanctioned and/or reciprocated, a relatively few examples of nonsanctioned noncooperation could change these expectations drastically. (pp. 206-207)

This fragile flaw in Miller's cooperative *equilibria* is due precisely to the fact that his incentive system model does not deal with the moral developmental limitations of "psychological egoism" and vested interest behavior at stage 2 of the Kohlberg scale. The latent truth is that the performance flaw can, at times, be reflective of behavior motivated by the individual's social psychological intentions to "look good" at stage 3. And this possibility is even more frequent at the highest levels of management superiority conventions, such as, the "games" that many executives "play" in terms of their vested interests in executive compensation and bonus expectation packages. His model is thus determined to level somewhere within the pre-conventional and conventional stages of two and three, as constrained by the social and economic conventions of corporate cultural externalities. This critique is evident from his analytical perceptions of the norm of reciprocity. In his game-theory analyses of work-team cooperation, it is to be noted that his explanations of reciprocity are *not formulated* at the levels of moral reasoning from which higher conventional and even post-conventional trust, role-taking initiatives and other-caring dispositions can be expected:

> reciprocity will be a strong norm in successful small work groups. It is worth repeating that cooperation in a repeated game need not be based on mutual altruism; it is based on the shared knowledge that each of us can punish the other (by future noncooperation) if either of us fails to cooperate in this period.   (p. 187)

It is evident that this explanation is only explicative of a second-stage *instrumental reciprocity* and vested interest exchange. The external inducements that he proposes like the "property rights" of employment security, team production compensation, profit-sharing and ownership equities, may indeed be incentives for intrafirm cooperation; but they do not by themselves generate higher-stage trust and commitment nor automatically set a moral climate for workplace justice and *caring reciprocity*. A socially just and interactionally reciprocal moral climate needs more than rationally induced incentives. Its organization atmosphere does not need the structural flaws of "moral hazards;" it rather needs the interactional strength of 5th stage contractarian reciprocity and 6th stage *caring* generosity.

Miller's instrumental reciprocity closes his incentive perceptions to worker occupational and corporate operational expediency perspectives. From these second-stage points of view, his game theories do not open his model to more advanced moral development contractarian perspectives. In the end, disparagingly enough, his incentive-building methods *do not hold any hope* for resolving the moral hazard "puzzles" with which he starts and certainly, by his own admission, do not generate the strengths of ethically principled caring reciprocity. The only hope left to resolve the "perennial problems" of "moral hazard" inefficiencies is MBE.

MBE SOCIO-ECONOMICS AND CARING RECIPROCITIES

The MBE *Socio-Economic Moral Incentive Model.* Taking ethics *more seriously* as a higher stage contractarian norm, caring reciprocity is fundamental to upgrade a moral incentive system model to the post-conventional levels of moral development. What is needed to build such an integrative *praxis* theoretical model that can deliver contractarian moral commitment in the workplace and principled ethical caring reciprocity in the marketplace is a MBE paradigm shift toward the integration of economic theory with theories of "evolutionary economics" and the *praxis* strategies of "creative destruction."[1] The ethical range of this paradigm is constructed not only to measure "economies of scaling" but also *deliver "moralities of scaling."* It is analogically pertinent to note that as a contemporary scholar of Lawrence Kohlberg in the early periods of his moral development studies, Bela Balassa (1961) Professor of Economics at Yale, was studying the economic "intra-plant economies of scale." The first of his scaling conclusions was defined in this way: "For various types of equipment, such as containers, pipelines, compressors, etc., cost is a function of the surface area, whereas capacity is directly related to volume. From this principle, engineers derived the .6 rule according to which the increase in the cost of equipment of this sort is given by the increase in capacity raised to the .6 power. (pp.121-2.)

Though this scaling simply represents a mathematic co-relational cost-value in production with relevance to the economies of scale, it is critically relevant to the integrative studies of economic theory that, in morally specific global needs, contemporary economists should give, at least, equal attention to the studies of ethical values with *moral development scaling* in economic policy formulations toward the integration of international market economies (see Krugman, on ethics and public policy, 2007). With moral concerns about critical global poverty problems in international economies, Helmut Hesse, renowned Professor at the Universities of Gottingen and Hannover states:

> As concerns poverty however, economists and ethicists could come to an agreement comparatively quickly. A basis for doing so is systems theory. This theory establishes that for the purpose of reducing and managing the world's complexity, it is necessary to break the world down into social subsystems. The subsystems have to perform specific tasks and thereby help to stabilize the system as a whole. The economy is such a subsystem. Its primary function is to shield mankind from poverty and economic distress, and to strengthen and secure the material foundations of society for every single person. It is the economy's business to do whatever is necessary to meet this moral commission. In this connection—as in other subsystems— the economy's workings have to be shaped according to their own purposes. In principle, these workings are outside the scope of morality. It is not

individual economic decisions that are subject to moral judgments, but instead *the total outcome of their interplay* (1994: p.174).

Economic Moralities and Eco-System Reciprocities. For more recent economic policy concerns on global poverty, eco-ethics and international political economies, see Alan Miller, 2003). Though "economies of scale," such as the above citations of Bela Balassa, are usually unrelated to moral problems, their practical interplay within the global problems of international economies and world hunger are analogically and ethically related to "moralities of scale" as an innovative critical *praxis* application of universal ethical principles and global moral responsible incentives. It is therefore hypothetically consistent to posit from such ethically integrative theoretical scaling that 6th stage moral development "extra-plant" economies of scale would have *morally incentive building power* as a socio-economic moral incentive model. From this hypothetical position as an ethical challenge to construct this socio-economic moral incentive model, it needs to be realistically understood that the study of economics, by its very nature as a structural and functional eco-system of local, national and global commerce of market exchanges, is focused on the practical operations of these exchanges especially in local structures and are thus predominantly operated by rapid mathematically driven exchange forces of bargaining interactions. As a functional consequence, these exchanges do not usually allow quantitative time for interpersonal moral proprieties, let alone for caring reciprocities and eco-system economies, due to the rapid production demands of global marketing economies of scale. But as a structural sequence, these exchanges, especially in the wider spheres of national and global marketing exchanges, where policy-making formulations are debated in the political spheres of national economies and transacted in global spheres of international market economies, there is a critical *praxis* need for qualitative time to review and ethically assess *economic moralities of scale* toward the re-awakening of *moral virtues* to achieve "economic prosperity" as the *ethical* "price of civilization" (Sachs, 2011). In addition, there is a critical practical need for ecological time to reassess ethical principles, economic moralities and environmental possibilities toward saving the ecology of the Universe. (See Orr on ethically keeping the *Earth in Mind*, 2004).

Ethical principles of market economies are theoretical; moralities of scale in *poverty economies* are practical, as *morally evaluated by these principles.* Professor Hesse argues for such a *moral imperative:*

> It seems to be very difficult to defend a purely market-based world economic order on ethical grounds. It might be advisable to enter into a discussion of the question of whether or not, in these extreme cases, rich countries should provide transfers if the recipient countries would in turn agree to certain conditions (1994, p. 178).

Such critically extreme conditions should be set within the socio-economic MBE archway of "moralities of scale," which would bear the ethical innovative flow of evolutionary management processes through morally developed socio-economic, social responsibility and financial ethical integration. (See Exhibit 6:1 Part B, p. 182; see also Hall, 2006 on the Ricoeur's "Economy of Gift.")

EVOLUTIONARY MANAGEMENT AND MORALITIES OF SCALING

A more active, unobtrusive way to initiate ethical discourse in a company, with the rational advantage of making corporate ethical sense out of strategic profit planning and "moralities of scale," is to utilize the "evolutionary management" advances of technology and interactive media in managing organization programming. These modern training tools are new symbols of management interaction processes, where socialization potential has yet to be tapped as far as ethical consciousness-raising techniques are concerned. The "Evolution Management" series of Van der Erve (1992, 1993, 1994), for example, are interactive computer programs designed to critically awaken the culture consciousness of managers through management perception analyses for the purpose of revitalizing companies and re-creating business enterprises. Van der Erve has constructed four graphic and animated software design modules that *identify prevailing dominant attitudes* in a company; *evaluate operational strategies* to uncover counter-productive behavior; *define strategic directions* from task-oriented enterprises to *culture-specific missions*; and *integrate* these analytical *perceptions into corporate cultural reformation and organization-set transformation.* (It is to be noted that this fourth module of "evolutionary management" would be interdisciplinary compatible with "evolutionary economics" and strategically directive toward defining the integration of "moralities of scale" with "economies of scale" in marketing "culture-specific missions," as proposed above.) With integrative vision, Van der Erve states "Our focus, therefore, should be directed toward the 'motion' or 'dynamics' of strategies and on the related *processes* which cause evolution to advance from stage to stage. . . . as a complexity-resonance continuum." (1994 p.10-11; see also 1998). His publisher states: "Traditionally books look at 'success', but the argument of this author is also concerned with 'failure' (as in the biological world) where new life forms are created from fundamental mutations, and a state of 'corporate failure' may be an important phase in the evolution of a successful corporate strategy" (1994 Jacket-Frontispiece). In the state of the global magnitude of *economic and corporate failures* of international economies and social class poverties, it behooves scholars to reflexively consider how much more *re-creatively* the MBE paradigm can begin to re-construct global economies based on *praxis centered moralities* than on structurally broken economies. The economic structures of both European and American economies and Asian and African societies are quaking before the political and governmental eyes of all countries blinded by uncontrollable poverties. With memory of Professor Hesse's moral warnings, "economists and ethicists could come to an agreement comparatively quickly. A basis for doing so is systems theory. . . . it is necessary to break the world down into social subsystems," where Van der Erve's evolutionary vision stimulates a *praxis* process strategy and a liberation theology for poverty stricken populations (1999, see p. 92, and Martin, 2008;[2] review Exhibit 6:1 on "global responsibilities" and "moralities of scale"). Although there is not much formal systematic ethical programing within these evolutionary management modules, they provide a compatible technological communication medium for dialectical system analysis and corporate reconstructive planning (see also Van der Erve's studies of 1994, ch. 9 on "[Re]constructing Business").

MBE ECONOMICS AND POST-CONVENTIONAL MORAL MANAGEMENT

As evolutionary corporate strategic instruments for the moral [re]construction of "economic and corporate failures," MBE ethical imperatives of interactional integration and value re-negotiation could constitute new order graphic symbols for re-animating operational functional systems with managerial ethical policy-making and *morally resonating* programing. (See Exhibit 7:1 in Chapter 7 of this book.) Through coordinated usage with value-system-rebuilding and ethical-discourse-management, these modules could help executives to *actively seize the time for* MBE *initiation* toward mobilizing their companies into *an advanced ethical identity and a morally productive future*. With evolutionary *moral management resonance*, it is plausible to [re]constructively plot that if the "economies of scale" bring the MBO business goals of a company and the customer's "situation specific" needs of purpose together in a functionally pre-conventional exchange location at stage 2 of the Kohlberg scale, *moralities of scale* could dialectically [re]develop the business operational [re]viewing policies of a company together with the customer's *ethically specific* satisfaction needs in a 5th and 6th stage post-conventional *morally economic* MBE exchange forum (see Rest's 1999 as an applied "Neo-Kohlbergian Approach"). Moreover, it is historically confirming to note that such *post-conventional moral development modules* are complementary developments of what Joseph Schumpeter had called for in his own economic *praxis* theories of the evolutionary processes of "Creative Destruction" in the Post World War II period of rebuilding democratic societies and political economies of scale through his innovative forms of "associative corporatism" (1942; see also Sievers, 1962). In heeding to respond to the urgency calls of global poverty, see the *associative 6th stage management* of Brian O'Hanlon (2012). His inventive model of *Ocean Blue Fish-Farming* and his "sustainability-daring" strategies of MBE *caring moralities* are managing the crises of global poverty on the "economies of scale" with economic *practical* strategies from his ethically induced incentives on the "*moralities of scale*."

Cross Cultural Ethics and Socio-Moral Economics. The international scope of global poverty, critically awakened by the socio-moral sensitivities of Professor Hesse in the International Workshop Forum of the Kiel Institute of World Economics 1993 (see ch. 8: pp. 233-238), has grown significantly worse through nearly two decades of world hunger and global poverty that challenges the need for *strategic critical praxis relief* from the pulverizing destructive power of international warfare and from the devastating pangs of poverty in the human diminishments of global hunger. Through this long enduring period of inhumanistic "immoralities of scale," with added imminent fears of global economic depressions, the continuing need for humanistic mercy and holistic charity rendered by international relief agencies, such as *Food For the Poor* and *Doctors without Borders*, presses on with unbending determination by the *sacred* services of the humane few for the inhumane many as the "suffering servants" of global humanity. The world needs not just devoted charity from cross-cultural ethics. It needs the *caring* economy of *multi-cultural moralities* to deliver a marketing economy that is capable of resolving injustices of inhumane markets and their morally dysfunctional "economies of scale." Only a dialectical solution of this devastating global social problem can be resolved by the universal principle of reversing failure and falsehood with the solutions of managing morally interactional models of "moralities of scaling" structured on following dialectical ethical patterns. Critically and practically important to these patterns, is the 6th stage ethical principle of morally interactional caring reciprocity as *motivating* "moralities of scale" in a *dialectical reversal process* of profit maximization toward *profit minimization*. It is only through such a *praxis* strategy of ethically sensitive generosity that the "moralities of scale" can be balanced by the caring reciprocities of MBE generosities.

MBE CARING RECIPROCITY AND HUMAN RESOURCE ECONOMY

Innovations for Productive Moral Reasoning and Reciprocity Interaction. It is the critical cognitive-emotive "solution" that turns productive reasoning into moral reasoning and impels individuals to translate philosophical principles into moral action (Boyd, 1984). Caring reciprocity is what generates the social caring power of virtues for altruistic cooperation and moral leadership. More simply stated, caring reciprocity is *moral power* generated by *ethical thinking*. As an innovative human resource power generator, caring reciprocity is not the same kind of power that is generated from prestige and wealth within the traditional power structures of corporate and government cultures, especially in the hierarchical management ranks of companies and government and military bureaucracies. These kinds of bureaucratic power organizations often contaminate the moral spirit of human resources and deteriorate employee workforces with fearful reflexes and inferiority complexes in interactional human discourse within hierarchical relations. They also tend to de-generate working incentives in the workplace and to disintegrate the spirit of cooperation in the workforce which, as seen in ch. 5, is so critical for the attitudinal advancement of workers and the *moral upgrading of a company's overall economic performance.* The power within the spirit of caring reciprocity is generated from the virtue of moral purpose and principled thinking which is what Professors Penn and McNeel were describing in the previous 5th chapter as the "power of ethical thinking." This kind of power generates moral incentives which induce motives for moral action and inspires workers to *cooperate* at the highest levels of moral development based on caring motivation. The ethical power within this spirit of caring reciprocity is "electric" in its human resource potential in igniting *praxis* change in organization cultures when people care about one another, CEOs caring about workers, and unions, about *human resource management economies.* This kind of MBE human resource economy was effectively reciprocated and affectively dramatized in the Congressional Hearings on the TARP "bailout" requests of the insurance and banking industries with the caring reciprocities of Warren Buffet of the Berkshire Hathaway Corp. and Bill Gross of the PIMCO Corp. for the U.S. Treasury, as analyzed in Chapter 3.

Intrinsic Value Motivation and Moral Incentive Building. In their 1985 study, cited in ch. 3 above, Higgins and Gordon did find that, in the Northern worker-owned company, the intrinsic motivation values of work quality, affiliations, and democracy, as an ideological governance form, constituted the stronger incentives than the extrinsic instrumental motivations of money and workplace convenience. They also found, however, that in the Southern company, the extrinsic instrumental motivations of making money outranked the more intrinsic motivations of democracy as a shared ethnic ownership form, and of work quality and affiliations. While they account for this reversal of incentive preference by reason of the company's location in a poor and rural high unemployment region and because of *depressed economic conditions* within the company's industry, they hasten to add that the *strong normative caring climate* within the organization and the internal ethnic incentives for moral role-taking, manifested by trust in management, ensured worker cooperation and company survival.

Moral Motivations and Reciprocity Building. Without further published replications of the Higgins and Gordon studies and their use of the Kohlberg scale, a much more recent and comprehensive study of worker motivation attitudes conducted by Lance Minkler (2002) found that moral motivations, *anchored in reciprocal trust* of management, engendered worker commitment to optimal performance effort in the workplace. This finding was significantly higher than other determinants of work performance, such as, monitoring and wage-raising incentives, peer- pressure relationships, and fairness motivations. It was also found that intrinsic motivations from interesting work ranked second among these work-performance determinants.

With a national survey of over 1000 adult members of workforces throughout the contiguous United States, Minkler and Miceli found that 82.7% of the respondents indicated that they were very likely to keep an agreement to work hard, if they agreed to, even if it was almost impossible for their employer to monitor them. This finding is a remarkable piece *of reciprocity trust data*, which disproves the "shirking propensity hypothesis" usually associated with an unmonitored work climate. The overwhelming positive results, moreover, support Minkler's own pre-data-gathering explanation of worker attitudes on performance reliability and personal integrity:

> Integrity can be seen as identity-conferring commitments to moral principles (like honesty). Thus, to violate one's own moral principles is to risk rendering one's own identity as incoherent—a loss of the most significant kind. It turns out that the existence of integrity influences both the propensity to make promises and then the likelihood of keeping them.. . . the existence of integrity implies that some will keep their word even if doing so is contrary to their material incentives. In the workplace, the existence of integrity means that some would work hard, *if they had agreed to*, irrespective of the external incentive mechanisms in place....
>
> The literature on moral motivation suggests that workers may provide effort if they see doing so as a moral duty (p. 9).

In this study, Minkler and Miceli also found convincing data on the relationship between moral and intrinsic motivations and job commitment in terms of honoring workplace agreements:

> Just under 2/3 of the respondents thought workplace agreements exist and are important (to honor).... The survey question on the existence of workplace agreements hints at a more important point. Perhaps the best way to induce both workers and employers to fulfil their consensual obligations to one another is to get them to realize their mutual commitments. Of the respondents who answered to (the importance of honoring workplace agreements), 87.5% also answered "very likely" to the question about working hard if they agreed to.... While the evidence suggests that a large number of workers already recognize a commitment to keeping agreements with their employers, there may be a real missed opportunity (to) get the others to commit. That won't happen until workers and employers each see the existence of workplace agreements, and also the importance of honoring them, even despite their imperfect enforceability. Finding ways of promoting honesty on both sides would be a good place to start (p. 19).

Their description of integrity as "identity-conferring commitments to moral principles (like honesty)" clarifies that the discussion here is not just about "promoting honesty on both sides" but on *reciprocally grounding* that honesty in the personal identity of the *worker's conscience* and in the company identity of the *corporate conscience*. This grounding is a better "starting place" because it *provides*, a deeper moral organizational framework for individual, collective and corporate *identities* to reflect with *integrity*, in a fifth stage consensual trust and a sixth stage *fairness reciprocity environment*, on matters of workplace agreements for making and *keeping* moral commitments. Thus, the breaking of workplace agreements on the part of the company would have the same *conscientious* effect as on individuals who violate their moral principles, i.e., the effect of rendering its corporate identity as "*incoherent*—a loss of the most significant kind." In contrast, the gain of the most ethical kind would be the *cohering* constitution of a reliable and caring workplace climate engendering *collective moral responsibility commitment* and enriching the gains of enduring *human resource economies.*

Workforce Commitment, Workplace Cooperation and Worker Caring Reciprocities. In an earlier and more specific occupational study, Sethia and Von Glinow (1985) demonstrated the positive co-relation between caring human resource cultures and intrafirm *cooperation* in high-tech companies. They found that when organization cultures integrate high concern for people with strong performance expectations, successful performance results for individuals, groups and even firms were long term (see also Von Glinow, 1988).

In a broader context, both Kohlberg *et al.* (1990) and Habermas (1990) claim that caring reciprocity is plausible in a moral atmosphere, wherein participants are not constrained by normative procedural agreements but are allowed to interact and communicate to a "moral point of view" through "ideal role-taking" interaction. This means that when workers are coached to universal reasoning to take the role of others by means of *imaginative* role-playing (as in Argyris's case-study write-ups, described in Chapter 4) of ideal caring reciprocity, they can come to realization of a sixth-stage "moral point of view," valuing universal care for everyone.

A most effective example of imaginative role-taking generating ideal caring reciprocity incentives was in the recent catastrophic terrorist attack on the innocent people residing in the Taj Mahal Hotel in Mumbai (Bombay) India. People of all faiths and every nation were so disturbed by the horror that they could not help but imaginatively role-play what their own behavior would have been, were they confronted by such barbaric and violent uncaring behavior in their work environments. The riveting descriptions and graphic scenes of the events *engendered* authentic interpersonal compassion and ideal caring reciprocity for the victims and for their families. These kinds of unforgettable events help to *induce* a "moral point of view" with focused everyone.

Applying this caring example of imaginative role taking in workplace environments also means that when organization hierarchies show concern for people and systematically encourage all their workers, even poorer performers, to reflect on their performance through private or collective discerning performance evaluation, as discussed in Chapter 4 with Argyris' simulated reflexive case study write-ups, they are actually cultivating a moral incentive climate and validating their policies on *human resource care* (as in Weiss's, 1986, validating management policies, cited in Chapter 2). Jurgen Habermas validates these kinds of *role-taking reflexivity discernments*:

> Because discourses are a reflective form of understanding-orientated action . . . their central perspective on moral compensation for the deep-seated weakness of vulnerable individuals can be derived from the very medium of linguistically mediated interactions to which socialized individuals owe that vulnerability. The pragmatic features of discourse make possible a discerning will formation whereby the interests of each individual can be taken into account without destroying the social bonds that link each individual with all others.   (1990, pp. 245-246)

CARING ASSOCIATIONS AND WORKPLACE TEAMS

These interlinking caring bonds of workforce reciprocities are what morally compensate for workplace vulnerabilities and constitute the ethically productive role-taking "architecture" of workplace teams. Through inter-active work information flow, they open communication lines for shared knowledge and create a moral atmosphere for mutual altruism. This moral climate is what provides the kind of *archway* incentives that *induce* every work-team "player" to take the initiative to back up the "plays" of the other for performance consistency and work integrity (Refer back to the "*ethical archway*" Exhibit on Moral Incentive Inducement Building at the beginning of this chapter to visualize the organizational structures of *teamwork associations*.) Hackman's (1986) airline case study of the behavioral signs of self-management performance in the realistic contexts of worker vulnerabilities and organizational inconsistencies places initiative-taking responsibility at the highest levels of work-team maturity development. His conclusions go beyond Miller's instrumental reciprocity, confirming the value of workplace altruism as an interactional strategy to maintain performance consistency: "People take initiatives to *help people in other areas* improve their performance, thereby strengthening the policies and performance of the organization as a whole" (1992, p. 97; see also Etzioni, 1988, for a review of empirical evidence on altruistic behavior, ch. 4). The value of workplace altruism could not be demonstrated more convincingly than in the aesthetic environments of the performing arts, as is consistently demonstrated in the theatrical and musical productions of the TONY Awards. The graciousness of the winning actors, performers, dancers, composers and directors recount the interpersonal caring of the company's team work and back up support in a litany of tributes with convincing emotions and committed gratitude to all the performing and directing artist team.

Caring Reciprocity and the Strength of Moral Commitment. Such a moral climate that offers the caring reciprocity of workplace altruism to strengthen corporate policy and organizational performance is one where deeper moral incentives can germinate. Since there is clear and relatively strong confirmation of the relationship between moral reasoning and altruistic behavior (Blasi, 1980), a lot of promise awaits the corporate ethical con-sciousness challenge to build *team-working moral climates*. The higher the *moral cognition* for helping other more vulnerable workers in an organizational climate of caring relationships, the deeper the incentives for collaboration persistence to compensate for work-team vulnerabilities and ultimately to promote *enduring cooperation* in the workplace. Emanating from the social system perspective of the *company's economic good* and, gradually as the moral climate develops, from the universal principle perspective of the cosmic and global social good, these morally internalized caring incentive inducements are more likely to motivate personal preferences for *cooperation* (Etzioni, 1988). "In short *moral internalization turns constraints into preferences*" (p. 46). Etzioni typifies this preference conversion process as "the power of internalized values" that can generate the deontological ethical conviction for action-value consistency from a sense of duty, reflecting the *enduring caring* "strength of moral commitment" (pp. 47-48). No greater examples of such caring strength are relevant than the ultimate moral commitment of the Nations' Heroes in the war-places of the military and the intimate caring work-places of CNN's Heroes in poverty stricken nations and sub-cultural deprivations. (For a lighter analogical reference on workplace teams and collective altruism, female gender leadership and nearly incalculable combinations of workforce efficiency, collegial commitment with "royal reverence" for queen-ship *bumble bees'* caring trust, see O'Malley, 2010).

MBE and *Moral Commitment Endurance*. It is worth stressing in this context that MBE moral commitment is much more than MBO job commitment which is based on external workplace inducements and dependent on moral reasoning climate fluctuations. In any case, job commitment is as strong and as enduring as the credibility of specific managerial strategies that control incentive inducements (Miller, 1992). As such, its value is *particularized*; and, moreover, its endurance span is fragile and can likewise be easily flawed by pre-conventional moral authority styles or management defection contingencies. As a *universalized* cognitive "meta-preference" (Etzioni, 1988, pp. 45-48) for the integrity of work itself and an internalized affective conviction (Haste, 1990) for the quality of its performance, MBE *moral commitment is an enduring dispositional virtue* that can be expected in post-conventional work climates which are striving to open a corporate "moral point of view:"[3]

> Internalized values have a significant impact on behavior. As to the suggestion that internalization is merely the result of conditioning, the findings suggest that once individuals internalize guides to behavior these become *generalized* to a variety of situations beyond those in which the individual was conditioned, and are not merely a reflection of prior rewards/punishments. Further, they *last* [emphasis added] well beyond what one would expect from prior conditioning. (Etzioni, 1988, pp. 47-48)

CONCLUSIONS

MBO POLITICAL ECONOMIC STRATEGIES OF SCALE
AND
MBE SOCIO-MORAL ECONOMIES OF SCALE

As a MBO political economic incentive system model, interlinking neoclassical economic and organizational behavior theories, Miller's job commitment design provides the appropriate socialization techniques and organization strategies for high-involvement management and work-team inter-dependencies, as discussed in Walton (1990) and Lawler (1986). But it is not the kind of model that will facilitate reciprocal role-taking cooperation in a decentralized hierarchical learning atmosphere where idea communication is shared and entrepreneurial leadership is encouraged (Maremont, 1993).

In contrast, MBE, as a moral behavioral incentive system model, engenders motivation anchored in internal ethical awareness dispositions rather than in external economic posturing calculations. As seen, it is an incentive inducement system design that can inherently broaden the morality scope of corporate governance and operationalize the ethical levels of *enduring* intrafirm cooperation, which produces the *holistic economic good. . .* "Organizations endure. . . in proportion to the breadth of the morality by which they are governed" (Barnard, 1938, p. 282).

In addition, as a cognitive morality model for human resource development in ethical reasoning, MBE's collegial learning designs can easily be integrated into other company incentive-inducement-building programs that pursue continuing professional management and competence education (Willis and Tosti-Vasey, 1990; Farr and Middlebrooks, 1990; Miller, 1990). Moreover, it would seem that some of these incentive programs could derive some practical benefit from MBE socialization methods. Farr and Middlebrooks (1990), for example, stress the need for intrinsic motivation in their use of expectancy theory to enhance and maintain competence. From this perspective, their approach to competence development, falling somewhat short of incentive internalization, could itself be enhanced within a MBE climate, where intrinsic motivation can secure anchorage to personal self-expectancy and collective responsibility incentives.

Similarly, as Von Glinow (1988) suggests the need for more meaningful and relevant incentives for high-tech professionals than traditional economic inducements, MBE can offer significant incentive levels of ethical meaning and *economies of moral purpose*. Her studies of this group conclude:

> It is fascinating to note, from a behavioral perspective, that no single stock incentive was ranked in the upper quarter by any age group in either my research or that of others (Griggs and Manring, 1986), for example, interested in determining reward salience (pp. 78-79).

She thus argues for new incentive schemes that relate to individual values and beliefs, such as ethical, collegial and autonomous work climates which value performance commitment. It would seem that MBE, in its reliance on moral reasoning for performance and on communication ethics for learning, could effectively contribute to the rebuilding of the suitable work incentive climate for this group. She concludes:

> Once they (managers) grasp the powerful impact that productive reasoning can have on actual performance, they will have a *strong incentive* (emphasis added) to reason productively not just in a training session but in all their work relationships (see also Argyris, 1991 p. 107).

Within this reforming moral scope of corporate governance, as broadened by the practical long-term planning for ethical consciousness development and by the ideal typical use and *praxis* application of the Kohlberg scale, MBE can provide the cooperative internalized moral incentives for *individual and collective competence and enduring optimal efficiency*. "This is only to say that foresight, long purposes, high ideals, are the basis for the persistence of cooperation" (Barnard, 1938, p. 282). Such a memorable reference to the morally high ideals of *cooperation persistence*, as projected by this eminent scholar during the early period when MBO became the functionally dominating paradigm of the industrialized global economy, is a prophetic reminder and an historical inducement incentive for MBE caring of others in crisis situations of economic poverty, catastrophic emergencies and workplace contingencies through the *praxis* economic strategies of *"moralities of scales."*

END NOTES

1. Evolutionary economics have been the research focus of Joseph Schumpeter (1883-1950) and his student, Wolfgang Stolper (1912-2002) from the mid-20th century of economic studies at Harvard University. The interdisciplinary range of this research field is more *practically* opened to the real meaning of integrative economics, as it analyzes the integration of market economies and production outcomes from the changing economic forces within complex organization environments. It is this kind of *praxis* integration that creates evolutionary industrialized and marketing processes of re-"creative destruction," social trends and organizational re-development patterns. See Schumpeter's classic works in these fields *Capitalism, Socialism and Democracy* (1942; and *Can Capitalism Survive? Creative Destruction and the Future of the Global Economy*; see also Stolper's *The Structure of the East German Economy* (1960), *Joseph Alois Schumpeter: The Public Life of a Private Man* (1994), and *Inside Independent Nigeria: Diaries of Wolfgang Stolper* (2003).

2. Martin describes Lonergan's evolutionary economics as a *praxis* methodology "of providing adequate economic knowledge to individuals, groups and governments so that they can exercise moral responsibility in their everyday economic decision making in ways that economics now does not" (p.163). Lonergan's "new paradigm *for economics*" traces the historical scientific and moral root system, as a seminal reference source for the *praxis* application of the *ethical innovative* paradigm of MBE.

3. For a discussion of managerial strategies, job design principles and human resource benefits in re-organizing hierarchies for commitment building and organizational competence, see (Walton, 1990).

CHAPTER 7

MBE ORGANIZATION GOVERNANCE AND RESISTANCE TO CHANGE

Opening "foresight" with the moral development scope of the MBE paradigm, with its "long purposes" for the "high ideals" of corporate governance and moral responsibility delivery, demands "the persistence of cooperation" to focus on several problems left unanswered in the Kohlberg empirical legacy. Two applied research problems, particularly significant for MBE as a moral education innovation toward inducing workforce moral incentives and motivating management ethical efficiency, are: (1) the problems of cultural hegemony in the moral development research legacy and (2) the problems of established realities in personal and organizational inconsistencies as resistance to moral development performance strategies.

CULTURAL HEGEMONY IN MORAL DEVELOPMENT

"THIS IS THE WAY MBO *OPERATES* AROUND HERE!"

Hegemony is a latent value system control phenomenon that develops over an historical period of time as an established way of thinking or doing things which often prevents organizations and their members from becoming openly critical of such established realities, let alone from actively promoting change toward innovative possibilities. For more on cultural and socio-economic hegemony, see note 1 in Chapter 3. The problem of moral under-development hegemony is provoked by practical hidden curricular determinants both in the research subjects and the research processes. Kohlberg himself recognized these determinants in the subjects, acknowledging the latent ideological power bases within educational systems (Power *et al.,* 1989). But his own persistence for justice education and democratic governance in schools was not enough to convert the macro-sociological power fortresses in wider global cultures, especially in political and economic domains which ultimately shape the agenda of corporations as well as the curricula of schools. From this critical *praxis* perspective, Kohlberg's justice education model may begin to stimulate post-conventional moral development in classrooms; but these higher stages may be quickly undermined when students graduate to the governance world of corporate economic power and experience the hegemonic cultural causes of value norm incongruences (see Emler and Hogan, 1991). Consider, for example, when such students who graduate from schools with high hopes to achieve post-conventional moral development in their careers enter a workforce, like one at Morgan Stanley during its 2004 sexism scandal, how vulnerable they become, noticing and hearing the following atmospheric symbolic construct: "this is the way things are done around here." With over three hundred women who experienced gender-ridden career advancement discrimination as well as sexual harassment and the denial climate created by the hierarchical power structure of management in the litigation process and even in the settlement statements, the whole workforce was gripped in hegemonic control at the lowest stages of moral *under*-development. Consider also the symbolic construct of settlements themselves in terms of maintaining the denial climate. It is commonly known among lawyers and judges, as part of the hegemonic culture problem, that "wrongdoing is never admitted" in the settlement process (CNBC law firm interview, 7/11/04). How can any corporation conduct moral reform, if the larger complex organizational environment of its organization set, in this case, namely, the judicial and legal system, participates in vested interest laden solutions at the second pre-conventional moral exchange stage of instrumental relativity?

ESTABLISHED REALITIES AND INNOVATIVE POSSIBILITIES

"THIS IS THE WAY MBE *GENERATES* AROUND HERE"

Moral Under-Development in the Marketplace. From the "critical practical" perspective, the analytical explorations need to address such latent socio-cultural anomalies and social system blockages that impair the full moral development of populations. The social psychological and anthropological dimensions of the MBE paradigm and its "revolutionary scientific" perceptions for socio-moral development demand critically reconstructive sets of questions (Kuhn, 1970), such as: What symbolic constructs within cultures and, especially sub-cultural entities, like corporations, co-exist with governance structures that might be influencing value-norm incongruences and moral inconsistencies and thus skewing moral development ratings? In another contemporary example, the past investigations of value incongruity and moral inconsistency in the New York Stock Exchange by the New York State Attorney General reveal serious hegemonic problems in the governance structures of the exchange as a non-profit organization. The NYSE Board of Directors itself, as a symbolic construct, manifests a low level of moral awareness when it argues that the chairman's executive performance justifies the exorbitant salary awards which he received. In making its justification argument, the board defended the salary awards by reason of his leadership performance during the 9/11 terrorist crisis. If the subject is about justification relative to socio-economic justice, comparisons of the salaries and the heroic performance of the Mayor and the fire-fighters of the city reveal grave value incongruence and moral inconsistency, if not flaws in the moral leadership of the NYSE Chairman and its Board of Directors.

Moral Under-Development in Environmental Space. Continuing with "critical practical" research questions, one may ask: Might the economic arrangements of the MBO corporate power structures of companies in some dependent local communities be determining the moral consciousness of citizens, the (*un*)healthy quality of their lives (see Adeola, 2012) and the social (*in*)equalities of their class (Anderson 1974; Krause, 1977; Walzer, 1983; see also Dahrendorf, 1959; Goldman and Van Houten, 1977; and Misgeld, 1991)? This question has long been salient since the days of Love Canal. In this case, it might provide some helpful insight to review the history of this environmental toxic waste disaster. Notice, for example, how the socio-economic forces of hegemonic "power" structures generated the best of electric power development planning and degenerated with the worst of moral development awareness at the turn of the 20th century. At this time, the Love Canal landsite had been planned to be built as a "dream city" by William T. Love on the eastern edge of the city of Niagara Falls. After Mr. Love had begun construction of a short canal between the upper and lower rivers in Niagara Falls to generate electric power to his "model city," Louis Tesla discovered how to transmit electric power more economically over long distances through alternating currents. This historical development ended Mr. Love's plans and eventually turned his landsite into an industrial chemical dumpsite, in the 1920's. Subsequently, the site was bought by a chemical company whose owners and operators covered the land with earth and sold it back to the city in 1953 for one dollar. In the later part of that decade, a working class community of one hundred homes and a school was in place directly on a municipal industrial chemical dumpsite (Beck, 1979). Twenty-five years later, this community awakened to a kind of "tsunamic" nightmare of hazardous degenerative health effects on its families from the toxic eruptive "lava" within the covered dumpsite. Eckardt Beck, who was the Administrator of the EAP for region 2 from 1977 to 1979, described the eruption as an eye witness:

> I visited the canal area at that time. Corroding waste-disposal drums could be seen breaking up through the grounds of backyards. Trees and gardens were turning black and dying. One entire swimming pool had been popped up from its foundation, afloat now on a small sea of chemicals. Puddles of noxious substances were pointed out to me by the residents. Some of these puddles were in their yards, some were in their basements, others yet were on the school grounds. Everywhere the air had a faint, choking smell. Children returned from play with burns on their hands and faces (1979).

He then outlined the "birth defects..., a disturbingly high rate of mis-carriages.... (and) a large percentage of people... (with) detected high white-blood-cell counts..." (1979).

This short case study of the "Love Canal Tragedy" reveals moral behavior at radically different polarities of the Kohlberg scale and illustrates the hegemonic problem in moral development. *First*, the "dream community" planned by William Love appears to have been an ideal 6th stage urban development plan based on the utilitarian ethic of a "model city" with a cost effective power industry generated by a short canal. His dream, however, was "short-circuited" by a utilitarian inventor, who seemed to have had at least a 5th stage practical plan to transmit power to much wider areas for the greater use of electric power and the industries of larger populations. Tragically enough, this case history of urban industrial development became contaminated by the "short"-sighted moral awareness levels of stage 1 and 2 pre-conventional municipal managers and chemical company executives motivated by latent fears of unknown consequences of irresponsible toxic-waste-dumping and short-shrifting 2nd stage instrumental expediency dealing. *Second*, the hegemonic problem in this moral under-development story is demonstrated by the power "blinders" of hierarchical civil officials and corporate executives whose decision-making incentives were induced by the expediency of MBO stage 2 pre-conventional functionality and conventional custom. Such "blinders" tend to fix an organization culture on "a way of doing business" expediently and conveniently, often, as in this case, to the detriment of corporate responsibility and environmental capability (see Thomashow, 1995).

With these critical reflections on this case study of Love Canal, a further "critical *praxis*" research question becomes practical: Might company policies and operational strategies, especially those shaped in traditional organization hierarchies by the functional imperatives of resource *adaptation, goal-attainment, integration* of operations and value *latency*, be binding decision-makers "to change the environment to meet the needs of the system" (Parsons, 1967, p. 493)? In effect, have not these functional imperatives "maintained the patterns" of Parsons' system *agility* at the expense of natural and organizational environmental immorality, as an un-natural disaster of a *Death Canal*? Are not these classic sociological models of structural-functionalism *system*-atically impairing individual and corporate performance from developing beyond the conventional moral stages? In short, is there not a *hegemonic lid* on moral development and corporate responsibility? "Yet on this most crucial of all questions for moral psychology research—who commands and what are their moral credentials?—has thus far shed almost no direct light at all" (Emler and Hogan, 1991).

(For some "indirect enlightenment" on such dialectical systemic processes in international policy-making and MBE diplomatic strategy-shifting relative to *moral development awakening* in the economic and military zones of the Far East, where the government policies of Myanmar have *systematically* shifted in favor of changing its international structural diplomacies with India, China and the United States to "morally meet the international humanitarian needs" of its own economies, see Fareed Zakaria's report on "The Global Public Square" CNN, Dec. 04, 2011).

Love Canal: Electric or Hegemonic Power? In dialectical contrast to the Parsonian AGIL functional model of "changing the environment to meet the needs of the system," the social psychological *imperative of ethical integrity* is the ultimate credential of *enlightened* leadership. As the latent value in the new MBE paradigm, it opens cultures and systems towards moral developmental governance and allows the freedom of ethical discourse and the *interactional integration of value negotiation through moral reflection.* Ethical integrity, interactional integration and value negotiation, all of which induce incentives for moral reflection, promote the AGILITY for corporate executives to make structural-functional and even *reparative* operative adaptations to organization systems. These integrative and morally reflexive negotiating processes require innovative symbolic interactional constructs, such as ethical discourse forums, to allow management decision-makers to reverse corporate *dialectical* priorities *to change the system to meet the needs of the environment,* especially in times of crisis (see Benson 1977 a and b). From these interactional imperatives, executives and managers would have a social psychological rationale and an organizational medium for reformulating company norms, re-prioritizing its value-system, and renegotiating corporate moral meanings. It is only from these *ethically illuminating* meanings that individuals and corporations can be stimulated to higher 6th stage moral performance ABILITY toward the development of *praxis* planning to meet the ecological needs of the global environment[1] (see Exhibit 7:1 and Thomashow, 1995).

Exhibit 7:1 DIALECTIC ORGANIZATION SYSTEM MODELS
AND
THEIR OPERATIONAL IMPERATIVES

AGIL Structural Functional Model	MBE Interactional Reconstructive Model

Changing the Environment to Meet the Needs of the System	Changing the System to Meet the Needs of the Environment

STRUCTURAL FUNCTIONAL IMPERATIVES	INTERACTIONAL ETHICAL IMPERATIVES
Functional AGILITY	Moral ABILITY
ADAPTATION of natural resources	ADAPTATION, REPARATION & PRESERVATION of natural resources
GOAL ATTAINMENT by profit-producing production	GOAL CONTAINMENT to *environment-inducing protection*
INTEGRATION of organization complexity	INTEGRITY of organization *reflexivity*
LATENCY of company-centric values	LATENCY of socially-centric principles
MORAL PERFORMANCE PLIABILITY stages: 1, 2, 3	MORAL PERFORMANCE PLAUSIBILITY stages: 4, 5, 6

Value-free research must admit that populations will never transcend conventional boundaries, if they are not socialized beyond the static conventions and the hegemonic implications of their institutionalized symbolic constructs (see Lifton, 1970). From this dialectical research perspective, it would appear that empirical testing of individuals in culturally bound social and organizational systems is doomed to yield "stable" scores with unimpressive stage 5 and unverifiable stage 6 post-conventional results.

> The most fundamental control device of any *stable* social system is not its use of crude force, or even of other, nonviolent forms of punishment, but its continuing distribution of mundane rewards. It is not simply power that a hegemonic elite seeks and uses, but an authority that is rooted in the readiness of others to credit its good intentions, to cease contention when it has rendered its decision, to accept its conception of social reality, and to reject alternatives at variance with the status quo. (Gouldner, 1970, p. 498)

The ethical challenge needs to move forward with a critical historical reconstructive vision to identify the "mundane rewards" and their double-edged symbols of hegemonic leadership inconsistencies that cut deeply into the social networking and moral fabric of organizations from Wall Street to Niagara Falls and now even to the environmental "falls" of the Gulf regions. It is these symbolic inconsistencies that are not only shaping the organizational realities and moral meanings of institutions but are determining the moral stages of its managers and members (see Emler and Hogan, 1991; see also Longstreth, 2011 for an holistic study of 6th stage "ecological rewards" in *changing* status quo systems through the ethical values of environmental restoration).

Lifting the Research "Hegemonic Lid." An earlier promising study by Minkler and Miceli cited in Chapter 6 (2002) offers some propelling hope for lifting the "hegemonic lid." His convincing findings of worker attitudinal integrity and commitment to optimal performance suggest that post-conventional moral awareness of workers is far more plausible than the Higgins and Gordon studies and those of Weber and Kohlberg himself would lead one to believe. It is critical to note: first, the study was conducted outside the organizational structural framework of the workplace culture, thus rendering any hegemonic influence on the respondents implausible; second, the study was conducted outside the parameters of the Kohlberg paradigm, thus allowing some conceptual cross-angulation of cognitive moral awareness terms and affective moral attitudinal dispositions; and third, this unintended cross-angulation demonstrates that moral development affective attitudes, immune from hegemonic power influences and "theory of the firm" shirking hypotheses, reveal a significantly higher capability of 5th and 6th stage moral aptitudes for optimal effort at work performance. To support these analytical conclusions, compare the findings of the Minkler Miceli study with Exhibit 3:5, as seen in Chapter 3. In this comparison, note that worker compliance and attitudinal commitment, in the Exhibit, are plotted at the 5th stage of moral development trust in worker-management relationships and that management supervision of fairness reciprocity, and at the 6th stage of moral development caring in collegial cooperative relationships. It was noted in Chapter 3 that the 4th, 5th and 6th stages of the scale were the hypothetical correlational plottings of the author. It now appears that these correlations are confirmed by the Minkler/Miceli study. In conclusion of this discussion on hegemonic workplace cultures, it also appears from the impressive results of *moral motivation preferences* of the comprehensive respondent pool of that study, that the "ideal" caring typification of 6th stage worker management relations, which appeared to be a capitulation by Professor Kohlberg for lack of empirical data in earlier moral development studies, can be typified convincingly as a *practical caring* stage. These conclusive results, moreover, encourage *praxis* oriented research endeavors in moral development pedagogies to break forth from any *inauthentic* gridlocks in moral measuring framed by the *politics of hegemony* toward pursuing more creative post-conventional social scientific management strategies through MBE "moral sources," and managing by the renovative *"ethics of authenticity"* (see Taylor, 2007 and 1991).

MBE RENOVATIONS OF ESTABLISHED REALITIES

Established Realities and Moral Inconsistencies. As Blasi (1980) and Haste (1990) have exposed some of the research limitation problems of the cognitive structural approach to moral development testing in terms of its failure to account for affective domain determinants, it would seem timely to consider other influences on moral reasoning and moral performance outcomes in terms of *organization domain determinants*. For example, research questions must begin to address judgment-action consistency problems at organizational levels of analysis in addition to individual management and worker levels. By opening methodology to collective units of focus, only initially begun by Higgins and Gordon (1985), as seen in ch.6, questions such as these need to be probed: what moral choices are available to corporations in culturally bound and morally undeveloped complex organization environments where established realities of a company's organization-set may bear differing economic determinants that influence production outcomes or restrict business options? It is clear that the moral choices of oil companies reveal gross personal and organizational ethical inconsistencies in the international organization-sets of their business operations with the astronomical profits from their production and the multi-million dollar salaries of their executives, while at the same time, boasting of their environmentally and morally sensitive ethic on their websites. During the early stages of the Gulf oil sub-sea disaster, the three companies of BP America, Transocean Ltd. and Halliburton, involved in the structural operations of the oil-rigging organization-set testifying before Congress were shifting accountability admissions with impunity digging their companies deeper in the immoral "muck" of organizational moral inconsistencies. And likewise, what moral choices are available to individual executives, managers and workers in culturally bound and morally undeveloped companies where the *management power structure* may bear *resisting economic determinants* that *impair moral performance* outcomes or restrict career advancement options? For example, it is clear that the moral choices of the three hundred women in Morgan Stanley were significantly limited and their career options effectively blocked by the economic and sexist determinants of stage 2 instrumental *using* and stage 1 emotional fear-*abusing* of these women by pre-conventional *under*-developed moral management. And again, if "domain consensus" is critical for the power relationships that form between an organization and its task environment (as seen above in Chapter 3), what is the relationship between domain and moral consensus in the overall context of company or departmental ethical discourse and interorganizational political processes? In this probative regard, it is clear that there was a dysfunctional relationship between domain and moral consensus in the overall infrastructures of the organization-set of the United Nations and its "Oil for Food" program. The power relationships which formed among the participating nations in the aftermath of the Gulf War during the regime of Saddam Hussein failed to identify grave moral performance inconsistencies in the trading processes of the program, thereby allowing the exchange agreement to operate at the lowest stages of the Kohlberg scale. More often than not, the organization power structures within corporate and government organization-sets are so framed in historical established realities of customary policies and functional and/or diplomatic procedures that hierarchical resistance to change is latently buried in the value-system of their MBO hegemonic cultures. To this day, this scandalous UN international management performance reflects not only morally inconsistent domain consensus but, more tragically, consistent immoral operational consensus. These kinds of questions on personal and organizational consistency matters could open more incisive "critical practical understanding" of actual organization-management moral, gender and power dilemmas that not only impair moral stage development but threaten organization stability and career survival. Had Enron and WorldCom enjoyed the benefit of empirical answers to these "critical practical" research questions for moral structural reform, the non-compliant *reflective* executives might have changed the hegemonic power centers of executive corruption, saved their organizations and their own careers as well as the 401K retirement investments of their workforces. The moral challenge thus is to awaken ethical reflexivity in the hierarchical governance structures of the corporation and to induce incentives of corporate accountability to change the established realities of personal and organizational moral inconsistencies. The MBE moral governing imperative is thus to develop post-conventional reformative planning toward corporate ethical identity consistencies by dispersing unethical hierarchy hegemonies and securing organizational ethical reliability democracies. With contemporary insecurities of complex organizational breakdowns in global societies and market economies, such as in the social unreliabilities of the insurance industrial complex and the Obama Affordable Care Act, there is an imminent need for ethical reliability and corporate social personhood.

Ethical Reliability and MBE Corporate Personhood

> In the narrowest sense, corporate governance addresses the problems of how to get managers to serve as effective and obedient agents for owner/shareholders, or principals. . . . In the broadest sense, then, corporate governance literature including the kind of popularized writing about corporate activity . . . constitutes a complex cultural discourse about what it means to be a person in a corporate society. . . . I argue here that anti-managerialism has developed a similarly romantic and exceptionalist understanding of corporate personhood, and that for this reason its critique of corporate power functions ultimately to legitimize corporate activity on new terms for a new historical moment. (Guthey, 2004, p. 325)

Corporate Governance and the Ethical Moment for MBE. From this "critical practical" perspective toward a new historical moment, further moral consistency research might consider the rather cognitively structured "role" that role-taking analysis has played in moral development studies. While this cognitive concept has been a central element in moral development theory building by Kohlberg and his followers in the context of the interactional analysis and hegemonic arrangements associated with social conformity and rule-governed behavior, the full social psychological implications of role-taking processes need to be explored in terms of reconstructing conventional stage development through innovative forms of post-conventional corporate moral activity with the new MBE paradigm toward achieving an *enduring* morally temporal period for the future of corporate behavior. Critical reconstructive research needs to explore what these wider implications mean for personal and organizational moral consistency. Role-taking is not simply a structured cognitive process for rule-conformity and institutionalized conventions. It is rather a dynamic interactional process and often requires an *affectively caring motivation* which impels individuals and collectivities to plan for change (Turner, 1962; see also Yussen, 1976; and Bennis, Benne and Chin 1969).

Planning for Change in Complex Organizations

Planning for Change with Affective Caring Motivation. A contemporary critical practical and enduring need to effect "planning for change" is demanded not only in hegemonic interactional arrangements of complex organizations but especially in the catastrophic environmental events of disorganized devastating disasters. An example of such complex

organizational disarray in responding to the emergency earthquake needs of
the masses of homeless people and displaced families of Haiti in 2010 reveal
the desperate need for *negotiated theory planning* throughout the multi-
organizational sets of the United Nations and the respective responder
countries paralyzed in the moral organizational complex of 1st and 2nd stage
ruling throughout the bureaucracy of the Haitian government and public
administration systems. With six months after the devastating quake
happened, only 2% of all the emergency donations of the relief funding
organizations and care giving institutions had reached the homeless people
and helpless children still trapped in the mud lanes of their sagging tent
conclaves. Media reports of the quagmire scenes and the pre-conventional
moral stages and even of the dysfunctional rulings of government and
customs agencies have recounted not only the rescue organizations' trapped
efforts for collective care delivery and funded infrastructure re-building but
have reported the imposition of appalling fines on these 6th stage international
volunteer associations (Cooper, 2010). What is clearly needed in the relief
paralyzing postures of these associations is for some applied planning to
break through these institutionalized blockages of 2nd stage morally inept
officials and 1st stage morally under-developed government structures and
bureaucratic organizations. What can be efficaciously implemented by a new
order for *corporate moral activity* is a concentrated effort at the highest levels
of international government, such as the United Nations and its mediating
associations (see ch. 8 below), to apply some fundamental principles and
interactional strategies of "negotiated order theory" processes (Day and Day,
1977).

The critical *praxis* challenge here is to negotiate a morally consistent,
legitimate agreement for affectively administering emergency comfort needs,
food and money to the displaced homeless peoples and especially to
abandoned children, over-riding conventional structured regulations in favor
of a post-conventional moral action. The negotiation of these agreements are
needed to authenticate the moral legitimacy of prioritizing personal emergent
care over the organizational inconsistencies of functional rules and
bureaucratically structured determinants. Through such symbolic coordination and the *affective sharing of reconstructed meanings* about rules and
regulations, the need recognition for compassionate caring 6th stage *moral
sensitivity* for pain, suffering and displacement is to be definitively stressed
and prioritized for the immediate relief delivery of the homeless earthquake
victims. Caring international government activity for such afflicted and
displaced individuals can change the established conventions of diplomatic
structures and border-controlled systems to integrate their own personal and
organizational moral consistency response to higher post-conventional moral
decision-making not just to form a "moral point of view" but to formulate a
moral plan of action (see Uhl, 2003). Plans of this kind could be immediately
effective for displaced starving refugees in cross-border exodus flights for

sanctuary from warfare and *emergency* for welfare, as seen in Somalia and Sudan. This strategy for organization change, grounded in *negotiated order theory*, can be operationally effective even when a given conventional management hierarchy, blocked by MBO blinders, fails to grasp the post-conventional moral viewpoint and the imminent need for MBE moral action delivery. Robert and JoAnne Day describe the organization change efficacy of this theory in these terms:

> In the case of negotiated order theory, the individuals in organizations play an active, self-conscious role in the shaping of the social order. Their day to day interactions, agreements, temporary refusals, and changing definitions of the situations at hand are of paramount importance. . . . Negotiated order theory downplays the notion of organizations as fixed, rather rigid systems which are highly constrained by strict rules, regulations, goals, and hierarchical chains of command. Instead, it emphasizes the fluid, continuously emerging qualities of the organization, the changing web of interactions woven among its members, and it suggests that order is something at which the members of the organization must constantly work. Consequently, conflict and change are just as much a part of organizational life as consensus and stability. . . . Hence, there is an implied dialectical relationship in which the informal structure of the organization acts upon the formal structure, producing social change (1977).

While their study is actually quite critical of negotiated order theory as an applied theory for political power change efficacy of the complex organization health care establishment in the United States, it does advocate the application of negotiating processes which address "the inherent contradictions and inconsistencies not only in the political economy of health care, but in the economic structure of American society as well" (p.140). This is exactly what MBE is addressing in the critical practical (praxis) terms of morally negotiating against the "contradictions and inconsistencies" of corporate economic power structures and industrialized morally im-practical realities of the MBO social networking establishment.

MBE PRACTICAL SOLUTIONS:

REALITIES AND POSSIBILITIES FOR CORPORATE ETHICAL DISCOURSE

Realities. As this study presents the "high ideals" of moral development for both corporate organization structures and economic incentive systems, it acknowledges the arresting evidence from research on the lower-level realities of morality in the informal structures of the workplace. It also acknowledges the real problems of individual and organizational consistency in value-system choices and moral performance records. Notwithstanding these prevailing realities, the study does conclude, from its critical review of organization cultures that the correlational domains of the moral research legacy of complex organization environments demonstrate that the lower the stage of ethical awareness, the higher the inconsistency problems for the moral performance of individuals and organizations. Executives and economists, therefore, need a certain philosophical realism to address these moral inconsistency problems rather than an experimental cynicism about ethical complications.

Philosophical Realism. Alfred North Whitehead (1938) suggested that the problems of inconsistency in social organization are inherently related to the natural order of finiteness and the natural dialectical processes of order versus disorder. Without leaving his readers to the boredom of abstract thinking and to the frustrations of concrete planning, he adds: "Our task is to evolve a general concept which allows room for both" (p. 50). As one who considers "process and reality" (1964), Whitehead defines inconsistency as ". . . the fact that the two states of things which constitute the respective meanings of a pair of propositions cannot exist together" (1938, p. 53). His practical approach to addressing these realistic incompatibilities is to offer an understanding of process that not only explains its relationships to inconsistencies but suggests a way of dealing with them. This is the *philosophical incentive relationship* that helps the executive's mind to accept the reality of dealing with inconsistencies in the workplace:

> Process, . .is a fundamental fact in our experience. We are in the present; the present is always shifting; it is derived from the past; it is shaping the future; it is passing into the future. This is process (pp. 52-53).

And this is the *organizational relationship* that helps the executive manage his or her expectations of attaining consistent quality performance with caring role-taking reciprocity:

> Again the attainment of that last perfection of any finite realization depends on freshness. Freshness provides the supreme intimacy of contrast, the new with the old. A type of order arises, develops its variety of possibilities, culminates, and passes into the decay of repetition without freshness. That type of order decays; not into disorder, but by passing into a new type of order (1964, p. 126).

This philosophy of managing organizational inconsistencies in the workplace is what was behind Weiss's (1986) second operational principle of value-system-building for Ameritech, namely, the principle of ambiguous reality. It is also what directs Bowen and Power's (1993) admonitions for the "moral manager" to strive for reasonable judgments rather than insisting on correct judgments in dealing with ethical inconsistencies from managerial decision-making uncertainties. "Do your utmost *moral best* and our corporate conscience will take *ethical care* of the rest...." (review Chapter 2).

Possibilities. If established realities persist within the old order without "freshness," executives and managers need to pass over to realistic possibilities. With the old order fairly well entrenched in the pre-conventional and conventional ways of doing business and running operations, according to the early workplace studies cited earlier, it would appear that moral development intervention, especially in change resistant organization hierarchies, might not be a high priority in corporate planning. The realistic possibilities for a new moral order in the workplace, therefore, might be few. But, in social movement organization process, new order change starts with social unrest (Guerrette, 1981, ch.1; see also Turner, 1969 and Lauer, 1976). And there is no question, at least, in the media that socio-moral unrest pervades throughout society and deeply within the corporate sector. If the culture has been searching for its "moral bearings" through the last century and has yet to find them in this new century, executives, managers and workers might be more ready than organization development planners. And again, if perennial ethical problems are so embedded in the organization structures of hegemonic systems (Gasparino, 2005), corporate culture will only find its "moral bearings" toward a new systemic order through the "moral compass" within the *corporate conscience*[2]. In social movement process to new order change, mobilization needs to follow social unrest. The strategic task to new moral order for corporate culture, therefore, is to mobilize the processes of possibilities, through the *praxis* theories of MBE to achieve the actuality of *socio-moral* realities. And that demands the "*freshness*" of *corporate ethical* discourse.

Corporate Ethical Discourse and Corporate Retreats. Initiating ethical discourse is a real possibility for any executive in any company. Timing for the initiation, however, is extremely important. As a moral leader, the executive needs to be sure of him/herself. One cannot mobilize others to "pass into the future," if one is not ready one's self. Ethical discourse must really start at home. It has to begin from within. Dialogue is needed between the assertive *self* and the *reflexive self.* One cannot hope to manage and direct a corporate conscience, if one is not in touch with one's own. Executives need to initiate an incentive for *self-mobilization* by inducing and developing a facility for comfort with reflexivity (see Griffin, 1993). They need to consider the importance of solitude for contemplating creative paths towards personal and professional change and for planning reconstructive tracks for organization development and corporate moral reform (Koestenbaum, 2002).

It might make sense in their busy lives and demanding organization schedules to slip away, from time to time, for private retreats, alone or with staff, where a refreshing contemplative ethical resource environment could help to expand their moral consciousness through reflexive pondering and aesthetic wondering. (see Chapter 10 below on "corporate and private retreats.")

Mitchell Thomashow, Co-chair of Environmental Studies at Antioch New England Graduate School recommends such retreats, especially for reflexive executives with a value-system consciousness in ecological studies and environmental programming:

> Depending on the size and mission of the organization, there are steps leadership can take to allow staff to confront some of these issues. These include periodic retreats affording the quiet and privacy in which people can discuss the difficulties and challenges of being an environmentalist; opportunities for discussing some of the moral dilemmas that occur when staff participate in controversial public issues; discussions of the various value conflicts that people confront on the job; and opportunities for the staff to take short natural history excursions together. These are means to incorporate reflective practice into the daily life of the environmental organization.   (1995, p.166)

In such a retreat center that offers the privacy of reading, thinking, planning and discourse with an ethical consultant, at one's own pace in re-creational leisure, "critical practical understanding" can open to a "moral point of view" and develop into a "moral plan of action."

Meanwhile, if the internal climate is still not yet actively disposed at the company for developing moral plans of action, let alone for environmental scans of learning, lower level executives and supervisors may be passively receptive to literature, lectures and consults with other morally developed executives. As in the case of the small family-owned refrigeration business above, interest, even from passive receptive levels, builds rapidly when ethics make sense and morals earn profit. When the interest builds to *active dispositions from reflexive learning* and the time to seize the new order arrives, the executive needs to act and that is when to begin the moral "freshness" of MBE and its socialization process for "passing into the future."

PASSING INTO THE FUTURE:
FROM CORPORATE ETHICS TO GLOBAL ETHICS

If there ever was a time to seize a new order in the world, especially after 9/11 and the terrorizing destruction of the twin towers of the World Trade Center, it is now. In an earlier reference to the work of Hans Kung and his decade long work of promoting a "new order for a global ethic," it was noted that, with the advent of the corporate conscience as the legal unit of analysis for corporate responsibility, it is indeed plausible to promote the advent of a *global conscience* as the moral unit of analysis for global responsibility (see note 3 in Chapter 1). Much more needs to be explored, however, about the applied (*praxis*) research possibilities between the "twin towers" of "corporate ethics" and "global ethics."

THE GLOBAL ETHIC FOUNDATION

Kung has spoken and written extensively about the need for a "new global order." In 1991, he began his mission to rebuild a new order for the world with his publication on *Global Responsibility: In Search of a New World Ethic*. In 1993, his *"Declaration Toward a Global Ethic"* was endorsed by the Parliament of the World's Religions (see Kung and Kuschel, 1994). Having begun an earlier scholarly ecumenical search of the world's religions as director of the Ecumenical Research Center at the University of Tubingen in Germany, he eventually published a trilogy of the world's monotheistic religions with *Judaism: Between Yesterday and Tomorrow* (1995), *Christianity: Its Essence, History and Future* (1996), and *Christianity and World Religions: Paths to Dialogue with Islam, Hinduism, and Buddhism* (et al., 1994). During this long period of his ecumenical search, he also published, with Julia Ching, *Christianity and Chinese Religions* (1989). This work focused on Confucianism, Taoism, Buddhism and Chinese folk religions, presenting them not as sectarian offshoots of Far Eastern religions but as independent historical faith traditions with equality to prophetic Semitic and mystic Indian religions. Subsequently, in 1995, with the support of Count K. K. von der Groeben, Kung established the *Global Ethic Foundation* in Tubingen and Berlin, Germany to conduct research on and promotional planning for this global ethic. Kung's vision for this universal ethical mission clearly manifests a purpose to awaken a 6th stage collective moral responsibility awareness on the part of world religions to lead the way to global peace by promoting this global ethic. In the promotion of this work, Kung himself has stated:

> The most fanatical, the cruelest political struggles are those that have been colored, inspired and legitimized by religion. To say this is not to reduce all political conflicts to religious ones, but to take seriously the fact that religions share in the responsibility for bringing peace to our torn and warring world (Global Ethic Foundation - Literature Website, p. 4).

For these reasons, Kung has been relentlessly attempting to bring the leaders of the world's religions together to lead them in collating common ethical standards and guidelines to promote world peace. Consequently, in 1996, having been a professor of theology for thirty years at the University of Tubingen and having directed its Institute for Ecumenical Research, Hans Kung retired as Professor Emeritus and expanded new dimensions to his research on world religions in the global context of international politics and economics. His publications in these interdisciplinary domains include: *Yes to a Global Ethic* (1996) in which, as editor, he invited contributions from heads of state, international organizations, religious leaders, and scholars to open their visions to a global ethic; *A Global Ethic for Global Politics and Economics* (1998) in which he examines with a critical ethical analysis the lack of a political and economic moral focus in the business world. In this work, he prophetically warns against the waves of growing financial scandals, which have since struck the global corporate shore lines with the force of tidal waves. In that same year, he published *A Global Ethic and Global Responsibilities: Two Declarations* (1998). In this publication, he collaborated with Helmut Schmidt, former Chancellor of the Federal Republic of Germany, as editors in producing, with other elder statesmen and public figures, a "Universal Declaration of Human Responsibilities" to justly and globally balance the United Nations Declaration of Human Rights for its fiftieth anniversary.

From this legacy of Kung's work, the Global Ethic Foundation has published on its website the "Text of the Declaration (on) The Principles (of a Global Ethic)". The text is composed of four major headings under which the principles of the global ethic are defined in multi-culturally specific detail. Essential elements of the specifications are herein presented, accordingly, as an analytical connection of the global ethic to the corporate ethic and to demonstrate the need for a corresponding global corporate conscience.

The great contribution of these following principles is that they specify at length in clear practical terms a contemporary global application of the two universal principles of equal justice and caring reciprocity cited in the sixth stage of Kohlberg's moral development scale. This author has seen nothing comparable in the moral development literature which specifies these principles so clearly and applies them so practically and extensively with relevance to contemporary political, social and moral problems. These principles are based on the following four fundamental values:

THE PRINCIPLES OF A GLOBAL ETHIC

1. NO NEW GLOBAL ORDER WITHOUT A NEW GLOBAL ETHIC
    (The ethic is specified as :) The full realization of the intrinsic dignity of the human person, the inalienable freedom and equality in principle of all humans, and the necessary solidarity and interdependence of all humans with each other.... By a global ethic we mean *a fundamental consensus on binding values, irrevocable standards, and personal attitudes*.

2. A FUNDAMENTAL DEMAND: EVERY HUMAN BEING MUST BE TREATED HUMANELY
    ....Possessed of reason and conscience, every human is obliged to behave in a genuinely human fashion, to *do good and avoid evil*.

    It is the intention of this Global Ethic to clarify what this means. In it we wish to recall irrevocable, unconditional ethical norms. These should not be bonds and chains, but helps and supports for people to find and realize once again their lives' direction, values, orientations, and meaning.

There is a principle which is found and has persisted in many religions and ethical traditions of humankind for thousands of years: *What you do not wish done to yourself, do not do to others.* Or in positive terms: *What you wish done to yourself, do to others.* This should be the irrevocable, unconditional norm for all areas of life, for families and communities, for races, nations, and religions.

3. IRREVOCABLE DIRECTIVES

COMMITMENT TO A CULTURE OF NON-VIOLENCE AND RESPECT FOR LIFE.

COMMITMENT TO A CULTURE OF SOLIDARITY AND A JUST ECONOMIC ORDER.

COMMITMENT TO A CULTURE OF TOLERANCE AND A LIFE OF TRUTHFULNESS.

This (specification of the ethic) is especially true:

- for those who work in the *mass media*, to whom we entrust the freedom to report for the sake of truth and to whom we thus grant the office of guardian. They do not stand above morality but have the obligation to respect human dignity, human rights, and fundamental values. They are duty-bound to objectivity, fairness, and the preservation of human dignity. They have no right to intrude into individuals' private spheres, to manipulate public opinion, or to distort reality;

- for *artists, writers* and *scientists,* to whom we entrust artistic and academic freedom. They are not exempt from general ethical standards and must serve the truth;

- for the leaders of countries, *politicians* and *political parties,* to whom we entrust our own freedoms. When they lie in the faces of their people, when they manipulate the truth, or when they are guilty of venality or ruthlessness in domestic or foreign affairs, they forsake their credibility and deserve to lose their offices and their voters. Conversely, public opinion should support those politicians who dare to speak the truth to the people at all times;

- finally, for *representatives of religion.* When they stir up prejudice, hatred and enmity towards those of different belief, or even incite of legitimize religious wars, they deserve the condemnation of humankind and the loss of their adherents.

COMMITMENT TO A CULTURE OF EQUAL RIGHTS AND PARTNERSHIP
BETWEEN MEN AND WOMEN

The relationship between women and men should be characterized not by patronizing behavior or exploitation, but by love, partnership, and trustworthiness. Human fulfillment is not identical with sexual pleasure.

Sexuality should express and reinforce a loving relationship lived by equal partners.

The social institution of marriage, despite all its cultural and religious variety, is characterized by love, loyalty, and permanence. It aims at and should guarantee security and mutual support to husband, wife, and child. It should secure the rights of all family members. All lands and cultures should develop economic and social relationships which will enable marriage and family life worthy of human beings, especially for older people. Children have a right of access to education. Parents should not exploit children, nor children parents. Their relationships should reflect mutual respect, appreciation, and concern. To be authentically human in the spirit of our great religious and ethical traditions means the following:

- We need mutual respect, *partnership* and understanding, instead of patriarchal domination and degradation, which are expressions of violence and engender counter-violence.
- We need mutual concern, tolerance, readiness for reconciliation and *love*, instead of any form of possessive lust or sexual misuse. Only what has already been experienced in personal and familial relationships can be practiced on the level of nations and religions.

4. A TRANSFORMATION OF CONSCIOUSNESS

In conclusion, we appeal to all the inhabitants of this planet. Earth cannot be changed for the better unless the consciousness of individuals is changed. We pledge to work for such transformation in individual and collective consciousness, for the awakening of our spiritual powers through reflection, meditation, prayer or positive thinking, for a *conversion of the heart.*

It is clear from this conclusion, that although Hans Kung did not specify the need for a global corporate conscience, he actually described the need for its "awakening" operations in terms of "collective consciousness" reflexivity. And even more recently, he has acknowledged *the need for a complex organization moral delivery system* to achieve the global ethic: "What's needed . . . is a *moral framework* which is both interactive and interdependent with the economic function of. . . markets, governments, civil society and supranational organisations" (2009).

(The complete text of the principles may also be found in *Yes to a Global Ethic*, Kung, ed., 1996, pp. 12-26 © Continuum, by permission of Bloomsbury Publishing Plc.. See also the more recent and comprehensive "Manifesto for a Global Economic Ethic" on PDF www.bbvaopenmind.com April 1, 2009).

THE MBE MORAL FRAMEWORK AND COLLECTIVITY STRUCTURES OF THE GLOBAL CONSCIENCE

Not only does the MBE paradigm offer this "moral framework" through moral development theory and socialization planning but it also contributes a scientific operational delivery system grounded in organization-management studies equipped to be "interdependent and interactive" with the economic functioning of markets in a global complex organization environment. It also offers a socio-economic moral incentive model for nations to induce moral performance delivery of the global ethic based on the operations of the corporate conscience model (see Chapter 6 above). Within this multi-national complex organization environment, there exists multiple possibilities for projecting the model of the corporate conscience operations within the collectivity infrastructures of global organizations. For example, inasmuch as there is no nation nor multi-national organization which is structurally or politically organized to currently operate a global conscience, all nations and multinational organizations can serve as multiple international collectivities with sector morally definitive and culturally specific "informed" educational MBE programs actively promoting the global ethic.

The United Nations and the Global Conscience. Accordingly, the largest multinational organization with structural and political formation to operationalize an actual *global conscience* is the United Nations. Although this organization has lost some serious credibility in its inability to deliver a unified political and diplomatic resolution over the Iraq war and more particularly in the gravely immoral shadows of the "Oil for Food" scandal which has hovered over its own organizational moral image, it still has a unique organizational status to operate a global organizational conscience. Within its democratic *collectivity infrastructures*, it has the capacity for implementing the MBE paradigm through its morally reflexive intra organizational units of its global structures, as ethically defined and morally tracked in this book for any organization culture. The gravity of need for developing this global ethical mission has been stressed by Dan Erikson, Senior Associate for U.S. Policy and Director of Caribbean Programs at American Dialogue, in the aftermath of the Haitian earthquake and the flow of funds from multilateral organizations:

> Tracking the money has really been a huge challenge. Everyone realizes that there needs to be accountability in aid, and that it's important to have a zero-tolerance policy for corruption. But as a practical matter, what you have in Haiti is so much money coming in from different sources—private sources, multilateral organizations, as well as the U.S. government and other foreign governments—it's going to non-governmental organizations, local governments in some cases, the national government. So as a result, it is really hard to get a clear picture of where all this money is going. There are some successes, some areas where aid has been quite effective, but at the macro-level, clearly it's failed to achieve any sort of sustainable development for the country. . . . So it's really been very difficult to develop a central source. I think this is an area where the United Nations could perhaps play a much more dominant role in the coming months. The U.N. could serve as a clearing house for this type of organization (2010).

In addition to this distributive justice "clearing" role as a global conscience function, the United Nations could exemplify an authentic *cleaning* role for organization moral behavior throughout its collectivity structures by implementing the MBE training programs within the departmental units of its own headquarters and *integrating its ethical focus with an aesthetically moral inspirational ethos.* In view of the advanced educational levels of its diplomatic corps and professional workforce, it is indeed quite plausible that that the implementation of the MBE training programs would be sufficient to sublimate the moral motivational and ethically incentive inducement building of the entire U.N. staff. That this staff is capable of the highest morally motivated performance and post conventional ethically induced incentives has been evident with its life-giving sacrificial heroism and care-giving committed service to the poorest "*anawim*" of the poor people of Haiti.[3]

Through their global infrastructures, notice how the United Nations *conscientiously* responded with the heroic sacrifices of the lives of their multiple executive officers and their working staffs in the recent earthquake disaster in Haiti. Though their organization headquarters in Port-au-Prince was demolished, their surviving staff workers stayed on to organize the international responder efforts from their member nations with 6th stage care-giving moral performance. In this catastrophic climate of intra and inter organizational chaos, this U.N. global conscience led the spirit of all the care-giving responding nations with post-conventional moral virtue for all other responder institutions in the global organization set during the aftermath of the quake.

CNN *and Its Global Conscience Networks.* One most visible responding organizational unit of this global set manifesting such virtue was the *corporate conscientious* media operations of CNN and its own global collectivity, CNN International, with their continuing reporting of the lifesaving events of rescuing teams from multiple nations and their organizational fund-raising programming for the Haitian people. The compassionate virtues of their reporting staff of Anderson Cooper, Dr. Sanjay Gupta, Gary Tuckman and Ivan Watson inspired their viewers with an exemplary 6th stage professional reporting team and post-conventional sympathetic concern for the shoveled remains of the dead and the wandering displacement of the living. This collective operational programming was a dramatic on site performance of how a global conscience can and should work through the telecasting corporate productions of the international media and the reflexivity awareness of their executives and leaders. More recently, during the catastrophic events of the "Holy Innocent" martyrs of the Sandy Hook children and their teachers, CNN reporters remained with the entire community of the Newtown Connecticut families and its citizens, conducting media interviews with 6th stage morally caring and compassionate coverage of the grieving parents and community responders. The programing was a media masterpiece of MBE managing performance of evoking responder priorities with morally caring bereavement needs for the families of the victimized children and of convoking responder priorities toward ethically invoking amendment needs for MBE governing policies of MBO gun-controlling lobbies.

The Clinton Foundation and Its Global Conscience Networks. Another morally reflexive executive and world leader who has himself passed over from political to ethical leadership since having left office is President William Clinton of the United States. Much in the ecumenical spirit and charismatic disposition of Hans Kung, President Clinton has innovatively moved the traditionally established Presidential Foundations beyond the immobile structures of the historical past to the morally transformative post-conventional stages of current exploratory global initiatives.

The Clinton Foundation and Its Global Moral Collectivities. The William J. Clinton Foundation is designed to open the boundaries of nations and religions to achieve the *harmonies of beliefs*, the *subsidies for health* and the *securities of peace*. Through his ethically sensitive leadership and exploratory global vision, the former President has expanded the technological and communication linkages of globalization in terms of passing into the future towards the phenomenological[4] experience of proactively building "a better future" into an "integrated global community." With this vision and purpose, President Clinton established the *Clinton Global Initiative* in 2004 as a global collective entity informing the global conscience and reforming its moral focus.

Conclusion: Partnerships for Global Moral Reform. The Global Initiative goals of *climate-change-responding*, *responsible governance*, *poverty elimination* and *religion reconciliation* clearly reflect 5th and 6th stage moral conscientiousness. Having launched this *Global Initiative* in September 2005 to coincide with the opening of the United Nations General Assembly, President Clinton has already secured voluminous numbers of high profile multinational corporate, government and religious leaders. In this practical (*praxis*) change endeavor, he has formed committees and partnerships among them to direct programs for planning and to *engage in commitments for action*. The commitment options contain an exhaustive list of *action projects* designed to address specific environmental and global philanthropic "focus areas" relevant to the *praxis* attainment of Initiative goals:

> By bringing together leaders from many fields whose voices, policies and actions have an extraordinary impact, the Clinton Global Initiative provides an unusual opportunity to stimulate change. . . . "Together, they contributed to a dialogue that has resulted in commitments that will change

the lives of millions of people around the world" (Clinton Global Initiative Website, September 20-22, 2006).

These kinds of global collective initiatives and moral performance engagements are what delivers corporate moral reform and global ethical transformation through "*inspiring change*" (see Exhibit 7:2).

Exhibit: 7:2 Clinton Global Initiative

CGI 2006: Sept. 20-22

OUR MISSION

Clinton Global Initiative: Inspiring Change
President Bill Clinton and the William J. Clinton Foundation have launched the Clinton Global Initiative to help our world move beyond the current state of globalization to a more integrated global community of shared benefits, responsibilities and values.

The mission of the William J. Clinton Foundation and the goal of this Initiative, is to increase the benefits and reduced the burdens of global interdependence; to make a world of more partners and fewer enemies; and to give more people the tools they need to build a better future. The Clinton Global Initiative is a non-partisan endeavor, bringing together a carefully selected group of the world's best minds and most distinguished problem solvers to focus on practical, ideological, religious, ethnic and geographical backgrounds—including current and former heads of state, top business executives, preeminent scholars and representatives of key non-governmental organizations.

The Clinton Global Initiative is a non-partisan catalyst for action, bringing together a community of global leaders to devise and implement innovative solutions to some of the world's most pressing challenges.

This Initiative is unlike other world conferences in one respect: it is determined to change things now, by discussing some of the world's most pressing problems; detailing successful responses to them; seeking the best now solutions; and most important, obtaining a specific commitment from each participant to take action in one of the topics discussed.

END NOTES

1. This dialectical schematic "borrowing" from the AGIL imperatives of Parsons' functionalism is not unmindful of the importance of his theory-building contribution to sociology in the last century nor is it meant to suggest that he was unmindful of natural environmental needs. Quite contrarily, he was so widely attuned to the social environment and its relation to the social system that he could have been called a pioneer of "open system theory." The "borrowing" here is simply used as a dialectic contrast of concepts to build a theory of corporate ethical action for the MBE paradigm. As Jonathan Turner describes, Parsons himself did the same kind of borrowing, ". . . using works (of others) and selectively borrowing concepts to build a theory of action" (1978, p. 42, note 6).

2. See *Time* (25 May 1987). This issue, written in the aftermath of the Wall Street and Contragate scandals, manifests the magnitude of socio-moral unrest. Its front cover poses the national moral dilemma and defines the need for a cultural moral compass: "What Ever Happened to ETHICS? Assaulted by sleaze, scandals and hypocrisy, America searches for its moral bearings" (cover piece).

3. *Anawim* is a Biblical Hebrew-Christian term signifying "servants of God." See *The New Jerome Biblical Commentary* on the Psalms, p. 532. Review also *The Treasures of the Church: A Theology of the Anawim*" by Eric Stoltz, Jan. 12, 2004: www.stbrendanchurch.org/deacon/pdf/anawim.pdf.

4. In the social scientific literature, this term signifies the purpose for which the Clinton Global Initiative has been established in relation to the critical practical (*praxis*) needs of "globalization" by *making things happen by living experiences* through engaging commitments and participatory action. (see Ricoeur, 1988)

CHAPTER 8

SOCIAL SYSTEM PROBLEMS AND GLOBAL MORAL REFORM

MORAL DEVELOPMENT PROBLEMS AND FAITH DEVELOPMENT SOLUTIONS

The Problem of Time. The innovative social scientific rediscovery of the corporate conscience and its operational location in the institutional structures of corporate and global organizations can open ethical reconstructive planning in applied organization science toward upgrading moral behavior in management leadership and workforce compliance; but it will not immediately deliver sixth stage post-conventional moral performance on organizational floors nor in market exchanges. The reasons for this are in the complexities of the *problem of time* emanating from the diversified realities of free markets which lead people to make choices, as the Kohlberg legacy has demonstrated, at the conventional levels of morality at best, for the most part, and at the pre-conventional levels at least, for the disturbing part. These disparaging market conditions have caused widespread global system problems with an erupting disintegration of *social faith* in the ethical foundations of market economies and the consequential breakdown of *public trust* in the international institutions of market securities. A contemporary example of how the problem of time can bear on moralities of choice is in market investing when global populations and financial institutions place their investments in international markets through multiple exchanges with unbalanced "economies of scale," as in the recent Euro Zones of Greece and Cyprus, with innocent investors losing their earnings as well as their social faith and public trust in these counter cultural exchanges operating at the pre-conventional levels of "moralities of scale." The problem of time for cultures to blend and markets to lend without a global corporate conscience and an ethical management leadership exposes corporations and investors to the problems of evil.

The Problem of Evil. Another reason for such social system problems and especially for the most serious social effects on the economies of scale with the consequential undermining of the public trust breakdown is the more serious *problem of evil*, likewise emanating from the unethical realities of institutionalized corruption, which commonly persuade morally under-developed investors to violate the moral law at the uncommon levels of immorality with bilking means and "ponzie" schemes. While the Kohlberg research was never designed to measure such radically immoral behavior, it was conducted to measure moral awareness and ultimately to upgrade moral performance. Furthermore, while the designs were set to evaluate universal moral developmental conclusions through multi-cultural longitudinal studies, they were never meant to reconstruct global societies or to regenerate market moralities. These tasks are set for the *critical practical* sociological reconstructionist who analyzes the ethical complexities of multi-cultural organizations and the problematic moral *under*-development of social system moralities.

ANALYTICAL THEORIES

Moral Development Reconstruction. To speak of the reconstruction of societies and the regeneration of moralities, especially in the global proportions which were outlined by Hans Kung, as noted above in Chapter 7, appears to be an insurmountable task, if not an impossible mission. But if one focuses on the economic theories of *moralities of scale*, as proposed in Chapter 6, and the *praxis* theories of Management by Ethics with applied moral development socialization, the task is clearly possible and the mission realistically plausible. The secret of this moral development reconstructive mission lies in the theoretical word "reality" or more *practically* with the phrase "in reality reconstruction" (Berger and Luckman, 1967) in the strategic terms of *Praxis and Action* (see Bernstein, 1971). These works open a reconstructive vision toward expanding practical strategies for the mission of social change through the *interactional* tracks of *social faith* and *public trust.*

Reality Re-construction and Organization Culture. To put it simply, if one is dissatisfied with a given reality, one needs to change the reality. Obviously, if one is to change a reality, one must understand how realities are constructed. Symbolic interaction theory in sociology explains this constructive process by demonstrating how the management of interactional symbols creates particular realities through the communication of *shared meanings.* Symbols, unlike signs, are not fixed nor static. They are fluent and changeable, as they depend for their constructive efficacy on the interactive shared meanings which two people or a group assign to a given object, incident or an experience. When shared meanings grow from this interactional base, organizations and their cultures of meanings form. People unite only through shared meanings; but since meanings are mental with internal cognitive significance, they need symbolic formation with external expressive interaction. The most common symbolic form of this interaction is language. Thus, the most common and constructive symbols of reality building or reality reconstruction are words. A stressful reality change and media wide example of the external power of words emerged in the first political campaign of Barack Obama and the shared meaning of the religious truths and liturgical rites which he and his wife and children had enjoyed for twenty years in the organization culture of a large Black church in Chicago. But when Obama became a candidate for the presidency of the United States, his shared meanings and symbolic realities magnified by global proportions. When his Pastor began to use language to define Black Liberation Theology in his church and in the public media with counter cultural and inflammatory words, Mr. Obama courageously changed his political organizational and ecclesial affiliation determinatively with the *symbolic power of his own words* to redefine his political focus and to reconnect *his shared meanings* of religious faith with the mainline parochial cultures of American Churches, Synagogues and Mosques.

In addition to the symbolic power of words, any object or subject or experience, etc. can become symbols when individuals or groups attach shared meanings to such entities. The tearful experiences of joyful gratitude of subjects like Jesse Jackson and Oprah Winfrey on the night of the first election victory of Barack Obama as the President elect of the United States became immediate symbols of Black pride with shared meanings of finally achieving the dreams of racial integration and the objective entities of equal justice for all Americans. So realities can and often do develop a constellation of symbols to express the shared meanings of peoples and organizations. Such a constellation of symbols is what constructs a shared reality and constitutes an organization culture.

Reality Re-Construction and Corporate Culture. Since every organization develops its culture through this simple social psychological formula of the sharing of meanings and expressing them through its ambient design of words (mission statements, employee regulations, codes of ethics, occupational, professional, business enterprises, etc.), they also utilize natural and human resources shaping the former to fit a product, while training the latter to conform to shared meanings of its production, its purpose and its profits. In sum, all of the above become the symbolic constructs of a company culture. To analyze more incisively, it can be specified that all of these constructs can be identified as internal symbols of a company culture. These internal symbolic constructs are commonly found on company websites and usually define a company ethic and trace its moral profile. But there are other powerful symbols a company can use to project its imagery beyond the internal constructs of its organization culture, such as, the external constructs of ethical company associations and environmental product advertising. Ben & Jerry's Ice Cream and its "Rain Forest" products are healthy ecological examples serving as an incentive flavor symbolism to promote external environmental associations for the training of its human resources and for the sharing of its internal ethical consciousness values with public touring customers in their Vermont corporate headquarters.

Recognizing an applied, practical understanding of symbolic interaction theory in reality construction processes, Robert Dilenschneider encourages the creation of "symbolic value" beyond one's operational role: ". . . an association with a big issue like trade or foreign relations is a good anchor. It's a symbolic association which can endure and support your [one's] public profile for a long time. . . . The symbolism of corporations is actively read inside and outside the company. . . . Managers scaling the rungs of corporate influence *must be concerned about these symbols* [emphasis added] because that's how the world reads corporations." (1990, p. 80)

Through these external zones of symbolic expression within and *beyond* company grounds through media communications, a multiplicity backfire, if not an "explosion," of company symbols can ultimately *disfigure* the company's shared meanings of its value-system and ethical realities toward a national ethnic and even toward international multi-ethnic global ranges. Notice, for example, the very clever use of media advertising of the British Petroleum Corporation. Its television ads described the company's petroleum products and briefly stressed its ethical concerns for the protection of the environment and for the solution of problems associated with global warming. The viewer was left with an imaginative "faith" challenge, wondering about the depth of meaning of the green-lettered logo BP and the words: "Beyond Petroleum." These ads were a most effective use of linguistic and projective symbolism to frame the ethical image of the company, to manage the impression of moral awareness reality in its value system and to stress the need for moral reality reconstruction in the corporate industrial culture of oil production. Behind the ads and the company's projected ethical image was an alert corporate conscience which was assumed to be reflecting on global warming and environmental protection. The company website described what BP was doing to achieve carbon reduction and atmospheric stabilization and in symbolic analogical terms suggested "what you can do" as a morally incentive inducement "to go on a *low-carbon* diet."

The *moral tragedy* of all this ethical good, however, was literally *exploded* in the corporate face of British Petroleum's symbolic imagery as an environmentally sensitive company with the catastrophic explosion of their deep sea oil rig in the Gulf of Mexico in the spring of 2010 with the death of 11 BP workmen and the "drowning" of their corporate ethical image. The company's linguistic use of the "beyond' symbolism projections were not given sufficient "scaling" concerns within the moral developmental "rungs" of its corporate conscience, as Dilenschneider was urging for management supervision. With hindsight review of management's performance during the

Gulf of Mexico oil-rigging disaster, however, the corporate conscience of the company clearly indicated vested interest relativity motivation at stage 2 with empty promising platitudes for the coastal peoples of the region revealing the ravishing "rungs" of their morally insensitive symbolism. In the aftermath of this largest environmental disaster in the history of the United States, with the atmospheric destabilization of the Gulf coastal regions and the economic destruction of their fishing and shrimp industries, the corporate ethical image of the company's reputation is for the public *beyond* belief in the veracity of all their statements about morally inducing retribution. In effect, the company is left with no "symbolic value" of credibility and is itself in desperate need of a *"high-ethically productive* diet" toward reality reconstruction and corporate moral reform. (For a critical *praxis* sequel to this critique, see below pp. 257-259).

Reality Re-Construction and Corporate Moral Reform. Company values and ethical realities, however, can and often disintegrate when employees and even management and owners differ and abandon the sharing of meanings. Case after case of corporate fraud and management greed have demonstrated the widespread breakdown of moral meanings, especially in the last several years. Congressional hearings, SEC investigations and the lineup of judicial trials have exposed the immoral and deceitful scheming of fraudulent meanings. As one watches the legal "line-ups" of executives, consultants, brokers and traders from courtrooms to prisons, one wonders how these "traitors" could have allowed themselves to fall from executive grace. This wondering about moral breakdown demands reflection about moral development studies. It is discouraging to note that there has been little or no research on moral *under*-development in the "scheming" terms of the corporate organizational climate of corruption undergrowth. What is salient in the experiences of moral breakdown is that the incremental process of moral development from a lower stage to the next higher stage revealed in the Kohlberg studies does not seem to warrant a corresponding hypothesis in the opposite morally detrimental direction. The Enron case, cited in chs. 2 & 3, is an example of the catastrophic loss of shared moral meanings in the hierarchy of the company while the rapid moral spin-down of the corporate leaders, entrusted with fifth and sixth stage moral responsibilities, crashed in the *immoral* undergrowth of corporate corruption at their worst with this fearful hierarchy hiding in stages one and two at their "morally" best. To prevent immoral "tsunamic" disasters such as this, and to address the problem of evil in organization structures, corporate executives seeking moral reform need to keep in mind one basic discovery in the moral development research, the simple fact that moral development is an incremental process with moral awareness advancement from one stage to the next higher awareness level. Thus, in their moral socialization roles, they first need to identify the stage of moral development of any given employee or group in the company and to acquire an operational understanding of the social structural *reality* of that employee or group. Only then, can they begin to calculate the exact plausible stages for moral advancement. (It is to be noted, however, that much of Kohlberg's studies were conducted with the younger educational populations of schools and that it is much more plausible that older populations of adult workers in factories and business environments would be much more alert to moral advancement inducement through the pre and post conventional stages.) This kind of interactional understanding requires a humanistic approach to management, allowing the leader to "pass over" into the social world of the subject(s) in order to perceive his/her/their realities. The pedagogical challenge here is to see how they *operate*—where they are coming from, what their symbols of interest and interaction are, what shared meanings these symbols express for them and how these meanings synchronize with or counter against company meanings. This moral evaluation search by the socialization leader does not take long. The art of passing over into another's world is simply the caring skill of taking the roles of others to achieve an understanding of their moral perceptions and a stage evaluation of their behavior. The simplicity of this moral role-taking search is manifested by the interactive sensitivity of *listening*. Authentic listening with caring sensitivity engenders openness and truthfulness in interactive discourse and prepares employees with motivation for moral advancement. In the case of the author's consulting with the owners and supervisors of the refrigeration company, cited above in Chapter 3, the supervisors of the service teams were advised to *listen* to their apprentices' accounts of how they spent the weekend, while on journey from job to job through the day. It was pointed out that they could quickly and quite accurately formulate a stage evaluation of the apprentices' moral awareness and even performance, learning how they treated their girlfriends on their dates, what bars they may have lounged in and how long, where they spent the nights, etc. Such symbolic revelations would ordinarily and clearly indicate whether their apprentices were *using* others or *caring* for them. When a supervisor, manager or executive is willing to reach out and so visit the social worlds of employees with authentic and sensitive listening, he or she will quickly and effectively learn what symbols and meanings constitute their realities and whether or not they are capable of sharing the moral meanings of company symbols and ethical realities, what stages are *operative* in their moral awareness spectrum and what stages are *plausible* for their advancement (see again Exhibit 4:1 in Chapter 4).

Why it is so imperative to grasp the external social realities of employees is *first* because these realities manifest a clear and dominant moral awareness which can be assessed as complementary or contradictory to company values and ethics; and *second*, one cannot expect from employees internal moral performance consistency in the workplace if there is external immoral performance inconsistency in the realities of their social environment. Thus, reality reconstruction and corporate moral reform are dependent on a clear and certain organizational and personal consistency of shared moral meanings among executives, line management and employees throughout a company. Within this kind of corporate culture, the interdependent linkage between organizational and personal moral consistency creates the ideal typical moral learning climate for the stage advancement of faithful and trusted employees, since they can be easily and simply coached to perform at the next higher stage through the powers of moral persuasion and the virtues of moral emulation. The same can be said for companies which have lost their moral integrity through the scurrilous scandals of the fraudulent few with new moral leadership personally directing corporate moral reform through the pedagogies and socialization programming of MBE. It's that simple—*involved and integrating personal moral leadership*—advancing the workforce stage by stage through the sharing of moral meanings and the reconstruction of authentic moral realities (see Chapters 9 and 10 for fuller descriptions of these models of moral leadership).

FAITH DEVELOPMENT SOLUTIONS

Social Faith Development and Social Trust Reformation. While the corporate moral reformer may be intent on the sharing of moral meanings in a company with personal and organizational consistency, he/she needs to be prepared to confront systemic operational problems. Such problems are provoked by the fact that not everyone in a company and its various multiple departments and divisions, especially in multi-national corporations, can perform consistently in the higher post-conventional levels of moral development. The reformer needs to recognize this fact along with the moral complexities of such organizations and even the moral relativities which often co-exist in pluralistic cultures. For instance, the international problem of moral relativism has persisted in global commerce for centuries and what may be considered legal and even ethical in one culture, may be unlawful or immoral in another (Hills, 1976).[1] With his global corporate counsel experience of dealing with cross-cultural organization climates and ethical decision-making, Dilenschneider writes:

> The growth of global business complicates ethics decisions. I meet with many business executives abroad. Once we get to know each other, they tell me they can't understand American righteousness. They don't understand why Americans expect that a globally uniform standard of values should exist. And, they ask, why especially should this standard be driven by U. S. administrative law rather than a time-honored religious or moral code? (1990, p. 35)

Cross-Cultural Bridges of Moral and Social Faith Development Paradigms. In this present time of history, with such contentious ethical realities of religious wars and the destructive operations of international terrorism, there seems to be little hope for the social and ecumenical reconstruction of global moral reform. With this recognition admitted however, it may be helpful toward achieving the goal of global ethics by a "time-honored religious or moral code," to explain the problematic relativities in the search for regenerative moralities through a sister paradigm of moral development, namely, *the paradigm of Faith Development*. The early work of Kohlberg (1981) in this area was inclined to view faith development as providing a higher order for moral reasoning and behavior and as generating more enduring incentives for moral performance consistency in terms of ultimate life-meaning. His studies concluded that highly developed moral reasoning, even at stage 6, does not appear to hold the virtue of moral consistency beyond the point of rational logic. For example, Kohlberg suggested one could pose the question to one's self, "Would I die for stage 6?" He claimed that philosophical rational logic would be prone to conclude: "No. The rational logic of stage 6 moral reasoning does not require the ultimate sacrifice of death beyond a justice or reciprocity level to reflect morally consistent judgment and action." This hypothetical question was actually faced by numbers of families during the devastating floods of the Gulf coastal regions in the aftermath of Hurricane Katrina. In a television interview of one such case, a married daughter responded with rational logic to such a life and death choice which she was forced to make by the rescue operations in her neighborhood which could not accommodate elderly bed-ridden people. The daughter explained that since her mother was confined to bed, she had to escape with her husband from the surging waters already in the home to save their lives, leaving her helpless mother alone to drown. Sixth stage rational logic would argue: "It makes no sense to lose three lives when one of the lives is already in its end-of-life period." Kohlberg's acknowledgment that inasmuch as faith development provides a higher order for moral reasoning and behavior and that as this order focuses on ultimate life meaning, *the virtue of faith* could impel one facing such a life and death choice to make the ultimate sacrifice and to lay down one's life for and *with* one's mother. By studying the lives of people who displayed such virtue, even to death, such as, Gandhi and Martin Luther King, Kohlberg described a certain "moral maturity" which allows people to transcend the limits of reason through a *faith vision into ultimate life meaning*. He concluded that this vision represents a more holistic faith development which projects one's moral commitment to a higher transcendental plane for moral consistency as anchored in religious meaning and life purpose. This conclusion might help some corporate executives to respond generously to the hypothetical, but *morally conscientious question*, of 2nd stage vested interest greed in executive compensation packages, provoked by the grip of third world starvation needs: "Would I contribute for stage 6?"

The Faith Development Paradigm. The work of James Fowler in faith development pursued more comprehensive interdisciplinary studies with the moral paradigm, even earlier than Kohlberg's, by linking theological ethics and moral development studies to developmental psychology and social psychology. As a qualitative research analyst, Fowler began his studies at Harvard Divinity School in the late sixties and early seventies gathering interview data on his subjects' life journeys in faith. From the breadth of his interdisciplinary insights, he formulated his faith paradigm by: (1) building a developmental psychology of the *inner self* grounded in the life stages of Erik Erikson (1963, 1968, 1977); (2) shaping a social psychology of the *outer self*-anchored in the social interactional studies of the mind by George Herbert Mead (1934); and (3) constructing a moral psychology of the *philosophical self-b*ased on the moral stages of Lawrence Kohlberg. This inter theory linkage provides more than adequate empirical scientific grounding for a comprehensive developmental psychology of the *holistic social self* (Fowler, 1981 and 2001). Such interdisciplinary vision into the practical interactional dimensions of the intricately complex personal and social self should silence some later postmodernists who have claimed that his faith development model lacks a developmental psychological understanding of the self and is more comprehensible as a system of types rather than a sequence of stages. In the author's own critical review of his response to his postmodern critics, it is incisive to note that faith development *per se* is socially linked to and contractually shaped by the moral domain of stage 5, which, in the Kohlberg paradigm, is the building stage for post conventional moral trust. And since there is an incremental four stage foundation in the moral development building process of achieving trusting behavior; and also since trust is not viable without faith, it makes no theoretical or practical sense to identify faith development in terms of types. Faith development is clearly a developmental stage process with psychosocial stage affinity ties to ego-identity building and moral awareness development. In conclusion to this critique, Fowler's work on faith development is more critical than ever toward understanding the complex reality correlations of moral and faith development stage sequences and their respective configurations for the corporate moral reality reconstructions of social trust reformation and public trust restoration. (More applied analysis of "faith development" is discussed below along with *praxis* interpretations of Fowler's 6th stage scale on p. 246).

Social Trust Reformation and Public Trust Restoration. With reference to the critical demands of reconstructing the corporate unethical realities and the inter-organizational moral complexities of the current socio-economic breakdown in market cultures with the loss of the humanistic virtues of social faith and the investing virtues of public trust, it is helpful to consult the incisively critical paradigmatic work of the Business Roundtable Institute for Corporate Ethics and the Arthur W. Page Society (Bolton R. et al., 2009). This study identifies three social psychological dynamics for businesses to restore the public trust in their markets in the aftermath of the widespread moral failures in corporate cultures:

For corporations to help restore public trust in business—and to capitalize
on the increased opportunities such increased trust would create—they will
have to do three things. They must identify values and interests that can
serve as a foundation for mutuality. They must assess and balance the power
of vulnerability of each party. And they must establish minimal safeguards
against bad actors to protect those willing to make themselves vulnerable.
(p. 22)

While the Business Roundtable Institute and Page report is reconstructively
helpful in its mechanically graphic terminology, it is especially important to
understand the essence of a social psychological ethic in mutual role-taking
sensitivities and their corresponding sixth stage moral reciprocities of *caring*
mutualities for achieving trust restoration. It is more radically important,
however, to identify the scientific *foundational root system* of the social
psychological and the interactional systemic processes of mutuality. It is,
moreover, to understand that this root system is philosophically embedded in
the *ethically principled* grounding "soul" of the *corporate conscience*.
Authentic and sincere mutuality is motivated by role-taking sensitivities and
generated by caring interpersonal affinities between and among interpersonal
individuals and interorganizational collectivities. In accordance with this
social scientific clarification, role taking sensitivity between and among
agents of business transactions and mutual caring interaction in the
commerce of their corporate enterprises will reset the moral egalitarian scale
for trust balancing evaluations toward restoring the balance of power in
global economies and the safeguarding of the public trust in their marketing
entities.

With further interdisciplinary constructive analysis of the Business
Roundtable Institute for Corporate Ethics and the Arthur W. Page report, it
should be stressed that, while public trust is specifically different from social
trust, as was clearly explained in the report, all forms of mutual trust
including public trust are grounded in social faith. *One cannot trust another
without faith in the other.* This simple critical interpretive explanation of the
social interactional reality of faith-rebuilding in transactional as well as in
contractual business arrangements is that one cannot generate trust
motivation unless the social psychological incentive of *believing* in the other
induces the corresponding moral virtue of trust in the other. With this
essential principled ethical underpinning of trusting transactions, it needs to
be clarified that social faith constitutes the fundamental paradigmatic
foundation of public trust.

In support of these conclusions and references, Fowler's own commentary
about the meaning of faith in terms of its multinational and global proportions
is consistent with the teachings of his theological mentor and social ethicist,
H. Richard Niebuhr (1991):

Niebuhr created an original synthesis of historical-critical, sociological, and psychosocial perspectives on the phenomenon of faith. Faith, for Niebuhr, was not limited to religious faith. He saw and illumined the relational structure of the kind of faith (or "good faith") that makes the flourishing of stable communities of strangers and neighbors possible. Faith involves ties of mutual trust and loyalty between persons and groups who commit themselves, explicitly and tacitly, to loyalty to and trust in shared centers of value and power. Shared commitments to the values of truth telling, fairness, *non-injury* (emphasis added), and the practice of procedures that guard and fulfill the common good, help to constitute a viable social faith. Religious traditions help to evoke and form commitments of this sort but also call their members to more specific commitments and visions, including those which can provide critical and transformative perspectives in relation to routinized or corrupted forms of societal faith (Fowler, 2001, pp. 168-169).

The consistency of these social faith teachings of Niebuhr and Fowler have been expressed more recently with a practical synthesis of their interdisciplinary relevance by the Network of Global Agenda Councils of the World Economic Forum and its "Discussion Highlights on Faith" at the Network's Summit in Dubai, United Arab Emirates, 7-9 November 2008:

> Religion is high on the global agenda. . . . Today's global challenges of war and peace, democracy and human rights, and economic and social development all have important religious dimension. . . . Faith is often part of the problem; tensions among religious communities can impede international cooperation, public stability, social cohesion and economic growth. But it is also potentially part of the solution: these communities are often among the most important forces mobilizing ground core values such as human dignity, solidarity and social responsibility. More than 80% of the world's population identifies with a religious tradition. The ethical resources of faith communities—a source of transcendent values—and their social influence are underutilized resources in building coalitions for positive change. Religious traditions prioritize human flourishing, a core value for the creation of a durable and legitimate global economic and social order.

> The Global Agenda Council on Faith proposes that religion can contribute . . . in the following ways. . . . For business:

> - The current global economic crisis extends beyond markets. It is also a crisis of confidence and a failure of values of transparency, integrity and the public good.
> - Religious traditions are reservoirs of ethical resources. Each tradition has its own perspective, but all speak to core values of economic and social life.
> - Dialogue among religious, political and business leaders can engage differences and highlight the shared values that inform the emerging global economic order.

- Educational institutions and the media should place more
  emphasis on the role of values alongside of material forces in
  economic life.   (World Economic Forum, 2008)
  (https://members.weforum.org/pdf/GAC/Reports)

These agenda highlights need to be underscored and integrated into the
curricula of all business, management, and administration and accounting
schools in the global business educational environment and in all the human
resource training sectors and divisions of corporate executive education and
corporate ethical learning institutes in their concentrated efforts to rebuild
the global social trust in business and the international public trust in
markets.

*Rebuilding Global Social Faith in Business and Cross-Cultural Public Trust
in Markets.* One of the most sensitive cross cultural areas for the rebuilding
of social faith in organization corporate cultures and for restoring public trust
in market investing subcultures is in the controversial common practices of
executive compensation and bonus distribution payments and their
demoralizing effects on the balance of power in corporate culture and
management leadership, as addressed above in Chapter 5. Heated media
discussions of these controversial practices often explode into irate political
persuasions and "low rate" critical de-constructive analyses and usually
blatantly expose political partisan subjective biases. What would
significantly contribute to these discussions of executive compensation and
bonus distribution practices is a more objective critical *praxis* understanding
of the moral and faith development scaling presented in this book toward
morally upgrading management leadership through the innovative MBE
paradigm.

While the faith development paradigm of Professor Fowler contains some
references to religious values and contemplative spiritualities at the higher
stage levels of ecumenical belief and transcendental insight, the median stage
levels open critical practical insights toward the *social mores and cultural
sources of social faith and religious ideologies*, as to be discussed below with
Exhibit 8:1 p. 246. It is within these developmental faith stages that one can
evaluate global starvation poverties on the "moralities of scale" from Chapter
6; and, with foresight, calculate 5th and 6th stage moral development solutions
to the socio-economic problems of the maldistribution of wealth, relative to
the ineffective conventional "economies of scale" with provisionary *post-
conventional praxis* planning for *delivery* solutions to global hunger. In these
tragically terrorizing and socially disruptive times, it is reassuring to
comprehend the *rebuilding power of social faith* and to *believe* in the
restoring virtues of public trust for the social and ethical reconstruction of
market economies.

MBE INNOVATIONS FOR SOCIAL FAITH AND PUBLIC TRUST

Innovative Action with Music for Social Change. Mark Johnson (2008) expanded a strategic vision for social change by focusing on an *aesthetic* "moral framework" toward reconstructing the infrastructures of global social system "realities" with the "power of ethical thinking" and the *virtue of moral leadership* in the performing arts with his musical production of *Playing for Change: Peace through Music.* As a producer, he selected the song "Stand by Me" and directed its performance into an integrated composition by multinational individual and group performers with brief continuing segments of scenes from subways to sidewalks through pastures and hilltops around the globe depicting singers and audiences gathering together to sing with and for one another un-endingly with the compassionate refrain of "Stand by Me" generating the ethical spirit of *universal caring reciprocity.* (See the performance on PBS.org under the *Bill Moyers Journal* on the Video and Transcript tabs, October 24, 2008; see also on *You Tube*). This work of moral leadership *germinated from* the symbolic constructs of the "sounds of music" and the symbolic processes of "imaginative rehearsal" role-taking among singers in subways and listeners on sidewalks has *flourished with* role-playing by musicians around the world with shared meanings of reconstructing peace and unity in a terrorized and divided world. It is a leadership call for people around the world with social faith and a MBE voice to Stand by Our global "Corporate US" to save the Planet and its ethical foundations of Public Trust in market economies with "moralities of scale."

Rebuilding the Ethical Foundations of the Market Economy. At this critical time in human history, the widespread universal social system problems, associated with the spreading anxieties of global hunger, demand world leaders to *act in concert* by taking the lead with international ethical policy planning to alleviate immoral poverty. As a socio-economic moral incentive model, MBE has been proposed above in Chapter 6 precisely to reconstruct the ethical foundations of the market economy for the *ultimate purpose of rebuilding public trust toward achieving global market moral reform.* To convince one of this desperate need for global market reformation, consider the scholarly work of world renowned economists, from the *Kiel Institute of World Economics*, who have been studying the problems of world poverty and global hunger for decades only to lock themselves in an outdated economic paradigm laden with the perennial controversies of private free market economies and social welfare state systems.

> Democracy and the market economy have survived the battle of the systems. The recent downfall of communism in many countries has shown the inferiority of the underlying economic system in supplying people with the means of material well-being. Nevertheless it has been doubted whether the market economy is able to successfully tackle the many economic and

ecological challenges ahead and it has been contended that the market
economy lacks the necessary moral underpinnings. This is why the Kiel
Institute of World Economics conducted an international workshop on "The
Ethical Foundations of the Market Economy," which took place on August
30-31, 1993.   (Siebert, ed., p. V, 1994)

Democracy and the market economy may have survived the "battle of
systems" *but the poor have not.* Poverty stricken people have lost social faith
in the politics of governance and the economies of markets. They have little
or no incentives, let alone opportunities, for economic advancement and
material well-being. So the moral question is: how can any incentives be
induced for them, when they discover their governments and their markets
operating at the lowest levels of the Kohlberg scale? In many countries of the
third world, the poor have experienced fear from the power and prestige of
their rulers and alienation from the privileged and well-fed employed elite
(stage 1). In most countries of the developed world, the poor have witnessed
the morally underdeveloped markets proliferate grave and expansive maldistribution of wealth through manipulative techniques of investing which
render market exchanges favorable to savvy traders and large institutional
holders (stage 2). These market conditions manifest a socially destructive
power imbalance between the privileged upper class rich and the destitute
lower class poor and constitute a prevailing economic climate of class
inequality and public trust debility. Notice, for example, how the common
practice of "short-selling" in the stock market to cover losses or to secure
gains resembles the betting in gambling casinos and disrupts the integrity of
investing hard-earned capital in unadulterated businesses. Gambling against
the pure purpose of a company's business ventures reflects a disingenuous
moral impunity and impairs the socio-economic faith of other investors, often
causing a run on the rapid trading of stocks and, at critical times, causing
uncontrolled panic-selling by ingenuous investors. In this kind of short-
selling investing climate, the devastating power of uncontrolled rumors can
spread so rapidly that even professional brokers and senior executive officers
of prestigious investing firms can be caught in a "tsunamic" onslaught of a
collapsing market with the breakdown of public trust, as in the recent case of
the collapse of the Bear Stearns Investment Banking and Brokerage Firm.
This kind of market investing behavior can be evaluated on the Kohlberg
scale at stage 1 (fear of punitive monetary losses) and stage 2 ("instrumental
relativity" exchanging). Distrustful market behavior of this kind is prone to
cause pockets of poverty among the non-savvy working class of investors
while damaging the integrity of the nature of investing and undermining the
ethical foundations of market economies. Such pre-conventional low level
moral trading without the public trust is certainly not driven by an authentic
utilitarian ethic. But more critically important for the ethical foundation of a
morally reformed market economy would be moral behavior motivated by a
deontological ethic.[2] This philosophically grounded ethic is ultimately

concerned about the moral integrity and the trusted reliability of the institutional nature of investing brokerages and the ethical operational processes of their trading mechanisms. The fact that the markets themselves do not have a deontological foundation is demonstrated by the papers presented at this international workshop. The only prominent ethical theory presented at this workshop was utilitarian theory. In view of the fact that this theory has an affinity to exchange theory in terms of the "instrumental relativity" of moral behavior at stage 2, as explained above in the moral judgment stages of Exhibit 3:1, its moral development scaling correlation to business operations and investing interests is actually measured in terms of the economic utility of market behavior. Accordingly, to more clearly explain the affinity, it needs to be pointed out that there is often a vested interest side of utilitarian theory identified as *act utility* in contradistinction to *rule utility* which is focused on the rules or norms of moral codes and values (see Beauchamp, 1983). Act utility is thus focused on actual situations, as for example, in the *situational ethical* arrangements of business deals, of corporate mergers and acquisitions, etc., dis-allowing a wider complex organizational scope for associated environmental and economic market conditions. While this application of utilitarian theory is less ethically relative and inconsistent with the theories of "situation ethics" (Fletcher, 1966 and 1967), it is inconsiderate of more comprehensive objective fluctuations of relative moral behavior in evaluating what conditions are generative for the optimal collective good. As such, not only is act utilitarianism closed to the problems of moral relativity in global international market economies; but it is susceptible to exclusionary enclosing within the internal spheres of calculating what is generative of the proximate company good. It is within this latter context that act utilitarian theory is directly related to the pre-conventional morality of exchange theory in deciding what is instrumentally generative for the vested interests of the profiting capacity good. This latter affinity is what reduces higher moral 5th and 6th stage altruism of post-conventional deontological theory to the lower moral 2nd stage individualism and instrumental relativity of exchange theory. And, thus, when workers or investors feel used or exploited by 2nd stage managers and markets, they lose *economic trust* in the systems. And when *the poor and the starving feel marginalized by economists' graphs and executives' greed*, who have not experienced hunger, and are deprived of material well-being by their corpulent war lords, they lose *humanitarian public trust* in market systems and political regimes. While the "Idi Amin's" did not care, the economists do; and while the workshop presenters did try to explain how the market economy functions in these systems and regimes, they ran "short" on post-conventional deontological ethical theory. Their pre-conventional moral development explanations, however, reveal how dysfunctional market behavior is, as "instrumentally irrelative" to the issues of poverty alleviation, income distribution and morally insensitive to egalitarian welfare transfusion, as an *ethical* hunger fix. The actual co-principal researcher of the historical country studies on growth, poverty and income inequality, Deepak Lal, alluded to the ineptitude of a *marginal utility* fix relative to the problems of egalitarianism:

> The alternative technocratic approach to poverty alleviation is, by contrast, necessarily infected with egalitarianism because of its lineage. At its most elaborate, it is based on some Bergson-Samuelson type of social welfare function. Given the ubiquitous assumption of diminishing marginal utility underlying the approach, any normative utility weighting of the incomes of different persons or households leads naturally to some form of egalitarianism. But this smuggling in of an ethical norm that is by no means universally accepted leads to a form of "mathematical politics" (1994, pp. 154-155).

And finally, with the empirical evidence of his studies, Lal concluded: "On the existing evidence, mass poverty can be alleviated by concentrating on the rapid, efficient (labor intensive) growth promoted by a market economy, and we need not worry about the distributional consequences" (1994, p.161).

Deontological Ethics and Market Moral Dynamics. If Deepak Lal is not going to worry about the distributional consequences, economists as well as executives and managers do need to worry about the moral *under-development* propensity of such 2nd stage MBO driven "laissez-faire" management presumptions and morally detached economic assumptions that labor growth intensity will alleviate mass poverty. New "existing evidence" conclusively demonstrates grave social anxieties about the rapidly spreading concerns of global hunger and the "ubiquitous" market realities of "distributional consequences" with the "diminishing marginal utility" of human life. These hunger consequences and human life diminishments, such as the catastrophic depleting "economies of scale" spreading through the EuroZones of Greece, Italy and Spain, demand post-conventional reconstructive market moral dynamics, such as the deontological ethical dynamism of "moralities of scale" presented in Chapter 6 on MBE socio-economics. (Review end-note 2 on deontological ethics.) The recent historical evidence for these concerns is alarmingly manifest, especially with the *public trust* breakdown in the American market economy since the failure of Bear Stearns in the first quarter of 2008. The liquidity collapse of this firm was so rapid in the vortex of the power of rumors and the panic of short-selling that the immediate subsequent events of the collapse appeared as an emerging crisis threatening the entire global market economy. These appearances forced the U. S. Federal Reserve Board to intervene with an unprecedented overnight limit loan of $30 billion to prevent the bankruptcy of Bear Stearns. The Federal Reserve underwrote the transaction with the acquiring J P Morgan Chase firm as a strategic defensive lending dynamic and as a postconventional preventive moral dynamic with a sixth stage caring ethic for the purpose of avoiding a multinational market crash and an international economic depression. In subsequent Congressional testimony, Alan Schwartz, CEO of Bear Stearns, explained the relentless force of the rumor tide and the consuming power of its short-covering mill in these terms: "I would just say that, as an observer of the markets that looked like more than just fear. It looked like that there were people that wanted to induce a panic" (CNBC Video April 4, 2008 video: *The Power of the Rumor Mill: Rumors and Short-Selling*, Thompson, Griffeth, Liesman and Kneale). In retrospective federal ethical review, it was this sixth stage moral power of the "Fed" that overcame the first stage unethical power of the "Mill."

It is not altogether certain, moreover, that there is pristine innocence in these events, let alone good faith in the executive principals of Bear Stearns. To be specific, it is quite evident that the company did not *bear* sufficient moral accountability in providing authentic transparency relative to its liquidity in the historical ongoing events leading up to the critical moments of the rumor mill and the short-selling panic run on its stock. Consider these further remarks of Alan Schwartz before Congress:

> The nature and the pattern of the rumors, I mean, one of the things we were trying to do was get facts out that discounted the rumors that were out there. And the minute we got a fact out, more rumors started—there were different set of rumors. So you could never get facts out as fast as the rumors. (Idem. CNBC video)

The panel on this video then began to discuss the moral accountability of Bear Stearns in terms of its transparency failure to disclose the facts of their own liquidity profile. Steve Liesman, economist analyst for CNBC, continued in an interview with Bill Griffeth:

> It's not clear to me if Bear Stearns may have been trying on Wednesday to get the facts out, where it was on Tuesday and the Tuesday before that? We got information yesterday that Bear Stearns liquidity dropped from $21 billion at the end of January down to $12 billion dollars on "D" day when it fell from 12 to 2. That's three months, not to mention the fact (Bill) that over the prior seven or eight months, rumors had been rifling through the markets about Bear Stearns. My interest in this story in sub-prime began a year ago when I heard a rumor Bear Stearns could not place its commercial paper. They had twelve months to get the facts out and the fact that they were besieged by rumors on one day shows they were late to the table. (Idem. CNBC video; see also Sorkin, 2008 for an inside transparent view of a lower-level morally conventional subculture in the power structure of Bear Stearns operational climate.)

It is not difficult to imagine what this table tardiness did to the *social faith* and *public trust* effects on the 14,000 workforce of Bear Stearns and on their client banking firms and their own shareholders, let alone to the hundreds of thousands of investors in the wider global market investment firms. But it is difficult to learn what such low moral accountability and loose moral, if not immoral, market manipulating behavior associated with short-selling and put-call options have done to the wider socio-economic markets of agribusiness and oil production in terms of food for fuel options and global hunger outcomes. The "ethical foundation of market economies" deserves a post-conventional reform ethic based upon the 6th stage universal principles of justice and reciprocity *rooted in the theory of deontological ethics* and the authenticity of respect for the honest nature of investing and the essential veracity of shared meanings in trading practices. The socio-economic reality reconstruction of this kind of market moral reform would terminate the speculative practices of gambling with market capital, eliminating the contradictory inauthentic realities of selling "equities" which "investors" do not actually own. These practices do not share the authentic meaning of investing. They rather violate the essence of an existing investment and the integrity of its equity, thereby undermining the shared meanings of committed investors and their *public trust* in the market *realities* of economic *securities*. These common speculative practices are essentially 1st and 2nd stage gambling transactions and thus belong in gaming and casino subcultures and not in market investment mainline cultures. Had these practices not been in place in the operational transactional realities of mainline market investment exchanges, Bear Stearns would not have become an investment banking victim of short selling and the panic fear of serious committed investors who lost their shared meanings of 5th stage authentically honest contractual investing. Neither would 14,000 of their workforce have lost their jobs and the shared meanings of *public trust* in their company ethic. Inasmuch as these gambling practices have been a part of the established realities of markets for years and influence the economy for better or worse, they cannot be reconciled with a deontological ethic. At best, they can only claim an exchange affinity with a "utilitarian act ethic" at the pre-conventional level of the second stage of the Kohlberg moral development scale. Commenting on these utilitarian actions in the context of the commercial currents of speculative markets and the pricing pressure of oil on the economy, a follow-up business news analysis on CNBC reported that in India futures trading has been shut down completely. On this news of trying to force speculation out of the market, guest analyst Daniel Dicker, President of Mercbloc, commented: "A sovereign democratic nation recognizing that speculation may be a key driver in the increase of prices in commodities is looking to do something in trying to alleviate some of that pressure" (Haines and Burnett, 2008, CNBC video May 12, "Nothing Stopping Oil"). With some astonishment, interviewer Mark Haines, posed the question, "How can we deal with this? . . . We don't want to negatively impact the liquidity." While this "negativity" might remain an exchange problem for utilitarian ethics and market economics to resolve with some situational relativities and rule-bearing shared meanings,[3] "we" do want to *positively* impact the integrity of world markets with *reliable* shared meanings of *social faith* and *public trust* in the secure symbols of *fluent* liquidity and *enduring* equities.

Deontological Investing, Market Securities and "shorting" Vulnerabilities. Reviewing the philosophical concepts of deontological ethics in Chapter One of this book would help to respond to the critical practical problems, raised by the late Mark Haines of CNBC, with the integrity of a *praxis* investing methodology in market securities and deontological strategies based on postconventional moralities. Such strategies simply require the social faith of believing in a company's product or business, trusting in its ethical security and promoting the endurance of its equities with shareholding fidelity. These are critically important strategies which many experienced investors believe in, with their own personal faith and social trust in "holding" securities against the shifting trade winds of market insecurities and "shorting" vulnerabilities. It is somewhat depressing to note how these critical ethical sensitivities are completely missing in the most important study of *The Ethical Foundations of the Market Economy*. Deontological ethics were not even cited in this otherwise excellent MBO study by the Kiel Institute of World Economics.

Social Faith and Public Trust Undermining of Global Markets. In order to deal with liquidity problems in market insecurities, it is analytically imperative that we first deal with the credit problems of *social faith* and the investment securities of *public trust*. The magnitude of these credit problems has been historically reviewed and critically analyzed by the CNBC documentary report on the frenzy of mortgage backed securities and CDO "insecurities", as collateralized debt obligations[4], through this ongoing decade and the eventual collapse of the housing market with subsequent foreclosures throughout the country (see Faber 2009). The documentary traces the breakdown of social faith and public trust from the period of the 9/11 World Trade Center terrorist attacks and the consequent market downturn which immediately pervaded through American investment cultures and gradually into global market economies. While this report micro-analyzes the stage 1 moral foreclosure fears of buyers and stage 2 grafting greed of morally uncaring bankers and unethical mortgage dealing in "bundled" markets, its concluding segment reflects impaired moral vision for the plausibility of any MBE moral reform insights toward social faith and public trust reconstruction. It is critically relevant to note how the morally limited MBO structurally functionalist value system admonitions of Alan Greenspan conventionally reflects a quasi-theoretical vision of socio-economic determinism associated with the *moral inadequacy* of MBO, as a reliable ethically based paradigm, to redeem the moral hazards of unprincipled economic planning and undisciplined market dealing. With, however, his economic wisdom, his prophetic vision has identified the problem of public trust without social faith. During an earlier interviewing discourse with David Faber on CNBC in 2008, Alan Greenspan explains how the second stage profit maximization policies of MBO have left the morally-limping markets depleted from the higher stages of post-conventional morally developed consciousness. With due respect for the record of his scholarly economic years in Federal Reserve leadership and his devoted noble service as Chairman of its Board, his *deterministic* conclusions have left the morally-limping markets with unanswered systemic retributional consequences and with a morally under-developed fractured economy as a hazardous and recessionary *bundled victim* of the prevailing state of the ethically less informed and morally conventional developed federal reserve conscience during that period of his service. (See "Sustainable Economics and Determinism" on www.examiner.com. January, 2014)

During an interviewing discourse with David Faber on CNBC, Chairman Greenspan acknowledged how the second stage profit maximization policies of MBO under-developed moral awareness still prevail among corporate executives and market investors. He even acknowledged that their awareness of investment risking and their calculative abilities to trade equities with full risking knowledge of the instrumental relativities of pre-conventional moral ineptitude. (See also his CNBC interview with David Faber, 2008)

As David Faber responded with a critical prediction of this under-developmental moral ineptitude, and his own critical analysis of executive leadership inaptitude, Alan Greenspan firmly acknowledged that the moral depravity of such management investing and financial planning was reflective of profit maximization greed. He convincingly admitted that such managerial legislative reform is inefficaciously and ethically inept.

In conclusion to this depressively and ethically impaired ineptitude, Alan Greenspan concluded that there is a vicious cycle of systemic historical determinism. His remarks throughout the interview clearly reveal that the problems of social faith and public trust are institutionally cyclical and are institutionally bonded by a MBO structural functional paradigm which impairs the social psychological components of organizational caring reciprocities. In the organizational and ethical realities of this "convicting" conclusion, it is the *convincing* conclusion of these studies that MBE offers a contemporary paradigm in management studies toward the rebuilding of the moral development values of social faith and public trust.

Social Faith and Public Trust Restoration. Pursuing the need for the restoration of socially reconstructive faith and morally reformative trust, Bill Griffeth, moderator of the panel presenters in the earlier CNBC video on "Rumors and Short-Selling," alarmingly noted that, with the social faith breakdown in the panic driven short-selling of securities, "there is an issue of trust as well." It is ethically imperative, therefore, to comprehend the *integral reliability bond* between the virtues of faith and the moralities of trust. It is, moreover, critically strategic that to reconstruct social faith in world markets, it is essential to [re]establish the *reliability* of institutionalized public trust in the complex multinational organizational environments of global socio-economic affairs. It is not just theoretically remarkable but actually admirable that *the social virtues of faith and trust hold world markets together* in reliably bonding forms of global cooperative policies in and through which international commerce thrives with shared economic meanings and multi-cultural benefits for humankind. This interactive socio-political bonding of *social faith and public trust* constitutes a socio-economic inducement incentive for all nations to cooperate in striving for the benefits of global market moral reform.

To induce these incentives, it is instructive to compare the works of Kohlberg and Fowler with ecumenical insight and socio-economic foresight. As Kohlberg himself discovered, faith development is truly an efficacious powerful incentive for the human spirit to perform altruistically and self-responsibly at the highest stages of moral development, inspiring the poor to believe in themselves as non-marginalized contributors to poverty alleviation and global market reform. In comparison with Kohlberg's empirical focus on moral reasoning, Fowler's faith development model analyzes people's images and conceptions in terms of more holistic reasoning stages with an ecumenical focus on socio-religious beliefs and transcendental mythical realities. He uses the faith reasoning variable as a religious belief or cultural myth which projects one's reasoning to ultimate holistic meanings (1983).

THE FAITH DEVELOPMENT SCALE

Like the moral development scale of six stages discovered by Kohlberg, the following variation of Fowler's original scale, who was one of Kohlberg's early associates, outlines six stages of faith development which evolve through an invariant sequence of higher level meanings (see Exhibit 8:1).

Chapter 8

Exhibit 8:1

Faith Development and Cultural Sources

Faith Development Stage	Socio-Cultural Sources	Transcendental Perspectives
1 Three to Seven Playful Age	Family Rituals and Childhood Literary Forms	Family Faith Customs
2 Seven to Twelve Socio-Religious Literature	Mythical and Festival Narratives	Symbolic Deity Artistic Forms
3 Adolescence Traditional Faith Reasoning	Religious Liturgies and Ethnicity Mores	An Interpersonal Architectural God
4 Personal Reflexivity Self-Identity Awareness	Symbolic Interactional Interpersonal Trust	Religious Faith Identity
5 Interpersonal Faith Awareness Realities	Socio-Ecumenical Public Trust	A Cosmological ALPHA God
6 Transcendental Ethos Spiritualties	Cosmic Onto-Theological Trust	A Mystical OMEGA God

The following explanations of his stages offer a critical practical narrative on applying his definitions to contemporary problems on religious beliefs and on social faith and public trust. Unlike moral development, though, faith development is experienced as a structural whole at each stage, supplying life meaning to a person in terms of an ultimate environment with parental and educators' guidance. Faith is thus like a beacon of light which guides a person through life by means of primary symbolic indicators, developmental conceptual imageries and spiritual religious references, signifying transcendental meanings along with social and cultural relevance. It is a virtue that is not dependent on moral reasoning, though it often encompasses moralizing cognitive processes.

These processes develop through life from *intuitional faith* in childhood fantasy as a *first believing playful stage* to a later childhood story-telling *second stage* evoking a *mythical-literary story-telling faith*. During adolescence and early adulthood, logical reasoning is contained to a *third stage un-reflexive traditional faith* at which level great numbers of a "silent majority" enjoy a simple surrendering faith with trust in social system authority leaders. Eventually, through cognitive progression and more incisive moral development awareness, increasing numbers of this majority subsequently open to a *fourth stage* reflexive reasoning awareness and begin to question the stabilized conventions of a functionally ordered establishment assuming the confidence *of a reasoning faith*. Subsequently, with expanding independence in transcendental interests, their deepening reflexivity opens their awareness to ultimate realities and stimulates an interest in philosophical *wonder* and a reverence for theological *mystery*. At these higher developed stages, philosophical wonder so informs a person's inner spirit as to clarify his/her vision with a *fifth stage communal faith* spiritually devoted to an immanent Reality and an ultimate Deity. Numbers of believers reaching this stage of critical creative reasoning often return to the roots of their pristine religious faith through *historical continuity awareness* (see Erikson, 1968)[5] and *eternal perpetuity hopefulness* (see Eliade,1959),[6] with some few leaping beyond history to a *sixth stage transcendental universalizing faith* through a spirituality of self-transformation in communion with the "commonwealth of Being." (See Fowler's original scale, 1981 and Snarey's 1991 study of faith development and Judaism.)

Faith Development Profiles and Dominant Conceptual Processes. The earliest stages of the paradigm descriptions trace early life exposure to "socio-cultural sources" with *obeying* and *conforming* profiles at stages 1 and 2, while the more developed stages manifest faith behavior as *consenting* at stage 3; *evaluating* at stage 4; *conjoining* at stage 5 and *transcending* at stage 6, as critical contemporary interpretations of the above scale. These brief descriptive insights are critically important because they allow the corporate moral reformer to understand how faith-believing people lock into conventions at stage 3 by consenting in the shared meanings of their *cultural motivational sources* and their corresponding symbolic constructs of authority systems and leadership hierarchies. Without questioning these hierarchical systems (such as, governments, political organizations, corporations, unions, social movements, religions, etc.) and their leaders, stage 3 people tend to consent in rational stage dependency in which case their dominant conceptual understanding of shared meanings is governed by "consenting unreflective conceptions," as Fowler described in his original scale. So much of organizational order in global social systems works this way with the consequent building of hierarchical power bases in corporate governance structures.[7] While these hierarchical structures benefit greatly from organizational stability in these respective sub-cultures, shaping a "dominant cultural process" toward a *faith*-ful stage 3 obedient public (as within *co-dependent* workforces an ecclesial congregations), fearful events, such as, repressive controls and/or voting irregularities, tend to awaken "critical reflexive conceptions" within stage 4 *protesting* minorities toward destabilizing the whole social system of political and public trust in the mainline authoritarian cultures. As analyzed in Fowler's original exhibit, the development process at this stage opens faith to "critical reflexive conceptions" with *independent rational thinking* often inspiring its believers with independent thinking, anti-structural symbolic language, (Turner, 1969) and social movement behavior (Guerrette, 1981) and sometimes even exploding with mobilizing discourse and revolutionary activity (Tilly, 1978). Faith stage development, however, can become strategically pivotal with such persuasive converting dialectics that can turn conventionalities into relativities empowering an eventual psycho-historical revolution (Lifton, 1970). In realistic actuality, though, such relative turning can take time and even years of political policy shifting between stages 3 and 4 before the independence of rational thinking and the faith virtues of political theological persistence prevail with ultimate liberation. Contemporary terrorist activities emanating from the fanatic subcultures of the Middle East war zones are frightening examples of stage 3/4 militants departing bravely but brutally from the conventional mainline cultures and faith systems of their respective religions and/or political parties. With the contemporary phenomenological spinning of the political theological views of martyrdom by the fanatic hierarchical power base of the militant leaders in the subcultures of Islam, the young silent awestricken conventional believers often find themselves inspired to lay down their lives for the "conventional" rewards of paradise with the blind unreflective obedience of stage 3. More often, than not, however, stage 4 people discover new shared meanings *conjoining* their beliefs with 5th stage companions in open congregations and more democratic or team-structured corporations, with whom they may even *transcend* to stage 6 with "universalizing faith." The martyred symbolic figure of the Iranian "Neda" who laid down her life for her redirected beliefs with her faith-driven *caring* reciprocity for justice and freedom motivated by her 6th stage religious beliefs in *Allah* as her cosmological Alpha God with her transcendental faith and social trust in her "mystical Omega God." (Review Exhibit 8:1 in *faith*-ful memory of "Neda" and the more recent memories of the families of Iraq and Syria.)

Faith Development Profiles and Cultural Motivational Sources. With synchronizing accord to the "cultural motivational sources" aligned in the 2nd column of the Faith Development scale of Professor Fowler, faith can be explained, for the purposes of this book, as the *theoretical and inspirational* generator of the "social system and cross cultural mores" and as the *practical and motivational* sources for "corporate culture and market moral reform." As such, faith at stage 5 is an intensive and probative faith process in search of ultimate meanings. It pursues this search relentlessly in "open system" research methodologies, as described in Chapter 2, *to change the corporate cultural system to meet the needs of corporate ethical environments.* It is thus a *conjunctive faith*—paradigmatically ready to accept other believers in quest to be connected with the ultimate spirit of *Ethical Being* and *moral becoming.* It recognizes truth as corrective and *transformative* and explores the proximate scientific wonders of the universe and ultimate transcendental mysteries of the Unknown.

Tony Blair's *Faith Foundation* is a paradigmatic example of the *conjunctive power of socio-religious faith* in search of proximate and contemporary meanings which open possibilities of social faith for practicalities of understanding and believing in ultimate meanings. As a renowned Prime Minister, Mr. Blair is a *praxis* leader who applies religious faith to change a warring world and its weary populations into social faith commitments to cure human suffering and to ensure social trust. The summary of his inspirational speech in launching his Faith Foundation, with Yale Divinity School and the School of Organization Management, outlines *conjunctive planning with "critical practical" works to empower social faith and engender social trust:*

> You cannot understand the modern world unless you understand the importance of religious faith. Faith motivates, galvanizes, organizes and integrates millions upon millions of people. Here is the crucial point. Globalization is pushing people together. I believe, as someone of faith, that religious faith has a great role to play in an individual's life. But even if I didn't, even if I was of no faith, I would still believe in the central necessity of people of faith learning to live with each other in mutual respect and peace. That is the "why" of the Foundation.
>
> Now, for the "what." There are many excellent meetings, convocations, conferences and even organizations that work in the interfaith area. We do not want to replicate what they do. We do not want to engage in a doctrinal inquiry. We do not want to subsume different faiths in one faith of the

lowest common denominator. We want to show faith in action. We want to produce greater understanding between faiths through encounter. We want people of one faith to be comfortable with those of another because they know what they truly believe, not what they thought they might believe.

There will be four specific aspects to our work on which we concentrate today. *First*, the Foundation aims to educate. We begin today with the association with Yale University. Yale's School of Divinity and School of Management will help to design a new course called "Faith and Globalization." It will run over three years. I will lead a series of seminars each fall, starting in September 2008. The idea is to create a course which, over time, can become an enduring part of Yale's teaching, can be spun off to other universities in different parts of the globe, can stimulate original research and be a resource for those working in this field. We are going to use new and interactive media to engage young people of different faiths. Annika Small, who has done such a brilliant job with Future Lab in the UK bringing together software and education, has agreed to head up this part of the Foundation's work. We are in discussion with leading publishers about a specific publishing imprint for the Foundation and with others to create a set of programs explaining the world of faith. We will make announcements of these partnerships later in the year. We will use the material we design not just for young people and faith communities but also for business and the worlds of commerce and politics. We cannot afford religious illiteracy. No modern company would today be ignorant of race or gender issues. The same should be true of faith.

Secondly, we are announcing the first of our partnerships to mobilize those of faith in pursuit of the UN's Millennium Development Goals. Today we call upon the 4 billion people of faith in the world to help do more to end the scourge of malaria that has killed so many millions of our fellow human beings and will kill many more unless eradicated. We are joining with the Malaria No More Campaign, a wonderful organization whose mission is to end death through Malaria in the next 5 - 10 years. Put simply, over one million people die of malaria each year. Their deaths are preventable. In Africa, 40% of victims are Muslim. But across much of Asia, malaria continues to strike and combating it is a huge opportunity for people across faiths - Hindu, Sikh and Buddhist as well as the Abrahamic faiths—to act in unison. The solution lies in disturbing bed nets and medicine. The resources are becoming available. But the need to get the bed nets and medicine to the people and see them properly used, is where the faiths, who are present in each of the affected communities, can help. Our purpose will be to help mobilize the different faith in pursuit of this goal.

Finally, we will help organizations whose object is to encounter extremism and promote reconciliation in matters of religious faith. Though there is much focus, understandably, on extremism associated with the perversion of the proper faith of Islam, there are elements of extremism in every major faith. It is important where people of good faith combat such extremism, they are supported.

To summarize, the possibilities of a world of change are enormous. This is a century rich in potential to solve problems, provide prosperity to all, to overcome longstanding issues of injustice that previously we could not surmount. But it only works if the values which inform the change are values that unify and do not divide. Religious faith has a profound role to play. For good of for ill. The Tony Blair Faith Foundation will try to make it for good. (30 May, 2008)

Tony Blair's own exemplary passionate commitment to this 5th stage *socially conjunctive* faith mission to the interreligious missionary spheres of the ecumenical world latently manifests a contemplative private spirituality and mystically active corporate charity which reflects his own stage 6 personal level of faith development. As a socio-religious and *practical* ecumenical faith "inspirational generator," he has opened this globalization mission to other universities around the world with 6th stage "universalizing faith" and "transcendental" wonder.

Ascetic Faith and Aesthetic Wonder. Faith at stage 6 is an externalized deepened faith enriched by creative contemplation of the Unknown with *wondering* exploration of the "mysteries of being" (Marcel, 1950) and of the "enlightenment of becoming" (Cohen, 2009). It is an internalized reflexive faith inspiring self-confidence of *how one can creatively believe* (Teilhard, 1969) in the mystery of the Divinity. It is a free faith—an interpersonal and socially imaginative faith. It is not statically bound by dogmatic revelation (Dewart, 1966) but profoundly open to critically reflexive contemplation (Merton, 1961, 2007 ed.). It is not fixed to theological teaching but compassionately transfixed on "social suffering."[8] It is not an antiseptic faith—C condemning others who do not believe; it is rather an *ascetic* faith *trusting in others* and their "theological traditions." It is a "metaphysical" faith with prayer for ecumenical unity in a secular world of ethnic disunities (Healey, 2013). It is hopeful for moral integrity in a global economy of unethical dishonesty. With a "transcendent community" consciousness and a cosmological exploratory awareness, this "universalizing faith" stage is graced with a spiritually developed understanding of extra-terrestrial "conceptions of mystery." Within and beyond these metaphysical spheres of philosophical cosmology and theological eschatology, this ultra-developed faith stage is focused on an intra-devotional *aesthetic wonder* about the *Beauty* of the "ultimate integrative Deity" and the corporate mystical unity within the divinely expansive *"Commonwealth of Being."*

If the CEO, as an involved, integrated moral leader and MBE reformer, exhibits a social and religious faith development at such "ultimate integrative" levels of stages 5 and 6 and encourages independent "consolidative" reflexivity among his/her leadership staff, he or she will create a "conjunctive" moral credibility in his or her own leadership image.

Moreover, if either manifests, at least, an authentic interest in ultimate meanings of company purpose as integrative with life purpose and sensitive to the *Commonweal of Being*, he or she will soon discover an incremental sharing of post-conventional moral meanings and a company reflexively and faithfully responsive to a transformative corporate ethic toward the *commonwealth of becoming*. (Review Exhibit 8:1 to contemplate the integration of socio-cultural sources and public trust commitment).

FAITH DEVELOPMENT AND THE SAFEGUARDING OF PUBLIC TRUST

Faith development is not just helpful to re-stabilize social faith—it is the *safeguard* for the public trust. It is critical for opening the reflexive powers of persons and corporations to global universal realities and ecumenical possibilities, once these companies and their personnel become open to stage 4 faith experiences. Such openings are becoming increasingly wider and more frequent in contemporary society and especially in corporate and government cultures where *faith reflexivity* has become critically imperative for public trust awareness and even for the safeguarding of political trust as well as for personal security and social system consistency.

Social Faith and Social System Consistency. Some conventions of corporate and governmental power hegemonies are now being shaken with the reflexive complaints of automotive workers over management trust-breaking strategies to significantly cut health care benefits and to terminate dealership franchises. The silent majority of working classes and even shareholders are now beginning to speak out with critical contesting power emerging from social unrest caused by such social system inconsistencies. The protesting voices of their trust reflexive thinking are objecting to what those kinds of cuts mean to social system conservancy in the complex organizational environment of industries as well as to the public trust masses of working class populations. It is, thus, of no ethical wonder that the socially protesting "Occupiers" of Wall Street persisted in their courageous efforts to change this morally imbalanced economic environment, while executives remain secure with their million dollar salaries along with their 2nd stage *moralities of scale* in their multi-million dollar stock investments and multiple seasonal mansions. (See Time Magazine, for its 2011 "Person of the Year" selections of social movement organizations as *corporate persons* of the year acknowledging that such "demonstrations against corporate and financial systems" are continuing globally throughout the world against the "power elite" systems embedded in economic "*immoralities* of scale").

Social System Consistency and Social Faith Reflexivity. Assessing these social system inconsistencies reveals that the symbolic language of workers or citizens demonstrates a break of shared conventional meanings with management or federal and local bureaucracies signifying social depressions of distrust and critical impressions of unjust economic power imbalances. The moral mandate to save the public trust in such complex organizational breakdowns of conventional meanings is to critically strive, with 5th stage contractual readiness on the Kohlberg scale, to search for reconstructive shared meanings which *reflect a social faith* in the workers' company and a public trust in the citizens' economy, on the Fowler scale, grounded in workforce dignities and in investment reliabilities. The persuasive insights of this faith paradigm indicate that 4th stage inducing incentives of "dominant conceptual process[es]" with *critical social faith reflexivity* constitute the symbolic interactional dynamics that are *ethically* needed to change the power imbalances of the social system to meet the needs of a morally investing environment and to rebuild the balance of power in the economy for the safeguarding of public trust in its markets.

GLOBAL NETWORKS OF PUBLIC TRUST

Mediating Institutions and Multinational Corporations. This faith development sister of the moral development paradigm constitutes a breeding ground for the formation of reliable moral leaders not just in corporations but in all the complex organization sets of mediating institutions. Line and staff personnel at every level of moral and faith development stages in these organizations need leaders they can trust and in whom they can believe. Fourth and fifth stage social faith development learning in human resource training programs in the overall context of moral development socialization programming provides these kinds of leaders who can execute moral reform on all fronts and deliver social faith and public trust in all the global networks of complex organizations. In the pursuance of this moral reliability goal throughout global complex organization environments, multinational corporations can assume a critically practical *harmonious* role toward integrating social system faith development change and systemic global moral reform by ethically balancing the public trust with the *praxis* strategies of the MBE *moralities of scale.*

An *inspiring* example of such reliable moralities and social faith practicalities is within the multicultural organization sets of the United Nations and the international leadership of President Clinton with his innovative mission of the *Clinton Global Initiative*, as described in the previous Chapter 7. The specific faith mission here bears the moral purpose of addressing the alleviation of third world poverty through the ethical cleansing of political corruption scandals in emerging democracies through accountable governance and *social faith reliability*. It is *critically constructive* to note that this ethical initiative is seeking "to develop systems of enforceable accountability" to eradicate corruption in emerging democracies (see Exhibit 8:2).

Exhibit 8:2 Clinton Global Initiative

CGI 2006 Sept. 20 - 22

COMMITMENT ANNOUNCEMENT

Focus Area: Governance, Enterprise and Investment
Project: Task Force to Develop Systems to Eradicate Corruption in
                   Emerging Democracies
Commitment By: Capri S. Cafaro
Value: $25,000

Objective: To address corruption in emerging democracies through the creation
of a Task Force to Develop Systems to Eradicate Corruption in Emerging
Democracies.

Commitment: To recruit and solicit Task Force participants, provide a conference
location in the Washington, D.C. area, facilitate travel arrangements and make a
financial commitment to assist in related expenses.

Background: More than a decade has passed since the fall of the Berlin Wall.
Today, it is poignant that corruption is pervasive in developing democracies from
Eastern Europe and Central Asia to Latin America and Africa. Corruption plagues
governmental structures and impedes good business practices throughout the
globe's new democracies.   In many of these nations, regime change came
abruptly, leaving many struggling to stabilize their domestic economies and to
establish systems of accountability with limited resources.

Corruption exists in developed nations as well as in transitioning democracies.
Yet the existence of corruption in emerging democracies tends to be the primary
hindrance to establishing a sound economy and functioning government. In order
to effectively strengthen our globe's newest democratic partners one must make
combating corruption a high priority. Strengthening emerging democracies
through anti-corruption efforts will also help deter activates such as selling
chemical or nuclear weapons on the black market, thus aid the global war on
terror.

The proposed Task Force to develop systems to Eradicate Corruption in Emerging
Democracies would take form of a collective of international experts from
academic, non-profit, multinational, and governmental entities that would
tentatively convene in Washington, D.C., in June 2006. The Task Force would
focus primarily on providing ideas to create a culture in which corruption becomes
unacceptable, as well as on systems of enforceable accountability that deter
corrupt activities in both government and enterprise. The Task Force would
provide a unique chance to bring together individuals of varying expertise to
approach anti-corruption efforts in an integrated and creative manner.
(Source: The Clinton Foundation)

Multinational Corporations as Mediators for the Public Trust. Political and corporate organizations in all nations and especially in emerging democracies are desperately in need of conscientious governance and moral leadership of this kind. Since there appears to be few faith-motivating leaders in the global organizational set, even among the religions, who can stop international terrorism, prevent global hunger, inspire planetary hope and deliver world peace, it is conceivable that the multinational corporations, with the socialization programing of the MBE paradigm, could provide new breeding grounds for "mediating" this kind of trusted leadership (Fort, 2001).[9] As private sector companies, these corporations already have access to the international structures of the organization sets of the United Nations for "creative partnerships" within these sets through the U.N. Global Compact Initiative established by Kofi Annan in 1999. Through these partnerships multinational corporations can thus *mediate the relieving of terrorizing tensions among nations, the feeding of starving populations within the third world and the reconstruction of global hope for the survival of the planet.* Carolyn Woo, former Dean of the Mendoza College of Business at the University of Notre Dame, Member of the Ethics Education Task Force of the International Association to Advance Collegiate Schools of Business, has been charged with the task of "identifying new issues and challenges in management education on a global basis." As Chair of the New Issues Committee of this Association and having recently addressed the Global Forum for Responsible Management Education at the United Nations, she has been a supporter of these partnerships between the United Nations and private sector multinational corporations. She stated:

> He (Kofi Annan) made the comment that business can play a very, very important role in stabilizing unrest and also contribute to economic development and the rebuilding of a country. This is an unusual statement in the sense that the U.N. had never really worked closely with business. So for him to make a declarative statement that business needs to be involved in an agenda of peace is a major step. These (multinational) corporations determine the development of economies, consumption, pricing and development of natural resources, as well as winners and losers in different economies. Their products embody social values and influence culture and the quality of life. (2008, pp.36-37)

These multinational corporations (MNCs) already have the international structures conducive for consolidative and ecumenical social faith development in their pluralistic corporate cultural settings and multi concentric organization sets for implementing MBE programing and moral development socialization. In response to the promotional support of Dean Woo and her above cited remarks from Kofi Annan, it is expedient to point out that the Department of Economic and Social Affairs of the UN, in response to the role of MNCs in world development, states that "The question at issue, therefore, is whether a set of institutions and devices can be worked out which will guide the multinational corporations' exercise of power and introduce some form of accountability to the international community into their activities"(Fayerweather, 1976, p. 16). The answer at issue therefore is that a set of ethical principles and moral stages balanced on economic *moralities of scale* can produce accountability to the international community of nations through the mediating institutions of MNCs. Such an introduction of MBE programing within the organization sets of the complex organizations of their global environments could readily influence higher scaled moral performance with principled thinking and accountable planning for *upgrading the quality of life in all economies* so all nations could be "winners" with no "losers" throughout global cultures. Consonant with this corporate ethical vision, it would be productive for such companies to perceive themselves as environmental organizations, committed to a global ecological mission to change the instrumental systems of corporate culture to meet the humanistic needs of global climates and world hunger (Werhane 1999).[10] Inasmuch as the complex organization literature has already developed conceptual constructs for analysis of organization structures, as seen in Brinkerhoff and Kunz (1972) and in Chapter 1, it is quite plausible and would be most productive for critical *praxis* engaging of organization interaction to so conceive and interpret these multinational corporations as "mediating" organizations with their respective governmental institutions and political regimes for global environmental and political moral reform (see Lal, 1994).[11]

A critical word of moral caution, however, needs to be addressed beyond such conceptions and interpretations relative to any moral hazard probabilities which could develop within the infrastructures of such large complexities and extensive bureaucracies of the organization sets of these multinational mediating institutions. Consider, for example, the morally vulnerable complexities of the merger takeover of the Merrill Lynch Investment firm by the international Bank of America and the moral hazardous outbreak which further damaged the public trust of the nation. One must comprehend that while a mediating organization can provide complex organizational structures of communication for the integration of the collective corporate conscience in an interorganizational sector, within which all the business enterprising units of the sector can reach higher post-conventional moral development public policy positions anchored in caring reciprocity incentives, some unpredictable hazardous marketing events can occur, at times, in larger interorganizational sectors of market economies which can create power imbalances resulting in moral hazard behavior. Such irresponsible behavior can cause devastating effects on the moral trust in the original organization set and even spread wider demoralizing effects to the public trust within governmental structures and federal regulatory agencies. These alarming contingencies were recently witnessed by the mass public with the dramatic media unfolding of hazardous moral behavior in the above cited case of Bank of America's mediating acquisition of the Merrill Lynch

Investment firm. Shortly after the merger settlement, moral hazardous behavior was discovered with the revelation of an exorbitant sum of over one million dollars spent of the remodeling of the Merrill Lynch CEO office of John Thain. This discovery manifested grave moral insensitivities of 2nd stage pre-conventional vested interest behavior causing a morally critical outrage throughout market communities with further social faith vulnerabilities to the public trust breakdown and the personal trust wavering over the moral reputation of Ken Lewis, Chairman and CEO of Bank of America. Subsequent moral hazardous events surfaced in the aftermath of the merger with media revelations of first stage moral behavioral intimidation of Ken Lewis, on the part of high level government officials of the Treasury Department and the Federal Reserve Board, as supervisory mediating organizations of the merger, warning him not to withdraw from its agreements for the purpose of preserving the stability of the economic system. The lesson learned in this scandalous case study is that the ethical heartbeat of mediating interventions must be monitored by the harmonious pulsating of morally developed motivations to prevent MBO "immoralities of scale." (See the latest work of Jonathan Macey who graphically demonstrates "How Integrity Has Been Destroyed on Wall Street.")[12]

Eco-System Harmonies and Cosmic Trust. Moral hazard, notwithstanding, it is time for multinational corporations and all other mediating institutions to take a moral stand, not just for the global integrity of the complex organizational environment but for the cosmological integrity of the complex natural environment. Accordingly, the expansion of this harmonious mission is to encompass a universal moral stand with an environmental ethical mandate for all multinational organizations to serve as mediating institutions toward restoring *public hope* for the planet by promoting the purpose of preserving stability for the eco-system. The fundamental logic of this ethical mandate for the global complex organizational environment therefore is to expand public realization that the ultimate multinational corporate responsibility in global moral reform is to rebuild *cosmic trust* in the planetary ecosystem for the restoration of the universal balance of all living beings.

While Mitchell Thomashow's following admonitions were written for leaders and staff workers of environmental practitioners in the specific disciplinary domain of environmental and ecological studies, they are in fact *critically practical*, in terms of interpreting the faith development paradigm with the transforming *praxis* of social, public and cosmological trust-rebuilding among all nations and with international mediating respect for consolidative religious and spiritual harmonies among global populations. These admonitions need to be followed by all leaders and staff of all corporate and governmental mediating institutions in the multinational organization and environmental domains of corporate culture and political practice:

An environmental organization cannot be successful unless there are shared goals and objectives, a willingness to work together, and an understanding of the personal and professional needs of staff and leadership. It is a place where people learn about their profession, the important public issues that surround their work, the way other people perceive their ideas, where ideas are shared and communicated or where various group decisions get made. Environmental organizations have an educational obligation to their staff and clientele to recognize the *moral and spiritual magnitude of their mission,* [emphasis added] to incorporate *reflective discourse* [emphasis added] as part of the job description (1995, pp.166-167).

It is thus important to note that such a universal magnitude of the moral and spiritual mission and the incorporation of reflective discourse within and through these multinational corporations, as environmentally and ecologically conscious organizations, will eventually engender sixth stage post-conventional awareness postures of the moral, faith and trust development paradigms. Notice, for example, the British Petroleum Corporation referred to above. This company has branches in over one hundred nations around the globe and already had an impressive ethical profile, especially in environmental and ecological ethics. This corporate ethical profile itself did reflect the "moral magnitude" of its environmental organizational image before the Gulf region disaster and projected an activated "discourse" in its ecological "mission" within and *beyond* its industries. While its ethical training program lacked the depth and breadth of moral development socialization, as presented in this book, consider what MBE training in such a multinational corporate organization setting of this size could have done toward preparing the populations of these nations for accepting and promoting the goals of a universal moral consensus and an ecologically environmental purpose. With the company's personnel representing virtually every religion in the world, it is reasonable to expect that the MBE paradigm could have configured a consolidative and ecumenical binding in post-conventional moral development and could have fostered an ecologically sensitive and morally consistent environmental ethic throughout its multinational structures. Sadly enough though, what is revealing about the company's doubled face ethical profile in the aftermath of its pathetic 1st and 2nd stage managerial moral performance in their environmental recovery efforts in the Gulf waters and their unfulfilled promises for the livelihood restoration of the coastal populations is that its clever ethical imagery shaped by the cosmic promising term of "beyond" was consistently projected in its media promotions without any moral development socialization in its company human resource training programs. Any company whose corporate ethic is anchored only in philosophical intentions or poetic promotions cannot withstand the transactional tidal waves of economic depressions or market contentions, let alone environmental disasters and marketing crashes. An efficacious corporate ethic needs the pedagogical grounding of involved managerial leadership based on moral development socialization and moral performance evaluation.

In conclusion to this multinational epic and corporate ethic tragedy, the caring ethical imagery of BP has lost its 6th stage mythical and moral profile as an environmentally sensitive company in the oil producing market and has been reduced to a typical 2nd stage instrumental morally performing corporation with depressive double-talking motivation unintentionally revealing what is really "beneath" its vested interests and what has actually been "behind" petroleum as a product for profit and returns from greed. If the market investments in and the innocent investors of this company, and especially its morally devoted workers along with the morally violated families and industries of the Gulf coast regions support its ongoing operational viability, the company owes an authentic faith commitment to rebuild its corporate moral face with the MBE paradigm. The reconstructive ethical and cosmological mandate for this company is to upgrade its corporate multinational conscience toward restoring the Gulf region trust and its eco-system harmonies. It is only through the *"corporate moral and social faith magnitude"* of this MBE mission that the global social system can restore the *public trust* and the global eco-system, secure the *cosmic trust*.

END NOTES

1. See also Reisman (1979) who examines "myth systems" and "operational codes" of doing business in pluralistic societies within the complex organizational sets of international governments and multinational organizations. He defines the former as *normative guides for appropriate conduct* and the latter as *actual conduct demanded by sanctioned expectations* in the real world of commercial operations (ch.1, pp. 15-36).

2. Beauchamp and Bowie (1983) present a different interpretation of the meaning of *deontological* in terms of a duty-bound obligatory significance from the Greek *deon*, as specified in the Encyclopedic Edition of *Webster's Dictionary*. This same edition, though, also lists the word *deontos* in parenthesis which, in effect, offers a more complete etymological relationship between the Greek and English root structures of the noun *deontology*. The actual Greek root of this word is *ontos* which signifies *being*; and, with its *logos* suffix, forms the word *ontology* designating the study of *essences*. For a more comprehensive understanding of deontological theory, especially for its ties to Kantian ethics and its *universal moral imperative to respect persons*, see pp. 31-40 in Beauchamp and Bowie. Finally, the importance of these etymological and deontological notes is to emphasize that moral awareness and especially moral performance, as motivated by *respect for the essences of being* and the *sensitive caring for persons*, are at higher and more virtuous levels of moral development at stage 6 than the duty-bound and obligatory motivation levels at stage 5.

3. It is noteworthy to perceive that the relatively large numbers of actual jobs lost at Bear Stearns as a result of the situational events of its impending liquidity crisis, as

opposed to the precipitous possibilities that a much larger number of networking investment firm collapsing throughout multinational markets with even more job terminations and much greater financial losses, demanded an imminent need for the Federal Reserve Board's morally motivated intervention. Upon critical analytical perception, however, it is encouraging to conclude that the Federal Board stabilized this pending global market "quake" by an exemplary blending of situational and regulatory utilitarian ethics.

4. As financial derivatives, CDO's are collateralized debt obligations utilized as a form of asset backed securities. In the current credit crisis, they have been evaluated as extremely risky funding instruments and can therefore be identified as an *insecurity*.

5. The late Erik Erikson best explained the latent ethical driving force of returning to one's faith roots through historical processes and generations of tradition to more completely understand and inform one's identity: "To enter history . . . each generation of youth must find an identity consonant with its own childhood and consonant with an ideological promise in the perceptible historical process. . . . Moralities sooner or later outlive themselves, ethics never: this is what the need for identity and for fidelity, reborn with each generation, seems to point to. Morality in the moralistic sense can be shown to be predicated on superstitions and *irrational inner mechanisms* which, in fact, ever again undermine the ethical fiber of generations [for a contemporary updating of the unethical dangers of *outlived moralities* from the "irrational exuberance" of contemporary market investing and the weaknesses of the free market system in "ethics and professional standards," see Shiller (2005, pp. 210-12)]; but old morality is expendable only when new and more universal ethics prevail. This is the wisdom that the words of many religions have tried to convey to man. . . . The overriding issue is the creation not of a new ideology but of a universal ethics growing out of a universal technological civilization. This can be advanced only by men and women who are neither ideological youths nor moralistic old men, but who know that from generation to generation the test of what you produce is the *care* it inspires. If there is any chance at all, it is in a world more challenging, more workable, and more venerable than all myths, retrospective or prospective: it is in historical reality, at least ethically cared for" (pp. 257-260). One 5th stage *faith-driven* middle-aged global moral leader who has passed the trans-generational tests of *caring* for others as an inspiring performing artist is Bono: "Africa . . . needs what only a certain kind of world figure can give—a call to conscience, an appeal to the imagination, a melody or a lyric you won't forget. The cause of ending extreme poverty . . . speaks to Bono's prophetic impulse. . . . Among his best work is the rallying cry. . . . 'My generation wants to be the generation that ended extreme poverty' " (Hanson, 2006, p.294).

6. Eschatology is the theological study of the end of time and the realities of eternity. The late Mircea Eliade, distinguished Professor of History of Religions at the University of Chicago, understood history as a theophany, i.e., God intervening in time until He comes in the *"eschaton"* (p. 130). His work is a classic treatise of a stage 5 faith thinker and believer. He described human suffering as a norm of historical existence which include catastrophic events, such as wars and terrorizing activities and natural calamities, such as Tsunamis, earthquakes, hurricanes, and even epidemics and pandemics. God's presence thus is in the suffering consequences of these historical episodes which is manifested as a theophany and an epiphany by the overwhelming charitable responses of international relief agencies of a global

community. "Faith, in this context, as in many others, means absolute emancipation from any kind of natural "law" and hence the highest freedom that man can imagine: freedom to intervene even in the ontological constitution of the universe. It is, consequently, a pre-eminently creative freedom. In other words, it constitutes a new formula for man's collaboration with the creation . . . . Only such a freedom . . . is able to defend modern man from the terror of history—a freedom, that is, which has its source and finds its guaranty and support in God. Every other modern freedom, whatever satisfactions it may procure to him who possesses it, is powerless to justify history; and this, for every man who is sincere with himself, is equivalent to the terror of history." (pp. 160-161)

7. For more on this subject of corporate governance and transnational social system environments, see the work of Fort and Schipani (2000).

8. A transfixing spiritual example of a sixth stage "universalizing faith" has been described in the following account on "Social Suffering" by Monsignor J. Messner in *Man's Suffering and God's Love*:

> Lord, have You not said that You have compassion on the multitude? Do You not see the masses of those who bear the toil but whose bread is always scanty, whose families never know a day without care, whose share of the earth, made for all men, is withheld from them, and whose appeal for justice does not really find a hearing?
>
> Yes, I do see the multitudes and their suffering. . . . The suffering of the poor will be a double blessing in the winepress of God. For, it flows unto those who give love for my sake and unto those who for My sake are in need of love. Yet, to these last who have thus become a call of love, this blessing will be the full measure of Love itself. (1941: 84, 92)

9. Timothy Fort's work "focuses on the legal and ethical frameworks necessary to regularize ethical business behavior with particular attention to how businesses can be constructed as communal 'mediating institutions'. . . (and) how a teleological goal of sustainable peace is a realistic contribution for businesses and an orienting mission that requires responsible business behavior . . . with an ultimate aim of contributing for global sustaining security" (2005, Business Roundtable Institute for Corporate Ethics).

10. This functionalist Parsonian reversal is demanded by the critical apocalyptic events of global warming, polar melting, animal starving (see Mansbridge, 2007) and human hunger (see Lal, 1994). It is thus ethically incumbent upon these international organizations and instrumental systems to *mediate* socially co-responsible initiatives with morally transformative *praxis* engagements (see Tracy, 1981 ch. 10: "the contemporary socio-ethical crisis and its demand for criteria of transformation and praxis. . . . is the risk of a creative, as both participatory and critical, interpretation of the event [and the traditions and forms mediating the event] in and for the interpreted situation." p. 406). To activate response to this crisis and to Tracy's demands for the "criteria of transformation and praxis," see Guerrette's related corporate art study as an *inspirational aesthetic medium* (2014, vol. II) which *creatively* induces motivation for a critical practical transformation of the apocalyptic

events of MBO global warming toward achieving the *praxis* ecological transforming effects through MBE *moral performing*. Many of these transformational effects can also be induced in corporate decision-making processes and even in complicated mediating encounters of these complex multinational organizations through the morally imaginative insights of business ethics and management scholar, Patricia Werhane:

> In managerial decision-making, moral imagination entails perceiving norms, social roles and relationships entwined in any situation. Developing moral imagination involves heightened awareness of contextual moral dilemmas and their mental models, the ability to envision and evaluate new mental models that create new possibilities, and the capability to reframe the dilemma and create new solutions in ways that are novel, economically viable, and morally justifiable.   (1999 p. 93)

11. Deepak Lal's studies on poverty and hunger demonstrate that "famines are caused by politics" and that the economies of political regimes are much more causative of famine than global environmental sources. He concludes that: "Increasing destitution has been due to political violence in post-colonial Africa, and not to the cyclical climatic factors that have always put some Africans (particularly pastoralists) at risk" (1994, pp. 151-152).

12. In more intensive analysis of social trust building in the complex organizational sets of interactional mergers in the MBO environmental regulatory processes of financial institutions, Professor Jonathan Macey, Yale economic scholar and Law School Professor, demonstrates how the moral developmental fracturing between "reputation and regulation" is systematically locked into the complex organizational systems of the MBO paradigm:

> First, and perhaps most important, reputation and regulation are substitutes for each other. Imagine—and admittedly this takes a healthy imagination— a highly regulated financial system in which regulation functions perfectly. In such an environment, firms would not have to invest in developing reputations for integrity. The value to financial institutions of investing in reputation declines as a regulatory system increases in effectiveness, because the investing community is able to rely on the extant regulatory regime. This eliminates the necessity for firms to invest in and to develop reputation in order to give investors the confidence and trust required to motivate them to engage in financial transactions. (p. 256)

Macey's critical MBO moral hazardous analyses demonstrate the paradigmatic need for *eco-system harmonies* and MBE *social trust economies*. This MBE paradigm feed can re-constitute the integrity of Wall Street and institute the *Resurrection* of Corporate Reputation.

THE CORPORATE CONSCIENCE AND INVOLVED MORAL LEADERSHIP

Moral Leadership and Personal Involvement. In the simple organizational environment of family life, parents intuitively understand the primal direct connection between personal responsibility and the individual conscience. In their leadership role of guiding their children, parents instinctively direct their children with the self-evident admonition, "let your conscience be your guide." They perceive their nurturing role as moral leaders, not just as overseers, but as instructive interacting evaluators in the moral development of their children. They thus become *actively involved* in the personal leadership of their children, arousing their moral sense and coaching them toward higher moral performance. They would not dare to think about delegating this leadership role to anyone else. Herein lies the naturally traditional analogical insight of activating the corporate conscience as a delivery system for corporate responsibility—with *the CEO as an actively involved personal moral leader.*

Active Personal Involvement. The following statement by Robert Dilenschneider, previously CEO of Hill and Knowlton and currently of his own Group in New York more than illustrates the critical efficacy of personal involvement in managerial leadership:

> Symbolic involvement is essential. The art of ritual delegation shows that the CEO at least handled the issue, but sometimes the CEO can't simply coordinate. *He must personally involve himself,* (emphasis added) especially if he wants something special from a supplier or customer. . . . If this personal involvement success is true for CEOs, you better believe it will be true down the entire marketing chain of command.
> (Dilenschneider, 1990, p. 78).

MBE STRATEGIES OF MANAGING INVOLVEMENT

Interpersonal Activity. Whereas personal involvement in corporate leadership can be a very complex process for engagement by the CEO and

Chapter 9

other executives and managers through the entire production chain of command and critically contingent upon multiple organization set variables, such as, task environment differences, organization cultures and even individual leader personality traits, the degree and depth of personal involvement tends to vary accordingly (see Schein, 1980). For example, the CEO of a health care facility may likely bear more outgoing personality traits to become interpersonally involved as a morally *caring* leader with his/her staff as well as with clients than a CEO of a steel industry company. But no matter what organizational type a CEO is leading or a personality trait he or she bears, the CEO has a "social faith" obligation *to become personally involved in setting the ethical policies and moral norms of his/her company and nurturing the management and workforce to abide by them.*

Leadership Involvement and Work-Team Cooperation. One exemplary strategy of creating high levels of workplace cooperation is through the interpersonal and interactive communication of participating in work-team associations, as presented in Chapter 6. When a CEO engages him-herself at this level of work-floor managing, workers become expeditiously impressed through these symbolic associations at every level of managing interactional relationships, thereby stimulating higher moral stage awareness and inducing incentives for communal participation. Such morally developed leadership planning can efficaciously create an organizational climate of interactional *caring* in the workplace and ultimate corporate responsibility imaging in the marketplace. This MBE plan would symbolically and efficaciously improve the workplace interactional *moral efficacy* of the MBO Leadership Planning programs of the renowned Management Consultant, Loreen Sherman (see her *practical* exemplary works on "Corporate Leadership Development Programs" 2010-2011).

Organizational Leadership Styles. In his studies of leadership styles and organization types, Edgar Schein, the eminent organization scholar states:

> The leadership problem is least troubling in *normative* systems, those types of organizations which are tied together by common causes and mutual goals, by high levels of moral involvement and a belief that what is being worked on is important and exciting. Authority in such organizations typically rests on the *personal* qualities of the leader, his or her charisma or basic expertise in solving some important shared problems. The leadership terms one typically associates with such systems are *entrepreneur, leader, messiah, savior,* but the terms *supervisor, manager,* or *executive* could fit this concept equally well if the subordinates saw their bosses as "real leaders." The fact that a limited number of people do have the particular personal qualities (charisma) to elicit strong emotional support from their subordinates at a given time and place further complicates the problem of analyzing leadership. It is all too easy to assume that all we need to do is to find more such charismatic individuals or to teach people how to become

more charismatic. We forget that many kinds of organizations do not involve tasks or missions that could elicit high levels of involvement in the first place, and that the presence of a charismatic leader (even if we could get one) would not change a fundamentally utilitarian organization such as a company manufacturing textiles or a government bureaucracy into a normative one. Leadership, then, is a partly cultural phenomenon and must be analyzed within a given cultural, political, and socio-economic context. (1980, p. 109-110)

COMPARATIVE ORGANIZATION LEADERSHIP STYLES

Creating Inspirational Leadership Involvement. While leadership may be a "partly cultural" phenomenon in organizational scientific terms, it is also an *integrative holistic* cultural phenomenon in sociological interactive and educational psychological terms. But interestingly enough, in comparing the utilitarian type of organization to the normative one, Professor Schein describes leadership involvement as the utilitarian type which refers to Etzioni's "calculative," authority types, as described in Exhibit 3:5 (ch. 3). Recognizing that this type of "impersonal" leadership is much more problematic, (precisely because of its instrumental-relativity-bearing, evoking no higher moral performance on the part of subjects than stage 2 of the Kohlberg scale), he asks in his own exhibit "how to create involvement" in these types of organization cultures. The answer is, by no means simple; but neither is it all that complex, as it can easily be *inspirationally* induced by 6th stage moral awareness role-taking emulation. *Inspiration ignites emulation.* This kind of role taking moral leadership is cultivated in the organizational climates of interpersonal caring reciprocities at the 5th and 6th stage levels of post-conventional morality, as described in chapters 3 and 4; but it is also so naturally and inspirationally induced in the interpersonal family climates of child-rearing parents, even without the benefits of charismatic leadership personality traits. These simple interactional traits emanate from the natural social psychology of parental leadership generated from instinctive inducement incentives of morally caring sensitivity.

Impersonal MBO Delegating Leadership. One such *impersonal morally aroused* CEO was Michael Capellas, cited above in ch.2, for his good faith efforts to change the moral climate, when at MCI, stated in a CNBC interview that he was open to "structural change on all fronts." His awakening, however, certainly did not open his consciousness about the corporate conscience and the need for internal structural change for its formation and nurturing. He made no reference to its concept, let alone its structure, either in the interview or on the MCI website. His focus on structural change was primarily external. Though his intentions may not have been to impersonally delegate the moral reconstruction of the company by establishing an Ethics Office and a Chief Ethics Officer, he clearly set the organization hierarchical lines for MBO *delegation*. Several attempts were made to compliment Mr.

Capellas on his reconstructive mission and to encourage him to consider the "critical practical" pathways to inner structural moral reform. Every call was redirected to the Chief Ethics Officer who was otherwise occupied with training or traveling. Certainly, one does not have to talk about the corporate conscience, if the company has an active one. But if one talks about "structural reform on all fronts" in the context of corporate moral reform, and does not mention the need for an inner moral structure of a conscience in a company, it is evident that one is unaware of its importance or even of its existence. Had he known about the corporate conscience and realized its operations as the inspirational heartbeat of a company's moral integrity, he might have been inspired to have recognized more clearly his role to become a *primary involved* moral leader, as more *directively engaged* in the formation of its inner and outer organizational structures and *personally associated* in the nurturing of its reflexive operations. Without such moral inspiration and the lack of leadership ethical consistency, the company eventually lost its operational integrity in the legal processes of bankruptcy.

Interpersonal MBE Integrative Leadership. Though most CEOs are parents, they come from a bureaucratic management tradition which values the function of delegation as a strategic use of efficaciously achieving objectives—the MBO way. The price of delegation, however, often becomes the cost of non-involvement. Furthermore, the remnant MBO class would not dare to think of running a corporation like a family in accordance with the ethically sensitive model of Warren Buffet's gracefully paternal style of 6th stage moral leadership of the Berkshire Hathaway Corporation. It is not, therefore, surprising to discover that very few CEOs are involving themselves in corporate moral reform, let alone in corporate ethical training. Although they may very well believe in the importance of such reform, they do still delegate the programing to lower level managers, usually in human resource training departments in order to keep their strategic attention on MBO goal attainment, economic profitability and stakeholder values (Freeman, Harrison and Wicks 2007). They are now beginning opportunely to learn how to change course, however, as they critically hear about the growing sense of *shareholder moral values* and integrative moral leadership strategies. They are awakening, thus, with some accord and with varying degrees of moral awareness, to the socio-moral unrest of investors who have lost their life savings and social trust because of contemporary publicized rates of corporate executive involvement in greed and fraud.

Another and more recent type of an impersonal executive and instrumentally authoritative leader at the second stage of moral development relativity driven by business exchange theory was Steve Jobs of the Apple Corporation. His brilliant style of leadership was highly effective for the profit maximization goals he set for the company with his dedicated performance of rebuilding the corporation that he founded with a commanding performance of MBO leadership and profit maximization of entrepreneurship. While his expert managerial authority style was certainly not disintegrative, his inventive genius was critically functional for integrating company profits and contributing to the cybernetic inventions of corporate and public global communications.

COMPARATIVE INTERACTIONAL EXAMPLES OF CEO LEADERSHIP STYLES

Interpersonal MBE *Integrative Leadership.* A most practical analytical comparison to functional success of Steve Jobs, is the morally developed leadership style of Jeff Bezos of the Amazon Corporation. Starting literally in the grass roots sections of Seattle, Washington with his successful focused business selling of on-line books and CDs, he built his company as a model T formation of workplace interaction among small groupings. Such an architectural interactional design promoted a conducive democratic involvement within his workforce. His morally caring 6 stage priorities are exemplified in the following workplace interview about his sale-force team:

> Sometimes, Bezos says, you can't rely on facts because it would be too hard to test an idea, or too costly, or you can't figure out how to do it. And "sometimes we measure things and see that in the short term they actually hurt sales, and we do it anyway," he says, because Amazon managers don't think the short term is a good predictor of the long term. For example, they found that their biggest customers had such large collections of stuff—especially CDs—that they accidentally ordered items they had already bought from Amazon years ago. So they decided to give people a warning whenever this was about to happen. Sure enough, the warnings slightly reduced Amazon's sales. But it's hard to study the feature's long-term effects. Would it reduce sales over a 10-year period? They didn't think so. They thought it would make customers happy and probably increase sales. "You have to use your judgment," Bezos says. "In cases like that, we say, 'Let's be simpleminded. We know this is a feature that's good for customers. Let's do it.'"   (Deutschman, 2004)

Bezos' decision was a small-business decision-making example of applying "moralities of scale."

Interpersonal MBE *Transformational Leadership.* Another such CEO, Howard Lutnick, (cited above at the beginning of Chapter 3 for his heroic faith efforts to "care" for the victims of the World Trade Center Cantor Fitzgerald workforce and their 800 grieving families with 950 children), affirmed in a CNN interview on the 3rd anniversary of 9/11 that the firm had already raised $147 million through the first two years of the Cantor Fitzgerald Relief Fund and the Charity Days. The Charity Days were for the purpose of donating 100% of worldwide revenues from the operating business lines of Cantor Fitzgerald, eSpeed and BGC Partners, on the anniversaries as a memorial observance of 9/11. They were also for the days on which the many employees of the company and from eSpeed would donate their entire Charity Day's salary allotment to the revenue proceeds in observance of the anniversary. This consortium of *care*-giving partnership companies and employees contributed $7 million in 2003, which was placed in the Relief Fund for the overall care of the families and children, including living expenses and health care without cost for 10 years following 9/11. These funds were, in addition to the pledges of a quarter of the company's profits, for a full five years through 2006 since 9/11.

This MBE concert of "caretaking" moral leadership by Howard Lutnick is an transformational model of an involved *caregiving* CEO with a practical "ideal moral point of view." His compassionate care for the workforce of the company and their families during this life and death crisis was instantly and spontaneously delivered and reflected a committed "moral plan of action." This plan was not only moral, it was reconstructive *praxis* model as an exemplary 6th stage moral financial plan through which he radically *transformed* the company and its morale from "ground zero" to the highest moral expressions of *interactive* justice and *interpersonal* caring reciprocity. (For more on interactional and interpersonal transformational leadership, see the morally sensitive *praxis* studies of Barbara Robinson, 2009.)

As presented in Chapter 3, Howard Lutnick's caring was a spontaneously corporate moral development plan emanating from a corporate cultural ethos and a grieving compassionate pathos for the loss of a devoted family workforce. This financial plan inspired pure altruistic moral behavior more *reconstructively* inflamed with inter-familial *caring* than the destructively burning plains and the smoking building remains of 9/11. It was post-conventional moral development at its best and *transcendental faith development* for eternal rest.

These conclusions are not speculative. They are based on the following close review of the events, the timing and the morally specific actions of the Cantor Fitzgerald CEO, his executive national and international associates and partners, and the morally sensitive responses of the grieving families. When Howard Lutnick first heard about the plane crash into the tower of the building where his workforce was located, he thought it was a small piper cub. . . but still hurried to the scene. Noticing the severity of the smoking tower and how close the point of the crash was to the five floors of his firm's occupancy, he rushed to the burning building, subsequently describing his frantic rescue chase on *Larry King Live*: "I just had to get down there as fast as I could. . . to make sure my people were getting out. I'd grab them (the exiting survivors) as they went by and ask, 'What floor are you on? What floor are you on?'"

The CNN website (9/20/01) continues this story:

> What he did not know was that his employees had their escape route cut off by the fire that erupted when the plane sliced through the building a few floors below. Among those at the firm was Lutnick's brother, Gary, who worked for the company on the 103rd floor. Lutnick learned that his brother had called his sister and told her: (Howard Lutnick's words) "he wasn't going to make it and the smoke was coming in and things were bad and he called and said good-bye and that he loved her and for her to tell me that he, that he loved me." Since last Tuesday, Lutnick said, his days have been filled with funerals and wakes and calls from many of his workers' wives. "They call me and say, 'How come you can't pay my salary? Why can't you pay my husband's salary? Other companies pay their [dead and missing employees'] salary, why can't you?' But, you see, I lost, I lost everybody in the company, so I can't pay their salary. They think we're doing something wrong. I can't pay their salaries," Lutnick said, again dissolving into tears: "I don't have any money to pay their salaries."
>
> (CNN's Larry King Live interview with Steve Lutnick, 2001)

Five weeks later, The New York Times followed-up on clarifying the timing of the halting of the salaries and the funding of family benefit planning:

> By late September, some affected families had grown suspicious of Mr. Lutnick's promises of help—especially after Sept.15, when paychecks for the missing workers were halted. But in recent weeks, the firm has begun to flush out its chairman's promises and communicate them clearly to the affected families. Since Oct. 15, Mr. Lutnick has met with hundreds of families, explaining the company's benefit plan.   (Friday, Oct. 26, 2001).

In this same article, the evidence of the company's corporate conscience and its authentic 6th stage moral performance became manifest in the *morally sensitive delivery system of the promised benefits.* On October 25, 2001, the company announced that it had started paying $45 million in bonuses to the families of lost workers:

> The first checks are going out this week to the families of employees whose compensation did not include sales commissions...Cantor has promised that bonuses for dead or missing workers who received commission income will be distributed at Thanksgiving, in advance of the traditional year-end bonus season on Wall Street.
>
> The announcement about the unusual posthumous bonuses demonstrated the firm's growing the effort to be clear with the families of its lost employees. The first round of bonus checks will typically be equal to last year's bonus, plus any accumulated 2001 vacation time, but no family will receive less than $5,000. . . In addition, Cantor has said it will allocate 25% of the

firm's profits—which senior partners say have typically been $140 million to $160 million a year—over the next five years to the families of lost employees. (Ibid.)

And finally, to conclude the evidence of the authenticity of Cantor Fitzgerald's stage five corporate moral reliability and its having earned the stage 6 trust from the families of the employee victims, its temporal website stated:

> On September 19, 2001, Cantor Fitzgerald made a pledge to distribute 25% of the firm's profits and committed to paying 10 years of health care for the benefit of the families and loved ones of its former Cantor Fitzgerald, eSpeed and TradeSpark employees (profits which would otherwise be distributed to the partners of Cantor Fitzgerald). Cantor Fitzgerald has distributed this 25% of its profits every quarter since, and will continue to do so until September 11, 2006 (http//www.cantor.com).

This close review of the desperate catastrophic events and the charismatic covenantal commitment of this morally involved parental CEO to the families of his firm reveal the deepest compassionate moral vision perceiving the emotional anxieties of their grief. His *care*-fully *transformational* reconstructive commitment plan reflected the moral authenticity of his sympathetic compassion to the highest ethical sensitivities of their incumbent needs inspiring exemplary fifth and sixth stage managing moral performance. And this: in the context of catastrophic terrorizing events with corporate genocidal losses of lives, and architectural and financial losses in devastating corporate ruins.

Executive Leadership Comparisons. The CEO of MCI, Michael Capellas, an honorable and sincere Chief Executive Officer, with a record of sound MBO leadership tried to place the company in an honorable ethical direction through the appointment of a Chief Ethics Officer. The symbolic interactional forms of this reformative attempt were contained in the traditional hierarchical structures of corporate executive appointments without any ethically efficacious spirit of corporate moral reform nor any morally involved leadership for executing this reform. The CEO's of Apple and Amazon corporations were exemplary corporate leaders in specifically different ways:

STEVE JOBS

was a passionate MBO leader

intensely involved with his inventive products

moving international corporate and consumer markets

with aggressive leadership in commercial networking and

production processing.

Consumed himself, in a desperate struggle with *time and eternity,*

he burned with passion for the "sequence of his next discovery"

with his last conscious breath and his final eschatological words:

"OH WOW. OH WOW. OH WOW."

! + !

Recorded by his sister, Mona Simpson, English Professor at the

University of California,

Los Angeles and holder of the Sadie Samuelson Levy Chair in Languages and Literature at

Bard College

(See Simpson, 2011).

As a "mythic figure" of his own fate (Shiller, 2012, p. 20), he learned with dispassion of

his self-*involved* mortality.

Intensely involved with his devoted family, he awakened to his personal encounter with

"The Hound of Heaven" chasing him to his very last conscious breath:

"Nigh and nigh draws the chase,

With unperturbed pace. . .

Ah! Must — Designer infinite! —" (Thompson, 1940, pp. 369-370)

POST CONVENTIONAL MORAL DEVELOPMENT CONCLUSIONS

With a paternally charismatic style of a friendly generous leader, Warren Buffet exposes a wide socially interactive profile of a caring MBE Chief Executive Officer of the Berkshire Hathaway Corporation. With a morally sensitive post-conventional leadership image, he traditionally invites all shareholders of his corporation from around the world to meet with him and his Board of Directors along with his management staff and employees for the annual reporting and convening procedures of his multinational company's business. He actively participates in these meetings with an exemplary fatherly style as a gracefully friendly and approachable leader. His 5th and 6th stage *honest* and *caring* moral leadership in "corporate governance" has earned him an iconic MBE imagery that is reflected throughout the media of corporate culture and management hierarchies. (See Buffet, 2008).

In contrast, Jeff Bezos is an equally passionate MBE leader intensely involving himself with his workforce teams engaging their collective participation in workplace democracy interaction building their interactional commitment to his company's caring for customer satisfaction. To this end, he promoted innovative online interaction with his customer base, allowing free reviewing of books before purchasing along with free shipping for purchases of books over $25, even at the expense of short term losses for long term customer returns. These policies of trust building with his customers as well as with his workforce express a social faith commitment from his teams and a public trust investment in his business from his customers as an involved caring leader.

The CEO of Cantor Fitzgerald, Howard Lutnick, a noble virtuous man of sensitive caring MBE leadership *involved* himself in the actual site of trade tower rubble desperately attempting to reach his workforce and his trapped brother in the trembling twin tower of the World Trade Center. As a morally engaged leader, he was forced to disengage himself from the rubble but only to re-engage his compassionate moral role-taking sensitivity with the families of his fallen workforce. He activated his role-taking sensitivity into care-taking generosity. Without clarity of the magnitude of the monetary losses, and the initial inability to respond to the anxieties of the families of their fallen beloved victims, he reformulated his care-taking calculations with expanded funding of longer term "family benefit planning." He *involved* himself with visiting these families and promising them generous "posthumous bonuses" to express his compassion for the losses of their loved ones. And finally, he pledged "to distribute 25% of the firm's profits and committed to paying 10 years of health care for the benefit of the families and loved ones of its former Cantor Fitzgerald, eSpeed and TradeSpark employees (profits which would otherwise have been distributed to the partners of Cantor Fitzgerald)."

POST CONVENTIONAL FAITH DEVELOPMENT CONCLUSIONS

This 5th and 6th stage moral development compassionate response of Howard Lutnick to the bereaving families of his fallen workforce was an emulating manifestation of *parental involvement as an elder and wise ethical leader* of his investment firm. His inspiration ignites emulation and ethically answers the question of "how to *definitively* create involvement" in corporate ethical leadership through the interpersonal spirit of a MBE *caring* parent. His "creativity and temperance" grounded in the strength of his "transcendental courage" guided his ethical managerial "caregiving" sensitivity toward moving the company forward with the wisdom of his transitional adjustments, reflecting *compassionate* love for the losses of his human resources. The interpersonal and familial authenticity of his compassion and the strength of his courage reflect the "appreciation of beauty and excellence" and the gains of his *aesthetic resources* in his transformational leadership of *caring* interaction for the *Beauty of Eternal Life.*

> The souls of the just are in the hands of God. . .
> In the sight of the unwise, they seemed to die;
> But they are in peace. . .
> (Wisdom III:1-3)
> (See the "Elder-Wise Model of Transformational Leadership"
> in Robinson, 2009, p. 156).

A more contemporary transformational leader, whose *caregiving sensitivity* reflects the post-conventional MBE moral and faith development models of leadership is Howard Schultz CEO of Starbucks. His global vision of doing business is not grounded on MBO profit maximization values and delegating traditional authority lines of hierarchy. His moral vision of interacting business has developed an holistic mission of *interpersonal transformational* commerce of *caring* not just for products but especially for *persons.* His commerce is globally managed by symbolic interactional values of engaging with customers by communally integrating with *persons.* His leadership strategies transcend the structural containments of bureaucracy and engage the interactive discourse of democracy:

> What we've built is not steeped in Americana any more. In fact, it's as relevant in Hangzhou as it is in Madrid. The relevancy is in the sense of community, bringing people together in a place where they feel comfortable celebrating coffee and conversation. It all starts with the culture and values of the company. *Bloomberg BusinessWeek*
> (See"Charlie Rose Talks:" Starbucks CEO, Howard Schultz, April 3, 2014)

Chapter 10

The Personal Conscience and Integrated Moral Leadership

The following poetic text of the World Trade Center Towers 9/11 moral collapse integrates the ethical inter-relationship need of the Personal Conscience informing the Corporate Conscience in corporate culture.

THE WORLD TRADE CENTER TOWERS

As Ground Zero has proudly completed the redevelopment of its

World Trade Center Towers

with dedicated symbolic memories of their ecumenically buried martyrs of 9/11,

from the losses of Cantor Fitzgerald and Holy Innocent victims with fire-fighting heralds,

the architectural structures and inspirational monuments are now in place

for an aesthetic Multinational Memorial toward inspiring

ethical integrity in leadership and moral reform in markets.

While the integrated moral leadership of the City of New York,

and the healing of bereaving bearers of the World Trade Center firms,

we all can sing with hopeful hearts. . . and pleading prayers. . . in concert with

America, the Beautiful

and her Integrative Search for Moral Leadership. . .

At Ground Zero, her "spacious skies" shall ever be a National Shrine

with heroic interpersonal memories of holocaust victims caring for one another

at the Foot of the Cross of a Metropolitan City where

MBE Pentecostal Towers

Overcame MBO holocaust(al) powers.

ETHICAL INTEGRITY IN LEADERSHIP

The Integration of Moral Leadership. Meanwhile, another reconstructive and integrative leader in the institutional academic sphere "had long since begun" the rebuilding of a monumental program in management education at Yale University. As Dean of the School of Management in the aftermath of that period, Joel Podolny introduced with his faculty a new MBA curriculum with specific focus on an "Integrated Leadership Perspective."

The *Yale Alumni Magazine* described the curricular reform in this way:

> A new core curriculum for first year students in the 2006-2007 academic year. While the management profession has changed profoundly in recent decades, management education has not. This interdisciplinary curriculum will provide Yale MBAs with skills to work effectively and lead in today's private, public, and nonprofit organizations. The new core will be divided into three segments: Orientation to Management, Organizational Perspectives, and Integrated Leadership Perspectives. Organizational Perspectives will replace traditional functional courses (Marketing and Finance, for example) with multidisciplinary courses structured around the constituencies a manager must engage and work with in order to solve problems—or make progress—within an organization. As news of the reform has spread, SOM (School Of Management) has seen a substantial increase in the percentage of admitted applicants who chose Yale over other schools. *Yale Magazine* Vol. LXIX, no. 6, "New Yale Curriculum" (September 5, 2006).

Upon these earlier beginnings, both at the World Trade Center Towers and in the Yale School of Organization Management curricular reforms, it is clear from the elevating academic interests of these student applicants that the ethical imperatives of *reforming* global social and political terrorism and of *informing* moral developmental curricular learning in graduate education demand the continuing upgrading of applied learning through the perspectives of the MBE paradigm, as presented in Chapter 5 in this book.

Upgrading Leadership Perspectives from Historical Learning. Inasmuch as this critical need still exists, especially in corporate Headquarters, it is compelling to review how the MBO paradigm has been historically responsible for constituting an hegemonic trap for many executives, caught in the functional grips of managing business affairs by exchange theory blinders, who are otherwise socially sensitive and morally responsible citizens in their private lives and interpersonal friendships. As a result of this internal personal moral development discrepancy, their leadership profiles have suffered from a lack of their ability to integrate their personal values toward connecting their conscientious moral sensitivities to their business affairs and management styles.

In a past *eNewsLine* article for the (International) Association for the Advancement of Collegiate Schools of Business AACSB, Joel Podolny critically addressed this inner personal value system and its outer professional role divide:

> We are all familiar with the saying, "It's not personal; it's just business." Think about what this means—that work is somehow not an implication of self. But if work is defined apart from the self, the self—with its values, its aspirations (work) has no bearing on professional behavior. We see this dissociation of self from professional behavior most clearly when there are ethical breaches. The central protagonists in the recent corporate scandals did not perceive themselves as "bad people." Rather, they defined themselves by their actions outside the world of work: they were philanthropists, community leaders, church-goers, and so on. Such ethical breaches are especially spectacular manifestations of the dissociation of self from professional conduct. But this dissociation occurs every single day when individuals simply fail to infuse the better qualities of their selves— their values, aspirations, and the positive aspects of their character—into their professional conduct. (2006b, p.1)

MBE AS ASSOCIATIVE INTEGRATION IN MORAL LEADERSHIP

This graphic contemporary description of the dissociation of self from professional conduct is clearly a prevailing problem of the *disconnection between the corporate conscience and the personal conscience.* Many, if not most, executives still bear this disconnection in their professional roles and often make moral decisions and contractual deals for their companies by exchange theory at stage two of the Kohlberg scale. Yet they direct their personal lives at a much higher altruistic level of stage five and six, morally sensitive to the values of trust and honesty and to the universal principles of distributive justice and caring reciprocity. This kind of *morally* "split personality" in an executive leader can cave into a *moral disintegration* within a company. This is exactly what happened at Enron. The late Kenneth Lay was a good man in his personal life. Therein he displayed the virtues of a well-developed socio-religious personality as a fifth stage faith-believing Christian and as a sixth stage morally developed philanthropist in the greater civic Houston, Texas community. Within the company, however, he yielded to the immoral forces of a corporate conspiracy as a way of "just doing business." David Luban (2006) typified this corporate conspiratorial *quake* as a "moral meltdown" and cleverly explained its *morally disintegrating disconnections* through cognitive dissonance theory:

> But none of this explains our original puzzle of why the crooks continue to think they are not crooks. Here social psychology offers an answer. The basic reason is cognitive dissonance. Whenever our conduct and principles clash with each other in a way that threatens our self-image as an upstanding person, the result is a kind of inner tension—dissonance. And dissonance

theory tells us that wired into us is a fundamental drive to reduce dissonance. How do you accomplish that? Obviously, you cannot change your past conduct. Instead, you change your beliefs. That is what fifty years of research has taught. In situation after situation, literally hundreds of experiments reveal that when our conduct clashes with our prior beliefs, our beliefs swing into conformity with our conduct, without our noticing that this is going on (pp. 67-68).

Cognitive dissonance disconnects the wires of conscience slowly and one step at a time (p. 74).

THE LEADERSHIP MODEL OF MANAGEMENT BY ETHICS

Re-Connecting the Personal Conscience and the Corporate Conscience. The ethical mandate of integrated moral leadership then is to *connect* the corporate conscience with one's personal conscience and to redefine one's work as *integrated with the moral self.* While Dean Podolny states that executives need to "infuse the better qualities of their selves—their values, aspirations and the positive aspects of their character—into their professional conduct," the MBE ethical mandate directs them to maintain and even foster an ethical and moral consistency between their personal lives and their professional roles. But first, they need to define the *virtue of integrity* in order to achieve the *power of integrated moral leadership.* Integrity must reside in the self, i.e. in the personal conscience, before it can morally motivate others in the collective corporate conscience through the influential organizational processes of integrated leadership.

Integrated Moral Leadership and Personal Integrity. Defining the virtue of integrity for the purposes of collating its inspirational relationship between the personal conscience and the corporate conscience in terms of integrated moral leadership in organizational settings cannot be done even in this book by references or citations, such as the most relevant "identity-conferring" definition of Minkler in Chapter 6 above, relating its virtue to work commitment. Rather, its definition, in the co-relational leadership roles in the organizational contexts of corporate and personal moral behavior, needs the depth analysis of intense social psychological perception and psycho-historical understanding, such as that offered by the classical work of Erik Erikson:

> In the aging person who has taken care of things and people and has adapted himself to the triumphs and disappointments of being, by necessity, the originator of others and the generator of things and ideas—only in him the fruit of the seven stages gradually ripens. I know no better word for it than *integrity.* Lacking a clear definition, I shall point to a few attributes of this stage of mind.

It is the ego's accrued assurance of its proclivity for order and meaning—an emotional integration faithful to the image-bearers of the past and ready to take, and eventually to renounce, leadership in the present. It is the acceptance of one's one and only life cycle and of the people who have become significant to it as something that had to be and that, by necessity, permitted of no substitutions. It thus means . . . an acceptance of the fact that one's life is one's own responsibility. It is a sense of comradeship with men and women of distant times and of different pursuits who have created orders and objects and sayings conveying human dignity and love. Although aware of the relativity of all the various life styles which have given meaning to human striving, the possessor of integrity is ready to defend the dignity of his own life style against all physical and economic threats. For he knows that an individual life is the accidental coincidence of but one life cycle with but one segment of history, and that for him all human integrity stands and falls with the one style of integrity of which he partakes. . . .

A meaningful old age, then . . . serves the need for that integrated heritage which gives indispensable perspective to the life cycle. Strength here takes the form of that detached yet active concern with life bounded by death, which we call *wisdom* in its many connotations from ripened "wits" to accumulated knowledge, mature judgment, and inclusive understanding. Not that each man can evolve wisdom for himself. For most, a living *tradition* provides the essence of it. But the end of the cycle also evokes "ultimate concerns" for what chance man may have to transcend the limitations of his identity and his often tragic or bitterly tragicomic engagement in his one and only life cycle within the sequence of generations. Yet great philosophical and religious systems dealing with ultimate individuation seem to have remained responsibly related to the cultures and civilizations of their times. Seeking transcendence by renunciation, they yet remain ethically concerned with the "maintenance of the world." By the same token, a civilization can be measured by the meaning which it gives to the full cycle of life, for such meaning, or the lack of it, cannot fail to reach into the beginnings of the next generation, and thus into the chances of others to meet ultimate questions with some clarity and strength.

To whatever abyss ultimate concerns may lead individual men, man as a psychosocial creature will face, toward the end of his life, a new edition of an identity crisis which we may state in the words "I am what survives of me." From the stages of life, then, such dispositions as faith, will power, purposefulness, competence, fidelity, love, care, wisdom—all criteria of vital individual strength—also flow into the life of institutions.

Without them, institutions wilt; but without the spirit of institutions pervading the patterns of care and love, instruction and training, no strength could emerge from the sequence of generations.

Psychosocial strength, we conclude, depends on a total process which regulates individual life cycles, the sequence of generations, and the structure of society simultaneously: for all three have evolved together (1968, pp. 139-141).[1]

THE INSPIRATIONAL POWER OF INTEGRITY

It is evident from this *personal* and social psychological definition of integrity that its virtue is to develop a corporate ethical spirit as a life cyclical and historically holistic endeavor. Furthermore, its *inspirational power* to deliver a morally integrated leadership can be efficaciously magnetic if it is connected to an "integrated heritage" of "*wisdom*" and an *historical* heritage of "living *tradition*." Accordingly, wisdom as a mental trait means more than just being smart and crafty as many corporate executives are. This critically interesting word comes from the Latin *sapientia* signifying a historically enriched body of knowledge drawn from the living traditions of the past, informing one's flow of experiential learning in the present, and integrally feeding the learning flow into the future for the "sequence of generations." This is the "integrated heritage" which Erikson is tracing and which forms over time an identity in a civilization, in a nation, in a corporation, and even in a global leader, as the humble Nelson Mendela's living holistic tradition.

Leaders sensitive to these historically holistic processes of "integrated heritage" and the learning flow of this kind of *wisdom* do understand Erikson's admonitions: "Not that each man can evolve wisdom for himself. For most, a living *tradition* provides the essence of it." And, furthermore, as they themselves develop a moral awareness spirit in their historical place within their own limited life cycle, they begin to appreciate the ultimate concerns of a *corporate ethical tradition* and become motivated to contribute to its flow into the *sequential moral life* of their respective corporations. Ultimately, for most of them, these leaders inspirationally recognize and intuitively know that *the generative power of this ethical spirit is integrity.* In a recent interview of Bill Gates on *CNBC*, Donny Deutsch posed this climactic question to the Chairman of the Microsoft Corporation, asking him, what was the most important and meaningful thing he had learned from his friendship with and admiration for Warren Buffet, the Chairman of the Berkshire Hathaway Corporation. Mr. Gates replied with one word—*"Integrity."*

MORAL LEADERSHIP AND CORPORATE INTEGRITY

Integrated Moral Leadership and Corporate Integrity. If "ultimate concerns" are evoked "for what chance man may have to transcend the limitations of his identity and his often tragic or bitterly tragicomic engagement in his one and only life cycle within the sequence of generations," how much more critical it is for the corporation to evoke *ultimate concerns* for what chance it may have to *transcend the leadership limitations* of its corporate identity—from any "tragic or bitterly tragicomic engagements" by any of its executives in the past life cycles of the corporation within the historical sequence of its ongoing generations. This critical point was clearly addressed by Erikson at the end of his lengthy definition of integrity when he concluded:

From the stages of life, then, such dispositions as faith, willpower, purposefulness, competence, fidelity, love, care, wisdom—all criteria of vital individual strength—also flow into the life of institutions. Without them, institutions wilt; but without the spirit of institutions pervading the patterns of care and love, instruction and training, no strength could emerge from the sequence of generations (idem, p. 141).

What this means for corporations in these times of corporate fraud and its "tragic" and even "bitterly tragicomic" engagements by the infrastructural betrayal of CEOs and other high level executives is that these defined dispositions of integrity, which continue to exist and flow within the ongoing corporate life and business operations of the institution from the historical and cultural traditions of a company, can be revived by the sequence of generations in that institution. But it also means that if the damage is so pervasive that a total institutional financial breakdown occurs, as in the case of Enron, the institution will wilt and fade away in the mournful memories of its disintegrated executive betrayers. Analogically, as in the case of the Apple Corporation, though there was no corporate fraud in the cultures of its business operations during its early growth period with the organization's transitional leadership problems within *its* "sequence of generations," the Board of Directors manifested pre-conventional levels of morality at stage 1 and 2, with the "firing of its founder," as the late Steve Jobs acknowledged in his earlier historical commencement speech at Stanford University. His privately wounded self-image and publicly healed discourse delivery projected a charismatic message of post-conventional corporate ethics at stage 5 and 6 to the admiring youthful graduates to pursue careers with commitment and *integrity*. And above all, his private and personal *aesthetic* life reflected an *integrative moral commitment* to his family steadfastly enduring his ascetic "now" with what rationally appeared to be his ultimate post-conventional discovery of the *eternal* WOW !

From the prosaic and poetic eulogy of his devout sister, it would appear that his "INVENTOR" saved His divinely forbidden "Apple" for his last conscious *faith* discovery in his *exclamatory* breath. (See her *Eulogy* for her brother in Mona Simpson, 2011).

Rediscovering the Praxis Reflexive "How." Realistically, therefore, the *practical* answer to these ultimate questions of generational concerns for the preservation of the ethical spirit of institutions, with a morally strong and integrated leadership throughout corporate culture, is to *synchronize* the *reflexive operations* of the executives' personal conscience with those of the corporate conscience. Only when these conscientious operations enjoy *ethically reflexive synchronicity* will executives reach beyond the dualism and dissonance of cognitive and moral inconsistency toward the timely *delivery of morally integrated leadership consistency.* In the "sequence of generations" between MBO and MBE, such an integrated model of executive moral leadership, as empowered by the virtue of integrity, is far from becoming the emulating post-conventional model of corporate ethical leadership. The sequential generations of morally conventional CEOs [as often disrupted by the MBO functional imperatives of goal attainment in their professional conduct (driven by business exchange theories from stages 2 to 4 on the moral development scale) while, at the same time, like Kenneth Lay, as morally disconcerted executive "class-mates," persisting to be ethically upright in their personal lives (at stages 5 and 6 of the scale but morally disconnected in their corporate spheres)] continue, in their pre-conventional leadership styles, through the *"contra"*-sequential instrumental relativity of 2nd stage cognitively dissonant deal-cutting transactions. While this dis-integrative MBO dualism does indeed often provoke a moral identity crisis in the aging run of their professional careers, the "psycho-historical dislocating" (Lifton, 1969) reflections within the inner depths of their personal conscience will hold them accountable for the *ultimate realization that they will be remembered by what survives them.* It is ethically imperative, therefore, that sooner rather than later in their careers, they need to strive to attain a moral integration between their virtuous personal lives and their dissonant professional conduct. One conveniently *learning* option for these executives to respond to this inner reflexive accountability is to explore the professional *leadership benefits* of a socio-therapeutic "insearch" experience[2] in the private context of a personal Executive Retreat or a collective interpersonal Corporate Retreat, such as, for the CEO, his/her potential successors, and/or a morally motivated and ethically interested Board Director.

AN INNOVATIVE SEARCH FOR INTEGRITY

Corporate Retreats: Learning the Wisdom of Ethical Reflexivity. When one ponders over the revelatory heuristic thoughts of Erik Erikson and wonders about his repeated references to "ultimate concerns," "meaningful old age," " *wisdom*," "living *tradition*" and "transcendence," one realizes that he is not only talking about reflexive thinking but is actually opening the vision of integrative tracing toward perceiving and *contemplating* ethical reflexivity. Furthermore, when one considers the multiple ongoing activities of CEO's and the sequences of their company appointments, their internal executive meetings and external professional engagements, one realizes how little time there may be for reflexive thinking and how unaccommodating their executive offices may be for ethical reflexivity. Within the corporate complexities of these invasive operational realities, finding a convenient time and discovering a peaceful place to rest within the quiet zones of a corporate retreat center would be most conducive to experience the transcendence of "ultimate concerns" and the solitude for *reflexive* thinking and *praxis* action.

Cultivating the Art of Ethical Reflexivity. One such corporate retreat model offering the transcendental *"wisdom"* of Erik Erikson and the inter-theoretical resources for rebuilding the "spirit of institutions pervading the patterns of care and love, instruction and training" so that moral "strength could emerge from the sequence of generations" is the EquiPax Center for Human and Ethical Resources in Newport, Vermont. EquiPax is a Latin term signifying "equal peace." The mission of this Center, as an open voluntary association, is to *share an inner peace* "equally" with every guest who comes to rest in its sanctuary. As a sacred architectural landscape within a private innovative environmental sanctuary, EquiPax shares its peace in three convenient settings: the retreat home, an art gallery chapel, and a public ecological lake-life habitat on the Northern Green Mountains of Vermont. The retreat home is a spacious and intimately secluded residence in Newport, Vermont overlooking the City Dock on Lake Memphremagog. Its interior domicile contains several private guest rooms, a specialized library collection in corporate and environmental ethics, organization-management science, socio-economics and ecumenical religious studies with a music-meditation room and an interconnected art gallery chapel for private prayer, communal worship and/or aesthetic contemplation. The art gallery chapel is an innovative design in liturgical architecture which holds a collection of environmental and corporate art and other selections of painting and sculpture with aesthetic variations on these themes. An upper gallery loft opens toward the lake with environmental seasonal views of the international waters and the Border Mountains of Canada and the United States. A lower gallery offers the comfort of a conference chamber where retreatants enjoy optional and free access to private and confidential consulting, counseling or social psychological and psychohistorical therapy work. The lake-life sanctuary spans thirty miles beyond the border with views of Bear Mountain in Vermont and Owl's Head Ski Resort in Quebec. The site offers seasonal opportunities for nature walks, bicycle-trailing, cross-border boating tours, ice-fishing, alpine and cross-country skiing and lake/landscape painting. The residential site of EquiPax, with its historical and architectural landmark significance, has been included in a national recognition award as part of the Newport Downtown Historic District which is listed in the National Register of the National Park Service, Department of the Interior in Washington, DC.

The mission of EquiPax extends to the promotion of peace and integrity within the corporate sector. To this end, its Center for Human and Ethical Resources has developed *consulting methodologies and management strategies for the cultivation of the corporate conscience* in the workplace and the socialization of moral development in the workforce, as presented in this book. Accordingly, it offers two consulting programs at executive leadership levels: the corporate retreat and the corporate seminar. These programs are designed to facilitate reflexive insight in the socio-economic dimensions of company operations and ethical foresight in the practical concerns of corporate production. With *critical practical focus*, they trace the procedures and *expand the pedagogies for the moral development training* of human resources in a company and ethical-consciousness-raising in its management operations. In effect, the programs at EquiPax apply *innovative* interactional and action-based learning with inter-disciplinary ethical reflexivity for environmental and ecological planning and corporate moral reconstruction, as called for by the Management and Ethical Education Task Forces of the International Association for the Advancement of Collegiate Schools of Business (Olian 2002, Phillips 2004; and Policano 2010).

These *innovative consulting programs* are based on the executive development and management training model of MBE as a socialization delivery system for the restoration of honesty and integrity in corporate culture. The system is relatively easy to introduce in either a corporate retreat modality or a small group corporate seminar process. The corporate retreat modality is privately designed for one or two executives and their spouses for a weekend or an extended weekend as an informal and reflexive introduction to MBE. The spouses are optionally invited to encourage their roles as morally reflexive partners with their executive marital mates designed to foster the re-integration between the private personal self and the corporate executive role so alarmingly and tragically divided, as seen in the descriptive cases cited in the previous chapter. They will be given the option to participate in the reflexive presentations or to spend their own personal time in the art gallery or visiting the EquiPax Gardens or the lake-life attractions and the mountainous sport activities at the Jay Peak Recreation Center. Had the spouses of their morally dissonant culprit executives from Enron to WorldCom and Tyco enjoyed a morally reflexive integrated association with their criminally convicted husbands in a private corporate retreat spiritual compound, the latter may not have suffered the career ending dissonance of a morally pathetic meltdown. At EquiPax, they could have rediscovered their pristine faith in their executive leadership roles, as traced in Chapter 9, toward inspiring their collegial Board Advisors and the entire personnel community of their respective Corporations with the *humility of dignity* and *the honor of integrity*.

The corporate seminar alternative is designed for executives and their human resource trainers for a more formally developed and applied introduction to the MBE socialization planning system through an extended weekend or five day period. The seminars openly discuss the six step intervention management plan for introducing and implementing the MBE model in the retreatants' companies and are open to address particular moral problems and/or ethical dilemmas which participants may have encountered in their specific assignments.

These consulting programs are effectively promotive of what the International Association for the Advancement of Collegiate Schools of Business (AACSB) is calling for in terms of updating more practical and expediently accessible doctoral and curricular resources for the corporate learning and management education of CEOs and their Human Resource trainers. Asserting its leadership role in responding to the contemporary challenges of business and management education, the AACSB—International has opened a focus on "innovation" in three areas of professional management education toward (1) developing new strategies and alliances through the convergence of degree and non-degree education; (2) expanding the boundaries of doctoral research and teaching to encompass multidisciplinary corporate learning; and (3) applying curricular relevance to global business issues in multinational contexts. Stressing the critical centrality of this innovative continuing education agenda for the AACSB - International, its Management Education Task Force concludes:

> This report is a call to action to engage the deans of business schools, their faculties, and their business partners, as well as university provosts and presidents, to confront the changing context in which business schools operate and to consider bold, new strategies and alliances that have been rare among business schools (Olian, 2002. p. 5).

Deans, faculties, provosts and presidents know only too well that the efficacy of any "call to action" emanating from any *innovative* forms of executive education and corporate learning must be radically related to the moral depths of ethical reflexivity in management education and business practice. What is challenging for them to perceive, however, is that they will comprehend the need for the radical *root re-orientation* of their MBO curricular programing toward a corporate learning convergence with MBE principles and practice, as critically and reconstructively reviewed in Chapter 5 and above in this chapter relative to the new core curricular reform program of the Yale School of Management. They themselves, as deeply committed educators and gravely pressured administrators, may need to retreat from time to time for replenishing their own ethical sense and moral courage through the art of personal academic leadership and corporate pedagogic reflexivity. In recent Task Force report, past Chairman of the AACSB, Andrew Policano, Dean of the Paul Merge School of Business University of California, Irvine evaluates the role of innovation with these critical *praxis* remarks:

> In the economic downturn, innovation is a key strategy for institutions to not only recover but thrive and sustain growth into the future. Despite widespread recognition of the critical role of innovation, the concept of innovation is deceptively complex and often misunderstood. This report explores this complexity and provides insights into both the innovation process and the role and value of business schools in this process.

Business schools play a pivotal role by developing effective leaders and providing support for the *engine* (emphasis added) driving sustainable growth in their communities and throughout the world (2010, p. 3).

At EquiPax, MBE is the "engine driving" mission of *Engaging Studies for Graduate Internship Programs*. With pedagogical sensitivity for the three Business School Reports of the AACSB International and their respective visions for innovative curricular reform, EquiPax has responded to the call of the Business Round Table Institute for Corporate Ethics (2007) "to provide research and internship opportunities for faculty and students interested in the study of applied business ethics." This innovation offers a direct entry into the experiential *praxis* domains of higher education for the learning of *practical* knowledge with interdisciplinary programs in the interrelated fields of corporate and environmental ethics. The internship programs are designed to be offered conjointly with or separately from the retreat programs for "graduate students and faculty." The joint option would be offered with a CEO or a corporate Human Resource Director selected by the University so that the graduate students would enjoy an integrated learning exposure to an executive in the applied corporate cultures of their choice.

Since EquiPax enjoys a convenient international cross-border location in Vermont, with access to the co-curricular projects of the *Nature Conservancy* of the State, it has designed the social psychological "engine" building methodologies "for starting the incentive inducement "motors" of the integrative learning of corporate and environmental ethics in its prime ecological setting in the Green Mountain Lake Regions of the Appalachian Trail. This setting is ideal for integrating science and religion as essential co-curricular components for sustainability methodologies and philosophical spiritualties in *praxis* learning for internship and executive leadership training (see Gordon and Berry, 2006; Redekop, 2010; Western, 2010; Becker, 2010).

GRADUATE INTERNSHIP LEARNING

Praxis Learning through the Art of Reflexivity. As a Center for Human and Ethical Resources, the education mission of EquiPax is to cultivate the *art of reflexivity* for executives and interns. With this corporate moral purpose, the retreat center provides a fourfold sanctuary fostering *educational, therapeutic, aesthetic and transcendental reflection*.

First, *educational reflection* offers instruction and training in corporate ethics with an historical breakaway from Management by Objectives (MBO) to a new orientation for advanced management studies and practice with Management by Ethics (MBE). The instruction and training focus on activating the role-taking sensitivities of the retreatants as a means of morally awakening the virtues of *respecting* the qualitative aspects of their work, of *caring* for the humanistic needs of their workers and customers and of *providing* for the ethical expectations of their collaborators in the company's organization set. The zoom of this training focus must be set in the reflexive lenses of the personal conscience of the executive that he or she, as the principal informant of the corporate conscience, may intuitively lead as well as rationally assess the ethical spirit of institutional policy formulations and the altruistic performance of the company's moral role-taking capacity. "Without the spirit of institutions pervading the patterns of care and love, instruction and training, no strength could emerge from the sequence of generations." (Erikson, above) With this kind of cultivated ethical depth reflexivity, EquiPax retreatants can return to the executive chambers and director boardrooms of their companies with moral action learning to direct the demanding traffic of the complex organization lanes of commerce *reflexively in-formed* by the spirit of corporate ethical perception and the moral strength of principled performance action for the "sequence" of their company generations; and the interns, for the "sequence" of their career aspirations.

Second, *therapeutic reflection* offers executives a private professional and experienced counseling forum in a psycho or socio-therapy engagement to reflect on and reveal any and all personal problems and especially those dealing with personal immoral behavior and/or corporate moral failure. Its purpose is to console a grieving executive with compassionate understanding and to counsel the corporate offender in a safe sanctuary setting with insightful reflexivity toward awakening motivation for personal rehabilitation and corporate restitution. This EquiPax forum is designed to release the executive from the shameful grip of guilt toward opening a holistic therapeutic recovery for personal healing and professional restoration with an inner liberating peace.

Third, *aesthetic reflection* opens the transcendental domains of EquiPax's inner peace reflexivity mission towards the environmental zones of natural beauty through the visual media of the fine arts. Its art gallery, as presented in Volume II of this study, is appointed with a permanent exhibition on "The Forest Mythos and the Corporate Ethos" and is presented to honor the *deciduous*[3] forests which are giving their lives for the comfort of the public and the commerce of corporations. The exposition has been conceived to awaken a corporate ethical consciousness from the natural intercultural resources of the forest in ecumenical/biblical and historical/mythological literature. The artistic production of the exposition is prosaically and poetically arranged to portray the rapacious commercial conflicts within the "suffering servant"[4] soul of the environmental forest in compassionately promotive planetary and cosmological defense against the heartless corporate culture of industrialized productive greed. The art and sculptural forms of the artists and the Chapel architectural form of the Gallery express the integral ecological relations of the forest with its natural environment, encouraging an "environmental stand" against the disintegrating industrial relations with its corporate "predators." The five conceptual thematic variations of the exposition—*The Mythical Forest, The Biblical Forest, The Liturgical Forest, The Commercial Forest,* and *The Ecological Forest*—create a *reflexive cosmic worry* over these de-consecrating relations and inspire a *critical ethical mythos* for ecologically re-consecrating innovations for a sixth stage *corporate ethical ethos.*[5]

Fourth, and climatically in concert with the faith development paradigm of Fowler in Chapter Eight and the life development stages of Erikson herein, *transcendental reflection* reaches to the "ultimate concerns" beyond historical ages. Probing deeply into the "spiritual life age" of "living" and "ascetical theological traditions," reflections at this level of transcendence activate memories of historical and biblical events with inspirations of "*Faith*" and meditations of "*Wonder*" in the Latin meaning of "mirabilia" (review Fowler's paradigm in Chapter 8 and the transcendental ethos of spiritualities and the cosmological sources of a mystical *Omega God* in Exhibit 8:1). EquiPax is a sacred seminal place for the *contemplation of mystery* and the *inspirations of wonder.* In addition to the corporate art collection in its Gallery Chapel, the Retreat Home is appointed with a biblical and liturgical art collection at the ethically *reflexive* center of which is a music meditation room with a repertoire of Gregorian and Byzantine chant and liturgical, classical, operatic and contemporary music selected to inspire a contemplative mystical spirit and a transcendental cosmic wonder.

This descriptive section of EquiPax is not presented as a vested interest promotion but as a restored paradigm for promoting an authentic meaning to the concept of a corporate retreat in search of a management ethic. When one searches the internet for the purpose of locating a corporate retreat center, one is overwhelmed by the numbers of sites primarily focused as a "playground" periphery in a plush management resort center. Inasmuch as the historical significance of the retreat concept evolved out of a need for people to withdraw "from the dangers or difficulties of life" to "a place to which one withdraws for peace" (Cayne, 1989), it is critical that this original meaning be restored to the concept of the corporate retreat and be promoted for executives who may find themselves immersed in the dangers and difficulties of their professional lives.

EXECUTIVE RETREAT LIVING

In this age of corporate ethical learning and interpersonal consulting needs, EquiPax living accommodates Chief Executive and Human Resource Executive Officers with two programs designed for either private and/or corporate retreats in human resource ethical learning and moral resource development training, as presented in this book. Both programs can be integratively accommodated to suit the interests of the respective retreatants.

The Private Retreat Option. This option is primarily focused on the private personal needs or interests of executives and their respective spouses. This interpersonal option is offered for the moral and spiritual development of retreatants in the Retreat Home of EquiPax with engaging discussions of personal moral interests and/or interpersonal moral leadership issues. As a private retreat, this option is designed to accommodate the private interests and needs of respective retreatants and is ecumenically open to executives of any and all faith persuasions and can be conducted as simply focused on business ethical practicing issues and/or developing managerial leadership exemplary profiles. This interpersonal private engagement opens moral development charismatic discourse toward MBE social organizational reconstructive planning and interpersonal involvement action. This private retreat option can be conducted on an extended weekend retreat or on any selected dating appointments conducive to one's personal traveling schedules.

The Corporate Retreat Option. This option is more extensively focused on corporate organizational needs and resource development tracks toward the environmental learning of corporate ethical strategies and ecological living. This option is designed to actively engage retreatants in exploring the comparative ecological environments of the Green Mountains of Vermont and the White Mountains of New Hampshire. The exploratory purpose of this existential retreat *living-learning* option is to engage younger Human Resource organizational trainers to actively experience ecological values *within* the environmental resources of the natural forestry toward applying MBE learning principles within the workforces of their respective training pedagogies among their corporations. This corporate retreat option requires one week of on-site moral development reflexive learning from Volume I with applied ethical learning and aesthetic moral reflecting in the Green Mountains of Vermont with the EquiPax Gallery collection, as viewed in Volume II, and within a climactic ecological tour of the Gallery's White Mountainous Extension Home in New Hampshire.

The moral benefit of these interpersonal MBE leadership options is for the *enduring sequence of their Corporations.*

EXECUTIVE RETREAT OPTIONS

A Retreat Sanctuary for Healing Peace. Had the criminally dissociated executives of this corporate scandalous era, especially the convicted and imprisoned former CEO of Tyco, whose "morally melted" conscience tempted him to the retreat "parties" of dissonant sub-cultures of Italy, retreated to EquiPax, in search for *healing peace*, they might have spared themselves from the prevailing shame of "immorally disturbing dissonance" and the wailing dread of punitive incarcerated existence. But the worst punishment of all the fallen executives of this scandalous era, to use the dialectic counterpart of Erikson's "identity crisis," is that: *"nothing survives of them."*

Survival of the Moral Fittest. As one may have noticed, however, from internet searches for corporate retreat centers, most listings present their promotions with little or nothing of the cultural depth and the morally developed range of the EquiPax offerings. Thus, the above description of these offerings are critically needed to address the socio-economic therapeutic problems of post-traumatic corporate ethical stress disorders which have been erupting within corporate culture throughout the world with moral meltdowns, as viewed with the Murdoch empire of incompetence, the Berlusconi vampire of governance and the EuroZone's breakdown of confidence. In conclusion, the ethical imperative of contemporary applied *praxis* scholarship is, first and foremost, to morally reform the ethos of the multinational corporate culture; and second, to offer business and management schools, with their graduates and interns throughout the world, a new orientation to management studies and curricular development; and third, to offer existing corporate retreat centers a model of ethical and cultural resources for the purpose of morally upgrading their own retreat programs toward the *moral* "survival of the fittest."

From WorldCom through Tyco to Enron and the EuroZone, the global social order has seen many of its corporate institutions wilt, leaving little or no ethical stance or moral strength for the *sequence of generations*. The authenticity of EquiPax as a center for corporate retreats where executives can insure their survival is that it provides instruction and training for *integrated moral leadership*. It is a center where they can "withdraw for peace," re-integrate their personal moral life with their professional management behavior and breathe the *spirit* of MBE into the institutional structures of their corporations. Like Howard Lutnick of Cantor Fitzgerald, a parentally involved CEO who loved his martyred workforce and cared for their bereaving families, as recounted in the last chapter, these *morally reformed* executives will bear an ethical stance and will trace a moral strength that will survive them, leaving a *lasting legacy of leadership integrity*: *"for the sequence of generations."*

END NOTES

1. This account of integrity is a dialectical description of the eighth stage of Erikson's psychosocial life cycle scale. This scale traces personality development through personal growth within the psycho-historical conflicts of one's own challenging situations perceived as critical turning points for "increased vulnerability and

heightened potential" (p. 96). In its developmental analysis, this life cycle scale enjoys some compatibility with the Kohlberg moral development scale, the most elemental and compatible stage of which is the virtue of trust. Identifying this virtue at the beginning of the life cycle as the first critical stage of an infant's need to bond with its mother, Erikson describes trust as ". . . an essential trustfulness of others as well as a fundamental sense of one's own trustworthiness" (p. 96). Justifying the critical importance of this stage at the beginning of life, he defines this basic trust as "the cornerstone of a vital personality" (p.97). As noted above in Chapter 3, trust is the bonding virtue of the social contractual stage 5 of the moral development scale and is vital to personal, social and corporate morality. (From: *Identity: Youth and Crisis* by Erik H. Erikson ©1968 by W.W. Norton & Company, Inc. Used by permission of W.W. Norton & Company.)

2. The insearch experience is a personal quest within the innermost zones of the reflexive self for the *rediscovery of the soul* through depth psychology, ascetic spirituality and the aesthetic beauty of the fine arts. Within the context of the private retreat, "rediscovery" is significantly more illuminating as a *personal and spiritual work of art itself* rather than a clinical analytical work of therapy. (For a critical read on these themes, see Hillman, 1967.)

3. This word is used here in its original Latin significance "to fall away" and in its analogical association with Biblical literature "to lay down" one's life for one's friends (see John 15:13).

4. This analogical description of these *aesthetic reflections* suggests countervailing Biblical themes of *ascetic reflections* based on the "suffering servant" poems in the Book of *Isaias* in Hebrew Scripture and projected to the "Suffering Servant" passion of the "Universal Christ" of the Christian Gospels analogously signifying the Saviour as laying His life down for the ecological salvation of the planet.

5. The EquiPax Gallery Collection holds, on permanent exhibition, a series of paintings and sculptures depicting the desecrated forest by its corporate predators and the re-consecrated forest by its corporate ethically sensitive artists. The exhibition features the works of its international roster from the United States, Canada, France, England, Switzerland, Germany and Romania. (See this International Exposition in the corporate art collection of this study (Guerrette, 2014 Vol. II) on *Ethical Theories and Moral Narratives in Art: A Gallery Tour through the Corporate Moral Forest.*

Managing Moral Development in Sexual Ethics

Inasmuch as the moral development studies of Lawrence Kohlberg are primarily focused in this Volume I on business ethics and applied throughout the MBE study of complex organization management issues and corporate policy formulations of human resources, it can also be particularly helpful for all readers to comprehend the overall holistic scope of *managing applied moral development studies* in sexual ethics within the smaller interactional domains of interpersonal family structures and the wider extra-personal spheres among social companion gender relationships of sexual moral behavior.

The following descriptions of sexual ethics case studies by Thomas Lickona, a contemporary innovative scholar of Lawrence Kohlberg's theories, have been composed with practical moral development analyses of gender relationships as applied sexual-moral interpersonal explanations of the five *praxis* stages of ethical awareness and decision-making activities with personal and individual moral developmental outcomes. These *graphic sexual inter-relational examples* along with the *aesthetic sexual studies* presented in the Appendices of Volume II on *Ethical Theories and Moral Narratives in Art* should help to inspire all readers to become moral leaders in their companies and especially morally sensitive and ethically compassionate parents in their families.

Stages of Moral Reasoning and Sexual Decision Making

Tom Lickona, SUNY Cortland, www.cortland.edu/character

Based on his 20-year longitudinal study and cross-cultural research, Harvard psychologist Lawrence Kohlberg described 5 stages of moral reasoning. See Kohlberg's chapter, "Moral stages and moralization: The cognitive-developmental approach, in T. Lickona, Editor, *Moral Development and Behavior*, New York, Holt, 1976. For a reader-friendly summary and application of Kohlberg's stages to parenting, see T. Lickona, *Raising Good Children*, Bantam, 1983.

Think of these stages as "theories of right and wrong" that we carry around in our heads as children, teenagers, or adults. Each stage or theory has a different idea of *what's right* and a different idea of the reason *why a person should be good.* Each new stage of moral reasoning brings a person a step closer to a fully developed morality of respect for self, others, and society.

The Stages of Moral Reasoning

Ages indicate reasonable developmental expectations for an individual of normal intelligence growing up in a supportive moral environment.

STAGE 0: EGOCENTRIC REASONING (preschool years; around 4)	What's Right:	I should get my own way.
	Reason to be good:	To get rewards and avoid punishments.
STAGE 1: "STAY OUT OF TROUBLE" (around kindergarten age)	What's Right:	I should do what I'm told.
	Reason to be good:	To stay out of trouble.
STAGE 2: LOOK OUT FOR YOURSELF; TIT-FOR-TAT FAIRNESS (early elementary grades)	What's Right:	I should look out for myself but also do for those who do for me.
	Reason to be good:	Self-interest: What's in it for me?
STAGE 3: INTERPERSONAL CONFORMITY; "WHAT WILL OTHERS THINK OF ME?" (middle-to-upper elementary grades; early-to-mid teens)	What's Right:	I should be a nice person and live up to the expectations of people I know and care about.
	Reason to be good:	So others will think well of me (social approval) and I can think well of myself (self-esteem)
STAGE 4: RESPONSIBILITY TO SOCIETY; "I SHOULD	What's Right:	I should fulfill my responsibilities to the social or value system I feel part of (church, my country, etc).

BE A RESPONSIBLE PERSON AND GOOD CITIZEN" (high-school years/late teens/college)	Reason to be good:	To keep society from falling apart and to maintain my self-respect as somebody who meets my obligations.
STAGE 5: RESPECT FOR UNIVERSAL RIGHTS (late teens, early adulthood and later)	What's Right:	I should show the greatest possible respect for the rights and dignity of every individual person and should support a system that protects human rights.

To illustrate Stages 1-5, below are various-stage responses to a moral dilemma: "Faced with pressure from a store's security officer, Should Sharon tell the name of her friend Jill, who has just shoplifted a sweater and beat it out the store?" Note that at the lower stages, the same kind of moral reasoning can be used to justify opposite solutions (we'll see the same thing with regard to sex), but at the higher stages, more mature reasoning points to responsible action.

Stage 1 ("Stay Out of Trouble")

"If Sharon doesn't tell, she's going to be in big trouble herself. She should do what the security officer says."

"If she tells, she's going to be in hot water with Jill."

Stage 2 ("Look Out For Yourself")

"Why should Sharon have to take the rap for Jill? Jill looked out for herself, didn't she?"

"It depends on whether she owes Jill anything. Or on whether she wants Jill to cover for her sometime."

Stage 3 ("What Will Others Think of Me?")

"What kind of a friend would rat on her best friend? Everybody will say she's a fink."

"If she doesn't tell, she can be charged with being an accomplice to the crime. What's that going to do to her reputation?

Stage 4 ("What If Everybody Did It?")

"What kind of a world would it be if everybody went around ripping off everybody else?"

"Friendship is important, but a true friend doesn't cover for you when you do the wrong thing. If Sharon gets caught now, maybe she'll straighten out."

Stage 5 (Respect for Universal Rights)

"Even if everybody didn't go around shoplifting, it would still be wrong. Shoplifting violates the storeowner's rights as a person. That's the reason for the law in the first place—to protect all of our rights."

"Sharon should think of how all people, including poor people, have to pay higher prices because of shoplifting. Jill is disrespecting their rights."

Kohlberg grouped his stages into three levels: *"pre-conventional"* (self-oriented), *"conventional"* (oriented toward the expectations of others), and *"post-conventional"* (oriented toward higher values of universal respect for, and responsibility toward, all persons).

These three levels, and the stages within them, can help us understand how people think about sex and make sexual decisions. In this paper, I'll give actual examples of reasoning about sex at the different levels and stages of development—as well as ways we can talk to young people that (1) connect with their current stage of thinking, and (2) help them grow toward a more mature stage. We'll also look at how adults sometimes reinforce low-level reasoning.

I. PRE-CONVENTIONAL LEVEL: Focus on Self-Interest; Relationships Seen as Tit-for-Tat Exchange

Stage 1: "Stay Out of Trouble"

High school counselor: "I see kids going to the nurse in schools, crying a day after their first sexual experience, and wanting to be tested for AIDS. For some, it's enough to cause them to avoid further sexual involvement."

Stage 2: Look Out for Yourself; Tit-for-Tat Exchange

Recreational sex:
"Sex is pleasure," "It feels good," "My hormones are raging," "I want to do it," "It's my body," "It's OK as long as you use protection"

Jason (28): "In high school, my question was always, 'How far can I go with this girl?' I didn't go all the way, but I used girls. Pornography had an influence on me."

How some adults (both parents and educators) enable early, Stage 2 sex:
Planned Parenthood's promotion of Stage 2 sex-is-fun on its "Teenwire" website (www.teenwire.com, 1998 post):

How are you supposed to ignore your sexual urges when they seem uncontrollably intense? There is a whole universe of sexual activity that doesn't involve penis-in-vagina sex but can be fun, exciting, and fulfilling enough to keep you busy for hours and leave both you and your partner grinning from ear to ear.
Avoid intercourse until you're ready. In the meantime, you have lots of ways to get busy without, y'know—getting busy! Things can get pretty steamy . . . as long as you keep in mind that you will not have intercourse.

Sex as tit-for-tat exchange
"If I give him sex, maybe he'll like me": "If a guy spends money on me or time with me, I owe him sex."

Dodie (20): "I wasn't allowed to date until I turned 16. My first boyfriend was 20. I just assumed I'd have to have sex with him in order to keep him interested. Sex took over every other fun activity; it seemed like sex was all he came around for. I felt used, but I kept hanging on because I felt I'd given him everything I had—myself."

College dorm director: "There are girls in our dorm who have had multiple pregnancies and multiple abortions. The ironic thing is that practically all of them say they *hate* the whole bar scene—if a guy just talks to you, it's like you owe him sex. But these girls have such low self-esteem, they'll settle for any kind of attention."

Stage 2 "hook-up" sex, as described in a New York Times Magazine article:

"If you want it to be a hookup relationship, then you don't call the person for anything except plans to hook up. You don't invite them out with you. You don't call just to say hi. You don't confuse the matter. You just keep it purely sexual, and that way people don't have mixed expectations, and no one gets hurt."

Stage 2 reasons NOT to have sex:

Mary (18), a single mom: "Raising a baby is hard. I have no time to socialize with the few friends I have, and what money I have goes to diapers and formula. You will be sleep-deprived and that once-beautiful figure you had will be replaced with huge hips and stretch marks. In most cases, the father will not be there. My son has not seen his father since the day he was born."

Abortion: Not a quick fix—Mary Paquette, M.D., quoted in *Just For Girls/Just For Guys* magazine, www.humanlife.org: "Abortion is often thought of as a quick fix. No one will have to know this, and you can get on with your life as if nothing ever happened. If this sounds too good to be true—it is. Abortion is a painful option. Women have described it to me as the most awful thing they have ever been through. Women often block out the memory of it and regret having aborted their baby. Not only do these women have lives haunted by their abortion, but they also have an increased risk of infertility, miscarriage, and premature babies. There is also an increased risk of breast cancer in women who have an abortion. If you have had an abortion, there is hope and help. Contact Rachel's Vineyard at:www.rachelsvineyard.org."

II. CONVENTIONAL LEVEL: Focus on Feelings, Relationships, Expectations of Others, Expectations of Self

Stage 3 Looking for Love, Wanting to Please

("I wanted to prove my love for him"), Wanting to Fit In, Wanting to Feel Good About Yourself

Amy (18), can't handle the peer pressure: "In junior high school, I was part of a group where everyone was having sex. I couldn't handle the pressure."

Stage 3 reasons NOT to have sex or to stop having sex

Concern for reputation: "I don't want to get a reputation for being 'easy.'"

A guilty conscience: A 16-year-old boy in California said he stopped having sex with girls when he realized and felt guilty about the pain he was causing: "You see them crying and confused. They say they love you, but you don't love them."

Strong moral values: At the lower, less mature stages of moral reasoning, people reasoning at the same stage can do right or wrong, *depending on their values* (what they consider important).

One Stage 3 teen, whose parents stress the importance of chastity and doing the right thing, might reason, "My parents would be very disappointed in me if they found out I was having sex."

Another Stage 3 teen, whose parents emphasize being popular, might think, "The cool crowd is doing it." Both teens care about the expectations of others, but the first teen orients more to her parents' values, the second teen more to the peer group's values. Wise parents maintain close relationships with their teens so they "have the inside track."

Dan (12), "has his values in place": In 2005, *People* magazine and NBC news conducted a poll of 1,000 American teens ages 13 to 16. By ages 15-16, the percentage of kids experiencing sexual intimacy had risen to 41%. The *People* report included a story about a Pittsburgh mother whose 7th-grade son Dan came home one day and said, "Mom, there is this girl who keeps asking to give me oral sex." He turned her down, but then the next day she *and* her girlfriend gave him another chance. He said no again. The mother said, "He has his values in place. We are parents who make a point of being in our kid's face. Still, I wanted to cry—in fact, I did."

Kurt (age 15), doesn't want to stand out, finds friends who are virgins: "My 17-year-old brother totally regrets having sex before marriage. He says he gets embarrassed when he sees girls at school that he's had sex with. I don't want to have to worry about things like that. I always tell my girlfriends from the beginning that I plan on staying a virgin until I get married. I don't tell too many guys, though. Sometimes it's awkward hanging out with kids who have had sexual relationships. I feel like I stand out. But most of my friends are virgins, so that makes me feel more comfortable."

Concern for the quality of the relationship, Amanda (20): "I lost my virginity when I was 15. My boyfriend and I thought we loved each other. But once we began having sex, it completely destroyed any love we had. I felt he was no longer interested in spending time with me—he was interested in spending time with my body."

Stage 4 of Moral Reasoning

Focus on Becoming Independent of Social Pressure; Maintaining Self-Respect and Self-Control; Having a Sense of Purpose, Responsibility to a Moral or Religious Belief System, and Deeper Understanding of Sex and Love

Mark (23), staying in control by avoiding sexy media: "There's a lot of pressure by the media to have sex, so I pay a lot of attention to what I will and will not subject myself to. I won't turn on steamy television shows like 'Sex in the City' because they're all about sex. I won't even watch certain movies because I know they'll include a sexual affair with some like Sharon Stone. There are simply some images I don't want to have to deal with when the movie ends."

Becoming independent of peer pressure: "Most of my friends know I'm waiting until I get married, and most of them think it's cool. I've had guys say, 'Man, I wish I could go back.' I've also had tons of people roll their eyes when I mention it, and that's fine."

Brandy (20), on the role of her growing faith: "For the past two years, I've been with a boyfriend who is one of the best things that's happened to me. About a year ago, I told him I didn't want to sleep together anymore. My decision had to do with religion. The more I went to church, the stronger my feeling became. The decision not to have sex has brought us closer together. It's something we're determined to accomplish together."

Advice That Supports and Develops Self-Respect Reasoning

Self-respect as "the ultimate contraceptive": "If you respect yourself, your body, and the goals you've set and choose not to have sex, you'll be respected by others for being strong enough to choose that. Self-respect is the ultimate contraceptive."—Susan Bankowski, Campaign for Our Children

A Future Orientation: Looking Forward to Marriage

Hugo (21), "If I can do this, I can keep my marriage commitment": "Sometimes it's tough to keep the commitment I've made to myself. I figure that if I can stick to it until marriage, then I'll have a much better chance of sticking with the marriage. It's almost proof that whatever I choose to do, I'm a strong enough person to follow through with it."

III. POST-CONVENTIONAL LEVEL: Focus on Universal Ethical Principles of Respect and Caring.

Stage 5 Deep Respect for the Rights and Dignity of All Persons

Understanding of Sex as Self-Gift—Part of a Total, Loving Commitment—and Desire to Save Oneself for That Relationship; Understanding of Love As Wanting What is Truly Best for the Other.

Conscience based on respect for others: "If you keep in mind the person you will someday meet and marry, you'll wait for them. In the meantime, you won't do anything to disrespect or hurt a person who will someday be another person's husband or wife. Keep in mind how you will expect a young man to treat your daughter one day. By listening to your conscience in this way, you'll have a good idea of where to draw the line."—Jason Evert.

"Preserve each other's dignity": In her book, *Keep Love Real*, Filipino author Lora Tan-Garcia writes:

If you're a guy, ask yourself, "Do I want some other guy putting his hands all over my future wife?" Then don't put your hands all over someone else's future wife. Same for women. Love each other enough, so that if you do not end up together, you can be proud that you preserved each other's dignity.

Respect for one's future spouse:

"I don't want my wife to sleep with anyone but me, and I want to give her the same respect."—Elijah Martin

Love as total self-gift:

"One of the greatest gifts I will ever be able to give my husband is the total gift of myself. To me it would be a lie to give myself totally to someone before we've made public our permanent commitment to each other. I believe sex is a deep communication, not just between two bodies but between the two complete persons involved."—17-year-old girl

What is the meaning of love? Love Waits (a pamphlet):

Love is patient; love is kind. Love wants what is best for another person. Love will never cross the line between what's right and wrong. It's wrong to put one another in danger of having to deal with hard choices, choices that could change your lives forever.

Having sex before marriage may feel right for the moment. But the possible costs of an unexpected pregnancy, abortion, and sexually transmitted disease—as well as the deep hurts that can come from a broken relationship—outweigh the feelings of the moment. The feelings are temporary; their consequences are long-lasting.

All good things are worth waiting for. Waiting until marriage to have sex is a mature decision to control your desires. If you are getting to know someone—or are in a relationship—remember: If it's love, love waits.

"If you care about your future children, you will wait."

Brad Wilcox, Ph.D., "A Scientific Review of Abstinence and Abstinence Programs" (2008): "Programs that present a clear and compelling normative [value-based] message to young people—e.g., that tell teens to abstain for the sake of their partners and any future children they might conceive—are more likely to influence sexual behavior than programs that just provide participants with information."

A growing body of research finds that children and teenagers who grow up in a marriage, with their biological father in the home, are more likely to: (1) do well in school; (2) achieve a higher level of education; (3) avoid being suspended or expelled from school; (4) stay free of drug abuse; (5) avoid teen pregnancy; juvenile delinquency, running away, and suicide; and (6) have generally better physical and emotional health.

Stage 5's Sense of Social Responsibility: "I am my brother's keeper."

"I stood by silently and watched two close friends wreck their lives because of the wrong decisions about sex. One got pregnant, struggled to raise her child, and had to give up her dreams of college. The other got pregnant, had an abortion, and had a mental breakdown from the guilt. When I saw how much they were suffering, I prayed for them— but also for myself. My previous silence on chastity no longer seemed to be 'tolerant' and 'open-minded.' It was actually cowardly and selfish—taking good care of myself while letting them risk their sexuality, their spirituality, and their futures. Might I have made a difference if I had said something? Shouldn't I have at least tried? I no longer subscribe to the idea that people who speak out about chastity are trying to 'force their ideas' on others. I *am* my brother's keeper."
(Mary Ann Kurey, *Standing With Courage*)

Recommended resources:

The War on Intimacy
How Comprehensive Sex Ed
Sabotages Committed Relationships
& Our Nation's Health

Richard A. Panzer, Ph.D. and Mary-Anne Mosack
©2009 Center for Relationship Intelligence LLC
Center for Relationship Intelligence LLC (cenedmedia@aol.com)

Sex, Love, & You: Making the Right Decision

Tom & Judy Lickona
William Boudreau, M.D.
Ave Maria Press (2003)

REFERENCES

Adeola, Francis O. (2012) *Industrial Disasters, Toxic Waste and Community Impact: Health Effects and Environmental Justice Struggles around the Globe*, Lanham, Maryland: Lexington Books.

Allport, F. H. (1962) "A structuronomic conception of behavior: individual and collective. I. Structural theory and the master problem of social psychology," *Journal of Abnormal and Social Psychology*, vol. 64, 3-30.

Amaeshi, Kenneth and Nnodim, Paul (2012) *Corporate Social Responsibility, Entrepreneurship, and Innovation*, London: Routledge.

Anderson, Carl (2010) *Shaping a Generation*, Closing Bell Interview with Maria Bartiromo, on the Knights of Columbus Marist Poll, January 22, CNBC.

Anderson. Charles H. (1974) *The Political Economy of Social Class*, Englewood Cliffs, NJ: Prentice-Hall.

Anderson, Ryan T. (2012) "Ethical stem-cell researcher wins Nobel Prize for Medicine" in The Foundry: The Heritage Network, Conservative Policy News Blog, October 9, The Heritage Foundation.

Arendt Hannah (1966) "On the human condition" in *The Evolving Society*, ed. Mary Alice Hinton, New York: Institute of Cybernetical Research, pp. 213-219.

Argyris, Chris (1990) *Overcoming Organizational Defenses: Facilitating Organizational Learning*, Boston: Allyn & Bacon.

————. (1991) "Teaching smart people how to learn," *Harvard Business Review* May-June, 99-109.

————. (1993) *Knowledge for Action: A Guide to Overcoming Barriers to Organizational Change*, San Francisco: Jossey-Bass Publishers.

Atran, Scott (2004) *In Gods We Trust: The Evolutionary Landscape of Religion*, New York: Oxford University Press.

Ayed. Nahlah (2010) *Catholic Church Scandal Hits Germany*, CBC.ca Video, March 28.

Baker, Thomas L. and Hunt, Tammy G. (2003) "An exploratory investigation into the effects of team composition on moral orientation," *Journal of Managerial Issues*, vol.15, 106-114.

Balassa, Bela (1961) *The Theory of Economic Integration*, The Irwin Series in Economics, Homewood, Illinois: Richard D. Irwin, Inc.

Barnard, Chester (1938) *The Functions of the Executive*, Cambridge, MA: Harvard University Press.

Baum, V. (1974) *Ethics as a Behavioral Science*, Springfield, IL: Charles Thomas.

Baxter, G. D. and Rarick, C. A. (1987) "Education for the moral development of managers: Kohlberg's stages of moral development and integrative education," *Journal of Business Ethics*, vol.6, 243-248.

Beauchamp, Tom L. (1983) "Ethical theory and its application to business," in Tom L. Beauchamp and Norman E. Bowie (eds.), *Ethical Theory and Business*, 2nd edn., Englewood Cliffs, NJ: Prentice-Hall.

Bebeau, Muriel J. (2002) "The Defining Issues Test and the four component model: contributions to professional education," *Journal of Moral Education* 31(3), 271-296.

Beck, Eckardt, (1979) "The Love Canal Tragedy," EPA Journal, January.

Becker, Corne J. (2010) "The turn to spirituality and environmental leadership" in Benjamin W. Redekop, (ed.), *Leadership for Environmental Sustainability*, London: Routledge.

Bennis, Warren G. (1966) Changing Organizations, Cambridge, MA: M.I.T. Press.

Bennis, Warren G., Benne, Kenneth D. and Chin, Robert (1969a) *The Planning of Change*, 2nd edn., New York: Holt, Rinehart and Winston.

Bennis, Warren G. (1969b) *Organization Development: Its Nature, Origins, and Prospects*, Reading, MA: Addison-Wesley Publishing Co.

Benson, J. Kenneth (1977a) "Innovation and crisis in organizational analysis," pp. 5-18 in J. K. Benson, ed., *Organizational Analysis: Critique and Innovation*, Beverly Hills, California: Sage.

————. (1977b) "Organizations: a dialectical view," *Administrative Science Quarterly* 22: 1-21.

Berg, Per-Olof (1986) "Symbolic management of human resources," *Human Resource Management*, vol.25, no.4, 557-579.

Berger, Peter L. and Luckman, Thomas (1967) The Social Construction of Reality: A Treatise in the Sociology of Knowledge, New York: Doubleday.

Bergson, Henri (1935) *The Two Sources of Morality and Religion,* London: Macmillan and Company.

Bernstein, Richard J. (1971) *Praxis and Action: Contemporary Philosophies of Human Activity,* Philadelphia: University of Pennsylvania Press.

Berry, Thomas (2006) *Evening Thoughts: Reflecting on Earth as Sacred Community,* Sierra Club Books, Berkeley: University of California Press.

Birsch, Douglas and Fielder, John H., Eds., (1994) *The Ford Pinto Case: A Study in Applied Ethics, Business and Technology,* Albany: State University of New York Press.

Bittle, Celestine, N. (1950) *Man and Morals: Ethics,* Milwaukee: Bruce Publishing Company.

————. (1953) *God and His Creatures: Theodicy,* Milwaukee: Bruce Publishing Company.

Blair, Tony (2008) *Tony Blair's Speech to Launch the Faith Foundation,* Tony Blair Speeches, Archives (http://tonyblairoffice.org) 30 May 2008, London: The Office of Tony Blair.

Blasi, Augusto (1980) "Bridging moral cognition and moral action: a critical review of the literature," *Psychological Bulletin,* vol. 88, 1-45.

————. (1984) "Moral identity: its role in moral functioning," in W. M. Kurtines and J. L. Gewirtz (eds.), *Morality, Moral Behavior, and Moral Development,* New York: Wiley.

Blenkinsopp, Joseph (1969) *Sexuality and the Christian Tradition,* Dayton, Ohio: Pflaum Press.

Blumberg, P. (1973) *Industrial Democracy: The Sociology of Participation,* New York: Schocken Books.

Blumer, Herbert (1947) "Sociological theory in industrial relations," *American Sociological Review,* June, 271-278.

————. (1969) *Symbolic Interactionism: Perspective and Method,* Englewood Cliffs, NJ: Prentice-Hall.

Bogle, John C. (2005) *The Battle for the Soul of Capitalism,* New Haven: Yale University Press.

Boje, David M. (1991) "Learning storytelling: storytelling to learn management skills," *Journal of Management Education,* vol. 15, no. 3.

Bolton, Roger (2009) *The Dynamics of Public Trust in Business – Emerging Opportunities for Leaders: A Call to Action to Overcome the Present Crisis of Trust in Business,* Business Roundtable Institute for Corporate Ethics, Arthur W. Page Society.

Bowen, Michael G. and Power, F. Clark (1993) "The moral manager: communicative ethics and the Exxon Valdez disaster," *Business Ethics Quarterly,* vol.3, no.2, 97-115.

Boyd, Dwight R. (1984) "The principle of principles," in W. M. Kurtines and J. L. Gewirtz (eds.), *Morality, Moral Behavior, and Moral Development,* New York: Wiley.

Boyett, Joseph H. and Conn, Henry P. (1988) *Maximum Performance Management: How to Manage and Compensate People to Meet World Competition,* Macomb, IL: Glenbridge.

Braito, Rita, Paulson, Steve and Klonglan, Gerald (1972) "Domain consensus: a key variable in interorganizational analysis," in M. B. Brinkerhoff and P. R. Kunz (eds.), *Complex Organizations and Their Environments,* Dubuque, IA: Brown.

Brinkerhoff, Merlin B. (ed.) (1984) *Work Organizations and Society: Comparative Convergences,* Westport, CT: Greenwood Press.

Brinkerhoff, Merlin B. and Kunz, P.R. (eds.) (1972) *Complex Organizations and Their Environments,* Dubuque, IA: Brown.

Brown, Paul B. (2006) "What's Off-Line," (Personal Business Page: Executive Pursuits) in *The New York Times,* December 30, 2006.

Buber, Martin (1958) *I and Thou,* 2nd ed., New York: Charles Scribner's Sons.

Buffett, Warren (2008) *The Essays of Warren Buffet: Lessons for Corporate America,* 2nd rev. ed. Lawrence A. Cunningham, ed., Cardozo Law Review: New York.

Candee, Daniel (1985) "Classical ethics and live patient simulations in the moral education of health care professionals," in M. W. Berkowitz and F. Oser (eds.), *Moral Education: Theory and Application,* Hillsdale, NJ: Lawrence Erlbaum.

Carlo, William E. (1967) *Philosophy, Science and Knowledge,* Milwaukee: Bruce Publishing Company.

Carlson, Allen (1984) "Appreciation and the Natural Environment," in Patricia H. Werhane, ed. *Philosophical Issues in Art,* Chapter 13: New Approaches in Art Theory, Englewood Cliffs, NJ: Prentice-Hall.

Cayne, Bernard, S. ed., (1989) *The New Lexicon Webster's Dictionary of the English Language,* Encyclopedic Edition, New York: Lexicon Publications.

Cohen, Andrew (2009 a) "Being and Becoming" *Enlighten Next Magazine* www.enlightennext.org Cohen, Andrew (2009 b) *Being and Becoming,* Enlighten Next, Jan. 10, YouTube.

Colby, Anne and Kohlberg, Lawrence (1987) *The Measurement of Moral Judgment*, vol .I, Cambridge: Cambridge University Press.

Collier, Myles (2012) "Vatican Denounces Sister Margaret Farley's Book on Sexual Relations: A Harm to the Faithful" in *The Christian Post* (North America) June 4, 2012.

Cooley, Charles Horton (1902) *Human Nature and the Social Order*, New York: Charles Scribner's Sons.

Cooper, Anderson (2007) "Planet in Peril," (AC 360), *A CNN World Wide Investigation: Anderson Cooper, Jeff Corwin, and Dr. Sanjay Gupta Explore the Earth's Environmental Issues*, Atlanta: Cable News Network.

————. (2010) AC 360 CNN News Report, July 12.

————. (2012) AC 360 CNN News Report, December 21.

Curwen, Lesley, (2003) "The Corporate Conscience: Sherron Watkins, Enron Whistleblower," *The Guardian*, June 21, 2003.

Cushman, Fiery, Young, Liane, and Greene, Joshua D., (2010) "Multi-system moral psychology," in The Moral Psychology Research Group, John M. Doris, ed. *The Moral Psychology Handbook*, New York: Oxford University Press.

Dahrendorf, Ralph (1959) *Class and Class Conflict in Industrial Society Stanford*, CA: Stanford University Press.

Davidson, Marilyn (1992) *Shattering the "Glass Ceiling": The Woman Manager*, London: Chapman.

Day, Robert A. and Day, Joanne V. (1977) "A review of the current state of negotiated order theory: an appreciation and a critique," in J. K. Benson (ed.), *Organization Analysis: Critique and Innovation*, Beverly Hills, CA: Sage.

Deetz, S. A. (1983) "Keeping the conversation going: the principle of dialectic ethics," *Communications*, vol. 7.

Dewart, Leslie, (1967) *The Future of Belief: Theism in a World Come of Age*, London: Burns and Oates.

Dilenschneider, Robert L. (1990) *Power and Influence: Mastering the Art of Persuasion*, New York: Prentice Hall Press.

Dill, William R. (1958) "Environment as an influence on managerial autonomy," *Administrative Science Quarterly*, vol. 2 (March) 409-443.

Doris, John M. ed., (2010) *The Moral Psychology Handbook*, The Moral Psychology Research Group, New York: Oxford University Press.

Drucker, Peter F. (1954) *The Practice of Management*, New York: HarperCollins.

———. (1985) Innovation and Entrepreneurship, New York: HarperCollins.

Duckett, Laura J. and Ryden, Muriel B. (1994) "Education for ethical nursing practice," in J. R. Rest and D. Narvaez (eds.), *Moral Development in the Professions: Psychology and Applied Ethics*, Hillsdale, NJ: Lawrence Erlbaum.

Edwards, Mark (2011) *Organizational Transformation for Sustainability: An Integral Metatheory*, New York: Routledge.

Eliade, Mircea (1969) *Cosmos and History: The Myth of the Eternal Return*, New York: Harper and Row.

Emler, Nicholas and Hogan, Robert (1991) "Moral psychology and public policy," in W. Kurtines and J. L. Gewirtz (eds.), *Handbook of Moral Behavior and Development*, Volume 3: *Application*, Hillsdale, NJ: Lawrence Erlbaum Associates.

Erikson, Dan (2010) *Haitian Money Trail* (CNN Interview by Anderson Cooper 360, February 11, Video and Transcript).

Erikson, Erik H. (1963) *Childhood and Society* (2nd ed.), New York: Norton.

———. (1968) *Identity, Youth and Crisis*, New York: Norton.

———. (1977) *Toys and Reasons: Stages in the Ritualization of Experience*, New York: Norton.

Etzioni, Amitai (1960) "New directions in the study of organizations and society," *Social Research*, vol. 27, 223-228.

———. (1961/1975) *A Comparative Analysis of Complex Organizations*, New York: The Free Press.

———. (1988) *The Moral Dimension: Toward a New Economics*, New York: The Free Press.

Evan, William M. (1972) "The organization set: toward a theory of interorganizational relations," in M. B. Brinkerhoff and P. R. Kunz (eds.), *Complex Organizations and Their Environments*, Dubuque, IA: Brown.

Faber, David (2008) CNBC *Interview with Alan Greenspan*, September, Englewood Cliffs, N.J.

Faber, David (2009) *The House of Cards* CNBC Documentary, Englewood Cliffs, N.J.

Farley, Margaret (2006) *Just Love: A Framework for Christian Sexual Ethics*, London: Continuum International Publishing Group.

Farr, James L. and Middlebrooks, Carolyn L. (1990) "Enhancing motivation to participate in professional development," in S. L. Willis and S. S. Dubin (eds.), *Maintaining Professional Competence*, San Francisco: Jossey-Bass.

Fayerweather, John, ed. (1976) "Multinational corporations in world development," Department of Economic and Social Affairs, United Nations, New York (1973) UN Document ST/ECA/190 in *International Business Policy and Administration*: A Compendium of Experience, Concepts and Research from *The International Executive*.

Ferguson, Naill (2008) *The Ascent of Money: A Financial History of the World*, New York: The Penguin Press.

Ferguson, Naill and Zacharia, Fareed (2008) Fareed Zacharia GPS (Global Public Square) CNN Transcripts (January 18).

Fletcher, Joseph (1966) *Situation Ethics*, Philadelphia: Westminster Press.

———. (1967) *Moral Responsibility: Situation Ethics at Work*, Philadelphia: Westminster Press.

Fontinell, Eugene (1986) Self, God, and Immortality: *A Jamesian Investigation*, Philadelphia: Temple University Press.

Forester, J. (1985) "The applied turn in contemporary critical theory," in J. Forester (ed.), *Critical Theory and Public Life*, Cambridge, MA: MIT Press.

Fort, Timothy L. (1998) "The brothers Karamazov: responsibility in business ethics," in *The Moral Imagination: How Literature and Film Can Stimulate Ethical Reflection in the Business World*, South Bend, Indiana: University of Notre Dame Press.

Fort, Timothy L. and Schipani, C. (2000) "Corporate governance in a global environment," in *Vanderbilt Journal of Transnational Law*, 33:829-876.

Fort, Timothy L. (2001) *Ethics and Governance: Business as Mediating Institutions*, Oxford University Press.

———. (2007) *Principles and Practices for a Model Business Ethics Program*, Business Round Table Institute.

Fowler, James W. (1981) *Stages of Faith: The Psychology of Human Development and the Quest for Meaning*, San Francisco: Harper and Row.

———. (1983) "Stages of faith," *Psychology Today*, vol.11, 56-62.

———. (1984) *Becoming Adult, Becoming Christian: Adult Development and Christian Faith*, San Francisco: Harper and Row.

———. (1986) "Faith and the structuring of meaning," in C. Dykstra and S. Parks (eds.), *Faith Development and Fowler*, Birmingham, AL: Religious Education Press.

————. (2001) "Faith development theory and the postmodern challenges," *International Journal for the Psychology of Religion*, vol.11, no. 3, 159-172.

Freeman, R. Edward, Harrison, Jeffrey S., and Wicks, Andrew C., (2007) Managing for Stakeholders: Survival, Reputation, and Success, New Haven: Yale University Press.

Fromm, Erich (1956) *The Art of Loving*, New York: Harper and Row: Colophon Books.

Galston, William A. (2005) "Catholics, Jews & Stem Cells: When believers beg to differ," *Commonweal*, A Review of Religion, Politics and Culture, May 20 vol. CXXXII no. 10.

Gasparino, Charles (2005) *Blood on the Street: The Sensational Inside Story of How Wall Street Analysts Duped a Generation of Investors*, New York: The Free Press.

Geertz, Clifford (1973) *The Interpretation of Cultures*, New York: Basic Books.

Gellerman, Saul W. (1986) "Why 'good' managers make bad ethical choices," *Harvard Business Review*, July-August, 85-90.

Gibbs, J. C. (1977) "Kohlberg's stages of moral judgment: a constructive critique," *Harvard Educational Review*, vol.47, 43-61.

Gilligan, Carol (1982) *In a Different Voice: Psychological Theory and Women's Development*, Cambridge, MA: Harvard University Press.

Goffman, Erving (1955) "On face-work: an analysis of ritual elements in social interaction," *Psychiatry*, vol. 18, 213-231.

————. (1959) *The Presentation of Self in Everyday Life*, New York: Doubleday.

————. (1963) *Behavior in Public Places*, New York: Free Press.

————. (1971) *Relations in Public*, New York: Basic Books.

Goldman, Paul and Van Houten, Donald R. (1977) "Managerial strategies and the worker: a Marxist analysis of bureaucracy," in J. K. Benson (ed.), *Organizational Analysis: Critique and Innovation*, Sage Contemporary Social Science Issues 37, Beverly Hills, CA: Sage.

Goodpaster, Kenneth E. (1983) "The concept of corporate responsibility," *Journal of Business Ethics*, vol. 2, 1-22.

————. (1984) *Ethics in Management* (Course Module Series), Division of Research, Harvard Business School, Boston.

Goodpaster, Kenneth E. and Matthews, John B., Jr. (1982) "Can a corporation have a conscience?" *Harvard Business Review*, January-February, 132.

Gordon, John C. and Berry, Joyce K. (2006) *Environmental Leadership Equals Essential Leadership*, New Haven: Yale University Press.

Gore, Albert, (2007) *An Inconvenient Truth: The Crisis of Global Warming*, New York: Viking.

Gouldner, Alvin W. (1969) "Anti-Minotaur: the myth of a value-free sociology." in Warren G. Bennis, Kenneth D. Benne and Robert Chin (eds.), *The Planning of Change*, 2nd ed., New York: Holt, Rinehart and Winston.

————. (1970) *The Coming Crisis of Western Sociology*, New York: Basic Books.

Goulet, Denis (1974) *A New Moral Order: Development Ethics and Liberation Theology*, Maryknoll, New York: Orbis Books.

Graves, Phillip E. (2007) *Environmental Economics: A Critique of Benefit-Cost Analysis* Lanham, Maryland: Rowman and Littlefield.

Griffin, Drew and Fitzpatrick David (2010) "Hero skipper ignored pirate warnings, crew says" CNN Special Investigative Unit, May 25.

Griffin, Emile (1993) *The Reflective Executive: A Spirituality of Business and Enterprise*, New York: Crossroad.

Griggs, Walter H. and Manring, Susan (1986) "Increasing the effectiveness of technical professionals," *Management Review* (May) 62-64.

Guerrette, Richard H., (1973) *A New Identity for the Priest: Toward an Ecumenical Ministry*, New York: Paulist Press.

————. (1974) "The Re-Identity of the Priest: An Organizational Solution," in The Church as Institution, Part III: The Sociology of Ecclesiastical Institutions, Gregory Baum and Andrew Greeley, eds., Sociology of Religion, Nijmegen: The Netherlands.

————. (1981) *The Emmanuel Servant Community: A Case Study of a Social Movement Organization*, unpublished doctoral dissertation, London, Ann Arbor, MI: University Microfilm International.

————. (1986) "Environmental integrity and corporate responsibility," *Journal of Business Ethics*, vol. 5, 409-415.

————. (1988) "Corporate ethical consulting: developing management strategies for corporate ethics," *Journal of Business Ethics*, vol.7, 373-380.

————. (1994) "Management by ethics: A new paradigm and model for corporate ethics," in Alan Lewis and Karl-Eric Warneryd (eds.), *Ethics and Economic Affairs*, London: Routledge.

————. (2014) *Ethical Theories and Moral Narratives in Art: An Aesthetic Gallery Tour through the Corporate Moral Forest*, Volume II, Lanham, MD: University Press of America, Hamilton Books.

Guthey, Eric (2004) "New economy Romanticism, narratives of corporate personhood, and the antimanagerial impulse," in (eds.) Kenneth Lipartito and David B.Sicilia, Part III: The Business of Identity, *Constructing Corporate America: History, Politics, Culture*, New York: Oxford University Press.

Habermas, Jurgen (1979) *Communication and the Evolution of Society*, Boston: Beacon Press.

————. (1984) *The Theory of Communicative Action: Reason and the Rationalization of Society*, Boston: Beacon Press.

————. (1990a) "Justice and solidarity: on the discussion concerning stage 6," in T. E. Wren (ed.), *The Moral Domain: Essays in the Ongoing Discussion between Philosophy and the Social Sciences*, Cambridge, MA: MIT Press.

————. (1990b) *Moral Consciousness and Communicative Action*, Cambridge, MA: MIT Press.

Hackman, J. Richard (1986) "The psychology of self-management in organizations," in M. S. Pallak and R. Perloff (eds), *Psychology and Work: Productivity, Change and Employment*, Washington, DC: American Psychological Association.

Hagar, Mark (1985) "Personification of the business corporation," University of Pittsburgh Law Review 50:2, 1471-1475..

Hall, W. David (2006) "The Economy of the Gift: Paul Ricoeur's Poetic Redescription of Reality" in *Literature and Theology* vol. 20, no. 2, June: 189-204.

Hamilton, Stephen F., Basseches, Michael and Richards, Francis A. (1985) "Participatory-democratic work and adolescents' mental health," *American Journal of Community Psychology*, vol.13, no.4, 467-486.

Hanson, Kirk O. (2006) "Perspectives on global moral leadership," in *Moral Leadership: The Theory and Practice of Power, Judgment, and Policy*, ed. Deborah L. Rhode, Forward by Warren Bennis, Jossey-Bass, Wiley Imprint:San Francisco.

Harding, Carol Gibb and Snyder, Kenneth (1991) "Tom, Huck, and Oliver Stone as advocates in Kohlberg's just community: theory-based strategies for moral education," *Adolescence*, vol. 26, no.102, 319-329.

Haste, Helen (1990) "Moral responsibility and moral commitment: the integration of affect and cognition," in T. E. Wren (ed.), *The Moral Domain: Essays in the Ongoing Discussion between Philosophy and the Social Sciences*, Cambridge, MA: MIT Press.

Hausman, Daniel M. and McPherson, Michael S. (1993) "Taking ethics seriously: economics and contemporary moral philosophy," *Journal of Economic Literature*, vol. XXXI, no.2, 671-731.

Healey, Joseph P. (2013) *The Last Lectures of William E. Carlo*, Immaculata University: Immaculata, PA. (library.immaculata.edu/HealeyJP2013.pdf).

Hertzberg, F. (1968) "One more time: how do you motivate employees?"*Harvard Business Review*, vol. 46, 53-62.

Hesse, Helmut (1994) "Comment on Deepak Lal, 'Poverty and development' " in Horst Siebert (ed.), *The Ethical Foundations of the Market Economy, International Workshop*, Kiel Institute of World Economics, University of Kiel, Tubingen: J. C. B. Mohr.

Hesselbein, Frances (2010) "How did Peter Drucker see corporate responsibility," *Harvard Business Review*" Guest Edition: "What Does Business Owe the World?"

Heydebrand, Wolf (1977) "Organizational contradictions in public bureaucracies: toward a Marxian theory of organizations," in J. K. Benson (ed.), *Organizational Analysis: Critique and Innovation*, Sage Contemporary Social Science Issue 37, Beverly Hills, CA: Sage.

Higgins, Ann and Gordon, Frederick (1985) "Work climate and socio-moral development in two worker-owned companies," in M. W. Berkowitz and F. Oser (eds.), *Moral Education: Theory and Application*, Hillsdale, NJ: Lawrence Erlbaum Associates.

Hillman, James (1967) *Insearch: Psychology and Religion*, New York: Charles Scribner's Sons.

Hills, Roderick M. (1976) "Doing business abroad: The disclosure dilemma,"*Yale Law Report*, Fall issue, p. 6.

Hirsch, Fred (1976) *Social Limits to Growth*, Cambridge, MA: Harvard University Press.

Hogan, Robert, Raskin, R. and Fazzini, D. (1988) *The Dark Side of Charisma*, unpublished manuscript, Tulsa Institute of Behavioral Sciences.

Holmstrom, Bengt (1979) "Moral hazards and observability," *Bell Journal of Economics*, vol.10, no.1, 74-91.

————. (1982) "Moral hazard in teams," *Bell Journal of Economics*, vol. 13, 324-340.

Horowitz, David (1970) "Social science or ideology," *Berkeley Journal of Sociology*, vol. XV, 1-10.

Jacoby, Jill B. and Jai, Xia (2010) "Artists as transformative leaders for sustainability," in Benjamin W. Redekop, ed., *Leadership for Environmental Sustainability*, New York: Routledge.

James, William (1892) *Psychology*, New York: Henry Holt and Co.

Johannesen, Richard L. (1983) *Ethics in Human Communication*, 2nd edn., Prospect Heights, IL: Waveland Press.

Johnson, Mark (2008) *Playing for Change: Peace through Music*, Transcript in Bill Moyers Journal, on PBS.org, October 24.

Jones, Alexander, Gen. Ed. (1966) *The Jerusalem Bible*, New York: Doubleday and Company, Inc.

Kanter, Rosabeth Moss (2009) *SuperCorp: How Vanguard Companies Create Innovation, Profits, Growth, and Social Good*, New York: Crown Business: Random House.

Katz, Claire Elise (2005) "Raising Cain: The problem of evil and the question of responsibility," *Cross Currents*, vol. 55, no. 215-233.

Katz, Daniel and Kahn, Robert L. (1972) "Organizations and the system concept," in M. B. Brinkerhoff and P. R. Kunz (eds.), *Complex Organizations and Their Environments*, Dubuque, IA: Brown.

Katz, Daniel and Kahn, Robert L. (1978) *The Social Psychology of Organizations*, 2nd edn, New York: Wiley.

Khuzami, Robert (2009) *Testimony Concerning Mortgage Fraud, Securities Fraud and the Financial Meltdown: Prosecuting Those Responsible*, United States Senate Committee on the Judiciary, December 9.

Kidder, Rushworth M. (2005) *Moral Courage*, New York: HarperCollins.

King, Leslie and McCarthy, Deborah eds. (2005) *Environmental Sociology from Analysis to Action* Lanham, Maryland: Rowman and Littlefield.

Klein, Donald (1966) "Some notes on the dynamics of resistance to change: The defender role" in *Concepts for Social Change*, Goodwin Watson, Ed. Cooperative Project for Educational Development Series, Vol. I. National Training Laboratories, Washington, D.C.

Koestenbaum, Peter (2002) *Leadership: The Inner Side of Greatness, A Philosophy for Leaders*, 2nd edn, San Francisco: Jossey-Bass.

Kohlberg, Lawrence (1971) "Indoctrination versus relativity in value education," *Zygon*, vol. 6, 285-310.

Kohlberg, Lawrence, Scharf, Peter and Hickey, Joseph (1972) *The Justice Structure of the Prison: A Theory and an Intervention*, Cambridge: Department of Education and Social Psychology, Graduate School of Education Harvard University.

Kohlberg, Lawrence (1973) "The claim to moral adequacy of a highest stage of moral judgment," *Journal of Philosophy*, vol.70, 630-646.

Kohlberg, Lawrence et al. (1975) *The Just Community School: The Theory and the Cambridge Cluster School Experiment*, Harvard University Graduate School of Education (ERIC Doc. Reproduction Services, ED 223 511), Cambridge, MA.

————, (1976) "Moral stages and moralization: The cognitive developmental approach in T. Lickona (ed.) Moral Development and Behavior: Theory, Research and Social Issues, Holt, Rinehart and Winston.

————. (1981, 1984) *Essays on Moral Development*, Vol.I: *The Philosophy of Moral Development*, Vol. II: *The Psychology of Moral Development*, New York: Harper & Row.

Kohlberg, Lawrence and Candee, Daniel (1984) "The relationship of moral judgment to moral action," in W. M. Kurtines and J. L. Gewirtz (eds.), *Morality, Moral Behavior, and Moral Development*, New York: Wiley.

————, (1986) "The just community approach to corrections,"*Journal of Correctional Education*, vol.37, no. 2, 54-58.

Kohlberg, Lawrence, Boyd, Dwight R. and Levine, Charles (1990) "The return of stage 6: its principle and moral point of view," in T. E. Wren (ed.), *The Moral Domain: Essays in the Ongoing Discussion between Philosophy and the Social Sciences*, Cambridge, MA: MIT Press.

Krause, Elliot (1977) *Power and Illness*, New York: Elsevier.

Krugman, Paul (2009) *The Conscience of a Liberal*, New York: W. W. Norton and Company.

Kuhn, Thomas S. (1970) *The Structure of Scientific Revolutions*, 2nd edn., enlarged, Chicago: University of Chicago Press.

Kung, Guido, (1985) "The postconventional level of moral development: psychology or philosophy?" in M. W. Berkowitz and F. Oser (eds.), *Moral Education: Theory and Application*, Hillsdale, NJ: Lawrence Erlbaum.

Kung, Hans, (1991) *Global Responsibility:In Search of a New World Ethic*, New York: Crossroad.

————. (1995) *Judaism: Between Yesterday and Tomorrow*, New York: Continuum.

————. (1996) *Christianity: Essence, History and Future*, New York: Continuum.

————. (1998) *A Global Ethic for Global Politics and Economics*, New York: Oxford University Press.

————. (2004) "Hopeful realist Hans Kung points pathway to global ethic" (Profile interview by Patricia Lefevere) in *National Catholic Reporter*, vol. 40, no. 38 (Sept. 3).

————. (2009) *The Global Economic Crisis Requires A Global Ethic: The Manifesto For A Global Economic Ethic*, no. 3 "A Failure of Moral Virtues", Symposium: Launching of the Manifesto, New York: www.globaleconomicethic.org).

Kung, Hans, and Ching, Julia, (1989) *Christianity and Chinese Religions*, New York: Doubleday.

Kung, Hans, van Ess, Josef, von Stietencron, Heinrich, and Bechert, Heinz, (1994) *Christianity and the World Religions: Paths to Dialogue with Islam, Hinduism and Buddhism*, New York: Orbis.

Kung, Hans, and Kuschel, Karl-Josef, (1994) *A Global Ethic: The Declaration of the Parliament of the World's Religions*, New York: Continuum International Publishing Group.

Kung, Hans, (ed.) (1996) *Yes to a Global Ethic: Voices from Religion and Politics*, New York: Continuum.

Kung, Hans, and Schmidt, Helmut (eds.) (1998) *A Global Ethic and Global Responsibilities: Two Declarations*, London: SCM Press, Ltd.

Kurtines, William M. (1984) "Moral behavior as rule-governed behavior: a psychosocial role-theoretical approach to moral behavior and development," in W. M. Kurtines and J. L. Gewirtz (eds.), *Morality, Moral Behavior, and Moral Development*, New York: Wiley.

Kurtines, William M., Mayock, Ellen, Pollard, Steven R., Lamza, Teresita and Carlo, Gustavo (1991) "Social and moral development from the perspective of psychosocial theory," in W. M. Kurtines and J. L. Gewirtz (eds.), *Handbook of Moral Behavior and Development*,. Volume 1: *Theory*, Hillsdale, NJ: Lawrence Erlbaum.

Ladner, Gerhart B. (1959) *The Idea of Reform: Its Impact on Christian Thought and Action in the Age of the Fathers*, Cambridge, MA: Harvard University Press.

Lal, Deepak, (1994), "Poverty and development," in Horst Siebert, ed.,*The Ethical Foundations of the Market Economy: International Workshop*, Kiel Institute of World Economics, University of Kiel, Tubingen: J. C. B. Mohr.

Lanza, Robert and Klimanskaya, Irina (2008) *Essential Stem Cell Methods*, New York: Academic Press Elsevier.

Lanza, Robert, Klimanskaya, Irina, et al. (2008) "Human embryonic stem cell lines generated without embryonic destruction," Cell Stem Cell 2 (2): 113-117, February.

Lauer, Robert H., ed. (1976) Social Movements and Social Change, Carbondale, Illinois, Southern Illinois University Press.

Lawler, Edward (1986) *High Involvement Management*, San Francisco: Jossey-Bass.

Lawson, Robert W. (1988) "Two men with a corporate conscience,"*Vermont Business Magazine*, May, 16-18.

Levinas, Emmanuel (1998) "Useless suffering," in *Entre Nous*, trans. by Michael B. Smith and Barbara Harshav, New York: Columbia University Press, 91-101.

Levine, Charles (1976) "Role-taking standpoint and adolescent usage of Kohlberg's conventional stages of moral reasoning," *Journal of Personality and Social Psychology*, vol. 34, 41-46.

Levine, Sol and White, Paul E. (1972) "Exchange as a conceptual framework for the study of interorganizational relationships," in M. B. Brinkerhoff and P. R. Kunz (eds.), *Complex Organizations and Their Environments*, Dubuque, IA: Brown.

Lewin, Kurt (1948) Resolving Social Conflicts, New York: Harper and Rowe.

———. (1951) *Field Theory in Social Science*, New York: Harper and Brothers.

Lickona, Thomas, ed. *Moral Development and Behavior: Theory, Research and Social Issues*, Holt, Rinehart and Winston.

Lifton, Robert Jay (1970) *Boundaries: Psychological Man in Revolution*, New York Vintage Books.

Lindesmith, Alfred R., Strauss, Anselm L. and Denzin, Norman K. (1975) *Social Psychology*, 4th edn., Hinsdale, IL. Dryden Press.

Lipartito, Kenneth and Sicilia, David, B. eds., (2004) *Constructing Corporate America: History, Politics, Culture*, New York: Oxford University Press.

Lipartito, Kenneth (2004) "The utopian corporation," in *Constructing Corporate America: History, Politics, Culture*, New York: Oxford University Press.

Lonergan, Bernard (S.J.) (1999) *Collected Works of Bernard Lonergan*, eds. Frederick E. Crowe and Robert M. Doran (S.J.) Vol.15, *Macroeconomic Dynamics: An Essay in Circulation Analysis*, eds. Frederick Lawrence, Charles Hefling, and Patrick Byrne, Toronto: University of Toronto Press.

Longstreth, Richard, ed. (2011) *Sustainability and Historic Preservation:Toward a Holistic View*, University Press Copublishing Division, University of Delaware.

Luban, David, (2006) "Making sense of moral meltdowns" in *Moral Leadership: The Theory and Practice of Power, Judgment and Policy*, ed.., Deborah L. Rhode, Foreword by Warren Bennis, San Francisco: Jossey-Bass, Wiley imprint.

Lutz,.W.D. (1983) "Corporate doublespeak: making bad news look good," *Business and Society Review*, vol.44, 19-22.

Lytton, Timothy D. (2008) *Holding Bishops Accountable: How Lawsuits Helped the Catholic Church Confront Clergy Sexual Abuse*, Cambridge, MA: Harvard University Press.

Macey, Johnathan R. (2013) *The Death of Corporate Reputation: How Integrity Has Been Destroyed on Wall Street*, Upper Saddle River, NJ: Pearson Education, FT Press.

Mansbridge, Peter, ed. (2007) *The Big Melt*, (September 24-26) Toronto: Canadian Broadcasting Company (CBC Television).

Marcel, Gabriel, (1982) *Creative Fidelity*, New York: Crossroad Publishing Company.

Maremont, Mark (1993) "Summing up: has your company unleashed the spirit of enterprise? Or is it too bureaucratic? Here's how to tell," *Business Week* - Enterprise, New York: McGraw-Hill.

Marshall, Alfred (1970) *The R. S. V. Interlinear Greek-English New Testament*, Grand Rapids, MI: Zondervan Publishing House.

Martin, Patricia Yancey (1989) "The moral politics of organizations: reflections of an unlikely feminist," *Journal of Applied Behavioral Science*, vol. 25, no.4, 451-470.

Martin, Stephen L. (2008) *Healing and Creativity in Economic Ethics: The Contribution of Bernard Lonergan's Economic Thought to Catholic Social Teaching*, Studies in Religion and the Social Order, New York: University Press of America.

Mayo, E. (1945) *The Social Problems of an Industrial Civilization*, Harvard Business School, Division of Research, Cambridge, MA.

McCarthy, Thomas (1978) *The Critical Theory of Jurgen Habermas*, Cambridge, MA: MIT Press.

McGraw, Harold III (2007) *Principles and Practices for a Model Business Ethics Program*, Business Round Table Institute.

McNeel, Steven P. (1994) "College teaching and student moral development," in eds., J. R. Rest and D. Narvaez, *Moral Development in the Professions: Psychology and Applied Ethics*, Hillsdale, NJ: Lawrence Erlbaum Associates.

McNichols, Thomas J. (1977) Executive Policy and Strategic Planning, New York: McGraw-Hill.

Mead, George Herbert (1934) *Mind, Self and Society*, Chicago: University of Chicago Press.

Melaver, Martin (2010) "Leadership for sustainability in business: it's all about the stories we tell," in *Leadership for Environmental Sustainability*, New York: Routledge.

Merton, Thomas (1961) *Seeds of Contemplation*, Abbey of Gethsemani; (1972) *New Seeds of Contemplation*, Introduction by Sue Monk Kid, New York: New Directions Publishing.

Messner, J. Monsignor (1941) *Man's Suffering and God's Love*, New York: P. J. Kennedy &Sons

Minkler, Lanse and Miceli, Thomas (2002) "Lying, Integrity and Co-operation" in Working Papers number 36: University of Connecticut, Department of Economics.

Miller, Alan S. (2003) Gaia Connections: An Introduction to Ecology, Ecoethics and Economics, 2nd edition, Lanham, Maryland: Rowman and Littlefield.

Miller, Donald Britton (1990) "Organizational, environmental, and work design strategies that foster competence," in S. L. Willis and S. S. Dubin (eds.), *Managing Professional Competence: Approaches to Career Enhancement, Vitality and Success throughout a Work Life*, San Francisco: Jossey-Bass.

Miller, Gary J. (1992) *Managerial Dilemmas: The Political Economy of Hierarchy*, Cambridge: Cambridge University Press.

Mills, C. Wright (1948/1970) "The contribution of sociology to the studies of industrial relations," *Berkeley Journal of Sociology*, vol. XV, 11-32.

————. (1956) *The Power Elite*, New York: Oxford University Press.

————. (1959) *The Sociological Imagination*, New York: Oxford University Press.

Misgeld, Dieter (1991) "Moral education and critical social theory: from the 'First World' to the 'Third World,'" in W. M. Kurtines and J. L. Gewirtz (eds.), *Handbook of Moral Behavior and Development*, Volume 3: *Application*, Hillsdale, NJ: Lawrence Erlbaum.

Mitchell, Donald (1995) "The Creating of the Eighth," in *Symphonie No. 8*, Deutsche Grammophon GmbH, Hamburg.

Moltmann, Jurgen (1967) *Theology of Hope: On the Ground and the Implications of a Christian Eschatology*, New York: Harper and Row, Publishers.

Morrison, Ann M. (1992) *Breaking the "Glass Ceiling": Can Women Reach the Top of America's Largest Corporations?*, Reading, MA: Addison-Wesley.

Muriel, Diana (2002) "Worst-hit firm rebuilds after 9/11," CNN.com, Sept. 10.

Murray, John Courtney, S.J. (1966) "The declaration on religious freedom," in *Vatican II An Interfaith Appraisal*, ed. John H. Miller, C.S.C., Notre Dame, Indiana: University of Notre Dame Press.

Nagel, Stuart S. (1980) "Introduction: Policy analysis research, what it is and where it is going," in *Improving Policy Analysis*, Stuart S. Nagel, ed., Beverly Hills, California: Sage Publications.

Niebuhr, H. Richard (1960) *Radical Monotheism and Western Culture*, New York: Harper and Row.

———. (1989) *Faith on Earth*, New Haven, CT: Yale University Press.

Nouwen, Henri (1979) *The Wounded Healer*, New York: Image Books, Publisher.

———. (1990) *The Road to Daybreak: A Spiritual Journey*, New York: Image Books.

O'Brien, George Dennis (2007) *Finding the Voice of the Church*, Notre Dame, Indiana: University of Notre Dame Press.

———. (2010) *The Church and Abortion: A Catholic Dissent*, Lanham Maryland: Rowman and Littlefield Publishers.

O'Hanlon, Brian (2012): *Ocean Open Raised: Safety and Sustainability* on: www.openblue.com

Olasky, M. N. (1985) "Inside the amoral world of public relations," *Business and Society Review*, vol.52, 41-44.

Olian, Judy D. (2002) *Management Education at Risk:* Report of the Management Education Task Force to the AACSB International Board of Directors, AACSB Publications (Online).

O'Malley, Michael N. (2000) *Creating Commitment: How to Attract and Retain Talented Employees by Building Relationships That Last*, New York: John Wiley & Sons.

———. (2010) *The Wisdom of Bees: What the Hive Can Teach Business about Leadership, Efficiency and Growth*, London: Portfolio Penguin.

Orr, David W. (2004) *Earth in Mind: On Education, Environment, and the Human Prospect*, Washington, DC: Island Press.

Orsburn, Jack D., Moran, Linda, Musselwhite, Ed and Zenger, John H. (1990) *Self-Directed Work Teams: The New American Challenge*, Homewood, IL: Business One Irwin.

Oser, Fritz and Schlafli, Andre (1985) "But does it move? The difficulty of gradual change in moral development," in M. W. Berkowitz and F. Oser (eds.), *Moral Education: Theory and Application*, Hillsdale, NJ: Lawrence Erlbaum.

Oster, Sharon M. (1999) *Modern Competitive Analysis*, 3rd ed., New York: Oxford University Press.

Parsons, Talcott (1956) *Economy and Society*, Glencoe, IL: Free Press.

————. (1967) *Sociological Theory and Modern Society*, New York: Free Press.

Payne, Stephen L. (1988) "Values and ethics-related measures for management education," *Journal of Business Ethics*, vol. 7, 273-277.

————. (1991) "A proposal for corporate ethical reform: the ethical dialogue group," *Business and Professional Ethics Journal*, vol.10, no.1, 67-88.

Payne, Stephen L. and Giacalone, Robert A. (1990) "Social psychological approaches to the perception of ethical dilemmas," *Human Relations*, vol. 43, no.7, 649-665.

Penn, W. Y., Jr., (1990) "Teaching ethics – A direct approach," *Journal of Moral Education*, 19(2), 124-138.

Perrow, Charles (1972) "A framework for the comparative analysis of organizations," in M. B. Brinkerhoff and P. R. Kunz (eds.), *Complex Organizations and Their Environments*, Dubuque, IA: Brown.

Pfeifer, Jeffrey and Owens, Katherine, M.B. (2002) *Military Leadership and Ethics*, (prepared for Canadian Forces Leadership Institute, Department of National Defense) Regina, Saskatchewan: Canadian Institute for Peace, Justice and Security.

Phillips, Derek L., (1971) *Knowledge from What?: Theories and Methods in Social Research*, Chicago: Rand McNally.

Phillips, Susan M. (2004) "Foreword," in *Ethics Education in Business Schools*, Ethics Education Task Force, St. Louis, MO: Association to Advance Collegiate Schools of Business.

Phinney, David (2005) "Boeing scandal part of deeper problems at Pentagon," www.corpwatch.org, January 5, Oakland, CA: CorpWatch.

Piaget, Jean (1965) *The Moral Judgment of the Child*, trans. Marjorie Gabain, New York: Free Press. http://Www.corpwatch.org

Podolny, Joel (2006a) "New MBA curriculum," in *Yale Alumni Magazine*, Vol. LXIX, no. 6.

————. (2006b) "Personal, Professional Behavior Inseparable in *Business Practice*," eNewsLine, AACSB International, vol. 5, issue 9, Association to Advance Collegiate Schools of Business, Tampa, Florida.

Policano, Andrew (2010) "Business Schools on an Innovation Mission," Report of the AACSB International Task Force on Business Schools and Innovation, Association to Advance Collegiate Schools of Business, Tampa, Florida.

Pollard, Steven R., Kurtines, William M., Carlo, Gustavo, Dancs, Mary and Mayock, Ellen (1991) "Moral education from the perspective of psychosocial theory," in W. M. Kurtines and J. L. Gewirtz, (eds.), *Handbook of Moral Behavior and Development*, Volume 3: *Application*, Hillsdale, NJ: Lawrence Erlbaum Associates.

Ponemon, Lawrence A. and Gabhart, David R. L. (1994) "Ethical Reasoning Research in the Accounting and Auditing Professions," in Rest, James R., and Narvaez, Darcia, eds., *Moral Development in the Professions: Psychology and Applied Ethics*, Hillsdale, NJ: Lawrence Erlbaum Associates.

Posner, Barry Z., Kouzes, James M. and Schmidt, Warren H. (1985) "Shared values make a difference: an empirical test of corporate culture," *Human Resource Management*, vol.24, no.3, 293-309.

Power, Clark (1988) "The just community approach to moral education," *Journal of Moral Education*, vol.17, no.3, 195-208.

Power, Clark F., Higgins, Ann and Kohlberg, Lawrence (1989) *Lawrence Kohlberg's Approach to Moral Education*, New York: Columbia University Press. *The Chronicle of Higher Education*, December 2, B 19.

Pruyser, Paul W. (1976) "Lessons from art theory for the psychology of religion," (Presidential Address to the Society for the Scientific Study of Religion, Milwaukee, Wisconsin, 25 October, 1975), *Journal for the Scientific Study of Religion*, vol. 15, no. 1-14.

Redekop, Benjamin W. (2010) *Leadership for Environmental Sustainability*, London: Routledge.

Redman, Chris (1980) "Indiana's Pinto trial may alter corporate responsibility in the U.S.," *Washington Star*, March 9.

Reisman, W. Michael (1979) *Folded Lies: Bribery, Crusades, and Reforms*, New York, The Free Press.

Rest, James R. (1983) "Morality" in P. H. Mussen (Series Ed.) and J. Flavel and E. Markman (Vol. Eds.), *Handbook of Child Psychology*: Vol. 3, *Cognitive Development* (4th ed., pp. 556-629), New York: Wiley.

————. (1986) *Moral Development: Advances in Research and Theory*, New York: Praeger.

Rest, James R. and Narvaez, Darcia (eds.) (1994) *Moral Development in the Professions: Psychology and Applied Ethics*, Hillsdale, NJ: Lawrence Erlbaum Associates.

Rest, James R., Narvaez, Darcia, Bebeau, Muriel and Thoma, Stephen (1999) *Postconventional Moral Thinking: A Neo Kohlbergian Approach*, Hillsdale, NJ: Lawrence Erlbaum Associates.

Richardson, John E. (ed.) (2004) *Annual Editions: Business Ethics 04-05*, Dubuque, Iowa:McGraw-Hill Dushkin.

Ricoeur, Paul, (2006) *Memory, History, Forgetting,* translated by Kathleen Blamey and David Pellauer, Chicago: University of Chicago Press.

Rioux, Marcel (1970) "Critical versus aseptic sociology," *Berkeley Journal of Sociology*, vol. XV, 33-47.

Roberts, Harold Selig (1986) *Roberts Dictionary of Industrial Relations*: Arlington, Virginia: Bloomberg Bureau of National Affairs.

Robinson, Barbara Mabbs (2009) *A Qualitative Study of Twilight Years: Transitions and Issues of Psychosocial Development in Elderly Women*, Doctor of Arts Dissertation, College of Graduate and Professional Studies, Franklin Pierce University.

Roethlisberger, F. J. and Dickson, W. J. (1946) *Management and the Worker*, Cambridge, MA: Harvard University Press.

Roguet, A. M. (1962) *Christ Acts Through the Sacraments*, Collegeville, Minnesota: The Liturgical Press.

Rose, Charlie (2014) *The Charlie Rose Show* with Lloyd Blankfein (June 10, 2014)

Rule, J. T. and Bebeau, Muriel, J. (2005) *Dentists who care: Inspiring Stories of Professional Commitment*, Quintessence Publishing Co. Inc.

Rusk, Tom (1993) *The Power of Ethical Persuasion: From Conflict to Partnership at Work and in Private Life*, New York: Viking Penguin.

Sachs, Jeffrey (2011) *The Price of Civilization: Reawakening American Virtue and Prosperity*, New York: Random House.

Sawyer, Christopher Glenn (2007) "Uncommon alliance: connecting faith and environmentalism," in Reflections, vol. 94: *no.*1 *God's Green Earth: Creation, Faith and Crisis,* New Haven: Yale Divinity School.

Schein, Edgar H. (1980) *Organizational Psychology,* 3rd ed. Prentice-Hall Foundations of Modern Psychology Series, Richard S. Lazarus, ed., Englewood Cliffs, NJ: Prentice-Hall, Inc.

Schroeder, Timothy, Roskies, Adina L. and Nichols, Shaun (2010) "Moral motivation," in The Moral Psychology Research Group, *The Moral Psychology Handbook*, John M. Doris, ed., New York: Oxford University Press.

Schumpeter, Joseph A. (1942) Capitalism, *Socialism and Democracy*, Cambridge, MA: Harvard University Press.

———. (2009) *Can Capitalism Survive? Creative Destruction and the Future of the Global Economy*, New York: Harper Perennial Modern Thought Edition.

Schwab, Klaus (2007) *World Economic Forum*, - Headquarters, Geneva, Switzerland on YouTube, July 17: 16 minutes.

———. (2008) "Global corporate citizenship: Working with governments and civil society," *Foreign Affairs*, January/February.

Schwab, Klaus and Hilde (2009) "The Schwab Foundation for Entrepreneurship," World Economic Forum, Geneva, Switzerland (http://www.schwabfound.org).

Schweiger, David M., Ridley, R. Russell, Jr. and Marini, Dennis M. (1992) "Creating one from two: the merger between Harris Semiconductor and General Electric Solid State," Susan E. Jackson (ed.), *Diversity in the Workplace: Human Resources Initiatives,* Society for Industrial and Organizational Psychology Publication, New York: Guilford Press.

Sethia, Nirmal and Von Glinow, Mary Ann (1985) "Arriving at four cultures by managing the reward system," in Kilmann, Saxton, Serpa and Associates (eds.), *Gaining Control of the Corporate Culture,* San Francisco: Jossey-Bass.

Sewell, William H. (1970) "Some recent developments in socialization theory and research," in G. P. Stone and H. A. Farberman (eds.), *Social Psychology Through Symbolic Interaction,* Waltham, MA: Xerox College Publishing.

Sherman, Loreen, (2010-2011) *The Book on Leadership Skills for Today: Corporate Leadership Training for Tomorrow's Success Stories,* Calgary, AB: Star-Ting, Inc.

Schillebeeckx, E. (1963) *Christ the Sacrament of the Encounter with God,* New York: Sheed and Ward.

Shiller, Robert J. (2005) *Irrational Exuberance,* New York: Broadway Books.

———. (2012) *Finance and the Good Society,* Princeton, NJ: Princeton University Press.

Siebert, Horst, Ed., (1994) *The Ethical Foundations of the Market Economy: International Workshop,* Kiel Institute of World Economics, University of Kiel, Tubingen: J. C. B. Mohr.

Sievers, Allen M. (1962) "Schumpeter the Conservative" in *Revolution, Evolution, and the Economic Order,* Englewood Cliffs, NJ.

Simpson, Mona (2011) *A Sister's Eulogy for Steve Jobs,* The New York Times Reprints: Oct. 30.

Snarey, J. (1991) "Faith Development, moral development, and non-theistic Judaism: A construct validity study," in W. M. Kurtines and J. L. Gewirtz (eds.), *Handbook of Moral Behavior and Development,* vol. 2: *Research,* Hillsdale, NJ: Lawrence Erlbaum.

Snider, Julie (2006) "Our view on executive pay: Wall Street's big holiday gifts hint at nation's wealth gap," in Business issues - Editorial, Pay/Income issues, *USA TODAY,* December 26, 2006.

Sonnenfeld, Jeffrey (1988) *The Hero's Farewell: What Happens When CEO's Retire,* New York: Oxford University Press.

Sorkin, Andrew Ross (2008) "JP Morgan Pays $2 a Share for Bear Stearns," in *The New York Times*, Business Section (March 17, 2008).

Stewart, Jim (1991) *Managing Change Through Training and Development*, Amsterdam: Pfeiffer & Co.

Stewart, John (1980) "Communication, ethics, and relativism: An interpersonal perspective," paper presented at Speech Communication Association, November, New York.

Stewart, John, ed., (1982) *Bridges Not Walls*, 3rd ed., Reading, MA: Addison-Wesley.

Stewart, John and D'Angelo Gary (1980) *Together: Communicating Interpersonally*, 2nd ed., Reading MA: Addison-Wesley.

Stolper, Wolfgang (1960) *The Structure of the East German Economy*, Cambridge, MA: Harvard University Press.

———. (1994) Joseph Alois Schumpeter: The Public Life of a Private Man, Princeton, NJ: Princeton University Press.

———. (2003) *Inside Independent Nigeria: Diaries of Wolfgang Stolper, 1960-1962*, Clive S. Gray, ed., Hampshire, England & Burlington, VT, USA: Ashgate Publishing Ltd.

Taylor, Charles (1990) *Sources of the Self: The Making of the Modern Identity*, Cambridge: Harvard University Press.

———. (1991) *The Ethics of Authenticity*, Cambridge: Harvard University Press.

———. (2007) *A Secular Age*, Cambridge: Harvard University Press.

Teilhard de Chardin, Pierre, (1955a) *The Phenomenon of Man*, New York: Harper and Row Torchbooks.

———. (1955b) *Le Christique* www.users.globalnet.co.uk/~alfar2/Christic.htm

———. (1964) *The Future of Man*, New York: Harper and Row.

———. (1969) *How I Believe*, translated by Rene Hague, New York: Harper and Row, Perennial Library.

Thoma, Stephen J., Barnett, D., Rest, J. and Narvaez, D. (1999) "What does the DIT measure?" *British Journal of Social Psychology*, 38, 103-111.

Thoma, Stephen, J. (2006) "Research using the Define Issues Test," in Killen and Smetana (eds.), *Handbook of Moral Psychology*, Mahwah, NJ: Lawrence Erlbaum.

———. (in press) "A review of the Defining Issues Test," in *Handbook of Psychological Tests*, Cambridge University Press.

Thomashow, Mitchell, (1995) *Ecological Identity: Becoming a Reflective Environmentalist*, Cambridge, MA: MIT Press.

Thompson, Francis (1940) "The Hound of Heaven" in *Prose and Poetry of England*, revised by Julian L. Maline and William J. McGucken, H. W. McGraw, ed. Chicago: L. W. Singer.

Thompson, James D. (1967) *Organizations in Action*, New York: McGraw-Hill.

Thompson, Mary; Liesman, Steve; and Kneale, Dennis (2008) "Rumors and short selling" in *The Power of the Rumor Mill*, on Power Lunch video, Bill Griffeth ed. New York: CNBC.com (April 4, 2008).

Tevino, L. K. (1986) "Ethical decision-making in organizations: a person-situation interactionist model," *Academy of Management Review*, vol.11, no.3, 601-617.

Tilly, Charles, (1978) *From Mobilization to Revolution*, Reading, MA: Addison-Wesley.

Tracy, David (1981) *The Analogical Imagination: Christian Theology and the Culture of Pluralism*, New York: Crossroad Publishing Co.

Tronto, Joan C. (1987) "Beyond gender difference to a theory of care," *Signs Journal of Women in Culture and Society*, vol.12, no.4, 644-663.

Tucker, Mary Evelyn (2003) Worldly Wonder: Religions Enter Their Ecological Phase, Commentary by Judith A. Berling, Chicago and LaSalle, Illinois: Open Court.

Tuckman, Gary (2010) *What the Pope Knew*, CNN Documentary September 25.

Turiel, Elliot and Smetana, Judith G. (1984) "Social knowledge and action: the coordination of domains," in W. M. Kurtines and J. L. Gewirtz (eds.), *Morality, Moral Behavior, and Moral Development*, New York: Wiley.

Turiel, Elliot, Smetana, Judith G. and Killen, Melanie (1991) "Social contexts in social cognitive development," in W. M. Kurtines and J. L. Gewirtz (eds.), *Handbook of Moral Behavior and Development*, Volume 2: *Research*, Hillsdale, NJ: Lawrence Erlbaum.

Turner, Jonathan H. (1978) *The Structure of Sociological Theory* (revised edn.), Homewood, IL: Dorsey Press.

Turner, Ralph H. (1956) "Role-taking, role standpoint, and reference group behavior," *American Journal of Sociology*, vol. 61, 316-328.

———. (1962) "Role-taking: process versus conformity," in A. M. Rose (ed.), *Human Behavior and Social Processes*, Boston: Houghton Mifflin.

Turner, Victor W. (1969) *The Ritual Process: Structure and Anti-Structure*, Chicago: Aldine.

Turner, Victor W. and Edith Turner (1978) *Image and Pilgrimage in Christian Culture*: *Anthropological Perspectives*, New York: Columbia University Press.

Uhl, Christopher (2003) *Developing Ecological Consciousness*: *Paths to a Sustainable Future*, Lanham, Maryland: Rowman and Littlefield.

Van der Erve, Marc (1992) *Evolution Management: Winning in Tomorrow's Marketplace*: (Software Program, EM Corporation), Geneva: KPMG Fides.

———. (1993) *The Power of Tomorrow's Management: Using the Vision-Culture Balance in Organizations*, 2nd edn., enlarged, Stoneham, MA: Butterworth-Heinemann.

———. (1994) *Evolution Management: Winning in Tomorrow's Marketplace*: Oxford: Butterworth-Heinemann.

———. (1998) *Resonant Corporations*, New York: McGraw Hill.

Velasquez, Manuel G. and Rostankowski, Cynthia (1984) *Ethics: Theory and Practice*, Saddle River, New Jersey: Prentice Hall.

Von Glinow, Mary Ann (1988) *The New Professionals: Managing Today's High-Tech Employees*, New York: Ballinger.

Vroom, Victor H. et al. (1990) *Manage People, Not Personnel: Motivation and Performance Appraisal*, The Harvard Business Review Book Series, Boston, MA: Harvard Business School Publishing.

Vroom, Victor (1995) *Work and Motivation*, San Francisco: Jossey-Bass.

Walker, Barbara A. and Hanson, William C. (1992) "Valuing differences at Digital Equipment Corporation," in Susan E. Jackson (ed.), *Diversity in the Workplace: Human Resources Initiatives*, Society for Industrial and Organizational Psychology, New York: Guilford Press.

Walton, Richard E. (1990) "From control to commitment in the workplace," in V. H. Vroom (Pref.), *Manage People, Not Personnel; Motivation and Performance Appraisal*, The Harvard Business Review Book Series, Boston, MA: Harvard Business School Publishing.

Walzer, Michael (1983) *Spheres of Justice*, New York: Basic Books.

Watkins, Tom (2004) "Stakes high for Big Tobacco in landmark trial," CNN.com, Sept. 21.

Weber, Max (1993) *The Sociology of Religion*, Boston: Beacon Press (with Introduction by Talcott Parsons).

Weber, James (1990) "Managers' moral reasoning: assessing their responses to three moral dilemmas," *Human Relations*, vol. 43, no.7, 687-702.

Weinreich-Haste, Helen (1984) "Morality, social meaning, and rhetoric: the social context of moral reasoning," in W. M. Kurtines and J. L. Gewirtz (eds.), *Morality, Moral Behavior, and Moral Development,* New York: Wiley.

Weiss, William L. (1986) "Minerva's owl: building a corporate value system," *Journal of Business Ethics,* vol. 5, 243-247.

Werhane, Patricia H. (1984) *Philosophical Issues in Art,* Englewood Cliffs, NJ: Prentice-Hall.

———. (1999) *Moral Imagination and Management Decision-Making* (Ruffin Series in Business Ethics) New York: Oxford University Press.

Western, Simon (2010) "Eco-Leadership: Towards the development of a new paradigm," in *Leadership for environmental sustainability,* Benjamin W. Redekop, ed., New York: Routledge.

Whitehead, Alfred North (1938) *Modes of Thought,* New York: The Free Press.

———. (1964) *Science and Philosophy,* Paterson, NJ: Littlefield, Adams & Co.

Willis, Sherry L. and Dubin, Samuel S. (1990) "Maintaining professional competence: directions and possibilities," in *Maintaining Professional Competence: Approaches to Career Enhancement, Vitality, and Success throughout a Work Life,* San Francisco: Jossey-Bass.

Willis, Sherry L. and Tosti-Vasey, Joanne L. (1990) "How adult development, intelligence, and motivation affect competence," in *Maintaining Professional Competence: Approaches to Career Enhancement, Vitality, and Success throughout a Work Life,* San Francisco: Jossey-Bass.

Winerman, Lea (2010) "Goldman Sachs, SEC reach $550 million settlement," The Rundown, July 15, PBS News Hour.

Woo, Carolyn (2008) "Being Carolyn," Interview by Sally Ann Flecker, *Notre Dame Magazine,* vol. 37, no. 2, 34-38.

Wood, John A., Longenecker, Justin C., McKinney, Joseph A. and Moore, Carlos W. (1988) "Ethical attitudes of students and business professionals: a study of moral reasoning," *Journal of Business Ethics,* vol. 7, 249-257.

Wood, Robert E. and Mitchell, Terrance R. (1981) "Manager behavior in a social context: the impact of impression management on attributions and disciplinary actions," *Organizational Behavior and Human Performance,* vol. 28, 356-378.

Wyatt, Edward (2008) "Managing the bailout: he'd do it for nothing," *New York Times* (Economy), September 25.

Yussen, Steven R. (1976) "Moral reasoning from the perspective of others," *Child Development* vol. 47, 551-555.

Zakaria, Fareed (2011) "The Global Public Square" CNN, December, 4.

————. (2012) "Tough Decisions: A Fareed Zakaria GPS Special" CNN, December, 22.

INNOVATIVE AUTHOR AND THEME INDEX
(Chapter Themes with Authors' Subjects)

This index has been composed on the literary principles of unity, emphasis and coherence toward integrating innovative *"Ideas of Reform"* (Ladner, 1959) with citations that *inform* readers of the book by Chapters listed with coherent themes and academic theories. The sequence of page numbers guides readers and scholars for an *integrated search of multi-disciplinary subjects* identified with their authors rather than by an unintegrated alphabet search.

Introduction:

The Reformation of Management by Objectives (MBO)

Werhane, Patricia, 2 (philosophical ethics and moral incentives);
Drucker, Peter, 3-4 (Management by Objectives and its MBO legacy)
Sonnenfeld, Jeffrey, 4 (managerial operational functional themes)
Kohlberg, Lawrence, 4-5 (moral development theories and scaling)
Rest, James, 4 (moral measuring methodologies)
Gilligan, Carol, 4 (interactional caring reciprocities)
Capellas, Michael, 5 (instrumental moral reconstruction and ethical codes)
Phillips, Susan, 7 (AACSB Ethics Education Task Force designs)
Bebeau, Muriel, 7-8 (ethical education interventions)
Poneman and Gabhart, 8 (business ethics education for accounting and
         auditing professions)
Olian, Judy, 8 (AACSB ethical delivery system for corporate learning)
Policano, Andrew, 9 (AACSB "Innovative Mission" for business education)
Ferguson, Neil, & Zakaria, Fareed, 16 (*Innovation* "The core, the heartbeat
         of economic growth")
Erikson, Erik, 18-19 (the "sequence of generations")
Guerrette, Richard, 19 (ethical theories and moral narratives in art)
Lipartito and Sicilia, 19 ("capitalistic" policies and enterprising ethos)
Geertz, Christopher, 19 (cultural ethos, ethical priorities and
         humanistic ecologies)
Pruyser, Paul, 20 ("exposure to great art" and the "shaping of culture")
Marcuse, Herbert, 20 ("The Aesthetic Dimension" in art)

Kuhn, Thomas, 20 (scientific revolutionary theories)
Taylor, Charles, 20 (philosophy and political economics)
Werhane, Patricia, 20 (management science, art and social change)
Erikson, Eric, 20 (life cycles and civilization)
Lipartito, Kenneth and Sicilia, David 21 (*moral* transformations
    of corporate cultures and market economies)

Chapter 1

The Implementation of the MBE Paradigm

Van Der Erve, Mark, 22 (evolutionary management in the marketplace)
Berger, Peter and Luckmann, Thomas, 22 (reconstructing social
    organization realities)
Edwards, Mark, 23 (opening meta-theoretical visions)
Taylor, Charles, 23 (finding authentic moral standpoints)
Moore, Michael, 23 (revolutionary planning: "Occupy Wall Street")
Kuhn, Thomas, 23 (revolutionary planning in social scientific research)
Redman, Chris, 24 (Pinto trial and corporate responsibility)
Graves, Phillip E., 29 (environmental critique of cost-benefit analysis)
Brinkerhoff, Merlin and Kunz, P. R., 31 (complex organization
    environments)
Brinkerhoff, Merlin, 31 (organizations as units of analysis)
Perrow, Charles, 31 (comparative analysis of organizations)
Levine, Sol and White, Paul E., 31 (interorganizational relationships)
Goodpaster, Kenneth and Matthews, John, B. 31 (moral responsibility
    and legal accountability of corporate behavior)
Goodpaster, Kenneth 31 (conceptualizing corporate responsibility)
Redekopp, Benjamin 31 (responsible accountability for ecological
    sustainability)
Edwards, Mark 31 (transforming organizations for sustainability)
Kuhn, Thomas 31-32 (corporate entities as models for scientific research)
Blasi, Augusto 32 (management planning for moral performance
    consistency)
Etzioni, Amitai 32 (moral dimensions for socio-economic reviewing)
Blasi, Augusto 32 (moral consistency in moral functioning)
Hausman and McPherson 32 (economics and contemporary
    moral philosophy)
Kung, Hans 32-33 (moral frameworks with functioning markets)
Beauchamp, Tom L. 32-33 (ethics as normative science)
Baum, V. 33 (ethics as behavioral science)
Doris, John M. 33 (social psychology of ethics)
Cooley, Charles 33 (human nature and social order)
Mead, George Herbert 33 (social psychology of human behavior)

Blumer, Herbert 33 (symbolic interaction theory and the
sociology of industrial relations)
Allport, F. H. 33 (structural theory and collective behavior)
Katz, Daniel and Kahn Robert, L. 33 (social psychology of organizations)
Kohlberg, Lawrence 33 (moral theories in educational psychology)
Rest, James 33 (post-conventional moral thinking)
Kurtines, William 33 (psycho-social role theories in moral development)
Katz, Daniel and Kahn, Robert 33 (open system theories in
human behavior)
Parsons, Talcott 33 (structural moral theory of system maintenance
and organization integration)
Weinreich-Haste, Helen 34 (socio-cultural moralities and
inter-organizational collectivities)
Katz, Daniel and Kahn, Robert, 36 (open system theory as a dynamic
inter-organizational concept)
Cushman, Young and Greene, 37 (the social psychological structure of
the corporate conscience)
Van Der Erve, Mark, 38n ("evolutionary management" and
"complexity-resonance continuum")
Lipartito, Kenneth, 38n ("corporate personhood")
Hagar, Mark, 38n (corporation business and personification)
Birsch, Douglas, and Fielder, John, 38n (Ford Pinto trial,
legal issues and applied ethics)
Bernstein, Richard, 38n (critical theory in philosophy)
McCarthy, Thomas, 38n (critical theory of Jurgen Habermas)
Gouldner, Alvin, 38n (reflexive sociology and critical thought)
Lewin, Kurt, 38n (force-field action theories and
organization interaction dependencies)
Kung, Hans, 39n (moral frameworks of the global conscience)
Kuhn, Thomas, 39n (structures of scientific revolutions)
Buber, Martin, 39n (philosophical values theories and social interaction)
Velasquez, Manuel G. and Rostankowski, Cynthia, 39n (systems of
social cooperation)

Chapter 2

The Dynamic Corporate Conscience

Marshall, 41n The Jerusalem Bible ("conscience" as "*cardia*"
residing in the heart)
Dilenschneider, Robert 42 (an inspirational ethos as the *integrity of truth*
in the corporate conscience"
Mead, George Herbert 43 (location of individual conscience:
the assertive I and the reflexive ME)

James, William 43 (psychosocial operations of the conscience)
Bittle, Celestine, N. 43 (the moral philosophy of reflexivity)
Gouldner, Alvin 43 (corporate conscience in strategic decision-making)
Cooley, Charles Horton 43 (identity-making attributes of
          the corporate self)
Taylor, Charles 43-44 (ethical sources of the "self")
King, Leslie and McCarthy, Deborah 44 (corporate reflexivity operations
          and environmental sociology)
Thomashow, Mitchell 46-47 (personal and collective operational reflexivity
          in environmental studies)
Weinreich-Haste, Helen 47 (culturally specific meanings
          and the organization self)
Berger, Peter and Luckman 48 (value-system-building and
          reality construction theory)
Guerrette, Richard, 48 (management reflexivity strategies
          of the organization self)
Carlo, William, 49 (philosophical grounding notions of essence and nature)
Goodpaster, Kenneth, 49 (critical ethical consistency of rationality
          and respect)
Kohlberg, Lawrence, 50 (ethical principles of justice and reciprocity)
Dilenschneider, Robert 51-52 (value-system-symbols of the
          "Corporate WE" and the "Corporate US"
Gilligan, Carol, 52 (interactional concerns of caring and sensitivity)
Zacharia, Fareed, 52 (managerial attitudes and performance at ALCOA)
Guerrette, Richard, 52 (art and architecture in the workplace)
Goffman, Erving, 53 (processes of impression management theory)
          (organization rituals and corporate value-systems)
Berg, Per-Olof, 53 (company image-building and symbolic fields of action)
Lawson, Robert, 53 (organizational ethical strategies and interactional
          festival rituals; economic planning and market profitability)
Muriel, Diana, 54 (Cantor Fitzgerald 9/1 moral heroism: corporate
          conscience and ethical identity)
Teilhard de Chardin, Pierre, 55n 3 (value-system-building and
          ecology)
Wood, Robert and Mitchell, Terrance, 55 (management behavior and
          social context)

Chapter 3

The MBE Paradigm: A Delivery System for Corporate Moral Reform

Lindesmith, A., Strauss, A. and Denzin, N., 57 (social psychology
          of care-taking)
Sewell, William H. 57 (social psychology and socialization agents)
Guerrette, Richard H. 57 (shaping worker attitudes for moral performance)

Mills, C. Wright 57 (moral significance and worker attitudes)

Mayo, E. 57 (industrial sociology)

Roethlisberger, A. J. and Dickson, W. J. 57 (humanistic management)

Blumer, Herbert, 57 (moral and political critique in industrial relations)

Blumer, Herbert, 57 (symbolic interactional critique in sociology)

Kohlberg, Lawrence, 57-61 (moral development stages of responsibility
    awareness)

Kohlberg, Lawrence *et al*, 61 (moral method consistency
    in moral judgments)

Rest, James, 61-62 (psychology and applied ethics)
    62-63 (psychological components for moral judgments)

Schroeder, Timothy; Roskies, Adina L.; and Nichols, Shaun, 62
    (moral motivation for *critical practical* moral judging)

Cushman, Fiery; Young, Liane; Greene, Joshua, 63 (psychological systems
    and moral judgments)

Kung, Guido, 63 (empirical significance verification of stage 6)

Guerrette, Richard, 63-64 (social system hegemonies impairing
    stage 6 possibilities)

Etzioni, Amitai, 64 (moral implications of socio-economic hegemonies)

Gouldner, Alvin, 64-65 (power and wealth and moral code conformities)

Phillips, Susan, 65 (business education and deficient moral codes)

Johannesen, Richard, 66 (open system reforms and communication ethics)

Stewart, John, 66-67 (ethics communication as person-building potential)

Habermas, Jurgen, 67 (moral structural reform and communication ethics)

Lewin, Kurt, 67 (moral points of view and culture changing strategies)

Baxter, G. D. and Rarick, C.A. 70 (managers in "care-taking" leadership roles)

Oser, Fritz and Schlafli, Andre, 70, (interventions to higher-level stages)

Rest, James and Narvaez, Darcia, 75 (defining issues of moral thinking)

Ponemon, Lawrence and Gabhart, David, 76-77 (principle moral reasoning
    impairments)

Rest, James, 77-78 (measuring moral stages by concepts of *co-operation*)

Higgins, Ann and Gordon Frederick, 79 (measuring the collective
    dimensions of the corporate conscience)

Evan, William, M., 81-82 ("organization-set" of interorganizational
    governing relationships)

Kurtines, William, 84 (authority-subordinate correlations and rule-)
    governing relationships

Emler, Nicholas and Hogan, Robert 84-85 (the efficacy of honesty and
    ethics in qualitative management)

Turiel, Elliot and Smetana, Judith, 85 (complex power domains and
    influences on workplace morality)

Gellerman, Saul, 85 (persistent hierarchical conflicts and
    personal performance goals)

Levine, Sol, and White, Paul, 87 (moral performance consistency problems
    and organization domains)

Dill, William, R., 87 (organization environment and regulatory groups)

Thompson, James, D. 87 (organization domain and cooperative associations)

Braito, Rita, Paulson, Steve and Klonglan, Gerald, 87 (domain consensus and power relationships)

Kohlberg, Lawrence, 88-89 (moral behavior and the teaching of "*virtue*")

Blasi, Antonio, 89 (bridging moral cognition and moral action)

Rest, James, 89 (moral character and ego strength)

Kohlberg, Lawrence and Candee, David, 89 (associated virtues of moral character; and moral value intuitions for moral action)

Haste, Helen, 89-92 (associative pathways to moral reasoning-moral action continuum: Enron Congressional Hearings case study)

Kohlberg, Lawrence, 93 (role-taking and moral development progression)

Guerrette, Richard, 95-96 (associative exposure and ethical-image projection)

Candee, David, 96-100 (intervention methodologies for internal corporate moral problems)

Galston, William, 98 (moral dilemmas of cloning and stem-cell research)
   99 (Jewish tradition: Rabbi Tendler)
   100 (Christian perspectives: Peters, Lebacqz, and Bennett)

O'Brien, George Dennis, 99n (moral insights in personal ethical decision-making)

Levine, Charles, 100 (meaningful justice in communal structures)

Power, Clark, 100 (shared consciousness as the real agency of moralization)

Higgins, Ann and Gordan, 101 (moral climate in work-place democracies);
   102 (organization environments as conducive to socio-moral development; managerial need to identify organization stress)

Kohlberg, Scharf and Hickey 102 (cooperative structures and job satisfaction)

Kanter, Rosabeth, 103 (vanguard companies and parallel structure strategies)

Payne, Stephen 103 (dialogical ethical sensitivities in parallel interactional structures)

Baker, Thomas and Hunt, Tammy 104 (gender and teams in workplace ethics: female teams and higher moral development performance)

Kohlberg, Lawrence and Colby, Anne 105-109 (moral management: heteronomous and autonomous authority types)

Gilligan, Carol, 109-110 (interactional arrangements and organization structures of a corporate caring ethic)

Chapter 4

MBE Moral Performance Evaluation in the Workplace

Boyett, Joseph and Conn, Henry, 114 (maximum performance management)

Vroom, Victor, 114 (managing people with motivation performance)

Orsburn, Jack, Moran, L. Musselwhite E and Zenger, J., 114 (self-directed work-teams)

Willis, Sherry, and Dubin, Samuel, 115 (maintaining professional competence)

Kurtines, William and Gewirtz, J. L., 115 (measuring socio-moral understanding and behavior)

Pollard, Steven and Kurtines, William et al., 116 (moral competency development for co-constructive performance planning)

Argyris, Chris, 117-118 (reflexive thinking for self-evaluation learning)

Allport, F. H., 120 (open system theory and moral reconstruction flow)

Phillips, Derek L, 121 (interpreting investigative data in formulating persons types)

Phillips, Susan, 121-122 moral managing as "ethical role models"

Oser, Fritz and Schlafli, Andre, 122 (four phases of moral transition: disequilibrium, dissatisfaction, integration, and reinforcement)

Turner, Ralph H., 125 (integrating performance evaluation with forums of) associative conferential learning)

Hackman, Richard, 125n (implementing self-appraisal evaluations)

Dilenschneider, Robert, 125-126 (managers as symbols of integrity and models of consistency)

Blasi, Augusto, 126 (moral identity and personal consistency functioning)

Hausman, Daniel M. and McPherson, Michael S., 128 (corporate moral responsibility activity and corporate ethical policy consistency)

Rule, J. T. and Bebeau, Muriel 131 (moral organizational consistency and affective health caring delivery)

Bowen, Michael G. and Power, F. Clark, 131-2 (corporate performance evaluation processes and moral interorganizational consistencies)

Pfeifer, Jeffrey and Owens, Katherine, 132 (moral military leadership and ethical policy-making management)

Shiller, Robert, 133 (irrational persistence of error and unethical consequences of behavior)

Argyris, Chris, 133-134 (immoral cover-up behavior and organization defensive routines)

Lytton, Timothy, 135 (clergy sex abuse and legal accountability)

Bennis, Warren, 135 (organizational planning for change)

O'Brien, George Dennis, 136 (the relation of morality and sin)

Guerrette, Richard, 137 (priesthood re-identification: organization solutions)

O'Brien, George Dennis, 138 (the authentic voice of the Church)

Ladner, Gerhart, B., 138 (*"vitalistic ideas"* of reform)

Parsons, Talcott, 138 (structurally functional managerial adaptations)

Guerrette, Richard, 138 (interactional practical pastoral integration)

McNichols, Thomas 138-9 (strategic importance of corporate integration)

McNichols, Thomas, 140 (corporate integration and managerial placement scanning)

Nagel, Stuart, 141 (strategic management planning and
        environmental monitoring)
Weber, Max, 146n (the aesthetic dignity of sexuality)
Farley, Sister Margaret, 143 (contemporary defining sexual ethics)
Blenkinsopp, Joseph, 143 (sexuality and the Christian tradition)
Schillebeeckx, E., 143 (sacramental encounters with God)
Roguet, A. G., 143 (sacramental acts of grace)
Bergson, Henri, 143 ("elan vital" of love)
Marcel, Gabriel, 143 (sacramental *open* applications of love)
Guerrette, Richard, 143 (an aesthetic erotic "Passion Play" of love)
Nouwen, Henri, 144 (healing the Corporate Body of the Church)
Evan, William, 145n (interacting networks and co-operational organizations)
McNichols, Stuart, 145n (social organizational trends and
        cultural directional changes)
Weber, Max, 146n ("the sublimation of sexual expression")
Fromm, Eric, 146n (*The Art of Loving* and the nature of love)
Mahler, Gustave, 146n (the Holy Spirit of love)
Goethe, Wolfgang, 146n (the romantic poetry of love: ontological beauty
        and analogical integrity)

Chapter 5

Moral Incentive Building in Workplace Associations and Academic Education

Rest, James, 147 (cooperative associations and moral upgrading)
        148 (moral conceptions of work associations)
O'Malley, Michael, 149 (social development of cooperation)
Rest, James, 149 (social interventions for advanced moral behavior)
        (coaching interventions for advanced moral performance)
Sherman, Loreen, 150 (practical guides of leadership worker coaching)
Mills, C. Wright, 152 (vested interest benefits of power elite behavior)
Snider, Julie, 152 (executive pay and nations's wealth gap)
Krugman, Paul, 153 (corporate boards and corporate profits)
Argyris, Chris, 157 (ethical inconsistency and
        "organization defensive routines")
Mills, C. Wright, 157 (ethical principles and "sociological imagination")
        158 (moral character and historically involved moral leaders)
Rest, James, 159 (measuring principle moral leadership profiles)
Olian, Judy, 163 (management education at risk)
Phillips, Susan M., 163 (ethics education in business schools)
Policano, Andrew, 163 (business schools on an innovation mission)
Penn, W. Y., 163-164 (moral learning through curricular intervention)
McNeel, Steven, 164 (pedagogy of moral development
        through direct moral learning)

Podolny, Joel, 165 (core curricular studies in management education)
    167-168 (new curriculum: Yale School of Organization
    Management)
Bernstein, Richard, 170 (ethical learning for practical moral judgments)
Oster, Sharon, 171 (core curricular viewpoints in management education)
    178 (caring ethics for persons)

Chapter 6

Socio-Economic Organization Structures for Moral Incentive Inducement Building

Ferguson, Naiil and Zacharia, Fareed, 182 (managerial innovation and
    economic growth)
Ferguson, Naiil, 182 (financial innovation and economic growth)
Holmstrom, Bengt, 184 (shirking behavior and performance inefficiency)
Miller, Gary, 185 (inspirational management, intra-firm cooperation and
    moral performance efficiency)
    185 (work teams and cooperative equilibriums)
Miller, Gary, 186 (stage 2 & 3 economic conventions of corporate culture)
    186 (critical evaluation of Miller's instrumental reciprocities)
Belassa, Bela, 187 (intra-plant economies of scale)
Krugman, Paul, 187 (ethics and public policy)
Hesse, Helmut, 187-188 (global poverty and international economies)
Miller, Alan, 188 (global poverty, economic policy, and eco-ethics)
Sachs, Jeffrey, 188 (re-awakening *moral virtues* and economic prosperity)
Orr, David, W. 188 (ethical principles for keeping the *"Earth in Mind"*)
Hesse, Helmut, 188-189 (the moral imperative for economic principles)
Van der Erve, Mark, 189 (economics and evolutionary management)
    190 (process praxis strategy for poverty populations)
Martin, Stephen, 190n (evolutionary economics and praxis methodologies)
Lonergan, Bernard, S.J., 190n (praxis methodologies for
    macro-economic dynamics)
Schumpeter, Joseph, 190 (economic praxis and associative corporativism)
O'Hanlon, Brian, 190 (associative 6th stage moral management)
Hesse, Helmut, 191 (international scope of global poverty)
Boyd, Dwight R. 191 (translating principles into moral action)
Minkler, Lance, 192-193 (trust reciprocity and optimal work performance)
Sethia, Nirmal and Von Glinow, Mary Ann, 194 (caring human resource
    cultures and intrafirm cooperation)
Kohlberg, Lawrence, et al., 194 (ethical value of caring for others)
Habermas, Jurgen, 194-195 (caring reciprocity and role-taking interaction)
Hackman, Richard, 195 (6th stage workplace altruism
    and performance consistency)
Blasi, Antonio, 196 moral reasoning and altruistic behavior
O'Malley, Michael, 196 (analogical collective altruism of "bumble bees")

Etzioni, Amitai, 196-197 (moral caring and cooperation inducements)
        197 (internalized values and enduring dispositional virtue)
Barnard, Chester, 197 (enduring intrafirm cooperation and
        holistic economic good)
Von Glinow, Mary Ann, 198 (moral purpose reasoning on
        productive moral performance)
Stolper, Wolfgang, 199n (evolutionary theories and integrative economics)

Chapter 7

MBE Organization Governance and Resistance to Change

Power, Charles, Higgins, Ann and Kohlberg, Lawrence., 200 (hegemony
        in research subjects and processes)
Emler, Nicholas, and Hogan, Robert., 201 (hegemonic culture causes of
        value norm incongruences)
Kuhn, Thomas, 201 (MBE paradigm and "revolutionary scientific
        perceptions for socio-moral development")
Adeola, Francis, 202 (moral consciousness, industrial disasters
        and environmental justice)
Anderson, Charles, 202 (moral consciousness and social class inequalities)
Krause, Elliot, 202 (power and illness inequalities)
Walzer, Michael, 202 (justice fears of inequalities)
Dahrendorf, Ralph, 202 (class conflict inequalities)
Goldman, Paul and Van Houten, 202 (workplace inequalities)
Misgeld, Dieter, 202 (moral education and third world inequalities)
Beck, Eckardt 202-203 ("Love Canal" and love-lacking inequalities)
Thomashow, Mitchell, 203 (corporate responsibility and
        environmental capability)
Parsons, Talcott, 203 (structural function imperatives and
        the "Love Canal" disaster)
Emler and Hogan, 203 (MBE and credentials of moral psychology research)
Zakaria, Fareed, 204 (morally meeting international humanitarian needs)
Benson, J. Kenneth, 204 (innovation in organization analysis: changing
        systems for organization environmental needs)
Turner, Jonathan, 204n (borrowing concepts to build theories of action)
Lifton, Robert, J., 206 (hegemonic implications of
        institutionalized constructs)
Gouldner, Alvin, 206 (hegemonic elite variances and status quo stabilities)
Emler, Nicholas, and Hogan, Robert, 206 (ethical challenging of hegemonic
        moral stage determinism)
Longstreth, Richard, 206 (changing status quo systems with
        holistic moral stage optimism)
Minkler, Lance, 206-207 (lifting the research "hegemonic lid")
Taylor, Charles, 207 (moral sources and the ethics of authenticity)

Guthey, Eric, 209 (corporate personhood and a new historical moment)
Turner, Ralph, 209 (role-taking process and caring motivation)
Yussen, Steven, 209 (moral reasoning from perspectives of others)
Bennis, Warren; Benne, Kenneth; & Chin, Robert 209 (planning for change)
Uhl, Christopher, 210-211 (formulating moral plans of action)
Day, Robert A. & Day, Joanne, V., 210-11 (negotiating organizational order
     in planning for change)
Day, Robert A. and Day, Joanne, V., 211 (negotiating processes in health
     care and economic structures)
Whitehead, Alfred North, 212 (managing *processes* in
     role-taking relationships)
Weiss, William, 212 (value-system-building and decision-making
     uncertainties)
Bowen, M, and Power, C., 212-213 (moral uncertainties and
     ethical consistencies)
Guerrette, Richard, 213 (social unrest and new order change)
Turner, Victor, 213 (structure and anti-structure)
Lauer, Robert, H., 213 (social movements and social change)
Gasparino, Charles, 213 (investing "blood" on Wall Street)
Time Magazine (5/25/86), 213n (the corporate conscience and
     moral compass needs)
Griffin, Emile, 213 (self-mobilization and executive reflexivity)
Koestenbaum. Peter, 213 (leadership and inner-self moral development)
Thomashow, Mitchell, 214 (developing moral ecological awareness)
Kung, Hans, 215 (The Global Ethic Foundation)
Kung, Hans, 215 (Global Ethic Declaration)
Kung, Hans, and Kuschel, Karl-Josef 215 (Parliament of World's Religions)
Kung, Hans, 215 (Triology of World's Monotheistic Religons)
Kung, Hans, and Ching, Julia 215 (Christianity and Chinese Religions)
Kung, Hans 215 (world religions, international politics and economics)
Kung, Hans, and Schmidt, Helmut 216 (global ethics and
     global responsibilities)
Kung, Hans, 216-218 (Principles of a Global Ethic)
Erikson, Dan, 219-220 (global organization conscience of the UN)
Cooper, Anderson, and Gupta, Sanjay, 220-221 (CNN's global conscience
     networks)
Clinton, William, J. 221 (Clinton Foundation and global moral collectivities)
Clinton, William, J. 221-223 (Clinton Global Initiatives: "*Inspiring Change*"
     climate change; responsible governance; poverty elimination; and
     religion reconciliation)

Chapter 8

Social System Problems and Global Moral Reform

Berger, Peter, L. and Luckmann, Thomas, 226 (reconstructing social
    interactional trust)
Bernstein, Richard, 226 (practical reconstruction *activity* planning)
Dilenschneider, Robert 228 (symbolic associations and public profiles)
Reisman, Michael, 228n (praxis "myth systems" for operational guides
    in cross-cultural commerce)
Hills, Roderick, M. 231 (moral relativism in pluralistic cultures)
Kohlberg, Lawrence, 232 (faith development as a higher order
    for moral development)
    (faith development and dying for stage 6?)
    (faith" and "ultimate life-meaning")
    (world starvation and stage 6?)
Fowler, James, 233 (faith development paradigm)
    (faith and Erikson's developmental psychology)
    (faith and Mead's social psychology)
    (faith and Kohlberg's moral psychology)
Niebuhr, H. Richard, 235 (synthesis of historical critical faith)
World Economic Forum, 235-6 (socio-religious faith syntheses for business)
Johnson, Mark, 237 (music for social change)
Siebert, Horst, 238 (ethical foundations of market economies)
Beauchamp, Tom, L. and Bowie, Norman E., 239n
    (rules and norms of moral value codes)
    (deontological ethics and universal moral
    norms of respect for persons)
Fletcher, Joseph, 239 (situation ethics and moral responsibility)
Lal, Deepak, 240 (growth, poverty and income inequality)
    (poverty alleviation and labor intensive growth)
Fowler, James 246 (the faith development scale)
Erikson, Eric, 247 (historical continuity awareness)
Eliade, Mircea, 247 (eternal perpetuity hopefulness)
Snarey, J. , 247 (faith development and "non-Theistic Judaism")
Turner, Ralph, 248 (independent thinking & anti-structural symbol language)
Tilly, Charles, 248 (mobilizing discourse and revolutionary activity)
Lifton, Robert, J., 248 (faith development and psycho-historical revolution)
Blair, Tony, 249-251 (Faith Foundation: conjunctive power of
    socio-religious faith)
Marcel, Gabriel, 251 (the "mysteries of being")
Cohen, Andrew, 251 (the "enlightenment of becoming")
Chardin de, Pierre Teilhard, 251 (the "mysteries of creatively believing")
Dewart, Leslie, 251 (socially imaginative faith)
Merton, Thomas, 251 (critically reflexive contemplative faith)

Messner, Monsignor J. 251n (social suffering and universalizing faith)
Clinton, William, J., 254-255 (Clinton Global Initiatives: *"eradicating corruption in emerging democracies"*)
Fort, Timothy, 255n (legal-ethical frameworks for conducting business)
Woo, Carolyn, 255-256 (UN and multinational organization partnerships)
Fayerweather, John, 256 (multinational organizations' moral accountability)
Tracy, David, 256n (humanistic moral needs: global climates & world hunger)
Mansbridge, Peter, 256n (global warming, polar melting, and animal starving)
Werhane, Patricia, 256n (managerial decision-making & moral imagination)
Lal, Deepak, 256n (causation politics and human hunger)
Thomashow, Mitchell, 257-258 (faith development and cosmological trust rebuilding)
Fort, Timothy, and Schipani, C, 261n (corporate governance and, transnational social system environments)
Guerrette, Richard, 262n (corporate art and aesthetic transformation)
Macey, Jonathan, 262n (corporate reputation and legal regulation)

Chapter 9

The Corporate Conscience and Involved Moral Leadership

Dilenschneider, Robert, 263 (personal involvement in managerial leadership)
Schein, Edgar, 264 (interpersonal managing)
Sherman, Loreen, 264 (leadership development programs)
Schein, Edgar, 265 (leadership styles and organization types)
Freeman, Edward; Harrison, Jeffrey; and Wicks, Andrew, 266 (delegating leadership and stakeholder profiting values)
Deutschman, Alan, 267 (interpersonal integrative moral leadership)
Lutnick, Howard, 267-268 (care-taking moral leadership)
Robinson, Barbara, 268 (interpersonal transformational leadership)
Jobs, Steve, 271 (his personal, final eschatological words)
Simpson, Mona, 271 ("A Sister's Eulogy for Steve Jobs")
Shiller, Robert J., 271 (the "mythic figure" of Steve Jobs)
Thompson, Francis, 271 (the "Hound of Heaven" *chase* of Steve Jobs)
Buffet, Warren, 272 (post-conventional moral leadership: honesty and caring corporate governance)
Lutnick, Howard, 272 (morally engaging leadership: role-taking sensitivity and care-taking calculations)
Robinson, Barbara, 273 (the "Elder-Wise Model of Transformational Leadership")

Chapter 10

The Personal Conscience and Integrated Moral Leadership

Podolny, Joel, 275 (New MBA Curriculum at Yale Management School)
        276 (self-dissociation management and ethical breaches)
Luban, David, 276 (cognitive dissonance theory and
        morally disintegrating disconnections)
Erickson, Eric, 277-280 (personal integrity, corporate integrity
        and the "sequence of generations")
Simpson, Mona, 280 (the "*aesthetic life*" and the integrative
        moral commitment of Steve Jobs)
Lifton, Robert, Jay, 281 (psycho-historical integration and
        moral leadership consistency)
Olian, Judy; Phillips, Susan; Policano, Andrew, 283 (AACSB Deans and
        action-based MBE *Internship Programs*)
Olian, Judy, 284 (innovative strategies and alliances for
        business school education)
Policano, Andrew 284-285 (innovation process and strategies
        for business school education)
Gordon, John, and Berry, Joyce, 285 (the essential role of
        environmental leadership)
Redekop, Benjamin, W. 285 (leadership for environmental sustainability)
Western, Simon, 285 (eco-leadership as a new paradigm)
Becker, Corne, J. 285 (spirituality and environmental leadership)
Cayne, Bernard, S., 287 (corporate retreats and withdrawing for "peace")
Erikson, Eric, 290n (Erikson's psychosocial integrity scale and
        Kohlberg's social trust morality scale)
Hillman, James 290n (rediscovering the soul within depth psychology and
        aesthetic beauty)

Appendix

Managing Moral Development in Sexual Ethics

Lickona, Thomas, 291 (graphic sexual inter-relational examples)
        292-302 (stages of moral reasoning and sexual decision-making)

SIGNIFICANT AUTHOR AND SUBJECT INDEX

Subject Themes of Cited Authors

Adeola, Francis	202	industrial disasters and moral consciousness of citizens
Allport, F.L.	33	structural theory and social psychology
Anderson, Charles	202	social class inequalities and moral consciousness
Argyris, Chris	118	teaching workers on reflexive thinking
	133	organization defensive routines
	157	ethical inconsistency and "organization defensive routines"
	185	self-interest motivation and defensive routines
Baker, Thomas and Hunt, Tammy		
	104	gender and teams on workplace ethics
Barnard, Chester	197	enduring intrafirm cooperation and holistic economic good
Baum, V.	33	ethics as a behavioral science
Beauchamp, Tom L.	32	applying ethical theory to business practice
Beauchamp, Tom, L. and Bowie, Norman E.,		
	239	rules and norms of moral value codes deontological ethics: universal moral norms and respect for persons
Bebeau, Muriel	7-8	professional education and ethical development
Beck, Eckardt	202	"Love Canal" and love-caring inequalities
Becker, Corne, J.	285	spirituality and environmental leadership
Balassa, Bela	188	intraplant economies of scale
Bennis, Warren	135	organizational planning for change
Bennis, Warren; Benne, Kenneth; and Chin, Robert		
	209	planning for change
Berg, Per-Olof	53	company image-building
Berger, Peter L. and Luckmann, Thomas		
	22	reconstructing social organization realities
	226	reconstructing social realities
Bergson, Henri	143	"elan vital" of love
Bernstein, Richard	170	ethical learning for practical moral judgments
	226	practical reconstruction planning
Bezos, Jeff	18	ethical sensitivity
Birsch, Douglas	21-29	product safety and cost-benefit-analysis
	38n	Ford Pinto Trial
Bittle, Celestine N.	43	moral philosophy of the individual conscience
Blair, Tony	249-251	conjunctive power of socio-religious faith
Blasi, Augusto	32	evaluating methods for moral performance
	32	moral consistency in moral functioning
	89	bridging moral cognition and moral action

	126	moral identity and moral functioning
Blenkinsopp, Joseph	143	sexuality and the Christian tradition
	143	eros and the Christian
Blumer, Herbert	33	sociological theory in industrial relations
	57	symbolic interaction in sociology
Bowen, M, and Power, C.		
	131-132	moral managing and communicative ethics
	213	ethical inconsistency and reasonable judging uncertainty
Boyd, Dwight R.	191	translating principles into moral action
Boyett, Joseph and Conn, Henry		
	114	maximum performance management
Braito, Rita, Paulson, Steve and Klonglan, Gerald		
	87	domain consensus & power relationships
Brinkerhoff, Merlin	31	organization self as unit analysis
Brinkerhoff, Merlin and Kunz, P. R.		
	31	complex organizations
Buffet, Warren	266, 272	inspirational leadership and shareholder moral values
Candee, David	89	moral intervention problems in organizational settings
Capellas, Michael	5	ethics education on company values: evaluation
Carlo, William E.	49	philosophy, science and knowledge
Cayne, Bernard, S.	287	retreat concept of withdrawing for "peace"
Chardin de, Pierre Teilhard		
	251	"mysteries of creatively believing"
Clinton, William, J.	222	Clinton Foundation and global moral collectivities
	223-224	Clinton Global Initiatives: "Inspiring Change" climate change; responsible governance; poverty elimination; and religion reconciliation
	253-255	Clinton Global Initiatives: "eradicating corruption in emerging democracies"
Cohen, Andrew	251	the "enlightenment of becoming"
Cooley, Charles H	33	human nature and the social order
	43	location of the corporate conscience
Cooper, Anderson, and Gupta, Sanjay		
	220	CNN's global conscience networks
Cushman, Fiery; Young, Liane; Greene, Joshua		
	63	human capacity for moral judgments
Dahrendorf, Ralph	202	class conflict inequalities
Day, Robert A. and Day, Joanne, V.		
	210	negotiating organizational order processes
	211	inconsistencies in health care and economic structures
Deutschman, Alan	267	interpersonal integrative moral leadership
Dewart, Leslie	251	socially imaginative faith
Dilenschneider, Robert	42	influence and integrity
	125	leadership with moral consistency
	231	cross-cultural climates and ethical decision-making
	263	personal involvement in managerial leadership
Dill, William, R.,	87	organization environment and managerial autonomy
Doris, John M.	33	social psychology of ethics
Drucker, Peter	3-4	ethical legacy: short on Moral Development training
Edwards, Mark	23	opening meta-theoretical visions
	31	transforming organizations for sustainability
Eliade, Mircea	247	eternal perpetuity hopefulness
Emler, Nicholas and Hogan, Robert		
	84	honesty and ethics in MBO hierarchical promotions
	201	hegemonic culture causes of value norm incongruences
	203	balancing moral development and corporate responsibility

	206	hegemonic moral stage determinism
Erikson, Dan	219-220	global organization conscience of the UN
Erikson, Erik	18, 20	ethical care for the "sequence of generations"
	247	historical continuity awareness
	277-289	(social-psychological root systems of personal integrity)
		(corporate integrity and the "sequence of generations")
	290n	psychosocial life cycle scale & Kohlberg's social trust stage of morality
Etzioni, Amitai	31	new directions for organizations and society
	32	moral dimensions for economic reviewing
	63-64	moral implications of stage 6 deference
	84	authority-subordinate relations in terms of authority styles and compliance patterns.
	111n	hegemony is described as culturally bound preferences
	196	initiating moral power of "internalized values"
Evan, William, M.	81-82	"organization-set" of interorganizational relations
Farley, Sister Margaret	143	morally reformative defining of sexual ethics
Fayerweather, John	256	multinational organizations' moral accountability
Ferguson, Niall	16	innovation: the heartbeat of economic growth
	182	financial innovation
Ferguson, Niall and Zakaria, Fareed		
	182	managerial innovation
Fletcher, Joseph	239	situation ethics and moral responsibility
Fort, Timothy	255	mediating trusted leadership
Fort, Timothy and Schipani C.		
	261n	corporate governance and transnational social systems
Fowler, James	233	faith development paradigm
	234	faith and Erikson's developmental psychology
		faith and Mead's social psychology
		faith and Kohlberg's moral psychology
	245-246	transcendental universal faith
Freeman, Edward; Harrison, Jeffrey; and Wicks, Andrew		
	266	delegating leadership and stakeholder profiting values
Fromm, Erich	146n	the nature of love
Galston, William	98-99	moral dilemmas of cloning and stem-cell research: Jewish tradition: Rabbi Tendler; Christian perspectives: Peters, Lebacqz, and Bennett
Gasparino, Charles	213	investing "blood" on Wall Street
Gellerman, Saul	85	"good" managers making bad ethical choices
Gilligan, Carol	4	interactional caring reciprocities
	52	caring and sensitivity
Goffman, Erving	52	impression management theory and process
Goldman, Paul and Van Houten		
	202	worker inequalities
Goodpaster, Kenneth	31	conceptualizing corporate responsibility
	49	critical ethical consistency and rationality and respect
Goodpaster, Kenneth and Matthews, John, B.		
	31	can a corporation have a conscience?
Gordon, John, and Berry, Joyce		
	285	environmental leadership as essential leadership
Gouldner, Alvin	38	corporate conscience in decision-making
	64	power and wealth and moral code conformity
	206	hegemonic elite variances and MBE alternatives
Graves, Phillip E.	29	environmental critique of cost-benefit analysis
Griffin, Emile	213	self-mobilization and executive reflexivity
Goethe, Johann, Wolfgang von		

	146n	ontological beauty and analogical integrity
Greenspan, Alan	243-244	profit maximization policies of greed and ethically impaired systemic determinism
Guerrette, Richard	19; 21	multidisciplinary aesthetic dimensions in corporate ethics
	48	management strategies for the organization self
	52	art and architecture in the workplace
	137	priesthood re-identification: organization solutions
	138	interactional praxis integration
	143	an artistic archetypal erotic "Passion Play"
	213	social unrest and new order change
Habermas, Jurgen	67	moral structural reform and communication ethics
	194-195	caring reciprocity and role-taking interaction
Hackman, Richard	117	psychology of self-management in organizations
	125n	implementing systems of self-appraisal
	195	6th stage initiative signs of responsibility taking
Haste, Helen	89-90	moral commitment interactional pathways

Hausman, Daniel M. and McPherson, Michael S.

	32	philosophical ethics and moral economics
	128	policy evaluations and moral appraisals
Healey, Joseph	251	metaphysical faith and ethnic disunities
Hesse, Helmut	187	global poverty and international economies
	188-190	moral imperative for economic principles
	191	international scope of global poverty

Higgins, Ann and Gordan

	101-102	moral climate in work-place democracies
Hillman, James	290n	rediscovery of the soul through depth psychology and aesthetic beauty
Hills, Roderick M.	231	moral relativism in global commerce
Holmstrom, Bengt	184	shirking behavior and performance inefficiency
James, William	43	psychosocial operations of the conscience
Jobs, Steve	18	leadership style
Johnson, Mark	237	music for social change
Kanter, Rosabeth	103	vanguard companies and parallel structure strategies

Katz, Daniel & Kahn Robert, L.

	33	social psychology of organizations
	33-36	open system theories in human behavior
	36	open systems for social interactional imperatives

King, Leslie and McCarthy, Deborah

	44	activating environmental sociology
Koestenbaum. Peter	213	leadership and the moral development of the inner self
Kohlberg, Lawrence	4	moral development theories
	33	philosophy and psychology of moral development
	50-51	justice and reciprocity
	59-60	moral development stages of responsibility awareness
	88-89	moral behavior and the teaching of "virtue"
	232-233	faith development as a higher order for moral development faith development and "would I die for stage 6? the "virtue of faith" and "ultimate life-meaning" world starvation and "would I contribute for stage 6?

Kohlberg, Lawrence and Colby, Anne

| | 58 | formal education and higher stage development |
| | 106-107 | moral management: authority types: [MBO] heteronomus and [MBE] autonomous types |

Kohlberg, Lawrence; Boyd, Dwight; and Devine, Charles

| | 58-61 | "the return of stage 6" |

Kohlberg, Lawrence, *et al*

	58	moral education in schools and prisons
	195	ethical value of caring for others
Kohlberg, Scharf and Hickey		
	102	democratic climate reform in prison
Krause, Elliot	202	power and illness inequalities
Krugman, Paul	153	corporate boards and corporate profits
	187	ethics and public policy
Kuhn, Thomas	20	historian of science
	23	revolutionary planning in social scientific research
	201	MBE paradigm and "revolutionary scientific perceptions"
Kung, Guido	63	empirical significance verification of stage 6
Kung, Hans	32	moral frameworks for economic markets
	215	The Global Ethic Foundation
	216	Global Ethic Declaration
		Global Ethic Voices from Religion and Politics
		Trilogy of World's Monotheistic Religions
		world religions, international politics and economics
Kung, Hans, and Ching, Julia		
	215	Christianity and Chinese Religions
Kung, Hans, and Kuschel, Karl-Josef		
	215	Parliament of World's Religions
Kung, Hans, and Schmidt, Helmut		
	216	global ethics and global responsibilities
Kurtines, William	33	psycho-social role theories in moral development
	84	psychosocial role theory and rule-governed relationships
Kurtines, William and Gewirtz, J. L.		
	115	moral behavior and development
Ladner, Gerhart, B.	138	historical ideas of reform
Lal, Deepak	240	growth, poverty and income inequality
	262n	politics and famines
Lauer, Robert, H.	213	social movements and social change
Lay, Kenneth	18	religiously faithful, morally divided leader
Levine, Sol and White, Paul E.		
	31	interorganizational relationships
	87	organization domains and task environments
Lewin, Kurt	67	moral points of view and culture changing strategies
Lickona, Thomas	291	managing moral development in sexual ethics
	292-302	stages of moral reasoning and sexual decision-making
Lifton, Robert, J.	206	hegemonic implications of symbolic constructs
	248	faith development and psycho-historical revolution
	281-282	psycho-historical integration and moral leadership consistency
Lindesmith, A., Strauss, A. and Denzin, N.		
	57	social psychology of care-taking
Lipartito and Sicilia	19; 21	"capitalistic" policies and enterprising ethos
Lonergan, Bernard, S.J.	199n	praxis strategies for macro-economic dynamics
Longstreth, Richard	206	ecological rewards of environmental restoration
Luban, David	276-277	cognitive dissonance theory and morally disintegrating disconnections
Lutnick, Howard	267	9/11 Cantor Fitzgerald 9/11 Relief Fund
	267-268	morally sensitive interpersonal delivery system of benefits
Lytton, Timothy	134-135	clergy sex abuse and legal accountability
Macey, Jonathan	257	the loss of integrity on Wall Street
	262n	moral development "fracturing" of reputation and regulation
Mahler, Gustave	146n	the romantic poetry of love
Mansbridge, Peter	261n	global warming, polar melting, and animal starving

Marcel, Gabriel	143	sacramental novel applications
	251	the "mysteries of being"
Marcuse, Herbert	20	social theorist of aesthetic dimensions
Martin, Stephen	190	evolutionary economics and praxis methodologies
Mayo, E.	57	industrial civilization and social problems
McNeel, Steven	164	defining ethical issues in moral development learning
McNichols, Stuart	145n	policy decisions and clergy appointment planning
McNichols, Thomas	138	strategic importance of corporate integration and managerial scanning
Mead, George Herbert	33	social psychology of human behavior
	43	location of individual conscience
Merton, Thomas	251	reflexive contemplative faith
Messner, Monsignor J.	261	socially suffering and spiritual transfixing faith
Miller, Alan	188	global poverty, economic policy, and eco-ethics
Miller, Gary	185	inspirational management incentive building
	186	work teams and cooperative equilibria
	187	economic conventions of corporate culture
	187	critical evaluation of Miller's instrumental reciprocities
Mills, C. Wright	57	moral significance of shaping worker attitudes
	152	vested interest benefits of power elite behavior
	157	ethical principles and "sociological imagination"
	158	moral character and historically involved moral leaders
Minkler, Lance	193	trust reciprocity and optimal work performance
	206-207	lifting the research "hegemonic lid"
Misgeld, Dieter	202	third world inequalities
Moore, Michael	23	revolutionary planning on Wall Street
Nagel, Stuart	141	policymaking stability and variation flexibility
Niebuhr, H. Richard	235	synthesis of historical critical faith
Nouwen, Henri	144	healing the Corporate Body of the Church
O'Brien, George Dennis	99n	moral insights in personal ethical decision-making
	136	the relation of morality and sin
O'Hanlon, Brian	190-191	associative 6th stage moral management
O'Malley, Michael	149	social development of cooperation
	196	analogical collective altruism of "bumble bees"
O'Neil, Robert P. and Donovan, Michael A.		
	146n	sexual masturbation and guilt development
Olasky, M.N.	54	inside the immoral world of public relations
Olian, Judy	8	Dean UCLA Task Force on Management Education
	163	management education at risk
Olian, Judy; Phillips, Susan; Policano, Andrew		
	283	AACSB and Internship Programs
Orr, David, W.	188	principles, economics and the environment
Orsburn, Jack, Moran, L. Musselwhite E and Zenger, J.		
	114	self-directed work-teams
Oster, Sharon	170	core curricular viewpoints in management education
	178	caring ethics for persons
Parsons, Talcott	138	functional adaptation
	203	"Love Canal" electric or hegemonic power failure?
Penn, W. Y.	164	moral learning through curricular intervention
Perrow, Charles	31	comparative analysis of organizations
Pfeifer, Jeffrey and Owens, Katherine		
	132	military leadership and ethics
Phillips, Derek L.	121	methods in social research
Phillips, Susan M.	7	AACSB business education report
	65	business education and deficient moral codes
	163	ethics education in business schools

Podolny, Joel 165 core curricular studies in management education
276 New MBA Curriculum at Yale Management School
277 professional behavior and self-dissociation
Policano, Andrew 9 and AACSB: business schools
163 on an innovation mission
Ponemon, Lawrence and
Gabhart, David 8 ethical education need in accounting and auditing
professions
Power, Clark 100 moral climate in school-place democracies
Power, C.; Higgins, A.; and Kohlberg, L.
59 cognitive learning of incremental stage reasoning
200 hegemony in research subjects and processes
Pruyser, Paul 20 Society for the Scientific Study of Religion
Redekop, Benjamin, W. 31 responsible accountability for ecological sustainability
285 leadership for environmental sustainability
Redman, Chris 24 Pinto trial and corporate responsibility
Reisman, Michael 259n "myth systems" in normative guides and actual conduct
Rest, James 4 moral measuring of cooperative behavior
33 post-conventional moral thinking
61-62 psychology and applied ethics
62-63 psychological components for moral judgments
89 moral character and ego strength
148 conceptions of work associations
150 social interventions for advanced moral behavior
160 measuring principle moral leadership profiles
Rest, James and Narvaez, Darcia
75 defining issues of moral thinking
Rest, James and Narvarez, Darcia
75-76 principle moral reasoning and scoring impairments
183 cooperative virtue
Ricoeur, Paul 190 economy of gift
224n ethical generosity giving
Robinson, Barbara 273 "Elder-Wise Model of Transformational Leadership"
Roethlisberger, A. J. and Dickson W. J.
57 management and the worker
Roguet, A. G. 143 sacramental acts of grace
Rose, Charlie 273 transformational leadership of Howard Schultz
Rule, J. T. and Bebeau, Muriel
131 professional commitment and moral caring
Sachs, Jeffrey 188 re-awakening moral virtue and economic prosperity
Schein, Edgar 264 interpersonal managing
264-265 leadership styles and organization types
Schillebeeckx, E. 143 sacramental encounters with God
Schroeder, Timothy; Roskies, Adina L.; and Nichols, Shaun
62 moral motivation
Schumpeter, Joseph 190 economic praxis and associative corporatism
Schwab, Charles 24 market investing paradigm change
Sethia, Nirmal and Von Glinow, Mary Ann
194 caring human resource cultures and intrafirm cooperation
Sewell, William H. 57 social psychology of socialization agents
Sherman, Loreen 150 practical guides of leadership worker coaching
264 leadership development programs
Shiller, Robert J. 271 the "mythic figure" of Steve Jobs
Siebert, Horst 29, 238 ethical foundations of market economies
Simpson, Mona 271 the final moments of the death of Steve Jobs

	280	"aesthetic life" and the integrative moral commitment of Steve Jobs
Snarey, J.	247	faith development and Judaism
Snider, Julie	152	executive pay and nation's wealth gap
Sonnenfeld, Jeffrey	4	structural-functional themes of management operations
Taylor, Charles	20	philosopher and political scientist
	23	finding authentic moral standpoints
	44	ethical sources of the "self"
	207	deepening moral sources in the ethics of authenticity
Thomashow, Mitchell	46-47	personal and collective operational reflexivity
	203	environmental reflexivity practice
	214	developing moral ecological awareness
	257-8	mediating institutions and multi-national trust building
Thompson, Francis	271	the "Hound of Heaven" chase of Steve Jobs
	271	the final moment of the last breath of Steve Jobs
Thompson, James D.	87	organization domain and cooperative associations
Tilly, Charles	248	faith development mobilization
Time Magazine (5/25/86)	224n	"America Searches for Its Moral Bearings"
Tracy, David	261n	humanistic moral needs of global climates and world hunger
Turiel, Elliot and Smetana, Judith		
	85	social knowledge & moral action in domain coordination
Turner, Ralph H.	125	role-taking in group behavior
	209	role-taking process versus conformity
Turner, Victor	214	structure and anti-structure
	248	faith development and independent rational thinking
Uhl, Christopher	210	formulating moral plans of action
van der Erve, Mark	22	evolutionary management in the marketplace
	189-190	economics and evolutionary management
Vieira, Meredith	99	regenerative medicine and stem cell research
Von Glinow, Mary Ann	198	moral purpose impact on productive reasoning
Vroom, Victor	114-116	motivation and intuitive rational processes
		intuitive motivational understanding
Walzer, Michael	202	justice inequalities
Weber, Max	143	historically defining sexual ethos
	146n	"the sublimation of sexual expression"
Weinreich-Haste, Helen	34	socio-cultural moralities in collectivities
		inter-organizational collectivities and MBO moralities
	47	culturally specific meanings and the organization self
Weiss, William	212	value-system-building and decision-making uncertainties
Werhane, Patricia	256	managerial decision-making and moral imagination
	261-262	moral imagination and corporate decision-making
Western, Simon	285	eco-leadership as a new paradigm
Whitehead, Alfred North		
	212	managing processes and role-taking caring relationships
Willis, Sherry, and Dubin, Samuel		
	114	maintaining professional competence
Woo, Carolyn	255	UN and multinational organization partnerships
Wood, Robert and Mitchell, Terrance		
	55n	management behavior in social context
World Economic Forum		
	235-236	socio-religious faith syntheses for business
Yussen, Steven	209	moral reasoning perspectives
Zakaria, Fareed	15-16	the heartbeat of economic growth
	183	managerial innovation

CHÂTEAU
—— *of* ——
SECRETS

**Center Point
Large Print**

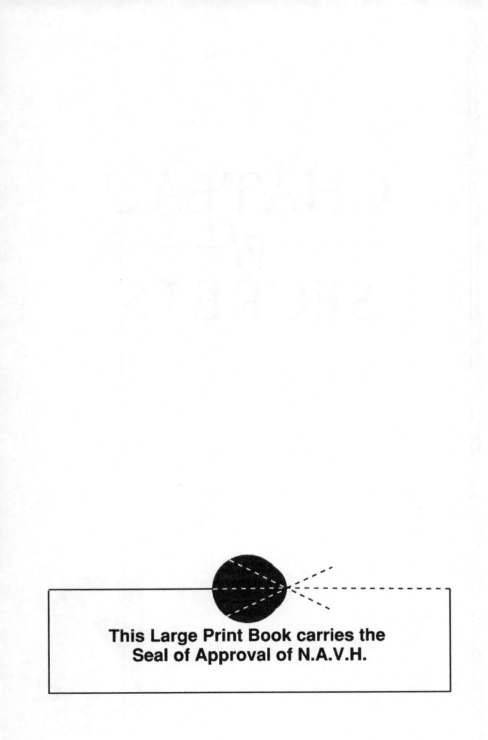

**This Large Print Book carries the
Seal of Approval of N.A.V.H.**

CHÂTEAU
—— *of* ——
SECRETS

MELANIE DOBSON

CENTER POINT LARGE PRINT
THORNDIKE, MAINE

This Center Point Large Print edition
is published in the year 2014 by arrangement with
Howard Books, a division of Simon & Schuster, Inc.

This book is a work of fiction. Any references to
historical events, real people, or real places
are used fictitiously. Other names, characters, places,
and events are products of the author's imagination,
and any resemblance to actual events or places or
persons, living or deceased, is entirely coincidental.

The text of this Large Print edition is unabridged.
In other aspects, this book may vary
from the original edition.
Printed in the United States of America
on permanent paper.
Set in 16-point Times New Roman type.

ISBN: 978-1-62899-145-1

Library of Congress Cataloging-in-Publication Data

Dobson, Melanie B.
  Château of secrets / Melanie Dobson. — Center Point Large Print
Edition.
  pages ; cm
  Summary: "A young noblewoman hides French resistance fighters in
tunnels beneath her home while Germans occupy her house. Seventy
years later, her granddaughter visits the family's abandoned château and
uncovers shocking secrets from the past"—Provided by publisher.
  ISBN 978-1-62899-145-1 (library binding : alk. paper)
  1. France—History—German occupation, 1940–1945—Fiction.
  2. World War, 1939–1945—Underground movements—France—Fiction.
  3. Nobility—France—Fiction. 4. Jews—France—History—Fiction.
  5. Family secrets—Fiction. 6. Large type books. I. Title.
PS3604.O25C47 2014b
813'.6—dc23
                                                        2014011824

Genevieve Marie Josephe de Saint Pern Menke
1922–2010

CHÂTEAU
— *of* —
SECRETS

PART ONE

*All the darkness in the world cannot extinguish
the light of a single candle.*

—ST. FRANCIS OF ASSISI (1181–1226)

Chapter 1

June 1940
Agneaux, France

Candlelight flickered on the medieval walls as Gisèle Duchant stepped into the warmth of the nave. The shadows in the sacristy were the only witnesses to her secret—no one but she and Michel knew the same small room that stored the vestments and supplies for their family's *chapelle* was also a hiding place.

She slid the iron gate across the entry into the sacristy, and after locking it, she set down her picnic hamper—emptied of its Camembert cheese and Calvados—and turned toward the pews.

Five women from Agneaux, the tiny commune at the top of the lane, knelt before the altar, the sweet fragrance of incense blending with the smell of cigarette smoke on their clothing. For centuries, women had visited this *chapelle* to plead with the Almighty to protect their husbands, sons, and brothers as they fought for France. Now they battled in prayer even as the men they loved defended their country against Hitler and his ploy to assimilate the French people into his Third Reich.

Gisèle slid her fingers over the amber rosary beads around her neck, gently fingering the ornamented handle of the brass crucifix in the center. A cross that was also a key.

"Secrets can destroy."

The words of her university professor echoed in her mind. If a secret was powerful enough, her philosophy professor had declared from his lectern, it could demolish an entire army. Or shatter the heart of a family.

The narrow pew creaked as she knelt beside it. Looking up at the crucifix that hung above the altar, she crossed herself and then whispered, "Our Father, who art in heaven, hallowed be thy Name."

Her mind wandered as the familiar prayer tumbled from her lips.

The healing powers of a secret intrigued her, the layers that sheltered families and nations alike. A secret could destroy, like her professor said, but it could also shield a family. Like the tangled hedge-rows of brushwood and bramble that fortified the nearby city of Saint-Lô, a secret could keep those you love from destruction.

When did a secret cross over the gray waste-land between protecting one you loved and destroying him?

Last month Prime Minister Chamberlain had evacuated all the British troops he'd sent to France, along with a hundred thousand French soldiers. Michel had been among those evacuated at Dunkirk, and Papa thought his son was safe in England.

But Michel snuck home after the evacuation, and she prayed God would forgive her for her trespasses, that her secret effort to save her younger brother's life wouldn't become a mortal sin.

The women whispered prayers around her, and like many of them, she couldn't confess her sin to anyone, not even to the priest who came once a week to preside over Mass. With the world in turmoil, they all had to guard secrets to protect the men they loved.

Aeroplane engines buzzed in the distance, and she shivered. The German bombers flew over them almost every night now, showing off their power for the citizens of Saint-Lô. Her country refused to be intimidated by their display.

Candles rattled in their bronze holders.

"Deliver us from evil," she whispered as the planes passed overhead. Then she repeated her words.

Unlike Austria and Denmark, France would fight the Nazis.

When the drone of engines settled into the night, the village women silently slipped out the door. Gisèle rose to attend to her duties.

Just as she was the keeper of Michel's secret, she was the keeper of the Chapelle d'Agneaux.

While other aristocratic women attended their formal gardens or antique collections, her mother had painstakingly cared for the *chapelle* for two decades. Instead of remembering her mother at the cemetery beside the *chapelle*, Gisèle liked to remember her inside these walls. When she was at the château, Gisèle unlocked the door of the *chapelle* every morning so villagers could pray, and every night she blew out the vigil candles and swept the stone floors.

Outside in the courtyard, the misty breath of the river Vire stole up and over the stone walls of the *chapelle* and the turrets of the medieval château that stood before her, the home of the Duchant family for more than three hundred years. While her family had lost sons and daughters to the guillotine during the revolution and to the wars that were waged across France, this fortress of stone towers and secret tunnels had sheltered many of her ancestors through wars and storms. It had been a solace for her mother. And for her.

Gisèle quickly crossed the gravel courtyard and hurried into the foyer of the Château d'Epines. Sliding off her red suede pumps, she padded across the marble floor in her silk stockings, the handles of the picnic hamper clutched in her hands. If she could store the hamper before she saw her father, she wouldn't have to lie to him.

She snuck past the staircase that spiraled up to the second floor and the entrance to the drawing room, but before she reached the door to the kitchen, her father called her name. Then she heard the heels of his sturdy Richelieus clapping across the marble floor.

She dropped the hamper and kicked it to the edge of the antique console table.

The sight of her father in his brown cardigan and trousers, the familiar scent of applewood and tobacco, usually comforted her, but tonight the fear in his blue eyes wasn't familiar at all. Papa—known in France as the esteemed Vicomte Jean-François de Bouchard Duchant—was never afraid.

She clasped the pumps to her chest. "What is it?"

His gaze wandered toward the tall window by the front door, like he was seeking solace from the *chapelle* outside as well.

"Hitler—" His voice cracked, and he hesitated as if he hadn't yet digested the news he bore.

"Papa?" she whispered, pressing him.

"Hitler has taken Paris."

Her shoes clattered on the marble and she stumbled backward as if the tiles had shifted under her feet. Her hands flailed, searching until they caught the banister.

Paris was a great city, the greatest in the world. How could it bow to a lunatic?

"But the war—" she stammered. "It has just begun."

Papa's shoulders dropped. "The government in Paris . . . they decided not to fight."

She squeezed the iron banister. How could the Parisians refuse to fight?

If the French resisted together, if they refused to cower . . .

They had to resist.

"What will happen?" she whispered.

"Philippe is coming to drive you south, to the manor in Lyon."

"I don't care what happens to me." Her voice trembled. "What will happen to France?"

He hesitated again, like he wasn't sure he should tell her the truth. He might still have thought her twelve, but she was twenty-two years old now. A graduate of the prestigious Université de Caen. She was certainly old enough to know the truth.

She willed strength into her voice. If he thought her strong, perhaps he would be honest. "You must tell me."

He seemed to consider her words before he spoke. "Hitler won't stop until he takes all of Europe."

She released the banister to pick up her pumps, her hands trembling. "I can't go to Lyon."

Compassion mixed with the fear in his eyes. "We must leave. Hitler seems determined to take London next, and his army will march through here on their way to the port at Cherbourg."

She rubbed her bare arms. Lyon was ten hours

southeast. "If they've taken Paris, it won't be long before the Germans take Lyon too."

"Perhaps." Papa tugged on the hem of his cardigan. "But Philippe can take you to Switzerland before then."

Hitler's appetite for power seemed insatiable. He'd taken much of Europe now, but she doubted conquering the rest of France and even London would satisfy the German führer. With the French government refusing to fight, they needed courageous Frenchmen—former soldiers like Michel—to stop him.

But ten years ago, before her mother died, she'd begged Gisèle to care for Michel. Even though she was just a girl, Gisèle had sworn, on the crucifix of her mother's rosary, that she would give her very life to watch over her brother. Michel may have been nineteen now, but he was just as headstrong as when he was a boy. How could she protect him from an onslaught of the German army and their bombs?

Papa rang a bell. "Émilie will help you pack your things for the trip."

Seconds later their housemaid rushed into the hall, her white apron tied over her black uniform and her graying hair pinned back in a neat knot. But instead of stopping, Émilie rushed past Gisèle to the front door, a valise clutched in each of her hands.

Papa called out to her. "Where are you going?"

Émilie set down one of her bags. "My sister just called from Cahagnes. German tanks are moving through the town."

Papa swore. Cahagnes was just thirty kilometers away.

As the door opened and then rattled shut, Gisèle slipped on her shoes. Before she left, she had to warn Michel that the Germans were near.

"You must pack your things," Papa said as he glanced at his watch. "Philippe said he would be here within the half hour."

Her chest felt as if it might explode. The Germans might kill them if they stayed, but she couldn't leave without telling her brother. He had to flee as well.

"I need more time," she pleaded.

"*Ma chérie*," he said tenderly as he reached for her hand, imploring her. "It is not safe for you to stay here any longer."

Her heart felt as if it might rip into two. How could she make him understand without revealing Michel's secret?

He nudged her toward the steps. "I will meet you in Lyon."

Still she didn't move. "You must come with us, Papa."

"I will follow soon, after I hide the silver and your mother's jewelry. If they arrive while I'm here—" He cleared his throat. "The Germans won't harm a member of the aristocracy."

She nudged her chin up. "Nor will they harm his daughter."

A siren wailed and the floor shook from more aeroplanes sweeping low in the valley. Hair bristled on the back of her neck.

Papa turned her shoulders toward the stairs. "Hurry, Gisèle."

"I can't—"

"You don't have a choice."

She knew he was afraid that he would lose her, just like he had her mother, but if she left right now—

She feared they would both lose Michel.

CHAPTER 2

June 2014
Richmond, Virginia

The clock at the back of my classroom ticked past the hour of four, and I shoved my MacBook into its pink-and-brown-striped case.

Don't be late!!!

Tommy Dawson, my favorite third grader, eyed the text on my phone. "Who is that?"

Mrs. Dawson nudged her son. "Miss Sauver doesn't have to tell you."

"It's Austin," I said before I turned off my phone. He was sending a car to pick me up at five for tonight's gala in downtown Richmond, and he hated it when I was late. It would take a good fifteen minutes to drive home and another forty-five to dress and do something decent with my hair, but I couldn't rush Tommy or his mother.

Tommy plucked his backpack off the hook one last time and lingered beside my desk for a final good-bye before summer break. Mrs. Dawson reached for Tommy's backpack and slung it over her shoulder before she turned back toward me. "When are you getting married?"

I smiled. "On August 10."

"I'm sure it will be a gorgeous wedding."

I maintained my smile, a talent I'd honed to perfection over the past six months. It had to be a dream wedding, the most beautiful one in Richmond that summer, or my first months of marriage would be a nightmare.

Mrs. Dawson handed Tommy a coffee mug, and he set it on my desk. After five years of teaching third grade, I had dozens and dozens of mugs, each one displayed on a shelf in my condo as a happy reminder of the student who'd given it to me. My students knew me and my passion for France well, gifting me every year with trinkets that displayed the Eiffel Tower or the Palace of Versailles or the Cathédrale Notre Dame in Paris. I admired the photo of Mont Saint-Michel on Tommy's mug and thanked him and his mother for the gift.

Then Tommy reached into his pocket and pulled

out a miniature plastic lion, the kind that comes in a box along with giraffes and elephants at the craft store. He lifted it up to show me.

"Who's this?" I asked.

"It's Aslan," he stated with certainty, as if I should know exactly who it was.

Mrs. Dawson flashed an apologetic smile. "He's been obsessed with Narnia ever since you read *The Lion, the Witch and the Wardrobe*."

"Narnia is one of my favorite places too." My gaze slipped down to Tommy and the lion clasped in his hand. "My grandmother used to read me the stories when I was about your age."

His eyes grew wide. "Have you been to Narnia?"

I almost laughed until I realized Tommy was serious. "Not yet . . . but perhaps one day."

He rewarded me with his grin.

"We'll both miss you." Mrs. Dawson glanced down at her son as he raced Aslan across the desk. "But I told him that he'd see you next year."

My poised smile began to crack. "Unfortunately, I won't be coming back to teach."

Tommy's lips trembled, and I leaned over, nudging his chin. "But I can still visit, can't I?"

He nodded and then hugged me. Mrs. Dawson finally coaxed him out the door, but the truth was, I didn't want them to go.

For the past nine months, Washington Elementary had entrusted twenty-seven students to my care. This year had been a challenging one, with two students, in particular, who felt quite confident in their leadership abilities. While I loved to teach—and loved the children—I hated conflict.

The year had been spent in a silent battle between two kids who were stronger than me in spirit. I'd had to feign confidence I didn't have, but in the end, I was stronger for it. Perhaps I wouldn't miss the demands of those two students, but I would miss the enthusiasm of the other twenty-five.

When I powered up my phone again, there was another text from my fiancé.

Chloe?

I typed back a quick response.

On my way.

I turned off the overhead lights and rushed to my car.

Thankfully the weeks ahead would be so full of wedding planning and campaigning, I wouldn't have much time to think about missing my kids. Then by summer's end, I would join Austin Vale and his political aspirations in matrimony. Come November, if public opinion held, I would be the wife of Virginia's youngest governor in history, and I'd promised Austin that I'd dedicate myself full-time to this new role. I would no longer be teaching elementary kids, but Austin and I both hoped parenthood would follow soon after our wedding.

My '68 Mercedes roadster had no air-conditioning

and the heat was as temperamental as Virginia politics, but the body was a beautiful burgundy color and the convertible top still worked. When I turned twenty-one, my dad had bought it just for me. The doors had gotten dinged up over the past seven years and the fender was slightly askew, but when my dad offered to buy me a newer model, I declined. I liked the mystique—the charm—of the old much more than the sheen of the new.

Austin didn't have the same appreciation or affection for mystique. He'd asked me twice to replace my vehicle with a newer model, something more trendy, like a BMW or an Audi. I'd compromised much in our relationship, but I wasn't trading in my car just because it had a few bumps and bruises. It had taken a few weeks of finagling, but Austin and I finally reached an agreement that worked for both of us. I drove the roadster to and from school. When he couldn't pick me up for political events or meals with his parents, he sent a driver in a shiny sedan.

The sunshine lit my path home this afternoon, and the river beside the road seemed to beckon me. *Come play.* But there would be no time to kayak this weekend. Almost every minute was scheduled. Tonight's gala. A luncheon tomorrow in the Fan. Dinner at the Vales' plantation home. Sunday would be church downtown with Austin and then a golfing fund-raiser at the country club. Every event, Austin said, was another brick mortared on the monument of his campaign, each stone solidifying what his manager told the press. Austin Vale may have been young, but he was passionate, articulate, and qualified to lead the Commonwealth of Virginia. And his future wife would be leading alongside him.

Event-hopping was exhausting at times, but I understood the importance of it. We were a team, working together to win this governorship. What bothered me most about the election process was when Austin and I talked about our wedding. Instead of a ceremony, sometimes it felt like he was helping me coordinate another meet-and-greet. With the bloated guest list, half of whom I didn't even know, we would be meeting and greeting half of Richmond the same day we said our vows.

The local media had been mesmerized by our story from almost our first date, a year ago. Austin Vale, the successful attorney and son of the Honorable Richard Vale, a justice of the Supreme Court of Virginia. Chloe Sauver, granddaughter of a French war hero and daughter of a French nobleman who now owned the largest investment management company in the Commonwealth of Virginia. My mom was an accomplished business owner in her own right, but the political powers that be ignored her successes with the popular Bliss Bakery.

Austin and I had met by accident, when he

literally bumped into me and my chai latte at a local coffee shop. When he asked me to dinner, I hadn't known he was being courted as a candidate and he hadn't known about my family. I'd fallen almost immediately for the charming attorney who brought me flowers on our first date and asked me a dozen questions, the man who stopped by every week for lunch at my school in those first few months of dating and called for no other reason than to inquire about my day.

The morning after Austin announced our engagement, the national media became fascinated with the minutiae of our relationship. The morning shows were enchanted by our wedding plans, speculating on the cake, the flowers, even our choice of music for the reception. But when the tabloids came out each week, my heart sometimes felt like it would bleed, the doubts inside me fighting against the truth. The tabloids couldn't have cared less about our wedding plans, speculating instead on our faithfulness, as if either Austin or I had the time or desire to be cheating on the other.

Thankfully, there would be no media on our honeymoon. I didn't know where we were going, but Austin had promised it would be a million miles away from cameras and campaigning. Secretly, I hoped he was taking me back to France.

I pulled into the garage under my condo.

Tonight I couldn't get hung up on the details for the wedding or our honeymoon. Instead I had to focus on getting ready for this gala. A new dress was waiting for me in my closet, a cobalt-blue affair that Austin handpicked in Manhattan, along with some strappy black stilettos to go with it. I tossed my casual skirt and blouse into the laundry bin and began the transformation.

Austin's driver was on time, but I wasn't. It took an extra fifteen minutes to finish my makeup and torture my long hair with the flatiron. The mirror displayed an elegant woman with eyes the color of her dress and blond hair tucked behind one ear, but I felt a bit like a broken gift hidden under pretty paper and a bow. Sometimes I felt . . . well, sometimes I wondered if I was the right woman for Austin Vale. And if he was the right man for me. He said he loved me, that he was confident in our relationship and our future. Why couldn't I be confident as well?

With our wedding a little over two months away, it was much too late to reconsider. Our months of dating had been a firestorm of sorts—a romantic inferno. He had literally swept me off my feet the night he proposed, wading across a reflecting pool at the Madison Inn to our dinner waiting on the other side. Dozens of candles reflected in the pool and rosebuds dangled along the patio's trellis, sweetening the air. Before we ate, Austin got down on one knee, and my doubts faded in the lights.

No one could ever guess at my fear of living in the spotlight for the rest of my life or my haunting doubts about Austin's love.

But tonight wasn't the time for soul-searching. I'd have to do that later on the river, a paddle in my hands.

As I slid out of the town car and into the lobby of the Jefferson Hotel, my cell phone began to play the first bars of "Do You Hear the People Sing?"—one of my favorite songs from *Les Misérables*. I glanced down at my mother's picture on the screen and stuffed my phone into my beaded handbag. I'd have to call her back later tonight. Or first thing tomorrow.

I rushed through the lobby, and by the time I entered the elegant ballroom, the orchestra had already started playing. Hopefully Austin wouldn't notice I was late.

Chapter 3

*P*hilippe tossed her two suitcases into the luggage compartment of his new cabriolet, and then he opened the passenger door, waving her inside. "Hurry, Gisèle."

Instead of moving toward the car, she turned

toward her father. He stood dazed in the court-yard, like one of the winged statues displayed at the Louvre. He should have been flying away from the château with them, but he couldn't seem to move at all.

Her cousin waved toward the car again. "We have to get through town before the tanks arrive."

The stained glass on the *chapelle* glowed in the moonlight, not twenty meters from where she stood. Michel had sworn her to secrecy, but perhaps she should still tell Papa . . .

Her father still hadn't moved. She understood the fear that seemed to paralyze him—more than twenty years ago, he'd lost both of his brothers and a cousin to the Germans during the Great War. Then, less than a decade ago, he'd lost his wife. Now the Germans were threatening his home and the rest of his family.

If Michel refused to leave, Papa wouldn't leave either.

Stepping away from the car, she pleaded. "I must visit the *chapelle*, Papa. One last time."

But it was Philippe, not Papa, who responded to her plea. "You can pray at a chapel in Lyon."

She shook her head. "I can't wait."

Philippe brushed both hands over his short hair, frustrated with her delay. "Then pray in the car."

"He's right, Gisèle," Papa said, urging her forward.

She eyed the *chapelle* one last time. She could

sprint toward it, but Philippe would follow her and so would Papa. She doubted they would force her into the car, but they would never allow her to be alone in the sacristy.

Papa finally stepped forward, kissed her cheeks. "I will see you before the week ends."

A bomb exploded to the east, the night sky sparking near the town.

"Come with us now," she begged her father one last time.

But he pushed her into the seat and closed the door.

"Soon," he mouthed on the other side of her window.

Over her shoulder, she watched him at the end of the drive, waving to her. She rolled down her window and waved back, her heart in shreds.

She felt like a coward, running away when her brother—and her father—needed her.

Philippe rode in silence beside her, under the long row of beech trees that lined the entrance to the château. His gloved fingers circled around the steering wheel, his eyes focused on the narrow road lit by the moon as he sped through Agneaux, turning left toward the city of Saint-Lô.

She and Philippe were distant cousins and they both looked like their ancestors with hair the chalky tan color of the Norman beaches and eyes the same light blue of the English Channel. Her father and his mother—Corinne Duchant Borde—

were technically second cousins, but she called his mother Tante Corinne.

Philippe's father had been killed during the Great War, but Tante Corinne and Gisèle's mother had been dear friends. Today Gisèle, Michel, and Philippe were the last descendants of the Duchant bloodline.

Philippe had asked her father twice to marry her, to reunite the Duchant family again through matrimony, but she didn't love him the way a wife should love her husband. Whenever Philippe brought up the subject, Papa had stalled, saying she must finish at the university first.

Now Gisèle had her diploma and her own desires for the future, desires that didn't include wedding her cousin. The Germans had muddied her plans to lounge on the beaches in Brittany for the summer and perhaps, to her father's dismay, obtain a position teaching literature in the fall. Papa couldn't understand why she would want to work, but the thought of living on her own, supporting herself even, thrilled her. And women did it these days. Her friend Odette had begun working in Paris last year and telephoned almost every week, begging Gisèle to join her.

Had Odette left Paris before the Germans arrived?

As lights flashed again in the distance, Gisèle retied the laces on her most sensible brogue shoes and clutched her sweater over her chest. They were two kilometers from Saint-Lô now, and on the other side of the city, the main road curled south toward Lyon. The Germans may have been bombing, but she prayed the tanks hadn't arrived in the town yet.

Philippe glanced over at her. "Your brother is the lucky one, hiding out in England with your mother's family."

"Lucky for him," she whispered.

"Your father should have sent you to England a long time ago."

"There was no reason for me to leave." She slowly unfolded her arms. Philippe didn't need to know that her father hadn't spoken to the Eckleys since her mother's death. "None of us guessed that Paris would surrender."

They rode through the forest and then over the stone bridge, the Vire flowing underneath. They trailed the river as they drove into Saint-Lô. Ahead was the tall steeple above the cathedral, a proud symbol of their faith in God and in France. Their government may have failed them, but she prayed God would not.

The main road was crammed with people. Dozens of cars and horse carts, bicyclists, and crowds of people fleeing on foot with their luggage in hand or strapped to their back. Her heart raced. How were they supposed to get out of town before the Germans arrived?

Philippe honked his horn, and the pedestrians

divided like the Red Sea. But a truck blocked the road.

Philippe opened his window. "Get out of the way," he shouted out, the gasoline fumes flooding into the *coupé*. The truck didn't move.

Another explosion ignited the sky, and Gisèle gasped. People fled from their automobiles into shops on both sides of the road.

Smoke poured into Philippe's window. Coughing, she waved her hands in front of her. "They're going to kill us all."

He honked again. "Now would be the time to pray."

She clung to the cross on her rosary beads and closed her eyes, begging the Almighty for a way out.

Something exploded on the left, and her window shattered. She froze on the seat, too shocked to even scream.

Philippe leaned over, pushing her door open. "Get out."

"But—"

"Please, Gisèle."

She stumbled onto the sidewalk, the smoke suffocating her. Villagers screamed around her, some colliding into each other as they fled. She didn't know in which direction to run.

"Philippe!" she screamed.

In the clamor of the crowd, she heard Philippe call her name, his voice muffled. She tried to run around the car, but the crowd pressed up against her and she tripped over the handles of an abandoned bicycle.

"Philippe," she said again, this time a whisper. It didn't matter how loud she screamed. He would never hear her.

In the blackness, the smoke, she ran west. Back toward the safety of her home, toward her father and brother.

Hundreds of people dashed back over the bridge alongside her, but on the other side of the river, she ducked into a narrow passage between the towering hedgerows. Her legs burned as she ran down another passage and then out into the forest of tangled hawthorns and apple trees.

Branches slapped against her body, the thorns snagging her arms and clothes. She shielded her face, rushing past the dozens of wooden beehives among the trees. She didn't stop until ahead of her, concealed in the forest, she saw a cottage. The home of her friends, André and Nadine Batier.

An aeroplane dipped over the trees, and she shivered. The château was still a kilometer away.

If the Batiers hadn't run away, perhaps she could wait with them until first light. Then she would meet Philippe back at the château.

CHAPTER 4

A crystal chandelier rained shards of light over the crowded ballroom. Columns of red, white, and blue balloons swayed at the front, on each side of the podium. There were two rows of chairs along the walls and in the middle of the room was an open space crowded with several hundred people. Under the archway at the back of the room, a buffet table teemed with hors d'oeuvres, but no one in the room seemed to be eating.

I eyed the table of food from afar. No one on Austin's staff wanted to insult me by explaining protocol, but on nights like this it would have been nice if Olivia Larson, Austin's campaign manager, handed me a brief list of the dos and don'ts. The most pressing question being, was the candidate's fiancée allowed to eat the stuffed mushrooms and crab wontons? Or was she simply to stand and smile?

It seemed such a waste to leave all that food on the table, especially when I'd had no time for either lunch or dinner. My tight dress wouldn't allow me to do anything except nibble, but it wouldn't pay for me to pass out during the function either.

Austin's parents were at the front of the room, and as I inched toward the buffet, Mrs. Vale eyed me from afar. With her slow nod of greeting, I knew she was scrutinizing my appearance as well, from my heels up to my hair. Like I was a package for display.

Perhaps I should have worn a bow.

Austin stood near his mother, hemmed in by admirers. With his wavy black hair parted on the side, his tuxedo a perfect fit, he breathed confidence. I admired him for a moment, like the hordes of women who gawked whenever we went out. Then I stepped closer.

His familiar laughter sounded genuine, his gaze focused on the man he spoke with, like his colleague was the only person who mattered in the world. The older constituents liked to compare his charisma and his appearance to JFK's. The younger ones said he looked more like Patrick Dempsey. Personally I thought he was even more handsome than either man.

When Austin's gaze met mine, he greeted me with his smile, his gaze admiring my dress. After clapping the shoulder of his friend, he turned and kissed me on the cheek. "You look amazing."

I smiled back. "Thank you."

"I was worried."

"I'm sorry." I reached for his hand, lacing my fingers through his. "Last day of school, you know."

"I thought your day ended at three."

"Tommy Dawson stayed after. He—"

Austin's attention wandered over my shoulder.

Fifteen seconds into the conversation, and I'd already lost him. He let go of my hand, stepping around me to greet one of the trustees from the University of Richmond. Sighing, I inched back toward the banquet table. Sometimes it seemed as if I was the only person who couldn't hold his attention.

But it was only a season. After the wedding, we'd have a whole week together, not a constituent in sight. And then a lifetime of nights to ourselves.

I reached for a plate on the table.

"Chloe!" Olivia, the thirtysomething woman whom Austin had hired to be his campaign manager, was barreling down on me. Olivia was an organizational wizard, but unlike Austin, she had little concern for her appearance. Her glasses had crept an inch or two down her nose, and the hair she'd tied back was falling out in frizzy chunks. It was as if she singlehandedly severed every ounce of stress that might infect Austin before it festered.

Olivia retrieved the plate from my hands and returned it to the stack. Then she reached for my wrist and tugged me toward the side of the room. "I've been looking for you."

"I was with Austin," I said as if I'd been hanging out for an hour.

"The program starts in twelve minutes," she rattled on. "Dr. Everett is going to speak about the future of the party for ten minutes, and then he'll introduce Austin. Austin will introduce you."

"I know." I shook my arm to free it from her grasp. "You emailed me the schedule."

"When Austin says your name, I want you to smile and give an elegant wave to the cameras on your left." Olivia attempted to demonstrate a wave that wasn't the least bit elegant.

"Like this." I showed off my well-rehearsed smile and wave.

"Exactly." Olivia glanced down at her tablet. "Austin will speak for a half hour and then the orchestra will start playing. You'll move up front for a dance with the candidate."

"Who is also my fiancé."

"Right." She tapped her tablet.

Of course I was right. Why did I feel like I had to convince Olivia—and Austin's family, for that matter—that I was more than a campaign volunteer? Austin was the one who'd pursued me. He was the one who'd proposed.

Olivia's phone buzzed and when she twirled on her heel, I leaned back against the column. Perhaps my "pretty package" analogy was all wrong. On nights like tonight, I was simply a prop. The room quieted when Dr. Everett took the stage. He leaned toward the microphone to introduce Austin, but before he spoke, the music from *Les Misérables* echoed across the room. Swearing under my breath, I dove into my beaded bag, muted my cell.

The doctor made a joke about the interruption, and my cheeks warmed as the people standing nearby chuckled. Hopefully Austin wouldn't find out whose phone disrupted his event. He wouldn't find it nearly as funny as my neighbors.

The ringing stopped, but the phone continued to vibrate in my hand. I glanced down at a text from my mom.

CALL ME! ASAP

The capital letters screamed back at me, and my heart began to race. What if something had happened to my grandmother?

With apologies to those around me, I ducked my head and carefully backed out of the crowd, grateful my new heels held steady as I exited through the arched doorway behind me. I would be back inside the ballroom in five minutes for my obligatory wave.

In the hallway, I called my mom back. She answered on the first ring.

"Is Mémé okay?" I demanded.

"As far as I know, she's fine."

"And Dad?"

"Chloe wants to know if you're okay," she called out. There was a muffled response in the background before she spoke to me again. "Your dad says everything is fine."

I took a deep breath, my heart slowing back to a normal pace.

"Where are you?" my mom asked.

"At the fund-raiser downtown. I have to get back inside—Austin's about to introduce me." I leaned back against a wall. "I thought it was an emergency."

"It is an emergency," she replied. "Is your passport up-to-date?"

"My passport?" I replied, agitated. Clearly we had different definitions of *emergency*. "My passport is not a matter of urgency."

"But is it current?"

"Yes." Just last summer, right before I met Austin, my best friend, Marissa, and I had kayaked through Costa Rica. But Mom and I would have to discuss my passport situation later. It wouldn't be long before Austin took the stage. "I have to go—"

The following sigh would have impressed all twenty-seven of my third graders. "Between school and the campaign, it's never a good time to talk with you."

"I'll have more time starting Monday."

"Oh, good." Mom paused. "Because your dad and I need you to do something next week."

I drummed my fingers against my dress. "What exactly do you need me to do?"

"We need you . . ." She hesitated. "Well, we need you to go to France."

"France?" The word came out as a shout. I stepped farther back into the hallway. My father was from France, and I'd spent two summers after college touring Paris and southern France. I loved everything about the country, but I couldn't go back now, nine weeks before my wedding.

My mom talked faster now. "Have you heard of Riley Holtz?"

"The name sounds familiar—"

"He's won all sorts of awards for his documentaries about historical events and he wants to film part of his new documentary at the château."

I switched the phone to my left ear, confused. The Château d'Epines was my grandmother's childhood home in Normandy, a grand fortress of beauty and legend that had captivated me since I was a girl. I'd only been there once, when I was eight years old. My grandmother wanted to honor her brother, Michel, with a tombstone in the family's cemetery, by the old chapel. My parents wanted to go with her, but for some reason, Grandpa hadn't been able to travel with us.

My family had spent an hour with a priest at a chapel, honoring Michel's life, and then we'd left without going inside the château. Philippe—my third cousin, multiple times removed—lived there with his wife and son. I remembered Dad saying he wished someone would remove Philippe from our family altogether.

But Philippe was gone now and so were the three wives he'd accumulated over the years. His son, Stéphane, had lived at the château until his father's death. After he moved to Paris, Stéphane sent regular letters to my grandmother, asking if he could return to the Château d'Epines.

My dad hadn't wanted to visit his childhood home since that trip years ago.

I tightened the grip on my phone, trying to focus. I only had two minutes, maybe less, before Austin took the stage. "What does the documentary have to do with the château?"

"Mr. Holtz wants to hear the stories from World War II."

I leaned back against the walls, which were striped with a muddy yellow and white. I knew plenty of stories about the château but very little from the years during the war. "I wish Mémé could tell him."

"Me too."

It was too late to ask her now. Even though her body was plenty strong, her mind had failed. "Why can't Stéphane handle it?" I asked. "Or the caretakers Dad hired?"

My mom cleared her throat. "Your dad doesn't want Stéphane back on the property, and this gentleman wants to talk to someone in the family."

"Then Dad should go—"

"He has to be in DC on Tuesday."

"This Tuesday?" My retort came out as more of a squeak.

"We thought you would be perfect—"

"I have nine weeks to plan a wedding!"

"The planning will be here when you return."

My mind whirled. Going back to the château was a dream of mine, but the timing was terrible. Austin would be frustrated if I even entertained the idea of leaving the country, and I couldn't blame him. The next weeks were pivotal to the campaign.

"I would go in a heartbeat if I could, Mom, but there's so much to do—"

"Your dad really wants you to do this," she whispered.

"But why now—" Austin's voice thundered over the speakers, and I rushed out of the hallway. "I really have to go, Mom. Austin's about to introduce me."

Slipping my phone back into my bag, I hurried back toward the ballroom, but as I neared the door, one of my stilettos rebelled and my ankle teetered. My hands flailed until I caught myself on a railing, and with my ankle throbbing, I reached down and freed my foot from the straps.

The audience laughed at Austin's opening joke, and for the first time, I hoped he would forget he was engaged.

Unfortunately, he didn't.

"It's an honor to introduce my lovely fiancée to all of you," he said. And then I heard him say my name. "Chloe Sauver."

Applause swept out the doors, into the hall. If I stumbled into the ballroom now, flustered and limping on one shoe, I would only create a spectacle, and there was nothing Austin hated more than attention being diverted from the campaign. Better for the audience to think—

Well, I wasn't sure what they would think, but they hadn't come to the gala to see me anyway. Austin would continue on just fine without me, and I would apologize to him after everyone was gone.

I leaned my head back against the wall. My parents' request had rattled me.

How could they ask me to visit France next week? They knew I loved France—that I'd dreamed about exploring the Château d'Epines—but life had collided with my dreams.

If I couldn't talk my parents out of this plan, Austin would do it with his perfect mix of charm and reason, explaining perfectly well why someone else would have to entertain this film-maker in Normandy.

Chapter 5

Gisèle woke with a jolt, sunlight stealing through the dormer window in André and Nadine's guest room. The room was quiet, but instead of celebrating the silence, it terrified her.

Where were the German bombers? And where were Papa, Philippe, and Michel?

Her arms and legs were bruised, and last night Nadine had helped her bandage her bloodied knees. Then her friend had loaned her a pink nightgown to wear to bed. On a chair near the window, Nadine had draped a fresh blouse and skirt for her to borrow.

Gisèle closed her eyes again.

If only she could be more like her mother—the former Lady Serena Eckley. The Vicomtesse Duchant after she married Papa. Her mother would have faced the Germans with courage and strength like she had in the previous war, but right now, Gisèle felt nothing but fear.

Forcing herself to rise, she smoothed her hair and stepped across the creaky floor to dress in her friend's clothes. They were a size smaller than what Gisèle wore but a much better alternative than the smoky, torn clothing she'd arrived in last night.

Her forehead against the windowpane, she scanned the tips of the trees for Nazi planes, but only puffs of cumulus clouds hung overhead. As if the heart of France hadn't changed overnight.

Had the Germans already taken Saint-Lô? The Batiers' property stretched into the trees, all the way down to the river, and collided with her family's property line. Most of the townspeople avoided this patch near the river due to the dozens of beehives along the path, some of them built centuries ago. Neither André nor Nadine tried to persuade them otherwise. The previous owner of their home had been an avid beekeeper, but André and Nadine had never officially kept bees. Even without the Batiers' assistance, the insects continued to flourish between the hawthorns.

André and Nadine had bought the house three years ago, days after André accepted a position as a teacher at the secondary school in Saint-Lô. The house had been a disaster with its crooked shutters and crumbling fireplace and unpainted wooden walls. Apparently the previous owner had been more enamored of beekeeping than housekeeping.

Michel helped André repair the fireplace, and in the following months, before Nadine's parents moved down to Grenoble, Gisèle assisted Nadine and her mother in painting the exterior a creamy yellow color, straightening the shutters, and planting a garden. There were few places more beautiful now than the Batiers' backyard in springtime, but she couldn't linger here.

In the clarity of morning, she knew what she had to do. She would sneak back to the château and tell Michel all that had happened. Then she would meet Philippe and leave with him and Papa—if Papa still remained.

Michel had enough food and apple brandy to last at least three days. Her brother didn't want to leave, but she would convince him to go to

45

Switzerland as well. Perhaps they could meet on the other side of the border. Or perhaps the British would come to their country's rescue and they could return home.

Her door inched open, and she turned to see her dear friend standing in the doorway.

"I didn't want to wake you," Nadine said. "But it's almost ten."

She glanced back out the window. "Do you have any news?"

"I'm afraid not much of consequence." She looked out the window. "The aeroplanes haven't returned this morning."

Gisèle pressed her fingers against the glass. "I suppose that is the best of news right now."

"Come eat." Nadine was small in stature, but André had nicknamed his wife "Flambée." Not because of her temper—Gisèle had never seen her friend angry—but because she was passionate about her garden, her home, her family. Her charcoal hair was coiled at her neck, and her olive skin was flawless. Years ago, she'd been confirmed in the Catholic Church, the faith of her community, but it would have been impossible to hide the Jewish heritage in her features.

The three of them had stayed up past four, until the skies grew quiet, listening to the BBC on the wireless even though there was little news reported during the night.

André and Nadine decided not to run—they had

no automobile and knew they wouldn't get far on their bicycles. Besides, André said, Nadine's family was in southern France and his family had moved to Morocco. There was no place for them to go. So they hunkered down in their cottage to see what would happen next.

Gisèle followed Nadine down into the living room. Nadine paused, lifting the corner of the curtain as if she were checking for the Germans before she turned toward Gisèle. "I'm afraid of what they will do if they stay here."

For a moment, Gisèle flashed back to her years in primary school, before Nadine and her family emigrated from Austria. Even though she preferred riding her bicycle up the long path like the other children, her father insisted that their chauffeur drive her to school. Most of the kids in her class shunned her, refusing to play with the "queen from the castle." She wasn't a queen and never thought of herself as nobility in those years. She viewed herself as a Norman girl who happened to live in a big house. A lonely Norman girl who had only her family and her father's horses for company.

Then Nadine arrived in Saint-Lô when they were both eight, and they became instant friends. They'd eaten lunch together every day, jumped rope on the playground, and stayed up late giggling on the rare occasions when Gisèle's parents allowed a slumber party in the château.

When Gisèle lost her mother, Nadine cried with her until no more tears would come, and even now, ten years later, Nadine sometimes mourned Gisèle's loss. But her mother wouldn't want them to grieve right now. She would want them to stand up to their enemy.

But how could they fight the Germans on their own?

Nadine rolled her hands over her belly and for the first time, Gisèle noticed the slightest bulge in her friend's abdomen. She met the eyes of her friend and saw the anxiety in them. "Nadine?"

She nodded toward the closed door of the office, the buzz of the wireless seeping out to the living room. "André doesn't know yet."

"Why not?"

"At first . . ." She swallowed. "At first, I wanted to be certain, and then when I confirmed it, I was scared. It's a terrible time to bring a baby into the world."

Gisèle thought of the joy a child would bring to all of them. "The baby won't know it's a terrible time." Just like she hadn't known there was a war when she was born. Until her mother died, she only remembered peace and happiness in her home.

"I pray the fighting will be done before she's born," Nadine said, the strength of her desire pressing through her words.

"How do you know it's a she?"

A gentle smile lit Nadine's face. "Just a hunch."

From the next room, she heard the crackle of a voice. Nadine nodded toward the office door. "André's been glued to the wireless all morning."

"Perhaps there is new information."

Nadine pointed toward the door. "You go listen with him. I'll bring lunch."

Gisèle knocked on the door, and André told her to come in. Nadine's husband sat on a padded footstool, his head almost resting on the small speaker of the wireless. His light brown hair was messy, and his wire-rimmed glasses crept down his nose.

The announcer said the French people were fleeing south by the thousands, the French army running alongside them. The French people had been assured that their army was strong enough to resist a German attack, yet everything was crumbling.

As the news broadcast ended, Nadine set a tray with small sandwiches on the desk along with a pot of coffee. "It is too late for us to fight."

André shook his head. "It is never too late. The people in France won't let the Germans stay here."

Nadine collapsed onto a chair. "But what do we do now?"

"We may not be able to fight them with weapons." André reached for his wife's hand, and with his other hand, he pounded his chest. "But we can fight them with our hearts."

Nadine shook her head. "The Germans care nothing about hearts."

"It doesn't matter if they care," André insisted. "It matters that we care about our country. About our fellow man."

Gisèle poured a cup of coffee and took a sip. "Sometimes, I fear, our hearts can steer us wrong."

"We will fight for the good in France," André said. "No matter what happens, we will know we did the right thing."

His words resonated with her. No matter what happened, she needed to fight for what was good as well.

They listened to the BBC, eating their chicken salad sandwiches, but it was the same news. France was still running, reeling, from the German blitzkrieg. And then there was news from London about Winston Churchill, the new prime minister in Britain.

She didn't want to know what was happening in England. She wanted to know what was happening right here, on the streets of Saint-Lô. And at the château.

When the announcer finished, Gisèle stood.

"Please stay with us," Nadine begged her.

"Philippe will be waiting for me," she said as they walked toward the front door. "And I must check on my father."

"Surely the Germans will be gone soon,"

Nadine said before Gisèle kissed both of her friend's cheeks.

Gisèle tried to smile as she whispered, "Long before your baby is born."

"I pray so."

"What will you name her?"

Fear flickered in Nadine's eyes before she returned Gisèle's smile. "It depends on André, of course, but if it's a girl, I want to name her Louise, after his mother."

Perhaps by the time Louise was born, the world would be righted again. "It's a beautiful name."

"With that name . . ." Pride flashed in her eyes. "No one will ever question whether or not my daughter is a Frenchwoman."

CHAPTER 6

Leaning my head back against the wall, I sank onto the floor of the ballroom and surveyed the damage. A half hour ago, Austin's supporters began trickling out, leaving behind a room littered with plates, napkins, and fancy toothpicks pierced into remnants of food.

At least someone had eaten tonight.

I tossed my sandal toward a chair but nailed a plastic cup on the floor instead. Red wine streamed onto the flecked carpet, and I watched, mesmerized, as the river grew hairline passages of fingers and toes. I should have run for paper towels, mopped up the mess before it stained, but it was half past two in the morning. Somewhere back around one, my energy had begun spilling out like the wine. Now there wasn't a single ounce left in me.

Closing my eyes, I breathed in the blessed silence. My hunger pangs had been numbed, the need for sleep replacing my need for food. Olivia drummed up a chai latte for me around midnight, but the effects had been minimal. No amount of caffeine could replace the benefits of a decent pillow.

The door creaked open on the other side of the room, and in the dim light, I watched Austin moving toward me. I'd botched up his introduction, but I made it for the first dance of the night. Barefoot. He hadn't said a word about either faux pas. Instead he smiled and I smiled, and for about three minutes, in the magic of the music and the lights, I had his attention.

"Dr. Everett was the last one to leave." Austin turned a chair around to sit beside me. "You think it was a success?"

Somehow his tux had managed to stay wrinkle-free for the entire event and his wavy black hair remained set perfectly in place.

"It was a blockbuster of a night," I said, coaxing my fingers through the stiff spray in my hair. "These people adore you."

He took a long sip from his bottled water. "I tried to introduce you, but you seemed to have disappeared."

A headache clustered over my eyes, and I pressed my middle fingers against my eyebrows. "I'm sorry."

The pout in his smile reminded me more of a kid like Tommy Dawson than of a confident candidate or movie star. "Better to ditch me here than at the altar."

"I didn't ditch you." I pressed harder on my brows, as if I could massage the pain away. "My mom texted and said she needed to speak with me. I thought it was urgent."

"Everything is urgent for your mom." He set his water bottle beside the chair and reached for my left hand, tugging it away from my face. Then he entwined my fingers through his. "What was it this time?"

"Something about a filmmaker shooting a documentary in France. Mom wants me to meet him at the château."

He leaned forward a few inches. "When does she want you to go?"

"Tuesday," I said, "but don't worry. I told her I couldn't do it."

He eyed me for a moment before speaking again. "Is this a documentary about World War II?"

At my nod, he leaned closer, his eyes intent on mine. "When will it air?"

"I have no idea, but it doesn't matter. There's no way I can travel to France next week."

His elbows propped on his legs, he held up my hand. "These are important details, Chloe."

"I have a thousand important details I'm trying to pull together. It's impossible to keep track of them all."

"That's why you hired a wedding coordinator. To help you with the details."

If only it were that easy. I, not the coordinator, would be responsible if everything went awry on August 10. Or, heaven forbid, if I picked out the wrong colors or plates or dresses for my eight bridesmaids—only two of whom were actual friends.

His eyes narrowed slightly, and I knew exactly what he was doing—developing some sort of a plan. "Would he be interviewing you?"

I wished I could read his mind. Why did he care if I did an interview on World War II? "My parents want me to tell him some of Mémé's stories, but it doesn't matter. I only have nine weeks to pull this wedding together."

Nine weeks to achieve perfection.

"So you run away for one of those weeks and get some rest," he said with a shrug. "You'll come back refreshed and ready to tackle what's left."

He drummed on my hand as I processed his words. He made it sound so simple, this running away. I cocked my head, studying him. "You really think I should go to France?"

"I think you should consider it."

Something else was going on behind that smile. I was exhausted, but if I was going to dig, I needed to do it now. Even though we'd be together all day tomorrow, we'd be surrounded.

"What's the real reason you want me to go?"

This time he shrugged. "I want my fiancée to relax."

"And . . . ," I said, pressing him.

He took a deep breath. "And that reporter at the newspaper keeps hounding Olivia for your grandfather's war records. No one can seem to find them."

I yanked my hand away from his grip. "It's none of the reporter's business—"

"That's not how he sees it, especially since we keep telling the press that you're the grand-daughter of a war hero." He put his hands on the floor. "If we tell him you're being interviewed for a documentary on the war, it might deter him for a bit, at least until after the campaign."

I rested my head back against the wall. I'd never asked Olivia to tell the media about my grand-father, but she wrote about him in my bio and then touted his military service.

I'd certainly never refuted his record, and it was much too late to tell Austin that Henri Sauver wasn't actually my biological grandfather. Henri was the only father my dad ever knew, and I was proud of him.

Grandpa had passed away fifteen years ago, but Mémé told me he was an officer in the Armée de Terre before the occupation—and a member of the French resistance after it. They'd met, she said, in Saint-Lô. Right after the war. And moved to Virginia.

I didn't remember Grandpa talking about his years before or during the war and as I grew older, I wished I knew more about his story—their story. Unlike Austin and the media, I didn't even particularly care about Grandpa's war record. I wanted to know the stories of how my grandparents met. And why they traded a château in France for a trilevel in Fairfax, Virginia.

Austin's reasoning for the needed PR was more viable than his urging me to vacate. He had no problem energizing the younger voters, but neither he nor Olivia was convinced that the younger crowd would turn out en masse at the polls. His competitor was a devoted family man with twenty-five years of experience, and Austin needed more than Virginia's millennials to elect him governor. The campaign needed to show that he was grounded. That he respected those generations who fought in the wars before him. His family's military roots were shallow—one grandfather was a conscientious objector and the other had married his first of four wives in order to dodge the draft for Vietnam. Even though the details were sparse, my grandfather's record provided Austin with at least the appearance of roots.

"You'll charm both the videographer and the viewers," he said.

"I'm no expert on World War II."

"I'll have Olivia put together a cheat sheet for you."

I cocked my head. "Methinks you are trying to get rid of me, Governor."

"I hate it when you call me that," he said, but he didn't mean it.

I glanced up at the light glowing from the chandelier. When Mom called, I thought traveling to France would be impossible until after the election, but perhaps it was plausible, even beneficial, for me to go.

Olivia was a pro at creating buzz even when there wasn't much to buzz about. A couple press releases about an upcoming documentary, along with an interview or two about the war, might convince Virginia's older generation that Austin was astute enough to be their governor.

"If Gisèle knows you're going, perhaps she would remember more stories," he said.

"Mémé rarely remembers anything these days, but I know a few stories about my grandfather."

"All we need are a few crumbs to throw to the media," Austin said as if he'd already decided I was going. "Then we won't have to worry about the records."

I wanted to know these stories, every one of them, but it had nothing to do with distracting the media.

"The château was magical," Mémé told me when I was younger, after she'd read me one of the Narnia stories. *"Like Cair Paravel."*

She'd told me stories about her and her brother swimming in the lake when they were children. About the gardens and her father's horses and the glowworms that lit their path in the summer. She told me about her parents and how she adored them, but whenever I asked her about the war, she would tell me about my grandfather's work. When I asked what she had done during the war, she'd change the subject.

Austin reached for my hand again and gently squeezed it. "Go and enjoy the French food and the wine and give this guy a few good sound bites for his show. You'll come back refreshed and ready for the rest of the campaign season."

"And for our wedding." I don't know why I felt like I needed to remind him, but I did.

"Of course." This time he let go of my hand. "The wedding."

Chapter 7

The relentless rhythm of jackboots pounded across the valley and latched on to the beat of Gisèle's heart. Even though an hour had passed, the rhythm still echoed in her mind, defiant and strong as the soldiers marched along the river path. The path that led to her home.

The soldiers were gone, but she remained hidden behind the swollen trunks of the beech trees, praying that Papa had fled and that Michel remained hidden.

She scanned the herds of butterscotch-colored cows grazing on the grassy hill across the river and the forest above them. To her right, the cathedral in Saint-Lô towered above the hills, and to her left, up on the cliff, was her family's château. Even though wars had raged in the valley for centuries, the Château d'Epines, protected by the forest and cliffs and stone walls, remained strong.

Before the French Revolution, her family's property had stretched across the Batiers' land, all the way to Saint-Lô. Life turned upside down during the revolution and several of her ancestors across the country had been beheaded. When radicals came for the head of the Vicomtesse Jeanne Duchant, she crawled into the hollowed-out trunk of an enormous elm tree and hid. Leaning back against the crusty bark of a tree, Gisèle petitioned the Blessed Virgin Mary for the protection and patience that had been gifted to her ancestor.

The French government had thought their country was as formidable as her family's château, but somehow the Germans had found a chink in their armor. Michel and other Frenchmen might have to hide now, but eventually they would fight. Like they had in the Great War.

Papa said there was no reason for the Germans to linger in Saint-Lô since they were intent on reaching Great Britain. The port of Cherbourg was a hundred kilometers to the north, and after the Germans took the port, they'd fight for England across the Channel.

But why were the soldiers still here?

A black speck appeared above Saint-Lô, and she ducked back into the forest. A yellow engine gleamed in the light as one plane and then a dozen of them flew low over the valley, each one touting a hooked cross on its tail as if they were fishing for the enemy.

Closing her eyes, Gisèle sank into a bed of leaves and buried her head. If they dropped a bomb on her beloved home, she couldn't bear to watch it.

And if they dropped a bomb—what would happen to Papa? And Michel and his men?

She prayed they were all safe, that Philippe had gotten out of Saint-Lô and Papa had fled during the night. And that Michel hadn't left the tunnel.

A minute passed, perhaps two, and the sound of engines had faded. She rose and looked back over the valley again.

On the other side of her house were fields to the north of the river—farmed by the Polin family, who rented the property from her father—and to the south was a forest filled with treasures: a small lake and caves and a medieval guardhouse that she and Nadine had deemed their meeting place when they were twelve.

The planes would spot her if she stepped onto the river's path, but in the darkness she could hide. She knew every step of the valley and the forest on the other side. If she waited until night, the Germans would never catch her.

She crept back under the cover of the hawthorn trees. They were in full bloom, the white petals like flakes of snow icing the thorns. Bees buzzed among the fragrant blossoms, and they seemed as unafraid of her as she was of them. As long as the sweetness of the flowers quenched their thirst, she didn't have to worry about the bees' sting.

Birds hid among the hawthorn branches, protected by the thorns, the melodies of their songs the only clue to their presence.

She wondered what it was they sang about. Perhaps it was their hunger or their fright or even their love. Whatever it was, they seemed oblivious to the dangers above them and on the ground. If only she could be oblivious alongside them. Still, the serenity of their song calmed the rhythm in her heart, the hours passing slowly as she waited.

The steady cadence of their song reminded her of her two years in the convent boarding school near Coutances, the familiar prayers flowing from their lips with the music. She hadn't appreciated the music as a child. Sometimes she and her friend Odette were downright awful.

The nuns in their boarding school had known French and Latin and a little English, but not a word of German. Odette had learned German from her grandfather and taught the basics to Gisèle so they could share their secrets without fear of a nun discovering their plans. They had been perfectly naughty during their middle-grade years—salting the porridge of the mother superior, hiding the prayer books of their classmates. When the others sang their morning hymns, she and Odette replaced the words with the lyrics from "Parlez-Moi d'Amour," giggling about treasures and kisses, bitterness and love.

The nuns may have suspected that she and Odette were the instigators of trouble, but they weren't caught until one windy afternoon in March when they were both fourteen. After they borrowed two horses from the stable—and got themselves lost in the forest—the mother superior whipped them both with a switch and sent them home for a week of reflection.

Papa spared her another round with the rod, but he insisted that Gisèle spend a miserable week in isolation and reflection. There had been no riding for her in the hills near their house, no wading in the lake below the château. Even Michel—the boy who'd never let rules stop him—was disappointed in her.

In hindsight, Papa was probably more afraid of her getting injured than disappointed in her for taking the horses. After a week of eating alone in her bedroom, she decided to tolerate the rules at school until summer break. The next year her father sent her to another boarding school, one where she rode horses every day.

During the summers, she'd ridden her horse up into the trees on the other side of the river. When she was fifteen, she'd been fond of a boy who lived in the woods—a boy named Jean-Marc Rausch. He and his parents used to come to the Mass at the *chapelle* long ago, but after she left for the university, she never saw him again.

Had he and his parents moved before the war? And what had become of him and her other classmates and of Odette in Paris?

The birds' song faded as darkness fell. Gisèle crept out of her hiding place and followed the river until she reached the steep bike path up to the château. In the moonlight, she could see the gray walls of the château, but there were no lights on inside. The other servants, she assumed, had fled like Émilie. Were Papa and Philippe waiting for her in the darkness?

She scanned the empty courtyard and driveway in front of the château. Perhaps Philippe had hidden his *coupé* in the carriage house or—she shuddered—perhaps he and Papa had gone on to Lyon without her.

Two towers soared over the stone castle, and she eyed the one on the far side of the house. Thorns from the rosebushes pecked at her arms as she snuck through the formal garden and around the old masonry oven that hadn't been used in a century or two. At the base of the tower, she clambered around the hedges and jimmied the top of a window until it opened.

The lock had been broken for years—it had been an easy way for her to sneak in and out at night to meet Nadine, before her friend married André. Her heart pounding, Gisèle lifted one leg onto the windowsill and then pulled herself through, into the small study.

"Papa?" she whispered in the darkness.

Accounting ledgers, newspapers, and the *Farmers' Almanac* were piled up on the side of Papa's desk, and his wireless stood against the wall beside it. When she was younger, she'd been afraid of the dark, and in the evenings, she'd often draped herself over the damask chair beside the desk and pretended to read while he pored over his books. Really she'd been watching him, fascinated as he calculated his figures and talked business on his black telephone and thumbed through *La Croix*. In the cadence of his work, she found comfort. After her mother passed away, she'd known her father would take care of her.

But if Papa had already left the château, she would have to care for herself. Like she'd wanted to do in Paris.

She lifted the telephone receiver from the cradle, to call Tante Corinne and see if she'd heard from Philippe, but the line was dead. Sighing, she dropped the receiver back onto the brass bands.

She leaned back against the open window, the warm moonlight casting shadows over the office. In the silence of her home, she listened to the sound of her breathing. Was Papa someplace inside the house? Or were there Germans hiding upstairs?

No matter how much she hoped the Germans had kept marching down the valley, she didn't know for certain, and she hated this, the feeling that her home was no longer a safe place.

Something moved behind the desk, and her breath caught in her throat. Clenching her fists, she willed herself to be strong, but her courage dissolved within her. She turned to flee back out of the window until she heard the softest of meows from under the desk. The trappings of her breath slipped out as she ducked under the desktop.

The source of her fear was crouched in the dark corner. A kitten.

"How did you get in here?" she whispered as she gently pulled him out into the light.

The kitten reached up with its paw and batted her nose.

She cradled him close to the window, brushing her face over his soft gray fur. On his neck was a white fleck in the shape of a star, and she could feel his tiny ribs through his skin.

"If Papa found you, he would put you right back outside where you belong," she said, scolding him.

She scratched his chin, and he purred back at her. A kitten could do nothing to protect her, yet somehow it made her feel more secure, bold even, to have it near. She dug through the top drawer of Papa's desk until she found the flashlight he kept for when the electricity failed. Then, the kitten in her arms, she crept through the large dining salon, past the long table and massive fireplace with the three lambs carved on the mantel. On her left side, a row of windows framed the courtyard, *chapelle*, and long drive. On the other side of the room four windows overlooked the river valley and the grassy hill and forest across the valley.

"Papa?" she called out again as she tiptoed into the foyer. No one responded, but the front door was partially open.

Had someone been here, or had Papa left the door open when he left?

She closed it.

On the other side of the foyer was the kitchen, and when she stepped inside, she flipped on the flashlight and set the kitten beside the brick fireplace. Copper pots hung neatly on each side of the mantel and two cast iron kettles rested along the hearth. The fireplace was built when the château was renovated in the seventeenth century, but their cook only used the white gas oven her parents had installed before she was born.

Gisèle stared at the spokes on the range and then looked at the three drawers beside it. She should make Michel some bread or something else, but how was she supposed to feed her brother when she didn't even know how to light an oven?

She sighed. Just because she wanted to help didn't mean she was able to do it.

Opening up the refrigerator door, she removed a pint of milk and trickled it into a bowl for—

She looked back down at the kitten as he lapped up the milk. "What should I call you?"

There were too many silly pet names—Fluffy, Tiger, Smudge. But this kitten was smart, hiding from the Germans. Shadow—that's what she would call him.

Then she scanned the contents in the refrigerator. There was a tub of butter, along with salami and cheese. On the counter was a half loaf of *pain noir*, the hardy black bread their cook liked to bake. It wasn't much food, but she hoped it would sustain her brother until the Germans left.

She set the flashlight on the counter and reached for a glass goblet to fill with water when the door to the kitchen swung open. Shadow leapt up on the counter, and she dropped the goblet as she whirled around, glass shattering across the floor.

Someone stood at the door, but she couldn't see their face. Sweeping the flashlight off the counter, she shined it toward the door.

"Émilie," she said with a sigh, her heart calming. "What are you doing here?"

The older woman tossed her valise onto the wooden table that stood before the fireplace. "I tried to walk to Cahagnes, but didn't get far."

Gisèle sank back against the counter. "I'm sorry."

"It's no matter," Émilie said, eyeing the salami and cheese on the counter. "I don't know what is to become of us, but in the meantime, I can help you and your father."

"I need you, but . . ."

Her gaze fell to the kitten lapping milk on the floor. "You better take that cat outside before Vicomte Duchant sees it."

"Papa's not here."

Émilie's eyes welled up with worry. "Where is he?"

Gisèle swallowed hard, trying to calm the fear that sparked fresh inside her. She didn't tell Émilie about the soldiers she'd seen marching toward the château. "He was planning to head south, after Philippe and I left, but we didn't get past Saint-Lô. I spent the night at the Batiers."

Émilie glanced back toward the door. "Is his automobile still here?"

"I haven't checked the carriage house yet."

"What about Philippe?"

"I don't know." She couldn't consider the possibility that he'd been injured, but the bombs had been falling and people stampeded in their frantic attempt to escape them.

"It will not be safe for you here," Émilie said.

"I'm afraid no place is safe in France."

"Perhaps I could stay and help you find your father?"

"I will go check the carriage house." Gisèle rapped her knuckles on the stovetop, the loneliness beginning to fade away. "Can you bake some bread tonight?"

"It doesn't seem right to bake . . ."

"I want to take it to those who are hungry." She paused. "Like my mother used to do."

Émilie tilted her head slightly, studying Gisèle's face. "Your mother used to take food every week to the children in the orphanage."

Gisèle nodded. When she was younger, she'd sometimes joined her mother to deliver the baskets of fresh vegetables and bread. "I'm not going to the orphanage."

Émilie opened the refrigerator. "But we can pretend you are."

Gisèle picked up Shadow. The world outside might be spiraling, but here inside the château, perhaps she and Émilie would find peace. Until Papa or Philippe returned, it would be their refuge in the storm.

CHAPTER 8

Saturday night's dinner was supposed to be a casual affair, but Austin's mother wore pearls with her ivory cocktail dress and coral cardigan. The table was set with antique silver and crystal goblets and folded napkins on the china plates. I wore the same yellow sundress I'd worn at today's luncheon, but still I felt underdressed.

Mr. and Mrs. Vale anchored each end of their dining room table. On one side, Mrs. Vale sipped a mint julep with shaved ice. On the other, Mr. Vale drank his bourbon straight up. I sat across from Austin's older sister, Lisa, and Austin faced his brother—a sixteen-year-old skateboarder officially named Lawrence, though for some reason unknown to me, everyone called him Vos.

Lisa's husband, Wyatt, was absent from the meal. I'd only seen Wyatt twice in the year since I began dating Austin, but in his absence Mrs. Vale touted his successes as a busy executive, as if the family could somehow take credit for his accolades.

Marissa had tried to talk me out of coming tonight, tempting me with an evening out at Tarrant's instead to celebrate the end of the school year. Marissa thought I spent way too much time pandering to Austin and his campaign. Before he proposed, she'd tried to talk me into breaking up with him, saying I should be with someone who loved me much more than Austin ever could. Now that we were engaged, she tolerated him, but sometimes I wondered if an undercurrent of jealousy drove her to dislike him. Still I missed hanging out with my best friend. I'd asked her to celebrate at the gala with me last night, but she declined. Even though we were on the phone, I knew the exact moment she'd rolled her eyes.

"A gala is work," she informed me. "You need an official 'Hooray—summer is finally here' party that doesn't involve politics."

I promised to celebrate with her next week, but now I'd have to reschedule. I didn't need a coordinator for my wedding. I needed one for my life.

Mrs. Vale cupped her manicured hands and held them out to her daughter. "Please pass the green beans."

Lisa reached for the bowl on the sideboard behind her and passed it along. The beans were followed by Virginia ham, rosemary potatoes, and French bread from Patty Wilson's chain of boutique bakeries.

Lisa began buttering her bread. "I wish I could go to New York with you on Tuesday."

I glanced up at her and then over at Austin, confused. Just an hour ago, after a conversation with both Austin and Olivia, I'd texted my mom with the go-ahead to buy plane tickets. She'd booked me on the first flight out on Tuesday, through New York, but I hadn't even told Austin it was a done deal.

Lisa smiled at me as if she was conspiring. "We could storm Fifth Avenue together in search of your trousseau."

"I won't have time . . ."

Lisa glanced at Austin. "Does Starla still own a shop in Manhattan?"

He choked on his bite of ham.

I poked my fork into a potato. "Who's Starla?"

Austin took a long sip of water, recovering before he replied. "An old family friend."

I turned back to Lisa. "I'm only flying through New York."

Now Lisa seemed confused. "Aren't you going with Austin to the fund-raiser?"

I put down my fork—I didn't know anything about a fund-raiser.

Austin lifted his glass of sweet tea. "Chloe's leaving for France on Tuesday."

In his ambiguity, it sounded as if I were going on vacation.

Mrs. Vale took the potatoes from Lisa. "Why in the world are you going to France?"

"I think it's fantastic," Lisa said. "You can storm the shops in Paris instead."

Austin winked at me. "An excellent idea."

"Perhaps I will," I said, trying to match my voice with the lightness in his, but I wasn't letting him off the hook. I'd wait and ask about the fundraiser when we were alone—there was no sense in pointing out my ignorance in front of his entire family.

Mrs. Vale dished a small serving of potatoes onto her plate. "Austin tells us the wedding plans are going well."

"Yes, ma'am," I replied.

Vos snorted at my formality, but even after a year of dating Austin, I wasn't quite sure what to call her. *Mrs. Vale* didn't sound right. Neither did *Katherine*. Austin and Lisa called her *Mother*, but I figured I needed an invite to use that title. And even if she suggested it, I wasn't sure I could say the word. Katherine Vale was nothing like my mother. For the moment, I was sticking with *ma'am*.

"Lisa can help you finalize the décor for your reception. She has excellent taste."

"Mother!" Lisa sputtered. "Chloe has wonderful taste too."

If Mrs. Vale had been sitting beside me, I was certain she would have patted my hand, but instead she indulged me with a strained smile. "I'm sure you do, dear, but it's good to rely on the experts for something as big as this."

Austin reached for my hand instead, as if his touch would erase her insult.

"Patty Wilson told me she will make your cake," Mrs. Vale said.

I glanced at Austin. "But my mother was planning—"

"For heaven's sake, Katherine," Mr. Vale interrupted, "it's her wedding. Let her choose who makes the cake."

Austin looked at his dad. "Patty and Robert are some of our largest contributors."

"And they will continue to contribute, even if Patty doesn't bake your damn cake," Mr. Vale said. "Robert has much bigger reasons to have you in office than to secure business for his wife."

Mrs. Vale stabbed one of her potatoes. "But Patty makes the best cakes in Richmond."

Heat rose to my face. It was one thing to insult me, quite another to insult my mother. "I don't think—"

Austin squeezed my hand a bit harder than necessary. "Perhaps this isn't the right time to have this discussion."

"It's only a cake," Vos said as he rolled his eyes. "I'll make it."

I slowly chewed a piece of the ham. While I loved Austin, dinners like these might drive me mad. Perhaps after the wedding I could use whatever excuse Wyatt had contrived to go AWOL. In my absence, perhaps Mrs. Vale would begin to sing my praises.

The doorbell rang, and the housekeeper bustled down the hall to the door. Seconds later, the former runner-up for Miss Virginia—Megan Browning— stepped onto a different kind of stage, the theater of the Vale family dining room. Her blond hair was smoothed back into a neat ponytail and she wore a fitted shirt over black leggings. Even though she was almost twice his age, Vos gawked at her.

Megan shifted her briefcase into her left hand, breaking the awkward silence. "I didn't mean to interrupt your dinner."

Mr. Vale threw his napkin onto the table and pushed back his chair. "Megan's helping me write an opinion for Monday morning."

"But you've hardly eaten . . . ," Mrs. Vale said.

He lifted his plate from the table. "I'll finish in my office."

Vos leaned slightly to watch Megan's backside as she disappeared down the hall.

"Lawrence," Mrs. Vale snapped from the other end of the table. "Pass the potatoes."

Vos glanced away long enough to retrieve the silver platter in front of him and pass it along to his mother. Mrs. Vale added another spoonful of potatoes to the pile already on her plate.

I shifted uncomfortably on the hard seat. The family liked to pretend Justice Vale wasn't sleeping with his law clerk, and I tried to ignore this fact with the rest of them. The thought made me queasy. Megan had graduated from George Mason University two years ago with her degree in law, but I doubted Justice Vale had hired her for the degree. Silently I wondered how much he paid her to assist him.

I glanced over at Mrs. Vale and her lips were pressed into a tight line. How could she live like this? How could they all continue to pretend? My parents had been married for thirty-two years, but if my mom thought Dad was cheating, she would never let him—and certainly not the woman he was sleeping with—back into our home.

Mrs. Vale stood and clapped her hands. "Who's ready for dessert?"

I looked down at my plate. Like the rest of the family, I'd barely begun to eat, but she left us no choice. "I'll help you clear the dishes," I said as I stood.

Twenty minutes later, Austin and I leaned against the banister of their deck, looking down at the lights of Richmond.

He reached for my hand. "You know I love you."

"I do, but I wish you'd told me about the fund-raiser in New York."

He covered my hand with his. "I thought I did."

"I would have remembered—"

"I'm sorry, Chloe. It's been so crazy." He squeezed my hand. "I wish you could go with me. It's a formal dinner and dance at the Plaza."

"Are you leaving Tuesday morning?"

He nodded.

I smiled at the thought of the two of us indulging in first class together, dreaming about where the future might take us. "Perhaps we can fly together. It would be like stealing away for a whole hour."

"I wish we could," he said, squeezing my hand again. "But my flight's going into LaGuardia."

I sighed. I had to go through John F. Kennedy for my connection to Paris.

"We'll drive to the airport together," he promised. "Just the two of us."

I heard Megan's laughter below the patio, and my stomach churned. I inched my hand away from his. "How can you tolerate your father's— *behavior?*"

Austin leaned forward, his arms resting on the banister, his voice low. "Dad will do what he wants to do."

"But he's cheating on your mom," I said, my voice clipped. I didn't care if Megan or Justice Vale or anyone else in the family heard me.

"It's not really cheating if Mom knows."

"That's disgusting, Austin. He's on Virginia's supreme court, for heaven's sake. He's supposed to be a pillar of all that is right."

He stood up, pulling me close. "It's how they do their marriage."

"It's not how we will do our marriage," I said, melting into him.

"We'll be more like your parents." He stroked my arm. "I need you, Chloe. You know that, don't you?"

"You just need a wife . . . ," I said, teasing him.

He kissed the top of my head. "You're stuck with me for life, for better or worse."

"Mostly better, I hope."

He pulled me in front of him, and I leaned back against his chest. "It will be the best," he promised.

And I believed him.

Chapter 9

*R*ain pecked at the dozen panes on Gisèle's bedroom window, and she pressed her nose to the glass, trying to spot any Germans patrolling the river valley below, but the valley was still. Her gaze went up to the gray sky and then to the tower of Saint-Lô's cathedral.

She'd slept little last night. The family's Delahaye was sitting in the old carriage house that had been remodeled as a garage, but there was no sign of her father. She tried to cling to the hope that Philippe had returned after the bombing and taken Papa away with him. Perhaps they were both searching for her. Once the telephone lines were restored, she told herself, both Papa and Philippe would call.

Still, she felt scattered, not knowing whether she should stay and wait for Papa and Philippe or go look for them. Life, it seemed, had tipped over on its side, cracking into tiny pieces. Somehow she had to fit it back together again.

After she went to the carriage house, she visited the *chapelle*—both to pray and to leave the black bread and a letter for Michel on the ledge, telling him all that had transpired. If he hadn't left yet, she would take him Émilie's food this morning.

Last night she'd taken a hot bath with lavender bath salts, cleaned her wounds, and washed her hair with the honey-scented shampoo her mother had loved before setting her hair with curlers. She had blue eyes, like her mother, but the skin under her eyes was tinted purple from her restless night.

This morning she splashed water on her face and quickly powdered her nose and cheeks before studying herself in the washroom mirror. It seemed trivial to be concerned with her appearance, but her mother would have told her to face this day—and any Germans in it—with dignity. She'd been born into an aristocratic family, Mother would have said, and the enemy would never respect the lineage of her family if she didn't respect herself.

She powdered her face again.

Émilie was already bustling in the kitchen, and Gisèle drank a cup of coffee before eating the last slice of bread, slathered with jelly made from the hawthorn berries. As the rain drizzled down the window, the two women kneaded the rye and wheat flour together to make four more loaves of bread.

It felt strange to be in the kitchen, working alongside the woman who'd been her mother's favorite servant. The camaraderie eased the loneliness in her heart, and Émilie seemed to be enjoying her company as well.

Émilie talked about her father, who'd worked at the Palais-Royal until his death in 1934, and about her sister and nephews, who lived in Cahagnes. They both talked of the family members they'd lost a little more than twenty years ago, when France defeated Germany during the Great War.

Gisèle had been born only three months before the Great War ended, so she only knew the stories her parents told her, but Émilie remembered well the horrors of that war, the millions of young men France lost to the battles, the blood of their countrymen spilling over French soil.

"We must defeat the Germans quickly this time," Émilie said as she pounded the dough in front of her.

Gisèle mimicked the way Émilie pounded her bread. "What will happen if we don't defeat them?"

She sighed. "I fear this Hitler will make us pay dearly for the past."

"Half of France wasn't even alive during the Great War."

"It won't matter to him."

Gisèle had read the first part of Hitler's book *Mein Kampf* when she was at the university. One of her professors extolled the honesty of Hitler's struggle, the fervor of his words, but the hatred in the man's writing—his soul—appalled her. Hitler asserted that the Aryan race—the blond-haired and blue-eyed men and women—was elite. The Jews were parasites, dirty, wily, repulsive, liars. The mortal enemy of the master race.

She couldn't finish reading the book.

Hitler might make the French pay for the Great War, but there was something more sinister about the man than revenge.

Gisèle turned over the dough in her hands. "I am going to bike into Saint-Lô this morning, to see if I can find a pay phone that works."

Émilie stopped kneading. "You can't go alone."

"I won't be gone long."

Émilie turned over the dough in her hands,

studying Gisèle for a moment before she spoke again. "What other food will you need to take to the orphanage?"

Gisèle pressed her lips together. The only thing her brother had ever requested was the local Calvados, but he couldn't live forever on apple brandy. "Some cheese, I suppose, and hard-boiled eggs or meat."

The exhaustion in Émilie's eyes fled with her smile. "You remind me of your mother."

Her words warmed Gisèle to her core. "Thank you."

"You must take more than bread and cheese." Émilie opened the pantry door and rustled inside it before she shut the door with a loud huff. "But we are lacking in almost everything."

"How do we get—" Gisèle started to ask, but Émilie kept talking.

Émilie moved up into the hall and Gisèle followed her to the front door. "I will go ask the Polins for some eggs and carrots from their garden and perhaps some flour."

The Polins lived farther up the lane, in the house where their family had lived for almost fifty years while they farmed a portion of the land for the Duchants.

"Will you return?" Gisèle asked. She hated this feeling of desperation, but she needed Émilie even more than she had the last time she'd walked out the door, on the way to her sister's house.

Émilie stepped outside and opened her umbrella. "I won't be longer than an hour."

The rain tapered into a drizzle until the summer sun chased it away. Gisèle zipped up her boots under her slacks and retrieved her bicycle from the carriage house. Months ago she would have put a saddle on Papillon Bleu, her Anglo-Norman mare, but Papa had sent away all their horses when Germany began to threaten the Maginot Line. In hindsight, Papa should have insisted their entire household relocate to Lyon when he sent away their horses, but he hadn't really thought the Germans would make it this far west into France.

She wouldn't linger in Saint-Lô this morning, only long enough to learn if the Germans were gone. And if they were, she would search for a working pay phone. If Papa were in Lyon, he would be worried sick about her.

The sun warmed her bare arms as she pedaled under the narrow lane of elm trees up into Agneaux. One main street divided the village, and it was strewn with clothes and toys and broken bicycle wheels. She pedaled quickly through the commune, along rue de la Cavée, until she crossed the bridge into Saint-Lô.

A rank of tangled hedgerows, twice her size in height, usually fenced in animals and gardens on both sides of the street, but she didn't hear the bleating of sheep or the bellowing of cows or even dogs barking today. Instead of automobilists and bicyclists clamoring up and down the road, automobiles sat abandoned in the middle of the road and bicycles lay on the sidewalk.

The earlier mayhem had diffused into an eerie calm.

Instead of pedaling into the town center on the road, Gisèle found a break in the hedges and biked along its bumpy backside. There was a telephone booth near the police station. She would call Tante Corinne from there.

Peeking through another break in the hedge-rows, she surveyed the cobblestone street between the shops and primary school. Glass and debris covered the sidewalks and empty vehicles.

Had everyone in town fled or were they all hiding in their homes?

A troop of German soldiers marched from around the corner, into the street, the silver butts of their rifles gleaming in the sunlight. Their heavy boots pounded together on the stone.

Then a dark gray tank rounded the corner, a soldier perched above an enormous machine gun.

She watched as the gunner scanned the high buildings on both sides of him first before turning toward the hedgerows. Gunfire popped on the street, and she ducked back under the thick hedges with her bicycle, losing herself again among the rows.

The Germans, it appeared, were in no hurry to leave Saint-Lô.

CHAPTER 10

"Hello, Mémé." I bent to kiss the bony cheek of my grandmother.

Officially, she was the Honorable Gisèle de Bouchard Duchant Sauver. Hers was a lofty title for a little woman, but in spite of her age and illness, my grandmother still had the elegance and often the attitude of a French noblewoman. The air of superiority sometimes flared in her later years, but we all adored her, even when she liked to tell us exactly what we should—or should not—do.

"She escaped again yesterday," Pamela James, her saint of an aide, said from the other side of the bed. "I found her petting a cat—"

"Not just any cat," Mémé said, spanking Pamela's hand. "His name is Shadow."

Pamela's smile was strained. "I found her petting *Shadow,* down by the pond."

"I went to see Papillon Bleu." Mémé scooted herself farther up on her mound of pillows. "But I wasn't going to ride her until today."

My grandmother hadn't ridden Papillon Bleu or any other horse in two decades, but I wasn't going to remind her. "Now, Mémé, you can't go riding without Pamela."

A stream of French poured from her lips, telling

me it was none of my business when she rode a horse or with whom.

"Pamela needs your help," I insisted.

Mémé scrutinized Pamela as if to ascertain whether or not the woman before her really required her assistance.

I sat down on the stool beside her bed. I had been glad to skip the golf tournament this afternoon to visit my grandmother. On the table beside her was a black-and-white photograph of our entire family, a small jewelry box, and a glass of water. "Guess where I'm going this week?"

"Who are you?" she asked.

I kissed her forehead. "Someone who loves you."

She looked over my shoulder like she didn't see me, toward the front door of her apartment at Meadow Glen. "I'm thirsty."

I held the water glass up to her, and her hands shook as she took a sip. Then she patted my arm. "Much better. Thank you, dear."

Pamela stepped toward the door. "I'll get her some lemonade."

I leaned toward my grandmother, whispering as if I had a secret. Like she used to do with me when I was in grade school. "I'm going to Normandy."

"Normandy?" Her eyes grew wide, and I could see the lucidity battle her confusion. "The Château d'Epines . . ."

Relief filled me with her words. For that fleeting moment, her mind was with me.

"There's a man meeting me in France." She was watching me closely, so I continued. "He wants to know what happened at the château during the war."

"The château is such a lovely place," she mused. "You must take your friend down to the lake. Most people don't even know it's there—"

"Did you meet Grandpa at the château?" I asked, trying to help her focus.

Her stiff fingers tugged at the blanket over her chest. "We used to swim in it."

"You and Grandpa used to swim?"

"No." She shook her head. "Me and Michel."

I smiled as I imagined her, years younger than me, splashing in a lake with the younger brother she adored. They probably jumped off logs and paddled in a canoe and hunted for frogs and perhaps even snakes on the shores. It seemed to me that Mémé wasn't afraid of anything.

"And Nadine used to swim with us too—before they took her away."

I leaned closer. "Who is Nadine?"

Her gaze wandered to the wall in front of her, to the cards and artwork drawn by the grandchildren of the many students and colleagues she'd befriended over the years, and her fingers began the familiar rhythm of moving the amber rosary beads that hung around her neck. "No one knows what happened at the lake."

Mémé began to rock against her pillow, and I

reached for her hand. I wanted to offer her comfort, not distress, but something I said had upset her. This was why we couldn't talk about the past. The memories confused her.

Tears began to fill her eyes. "Poor Papa. He . . ."

I wanted to probe, but the pain in her eyes pressed me to stop. "We don't have to talk about it."

"There was nothing but good in him," she said, rocking faster now. "Nothing but good . . ."

Pamela shuffled through the door, and I turned around. Worry creased her eyes.

I gently stroked my grandmother's hand. "It will be okay, Mémé."

She jerked her hand away and threw off the blanket. Then her gaze found my face. "We must find her."

I looked up at Pamela again, wondering who we must find, but she seemed just as confused as me.

I tucked the blanket back across Mémé's chest. "Do we need to find your friend?"

"No." Her small hand reached out and took my arm, the strength in it surprising me. "We must find Adeline."

I swallowed hard. "Who is Adeline?"

"The girl." Her voice grew more insistent. "You must find the girl."

"Where should I look for her?" I asked.

Her blue eyes seemed to pierce me. "In the hawthorn trees."

Her head fell back against the pillow, and she swept her hand from mine, bracing it on her chest as the fire in her eyes began to dull. Her eyes closed, and I watched the blanket slowly rise and fall. Then her eyes fluttered open again, and her gaze darted back and forth between Pamela and me before it settled on my face.

She tilted her head. "I'm sorry, dear. Who are you?"

I picked my handbag off the floor. "Michael's daughter."

She looked over at Pamela again, confusion wrinkling her forehead. Pamela leaned down and pulled the blanket back over her chest. "You must rest, Mrs. Sauver."

She threw the blanket off her chest again. "But it's time for us to ride."

I kissed her cheek, blinking back my tears. "Perhaps you can go riding tomorrow."

Chapter 11

The ring of the doorbell startled Gisèle, and she almost sliced her finger with the paring knife. Across the table, Émilie was chopping leeks, and Gisèle saw the fear mirrored in her eyes. But perhaps the news wasn't bad this time. It could be the Polins or even Nadine with good news for them.

"Be careful," Émilie warned her, as if Gisèle could somehow ward off the Germans with her caution.

Shadow trailed her to the window beside the door. There wasn't an automobile in the courtyard, but she saw a bicycle. And the blond curls of a young woman standing on the flagstone outside.

Opening the door, she hurried the woman inside. Lisette was barely seventeen, but she had stolen Michel's heart two years ago. When Michel left with the Armée de Terre, Lisette began coming by often to visit her.

Gisèle kissed Lisette on both of her cheeks and then escorted her into the salon.

"Have you heard any news of Michel?" Lisette begged as she sat on the couch across from Gisèle.

She wished she could offer her the comfort of the truth. Instead she shook her head.

Lisette dabbed her cheeks with a white handkerchief. "I wish he would send a letter."

"We haven't received a letter from England in months," Gisèle said.

"Surely the Germans will let us get mail."

Gisèle hated the resignation in Lisette's voice, as if the Germans would bring an end to their problems. "The Germans will be gone soon," she insisted.

"I don't think so." Lisette folded the handkerchief on her lap. "They've begun moving men into the courthouse in Saint-Lô. They want to make it their headquarters for all of La Manche."

Gisèle shuddered at the thought of all those soldiers she'd seen remaining in the city. "How do you know?"

"Someone told them my uncle had been a translator during the Great War so they knocked on our door. He was too ill to leave the apartment, but I could translate for them."

The telephone rang out from her father's office. For a moment, Gisèle ignored it, as if Papa would answer the call. Then she leapt to her feet.

The telephone lines had been restored.

She excused herself and hurried toward the office.

Trepidation filled her along with a bit of excitement as she reached for the black receiver. "Hello?"

"Gisèle?" It was Philippe on the other end of the line.

"It's me!" she exclaimed, so glad to hear his voice. "Is Papa with you?"

"Are you safe?"

"Yes, but I—"

"I've been trying to call." His words rushed out. "I searched all over for you."

"I went to the Batiers' house."

The line clicked. "Who?"

"My friends' home. Is Papa with you?"

There was a scratching sound on the line and then she heard a muffled voice. The Germans may have restored their telephone lines, but it seemed they might be listening to their calls as well.

"What did you say?" he asked.

"Papa," she repeated again. "Is he with you?"

"No," he said. "I haven't seen him."

Her excitement leached out of her. "Are you in Lyon?"

"Yes."

She fell back into her father's chair, and Shadow jumped on her lap. If Papa wasn't with Philippe, where had he gone?

Lisette stepped into the office. "Is it Michel?" she mouthed.

When Gisèle shook her head, Lisette retreated back into the salon, leaving her alone with her cat and Philippe's voice.

"Did the Germans bomb the château?"

"No, the house and property are safe."

"Good," he said. "Quite good."

"Is your mother safe?" she asked.

"She's right beside me." Another crackling sound on the line interrupted his words. "We're trying to figure out how to get you here as well. We could marry—"

"I can't leave the château," she interrupted. Her stomach coiled again at the thought of marrying him. "Not until I find Papa."

Then her heart began to beat faster. What if her

father was trying to call her right now? "I must get off the line."

He pressed through her retort. "The Germans aren't marching toward the south of France," he said, and she wondered how well those who listened to their conversation understood French. "You will be safe here."

"Papa and I will come soon."

"Gisèle—"

"I must go," she said. "In case he's trying to call."

After she hung up the receiver, she waited by the phone. How could Philippe talk of marriage when her father was missing? He didn't seem to care . . .

Lisette wandered back into the room and sat down across from her. "Was that Philippe?"

She nodded her head, stroking Shadow's fur.

"Michel doesn't like him," Lisette said.

She managed a weak smile. "He and Michel used to fight as children."

"Michel said his cousin will do anything to get ownership of this château."

It was ludicrous to consider Philippe obtaining their property. Papa wasn't even fifty yet, and even when he was gone, Michel would inherit the place, and Lisette would be the new vicomtesse. Decades and decades from now.

And she would come regularly from Paris to visit them and their children, long after the Germans were gone.

CHAPTER 12

Light dappled the ripples in the murky lake water, twinkling like a thousand fireflies at twilight. I dipped my paddle into the sea of lights and pushed the kayak smoothly through it, the steady motion soothing my nerves. For the first time in weeks, I was free—liberated from responsibilities and obligations and all that was required of me.

A small catamaran sailed across the lake from me, its red-and-blue-striped sail fluttering in the wind. The city had been sweltering today, but the breeze drifting over Lake Kendall felt blissfully cool.

Perhaps I should have felt guilty for my desire to escape, but I beat away the guilt with every stroke of my paddle. For this rare hour, I wasn't the fiancée of Austin Vale or the daughter of the Sauvers or even a third-grade teacher at Washington Elementary. For this hour, I could simply be.

When we met, Austin had captured me with his vision of the future—our future—but somewhere along the line, I'd forgotten exactly who I was, silhouetted by those with greater dreams than my own.

Chaos—in the best sense of the word—had been the backbone of my family life growing up. My dad was raised by parents who loved him but struggled to survive in the United States. He had always been fascinated with numbers. When he was twenty-five, he started his first business—a coin-operated Laundromat that quickly turned a profit. He used the flood of revenue to purchase a second Laundromat a few months later, and then for the next decade, he bought another business each year. When he turned forty, he sold everything and launched a company to invest in other people's businesses.

My parents met when Dad was forty-three. And a multimillionaire.

Growing up, it seemed as if my father was as old as some of my friends' grandfathers. He spoiled me as a child, but thankfully my mother, as she liked to say, kept me from going rotten.

When my parents married, they both were already business owners. Even though their ventures were polar opposites, the world of self-employment required them to work nights and weekends, when they were eating, and practically when they were sleeping. The results of their enslavement were ridiculously successful careers. And a life with few memories outside their work.

Instead of a hectic life like my parents, I'd craved a more simple one, time to enjoy the water and my family and my students. For as long as I could remember, I'd wanted to teach children, discovering ways to make learning stick for a lifetime. Teaching invigorated me, the opportunity to help provide a foundation of education for the kids in my community. Then each summer, I traveled someplace new, steeping myself in history and culture and local food.

But it seemed my destiny wasn't going to involve much simplicity. As long as I could continue to carve out chunks of time like this to savor, I would enjoy the more public ride with Austin.

A branch draped low over the cove, and I ducked under it before sinking my paddle into the water again. The edge trailed in the water, the ripples blending with the light. Mesmerized, I watched as the light danced along the top of the brackish pool.

I hadn't planned to be on the water today, but when I arrived at my parents' summer home, neither of them was here yet. Instead of waiting inside, I hauled my kayak out of the boathouse and paddled across the small lake to an overgrown cove that seemed a million miles away.

And as I paddled, I mulled over my family's stories.

Mémé was usually confused these days, but this afternoon she'd seemed lucid when she begged me to find Adeline. Who was this girl who seemed to haunt her? And what happened to my great-grandfather during the war?

My grandmother had seemed afraid until the

sadness overtook her. Something terrible must have happened to her father. If only she had told me years before, when she told me my grandfather had fought the Germans.

Unlike my father's side of the family, the history on my mother's side flowed like a rapid river current. My mother's parents—Lionel and Grace Bishop—had seemingly endless tales from their year of courting. Every payday in the winter of 1954, Lionel had shown up at the bakery to buy a dozen of Grace's coconut macaroons. It took him a solid six months to muster enough courage to ask her for a date, but after another six months, he proposed and they married in an old church in Bethesda. To celebrate every anniversary, Grace still made him macaroons.

My grandparents on my father's side loved each other deeply, but all I knew about their courtship was that they'd met in a café. They'd told me no stories about their wedding day.

I remembered a little about my grandpa—the cinnamon candies he'd kept in his pockets and his fascination for anything that flew. He had a remote-control plane and during the summer, I spent hours at the park with him, flying it above the trees. His knowledge of history inspired me to love education, but somehow the history he discussed never encompassed his own story and I was too young at the time to think about asking for more. It was my grandmother who told me about his service in the military and resistance.

One specific memory from the years before Grandpa passed on rose to the top. It was my grandparents, holding hands as I joined them for a walk along the Atlantic coast. Mémé swatted Grandpa away playfully when he tried to steal a kiss. Then they'd escaped around a dune, ahead of me. When Mémé thought no one was looking, she kissed him back.

I smiled at my treasure of a memory—a simple, stolen kiss that sealed their enduring love, a love that lasted almost sixty years.

Near the shore, I saw the flat head of a snake and then the black sheen of its body trailing behind it. With swift strokes, I paddled away. While I loved the water, I wasn't thrilled about sharing it with a moccasin. Few things above the water scared me, but I was scared of what swam underneath it. Especially snakes looking for trouble.

Perhaps that was why I had a deep appreciation for the kayak. I could play on the water without diving in.

As I neared the dock, my mom waved from the patio of the house.

"Ahoy!" she shouted as she descended the path down to the water, a cooler in her hand. Her ash-blond hair was twisted back into a knot, and she wore a sleeveless blouse that showed off the bronze color on her plump arms. My mom was sixty-four, but she believed that age was relative.

A state of mind. Oddly enough, her mind insisted that she hadn't yet hit the big 4-0.

After I beached my kayak, she greeted me with a giant hug. I pulled a chair under a yellow umbrella and kicked off my flip-flops. "I'm glad to see you're pretending to retire."

"We are retired," she said. "On the second Sunday of every month."

I rolled my eyes. "I guess that's progress."

My parents were supposed to be easing their way into retirement, though the pace of their professional lives didn't seem to be letting up. I couldn't envision either of them fully retired.

A catamaran sailed toward our side of the lake, and I could see the chalky outline of a sailor leaning into the wind. Her eyes on the sailboat, Mom reached into the cooler and pulled out a Perrier for me. "Are you excited about France?"

"I'm excited to return to the château," I said. "But I don't know what I'm going to say in an interview about World War II."

Mom pulled a Tupperware container from her cooler and propped it on her lap. "Just tell Mr. Holtz the stories you remember about your grandfather."

She opened the container and took a strawberry from the pile of fresh fruit. It seemed ironic to me that she—the owner of Bliss Bakery—abstained from all refined sugar and artificial colors. Most of her cakes and cookies were chock-full of the processed stuff, but these days she let others bake while she met with brides who wanted one of her prized cakes.

Except for my wedding cake. She was planning to bake it herself. I wasn't sure how I was going to tell her that Austin's mother had asked Patty Wilson to bake one as well.

My mom held out the container, and I popped several blueberries into my mouth. "Perhaps Grandpa has family I can visit while I'm in France."

She shook her head. "He was estranged from them long ago."

The catamaran drew close, and I realized the man sailing the boat in long board shorts was my father. "What is Dad doing?"

"He decided to take up a new hobby."

I understood my dad's love of the water, but he was much too old to be out sailing by himself. "Can't he take up golfing or—I don't know— bunco?"

She laughed. "He'd be bored out of his mind."

Dad lassoed a post on the dock and pulled in his catamaran before retrieving a towel and T-shirt from the dock. He wiped his tanned face with his towel. "I'd give you a hug, but . . ."

I waved both hands. "There's no need."

Mom scooted the cooler toward him with her toes. "Drink something, Michael."

"When did you get a sailboat?" I asked.

"Two weeks ago." He plucked a vitamin-infused water out of the cooler and then he winked at me. "I'm planning to go pro."

Mom rolled her eyes. "He thinks the catamaran scouts are coming for him."

Dad pulled over a chair to sit beside me. His silver hair glistened in the sunlight, but besides his hair, few people would probably have guessed he was pushing seventy-six. He was in better physical condition than half the guys my age, and he worked harder than any other man I knew. "Thank you for doing this interview."

I leaned into the shade of the umbrella. "I wish you could go with me."

He took a long drink and then put the bottle back down on the glass table. "Not this time, I'm afraid." He always seemed to have an excuse as to why he couldn't return to France, but he never explained it to me. "Perhaps someday we'll all go back again for a visit together."

"I saw Mémé this morning." I slowly twirled my toes. "I told her I was going to Normandy."

Dad twisted the water bottle. "What did she say?"

"She talked about the château and her father and then she asked me about a little girl named Adeline."

My parents shared a glance, and I looked between them.

"What are you keeping from me?"

"We're not keeping anything," Mom said. "It's just that Gisèle has mentioned this Adeline a few times recently."

"So you were keeping it from me."

Dad shook his head. "She says a lot of things that don't mean anything. We thought she was confused."

"She seemed quite intent on it today."

"I've never heard of anyone named Adeline," Dad said.

I sipped the bubbly water. "She was afraid for her father as well."

Dad glanced back out at the lake. "My grandfather died at the beginning of the war."

"Do you know how he died?"

After Dad shook his head, Mom slipped off her sunglasses and placed them on the table. "Tell her what Mr. Holtz said."

Dad leaned toward me, his eyes intent. "He seems to think something significant happened at the château."

"Like what?" I asked.

"He didn't expound."

I sighed. "I wish he could have given us a little lead time to gather material."

"Apparently he was just able to track us down," Mom said.

"Maybe Stéphane could tell me some stories—"

"That man is not to be trusted," Dad said.

"Why not?"

"His father lost their family's home in Lyon and then he spent a lifetime trying to steal the château from my mother, even as she allowed him to live there without paying a dime of rent." Tears welled in his eyes, and I loved how much he still loved Mémé. Her mind might be slipping, but Dad remembered everything good about her. "Philippe despised her, but she didn't turn him away."

"What was it like growing up in a château?" It was the same question I'd asked when I was younger, but this time I hoped for a better answer.

"I don't remember much," he said, his voice quiet. "I was barely six when we moved to the States."

I had so many memories from my early years of life—coloring with my friends in kindergarten, playing in the ocean in Virginia Beach, my dog who died when I was five. "Surely you remember something," I said, pressing him.

"My mother tells the grandest stories of my childhood there, but all I recall are the tall stone walls." His gaze wandered toward the water. "And a room filled with children, dozens of them . . ."

I glanced up at the contrails of a plane in the sky. "I suppose it's hard to tell the difference between a childhood dream and a memory."

He looked back at me. "Dreams and blurry memories should never be trusted. And neither should the Bordes."

Chapter 13

*T*he spicy scent of incense lingered in the *chapelle*, and the stained-glass windows gleamed from the setting sunlight, warming the blond wood of the benches. Near the altar was a statue of Mother Mary holding her baby, and pictures lined the walls—scenes of Saint Francis holding a lamb, Saint Michel defeating the dragon, Jesus carrying his cross to Calvary.

With the handles of the picnic hamper strung over her arm, Gisèle unlocked the gate across the sacristy and then relocked it behind her. A cabinet to the right stored linens and beside it was a locked closet for vestments. Usually she came to the sacristy after dark, when those who prayed couldn't see what she was doing, but she couldn't wait until nightfall to find Michel. She needed his help to find Papa.

The skeleton key that hung on her rosary also unlocked the large closet in the sacristy, and she pushed aside the tunics, stoles, and robes until she felt the wooden panel in the back. When she pressed on it, the wood swung inward.

Turning on her flashlight, she shone it onto the ledge and saw the food she'd left last night in the picnic hamper was still there, along with her letter. She stepped inside and closed the panel behind her before picking up the hamper.

Steps led downward from the ledge, into the darkness, and her skin bristled as she shined her light below.

Her father used to tell them legends about a tunnel under the property, a place where their ancestors hid during the French Revolution, but she had never known where the entrance was until Michel returned last month from England and begged for her help. Her brother made her swear not to tell anyone, especially their father, that he'd found the tunnel.

Breathing in the cool air, she began her descent. The dirt walls circled around her. She much preferred the open lands around her home to dark, tight spaces like this, but she forced her mind to wander away from its panic, to wonder at those who had come down here long before her. Perhaps the Vikings had built the tunnel after they raided this land, or maybe the Romans built it in the earlier centuries after Christ's birth. Perhaps it had been used as a catacomb.

She shouldn't let her mind wander.

The passage tapered, the cold air chilling her skin, but even with the drop in temperature, her hands were clammy. The sooner she found her brother, the sooner she could get back to the warmth on the surface.

"Michel?" she called out.

There was no answer.

The tunnel diverged into two passages, and she shone her light down both sides. On both sides, the darkness swallowed up her ray of light.

She chose the left passage at first, but it dead-ended into a dozen stone steps, a small pocket door at the top. Curiosity spurred her forward and she tugged on the metal pull. The door cracked open, but it was the tiniest sliver. On the other side was some sort of barrier.

Her breathing grew faster now. What if she was trapped under the earth? What if she lost her way and couldn't get back to the *chapelle*?

What if someone locked the closet door from the outside and she couldn't open it?

What if her brother was gone—and someone else was here instead?

She had to find him quickly and get back up the stairs.

The tunnel sloped downward as she crept forward, and she wondered if she was descending in the direction of the forest or the river. She knew every step of their property aboveground, but it felt so strange to be far below all that she knew.

When the path flattened again, she paused by a small room cut out of the dirt. Blankets and cigarette butts littered the ground. She passed by the room, but voices echoed farther up the tunnel, and she froze, listening to the sound. Then she turned off her flashlight.

Light continued to illuminate the walls in front of her, and she prayed her brother was with the light.

"Michel?" she called again.

The voices stopped, and for a moment, all she heard was her breathing.

"Is that you, Gigi?"

At the sound of her brother's voice, her heart returned to a steady pace. Only Michel was allowed to call her that name. "It's me."

"It's not safe for you to be here." The sternness in his voice frightened her.

She squinted into the light but couldn't see him or anyone else, so she stepped toward the lantern. "I've brought your food."

"Leave it where you are," he said.

"But I need to speak with you."

The shadow of a man emerged in front of her, and she flashed her light on him. Her brother, dark and swarthy, walked toward her as if he were Clark Gable or another one of America's stars who dominated the silver screen. Many of the young women in Normandy pined over Michel Duchant, but he'd always been more enamored of his motorcycle than the idea of marriage—at least until he met Lisette.

He'd been conscripted into the Armée de Terre before he graduated from *lycée* and reported to duty on his eighteenth birthday, ready to slay the dragons like the saint Mother named him after. Sometimes Gisèle wondered if anything ever frightened her brother.

"You can't see the other men who are with me," he said.

She set the picnic hamper on the ground. "I wouldn't tell anyone who they are."

"We're in a war," he said, his voice sad. "None of us can be certain what we will or will not do."

As he drew closer in the tunnels, she could smell sweat and brandy and cigarette smoke, but she didn't care. She hugged him.

When he released her, he clamped his hands on her shoulders. "What is it, Gigi?"

"Émilie and I baked you bread." She nudged the picnic hamper toward him. "You must check the ledge, Michel. I left you a letter last night."

"I thought you'd fled," he said. "We heard the bombs two nights ago. One of our men went out—" His voice cracked with emotion. "He hasn't returned."

She took a deep breath. "The Germans have taken Paris."

His fist shot out, hitting the wall. "This is what we feared," he said as he pulled his fist back into his chest. "The worst of our fears."

"I am afraid for you, Michel."

"Where are the French soldiers?" he asked, rubbing his hand.

"The wireless said they were running south."

"Our government—they are all cowards."

"No one wants the Germans here," she said.

He shook his head. "Some do. They think it will bring peace."

"How can bombs bring peace?" she asked.

"It all depends on who is dropping the bombs." His voice grew stronger. "If our army can't stop them, then we will have to."

His declaration made her shiver, and she trembled. His fervor, she feared, might get him killed. "You must leave here too. Papa said we could get to Switzerland."

"I will not run away." He paused. "Why are you still here?"

She forced a smile. "I promised Mother that I'd take care of you."

"That was ten years ago," he said. "You must leave, Gigi. We will find food another way."

"How many are down here?" she asked.

"Four right now, but with this news . . ." He unclenched his hand. "There will be more."

"Then you will need more food." When they found Papa, he would agree with her.

"I can't put you into harm's way. If something happened to you, Papa would never forgive me, and I—I would never forgive myself." He paused again. "Why hasn't Papa made you leave?"

Tears began to well in her eyes. "He's gone, Michel, and I don't know where he went."

"He left without you?"

"He stayed behind to hide the silver and Mother's jewelry. Philippe came to get me—"

"Where is Philippe now?" he demanded.

"We got separated in the bombing," she explained. "But he called today, from Lyon."

"He is just waiting . . . ," Michel muttered.

"Waiting for what?"

He shook his head. "Nothing."

"You must tell me, Michel."

But he didn't speak anymore about Philippe. "Papa would have tried to hide the valuables down near the lake."

She took a step back. "I will go look for him."

"Not by yourself, Gigi." He glanced back over his shoulder, at the dark corridor. "I will go with you tonight."

"Do you think . . ." She couldn't bear to finish the question, couldn't bear the thought that he might be lying wounded by the bombs.

His voice dipped low. "I don't know what to think anymore."

CHAPTER 14

Austin turned off the ignition in the airport parking garage and intertwined his fingers through mine. "I am the luckiest man in the world."

I glanced out the window, at the red and blue

lights flashing along the cement wall. "The security cameras are watching."

He pulled me closer. "I don't care if the whole world knows how much I love you."

His kiss reminded me of all I loved about him—his confidence and passion and fervent dreams for our future. As I sank into him, in the privacy of the parking deck, he held me as close as he could with a console stuck between us.

What was I thinking, going to France weeks before my wedding? Even with Austin's encouragement, even with the allure of visiting the château, I didn't want to leave.

"Perhaps I shouldn't go—" I began to say.

Austin hushed me with another kiss, one that made my toes tingle. "I'll be waiting here when you return," he said. "And then next time you travel to France, we'll be together."

"You will love it in Normandy," I said.

Grinning, he brushed my long hair back over my shoulder. "I would love anyplace if I'm with you."

I kissed him one last time, and with a glance at the dashboard clock, began to inch away. I didn't want to step outside, but my flight left in an hour.

As he removed our luggage from his trunk, I reapplied my lip gloss and we strolled into the Richmond airport like an old married couple, side by side about three feet apart. Together but distracted.

Before we made it to security, a young couple

stopped Austin. Nervous, they began to gush about their desire to have him as their next governor. His smile charismatic, he thanked them and then disarmed them by asking the questions he asked of everyone—where did they live and what did they want for the future? As they chatted, I discreetly checked the time on my phone. My flight left in thirty-five minutes now, his in an hour.

He introduced me as his future wife, the third-grade teacher who would champion education reform. I smiled politely and then stretched my fingers over his arm. A gentle tug brought him back to the reality that we were in an airport, trying to catch two separate flights to New York. Others might wait for the candidate, but I was pretty sure the commercial airlines would not.

By the time we arrived at the gate, I was out of breath and the attendant was calling for final boarding.

"Did Olivia send you the research notes?" Austin asked.

I tapped my briefcase. "They're all on my iPad—I'll read them on the plane."

"I'm going to miss you," he said.

I'd only be gone a week, I told myself. After that we had a lifetime together. "I'm going to miss you too."

He pecked my cheek. "Call me when you get to Paris."

I smiled. "I'll call you when I land in New York."

Worry flashed in his eyes. "Someone from the party is picking me up at the airport. I'm afraid they have meetings planned all day for me."

My smile fell. "Of course."

"But I'll send you a text."

I slid my boarding pass out of my purse. "Good enough."

"I'm sorry, Chloe. I wish you were going with me."

I didn't mean to be insensitive to his commitments. I just wasn't quite ready to say good-bye.

"No stress," he commanded, "for an entire week."

The attendant called my name from the podium, and Austin stepped back, pointing his thumb over his shoulder. "I suppose I should catch my flight too."

I shooed him away. "Go."

Before I stepped onto the Jetway, my fiancé was gone.

Steely clouds anchored themselves above the New York skyline, dark and foreboding. Our plane circled the airport three times before the pilot was cleared to land. After the plane parked, hail began to pelt the windows, and inside the terminal the attendant informed me and every other passenger on my flight that we were grounded until the thunderstorm cleared. Pending weather, the next flight to Paris would leave tomorrow morning at ten.

I glanced around the lobby. People were already draped over most of the seats, and both luggage and children had strayed onto the walkway. The weather might keep me out of the skies for the next twenty-four hours, but it didn't mean I had to stay off the roads.

Perhaps I could join Austin at the Plaza.

I wasn't naïve enough to think it would be a romantic evening, but I much preferred spending the night at the Plaza than at the airport. And maybe Austin and I could duck out after the event for a walk in Central Park or even a midnight carriage ride.

I called Austin's number, but his phone went straight to voice mail. He'd probably been whisked off to a meeting the moment he landed.

My luggage would be transferred to my next flight, but I could secure an elegant dress and shoes on Fifth Avenue. And if I called ahead, perhaps I could make an appointment with a stylist to do my hair and makeup.

Smiling, I climbed into the cab. I wouldn't try to call Austin again.

Instead I'd wait and surprise him at dinner.

Chapter 15

Gisèle slipped out of the château after midnight and hurried west, toward the forested hill that dipped down to a lake and ancient caves where Michel loved to hide as a child. Her flashlight trembled in her hand, but she didn't dare turn it on.

The narrow path wound under the stone walls of an old guardhouse to the brick wall that separated the landscaped lawn from the towering oak and beech trees. A rusty iron gate linked the wall, and the hinges creaked when she edged it open.

An aeroplane flew over the château, and she ducked under the canopy of branches until she heard a low whistle filtering through the trees. She whistled back.

"Gigi," Michel whispered.

"I'm by the gate."

Her brother crept up beside her. "We must hurry," he said.

She followed him down the winding path that descended to the lake. Every minute or two, the beam from his flashlight swept across the floor, and then they were covered in blackness again.

"Lisette came by today," she whispered as they walked.

He slowed his pace. "What did she say?"

"She's worried about you."

"You can't tell her where I am," he said, worried.

"Can I tell her you are safe?"

He shook his head. "She must forget about me."

"None of us will forget about you, Michel."

He flashed his light again and they scanned the fallen branches and overgrowth on the forest floor.

"Why don't you like Philippe?" she asked as they neared the lake.

"I want you to marry someone who loves you."

She stopped walking. "You don't think Philippe loves me?"

"Not like he should." He hesitated. "He wants the château."

"But the château will be yours one day."

"Philippe is a gambling man."

Michel resumed his walk, and she fell behind him, trying to sort out the implications of his words. What was Philippe betting on?

The trail flattened, and ahead of them, moonlight trailed across the small lake, like the filmy train of a bride. As they rounded the edge, Michel scanned the rocks and downed logs along the shore. On the other side of the lake was the shadowy entrance to a cave.

Michel ducked inside, and when he flicked on his light, she stepped in behind him.

"Stop!" he yelled, but it was too late.

Against the wall was her father, and she rushed forward. Dark bruises circled around his eyes. Dried blood caked his ears and cheeks. "Papa," she whispered, shaking him.

Michel placed his hand on her shoulder. "Gisèle."

She pushed her brother away. "No . . ."

Her head dropped to her father's chest, listening for the whisper of his heartbeat, but his body was still. "Papa!" she yelled, shaking him as if he might wake again, but there was no life left in him.

Rushing outside, she retched in the bushes.

Papa had said the Germans would respect the aristocracy, that he would follow her to Lyon. That he would be safe.

Michel was beside her again, but this time she didn't shake him away. He put his arms around her and she sobbed on his shoulder.

Had the Nazis killed him for the silver? As if silver was worth more than the life of her father, a hero of a man. How could Hitler's soldiers kill good men, innocent men, as they plundered Europe?

Her entire body trembled as she collapsed to the ground. "I shouldn't have left the château without him."

"This isn't your fault."

She clutched the crucifix that hung around her neck. "They murdered him."

"And they will pay for it," he said, anger teeming in his voice.

She curled over her knees, rocking back and forth. "We must bury him."

"The others will help me retrieve his body. We'll bury him beside Mother."

Michel stepped back into the cave, but she couldn't go back inside. Her hands clasped around the cross, she whispered her prayer as she counted the beads.

> Our Father who art in heaven,
> Hallowed be thy name;
> Thy kingdom come
> Thy will be done
> On earth as it is in heaven.

Michel appeared back at the entrance, his hand outstretched. She looked down at his palm in the flashlight beam and saw an onyx-and-gold cuff link with a tiny diamond in the center.

He folded his fingers around it. "I'll kill a hundred *boches* to avenge his death."

Her heart seemed to collapse within her. As much as she wanted revenge, she couldn't lose two of the men she loved. "It won't bring him back," she said. "We should both go to Lyon."

His eyes seemed to blaze. "I won't cower, Gigi."

She didn't want him to cower, but she had to

protect her younger brother. If he went into Saint-Lô now, the Germans would surely kill him.

"You must wait," she begged.

"You can go with Philippe," he said, his voice broken. "But I have to stay here. I have to fight them."

Her anger collided with her fear as she walked back up the trail beside him, her body numb.

"I will help you," she said before he slipped back into the shadows.

She wouldn't leave her brother here alone.

CHAPTER 16

After the rain stopped, I reemerged onto Fifty-ninth Street, a chai latte in hand. Ahead of me was Central Park, along with the elegant façade of the Plaza, overlooking the trees. Storm clouds still threatened the shoppers who paraded along the sidewalk, but at least I could walk to the hotel without getting drenched.

On my cab ride from the airport, I'd secured a hotel room for the night, along with an appointment at their salon. After checking in, I had four hours to find the right dress and shoes before the artisans began working their magic on my makeup and hair. It was almost impossible to surprise Austin—I couldn't wait to see his face when I walked into the ballroom.

As I crossed Fifth Avenue, a black limousine rolled up to the curb next to the hotel and a bellman rushed forward to open the door. Austin emerged from the car, and my heart leapt. Perhaps it would be just as fun to surprise Austin now, away from the spotlight. In the timing of providence, perhaps, instead of my own.

I pulled my phone out of my bag and quickly typed.

Turn around.

Smiling, I lifted my finger to send my message, but before I sent it, I glanced back up. Instead of walking into the Plaza, Austin extended his arm back into the limousine. Another figure emerged on the sidewalk beside him. A woman.

And she was stunning.

I watched with a mixture of awe and horror as she reached for Austin's hand.

Dropping my phone back into my purse, I watched them laugh together as they strolled up the front steps. What if someone recognized him?

I supposed it didn't matter. Surely she was only a colleague from the party headquarters in New York.

The woman's ebony curls bounced with her laughter, and her white summer dress glided behind her like that of a Greek goddess. I glanced down at my navy capris, wrinkled from the plane ride, and tan-colored blouse. There was no comparison between me and a goddess.

But it was Austin who had kissed me this morning, three hours ago. It was Austin who told *me* how beautiful I was and how much he loved me. As I watched him with this other woman, my head felt like it was about to explode.

There had to be an explanation—but why didn't he let go of that woman's hand?

The bellman opened the door to the lobby, and Austin and his escort disappeared under the golden lights.

Hiking my handbag over my shoulder, I rushed toward the hotel, and the same bellman who'd opened the door for Austin opened it for me. The lobby radiated elegance, with its marble columns and oriental rugs. To the right of the registration desk was a giant fern. I didn't exactly hide behind it—I merely paused beside it and no one seemed to notice, perhaps because they were all staring at the eye candy dangling on Austin's arm.

And how could they not stare? She was more striking than the gold encrusted around the lobby's windows and doors.

I clutched my handbag to my chest. My dad would tell me not to be impulsive, to wait and make a decision after I had all the facts. The woman was probably a campaign manager for a candidate in New York or someone's assistant sent to escort Austin to his meeting. In a few minutes, the three of us would be laughing about the misunderstanding. It would be awkward but understandable. If she wasn't a business associate . . .

I couldn't allow myself to linger on that possibility.

The man at the registration desk slipped Austin an envelope and told him his room—the Edwardian Fifth Avenue Suite—overlooked the Pulitzer Fountain from the eighteenth floor. Austin turned to pick up his suitcase, and I almost wished he would glance up and see me hovering beside the fern.

He didn't notice me.

Now that he had his hotel key in hand, I prayed he would say good-bye to the woman. Bid her a good day. But there was no handshake as they parted ways. Or the kiss of the French on both cheeks. The woman trailed Austin to the elevator and slipped inside.

As the doors began to close, I saw Austin lean down. Even though I knew the scene would haunt me, I couldn't look away. Before the doors shut, I watched the man I was supposed to marry kiss her lips.

The bright colors of the lobby fused together and I felt as if I might faint. *Air.* I needed fresh air. Rushing back out the lobby doors, I collapsed against a column and pounded my fists against the stone, gasping the warm, fume-laden air. The relentless horns of taxis rattled my head. Messy tears flooded my cheeks.

How could I have been so stupid?

I punched the column again. I'd known something was off the moment Lisa mentioned the trip to New York. Or perhaps it was before, when Austin lectured me on the importance of my commitment and then put me on a plane to France.

No wonder he hadn't wanted me to call him during my layover. And why he'd neglected to invite me on this trip. His *meeting* would indeed encompass all of his time.

My head whirled as I pressed against my brows. It was too much to comprehend.

"Are you all right, miss?"

I looked up at the tall form of a uniformed bellhop. My body shook as I tried to right myself. "It's just a headache," I said, pointing to my forehead.

What else could I tell him—that I feared my fiancé was sleeping with another woman? That my relationship, my future, was crumbling before me? He might tell me to ditch the guy, but it wasn't that easy.

"Can I get you some Advil?" he asked.

When I shook my head, he backed away.

I'd given my heart, along with my dreams, to the traitor upstairs. If I ended our engagement now, the media would feast on the story of Austin's indiscretion. My closest friends would pity me, while those who didn't know me—including the hundreds who'd already received a wedding invitation—might wonder what I'd done to make my fiancé unfaithful. Others might joke about a last fling before he tied the knot.

I thought Marissa had been jealous of what Austin and I had, but I'd been a fool. She and my parents would tell me to march upstairs and break it off.

Instead of confronting him, I could take a taxi back to the airport for the night and then fly on to Paris in the morning. Pretend I never saw him kissing that woman. Guzzle mint juleps all the way across the Atlantic until my heart was numb.

A picture slashed violently through my mind. It was me, thirty years from now, the miserable Mrs. Vale. Like Austin's mother, I would have to tolerate his sorties for the sake of—for the sake of what? Being the wife of a politician or the money that came from being married to a successful man. Or to hold my broken family together by pretending that everything was fine and then demanding that everyone join me in looking the other way while my husband flaunted his latest affair. Instead of standing up to my husband, I would ask our precocious son to pass the potatoes.

No one respected Mrs. Vale—including Mrs. Vale. If I tolerated Austin's unfaithfulness, I would never be able to respect myself either.

If I broke our engagement, I'd be the punch line of late-night jokes and tabloid headlines, but better to be a punch line than the miserable wife of a man who preferred to be with other women.

I wanted to scream. Hurl something through the window. Run.

So many people had compared Austin's charisma and charm to John F. Kennedy's. Is this what Jackie felt like the first time she found out about her husband's affairs? Angry and ashamed.

Perhaps she felt trapped in their marriage, but I wasn't trapped. There was still time for me to walk away.

My heart heavy, I wiped away my tears and stepped back into the lobby. My father and Marissa had both warned me that Austin might be hiding something, but I'd ignored the waving of their red flags.

The elevator delivered me to the eighteenth floor, to a long hall lit with golden wall sconces and masked with mirrors. All it needed was smoke to complete the illusion.

My stomach rolled when I heard a woman laugh in the Edwardian Fifth Avenue Suite, like Megan laughing in the Vales' home. In front of the suite was an alcove with a stiff leather bench, and I sat, wishing I could break down the door.

Instead I pulled out my phone, looked at the text I'd almost sent on the sidewalk. The one asking Austin to turn around.

If I'd sent it, he might have turned and slammed the car door before I saw the woman with him.

Years or even decades might have passed before I learned the truth.

My stomach curled at the thought.

Austin's mother might have tolerated her husband's infidelities. Countless politicians' wives before me might have looked the other way. But I could not.

Slowly I began to delete each letter in my original text. Then, taking a deep breath, I began to type again.

I made it to NYC, I wrote. *You here?*

This time I heard his laugh blending with hers. Were they mocking me? I wiped away the last of my tears.

A few minutes later, he texted back.

Crazy storm, huh? I'm here. In meetings already.

So this is what he referred to as a meeting? Bitter, I joined in their laughter.

My phone flashed again with another text.

I miss you.

His audacity infuriated me.

Right . . . I typed. Casual bait to catch my fish. *Whatcha meeting about?*

He texted right back. *Budgets. Boring stuff* . . .

Doesn't sound a bit boring to me.

His reply came at lightning speed. *U ok???*

I stared at the phone for a moment, and the aching in my heart almost drowned out the anger. There was still time to run away. Pretend that everything was fine.

Yet I couldn't do it. Perhaps the meeting really was providential.

I leaned back against the wall and closed my eyes.

Laughter no longer bled through the door in front of me, and I wondered what might be going through Austin's head. Usually he knew the game plan of each player around him before he calculated his next move. Perhaps it was good to make him a little nervous.

Slowly I began to type again, anger fueling me. *I'm just great. When were you planning to tell me?*

Sorry, he wrote. *I didn't think budgets interested you . . .*

They do now.

What do you want to know?

This time I didn't hesitate as I typed. *I want to know the name of your girlfriend.*

I leaned back, relief filling me as the words vanished on my screen. The truth was the only thing that would free both of us.

Where are you?!?

I took a deep breath before I texted him back. *Sitting outside your door.*

Seconds later, Austin Vale stood before me in the doorway, dressed in a white robe, the Plaza insignia embroidered on his chest.

"What are you doing—" he demanded, stumbling over his words. I'd never seen Austin flustered before.

"I was going to surprise you." I tucked my phone back into my purse. "Apparently I succeeded."

His mouth gaped open. I'd never seen Austin at a loss for words either.

Standing, I eyed his attire. "Do you always conduct budget meetings in a bathrobe?"

He glanced down at the robe as if he'd forgotten it was on, and then he raked his fingers through his dark hair. What had appeared so handsome to me hours before suddenly looked fake. Plastic. Why had I kissed those lips with such fervor? Lips that told me they loved me and then lied.

He motioned back into the room. "I was just getting dressed for a meeting. I didn't mean to confuse you—"

Inside my heart was crumbling, but I had no choice—I had to cling to the thread of strength dangling within me. "What's her name?"

"I don't know who you're talking about—"

Then she—the woman he didn't know—stepped into the doorway behind him, wearing a matching robe. Her triumphant smile was nauseating. "My name is Starla," she said, mocking me. "Starla Dedrick."

Austin ignored the woman, his eyes focused on me. "This is not what it looks like."

"Of course it is." The bitterness in my laugh made him wince. "How much are you paying her?"

Starla's smirk began to fade. "I think I'll let you two work this out alone."

Austin glanced both ways before stepping into the hallway. Then he shut the door behind him. "You are supposed to be on your way to Normandy," he said as if this problem was somehow my fault.

"You are supposed to be faithful!"

"I don't love her—not like I love you." He looked so genuine, so pathetic. I didn't feel sorry enough to run back into his arms, but I wavered. For the briefest of moments.

Then I remembered. Lisa had asked if I was meeting Starla—the old family friend—to shop in New York. My hands sank to my sides. "How does your sister know her?"

Austin dug his hands into the pockets of the robe. "Starla and I dated in college."

I almost wished that he'd hired her for the day.

"I love you, Chloe." He reached for my hands, but I yanked them away. "Truly."

I wanted to pull every hair out of his head. One at a time. "I can't believe this, Austin."

"I'll never do this again." He took another step forward. "Nothing will change between us."

I picked up my handbag off the bench. "It's already changed."

I rushed back toward the elevator doors. Thankfully, they opened right after I pushed the arrow.

The last sound I heard from the eighteenth floor was Austin Vale, the distinguished gubernatorial candidate from Virginia, banging on his hotel room door, begging his girlfriend to let him back inside.

PART TWO

*Do not judge your fellow
until you have stood in his place.*

—RABBI HILLEL
ETHICS OF THE FATHERS

Chapter 17

August 1942

Juif. The vile word was woven into the star on the boy's black vest. Eyes wide, the boy stared into the window teeming with croissants and bread, but the branding prevented him from entering the bakery in Saint-Lô.

When the child lifted his head, Gisèle met his gaze. He couldn't have been four years of age, but his face was gaunt, his eyes flush with fear, like one of the prisoners she'd seen laboring along the road into town.

She lifted her hand to greet him.

"Don't encourage him." Turning, Gisèle watched the baker lift a woven basket onto the counter.

"But he looks so sad," she said as she handed him her coupon for bread.

Monsieur Cornett glanced down at the coupon and then looked back at her. "He's manipulating you."

"How do you know?"

"Because he's a dirty Jew."

The baker's words made her cringe, as if the child were a dog or a maggot instead of a hungry boy.

For decades France had been a haven for the Jewish people escaping persecution in Germany and Austria. Thousands of Jews—like Nadine's family—found refuge among the French, but since the Germans had *liberated* the northern districts of her country, they'd inundated France with propaganda about the threat of Jews.

How could anyone believe the Nazis' propaganda, the wretched manipulation and lies? Their frightening obsession with harassing even the youngest and oldest Jews had infected some of her neighbors, their blatant hatred sickening her.

The baker brushed the flour off his apron and disappeared into the back room to retrieve her ration.

The Germans seemed to be everywhere now— living uninvited in the homes of people in Saint-Lô, playing like chums with the children after school, patrolling the streets of the city to enforce order during the day and the curfew at night. They'd set up a headquarters in the town center for the entire French district of La Manche, across from the prison that they'd filled with people brave enough to resist their occupation. And even before her uncle passed away, they'd forced Lisette to work for them.

Still she feared that too many French people had begun to identify with their occupiers instead of fighting against them. Some French men and women were simply resigned to the occupancy, while others joined their occupants in despising the Jewish population, fanning the flames of bitterness until it raged in their hearts. Hatred, it seemed, was a powerful unifier of even the greatest enemies.

Hatred for the Nazis had also unified those resisting them. The more regulations the Germans inflicted on them, the faster Michel's resistance cell grew. Her brother's group now included dozens of men, former business owners, farmers, soldiers, schoolboys who'd become men during the occupation. They left for weeks at a time, wreaking havoc on their occupiers across France.

The Nazis had confiscated most of the wirelesses in the town, but Gisèle had kept hers, listening to it in Papa's office and relaying the information to her brother. Charles de Gaulle was hiding in London, but he spoke regularly to the people of France on the wireless.

"France is not alone," he'd pronounced. "She has a vast empire behind her."

When Gisèle heard his words, hope rekindled in her heart. Perhaps the entire world hadn't given up on them. With the help of others, perhaps they did still have a chance to win back their country.

"Whatever happens, the flame of the French resistance will not be extinguished," de Gaulle had said. Then he urged the resistance to cut telephone wires, sabotage the railways, print underground newspapers that promoted freedom for the French people.

Her brother and his men continued to stoke the embers of their freedom, and when they returned to the tunnels, she provided food and water for them.

The Nazis tried to regulate what the French people planted and what they ate, even from their own gardens. But no matter how hard they tried, it was impossible to monitor every apple and carrot stick.

She and Émilie didn't need bread from the bakery—the families who farmed their property continued to supply flour and cheese and vegetables to Gisèle and Émilie in abundance—but they had to use their ration coupons so the Germans wouldn't suspect. As the months passed, Émilie had taught her how to bake bread and cook the leeks, potatoes, and cabbage. Émilie knew the food they prepared wasn't for the orphanage, but she didn't ask questions. It seemed best for all of them not to question.

She glanced back out the window again and saw the child peeking around the glass. Where were his parents?

Last month the Germans mandated that the Jews living among them—even those born in France—wear the stars on their coats. If Jews refused to wear it, the Germans threatened a penalty of imprisonment, but Nadine thought wearing the badge was a greater threat than refusing. Gisèle was terrified as to what would happen to her friend Nadine if she didn't wear the star. Her daughter, Louise, had been born more than a year ago now, and Gisèle had tried to convince her friend to wear the star for Louise's sake, but Nadine refused.

Until the government began requiring the badges, Gisèle hadn't realized how many Jewish people lived near Saint-Lô. Now their city seemed to glow yellow from the fallen stars. Instead of finding safety, their haven had crumbled.

People wouldn't hate the Jewish people if they were blessed with a friend like Nadine. Nadine Batier was a French citizen, a devout Catholic. Her husband had been one of the favorite teachers at the secondary school until the headmaster in Saint-Lô terminated his position last term, citing the fact that he was no longer qualified to teach. They all knew the truth—the administration didn't want the husband of a Jewish woman teaching their children.

She couldn't comprehend why they would dismiss André because of the blood in his wife's veins. How was his family supposed to survive without work? But the Germans had taken his job away and now they wanted to brand his family.

When Monsieur Cornett returned, he glanced back out the window. "Why is he still here?"

The boy looked away. "Perhaps he's waiting for his parents."

"They were probably arrested last night."

A tremor of fear flared up her spine. "Why would they be arrested?"

"How would I know?" he replied. "They rounded up dozens of people around Saint-Lô."

He handed her the bread and she tucked it under her arm. "Where did they take them?"

The baker shrugged.

She shivered. There had been rumors of the Germans rounding up Jews in Paris, and she'd been afraid they would begin to gather the Jews here as well. Had André and Nadine heard what happened? Probably not—they rarely left their home these days.

She had to warn them.

As she moved toward the door, she ripped a large piece of bread from her loaf and held it out to the boy on the street. The boy stared down at her offering. When his gaze bounced back up to her, she saw fear mirrored in his eyes. Purple remnants of a bruise circled his eye, and for a moment, she flashed back to that horrific night when she and Michel had found Papa's body by the lake, his face battered by the Germans.

Had they beaten this boy as well?

Her heart felt as if it would rip into two pieces.

Instead of taking the piece of bread, the boy turned and ran. Stunned, she stood and watched him disappear into an alley.

Did he think she was trying to trick him?

Someone brushed up against her, an old woman wearing a brown-and-green scarf over her head. She kissed Gisèle on one cheek, and as she leaned to kiss her second cheek, she whispered, "He is afraid."

Gisèle clung to the woman a moment longer. "But why?"

"Because they are watching him."

The old woman continued her walk, swinging a basket in her arms. Gisèle looked up at the windows across the street and then down the lane of shops. Two soldiers stood on the street corner, guns at their sides to maintain order.

Since the occupation, the German soldiers had stood alongside the Russians forced into servitude as guards or soldiers for the Wehrmacht. After two years of *captivité*, the unwelcome presence of both the Germans and the Russians seemed permanently etched into the streets.

Sirens blared around the corner and an ambulance rushed toward her, the lights flashing. She hopped back onto the sidewalk and watched it race up the hill, toward the hospital.

The baker's words echoed in her mind. How many Jews had the Germans taken away last night? And where had they gone?

She prayed the Batiers, like the boy in Saint-Lô, hadn't been among them. She had to check on André and Nadine, but yet . . .

Her gaze wandered back to the alley where the boy had run.

The soldiers were everywhere, and the familiar fears threatened her. But she could not succumb to the paralysis of fear, not if the Germans were planning to take this child too.

Setting the bread in her basket, she waited until the soldiers shuffled down the street, and then she pushed her bicycle into the alley. The boy cowered beside an empty trash can, his head tucked into his knees. As if he could shrink into the wall and she would never know he was there.

She sat down beside him and held out the bread again.

This time he took it.

"Where are your parents?" she asked.

He wiped his face on his sleeves. "They had to leave."

"Are they coming back?"

"I don't know," he said quietly. "They said they couldn't take me with them."

As loudly as her heart cried out for her to hurry to Nadine's, she couldn't leave this child here, alone and hungry.

"Outside of town," she whispered. "There's a home for children."

He shook his head. "Not for children like me."

She swallowed. It was a Catholic orphanage, but surely they would take in an abandoned child, no matter his religious background.

When he finished his piece of bread, she offered her hand. "I cannot leave you by yourself."

He eyed her hand for a moment. "What if they don't want me?"

A tear fell down her cheek. "Then I will find another safe place," she promised.

He took her hand.

CHAPTER 18

"Pretty Woman" blared on the cab's radio as my driver navigated the streets of Paris. "*No anglais*," he'd said when I climbed into the car at the airport, yet as he maneuvered through the morning traffic of Paris, he had no problem belting out the English lyrics to this song.

It seemed so surreal—cruising past the celebrated museums and architectural treasures of this great city as we listened to American pop songs.

From Gare Saint-Lazare, I would board a train to Carentan in Normandy, and Marguerite, the woman hired to care for the château, was supposed to pick me up at the train station. Riley Holtz would arrive tomorrow afternoon to begin filming.

Between my confrontation with Austin and my lack of sleep, my head felt like it had been crushed. My mind raged with anger, but my heart wouldn't cooperate. It just felt shattered.

My phone lit up again, and I glanced down at Austin's number. I'd lost track of the times he'd called and texted since I left the hotel last night. Or was that two nights ago? I'd lost track of time altogether.

I declined his call.

As the cab crawled through a narrow street, I rolled down my window, and the aroma of warm pastries and strong espresso wafted into the cab. Morning had dawned in France.

I was supposed to be calling Austin, telling him I'd arrived, telling him how much I missed him. Instead he was texting me, in the middle of the night from New York, begging me to forgive him.

The memory of him kissing the lips of Starla Dedrick in the elevator looped through my mind. Was she sleeping beside him now as he texted me? Or had he snuck away while she slept?

The moment I saw Austin with Starla at the Plaza, my perfectly structured future had crumbled. I didn't know when I would speak to him again—if I would speak to him again—but there was so much more I wanted to say, conversations I'd rehashed over and over during my excruciatingly long flight across the Atlantic. None of it would change the fact that our engagement was over. There would be no wedding now. No marriage. Austin might become Virginia's governor, but I would not be the governor's wife. In hindsight, I knew I should have seen this coming, but I had thought his indifference to me in the past months was due to the busyness of his campaign. Apparently he had plenty of time for recreation. It just didn't involve me.

How could I have been so stupid?

I closed my eyes, imagining for a moment how he would position this new wrench in his campaign. Olivia would have a cow, no doubt. He'd probably make her handle the announcement of our breakup to the media and his staff. Still, the media would have questions that only he could answer.

Somehow Olivia and Austin would spin this in a positive light, probably making me look like a fool in the process. I shouldn't have cared, but I did.

How long had he been sleeping with Starla? For all I knew, they'd never even broken up after college. Perhaps Olivia had been covering for him all along.

All it would take was a call from me to one of the morning shows to set a scandal in motion. Or I could sell the gritty details to a tabloid. I had contemplated that very thing on the plane, the sweetness of letting the world know that Austin was scum.

But what woman really wanted to let the world know her fiancé had rejected her? It would be bad enough to tell my parents what happened. I didn't want to be part of the world's analysis of why my fiancé had cheated on me. The sweet taste of my revenge would sour quickly and somehow Olivia would position me as the villain instead of the victim.

Is she walking back to me? Yeah, she's walking back to me.

The driver grinned as he sang the final lyrics to "Pretty Woman," and when I glanced up at the rearview mirror, he winked at me. Cringing, I leaned my head back on the seat and gazed out the window at the crowds of Parisians emerging for work. Thanks to my grandmother and my college professors, I spoke fluent French, but I didn't want this man to know I could speak his language.

I wouldn't be walking back to Austin, nor did I have a job to return to in the fall. At some point I'd have to call Marissa and my other bridesmaids to let them off the hook in August, but I would start with my parents.

Still, how did you tell your family that the man you planned to marry was sleeping with another woman? That he had probably loved her all along?

The driver pointed up and I saw the golden Flame of Liberty before we descended into the infamous Pont de l'Alma tunnel where Princess Diana's car crashed when I was in elementary school. In that moment, my heart empathized with the princess—a young woman chosen to marry the future king of England, a devoted wife and mother who played her part well for fifteen years, smiling for the cameras even as her marriage was disintegrating.

Had the prince swept Diana off her feet even as his heart belonged to another woman—a woman the Crown wouldn't permit him to marry?

The next time my phone rang, my mom's picture flashed up on the screen. Either she was worried about me or she knew something—it was two in the morning there and my mom rarely stayed up past eleven.

With a cleansing breath to calm myself, I answered her call.

"Austin was just here, looking like heck," she said. "What happened?"

It took a lot of gall for him to petition my parents. "You don't want to know."

"I do want to know," she replied. "He said you'd fought . . ."

"Did he happen to say about what?"

"It doesn't matter, Chloe. Everyone fights before their wedding. That's why they call it jitters." A woman rode up next to the cab on a bicycle, a girl strapped in a seat behind her. The child's hands were stretched out to reach around her mother's back. "Austin said he's still planning to marry you."

I groaned. "That's awfully kind of him."

"He thought your dad and I might be able to convince you to reconcile."

The driver watched me in the mirror, and I

highly doubted his insistence that he didn't speak any English. "We're not reconciling."

"He said there was a misunderstanding. Surely it can be resolved—"

I stopped her. "I don't think so, Mom. I found him in New York with an old girlfriend."

Silence reigned on the other end of the line before she spoke again. "Having dinner together?"

"They weren't dining when I found them."

"Oh my—"

"And he didn't seem the least bit remorseful about their pillow talk at the Plaza."

"I'm—I'm so sorry, honey."

"Me too."

The shock in my mother's voice turned to anger. "If he can't be faithful now, he never will be."

I knew I'd made the right choice, but why did my heart still ache?

When we ended the call, the taxi driver glanced in the mirror. "Do you want to get a drink?" he asked in French.

I continued pretending not to understand him, like he pretended not to understand English.

"Thriller" started playing on the radio, and his attention was diverted to the song. As he drummed his thumbs on the steering wheel, my phone flashed again.

We need to talk, Austin wrote.

I powered off my phone and stuffed it deep into

my handbag. Part of me wanted to speak to him again, to say everything I'd forgotten to say at the Plaza, but the thought of talking to him made my stomach churn.

In France, I would have to forget about Austin.

In France, perhaps I would find a little bit of myself.

And for Mémé's sake, I hoped I would find out what happened to the girl she'd lost.

Chapter 19

*T*he boy clung to Gisèle's hand in the alley as she smoothed back his messy hair. Then she removed the identity document, stamped with an incriminating *J*, from around his neck and ripped it into tiny pieces.

He didn't want to take off the vest, but she finally coaxed him to remove it. She used it to wipe the smudges of dirt off his face before stuffing the vest and slivers of paper deep into the trash can.

"What is your name?" she asked.

When he didn't answer, she knelt beside him. "Are you scared?"

This time he gave her the slightest of nods.

She was terrified, but she didn't tell him.

Instead, she gently squeezed his hand. "If anyone asks, you must say you're my brother."

Gisèle prayed quietly as she pushed her bicycle slowly through the town center. The boy walked beside her, clutching her hand, her bread displayed prominently in the basket so the Germans knew the reason they were here.

There were no automobiles on the street; the government was rationing gas along with food. She didn't care much about the gas—she had no need to go anyplace farther than a bicycle ride— but she missed sugar and coffee. Though she could hardly mourn such things when the boy beside her didn't even have bread.

They neared the town center. The stone courthouse that the Germans had taken for their headquarters was on one side of the street, the gray prison on the other. A long red banner was draped over the front windows of their head-quarters, displaying a black swastika.

Two soldiers guarded the entrance to the head-quarters while three soldiers smoked nearby.

She refused to look at the soldiers, but she knew they were scrutinizing her and her com-panion. A smile on her face, she leaned down to the boy and whispered for him to laugh. While the soldiers watched, they both forced their quiet laughter.

The Jews in Saint-Lô no longer laughed.

"Halt!" a soldier ordered, and she tightened her

grip on the boy's hand as fear gripped her heart. She'd worked hard the past two years not to draw attention to herself, to appear as if she was complying with the law of their occupiers even as she worked covertly to help those resisting. She'd yet to have to stand face-to-face and confront their enemy.

Her teeth chattered as she smiled at the soldier. He looked to be about her age. "Yes, monsieur?"

He held out his hand. "Your papers," he demanded, his French poor.

She opened her satchel and pulled out her identity card. He scanned it quickly and then looked at the boy's neck for his document. Only the smallest children weren't required to wear their papers. "Where is his *Kinderausweis*?"

She sighed. "We left it at home," she explained in French. "I keep telling my brother that he has to wear his card, but you know boys—"

He stopped her and lifted a small radio, asking for a translator. She pretended not to understand his German.

Moments later, a woman stepped out of the headquarters, her yellow scarf flapping behind her. Gisèle's heart plummeted when the woman waved. She'd known Lisette had been conscripted to work as a secretary for the Germans, but she hadn't spoken to her in months. As Lisette rushed up beside her, she prayed the younger woman wouldn't betray her and the child.

Lisette spoke to Gisèle instead of the soldier. "What happened?"

Gisèle pressed her lips together before she replied, trying to steady her voice. "My little brother and I came to town to buy bread."

"Your little bro—" Lisette's gaze dropped and a soft gasp escaped her lips. "He looks like Michel."

"Could you please tell this man—"

The soldier stepped between them, talking rapidly in German to Lisette. Her friend turned back to her. "He's asking about his identity card."

"We forgot it," Gisèle said.

Lisette's eyes grew wide. "You can't forget your papers!"

"But I did."

Lisette chewed at the edge of a fingernail before addressing the soldier again. "She said she will bring the document back to you."

He eyed Gisèle again, ignoring the boy, and she cringed at the lust in his gaze. She'd heard horrific stories of what some of the Nazis had done to the Frenchwomen. A few wooed the local women. Others forced themselves on them.

"Where does she live?" he asked.

Before Lisette could translate the man's words, a dozen soldiers poured out of the prison, and Gisèle stared as they crossed the street. In the midst of them were four men in tattered clothes, their hands tied behind their backs, heads bowed.

Her heart raced even faster as she stared at the prisoners, trying to see their faces.

What if they'd caught Michel?

One of the men glanced over at her, and she recognized him—a former banker in Saint-Lô. He seemed defeated with his head down, but fire blazed in his eyes.

The soldier before her stopped one of the guards. "Who are they?"

"Resistance," the man spat.

With that single word, her interrogator grunted at her, telling Lisette that Gisèle must carry her brother's card with her. Then he followed his fellow soldiers and the prisoners away from the town center.

She turned to Lisette. "Where are they taking the men?"

"It doesn't matter," Lisette whispered, nudging her down the sidewalk. "You have to get that boy away from here!"

With a quick nod, Gisèle tugged on the child's hand. They hurried to the north edge of town, trailing about three hundred meters behind the pack of soldiers. She had to get this boy to safety, had to visit Nadine, but her priorities shifted again. Before she did anything else, she needed to make certain her brother wasn't among the prisoners.

The soldiers turned down a narrow lane between the trees, and she hid her bicycle behind one of the hedgerows. She and the boy trailed far behind them, walking among the trees instead of using the trail. The men stopped in a clearing, and she backtracked with the boy almost a hundred meters.

"Wait here," she said, hiding him behind a bush.

The boy didn't argue with her. Instead he sat down and pulled his knees to his chest. She snuck back toward the clearing and watched in horror as the soldiers tied the men against four poles.

She could see the men's faces now. Her brother wasn't among them, but her relief was fleeting. All of these men had families who loved them.

Were the soldiers going to torture these men where no one could hear their screams?

Her stomach reeled again; she felt as sick as she had the night they found their father.

She glanced at the tall oak trees around the clearing. If only there was something she could do. Distract the soldiers in some way and help these men escape. What if she screamed and ran away? Would they follow her?

Perhaps the Frenchmen could run away as well.

But what if the soldiers found the boy in the brush? They would kill him too.

Clutching her arms around her chest, she rocked back and forth, helpless. Was there nothing she could do to stop the Germans?

This time the fear paralyzed her.

The crack of a gunshot exploded in the forest, and the head of one of the men pitched forward.

At the second shot, she ran, fear clinging to her like the talons of a hawk.

She would never be able to fight the dragon.

The boy was where she'd left him, his eyes wide.

She held out her hand. "We must hurry."

Together they rushed down the lane, away from the madness. A few kilometers down the road, she found the path where she and her mother had once walked hand in hand, when the world seemed to make sense. She and the boy turned, and ahead of them was the tower of a stone manor peeking out above the trees.

For the first time, she felt his hand tremble in hers. She might not be able to fight the dragon, but she prayed she could rescue this boy.

CHAPTER 20

The Château d'Epines rose majestically above the trees that sheltered it, and I leaned back in my car seat to soak in the beauty—the magic—of the medieval château. Intricate strands of ivy wove around two turrets that climbed above the three stories of stone, and dozens of glass panes shimmered peach in the setting sunlight.

I remembered sitting here with my parents and my grandmother twenty years ago, soaking in the mystery of it all. The château hadn't lost the wonder for me, but after all these years, I still didn't understand. On that trip long ago, why had Mémé and my father refused to go inside?

Marguerite, the caretaker of our family's property, parked the station wagon in the courtyard. She turned off the ignition and stared up at the château beside me. "It is lovely, yes?"

I opened my door and the breeze awoke my senses. "Breathtaking."

"It was even larger, you know, before the war."

"I didn't know."

Marguerite pointed toward the left. "There was another wing on the west side of the house, but Allied pilots bombed it during the German occupation."

"It's so sad . . ."

She nodded. "Thousands of civilians died in Saint-Lô, but the Allied forces had no choice. The Germans refused to leave."

"Refused to leave Saint-Lô?"

Marguerite dumped the keys into her pocket and opened her car door. "They refused to leave our city and they refused to leave the château. The Allies had to almost flatten Saint-Lô and the surrounding villages before the Germans fled."

I needed to read the material Olivia had compiled for me. "I can't imagine how horrible it must have been to have the Germans occupying the town."

"At first, people were shocked by the blitzkrieg,"

Marguerite said, "but then Hitler commanded his men to be friendly to the French people and win them over with food depots and such until they decided that collaborating with the Nazis would be to their advantage. For two years, they were more like annoying neighbors than tyrants to the people here."

"What happened after those first two years?" I asked.

Marguerite's eyes focused back on the château in front of us. "The Nazi Party began to unravel."

My head tilted back again as my hostess stepped out of the car, my brain dazed from the shock of Austin's betrayal and my few, fitful hours of sleep. Did the filmmaker want to know the stories about the German occupation? If so, I was afraid I didn't have anything to tell him. Once again, I wished my dad had been able to make the trip.

I stepped out onto the gravel drive and glanced behind me. The château wasn't alone on the property. Along the driveway was a second house, a smaller, rambling structure where Marguerite and her husband lived, surrounded by a half-dozen outbuildings. Across from the château was a chapel. The cluster of old buildings reminded me of the ceramic French village Mémé used to display each Christmas on her mantel.

My gaze shifted back to the forest that curved around the back of the house like a warm stole. I wondered if the lake Mémé had told me about was still there in the trees. In the morning, perhaps I could find her favorite place and quiet the racing in my mind.

Marguerite slammed her car door and crossed over to my side. Her trousers and vest were a mossy brown color, her bushy eyebrows hedged above her green eyes. She was a large woman, but the extra pounds didn't seem to do anything to diminish her energy. In exchange for a place to live and a monthly stipend, she and her husband had been entrusted to care for the property and keeping squatters from sneaking into the house.

I slung my handbag over my shoulder. "Do you know where the lake is?"

Her eyebrows slid up. "Do you mean the river?"

I shook my head. "My grandmother said there was a lake in the forest."

She pointed left. "There's a small lake over there, but the path is overgrown."

I heaved my suitcase out of the back of the station wagon and set it upright on the gravel. The pewter-colored cover seemed to be made of titanium, and in my rush to get to France, I'd brought a hodgepodge of stuff—shorts and T-shirts, skirts, dress pants for the interview, even an evening dress, just in case I had a night out in Paris.

When I arrived at the train station in Carentan, a fellow passenger took pity on me and my mammoth bag, carrying it down to the platform.

Rolling it to Marguerite's waiting car had been a simple affair, but it had taken both of us to lift it into her car. Now I eyed the three floors of the château, wondering on which floor I would find my room.

"Are you certain you don't want to stay with us in the farmhouse?" Marguerite asked.

I thanked her and then reassured her that I wanted to sleep in the house where my grandmother had lived.

"I don't think anyone has slept here in several years, but I've cleaned the main rooms for you."

A new thought flashed into my head, one I should have considered before I insisted on staying in the house. "What about the utilities?"

"We've kept on the water and electricity, but there's nothing fancy like Wi-Fi."

"That's okay." I had Internet access on my phone and iPad, but the less connection I had to the outside world, probably the better.

Marguerite glanced down at the behemoth of a suitcase. "My husband can carry that up the stairs for you."

"There's no need for him to help—" I started to say. Her eyebrows rose in question as she slid her cell phone out of her purse, and I realized the ridiculousness of my words. "I would be grateful for it."

When she lifted her phone to her ear, I leaned back against the car. I was supposed to be here two full days before the arrival of Riley Holtz to overcome my jet lag and acquaint myself with the château, but with the delay in my flight, it was already Thursday. He would be here tomorrow.

My body was exhausted. My broken heart felt numb. How was I supposed to smile for his camera?

Being here, though, was much better than being at home. My phone hummed and I pulled it out of my purse. This time Olivia was texting me.

Call me, Chloe! We will work this out before the wedding.

My harsh laugh earned me a look of concern from Marguerite, as if she were trying to determine my mental capabilities. I mustered a smile. Olivia was a campaign manager, not a counselor, and there was nothing for her or us to *work out*.

I texted back. *The wedding is off!*

A flood of texts followed, begging me to call her, telling me the wedding could be postponed, not canceled. But standing outside Austin's room at the Plaza, my fingers pressed against my phone, I had made my decision not to overlook Austin's liaisons now or in the future. No matter what Olivia said, I would never marry Austin. The publicity might be messy, but I had no doubt that she had cleaned up bigger messes in the past.

If only Olivia would insist Austin clean this mess up on his own. Perhaps he would change his behavior.

Marguerite closed her flip phone, and I powered mine down. "You need to get some rest," she said.

I reached for the handle of my suitcase. "I'd like to sleep in my grandmother's room."

"I don't know which room was hers, but we've set you up in the master suite for tonight." She pointed at my bag. "Pierre said he will carry it up to the second floor."

Seconds later, a man came rushing toward us, a grasshopper sort of fellow—tall and thin with a white button-down shirt streaked with dirt and underarms soaked with perspiration. The grin spread across his thin lips was so friendly, I couldn't help but smile back at him.

Marguerite introduced us, and Pierre pumped my hand with enthusiasm. "It is a pleasure to meet you. A real pleasure."

"You as well."

He kept shaking my hand. "I hope you find the house to your liking."

"I'm sure I will like it very much."

Pierre's smile started to fade when he looked down at my suitcase and then it dissolved altogether when he tried to pick it up. He set it back on the gravel. "Did you pack a refrigerator?"

I smiled again. "I thought it might come in handy . . ."

He tried to lift it again. "Perhaps you packed two."

Marguerite scolded him. "Stop harassing her."

He wiped the sweat from his brow and heaved the suitcase off the ground before he lugged it across the stone pavers. Marguerite reached for the iron handle on the front door and opened it for him.

I hadn't known what to expect, but my mouth gaped open when I stepped into the entryway of the house. The home might have been vacant, but the elaborate décor remained in residence. In front of me, the hall rose three stories, with a giant tapestry draped over an arched doorway on my right. Beside it, a staircase spiraled up to balconies on the second and then third landing. The marble floors were adorned with oriental rugs of rich indigo, blood red, and deep evergreen.

For a moment, it felt as if I were back in the Plaza.

Marguerite flipped a switch and light cascaded down from a wrought-iron chandelier with electric candles. "The salon is through the arch," she said before pointing left. "And the kitchen is stocked—"

"The woman doesn't need food," Pierre teased. "She carries a refrigerator with her."

Marguerite ignored him. "I'll bring you up a dinner tray."

"That would be wonderful."

While Pierre fiddled with something in the kitchen, Marguerite gave me a quick tour of the rest of the house. There were a total of ten bedrooms on the upper levels, some with furnishings, others filled with boxes, two completely empty. Almost all of them were covered with a layer of dust.

On the main floor, the windows in the salon overlooked a lush valley and river. On the other side was a grassy hill topped with trees.

The salon, Marguerite said, could be transformed into a ballroom or a dining hall, and then she showed me the library, an office tucked into a turret, the drawing room, and a kitchen with a medieval fireplace. I asked Marguerite if I could try my hand at cooking over the fireplace. She said she didn't know—I would have to ask my dad.

Behind the kitchen was a small door, and I followed her downstairs into a wine cellar. There were circular brick bins on the walls that reminded me of a red-flecked honeycomb and large casks of wine stacked on the far end of the wall.

"It used to be a prison," Marguerite said. "Until the Duchants turned it into a wine cellar."

I rubbed my arms. "It feels strange down here."

She flicked off the lights. "The ghosts refuse to leave this place."

I hurried back up the stairs. That's just what I needed in the middle of the night, to be thinking about the ghosts.

Pierre pulled and I pushed my suitcase up the winding stairs of the turret. Then I followed him into a large room in one of the turrets, complete with a sofa, desk, and canopied bed with wrought-iron posts. Exposed rafters lined the ceiling and a dozen narrow windows lined the walls. Pierre set my suitcase near the armoire, and with a quick nod, he scurried back through the door as if he was worried I might ask him to lift something else. When he was gone, I stepped toward one of the windows to see the view, but all I saw were tree limbs and gray shadows from the fleeing sun.

Sinking back into the cushions of the sofa, I stared up at the rafters. The past twenty-four hours had been torture—trying to keep myself from melting down as I traveled across the ocean. Now I had no plane to catch, no taxi to find, no train to ride. And no one around to see me cry.

Tears drenched my cheeks.

I hated this feeling, this not knowing who I was without Austin Vale. I had no idea where I was going. For an entire year, my identity had been entwined with his, and now—now I felt like a lost soul.

Perhaps I shouldn't have gotten on the plane to France—I could have gone to my parents' house on the lake and hidden away for a few weeks. But Austin would have found me there in days, if not hours, and I couldn't face him or my family or friends yet. My family would be kind, telling me things like Austin didn't deserve me or someone better would come along, but I didn't want to hear that. The problem was, I had no idea what I wanted.

The aching in my heart returned, and I lay on the bed, my arms splayed out on both sides.

Austin swooped into my life last summer with an intensity that swept me away, a handsome, charming politician who seemed to be as fascinated by me as I'd been by him.

Perhaps he had found me attractive early on. He certainly acted as if he had, though he rarely pushed the limits of the boundaries we'd set for our physical relationship. I thought he was respecting my desire to wait until we married, but really he hadn't needed to be physical with me. Instead he needed the other assets I brought to the table as his fiancée and wife.

The daughter of a wealthy businessman who contributed heavily to his campaign and would pass along a considerable inheritance to his only daughter and son-in-law.

The granddaughter of a World War II hero.

The elementary schoolteacher willing to give up her career to tout his education reform and raise his children.

The woman who would dote on Austin and smile at dinners and dances and golf tournaments for decades to come.

The wife who would entertain herself while her husband took weekend trips to New York.

I felt sick.

Had Austin seen dollar signs when he looked into my eyes? Had he and Olivia compiled lists of single women in Richmond and narrowed it down to the final three? The morning we'd met in the coffee shop, when he'd spilled my latte . . .

The memory pricked my mind, clearing the fog.

That was why our engagement had been so swift. He and Olivia must have orchestrated our meeting.

A single man his age would probably never be voted in as governor, especially when he was running against an older, much wiser family man. The past year had been a façade concocted by him and Olivia and maybe even Starla to make the media think he was a mature man committed to government and family, and I—

I was nothing but a campaign pawn in order to get him elected.

When I'd agreed to his proposal of marriage, Olivia had rolled me out with great fanfare to the media, and I'd been blinded by all the lights, painfully ignorant of the casting call for a governor's wife. It was as if I were a contestant on *The Bachelor* but no one bothered to tell me about the invisible strings pulling my arms and legs and even my mouth.

What was Austin planning to do with me postelection? Show me off like a horse in an arena? Olivia could braid my hair and decorate my tail with ribbons and parade me around for everyone to see. Then they'd probably put me back in the stall until the next show.

Whether or not he won the governor's house—and whether or not he married another Virginia girl—I suspected Austin would continue to indulge in his trips to New York.

A light blinked outside the window, and it took me a moment to realize that stars had appeared. The château, in all its glory, was a lonely place, and I felt the pangs of loneliness along with the ghosts of the past.

But I couldn't wallow in my pain. I had to press through it.

My eyes grew heavy.

This trip was no longer a favor for Austin—I didn't care one bit about the documentary and its benefit to his campaign. But I was in France and curious about my roots, curious about the echo of stories in the château, curious about the girl Mémé thought she'd left behind.

I had intended to stay awake until Marguerite brought up a tray of food, but if she knocked, I never heard her. Exhaustion won out over my hunger, and I drifted off into blessed sleep.

Tomorrow I would search for answers.

Chapter 21

Gisèle and the boy scuttled through a pair of lofty iron gates, into a grassy courtyard. Three children played on a metal merry-go-round, but when she and the boy approached, the children raced inside the manor.

It didn't deter Gisèle. With the boy's hand cocooned inside hers, she led him to the back of the house and knocked on the wooden door. The curtain lifted in a window by the door, and the eyes of a little girl looked back at her. Gisèle waved at the girl, and moments later, the curtain fell back into place, the lock on the door sliding back.

A nun in a black habit and white veil answered Gisèle's knock. She looked like she was in her midthirties, her face pale without any makeup, her smile kind. Behind her, dozens of children crowded around roughly hewn tables, eating from tin bowls.

The nun's gaze rested on the little boy. "My name is Sister Beatrice."

He gave her a slight nod.

"Are you hungry?" she asked.

When he didn't respond, Gisèle inched him forward. "He's hungry."

The nun put her hand on his shoulder. "One of my sisters will get you some stew."

The boy hesitated until another child came forward and led him to a table.

"Where did you find him?" Sister Beatrice whispered.

"He was in Saint-Lô. His parents . . ." She stepped into the house beside Sister Beatrice. "They can no longer care for him."

The nun watched him sit with the others. "He is one of God's children," she said, resolute.

"He is," Gisèle whispered. Though he no longer wore his star. Gisèle looked back at Sister Beatrice. "My mother was Vicomtesse Duchant from the Château d'Epines. She used to bring food for the children here."

Sister Beatrice smiled. "I remember your mother well. You are blessed with her eyes . . . and her heart."

The nun's words warmed her, but the woman had no idea of the fear that clutched at—poisoned—her heart as well.

"Can this child stay with the others, until his parents return for him?"

Sister Beatrice stepped closer to her. "Why don't you take him home?"

The gunshots from the forest seemed to echo in her mind. The soldiers were prowling the town and the countryside, searching for members of the resistance. If the Germans found the cell hiding under her house, they might kill all of them, including the child.

"I fear it won't be safe for him, so close to town." She looked across the great room again, at the children finishing their stew. The boy picked up his spoon and began to eat. "All he needs is a place to sleep and something nourishing to eat."

Sister Beatrice gently touched her arm. "A child needs more than that."

"That's part of the problem, she said with a sigh. "I don't know what a child needs."

"If his parents were part of the roundup, the police may come looking for him here. And if they find him—" Sister Beatrice's voice cracked. "The French think it is admirable to keep families together when they send them away, but if his parents are gone, they would send him away by himself."

The thought made Gisèle tremble, for André and Nadine and the little girl they adored. "Where are they sending these families?"

"I'm not certain. Perhaps to one of the work camps."

"He is too small. He'd be of no use to them—"

Sister Beatrice's voice dipped so low that Gisèle had to strain to hear her. "The Nazis have no patience for people who aren't useful, especially the Jewish people."

Gisèle thought back to some of the bitter reflections she'd read in *Mein Kampf*, to the deep loathing in the author's heart. "I don't understand why Hitler hates the Jews—"

"It isn't just Hitler," Sister Beatrice said. "He is only unifying all those in Europe who think the Jewish people flaunt their wealth."

The only Jewish people she knew well weren't wealthy, nor could she imagine Nadine or her parents flaunting the little they did have, but Gisèle understood the misperception. Since childhood, she had borne the brunt of meanness from people who'd thought the Duchants needed a good dose of humility. "But there aren't many wealthy Jews in France . . ."

Sister Beatrice folded one of her hands over the crucifix that hung from her neck. "Others hate the Jewish people because they claim to be God's chosen people and then others, I'm told, have hatred in their hearts because Jews were responsible for the crucifixion of Jesus."

Gisèle leaned back against the wall. "It's strange to think that an event that happened almost two thousand years ago could breed such hatred today."

This time a whisper of a smile crept up on Sister Beatrice's lips. "Almost as strange as an event that happened almost two thousand years ago healing lives today."

Gisèle rubbed her hands together. "Can I leave this boy with you?"

Sister Beatrice glanced back at the children.

"I will bring you food and—"

Sister Beatrice interrupted her. "You mustn't bring us any food. In fact, you mustn't come here anymore, at all. Someone may follow you."

"You will take him?'

"We will take him," Sister Beatrice replied. "But we aren't able to care for any more children."

A little girl with blond pigtails stepped up beside her, a bowl of stew in her hands. She held it out to Gisèle.

"Thank you," Gisèle said, smiling at the child. She ate rapidly, the broth warming her, the vegetables giving her strength. She would need it to pedal back to André and Nadine's.

Before Gisèle left, Sister Beatrice took both her hands, and the nun prayed with fervency, pleading with Jesus to protect Saint-Lô's children from the evil in their midst.

But Gisèle feared the Spirit of God had already fled Saint-Lô.

CHAPTER 22

A breakfast tray fit for the queen of England arrived at my door, a few minutes before eight. This time I heard the knock, and I would have answered it except I was in the midst of trying to wash my long hair under the bathtub's finicky spigot. The water did indeed work, and for that I was grateful, but it fluctuated from cold to hot as quickly as the polls in Virginia swung between Austin and his opponent.

With my wet hair wrapped in a towel, I retrieved the tray of food, placed it on the coffee table, and breathed in the aromas of dark espresso and apple butter. Piled onto the tray was a basket of warm croissants, prosciutto sliced so thin it looked like pink tissue paper, slices of honeydew melon, and little white tubs with butter and jam and soft cheese.

As I cut open a croissant, its breath warmed my face, and I slathered it with the butter and then the strawberry jam. While in France, I would not count a single calorie. It was Austin himself who had told me to enjoy the food. Immerse myself in the past. He and Olivia could sweat the future.

When I finished my breakfast, I took the tray down to the kitchen. "I'm so sorry," I said. "I fell asleep last night."

Marguerite waved her hand. "Please don't worry. I had an urgent call and brought it up late."

"I didn't even hear you knock."

"Riley Holtz is scheduled to arrive in Carentan this afternoon," she said as she piled the dishes in the sink. "Do you want to ride to the train station with me?"

I declined. Instead I would search for Mémé's lake.

I found a path on each side of the house—a wide

path that appeared to go down to the river and a sliver of a path that slipped back into the forest to the west of the house. I took the path west.

I'd only walked a few yards when I discovered an iron gate, its base anchored in mud. I lifted and pushed until there was finally enough space for me to squeeze through. The trail zigzagged down the hill, and I saw a glint of water at the bottom.

Several trees dipped low over the banks of the lake, while others had tumbled into the water. Sunlight streaked through the leaves above and glistened on the coats of moss below. Magnificent greens and yellows ornamented the browns.

I sat on a flat stone and curled my knees up against my chest. A turtle peeked its head out of the water and then glided along the surface.

I could almost imagine Mémé as a child, skipping along the stones, balancing herself on the slippery trunks that rested in the lake, splashing water at her brother, or sneaking down here to enjoy the solace. Cell phone reception had been sketchy in my room, but down here, there was none at all. I relished the sunlight that snuck through the trees, the simplicity of the warm breeze tickling my neck.

I wished I could paddle around this lake in a kayak or even a canoe, but for the moment, I would simply savor the quiet.

Closing my eyes, I remembered Mémé's laughter when she used to take me to the stables in

Virginia where she boarded her two horses. We would ride through the forest outside Fairfax, and she would tell me the stories of Normandy and the hours she would ride her horse along the river Vire.

Grandpa had been the vice president at a local bank and Mémé taught French literature at George Mason University. Every June, when school ended, I would spend two weeks at their house, riding horses, cooking comfort food like coq au vin and bouillabaisse alongside Mémé, paddling on the river nearby. Every Sunday, she took Grandpa and me to Mass, and before I went to bed, she quoted Scripture along with wisdom from her writing heroes.

You've never lived until you've almost died.
—GUY DE MAUPASSANT

I have learnt that all men live not by care for themselves but by love.
—LEO TOLSTOY

For there are many great deeds done in the small struggles of life.
—VICTOR HUGO

And her other favorite quote from Victor Hugo: *France is great because she is France.*

I wished I could call her now and tell her that I

was at the château. That I'd broken my engagement and didn't know what my future held. I could almost hear her say, "*Ma chérie*, your life is not over. It has only begun."

And then she would say something brilliant, influenced by all the writers she loved. Something like, "But don't live to bring happiness to yourself, Chloe. Live to bring joy to all those around you."

In the distance I heard the chiming of church bells. And I opened my eyes.

Had Mémé lost herself here when she was a girl?

Or perhaps she hadn't lost herself at all. Perhaps she'd found herself by the water.

Perhaps here she'd learned to give her life for others.

I slowly rose to my feet, my sweet memories fading. Riley Holtz would be here in two hours, but we weren't scheduled to meet until tomorrow morning at nine. This afternoon I would explore the property and read Olivia's notes about the war.

A second path meandered up the cliff and I followed it to the south of the house. It ended at a brick wall with another iron gate, but this gate was padlocked shut. I trailed the wall until I reached a portion that had collapsed. Heaving myself up, I climbed over it and began to wade through the tall grass.

On the other side of the field was another brick

wall, and behind that the stone chapel with a small cemetery to its side. A girl skipped past the church, her ponytail bouncing behind her. Then I saw an elderly man with denim overalls perched against the brick wall, about thirty yards away.

When I was about halfway across the field, the older man called out to me in French. "You'd best take care where you step."

I froze, lifting my eyes again to meet his gaze. "Why should I be careful?"

When he grinned, I saw a chipped tooth under his dried lips. "You're walking across an old minefield."

What was wrong with this man, smiling at me like that? And why wasn't the minefield surrounded by an electrical fence? Or marked by a giant, flashing Danger sign?

Perhaps there was a sign along the road. Probably no one else ever came up the back way from the lake.

Should I follow my footsteps back to the wall or continue forward?

Before I decided, the girl called out to me. "Don't mind Monsieur Lavigne. He likes to scare people."

I eyed the man again and then the girl, farther down the wall. She couldn't have been more than ten or eleven, but between the two of them, I decided to trust the child.

I quizzed her. "It's not a minefield?"

"It was, a long time ago, but the mines were taken out after the war. There is no need for worry—you won't lose a leg or anything now."

I wasn't sure if that was supposed to comfort me. I didn't want to lose a toe or a foot or any other body part either.

"Come this way," the girl instructed in French, waving me forward.

I took a small step as if to test the ground. "Are you certain the mines are gone?"

She nodded. "Unless you have tremendously bad luck."

I grimaced. "I'm afraid bad luck is chasing me."

She laughed. "You're funny."

I proceeded cautiously until I came to a muddy rut in the field, not ten feet from where she stood. I glanced back up at her before I walked through it.

"A bomb made that hole a long time ago," she said in English. "Nothing will grow on it."

I thought back to the crumbling wall by the gate and recalled Marguerite's words about the bombing of the west hall. "Are there a lot of these holes left?"

The girl shrugged. "My great-grandmother says that one is too many."

"Your great-grandmother is a smart woman."

When I reached the other side of the field, I took a deep breath and settled with my back against the wall. The elderly man had wandered away, but the girl remained, sitting on a log to tie her black shoes. The light brown hair in her ponytail curled down her back, and she wore a short plaid skirt with tights and a red blouse.

"Are you from Saint-Lô?" I asked.

"My great-grandmother lives down near the river." She pointed east. "I stay with her in the summers."

"I used to spend part of the summer with my grandmother." I brushed off my jeans. "Your English is perfect."

She smiled. "What is your name?"

"Chloe—Chloe Sauver. My grandmother lived here as a child."

She popped up from the log. "In Agneaux?"

"In the château. Her name was Gisèle Duchant before she married."

"Grand-mère said she used to be friends with the woman who lived here."

My heart quickened. Perhaps her great-grandmother could tell me more about Mémé's story. Perhaps she even knew Adeline.

"My name is Isabelle," the girl volunteered.

"That's a beautiful name." I stuck my hands into my pockets. "How old are you?"

"Almost eleven."

"It's good that you're learning English."

She twisted the hem of her skirt. "Grand-mère says I don't have a choice."

It was a bit strange to think this girl's great-grandmother and my grandmother were the same age, but since my father was older than most dads, I was used to the gap.

"What is your great-grandmother's name?" I asked.

"Madame Calvez."

"I would like to meet your great-grandmother."

Isabelle checked the watch on her wrist. "She'll sleep for another hour."

"Where were you going now?"

She nodded up the lane, toward the village at the top. "Up to Agneaux to buy bread." She paused. "When I get back, I could take you to meet her."

I wondered what Madame Calvez remembered about my grandmother.

Chapter 23

Gisèle turned onto the empty rue de la Vire and then pedaled toward the river as fast as she could, the words of the baker and then Sister Beatrice ominous in her mind. Leaning her bicycle against the Batiers' garage door, she glanced over at the lacy white curtains that concealed the living room. Nadine usually waved at her through the window, but this time she didn't see her friend.

"Gisèle!" a voice called, and she turned to see

Lisette pedaling quickly down the lane. She waited until Lisette stepped off the bicycle.

Her breath came in short heaves. "You pedal too fast."

"I didn't know you were following me," Gisèle said.

"For at least half a kilometer." Lisette patted her curls and then straightened the navy blue scarf around her neck before kissing Gisèle on both of her cheeks.

"Aren't you supposed to be at work?"

"The commander sent me on an errand." The woman's blue eyes implored her for information. "Have you heard from Michel?"

Gisèle shook her head.

"How about Philippe?" Lisette asked.

The Nazis had overtaken northern France, but in the south, they'd left France unoccupied in an area known as Vichy. De Gaulle called it a "puppet government," Hitler's cronies pulling the strings, but Lyon, where Philippe and his mother lived, was in Vichy.

"He tries to call about once a week," she said. Though lately it seemed to be more like once a month, and with the Germans listening, they never talked about anything of consequence. She'd stopped waiting for him to return to Saint-Lô a long time ago.

"I keep hoping . . . ," Lisette began. "I just want to know if Michel's still alive."

"You must keep praying that he's alive." Gisèle swallowed. "Thank you for helping me at the town square."

Lisette shook her head. "I don't want to know who that child is—"

"I won't tell you," she said even though she didn't know anything about him.

Lisette glanced up the lane behind her before she looked back at Gisèle. "Is the boy safe?"

Gisèle nodded as she stepped toward the house.

Lisette eyed the front door. "We shouldn't be here."

"André and Nadine are my friends."

Lisette lowered her voice. "Nadine may not wear her star, but the officials know about her parents."

"Her family is Catholic. And French."

"Before she became French—"

Gisèle stopped her. "It shouldn't matter about before."

Lisette waited by her bicycle as Gisèle walked through the picket gate and up the stone pavers that wove a path through the trellises of roses in the Batiers' front yard. She knocked on the front door, her fingers drumming against the frame as she waited impatiently for Nadine to swing it open and kiss her on both cheeks. When no one responded, she knocked again.

Stepping to the side, Gisèle tried to peer through the window, but the curtain covered the inside.

Perhaps André had been able to secure bus passes to Grenoble, where Nadine's parents lived. Or perhaps they had simply taken a walk down to the Vire.

She glanced over her shoulder at Lisette. "They must be out back."

Lisette looked skeptical, but she trailed her through Nadine's garden, to the edge of the property. Red berries ornamented the hawthorn trees, and the air smelled of wood smoke and rain.

"Nadine?" Gisèle called into the trees.

A bee buzzed past them, and Lisette shrieked. Then she pulled her scarf up over her head as she eyed a row of old wooden hives tucked back in the forest. "This place is creepy."

"As long as you don't harm the bees, they won't hurt you," Gisèle said.

"You don't know that."

Gisèle called André's name this time, but still there was no response.

Lisette stepped into the garden. "Perhaps they left before the roundup."

Gisèle had to cling to that hope—she couldn't let herself consider the alternative.

A goldfinch fluttered between the trees, and then she heard a noise. A cry. She swiveled toward Lisette. "Was that a bird?"

Lisette's eyes were wide. "It sounded like a baby."

There was a second cry, dull but persistent.

If it was Louise, why weren't André and Nadine answering her cries?

Turning, Gisèle raced back toward the cottage. On the second floor, one of the bedroom windows was cracked open. She reached for the knob on the back door, expecting to shove it, but the door was already open. She stumbled inside.

The living room looked as if a German tank had plowed through its center. André's prized books had been flung across the floor, torn pages crumpled, as if someone planned to build a bonfire. Legs had been hacked off the wooden furniture, the upholstered pieces slashed, dishes shattered on the floor.

Lisette cursed.

Gisèle steadied herself on the windowsill, trying to force her thoughts to stay present, but they refused to cooperate. Her mind flashed back again in rapid sequence to that terrible day two years ago when she found her father's bloodied body in the forest. The loss that had seared a hole in her core.

The room swayed.

Would she find André and Nadine as she had Papa? She didn't think she could bear the loss of someone else she loved, seeing them bloody and bruised. She knew it didn't really matter how much she could bear, but still, the thought of losing her friends was heart-wrenching. Overwhelming. Whatever she found, she would try to bear it, for Louise's sake and for the sake of her friends, but still—it seemed too much.

Lisette rushed toward the kitchen, and Gisèle yelled for Nadine as she hurried upstairs to the bedrooms. Louise's small bed, carved by her father, was empty, the pink spread unwrinkled on top. Her toys were in a wicker basket in the corner, under the lacy pink curtains that fluttered in the breeze.

In the next room, the bedcovers on André and Nadine's bed were balled up on the floor, clothes piled on top of it. Gisèle looked under the bed, as if a child was stowed underneath, but it was empty.

"Louise!" she shouted.

The child had just begun to walk. Had she toddled downstairs alone? But if the Germans had come, surely they would have taken her with her parents . . .

She found Lisette on the bottom step, a cigarette trembling in her hand. "You wanna smoke?" Lisette asked, holding it out.

Gisèle took a long drag, but the tobacco did nothing to calm her. They had to find Louise.

"I despise them all," Lisette said, her voice shaking along with the cigarette.

"Me too."

Lisette took another drag. "We heard a baby's cry, didn't we?"

"I pray so," Gisèle said as she moved toward the back door.

"And the Germans wonder why the resistance wants them dead." Lisette lowered the cigarette to her side. "If Michel were here, he would know what we should do."

The two women searched the garage, the garden, and back among the hawthorns again. They called for Louise all the way to the river, just in case she'd wandered away, but they didn't hear another cry.

Discouraged, the two women trudged back to the house. Gisèle collapsed against the side of the garage, wiping the sweat off her brow with her sleeve. She would never forgive herself if she left Louise here alone.

Lisette climbed on her bicycle. "I must return to work."

Gisèle kissed her friend's cheeks, but before Lisette began to pedal down the lane, the cry echoed again. Lisette threw down her bicycle.

Gisèle pointed left toward the river. "It sounded like it came from that direction."

Another scream erupted in the forest. "*Maman*!"

Lisette followed Gisèle into the forest, scouring the overgrown tangle of trees until they discovered what looked like an old root cellar among the beehives and brush, camouflaged with river stones and branches. On the moss-covered door was a rope handle.

Gisèle leaned down and yanked it open.

CHAPTER 24

Isabelle led me down to the river, to a paved path alongside a grove of white-tipped trees. Graying wooden hives stood among the trees, their resident bees congregating in the neighborhood outside. Last year one of my students had brought *The Life and Times of the Honeybee* to read to the class, and I had been just as fascinated as my students with the world of beekeeping.

I stopped for a moment, sniffing the blossoms. The scent reminded me of the sweet almond smell in marzipan. I reached for a branch, pulling it closer. Until it stung me.

"Ouch!" I said, shaking my fingers.

"The trees have thorns."

I rubbed my hands together. "I figured that out."

"That's why they call them hawthorns."

With a shiver, I recalled my grandmother's words about losing a baby. In the hawthorn trees. How exactly did one lose a child in these trees?

Not that Adeline would still be here, seventy years later, but I was curious to know where my grandmother's mind wandered and what she remembered. And what happened to this girl.

Isabelle chattered with a seamless mixture of French and English. About her school in Paris and her twelve cousins and how she planned to visit

America with her mother when she turned sixteen.

A bee buzzed past my ear, and I almost leapt into the river.

Isabelle laughed at me. "They won't sting you this time of year."

I waved my hands across my face. "You can't possibly know that."

"They've never stung me."

"That's because you don't look threatening to them."

"What does *threatening* mean?"

I stretched out my arms overhead. "Big and scary."

She laughed again. "I don't think you look threatening."

In less than a half mile, we veered away from the river and took a small path between the trees. Old hives clung to tree trunks on both sides. Isabelle didn't seem the least bit concerned about trekking through the city of bees, but I prodded her forward, practically stepping on her heels.

We passed an overgrown vegetable and then flower garden before we reached a white cottage adorned with peeling shutters, the color of their paint blending with the trees. A swing set had been built among the gardens and on the back patio of the house was a glass table with two vinyl chairs.

Isabelle slid open the glass door and slipped inside.

When she reopened the door, she didn't step

back onto the patio. Her sweet smile was gone, and worry tugged at her eyes.

"Is something wrong?" I asked.

She tilted her head slightly. "Grand-mère says she can't visit with you."

I tried to hide my disappointment. "Did you tell her that Gisèle Duchant is my grandmother?"

Isabelle nodded her head. "She doesn't want to talk about Madame Duchant."

I smiled at the girl. "Thank you for asking. Perhaps I can come back—"

"She said that you shouldn't return," Isabelle said in a louder voice. I assumed so Madame Calvez could hear.

In the window near the patio, I watched a face peek from behind the curtain. I lifted my hand to wave, but the face disappeared.

"I'll be here for a few more days," I told Isabelle as I backed away from the patio. "I'd love to visit her anytime."

I hurried back through the maze of beehives and trees.

What had happened between Madame Calvez and my grandmother?

I called Marissa and in lieu of being a bridesmaid, I asked if she wanted to go kayaking with me on August 10, far away from Richmond. My friend commiserated for an hour without reminding me even once that she'd told me so.

Then I tucked myself away in my room and searched online for the records of an Adeline who had lived in Agneaux or in Saint-Lô. Nothing emerged so I expanded my search through Normandy and discovered an Adeline who'd been born near here. In AD 980.

The other Adelines I found proved equally futile.

I hadn't expected an easy answer, but like my parents, I began to doubt the validity of a quest for a girl that Mémé remembered only after her mind began slipping away.

Outside the window, a cloud of dust trailed Marguerite's station wagon down the drive. I closed my iPad case and watched as a man stepped out of the car and took off his dark sunglasses to gaze up at the château. He looked to be in his early thirties, and he wore a brown bomber jacket even though it must have been at least seventy degrees outside.

When I realized he might see me, I started to step away from the window but it was too late. The man I assumed to be Riley Holtz waved up at me, and I had no choice but to wave back. Then Marguerite motioned toward the farmhouse and Riley followed her away from the château.

There was no reason to rush out now and greet him. I'd promised two hours tomorrow morning for his documentary, and I'd keep my word.

Chapter 25

Gisèle descended back into the tunnel, but this time she wasn't alone. Louise was in her arms, whimpering in the darkness as Gisèle stroked her soft wisps of hair.

She didn't know how long the child had been alone in the cellar, surrounded by the old equipment of a beekeeper, an emptied bottle in the playpen beside her. If André and Nadine had put her there before the raid, it would have been almost twenty-four hours.

Had the Germans wrecked the Batiers' house, searching for André and Nadine's baby? Her friends must have foreseen what might come, but why hadn't they hidden as well? And why had they left Louise in an abandoned basement instead of someplace she'd be more likely to be found?

When she brought Louise home, Émilie filled the child's bottle with warm milk. Louise guzzled the warm milk and slept beside Gisèle until dawn. Then she crawled into Gisèle's arms.

"*Maman*?" Louise had asked, her eyes wide with wonder.

"Your mother is on a trip," Gisèle said, not

knowing how much the girl understood and yet wanting to reassure her.

Louise nodded, her eyes still filled with expectancy. "Papa?"

"He is with your mother."

Gisèle's words seemed to comfort her. Or perhaps it was because Shadow snuggled beside her. Gisèle lay back on the pillow and watched the sunlight dance on the walls until Louise stirred again. In those early hours, she decided that she must hide Louise until André and Nadine returned.

When the tunnel split, Gisèle took the right passage. A voice echoed up the passage, and Louise flinched, knocking the flashlight out of Gisèle's hand. When it clattered to the ground, the tunnel faded into black and the child's cries echoed through the darkness.

Gisèle tried to comfort Louise, but this time she could not be consoled. Her parents were gone, and now Gisèle had her down in this cold, dark tunnel, just like the root cellar where she'd been hidden.

Gisèle fumbled for the flashlight until she found it and when she turned it on, Michel was standing in front of her.

At the sight of the man, Louise's cries turned into shrieks.

"Stop screaming," Michel demanded.

Gisèle bounced Louise on her hip. "Hush," she said softly. "He won't hurt you."

The girl pressed her face into Gisèle's shoulder as if she could burrow inside and disappear, her cries sinking to a whimper.

He eyed the back of the child. "Who is she?"

Sorrow passed over her again at the state of their world. Michel should have been smoking cigars with André the day Louise was born. He should have joined them at the cathedral in Saint-Lô on the day of Louise's baptism. He should have been visiting the Batiers on the weekends and getting down on his knees and playing with blocks alongside her, like any godparent would do. But he didn't know Louise, and she was terrified of him.

"This is André and Nadine's daughter," she said.

The edge in his voice softened. "Louise?"

She nodded.

"Where are André and Nadine?" he asked, his voice laden with worry.

She would have given just about anything to tell him she was caring for Louise for the night, that her parents were out picnicking or on an overnight visit to the shore, that they would return in the morning.

"I don't know. I visited this afternoon, and their house was in shambles. I almost left but—" She swallowed. "Lisette was with me. We heard her cry and found her in a cellar behind her home."

"Lisette helped you?" he asked.

She nodded, and he grew quiet for a moment.

"André must have hidden her before—" His voice cracked. "Before they took both him and Nadine away. They knew I would find her soon."

"But how would you find her?" she asked.

"Gigi," he said slowly. "Our ancestors were beekeepers."

Her mind flashed. She'd known there was another entrance to the tunnel, away from the house, but she'd never known where it was.

Louise clung to her neck. "Why didn't André and Nadine wait in the cellar with her?"

He reached out, and for a moment, she thought he would take Louise's hand, but then he pulled back as if he were afraid of her, as if caring for her could destroy everything he was doing. He put his hand back in the pocket of his ragged cardigan. "The officials would have searched until they found the whole family. Perhaps André and Nadine thought if they just hid Louise, she would have a chance."

She put her hand on Louise's back. André and Nadine had sacrificed themselves for their child. "God forgive me, Michel, but I hate the Nazis. Every one of them."

"The Nazis didn't take them away." His voice grew sad. "It was the gendarmes."

It felt like he had punched her in the gut. How could those hired to protect the French people send innocent citizens away?

"Where did they take them?" she asked.

He shook his head. "I don't know."

She heard the low murmur of voices behind them. "Can you keep her down here?"

He stepped back. "It's not possible."

"But they thought you could protect her," she insisted.

"They thought I would bring her to you."

She trembled. "I can't keep her in the house."

"My men and I are leaving soon, Gigi, but even if we weren't, someone above would surely hear her cries. It would destroy our operation."

"But if the police are looking for her, they will search for her in the château."

"Perhaps Lisette could care for her."

Gisèle shook her head. "She works at the headquarters office all day, but even at night—her neighbors would question where she got a child."

"There must be someone . . ."

Sister Beatrice had asked her not to come back, but perhaps she would change her mind. "I will take her to the orphanage."

"Thank you, Gigi."

"André and Nadine will return, won't they?"

"You must pray for them," he said, but there was no hope in his words.

The burden of war weighed heavily on her. "When will this be over?"

"De Gaulle says soon, as long as we keep fighting the Nazis from the inside."

"And when we do beat them, what will happen?"

She wanted to hear her brother say everything would return to how it had been before the war, but she knew he couldn't promise that—not with their father gone and the country wrecked.

"We will be free again," he said. "But until that happens, we can't stop fighting."

She told him about the men she'd seen killed in the forest, and his temper flared. He asked her a dozen questions, and then, as she pulled Louise closer to her chest, he disappeared back into the shadows.

If André and Nadine had risked their lives for Louise, she would do nothing less to keep her safe, out of honor to them and because, frankly, she adored their daughter.

CHAPTER 26

Marguerite discreetly suggested that I venture up to Agneaux for dinner, recommending two restaurants she thought I might enjoy. Then she offered me the use of their vehicle.

I didn't expect her to cook for me during my stay, but I was in France, and the thought of eating out alone was akin to torture. I envisioned myself surrounded by adoring couples, laughing and lingering over bottles of local wine. And then there would be me, alone for hours with my three or four courses and, even worse, my thoughts.

Scrounging through the refrigerator, I found some leftover ham, cheese, and fruit. And a bottle of red Bordeaux. As I poured a glass, a bell rang overhead, and with my wineglass in hand, I wandered up the three steps and across the hall. When I glanced through an oval window by the door, I groaned. I didn't want to be alone, but neither did I want this filmmaker to invade my space. I moved away from the window hoping he hadn't seen me.

Tomorrow morning, I would put on a skirt and flatiron my hair and perfect my smile. Then I would do his interview and move on.

I stepped back to hide in the kitchen until I heard the grate of the front door. Swiveling, I watched Riley Holtz step into the foyer, and my mouth dropped open.

With a sheepish grin, he pointed at the door handle. "You left it unlocked."

I didn't reply, too stunned to speak.

"It's probably not safe," he said, "considering all the thugs who live around here."

I regained my voice. "So you feel entirely comfortable with breaking into someone's house?"

"It's not really breaking in when the door is unlocked." He smiled again. "I saw you through the window and wanted to introduce myself."

"There was a reason I didn't answer the door."

He stuck out his hand. "You must be Chloe."

I stared down at his hand. "You're a smart man."

He dropped his hand back to his side, eyeing my wineglass. "Drinking alone is a terrible habit."

"Smart and cocky . . ."

I hadn't meant it to be funny, but he laughed anyway.

I put the glass down on a sideboard. "I was only drinking one glass. We're in France, you know."

"Indeed."

I leaned against the wall and studied the man for a moment. He was handsome in a rugged sort of way, with his green eyes and goatee. Nothing like Austin's polished persona. His smile seemed genuine. "Aren't you supposed to be sleeping off your jet lag?" I asked.

He eyed what looked like a diver's watch. "It's only seven and I can't start sleeping until at least nine or I'll be groggy for days."

"I was planning to do the interview with you tomorrow."

"I don't want to work tonight, but I'm starving." He glanced at my wineglass again. "Did you eat dinner yet?"

I nodded back toward the kitchen. "I was just getting ready to put something together."

"Why don't we go out instead?" His smile grew an inch wider. "We're in France, you know."

The way he said it was so casual. Unassuming. I felt guilty for a moment for making the "cocky" comment. I knew I should apologize, but at the moment I wasn't very fond of single men.

But then again, I was assuming that Riley was single. As he waited for me to answer, he looked up at the tapestry that hung from the wall and I dared a glance down at his left hand. His ring finger was empty.

An empty ring finger didn't mean anything, of course. A lot of married men didn't even wear rings. Riley probably had a wife or girlfriend back in California—or wherever it was that he was from.

"I promise not to keep you up late," he said. "We can talk about the documentary if you want. Or we can not talk at all."

As long as he kept the conversation focused on business, I supposed it was fine.

While he waited, I tossed the food back into the refrigerator and drained the last of my glass. Marguerite had suggested a café less than a mile away, so we strolled up the long drive, under the lofty beech trees. The evening light warmed our path and cast webbed shadows around our feet.

In my fog yesterday, I hadn't noticed the cow grazing on each side of the drive or even the village at the end of the road. Time may have stolen the life out of the château, but the land around it seemed to be thriving with the passage of the years.

The restaurant was in a stone house draped with ivy. Two iron lamps lit the stone walkway, beckoning us toward the dark-stained door. Inside, the owner led us upstairs to a room that overlooked a narrow alley. Four tables were crowded into the room, positioned like jigsaw pieces ready to snap together, but we had the room to ourselves.

Each table was clothed in white with two wineglasses by each plate, ready to top off what I'd already consumed at the château. Our server brought us two menus and a bottle of San Pellegrino. I sipped the bubbly water while Riley eyed the menu.

"Are you a fan of *escargot*?" he asked.

"Not particularly."

"Good." His smile eased onto his lips again. "I get concerned when people eat snails."

I glanced down the menu. "What about chicken?"

"I'm not as concerned."

"Then I'm going to order the *poulet à la fermière*."

"What is that?"

I glanced back down at the menu. "It's chicken with cream sauce. A farmwife's bounty, it says, with vegetables and fresh herbs."

"Impressive. Did you learn French from your grandmother?"

"My grandmother and then my dad. He and my grandmother always spoke to each other in their native language and then I minored in French in college."

Our waiter poured us each a glass of red wine

and then brought pea soup for our first course. Riley watched me stir my soup, the thin veil of steam rising between us.

"What?" I asked, self-conscious as he studied me.

He picked up his spoon, shrugging. "Nothing."

"What is it?" I demanded.

He took a sip of his wine, and I saw a tattoo etched under his wrist. "I just thought you would be different."

I pushed my hair behind my ear. "Different how?"

"I don't know," he said. His constant smile was beginning to irritate me. "More buttoned up, somehow."

"Like a politician's wife?" I asked.

He shrugged. "I hate stereotypes."

"Agreed." I lifted my wine in a salute. There was no reason to educate him on how I'd ended my engagement with Austin. This way it would be harmless—no questions. "I hate stereotypes and I hate trying to live up to them."

"Fair enough," he said. "Why don't you shatter the stereotype and tell me about your life instead?"

I was supposed to talk about my grandparents, not talk about me. We had the room to ourselves, but I had no desire to tell a filmmaker—and a stranger—my story.

I swirled my wine in its glass. "I'd like to hear about your documentary."

He ignored my snub. "I'm profiling the stories of some of the German soldiers."

His words took me aback. "The German soldiers?"

He nodded.

"But you're in France."

"I've already done my filming in Berlin."

A breeze wafted through the open window and rustled the sleeve of my blouse. Something about the way he said it—or perhaps it was because he folded his arms across his chest—made it seem as if he were hiding something. I refused to be played again. "After all the Germans did, I don't know why you want to do a documentary on them."

The fire in his green eyes relaxed in the flicker of the candlelight. "Hitler was an evil man, but not all the men in the Wehrmacht were evil."

"The Wehrmacht?"

"The German army."

Outside the darkened window a streetlamp glimmered. It reminded me of the lamp in Narnia—the one that beckoned the Pevensie children and lit their path as they returned home. The children confronted evil, but not on their own. They needed the tools gifted to them. They needed one another, and in their darkest hours, they needed Aslan, but Aslan had seemed distant at times in the book.

The novels were inspired, in part, by the three

young evacuees C. S. Lewis's family hosted during World War II. Perhaps it was Lewis's own journey of trying to process all the evil that happened in Europe. By the end of his stories, good had triumphed over the evil, but the lives of good people were also lost in the battle. It was a tumultuous journey for those who clung to all that was good.

When I looked back at Riley, he was watching me intently. "What are you thinking about?"

"Narnia," I replied. "My grandmother read the series to me when I was a girl, and I've read one of the books to my class each year."

"They were some of my favorite books as a kid too. We had a big wardrobe in my parents' room, and I kept knocking on its back wall when I thought no one was around."

"What does your documentary have to do with the Château d'Epines?" I asked.

"I'd like to talk to you about the German occupation."

Now I folded my arms. "I didn't even know the Germans occupied the château until yesterday."

"I'll have more general questions for you." He nudged his empty soup bowl to the side of the table. "Then perhaps you can give me a tour."

"Why are you doing this——" I started to ask, but our waiter walked into the room. He cleared our bowls and replaced my soup with a plate of creamy chicken with baby potatoes, carrots, and leeks. In front of Riley, he set fillets of red snapper, the fish ornamented with sprigs of rosemary and wedges of lemon.

The aroma was intoxicating, but I didn't begin eating. "What inspired you to do a documentary about German soldiers?"

"My grandfather flew a B-24 during World War II." He glanced out the window at the streetlamp glowing across from us. "And I suppose I've always been intrigued as to what sacrifices people will make to protect themselves and those they love. It tells a lot about a person when you find out what or who they're willing to die for."

When he smiled again, I wondered if he was always this cheerful.

"I still don't understand why you want to feature the Germans."

Riley's head tilted left, confusion filling his eyes. "Why don't we talk more about it tomorrow?"

My knife slid through the chicken as smoothly as if it were softened butter, and the meat tasted as if it were soaked in butter as well. Ah, well, when in France . . .

He held out his fork with a piece of baked fish on it. "You have to try this."

Wary, I eyed the oil puddled on his offering.

He persisted. "It's my clean fork."

In that moment, I realized that I was still playing for the cameras. Chloe Sauver, the candidate's fiancée, would be obsessed with her image and how she portrayed her future husband and family for the documentary. She would never trounce through France wearing jeans and flip-flops. And she certainly wouldn't eat a bite of fish off a stranger's fork.

But I was no longer the candidate's fiancée. There were no cameras here and no one but me seemed to care a thing about image. No longer did I have to play by the campaign rules.

I accepted his offering and enjoyed the tangy mixture of flavors on my tongue. Then I offered him a bite of the creamy chicken.

"Are you interviewing anyone else in Normandy?" I asked.

"A woman named Calvez," he said. "She lived at the château during the occupation."

I put down my fork. "I tried to visit a Madame Calvez earlier today."

Riley's face flooded with concern. "Did something happen?"

I glanced out the window before looking back at him. "She refused to see me."

He didn't seem surprised.

Over our third course—an assortment of breads and cheeses—I tried to probe further into Madame Calvez's story, but Riley refused to say anything else. It was for each person to tell their own story, he said, and his job to honor it. According to him, almost everyone wanted to share their story—eventually. When they were ready to talk, it was his job to share it with the world.

Why had Mémé hidden part of her story from me, until it was too late for her to share it? If only Madame Calvez would talk to me as well as to Riley. It wasn't too late for her to share her story.

Chapter 27

With Louise on her hip, Gisèle picked up the empty picnic basket and began to walk back across the yard from the *chapelle*. They would leave before lunch to cross the river and climb the hill, taking the path through the forest to find the orphanage. Somehow she would have to convince Sister Beatrice to keep Louise. If not, she feared the gendarmes would search for her here.

"I will miss you," she whispered to the little girl. She'd swept Louise's curly brown hair up into a ponytail. Thankfully the child had her father's blue eyes, the eyes of a national.

Louise clutched a fistful of Gisèle's hair in her hand. "*Maman*?"

"She'll be here soon," Gisèle lied. She didn't know what else to do. "In the meantime, you can stay with me."

"More milk," she begged.

"Of course, sweetheart. You may have all the milk you'd like."

She hummed to Louise as they moved across the morning shadows of the château, to the safety of the house.

If Sister Beatrice refused to take Louise, perhaps she could get a pass to take a bus down to Lyon. When Tante Corinne saw Louise, she would surely take her in. No one needed to know her mother was born into a Jewish family.

The low hum of an automobile startled her, and she turned around. Dust ballooned on the driveway, tires rumbling across the gravel, and she grasped Louise close to her as she squinted down at the brown cloud that obscured the vehicle.

Had the gendarmes already come?

She didn't want to see anyone today, not while she held Louise in her arms. A black sedan rolled into the courtyard and stopped near her. She glanced wildly around her, searching for a crevice or rock or someplace to hide her empty basket. And stash a child.

But it was too late.

She knew most of the gendarmes in Saint-Lô. How could she explain away picnicking with a child who wasn't hers?

Louise pulled Gisèle's hair as she swiftly calculated her options. There was nothing she could do except stand strong against whoever was in the sedan.

Pushing back her shoulders, she tried to appear taller than her small height. No matter what happened, no matter who emerged from the car, she wouldn't cower.

When the driver's door opened, a young German soldier stepped out, his uniform fitted snug over his slender shoulders. His hair was trimmed short, and he looked like he should be wearing knickers and knee socks.

The soldier didn't acknowledge her, reaching instead for the handle of the door behind him and opening it. A much older man stepped out into the courtyard, his gold-tipped walking stick crushing the gravel beneath it. His uniform was decorated with ribbons and medals, and he had the air of a weathered officer who'd fought many battles. And won.

Tapping his walking stick on the gravel, the officer surveyed the property—the fields laden with flax and wheat, the apple orchard and stone barn. He scanned the château and the *chapelle*, and then his steely gaze focused back on her and her basket. And her baby.

Silently she petitioned Saint Michel for strength.

Towering over her, the officer lifted his black stick and rapped it against his glove. She put her hand over Louise's back, afraid he might poke her with it. "Who is this child?" he asked in German.

She feigned ignorance. They needn't know that Odette taught her the German language a long time ago.

The officer mumbled something about the stupid French, and then he waved another man out of the car. This man's eyes were on the ground, but she recognized the civilian clothing of a Frenchman.

Traitor, she wanted to hiss, but she held her tongue.

The German barked at the shorter man as if he were an animal who could only understand commands. Loud, harsh ones.

The Frenchman faced her, and her heart filled with compassion when she saw the sorrow in his eyes. She had no idea what the Germans had done to him or his family.

The officer continued to shout in the man's ear. When the officer finally stopped, the Frenchman looked back up at her. A hint of amusement replaced the sorrow in his eyes. "The stupid German would like to know about the child in your arms."

"She is my daughter." The lie slid off her lips as easily as the one she'd told Louise about seeing her mother.

The Frenchman translated her words, and then they began to volley the translated words.

"What is the name of your daughter?"

She almost blurted out, "Louise," and the way

the major looked at her, it was as if he were waiting for her response in German as well. But she turned back to the Frenchman again. She had to take extra care in maintaining her ignorance. The French and possibly the Germans would be looking for Louise Batier.

A name rolled off her lips in response. "Adeline," she told him. "Her name is Adeline."

It was a name that reminded her of André and Nadine, a name that would honor both of them. In order to protect the child, she must pretend Adeline was hers, for as long as André and Nadine were gone.

"And where is your husband?" the officer asked.

Both of her parents—and the nuns at her boarding school—had impressed on her the virtues of an honest woman, but in the clarity of this thin moment, she knew she had to pretend with all that was within her that she had a husband. And that he had gone away.

"I don't know."

"*Maman*?" Louise—Adeline said again, but the officer didn't seem to hear the questioning in her voice.

The officer scrutinized the basket in Gisèle's hands and then looked up at the gray mantle in the sky. "Are you picnicking today?"

After the Frenchman translated for her, she replied, "Please tell him I help feed people who have no food."

"Where are these people?" the German asked.

"At the top of the hill," she told the Frenchman. "In Agneaux."

And then she wished she hadn't said that. What if he checked her story?

"Why are you feeding them?" the officer demanded.

"They are invalids," she said. "If I don't feed them, no one will."

The German officer looked over her shoulder as if he were trying to determine where she had come from.

"Would the officer like me to take him there?" Her heart pounded with her words, but she needed to proceed with confidence, as feigned as it may have been. Surely one of the Frenchwomen would corroborate her story for her.

The Frenchman spoke to the officer, stretching her story as he relayed it. "She said she would gladly take you there. They are all sickly people, but she said not to worry. Only a few of them are contagious."

The officer took a step back from her, as did his driver. "Perhaps we will go later."

"Certainly." She put down the basket and switched the child to her other hip. Adeline seemed mesmerized by the decorations on their shoulders—or maybe she was afraid as well. As the two German officers conversed, she bent toward the Frenchman. "What is your name?"

"Lucien."

"Why are you here?" she asked.

He shook his head. "I have no choice. My family tried to run from Paris when the bombing began, but the bombs killed my wife and daughter. When the Germans caught me, they almost killed me as well until they discovered I knew German."

"They killed my father during that raid."

Sorrow filled his eyes again. "I'm sorry."

"Stop talking," the German officer snapped at them. "Tell her we have come to visit her house."

The Frenchman hesitated. It seemed as if he was unclear as to whether or not he was supposed to speak again. As she waited, a hundred questions raced through her mind. What did it mean for the German officer to visit? And how long did he plan to stay?

"Tell her," the officer demanded.

The thought of having them in her house for even a moment revolted her. She didn't want to let them inside the front door—their stench, she feared, would linger long after. And how could she entertain the Germans as she cared for Michel?

"You have no choice," Lucien said after he relayed the officer's words.

She stood tall again. Perhaps if she played hostess instead of victim, they would treat her as such. "Tell him if they intend to spend the night, there are empty rooms on the third floor of the servants' quarters and in the west wing of the house."

They would probably take whatever rooms they wanted, but the thought of them sleeping in Papa's room or even Michel's room made her skin crawl. And she didn't want them anywhere near her chamber.

She pointed toward the house. "My servant and I will need an hour to prepare your rooms."

The officer ignored Lucien's words, marching across the courtyard instead.

She kissed Adeline's head as the child played with her sleeve. She didn't have any choice, did she? Not if she wanted to remain alive to care for Michel and the child in her arms. But what would Papa say to her allowing German officers inside?

He would probably tell her to do what she could to survive. Her mother would tell her to demand respect. If they respected her, they wouldn't harm her or Adeline.

She rushed around the officer and put her hand on the doorknob before he touched it.

Then she opened the front door and let the Germans inside.

CHAPTER 28

GUBERNATORIAL CANDIDATE DUMPS FIANCÉE.

I wanted to hurl my iPad across the room, but instead of throwing it, I clenched it in my hands, stared at the lie of a headline on the news site and the picture of Austin and me in front of the Byrd Theatre this past spring. His arm was around me, communicating to the world that we belonged together. Or at least that I belonged to him.

Austin and Olivia and the rest of his staff had probably huddled together in his war room for hours, trying to concoct the best way to announce the end of our engagement. I could almost hear the indifference in their discussion—was it better for Austin to be the victim of a breakup or the instigator? Would he seem cruel to break up with me prior to an election? If he was a victim, it would make him look weak, though some might take pity on him.

Austin wouldn't want pity.

Switching over to Austin's campaign site, I read the statement on his front page, and it was much more nuanced than the news headline.

Due to unforeseeable differences, my fiancée and I have mutually decided to postpone our wedding until after the election. A campaign is a rigorous affair and I am focusing my attentions on preparing to become the best governor for Virginia. This is a private matter between Miss Sauver and me, and we both respectfully ask that you allow us time and space to focus first on the election.

Mutual postponement, my foot.

Austin and Olivia had gambled that I wouldn't retaliate by dragging his reputation through the mud on the talk shows. And even if I decided to tell the truth, it seemed these days that even the career of a married politician survived an affair or two. My story might only benefit Austin in the end and pigeonhole me as a lunatic. A jealous lover's rage over her handsome fiancé's last fling. Some might even cheer him on.

I skimmed the statement again. Ironic that he had used the word *affair*.

Swiveling in the chair, I faced the dark windows. I needed to do something, anything, other than surf for news about the end of my engagement.

Riley had researched me before he came to France, so it was fair game, I supposed, for me to search for more information on him as well. Hundreds of results came up on my screen. My mother was right—Riley had won a bunch of awards for his work, including an Oscar a few years ago. It seemed that he had a fascination for documenting the secrets of World War II, and an even greater fascination for the women he met along the way.

I groaned as the first image filled my screen: Riley cradling a beer bottle in one hand, his arm wrapped around a blonde in a skimpy dress.

I skipped to the next picture. And then the next. Multiple pictures showed him partying with women in various states of undress. A slightly older version, it seemed, of Austin's brother. Or the secret life of my former fiancé.

Riley might have come across as charming, but like Austin, Riley was hiding his true self from me. And, I suspected, he was hiding the real reason he was doing this documentary.

I turned off my iPad and tossed it onto the bed.

I was tired of people trying to hide things from me. Tired of lies.

Instead of being angry at Austin's deception, perhaps I should be thankful that he showed his true self before we married. I should be grateful that he had gotten careless—or cocky—and I caught a glimpse of the destruction of my future before we proceeded with our marriage.

But right now I wasn't feeling very thankful.

Closing my eyes, I replayed the conversation I'd had with Riley tonight. He had hinted at my engagement, but I supposed I hadn't been honest with him either. I was so frustrated about my suspicions that I'd never stopped to consider that I was hiding information from him as well.

I rolled over on my pillow. It was the second time I'd gone to bed and still I wasn't able to sleep. In contrast to Riley's determination to fight jet lag, I had taken a long nap to fight the change in time, so now, long past midnight, I was wide awake.

It was a good time, perhaps, to explore. Before the interview tomorrow morning.

Pulling on a pair of socks, I padded out into the hallway in my long T-shirt. The light bulb in the hallway had burned out, but in the faint beam of my cell phone's flashlight, I puttered across the second floor, trying to locate my grandmother's bedroom.

I opened two doors, and in each room was a time capsule from the past—some of the décor seemed to be from the past twenty years, while some of the pictures looked as if they hadn't been updated in hundreds of years. Portraits of both men and women hung on the walls, some of them with ruffled collars and powdered wigs. Other pictures were of men and horses alongside their hunting dogs. As I stared into their faces, I wondered which of these people were my ancestors. It was a bit unnerving to see the people who'd gone before me all hanging on the wall, as if they were keeping tabs on their descendants.

As I crept to the third door, I imagined myself to be Mary Lennox in *The Secret Garden*, a stranger to the mysterious Misselthwaite Manor, walking down the dark corridor. Since Mémé couldn't tell me her stories tonight, I pretended she was here, sharing her favorite memories. The wonder of Christmas mornings in the château. The ornery escapades of her brother. The weekend parties her mother used to throw with their friends from Paris. The walls might have wanted to whisper more stories to me, but I couldn't hear them.

"The ghosts refuse to leave this place."

Marguerite had said it so matter-of-factly, as if the talk of ghosts was normal, but in these dark corridors, under the scrutiny of the portraits, my imagination raged. What if the ghosts of the past really were here? What would they say?

I didn't believe in ghosts, but I could almost imagine them watching me here. Perhaps they too were each clamoring to tell their own stories.

The door in front of me creaked open, and my inadequate cell phone light faded out in the vast space of the room. I flipped on the light switch by the door, and the bulb in here worked.

To my right was a canopied bed, and as I stepped left, I saw an antique dresser with rounded edges and a painting of faded flowers on the drawers. On top of the dresser were two tarnished candlesticks and a black-and-white photo of two young women smiling atop their horses. The woman in a light, button-down blouse looked like Mémé.

This must have been my grandmother's room. It seemed untouched, as if Stéphane and his father never stepped inside when they'd occupied the château.

I picked up the wooden frame from the dresser, examining the other woman. Could it be Isabelle's great-grandmother with her? As I studied the photo, their laughter captured on film, I was glad they had no idea about the destruction that awaited France.

But if this was Madame Calvez, playing with my grandmother, why wouldn't she welcome me into her home now?

Opening the armoire, I discovered a dozen colorful hatboxes in two neat stacks. I opened several of them, and spread the hats across the bed—there were felt hats with bows and flowers, a chic black velvet hat, one with netting in the front and daisies on the side. Mémé was always elegant in my eyes, even in these twilight days of her life. I could imagine her sporting any of these hats with a tailored suit or evening gown.

I picked up an ivory hat with a scalloped trim and copper-colored ribbons plaited in the front. Putting it on my head, I posed in the mirror, pretending I was a vicomtesse from long ago, preparing for a visit from a French king and queen. Then I opened another box and found a smart little navy hat. As I lifted it, I realized there was something underneath. A photo album.

The house creaked, and I jumped. I could almost hear the German soldiers shuffling on the floors above and below me.

Was Mémé alone in this house with the soldiers?

She had always seemed strong, but with the Nazis under her roof, she must have been terrified.

Shivering, I snagged the photo album and bolted back to the master suite, locking the door. I opened the album and began flipping through the black-and-white pictures, each one secured by faded white corners. There were cursive captions below many of them.

Mother bringing me home from the hospital.

Papa holding me in his arms.

Michel and I collecting Easter eggs on the front lawn.

Nadine and I diving into the lake.

Riding Papillon Bleu.

I held up a picture of Michel beside an old roadster. My great-uncle was a handsome fellow when he was young, his curly hair dipping over his eyes. Mémé said he'd died during the war, but like so many of the other stories, the end of his story was lost, at least to me.

I put down the photo album and opened up my iPad again, to the notes Olivia had compiled for my interview. She'd detailed the German occupation in Normandy and then the destruction of Saint-Lô. Once the Allied troops landed on the Norman beaches, she wrote, Hitler and his men knew defeat was inevitable, yet he refused to surrender. Until he took his life—if he took his life—Hitler had refused to be wrong.

The Nazis wouldn't relinquish Saint-Lô. The

Allies initially tried to chase them out of the area from the air, but they ended up fighting a bloody battle in the hedgerows that surrounded the city. Even as the French rejoiced that their enemy had been defeated, thousands of their civilians lost their lives in this final fight.

The darkness of what men could do to one another disturbed me deep in my soul. I had no desire to even try to understand a man like Hitler, but I was intrigued by Riley's idea to document the stories of some of the German soldiers. What if some of them hadn't wanted to fight? What if some of them tried to run?

I turned to the last pages of Mémé's photo album and several colored papers flitted out, falling onto the floor.

I picked up the top one and scanned it. Then I picked up the next one.

Chapter 29

*T*he German officer with the golden stick— Major von Kluge—toured the Château d'Epines as if he were the owner surveying his property. He flipped light switches, opened closets, prodded the carpets with his walking stick, all while telling three soldiers about his exploits in the Great War.

The soldiers swarmed around him like mosquitoes on a horse's rear, and Gisèle wished she could swat them all away from him and from her house.

After the arrival of the automobile this morning, three canvas-covered trucks had deposited dozens of officers and soldiers onto the château's front lawn. They descended into the crevices of her home like a plague of green locusts. Then the major ordered up dinner. As Émilie scrambled to make a simple meal, Gisèle followed the locusts and their leader through the corridors, lest they forgot they were guests in her home.

At Major von Kluge's command, the men scuttled into the dining hall. The officers took the chairs and the soldiers found their seats on the stone hearth of the fireplace, in cane chairs along the wall. As Gisèle served the men bread alongside sautéed zucchini and squash from the farmers' gardens, she tried to listen to the conversation, but even though she knew German, she couldn't understand the men. They spoke in low tones as they pointed toward the paneled windows that overlooked her valley, her serene oasis of river and trees. The lush hill across the river, the forest above that crowned the beauty—it all felt contaminated by their stares.

When they finished their food, the major pounded the tip of his walking stick on the table as if it were a bell, and when she responded, he sent her to fetch coffee and cognac and cigars, as if no one had informed him of the rationing they'd mandated in Normandy.

At least Adeline was safe from these men. The child played happily in the pen Gisèle and Émilie had found for her in the attic. Each time Gisèle returned to the kitchen, she pecked a kiss on the child's forehead.

The major pointed at his coffee—made from ground acorns since real coffee was scarce. "*Sucre?*"

She shook her head. "No *sucre*."

It fascinated her that one of the few French words the German man knew was sugar.

"*Oui,*" he demanded.

She turned to Lucien and explained that all their food supplies were low, and just like they had no meat to serve the men, they hadn't had sugar for months. Major von Kluge wasn't pleased when Lucien translated her words. She retrieved a little cream from the supply the farmers brought for them, but she reserved the milk for Adeline.

As she set the cream on the table, she studied the faces of the men around her—some didn't look much older than sixteen, while others, like the major, bore shoulders heavily laden with ribbons and medals. None of the men smiled. Their clean-shaven jaws were set in a grim pattern, their hair shaved at their collar and above their ears.

Could these men in her house, drinking cognac purchased by her father, smoking his favorite cigars, be the same men who had killed him? Hatred welled inside her again—hatred at them and hatred at herself for serving them.

She scanned their sleeves, searching to see if any of them wore an onyx-and-gold cuff link like the one she and Michel found by her father's body, but all of these men wore silver cuff links on their wrists. She didn't know what she would do if she came face-to-face with the man who'd murdered him.

Her glance turned toward Lucien, sitting on a chair by the door, clinging to the cup of tepid coffee she'd brought him. He was stuck, just like her. The Germans had killed his family, just like they killed her father, and then forced both her and Lucien to serve them. If she refused, they might kill her as well. And Émilie and Adeline.

Should she stand for all that was good and refuse them, even if it cost her her life? Or should she continue to compromise her morals to save her life—and the lives of those in her care?

The major commanded his men to follow him out into the main hall and then the dining hall was quiet. She knew not where they went, but after the room emptied, she and Lucien were alone.

Lucien glanced at the open doorway before whispering to her, "There are rumors of people resisting."

She nodded, wishing she could take the man into her confidence and tell him those who resisted were living below their feet. "I have heard them."

"It is making the Germans nervous. They pride themselves on maintaining control, and the more people resist, the harsher they will become. It is not only the Jewish people they will punish . . ."

She glanced toward the doorway. The hall remained quiet. "Do you know where they take the French Jews?"

His eyes heavy with sadness, he gave the slightest nod. "To an internment camp called Drancy."

Her heart began to race. If André and Nadine were waiting at this camp, she could petition the government for their return. Perhaps she could even have someone drive her there to retrieve them. If the French officials knew they were loyal citizens, if they knew they were good parents and André a schoolteacher, if they knew André wasn't even a Jew and Nadine had converted, surely they would let them return to Saint-Lô.

He rubbed his hands together. "No one stays in Drancy for long. They are deported to Germany."

She stood. There was no time to delay then. Father had once had many friends in the government. If any of them remained in the Vichy government down south, she had to contact them right away. If none of them were left, perhaps Philippe could help her. "Where do they go in Germany?"

He shrugged. "They don't talk about it when I'm around." He glanced back toward the door and then spoke again, his voice barely a whisper above the silence. "When we were at the police headquarters, I heard the gendarmes speaking of a baby missing from one of the Jewish families. Her name was Louise."

She shivered.

"They were angry about what happened but too proud to tell the Germans of their loss."

"They can't find out . . . ," she pleaded.

Her worry was mirrored in his eyes. "If you contact the authorities about Drancy, you would bring suspicion on yourself."

She thought of Adeline and how Major von Kluge already seemed to suspect something was amiss. André and Nadine hid their daughter for a reason. She couldn't point the police back to what they'd lost.

Jackboots hammered across the hall, outside the door, and she sprang to her feet, snatching a plate from the table and stacking it on another. Lucien seemed to shrink back into the plaster wall, as if the house might swallow him.

Major von Kluge marched into the room, his eyes sparking like flint when he saw her. Then, in spite of Lucien's attempt to disappear, the officer motioned to him. "Come with me," he demanded. "Both of you."

Lucien went first, and with trepidation, she

followed him through the hall and down the narrow steps that led into their cool wine cellar—the *cave*. Two light bulbs illuminated the bricks that lined the arched ceiling, the rounded brick bins on both sides of the narrow hall, and the wine casks stacked in the back.

This underground fortress held Papa's brandy and what remained of the family's vintage Bordeaux. The walkway between bins was only about two meters across and six meters long. The wooden door at one end led up to the house, and the room was filled with thirty of the brick bins on each side. The soldiers were removing dozens of bottles from each one. Another soldier had begun to roll aside the casks, but there was no other place to stack them in the narrow room.

Major von Kluge motioned Lucien forward, around the two soldiers who remained in the *cave*, until Lucien stood under the arch. "Listen!" the major commanded.

The room grew quiet, some of the soldiers cradling the wine bottles in their arms, as they listened to the brick.

"I heard voices," he insisted.

Gisèle placed her hand on the curve of a bin as Lucien translated. Was it possible they could hear the men hidden in the tunnel? After Michel had told her they couldn't keep Nadine's child because of the noise, his own men might betray him.

"Voices?" she asked dubiously, searching the

walls alongside Lucien even as she prayed that the men below wouldn't speak again.

Major von Kluge tapped his walking stick on the ceiling and then on the inside of an empty bin. "There were people talking somewhere down here."

"Perhaps it was the wind," she told Lucien.

"No!" Major von Kluge barked after Lucien translated. Then he began to falter, as if he realized how ludicrous his words sounded. "There were voices—muffled voices."

"Ghosts haunt these walls," she said, but the major shook his head, the suggestion of the supernatural seeming to make him even more angry. Sometimes it did seem to her as if the house groaned, as if it couldn't help but tell its story even if those who listened were invaders, but she doubted the noises today were from ghosts.

Lucien pointed at Gisèle. "Perhaps you heard her speaking overhead—with her housekeeper."

A sound from one of the bins startled her, and she held her breath.

What if one of the entrances to the tunnel was in here? What if one of the members of France's resistance stuck his head into a room filled with Germans? Surely none of them would be so stupid . . .

But they had no way of knowing the Nazis were here, on the other side of the wall.

She and the soldiers stepped away from the bin,

though Lucien remained, as if nothing could surprise him.

They heard the sound of a bottle rocking back and forth across the ruts in the brick, and one of the men gasped. She held her breath, praying that no one would enter the room. Then she watched as a gray paw stretched out from the depths.

Her cat hopped out, and the soldier next to her leapt backward. With a long meow, Shadow seemed to scold them for waking him from his nap. Gisèle suppressed her grin as he brushed against her leg. She glanced up at the soldier who had jumped, and in the dim light, she saw him trying to bite back a smile.

"She can be a noisy sleeper," Gisèle said, but Lucien didn't translate for her this time.

Major von Kluge's eyes narrowed again into slits, his finger on the revolver at his side. Swallowing hard, Gisèle plucked her cat off the floor and edged toward the entrance. Being insulted by a cat seemed to muddy the major's thinking. If he pulled the trigger, a bullet would surely ricochet off the bricks until it lodged itself into Shadow—or a person.

She rushed up the stairs and the soldiers followed her. They waited in silence in the lobby until minutes later, when the major emerged. His face was flushed red, but his thinking seemed to be clear again. He spoke directly to Lucien. "Tell her we will return in two days."

A hundred questions flooded her mind, but she waded rapidly through them, afraid her intrusion of being too inquisitive would muddle his thinking again. The most pressing question she dared to ask. "How should I prepare?"

He didn't answer her.

She stood in the doorway, watching their trail of dust as they drove away.

If only she knew what God required of her . . .

CHAPTER 30

I lifted the paper from those slipped into the back of the photo album. It was a faded marriage certificate between Gisèle Duchant and Jean-Marc Rausch—my biological grandfather. It was strange to see his name in print, the only link I had to the man who fathered my father.

Out of respect for Grandpa, I suspected, Gisèle never talked about her first husband, even after Henri passed away. But I did wonder sometimes what he must have been like. I had my mother's eyes and Gisèle's wavy hair and my father's love of the water. Did Jean-Marc pass along any of his features or traits to me?

If only there was a wedding picture in this box as well.

I placed the certificate on the desk and picked up another one—a diploma from the University of

Caen with Mémé's degree in literature. This I knew about, but why hadn't she taken her diploma when she moved to the States? Perhaps when her first husband died, she no longer needed their marriage certificate, but surely she would have wanted the diploma.

The last certificate was a pink color. A certificate of birth. The names were poorly written, and I leaned closer to the light, trying to read the scrawl. At first, I assumed the certificate was for my dad, but as I read the names, I realized it was for another child of Gisèle and Jean-Marc Rausch.

Adeline Rausch. The baby lost in the trees.

The print swam together in front of me. Mémé had a daughter?

No wonder she was tormented. Adeline would be my aunt. Dad's younger sister.

I thought of my grandmother, begging me to find Adeline. How had she lost her daughter? And after all these years, how could I possibly find her?

I stared down at the name as if Adeline's story might appear on the paper, like the stories on my iPad.

Did my dad know he had a sister? Clinging to the certificate, I picked up my phone and called him.

"It's the middle of the night there," he said with a laugh.

"I'm still on Virginia time," I said, collapsing

back against the cushions of the couch. "How is Mémé?"

He paused. "Pamela called this morning. She said my mother keeps asking about Adeline."

"About that . . ." I slid my hand over the certificate. "I found something."

"What did you find?"

"A birth certificate for Adeline."

He hesitated before asking, "Who are her parents?"

In his hesitation, I realized that my dad was afraid of the answer.

"Gisèle and Jean-Marc Rausch." The silence was heartbreaking. "Dad?"

"Gisèle Duchant Rausch?" he asked slowly.

"That's what it says." I skimmed the certificate again. "Adeline was born in February 1941."

"That would have been . . ." He paused again. "I would have been three years old when she was born."

He didn't say it, but I knew what he was thinking. He should have remembered his sister.

I reached for the faded green marriage certificate. "You were born in 1938."

"That's right."

"I found the marriage certificate for Jean-Marc and Gisèle as well. It says they were married in June 1940."

He didn't say anything for a moment, and I

feared it was too much. "I didn't know—I was born two years before my parents married."

Was that why Mémé kept her secret? Perhaps she was embarrassed that she had a child before she was married, a child that might not even have been her husband's. I didn't say anything to Dad about the man he thought to be his father. In his silence, I knew he was already considering this shift in his story.

"But you don't remember Adeline?" I asked.

His voice sounded broken. "My memories are like a shattered picture, Chloe. There are all sorts of little pieces, but I don't know how they fit together."

"What did Mémé tell you?"

"That I was born in the château before the war, and my first years were happy. She has pictures of me playing on the lawn and one in a swing."

She had shown me those pictures too. "She must have taken your birth certificate when you moved to the States."

"I have it now," he said. "But I wish I could remember more of my childhood in France."

"What do you remember?"

"I don't know what was a memory and what was a dream, or even bits from a book I read and made my own."

I stared down at the birth certificate again. "Perhaps I could help you piece some of it together."

Instead of answering, he changed the subject. "Your mother wants to know what you think of the filmmaker."

I tapped my iPad and glanced at Riley's cocky smile. And the beautiful woman entangled in his arm. "I think he is competent." I propped my feet on the small table. "Why does Mom want to know?"

"Your mom enjoyed talking with him on the telephone." Knowing Dad, he'd probably shrugged as he said this. He might act casual but something was brewing in his mind. "When she found out he was single . . ."

I shot up. "You set me up!"

"I had nothing to do with it. Your mom thought it would be nice for you to meet Riley before your wedding day."

I groaned. As if I needed my mom's meddling in my relationships. She must not have looked at his pictures online. "Please tell her that it's easy for someone to be nice when they want something from you."

"When are you doing the interview with him?"

"Tomorrow."

"Then why don't you come home right after it?"

As I lay down, I mulled over his words. But I knew I wasn't ready to return home yet. Not just because I wanted to stay away from the media and Austin. I wanted to dig a little deeper here, find out what happened to Adeline Rausch. Was it her presence that seemed to haunt the house?

A breeze came through the open window and I jumped as it ruffled the bedcoverings. Standing up, I shuffled toward the window and closed it, clasping it shut. With the lights off, I looked across the hill and saw a light on in the farmhouse.

Was Riley awake as well?

It didn't matter one bit to me.

Leaning back against the pillows, I began to drift to sleep. The breeze skipped across my eyelashes, my cheeks and forehead, as if they were stones in a puddle. In the coolness, I slept, and it wasn't until morning that I remembered I'd closed the window before going to bed.

Chapter 31

*D*esperation drove Gisèle to the *chapelle*, Adeline strapped on her back. The major and his men had left last night, but they said they'd return tomorrow. To take over her home.

How was she supposed to entertain their enemy, the very men who had killed her father?

As two of the village women prayed near the altar, she lit candles for both her mother and her father and then knelt with Adeline beside a pew.

Her mind racing, she begged God for wisdom, strength, and, most of all, courage in whatever it was that He required of her now.

For so much of her youth, she'd focused on what she wanted—riding her horses when she was a girl and then going to Paris. And one day perhaps marrying and becoming an elegant noblewoman like her mother, returning each year to visit Michel and his family at the Château d'Epines.

The Germans had changed everything. After her father's death, she knew she must care for her brother until the Nazis left France, but how was she supposed to do that with the enemy under her roof?

Above the pew was a stained-glass window, orange and red and cobalt blue. The pieces of colored glass melded together to form a picture of the body of Christ, broken and bloody after being taken down from the cross. The Roman soldiers beat Him terribly and yet He forgave them.

Her eyes wandered to the front of the room and the statue of Mary holding Jesus. Had Christ's mother forgiven the soldiers as well?

Love your enemies and pray for those who persecute you.

The Germans had killed her father and now they were destroying her country. How was she supposed to care for the men who had killed him? And even more, how was she supposed to love them—love evil? She despised everything they were doing.

Jesus had resisted the devil in the desert, but then He showed love to the men who tortured Him, forgave those who killed Him. When was she supposed to love her enemy and when was she supposed to resist? And somehow, in the great mystery of faith, was it possible for her to do both?

She asked God to take her pride and, trembling, she asked Him to take her very life if He had to, like Christ had done, in order to save those in her care from destruction on this earth. But if He didn't take her, she would cling to the hope of her future, that one day God would right all that had decayed in this world.

Her thoughts and prayers wrestled together. The commandment from the Scripture weighed against what she thought God would have her do.

She didn't think it was possible for her to love the Nazis, but perhaps she could pray.

As rain trickled down the stained glass, tears trickled down her cheeks. She wiped away her tears and crossed herself.

In the name of the Father and the Son and the Holy Spirit.

Her eyes closed, Adeline squirming beside her, she recited one more prayer—a petition to Saint Michel.

Saint Michel the Archangel, defend us in battle,

be our protection against the wickedness and snares of the devil.

May God rebuke him, we humbly pray; and do thou, O Prince of the Heavenly host, by the power of God, cast into hell Satan and all evil spirits who wander through the world seeking the ruin of souls.

Was it possible to love your enemy even as you hated—as you battled—the wrong that drove them? Perhaps that was what Jesus did on the cross. He forgave those who killed Him and in his death, He also defeated the sin that blinded them.

She could pray for her enemy, but she also had to fight against evil, and she had no doubt that the Nazis embodied the hatred of their führer. Lucien had said she must care for the men or they would claim her property and perhaps send her to one of the work camps as well.

What would Papa think, knowing the Germans were going to stay at their house, and knowing that Michel was planning to resist them? Her heart ached at the loss of the man who had wanted to protect her from all this.

She was glad she didn't go to Lyon so long ago, but sometimes she wondered what would have happened if she had made that choice. Papa would want her to take charge of the property now, and Michel was relying on her for food.

Perhaps in love she could fight.

When she finished, she opened her eyes. One of

the women was gone. The other was an old friend of her mother's, Madame Fortier.

Madame Fortier eyed Adeline. "Who is the girl?"

"My dau—" she began to say, and then stopped. The people in Agneaux knew she didn't have a child. "I have told the Germans she is my daughter."

Her eyes widened with horror. "Oh, Gisèle, you must hide her."

Gisèle gazed at the candlelight flickering on the stained glass, the warmth of the blond wood. This was her hiding place, her protection. Those who came here worshipped the same God she did. They were like family. "But no one here would say anything—"

"They might not want to bring harm on you or this child, but if they are questioned . . ." She glanced back toward the door. "They might stumble with their words."

"I will tell them I've hidden her for the past year," she said. "I married a French soldier right before the Germans came, and I feared for her life."

Madame Fortier brushed a lock of brown hair away from Adeline's face. "And now?"

"Now the Germans are coming to occupy the house, and no matter my shame, I must speak the truth."

The woman eyed her again, and Gisèle knew

that Madame Fortier was keenly aware of the consequences for repeating this lie.

"I will spread your story, but still, you shouldn't bring her here," she whispered. "People will ask too many questions."

She nodded. "Thank you."

Madame Fortier bent her head toward Adeline and then studied Gisèle's face. "You have the same eyes—I will tell my friends of the similarities."

Adeline rested her head against Gisèle's shoulder. "I pray the Germans will be too busy to concern themselves with her story."

"I wouldn't be too certain." Madame Fortier glanced back at the door. "I fear they may go to great lengths to demonstrate their power, both big and seemingly small."

It was possible that Major von Kluge and his men wouldn't return to the château. Perhaps they would march on to Cherbourg, or perhaps their entire convoy would be destroyed by Allied bombers. She'd heard on the wireless that the Allies were fighting against the Germans. And that the number of people resisting inside France was growing.

But if the Germans did return, she had to be prepared.

After Madame Fortier left the *chapelle*, she almost slipped down into the tunnel, but Michel would be angry if Adeline began crying again. She would go down in the morning and warn Michel before the Nazis returned. The next time Major von Kluge heard voices, he wouldn't believe it was a cat.

She left Adeline in the kitchen, with Émilie, and slipped back down into the *cave*. The light bulb flickered on in the cellar and she wandered down the passage, pressing against the brick and peering inside the bins. The room smelled of damp earth and old wine.

In the casing of cool bricks, she could hear the echoes of voices, muffled shouts of men below or beside them. The ghosts in the tunnel.

Michel had said he was going to leave soon, but when he returned, she feared it would be too difficult to feed him and the other men through the hiding place in the *chapelle*. If she could find another entrance to the tunnel in the house, she wouldn't have to go to the *chapelle* for any other reason than to pray.

Minutes passed as she searched, the faint voices in the tunnel no longer audible. Feet shuffled down the steps, and she turned, thinking Émilie had come with Adeline. But a man stepped through the doorway instead, his wide shoulders ballooning across the doorframe.

The man wore the grayish-green uniform of a German officer, his hair black as ink, his eyes brown. Instead of the Aryan people the Nazis idolized, he looked more like the pictures she'd seen of Hitler.

Her mouth gaped open, but no sounds came out. The Germans weren't supposed to return yet, not until tomorrow night at the earliest.

"What are you doing down here?" the officer demanded in German.

She pressed her lips together and swallowed hard before she replied in French. "*Je ne comprends pas.*"

I don't understand.

She hoped he would stomp away in frustration. Or find Lucien to translate.

His torso turned back toward the steps as if he was considering a retreat back up to the dark entrance.

She shifted herself to the center of the passage, ready to hurry upstairs behind him, but he didn't leave. When he looked back at her, she shuddered. In his eyes was something more sinister than desire, like she'd seen in the eyes of the soldier in Saint-Lô. It was a thirst for power. Conquest. And the only thing to conquer in this *cave* was her.

Everything within her cried out for her to run, but it would be impossible to get around this giant of a man. *A man will only respect you if you respect yourself.* Her mother's admonition flooded her mind, and she rolled her shoulders back, trying to maintain the Duchant dignity.

She slid a bottle of wine out of a bin and, clutching it in her hand, took a small step toward him and the exit. "If you would excuse me . . ."

His hulking form loomed over her. She tried to muster confidence, but inside her stomach clenched with terror. If he attacked her, no one above would hear her scream.

Her fingers tightened over the bottle. Her only weapon. What would the major do if she killed one of his men?

Before she could lift the bottle, the man stepped forward and grabbed her arm. The bottle shattered on the floor. Wine splashed across her stockings and shoes.

She shoved him away, commanding him to halt, but he ignored her, pressing his body into hers, pinning her against the jagged edges of the bricks. When he reached for her blouse, she screamed.

He pressed his hand over her mouth. "You scream again, and I will kill you."

She held her breath.

He slid a knife from his sheath and pressed it against her neck. The blade piercing her skin, she began to pray again—to Saint Michel, to the Virgin Mary, to God Himself if He was listening.

"Defend me," she whispered in French. "Protect me against the wickedness."

He pushed the knife deeper into her skin. "Shut up."

Her lips silenced, her eyes closed, she continued mouthing the words. And she pretended that she was far, far away, on the fields behind their house, cantering with Papillon Bleu along a stream. She was far from this madman who wanted to destroy what she'd saved for her wedding night. And probably take her life with it.

His knife slit open her blouse before the blade clattered against the brick floor. She gagged as he groped her skin. The stream—she could see it in her mind's eye. The breeze fluttered over her face and comforted her. She was transported in her mind, hidden in her place of refuge. Secure with her mother and her father and all who had gone before her.

"Halt!"

The command was so powerful, so loud, she thought for a moment that it had escaped her own lips, but she hadn't spoken a word. The man who had assaulted her shoved her to the ground, and she snapped back into the present, her hands sticky with wine, glass cutting her left palm as she hovered over the floor like a dog, her blouse in tatters, her breasts bruised.

In the doorway stood another man. A fellow German officer. Would he join his comrade in humiliating her?

Her mind began to wander again.

The enemy pressed his hand into her hair, her chin digging into her neck. "This doesn't concern you."

"The major said not to harm her."

"He does not care—"

"He wants her to make dinner tonight, and he

will care very much if you detain her." The officer's voice was hard.

Her neck screamed in pain as the men argued, her knees and palms ached, but she didn't dare make a sound. Then her attacker picked up his knife and shoved it back into the sheath before his footsteps echoed up the stairs.

She hesitated for a moment, uncertain if he would return, but then she reached for a bin and pulled herself off the floor. Mortified, she wrapped her arms across her bare chest. The officer before her—her rescuer—looked down at his boots.

He could have ignored her scream, could have looked the other way like she'd done in the forest. So many of them had to look away. The other man could have raped her—killed her even—and she doubted the major would care.

Her body trembled as she stood before him. "*Merci.*"

"Are you injured?" he asked.

She shook her head.

"You must stay away from the cellar until we are gone." The officer stepped back toward the exit. "I will have your housekeeper bring you another shirt."

"Will he bring you trouble?" Too late, she realized she had spoken in German.

"I'm not concerned about him," he said. "As long as you are useful to Major von Kluge, you will be safe."

Safe.

It was a strange word to use. She doubted she would ever feel safe again, at least not in her home.

She switched back to French. "What is your name?"

Instead of answering, the man bowed his head to her one more time. And then he disappeared.

CHAPTER 32

Someone pelted pieces of gravel at my window five minutes before eight. I pulled my hair back into a ponytail and crossed the room to reopen the window. Fog settled over the driveway and Riley stood in the midst of it, a backpack slung over his shoulder.

I leaned against the windowsill. "What are you doing?"

He grinned. "Waking you up."

I rubbed my eyes, the images flashing through my mind of him with his arm around multiple women. And his bottles of beer. His smile irritated me even more, as if I would swoon under his charms like the women in the pictures.

I crossed my arms. "Why do you feel compelled to wake me?"

"I thought we could get a jump-start on the interview."

"I'll be ready at nine," I insisted.

He glanced down at his watch. "How about eight thirty?"

"Nine!" I shut the window, refusing to be disarmed.

Slowly I took a bath and washed my hair. The cool temperature of the bathwater revived me, and I dressed in a black skirt and a teal blouse. Then I checked my voicemail messages—eleven of them from friends and fellow teachers who'd read the news. Some offered sympathy while others, it seemed, called mainly out of curiosity. Later I would return the calls to those who cared.

At 9:10, I sauntered down the staircase.

Riley was waiting on the bottom step, wearing jeans and a dark brown T-shirt under his bomber jacket. He seemed like such a different person from what I'd seen in the pictures, but I knew well that appearances could be deceiving.

He held out a white paper bag. "I thought you might be hungry."

I peeked inside to see a chocolate croissant. "Where did you get this?"

He shrugged. "I walked to the village while you were getting ready."

With a quick thank-you, I focused my attention on the pastry he brought. The flavors melted in my mouth—warm chocolate and melted butter and the flaky sweet crust. This was what I loved about France. A keen appreciation for the simplicity and sweetness of life. The French seemed to savor their minutes along with their food.

I leaned back against the railing as I ate. A few moments passed before I realized Riley was studying me. "What?"

"I asked if you wanted me to make some coffee."

"I'm sorry—"

He balled up his bag. "Is everything okay?"

I was so tired of people refusing to tell me the truth. As much as I wanted to tell him nothing was wrong, I would have been doing exactly what was frustrating me. "I couldn't sleep last night."

He leaned back against the steps. "All night?"

"Until about two." I paused. "I decided to hunt around online a bit to uncover your story, since you've already uncovered mine."

His smile faded. "I hate to think of what you found."

"A man who likes to party."

The intensity of his eyes unnerved me. "I'm not that man anymore—"

"You don't have to explain," I said.

He stood up and smiled again, but his smile had lost a bit of its charm. "Grace is a gift I don't take lightly."

He was baiting me, but still I asked. "Why do you need grace, Riley?"

Instead of answering, he picked up his backpack off the ground. "What do you like to do, Chloe?"

"What do you mean?"

He slung the strap of the backpack over his shoulder. "I mean what do you enjoy doing, more than anything in the world?"

I leaned back against the banister. "I like to kayak."

The green in his eyes shone. "If I can drum up two kayaks, will you paddle the river with me?"

I crossed my arms. "You're supposed to be interviewing me."

"I will," he said before stepping toward the front door.

I followed him. "From a chair."

He shrugged. "Chairs usually make for dull interviews."

I wanted to give a decent interview to honor my grandparents. And I wanted to kayak. So I changed my clothes again, this time into my paddling shorts and an REI T-shirt.

A friend of Pierre's loaned us two kayaks, and Riley and Pierre transported them in the station wagon from Agneaux to the river. After Riley stored his camera in a dry bag at his feet and his aluminum tripod in the storage hatch, we began to paddle.

Geese scattered as Riley and I kayaked under a stone bridge, the river meandering through the still morning. Fog swayed in front of us like a sheer veil hiding the pristine valley and the promise of warmth.

I didn't mind the coolness. Sometimes it was easy to settle into comfort, like a lobster swimming in a pot of warm water, minutes before it begins to boil. The bite in the air breathed life into me. I was made for this, the strain on my arms, the pounding of my heart as I cut through the water.

The château was hidden by the fog, but we paddled past the jagged cliffs underneath. As the river cut through farmland on the other side, Riley pulled up his sleeves, and I saw an odd mix of scribblings tattooed under his forearm.

I pointed at the tattoo. "What does that say?"

"It's a word from the Hebrew Scriptures. It means 'revelation' or 'unveiling.' "

"Very mysterious," I replied, but didn't probe.

It was an odd amalgam—a man tattooed with a Hebrew scripture, doing a documentary on German soldiers.

"I have a few questions for you," he said.

I glanced over at the waterproof bag at his feet. "Aren't you supposed to be filming?"

"In a bit."

I shrugged. It was his documentary. "Where do you want me to begin?"

He placed his paddle across his lap and floated beside me. "What do you love about kayaking?"

A bird trilled in the nearby trees and shards of sunshine cut through the mist as I leaned back to savor the morning again, the promise of a slate wiped clean, new beginnings. I stole a glance back over at him. "Being outside on the water and enjoying each minute as I paddle instead of striving to accomplish something new."

"Does your fiancé enjoy these minutes with you?" he asked.

He must not have read the news in the States today—at least not political news. Or were Austin and my breakup considered entertainment?

"Not particularly." I took a deep breath. "And Austin and I aren't getting married after all."

Silence was his response, and I wanted to flee. I'd poured out just a drop of my story, and he was letting it spill all over the ground.

He dipped his paddle back into the water, moving closer to me. "I'm sorry," he finally said. "Ending a relationship with someone you love is gut-wrenching."

We floated past crisscrossed wooden fence posts, and I wanted to run and hide behind them, not from Riley as much as from the torment of the emotions that crashed within me. "It's not so hard when you find the man you planned to marry sleeping with another woman."

His mouth dropped open and then he caught himself. "Chloe, I'm sor—"

I lifted my paddle and waved it slightly to stop him. "You don't have to apologize. I'm really not angry at all men—just Austin."

I shuddered as we floated through another curtain of mist.

"Let's not talk about Austin Vale," he said. "Why don't you tell me about your life pre-Austin?"

I dipped my paddle back into the water and flowed with the current. What was my life like before I met Austin? It had only been a year since the coffee shop fiasco and yet it seemed like a decade ago. I had enjoyed my freedom during those single years, but as my friends began to marry, I'd longed for a husband and children of my own. A part of me had felt like I was in a holding pattern since college, like life wouldn't begin until I met my Prince Charming.

Like Riley, I had once dreamed of the power of story—of using stories in the lives of children to inspire them—but I'd lost my dreams to someone else. To an opportunity that seemed too good to be true, with a man who'd swept me off my feet.

Riley paddled again. "I'm not going to let you off the hook about your story."

I dug my paddle into the slow-moving water and the motion calmed my nerves. I didn't want to tell him my story and yet I was spending these weeks trying to delve into the story of someone I loved who kept her story locked inside her. I didn't want to share my story with a man I didn't trust, but I didn't want to hide either.

"Until last week I was a third-grade teacher and I loved helping children learn new things," I said. "I loved watching when that proverbial light bulb went off and their eyes grew wide as they mastered a hard concept or learned something that ignited their world. In the summers, I used to travel with my best friend and sometimes by myself so I could learn as well, but when I was home, I spent most of my free time kayaking in Virginia."

"I read that your dad owns the top investment company in Virginia."

So many people knew *about* me but few actually knew me. It was easy to read a profile online, but that hardly told you what a person was like. "My parents are both successful because they love to work and they both do what they enjoy. Not because they want to be wealthy."

"There is nothing wrong with being wealthy, Chloe."

And yet there was. Even though my parents never flaunted the money they'd made through their successes, there was a stigma attached to it. They might have been oblivious to it or so wrapped up in their careers that they didn't care, but I felt it when I was in school. It seemed people were either criticizing me or judging me or holding me up to impossible standards. I never wanted the attention, good or bad. When I moved out of our home, I was comfortable in my modest condo by the river and in the steady pace of my work.

A tiny village lay to our right, the stone houses clustered together above the riverbank, and a grove of tall trees stood on the far side of the town, the branches barren except for giant balls of leaves that ornamented them. I pointed toward one of the trees with my paddle. "What do you think that is?"

"Mistletoe," he said. "Should we paddle under them?"

I turned back to him and saw his wide grin. Then I splashed him with my paddle before turning my kayak around. Laughing, he returned the favor.

After today, I would never see Riley Holtz again and I was glad about it.

Together we kayaked back toward the château. The fog had lifted, and we peered up at the castle on the cliff, surrounded by trees. It looked so majestic, like a gateway to the heavens. There were clusters of trees below the house as well.

When I looked back toward Riley, he had his camera out now, filming the château above me. Then he lowered the camera. "You ready to do this?" he asked.

I put my paddle on my lap. "As ready as I'll ever be . . ."

I clipped on the microphone he gave me, and then he lifted the camera again, training it on my face. I pretended I was back in my classroom, ten hands raised to ask questions. This time I would pick Riley.

"What do you know about the history of your family's château?"

I glanced up at the house and then looked back at Riley.

Olivia had put me through hours and hours of exhaustive media training. For my interviews, presentation was more important than content, the trainer had said. I'd memorized the campaign talking points in about an hour, and then the trainer had worked with me on the position of my shoulders and legs, the tilting of my head, the tone of my voice. In front of a mirror, he showed me the differences between a comfortable, warm smile and a strained one.

But there was no studio around me now. No chair.

I flashed what I hoped was a warm smile and began. "The first walls were probably built about a thousand years after Christ, during the reign of William the Conqueror. They named the area Agneaux because legend has it that Saint Martin of Tours prayed for the dead sons of the first Norman family who lived here. After the twins were restored to life, they were known as the Lambs—*les agneaux*—of St. Martin.

"The house probably harbored knights at one time, but three hundred years ago, King Louis XV gave the property to the Duchant family as a reward for fighting alongside him." I pointed toward the river. "Before the French Revolution, our property stretched all the way down to Saint-Lô."

"Did your family live here during World War II?" he asked.

"My grandmother was only twenty-two when the war started. Her mother had already passed away, but her father died during the war and her first husband was killed during a battle."

"Was your father born here?"

"He was, but he moved to the United States when he was six."

The current pushed us away from the château, and he put down his camera. "Should we continue onshore?"

"Sure." I dipped my paddle back into the water, and when I reached the edge, I pulled my kayak onto the grassy bank. We were at the base of the trees and cliff, and Riley set up his tripod and had me stand where he could capture the trees and river behind me. I readjusted my microphone and he began filming again.

"You said your grandmother was a widow at the end of the war," he said, prompting me.

I nodded. "My father was a young boy in 1944 and Mémé was a widow. A friend introduced her to Henri Sauver right after the Allies defeated the Germans in Saint-Lô, and they married about a month later. Henri adopted my father, and their family immigrated to the United States that same year."

"What did your grandfather do during the war?" he asked.

"At first, he fought with the French army as a captain until the Germans defeated them. Then he joined the French resistance. My grandmother said he used to travel all over Normandy and wreak havoc on the Germans."

Riley crossed his arms. "What sort of havoc?"

"He and his men disrupted the German phone service and telegrams and other means of communication."

"With bombs?"

"No, they snipped the lines."

"Did he bomb the railways?"

Mémé once said he did, but I wasn't sure she would want me to broadcast that on national television. Nor was I sure what the resistance had to do with a documentary profiling German soldiers.

I decided to redirect the conversation, a skill I'd acquired both from my media training and in negotiating disputes among third graders. "My grandfather was good at accounting and record keeping. My grandmother said he kept their records in a way no German could decipher, in order to protect all the men in their cell."

"What did your grandfather say about the resistance?" Riley asked.

My own questions resurfaced. I wished Grandpa had told me his stories before he passed away.

But I didn't have to prove anything to Riley or the reporter in Richmond or to anyone else.

Mémé was proud of Henri Sauver's military and then resistance record, and so was I. "My grandfather didn't like to talk about the war."

"I wonder why not," he said.

He waited for me to respond. Defend my grandfather perhaps.

I wanted to cross my arms like Riley, but instead I smiled at the camera. My media trainer had shown me dozens of clips from people who'd screwed up their interviews, usually by getting defensive with their body language. Others by stomping off in a huff. "Do you have any other questions for me?" I asked, even though I wanted to stomp off as well.

"How did you say your grandmother met Henri Sauver?"

"On a blind date, at a café in Saint-Lô."

"But after the war . . ." He tilted his head. "There were no cafés left in Saint-Lô."

I'd read about the bombing of the city but had never thought to question Mémé's story. Perhaps I'd heard wrong. "It might have been near the end of the war instead."

He watched me for a moment, and I expected him to ask why a member of the French resistance would be on a blind date, at a public café, while the Germans still occupied the town. Instead, he asked, "Was your grandmother part of the resistance?"

My lips pressed together for a moment before I

remembered to smile. "The Germans stayed at the château during the war," I said. "I'm sure she resisted them in her own way."

"Did she ever talk about the German soldiers in her house?"

My smile widened, hoping to engage him along with the camera as I spoke. "Can I ask you a quick question?"

"Of course."

I nodded casually toward the tripod. "Off camera."

His eyes on me, he turned the camera off. My smile collapsed, hardening into a grimace. This time I crossed my arms. "What are you keeping from me?"

"I'm trying to put together a documentary."

"But you know something I don't . . ."

He glanced up at the rocky cliffs towering above us and then looked back at me. "My grand-father flew a B-24 during World War II. He hid in a tunnel under the Château d'Epines with some members of the resistance."

My heart quickened. I didn't know any of the old tunnels had remained through the war. Or that the resistance had hidden in them.

"His plane crashed near a river outside Saint-Lô." Riley glanced back to the fields across the Vire. "He said Gisèle rescued him and brought him into the tunnel."

My gaze roamed over the hillside again, and I

wondered at my grandmother rescuing the pilot of a downed plane.

"Was my grandfather there?" I asked.

He shook his head.

"Where is the tunnel entrance?"

"Someplace in the forest." He took his camera off the tripod and began to pack it. "When my grandfather told me his stories, I was at rock bottom and didn't listen to the details, but I heard about redemption through everything he told me. There were second chances for him and others who survived the war."

I eyed him again. Was it possible the man before me was different from the man in the pictures? I hoped he had changed, for his sake, but still I didn't trust him.

He glanced at his diver's watch. "I'm supposed to interview Madame Calvez in an hour."

Madame Calvez had asked me not to return, but perhaps if I was with Riley she would change her mind. Or if she was like my grandmother, she might not even remember that I was Gisèle's granddaughter.

"Can I tag along with you?" I asked.

He raked his fingers through his thick hair. "I suppose, if you let me ask the questions."

I readily agreed.

Chapter 33

*H*er rescuer was named Hauptmann Milch. Lucien said the officer had a family in Berlin and was respected among most of his fellow officers, but Lucien knew little else about his background.

Gisèle didn't tell Lucien or even Émilie what had happened in the wine cellar. It was much too humiliating to share with either of them. The only ones who would ever know were Hauptmann Milch and Viktor Braun, the *Fähnrich*—sergeant— who attacked her. Lucien said Braun was a bitter man. He'd asked to join the Luftwaffe to fight Hitler's war from the sky, but he'd been assigned to act as a warden to the people of France.

Even after she bolted her bedroom door—and pushed her dresser across it—Gisèle hadn't slept well. With Adeline in the bed next to her, she replayed her minutes in the cellar over and over. Had her solitude been some sort of invitation to that man? The thought of what might have happened terrified her. If Milch hadn't rescued her, she might have been killed.

How could she live in her home with these men here? She would never feel secure again.

She ripped her soiled blouse into threads. It

would be impossible to replace, but even if she could patch it, she would never wear it again. Nor would she ever return to the *cave*.

The morning light brought tepid comfort, enough for her to get up and dress Adeline for the day. As she prepared breakfast, Gisèle determined to avoid both Milch and Braun—one because of her humiliation and the other because she feared what he would do the next time he found her alone.

While Émilie tended to the laundry, Gisèle began making scrambled eggs from the supplies the Germans had carried into her home last night. Not only had they secured eggs, they'd brought a ham smoked in ash, crates filled with vegetables, and bags of flour to make biscuits. She hadn't seen this much food since the war began and didn't dare ask where they had obtained it.

Adeline was sucking her bottle in her playpen when Lisette strolled into the kitchen and hopped up onto the counter, her legs dangling over the linoleum.

Gisèle cracked eggs into a porcelain bowl. "What are you doing here?"

"The Germans requisitioned me to work here instead of in Saint-Lô." Lisette glanced around the kitchen. "Please give me a job."

"Don't they need you to type or translate?"

She shook her head. "One of the new men does most of the typing so I won't see their correspondence with Berlin, and others can translate for them. If I'm no longer useful, I'm afraid they'll send me to work in Germany."

Earlier this year, the government had enacted the Service du Travail Obligatoire—Compulsory Work Service—to force hundreds of thousands of young Frenchmen and women to join their labor force. Lisette would be safer here, under the roof with the German occupiers, than living at a camp in Germany, as long as she avoided places like the cellar.

"I can't go to Germany," Lisette said, her voice trembling.

Adeline began to cry, and Gisèle wiped her hands on her apron so she could pick her up. Their guests didn't need any more reminders that there was a baby in the house.

Lisette reached into the pen. "I can hold her."

Gisèle wiped her hand under the *couvre-chef* that held back her hair. "Thank you."

"It's so sad about her par—"

Gisèle stopped her, pointing to the ceiling. "I told them her name is Adeline."

"Adeline." Lisette offered her a piece of a biscuit. "It's the perfect name."

"They think she's my daughter."

Lisette paused. "I suppose they should think that. I will keep your secret as well."

Émilie breezed into the kitchen. "The major said we should not be late with breakfast."

Gisèle sighed. The Germans were punctual

about everything, as if the war would be lost if everything from meals to bedtime were not observed at the precise hour.

Émilie began whisking the eggs, and Lisette sat down at the table with a bottle to care for Adeline. Gisèle was grateful for two women she could trust. None of them wanted to serve the Nazis, but they each had to do what they could to survive.

When the eggs were almost finished, Gisèle retrieved the ham from the oven and sliced it before taking the platter upstairs. Then she came back down for the coffeepot, eggs, and biscuits.

As she served breakfast to fifteen men, she was relieved that Viktor Braun wasn't among them. The *Hauptmann* was there, but she didn't dare steal a glance at him. Part of her feared any acknowledgment from her would put him in jeopardy with his commanding officer. And part of her was ashamed of what he had seen.

She prayed he didn't think she had been flirting with Viktor Braun. From her scream, Hauptmann Milch must have known that she was scared, and yet she hoped he didn't think she had invited the trouble. She shouldn't have cared what he thought—he was a German, her enemy. But even though he was a German, he'd risked his life to rescue her.

The coffeepot in her hand, she filled the cups and stepped back from the table.

An *Oberst*, the major's commanding officer,

joined the men for breakfast. Seidel was his surname. The Germans had taken over her father's office, including her *verboten*—forbidden—wireless, but she listened as Oberst Seidel told the soldiers of news from Germany, of the victories they'd had in Italy and the nearby islands. He paid no attention to her as he spoke. Either the major had told him she couldn't speak German or he thought her ignorant.

Fear clenched her stomach again. The men before her really believed they would take over the rest of Europe and then conquer the world. What if the Germans never left? What if this was the rest of her life—serving food to her enemy while she worried about her brother's life?

A few weeks ago, she'd heard a news broadcaster read a speech from Winston Churchill to the people of the United States. "If we are together nothing is impossible," he said. "If we are divided, all will fail."

What was the rest of the world doing right now? She prayed Great Britain and the United States remained strong. Churchill was right. They—the British and the Americans and the Free French—must battle this evil together to be victorious. They could not fail.

Evil would oppose all that was good, she supposed, until the very end of their world, but in the end, she believed with all her heart, good would ultimately win.

She began refilling a cup of coffee for Oberst Seidel.

"We are bringing another convoy from Berlin. The train will arrive in Saint-Lô on Friday." He looked up at her, switching easily to French. "Thank you for your hospitality."

She acknowledged him with a nod, and she felt the stares of all the men on her.

"After breakfast, I must see you in my office," he said.

Questions collided within her as she poured the coffee and she swayed back on her heels, the tiny ripples of coffee splashing against the edge of his cup.

Why did he want to see her?

"*Fräulein*—I believe that is enough," he said. "Fräulein?"

He tapped on her hand, and she jerked back the pot, spilling brown drops on the white tablecloth. Did he want to question her about the incident in the wine cellar? Or did he know something about Michel . . . or Adeline?

If he asked about Michel, she would have to smile politely and feign ignorance. She must convince him that she knew nothing. That she was slow in the mind even. No matter what happened, she mustn't draw attention to herself by acting nervous or scared. It was only by becoming as invisible as possible that she and Adeline—and Michel—would survive.

After she cleared breakfast—and cleaned the coffee stains—Gisèle met Oberst Seidel and two other officers in Papa's crowded office. The wireless was still near the window, but they'd moved his almanacs and maps, replacing them with neat stacks of manila folders and a lone copy of *Mein Kampf*.

From behind the desk, the *Oberst* motioned for her to take a chair as if he were the king of this castle and she his subject. Major von Kluge and another officer stood by the desk, and when the door opened, a third officer joined them—Hauptmann Milch. Even though she didn't acknowledge him, there was comfort in his presence. Still, she prayed he wouldn't tell the others that she knew how to speak German.

Oberst Seidel glanced over her shoulder at the dining hall beyond as he spoke to her in French. "This building is much too large for just you and a housekeeper, no?"

"I don't think of it as a building, Monsieur. It is my home."

He placed his monocle on top of a manila folder. "We have outgrown our headquarters building in Saint-Lô. From now on, we will be using the château."

A protest formed on her lips, but she swallowed her retort. Like Lucien, she was trapped in this web.

If Lisette helped her care for Adeline, hidden

away from these men, perhaps the Germans would forget about the child. But how would she continue to care for Michel with German soldiers living and working above the tunnels?

The officer's attention turned to the papers on his desk, and as he skimmed them, she thought of her father sitting in that chair, smoking a cigar as he read one of his newspapers. The images of the Nazis were replacing what she remembered of her father.

How would she be able to erase these memories?

She wanted to cling to the good memories of her home, to the days when she was a child and her father twirled her around the main hall as they listened to jazz music on the gramophone, to the laughter of her mother before her death, the afternoon they tried—and failed—to outrun a rainstorm on their bike ride back from Agneaux. In their drenched clothes, their hair clinging to their faces, she and Mother couldn't stop laughing. She wished the laughter never had to end.

Oberst Seidel opened another folder.

She could almost hear the tinkling of glass as her family and friends celebrated her graduation from the university more than two years ago. They had danced under a tent outside and talked of war, though no one believed that Germany would ever defeat France.

At one time, she'd dreamed of going to the

United States after Paris, visiting places like New York City and Los Angeles. When the war was over, she would run away from this château and all the bad memories that were replacing the sweet ones. She would preserve all that was good here in her heart and try to forget all that had been stolen from her.

"Fräulein." Oberst Seidel glanced up and studied her face. "Pardon me, mademoiselle—"

"Madame," she said, correcting him.

"Madame," he repeated as if he were willing to accommodate her in the smallest of ways but didn't seem to put much faith in calling her by the married title of a Frenchwoman. "While I appreciate your service for us, you cannot lie to one of my men. Ever."

She nodded her head.

"And you will not lie to me." He tapped the desk. "People who lie to me are sent away. And they never return."

She looked him directly in the eye. "I understand."

His demeanor was a frigid calm, his gray hair icing the coldness in his voice. Unlike the *Hauptmann*, Oberst Seidel seemed the kind of person who would stand by and watch unaffected while his men murdered Frenchmen tied up in the forest.

Oberst Seidel looked down at the papers on the desk again and then back up at her, continuing to speak to her in French. "I am concerned about some of the facts you have relayed to Major von Kluge."

She tried to recall the details that she'd contrived when she met him in the courtyard. "I will answer any questions you have."

"We have been searching for your brother." He riffled through the papers. "What is his name?"

"Michel."

He looked back up at her. "Ah, yes, Michel. Do you know where we can locate him?"

She balled up her fingers so the men around her wouldn't see them trembling. She wasn't as strong as Michel, but she had to pretend in order to protect all of them. "Why are you searching for my brother?"

"We have pressing business we must discuss with him." He laced his fingers together on the desk, leaning forward. "We fear he is in danger."

The gunshots in the forest seemed to deafen her ears. As if these men would protect him. "Last I knew he was in England with my mother's family."

"Where in England?"

"Kennington." Now she allowed the anxiety to flood her face. "I do not know if he is still there, but when you find him, I would like to speak with him as well."

He sat back a few inches and studied her face again, trying to unnerve her. But she didn't falter.

Instead she stared back into the emptiness of his pale green eyes.

"Did you and your brother part on bad terms?" he asked.

She contemplated her answer. "I love my brother, sir, but we did not always agree."

"What was your source of disagreement?" he asked slowly, as if they were chatting by the fireside, sipping afternoon tea.

She tried to mirror his placidity. If he didn't want to rush his words, neither would she. And she needed time to think. The man in front of her seemed to admire strength, and yet if she appeared too strong, he might crush her instead. If she said the disagreement between her and Michel was political, the *Oberst* would think she was pandering to him. "Neither my father nor I wanted him to join the army."

"And he joined anyway?"

She nodded.

"Why didn't you want him to join?"

"I—I was afraid he would be killed."

The *Oberst* pointed at the man standing beside him. "Major von Kluge says that you are married."

"I—"

He didn't let her finish. "Yet my men have found no record of your marriage."

She put her hands behind her back. "There should be a certificate in Saint-Lô."

He reached for a pen. "What is your husband's name?"

Her heart clutched. The name should have been ready on her lips and yet her mind was a blank.

"His name, madame," he repeated.

Then she remembered the boy who had intrigued her in town, the one who she hoped had left Saint-Lô long ago. "Jean-Marc," she blurted. "Jean-Marc Rausch."

The captain's eyes narrowed. "Rausch?"

"Yes, monsieur."

"Good." He tapped the pen on the desk. "I don't have time to spare one of my men to search for your marriage certificate in Saint-Lô, but I assume you have a copy."

"I'm not cer—"

He had no patience for a protest. "Where was your child born?"

"Here," she said. "In the house."

"Then you must have a certificate for her birth as well."

"Of course."

"Excellent!" He put the pen into the top drawer of the desk. "Please retrieve them for me."

She hesitated. "I will have to search for both certificates."

"I'm certain they are not far away," he said. "I will need them by morning."

CHAPTER 34

Isabelle's left eye twitched as she glanced between Riley and me, the door behind her pressed against her back. "I'm afraid Grand-mère can't talk right now."

"You must be the young lady I spoke to on the phone," Riley said.

She smiled at him.

Riley checked his watch. "Perhaps we can visit later today."

"I don't think—"

I stopped her. "I don't need to be here for the interview."

Neither of them protested as I stepped back. Whatever happened in the past must have angered or scarred Madame Calvez for life.

But before I walked away a shaky voice spoke from behind the door. "Let them in, Isabelle."

Riley glanced over at me, and I shrugged. Isabelle slowly opened the door, and Riley followed me inside.

In the living room was a woman crouched over a walker, scooting across a hardwood floor. Her short, white hair was curled neatly and she wore a tailored suit with hose and sturdy shoes.

Riley stepped around Isabelle. "You are Madame Calvez?"

Lifting her head, she flashed a tentative smile. "You must be Riley Holtz."

Riley moved quickly across the floor and kissed both of her cheeks like a seasoned Frenchman.

Then she motioned to me, squinting into the light. "Come closer, child. Age has stolen away my vision."

"I'm Chloe Sauver. The granddaughter of Gisèle Duchant Sauver."

As I walked toward her, she examined my face. "You look like your grandmother."

I kissed both of her cheeks, and then she turned away from me.

Isabelle put her arm around her great-grandmother's shoulders. "Monsieur Holtz wants to interview you about the war."

She nodded.

Riley glanced around the small room, most of the surfaces covered with used cups and dishes. Then he glanced out the window. "Why don't we talk outside?"

He opened the sliding door, and then he lifted Madame Calvez's walker so she could step onto the patio. Riley reached back to grab the backpack he'd left inside.

"It will only take me a few minutes to set up my gear." His eyes met mine. "Will you help me?"

So I stepped out onto the patio, Isabelle behind me. Madame Calvez sat beside a glass table, her walker hidden behind Riley's lawn chair and the bomber jacket he'd slung over the back. A small jungle of potted plants were crowded together on the patio and a sparrow dipped in a bath outside the kitchen window, seemingly undaunted by the visitors in its backyard.

I clipped a microphone on the lapel of Madame Calvez's jacket as he set up his camera on a tripod, chatting with the older woman about her plants. Isabelle brought me a stool, and I sat beside her, close to the sliding glass.

Riley pulled a Moleskine journal from his pack. He opened the journal beside him, and I saw a list of questions that he'd prepared.

Madame Calvez's finger, slightly crooked, pointed at the chair. "Where did you get your coat?"

"It was my grandfather's. He was a pilot during the war."

"From America?"

He nodded.

"The Allied airmen were very brave," Madame Calvez said. "Is he still alive?"

Riley shook his head. "He passed away three years ago, but he told me a few of his stories. Madame Calvez, may I ask—"

She stopped him. "You can ask me anything you want, but I can't guarantee you an answer."

He glanced back down at his notes. "When did you live at the Château d'Epines?"

She fidgeted with her fingers for a moment, and

when she spoke again, her voice sounded a bit sad. "I never technically lived there," she said. "Until the end of the war, I kept an apartment in Saint-Lô."

"Did you work at the château?" he asked.

"I was a secretary to the Germans in Saint-Lô, and when they moved their headquarters to the château, I helped at the house."

I leaned forward on the stool, intrigued about what she would say. Perhaps she could give all of us a glimpse into my grandmother's years during the occupation.

"So that would have been in 1942?" Riley asked.

"That's right. Two years before the Allies landed on the beaches. We had no idea, of course, that the end was near. We thought the Germans would be here forever."

"Did you know many of the German officers?"

"Of course." Madame Calvez looked over Riley's shoulder, at the bird playing in the water. "They were my employers."

"Did you have Jewish friends in Saint-Lô?"

"I had acquaintances but no friends. My father had been a farmer on the other side of France, and he didn't like the Jewish people. It wasn't until—" The strength in her voice slipped. "I didn't have any Jewish friends until after the war."

When he glanced over at me, I scooted toward Madame Calvez. "Can I get you something to drink?"

She shook her head, but I still stood up. Isabelle helped me pour two glasses of lemonade and deliver them back outside.

Riley took a long sip before continuing. It seemed as if he was trying to proceed with care, trying to understand her story without pushing too hard. "I read that some Jewish men served in the Wehrmacht," he said.

His words sounded odd to my ears. The Jews were the victims in this war. Why would they be in the German army?

Her gaze wandered to a bird diving his head under the water of the birdbath. "Some were full Jews, but mostly it was *Mischlinge* who served."

He jotted a note in his Moleskine before he continued. "What is a *Mischling*?"

"A partial Jew."

"My grandfather said he would never forget one man he met when he came to Saint-Lô—a Jewish captain named Josef who helped him get his identity card so members of the resistance could smuggle him through France."

Her hands shook as she reached for the lemonade. Isabelle helped her sip it. "So many officers came through here during the occupation," she finally said. "I can't remember all of them."

"Which officers do you remember?" he asked.

Her eyes glazed for a moment and she tugged on the sleeves of her jacket. "None worth talking about."

"I understand if it is too difficult."

Her lip quivered. "I don't believe you do . . ."

I glanced at him to see if she'd insulted him, but he seemed completely engaged. Instead of probing her for his agenda, he was probing her for her story, allowing her to lead him as well.

"You are right," he said, and I was touched by the kindness in his voice. "There is no way that I could understand."

She brushed her wrinkled fingers over the ridges on the glass table. "Some of the soldiers in Saint-Lô were prisoners themselves. They didn't want to be in the army—like most of the Jews."

Riley glanced down at his journal. "What happened to the *Mischlinge* who weren't in the army?"

"They were sent to the concentration camps." Sorrow locked her gaze and for a moment, it seemed she had gone to another time and place. Watching her, I wondered where she had gone. "So many people were hurt during this war. So many of us did things we would never have imagined we'd do—" Her eyes filled with sadness. "You cannot understand."

He agreed. "I cannot."

"It was a terrible, terrible time." She turned toward me. "What did Gisèle tell you?"

"She said very little about the war."

Madame Calvez folded her wrinkled hands together. "Gisèle never forgave me, but she didn't know what happened during the occupation—not the whole story."

Riley didn't move, not an inch, even though I knew he must have been dying to hear the whole story. "Would you like to tell me what happened?"

Isabelle's chair squeaked, and Madame Calvez's eyes flew to meet her great-granddaughter's. When she turned back to Riley, it seemed she was no longer dreaming about the past. "I only remember small bits and pieces now. The rest has faded away."

Riley leaned forward, trying to engage her again. "I want to tell people what you remember of your story, so we don't forget."

"If only Gisèle were here, she would tell you much better stories than I could. And she would probably remember your soldier."

I didn't have the heart to tell her that Gisèle had forgotten most of her stories.

"My grandmother mentioned the name of a child she was searching for," I said, glancing over at Riley before I looked back at Madame Calvez. "Did you know a girl called Adeline?"

Madame Calvez's eyes turned glossy again and it almost seemed as though she looked right through me. "I am sorry—I'm getting tired."

I wanted to ask her again, but Riley's glance silenced me.

"Forgive us," he said as he turned off his camera. "We've kept you too long."

Chapter 35

Gisèle slammed the door shut and collapsed on the floor of her bedroom. Pulling her knees to her chest, she struggled to breathe.

For two years, she and Émilie had maintained the château and fed the men in the tunnels without drawing attention from the Germans. Now their enemy had turned their cruel spotlight on her, and they wouldn't stop searching, she was certain, until they found out the truth about her and Adeline. People didn't lose their marriage and birth certifi-cates unless they were running—or perhaps their house burned down.

She could still say she'd misplaced it, but the *Oberst* wouldn't stop there. He would ask for the name of her doctor.

There was a whole war to be fought, continents to be conquered, and these men were fixated on the birthdate of one child and the marriage of her parents.

She hated living in a world like this—where the officials were more concerned about controlling people than caring for them—but there was no escaping this nightmare. Even if she took Adeline back down into the tunnel, Michel wouldn't let the child stay. It would ruin all he and his men were doing to resist the enemy.

She paced the floor in front of her bed.

How was she supposed to obtain a marriage and birth certificate by morning? The *Oberst* had made it clear what he would do if he caught her in a lie. Perhaps she could stall at finding them. Or perhaps he would be distracted by the convoy, at least until Friday.

But then again, if something happened to that convoy, he might take it out on the rest of them anyway.

She couldn't stay and let these men harm Adeline. If Sister Beatrice would let them spend the night at the orphanage, she could figure out transportation to Lyon tomorrow. The last time they spoke, Philippe had hinted again at marrying her. Perhaps she should tell him the truth— Adeline had lost her parents in the war. If they married, Philippe would protect Adeline.

Her gaze roamed over the grassy hill and trees behind the house. The Germans didn't know the countryside like she did. She was a Frenchwoman with a French daughter. Even if she didn't have papers for Adeline, she could carefully find her way among her people.

Autumn air chilled the room when she opened the window. It would be hard traveling with Adeline in the darkness, with the night patrols guarding the river and valley and the perimeter of the town. Adeline's cries would alert the patrols for ten miles around them.

Perhaps Émilie could give Adeline something to help her sleep.

They would have to leave tonight or it would be too late to run.

CHAPTER 36

"You weren't supposed to ask questions," Riley chided as we walked past a row of brick shops in Saint-Lô. Instead of returning along the river path, we'd followed Isabelle's directions into town to get some coffee and a late lunch.

"I'm sorry, I . . ." But I had no real excuse except that I wanted to know the truth.

Riley stuck his hands into his pockets as we climbed a hill. "Who is Adeline?"

"I believe she's my aunt, but Madame Calvez seems to be hiding the truth."

"People usually hide what they're ashamed of."

His words resonated with me. We were talking about Madame Calvez, and yet as he spoke about shame, I realized that I was hiding too—at a château in France instead of facing the media questions and Austin back home.

I had thought Austin loved me for who I was, not for what I brought to his campaign. I'd put him up on a pedestal in my heart, and when he fell, he hurt my heart along with my pride. Now I was hiding because I was ashamed of what my fiancé had done. And I was embarrassed that I'd been blind to his wandering.

Riley waved his hand in front of my face. "You with me?"

"Sorry." I blinked. "I was back in Richmond for a second."

"Better company there?"

I shook my head. I had to stop thinking about Austin and focus on the person with me.

"Not at all." I tugged my sunhat down on my forehead. Without the tree covering, the sun scorched my skin. "What were you saying?"

"That people who hide a portion of their story are usually either ashamed or they're protecting someone else. It takes a little time, but if I listen well and try not to judge them for what they've done, people will usually tell me the truth."

"Who do you think Madame Calvez is protecting?"

"I don't know."

Saint-Lô had been rebuilt after the war, but across the street were the remains of a medieval wall that had fortified the hillside in the center of town. We strolled up the steep sidewalk, and the bombed façade of a cathedral and a maze of winding slate streets overlooked the shops.

Riley ordered two *café au laits* at a small café, and as I waited, I imagined my grandparents here, meeting over coffee and cream. But Riley was right. The Allied pilots and soldiers—men like Riley's grandfather—destroyed almost everything as they fought to liberate this town.

Perhaps Mémé got the location wrong. Perhaps they met in another town.

I sipped my creamy *café* as we descended the hill and began our walk toward Agneaux. What would it have been like to live in one of the apartments over the shops during the occupation, German soldiers patrolling the streets below? The people in this town must have been scared to leave their homes, especially those who were Jews.

Did the Jewish people here know there were Jews fighting in the German military? Until Riley and Madame Calvez discussed it today, I hadn't known about it, and I was still trying to sort out the schism in my mind.

"Do you know how many Jews fought in the Wehrmacht?" I asked.

"Some put the number at a hundred thousand."

"But Hitler was trying to kill the Jews—"

He glanced down at the Vire as we crossed the bridge over it. "It's ironic, isn't it? On one hand, he was exterminating the Jewish people, and on the other, he was using them in his army. Sometimes he even 'Aryanized' them."

"How exactly does one Aryanize someone?"

"Hitler declared his Jewish soldiers had German

blood, and magically, by the power of Hitler, they had new genes."

"He thought he was God."

Riley nodded. "And the Nazi leaders encouraged his delusion. He was power hungry, but he was also pragmatic. The army needed more soldiers, and if the Jewish men were willing to fight for him, Hitler and his top men were often willing to look the other way. The families of these soldiers were a different story . . ."

We waited at a stoplight before crossing the street with a handful of pedestrians, their arms filled with fresh flowers and bread. "It's heartbreaking."

"Hitler had the power to give life or take it, or, in his eyes, change someone's genes. There is a reason why so many people thought he was a lunatic. Those who confronted him, though, lost their lives."

I took another sip of the *café*. "What I don't understand is after all the terrible things Hitler did to oppress the Jewish people, how a Jewish man could serve under him?"

"An excellent question, and that's exactly what I'm hoping to find out for this documentary."

"I thought you were profiling German soldiers."

"German soldiers with Jewish backgrounds," he said slowly.

So he had been hiding something from me.

"Some of them kept their Jewish roots a secret for the rest of their lives," he continued.

I glanced over at him. "Why didn't you tell me you were going to profile the Jewish soldiers?"

"I didn't want it to taint your answers."

We walked another block before I spoke again. "Are you doing this story because of the man who helped your grandfather?"

"Partially," he said. "My grandfather hated all the Germans until he met Josef and realized that not all of them were evil."

"What was Josef's surname?"

Riley shook his head. "My grandfather never knew."

Chapter 37

Gisèle gathered a small bundle of warm clothes and stuffed them into a satchel. It would be hard to carry Adeline along with the clothing and some food, diapers, and a bottle, but she would do what she must. She'd already poured a little brandy in Adeline's bottle before putting the child to bed and then tucked a flask of it into the satchel. As long as she could keep Adeline quiet, they would be safe for the night.

Shadow meowed at Gisèle as she packed, and then he kneaded the bedcovers with his paws and settled back in again. In her absence, she hoped he would continue to frighten the Nazis. Or perhaps Lisette would take him home.

He would find plenty of food and water near the river, but it made her feel better to think of Lisette caring for him.

Lisette had left hours ago to return to her apartment, and Gisèle and Émilie spent a long evening cleaning up after the officers. Émilie knew something was wrong with her, but she couldn't tell her friend what she planned. When the Germans interrogated them, neither Émilie nor Lisette would have any knowledge of her departure.

When she had gone to the chapel earlier that evening with the food and a letter for Michel, she'd slipped down into the tunnel to find him one last time. The corridors were empty, and in that moment, her scrambled plans became clear. She and Adeline would sneak out to the *chapelle* and take the tunnel back to the beekeeper's cellar. Then they'd escape to the orphanage until she found transportation to Lyon.

But a war still waged inside her, as daunting as the war waging in their country.

How could she leave her brother without someone to help him on the outside? And if she didn't leave, how could she protect Adeline?

"People who lie to me are sent away."

She wanted to rescue Michel and Adeline and all those being hunted by the Nazis, but she wouldn't help anyone if the *Oberst* sent her away. And if Michel knew what was happening, he would insist she run far from here, to save herself and Adeline.

When she emerged from the *chapelle*, the guard watched her kneel in the cemetery, pressing one hand on the patch of weeds on her father's grave and the other on her mother's tombstone as she said good-bye. Her heart ached at the thought of leaving her brother and Émilie as well without telling them good-bye, but she had no choice.

Back in her bedroom, she dressed in black pants and a gray sweater to blend into the night. When her clock ticked past one in the morning, she picked up Adeline and carefully unlocked the door. With Adeline asleep in one of her arms and the satchel secured in her other hand, she snuck down the back staircase to the main floor.

In the dining hall, she stopped, listened for voices, but the night was quiet. She prayed the brandy would keep Adeline silent. If something startled her, her cries would wake the entire house. Then she would have to fabricate yet another lie, that she was going to get warm milk or something else. The Germans would inquire about her attire and the satchel, but after what had happened in the cellar, she would never consider wearing her robe down to the kitchen at night.

She wasn't certain how to explain away her satchel.

The windows on the north side of the hall

looked out over the cliff—much too high for her and Adeline to jump—and there were no shrubs to hide behind along the windows that overlooked the courtyard.

She and Adeline would have to sneak out of the window in Papa's office, the one concealed by the hedge. They would wait until the night guard made his next round through the courtyard and then they'd run across to the *chapelle.*

The office door was closed in front of her, and as she neared the door, she heard a voice, low but stern, coming from the other side.

It was the *Oberst* speaking.

"The tracks were destroyed on this side of Caen," he said. "It will take an extra day to fix them."

Then she heard the voice of Major von Kluge. "We must stop these men. They will ruin everything."

She froze beside the door. Was that why the tunnel had been empty tonight? She prayed the Nazis didn't know who was thwarting their plans.

"Our men spotted a half-dozen men running into the woods."

"Did they shoot them?" the major asked.

"Only one," he replied. "But he had no papers to identify him."

She shivered. Michel would never tell her where he was going, but she knew he wouldn't shy away from danger—like blowing up railroad tracks or a bridge so the enemy's train couldn't pass.

"You have his body?" the major asked.

She didn't know if the *Oberst* nodded in response or shook his head. What would they do with the body?

"They cannot stop our convoy on Wednesday," the *Oberst* said. "We need the munitions in Cherbourg."

"That's what I told my men. We don't have enough men to watch every inch of the tracks, but we have ten soldiers guarding each car. The rebels don't have the manpower to fight all of them."

"I wouldn't be so certain," the *Oberst* said. "We don't know how many men they have."

Adeline began to squirm and Gisèle quickly backed away from the door before racing back up the steps.

Her hands trembling, she opened the door and placed Adeline on her bed. Then she slumped against the bedpost. What was she going to do now?

Even if the *Oberst* was distracted by the delay of their convoy, she doubted he'd forget her certificates.

The blackout curtains over her windows extinguished the stars, but she unhooked one of them and looked outside. The crescent shape of the moon seemed to rock in the sky and below it was a narrow strip of rocky land between the back of the house and the cliff that sank into the valley.

Could she throw her satchel out the window and escape? If it was just her, she might have been able to shimmy down a strand of sheets, but even with the brandy, Adeline would never stay quiet. And if the sheets tore . . .

She should run away while she had the opportunity, before the *Oberst* discovered she didn't have the papers. But she couldn't leave Adeline with these men. André and Nadine had to leave their daughter in order to save Adeline's life, but if Gisèle left her now, it would only be to save herself.

Closing her eyes, she leaned back against the windowsill and begged God for help. With so much evil in their midst, it seemed as if God was far away, but she couldn't give up hope that His spirit lingered. He had been in the cellar with her, and she was certain that He was here in her room. She may not have a sword to fight the dragon like Saint Michel, but she could battle with prayer.

Something shuffled outside her door, and her heart pounded again. Had she locked it on her return? She didn't move for fear someone outside was listening for her steps. If the door was unlocked, if an officer opened it, he would find her dressed, a satchel beside her.

But why would one of the men be opening her door at this hour? Perhaps Viktor Braun—the man from the cellar—was coming to finish what he'd started.

She eyed the knob in the moonlight and then carefully reached into her satchel and pulled out her father's knife.

There was a rustling sound outside the door and her gaze dropped to the floor. In the dim light, she saw a brown folder. Slowly she tiptoed across the hardwood and picked it up. Then she hid her satchel in the armoire and turned on the lamp beside her bed, not caring one whit if the Allied planes saw it.

She opened the folder, and her mouth dropped when she saw the green certificate in her hand.

Certified Copy of an Entry of Marriage
Marriage Solemnized at Chapelle d'Agneaux
May 7, 1940
Jean-Marc Rausch, 25
Gisèle Duchant, 22

She shivered. The date of their marriage was weeks before her fictitious husband disappeared. Below the marriage certificate was a pink one.

Certification for Birth
Château d'Epines, February 25, 1941
Adeline, Girl
Daughter of Jean-Marc Rausch
and Gisèle Duchant Rausch

The name of the registrar was a scrawl.

Her hands clutching the certificates, she stared at the crack under the door. The only people who knew about her need of papers were the men in her father's office.

Had Hauptmann Milch rescued her again? If so, where had he gotten the certificates?

It didn't matter, she supposed. As she clutched the papers to her chest, she blessed him or whoever had come to her rescue. She would stay at the château and continue to pray that the Lord would blind the Germans' eyes.

Gently she brushed her hands over the baby's soft hair.

Adeline Duchant Rausch.

The name fit her beautifully. With these papers, perhaps neither of them would have to run away. The Germans would never have to know the truth, and through her deception—*their* deception—they would save Adeline's life and perhaps the lives of many more.

CHAPTER 38

Riley and I found a quiet park in Agneaux and settled under the shade of a tree to eat—two baguette sandwiches and orange sodas from the bakery where he'd found the croissants. On the other side of the fence were three cows, their skin mottled black and pink, grazing in a pasture beside the park.

Riley handed me a sandwich.

"Why don't you tell me your story?" I asked.

"It's messy."

I smiled. "So is mine."

Whatever his story, there seemed to be few similarities between the man beside me and the stereotype of the man I'd seen in the pictures online. I'd asked him to see past the stereotype of a politician's wife. Perhaps I needed to see past the stereotype I had of him as well.

I leaned back against the jagged bark of the tree. "Where does the life of Riley Holtz begin?"

"I grew up outside Detroit," he said as he unwrapped his sandwich. "My dad and grand-father both worked in an auto plant, and by the time I was in middle school, I'd already decided I didn't want to be like them."

He took a bite of his sandwich before continuing. "I had a little success with acting while I was in high school, and I'd convinced myself that I was going to be the next Brad Pitt, so the summer before my senior year, I packed my car and drove to New York."

I eyed him for a moment. He certainly looked like he could be a movie lead and had the confidence that went along with it, but as he lay on the dry grass, relaxed, I couldn't imagine him under the lights of Hollywood.

I bit into my baguette sandwich, bulging with fresh mozzarella, tangy basil, and sweet tomatoes. I could have eaten this sandwich every day and been happy. "What did your family say?"

"They were devastated, but at the time I didn't care. I was thrilled to be leaving town. A long time passed before I looked back, and my regrets were too many to count."

I smoothed my paper wrapping on the grass and set the rest of my sandwich on it. For some reason, I'd expected him to downplay the bad in his life and tell me how incredible he was. It was refreshing to hear the authenticity in his story.

"New York wasn't quite as enamored with my acting abilities as my high school instructor. After a few weeks there, I sold my car to pay for rent and hopped on the treadmill of auditions—I kept running faster and faster but never seemed to get anywhere. When I wasn't auditioning, I was waiting tables to pay for food and a crummy apartment on the Lower East Side.

"It took a full year before I landed a role in a small film. It's not a role I'm proud of now, but I fooled myself into thinking I was a celebrity and began partying like one."

His smile dimmed.

"After that film, I had a few small gigs on the stage. It was enough to keep me pressing on. I was certain the powers-that-be would soon discover I was a star in need of a place to shine.

"The city is filled with lapdogs who lick the crumbs off the floor of the entertainment industry and then wag their tail as they wait for more. I was surviving on the rumors I'd heard about celebrities who'd been discovered off Broadway, but by the time I was twenty-four, I was desperate as well. I didn't realize it then, but I'd begun to hate myself for who I was becoming."

I sipped my orange drink, my legs crisscrossed in front of me. I couldn't imagine this man across from me being desperate enough to eat crumbs from anyone. He was confident like Austin, and yet he was authentic as well about his weaknesses. Austin had always been more focused on my weaknesses than on his.

Riley leaned back on his elbows, his legs outstretched. "At the same time my life seemed to be falling apart, I was hired to work as a host on a documentary. I thought it was my ticket to stardom, but I had no idea what was about to happen."

I leaned forward, curious. "What sort of documentary was it?"

His familiar gaze returned alongside his grin. "A documentary that was supposed to prove once and for all that the resurrection of Jesus Christ was a sham."

I leaned back against the tree again, wringing my hands together. I don't know why I felt so uncomfortable talking about the life of Jesus. I believed Jesus was the Son of God. I believed in the resurrection. I'd attended church every Sunday beside Austin for the past year, but church had become part of the show—like his concern for his constituents, like having a wife.

In essence, Austin Vale worshipped himself, and somehow—like Olivia and the others—I had changed my allegiance to worship alongside him.

I knew the pat answers on religion that Olivia had concocted for Austin and me. Answers that would appeal to those constituents who believed in God but wouldn't scare those who didn't believe.

But Riley, I feared, would see past my script. He was well acquainted with acting, and he could tell pretty quickly that I was a poor actress. If Riley asked me a genuine question, I might fumble.

Instead I would keep the spotlight on him. "Did you go to church when you were a kid?"

He nodded. "But our church preached more about judgment than mercy. My parents followed all the rules set out by our church, and I loathed the anger and perfectionism that masked itself as righteousness."

"So you turned away from your faith?"

"I fled from it," he said. "When I was in New York, I discovered I could pretend to be anyone I wanted, and the last person I wanted to be was the kid who grew up in church or the man who still had questions about his faith. Even after all those years away from home, a quiet voice still beckoned to me. For a long time, I plugged up my ears and refused to listen to its call."

I leaned forward, intrigued now by his story. "What was this voice saying?"

" 'Return to me.' " He glanced up at the clear sky. "I was desperately seeking peace, but I had no idea where to find it. I should have gotten on my knees and begged for His help right then, but I wasn't ready."

I took another long sip of my Orangina and glanced back at the cows. They had wandered far away from us, close to the playground at the other end of the park.

I couldn't decide if this guy before me was real, nor did I trust myself to make this decision. The pictures online of him and the multitude of women were proof that he'd had a wild side. I'd seen no pictures that spoke to his reform.

Was he weaving together a tale like Austin had done at our "chance" meeting in the coffee shop? But there was no reason for Riley to impress me.

I could be intrigued by his story, though, without trusting him. It wasn't like with Austin—my heart was too scrambled now to even consider romance.

"What happened next?" I asked.

"While I was filming the documentary, my grandfather came to visit me in New York. I had always admired him and his war stories, and as we talked about faith, he challenged me not to rely on what my parents or friends said about Jesus. He challenged me to find out what I thought about Jesus on my own.

"He also said something I'll never forget—he said we never know what we truly believe until we are standing in a trench, surrounded by the enemy. My trench came two weeks later. After spending the little money I had on alcohol and painkillers, I didn't have enough to make rent and was evicted from a pit they called an apartment during a snowstorm. I had no choice but to spend the night in a homeless shelter, and the next morning, I woke up shaking from a nasty cocktail of freezing temps and withdrawal.

"I'd been offered a job in a movie I knew I'd regret, and in that shelter, I realized I had to choose what I believed in—whether I would sacrifice everything for this obsession of mine or if I would choose to do what seemed right in my heart. I got down on my knees on that cement floor and asked God to reveal Himself. Thankfully, He did."

"And the documentary?"

The familiar smile returned. "The producer never finished it. He was determined to find solid evidence that the stories of Jesus were fiction, but after three years of working on it, he couldn't find the evidence he needed."

Two kids climbed up the monkey bars behind Riley and began swinging. "Did you return to acting?" I asked.

"No. I caught the bug for truth and started work behind the scenes on another documentary. A couple more years passed, and I started producing them on my own."

"So you converted?" I blurted before I realized it sounded like I was accusing him of failure. "I'm sorry—"

"God revealed Himself to me, just as I asked." He tapped on his tattoo. "It was the most painful experience of my life, but the healing started in the midst of the pain."

He tossed his ball of sandwich paper into a nearby trash can.

"My story is dull compared to yours," I said.

"I skipped over the dull parts."

I heard someone laugh, and when I turned, I saw a dozen kids lined up behind the low hedge, ready to invade the park. Riley hopped up and reached for my hand. His demeanor seemed to shift again. "We should probably let them play."

"I don't think they'll kick us out," I quipped. "We're bigger than they are."

He didn't acknowledge my joke, pointing instead to another gate at the back side of the park. "Why don't we go out that way?"

For a moment he reminded me of Sulley, the monster in *Monsters Inc.* who had been terrified of little Boo. "You're not scared of kids, are you?"

His smile was forced. "I'm scared of plenty of things."

I didn't ask, but after all he had been through, I was curious to know what could possibly frighten this man.

I gathered up my sandwich and he reached for my hand, urging me toward the door. I followed him out the gate and it wasn't until he shut it that I let go of his hand.

Chapter 39

The clock ticked mercilessly behind her father's desk as Oberst Seidel donned his monocle. Gisèle held her breath as he examined the certificates, awaiting her fate. If he didn't believe her . . .

There was nothing she could do if he didn't believe her.

He studied both of the papers closely. Then he slid them across the desk to Hauptmann Milch.

Hauptmann Milch lifted both papers and held them up to the light, scrutinizing them even longer than his commander had done. "They are in good order," he finally said.

She bit her lip to keep all her breath from escaping at once.

Oberst Seidel handed the papers back to her. "Do you have a death certificate for your husband?"

"I am not certain he is dead."

He set his eyepiece on the desk. "You have heard of the Compulsory Work Service."

"Yes, sir."

"Instead of sending you away, you and your housekeeper will work for us here along with that woman who was a secretary at our headquarters office."

"Lise—" She stopped herself. "Mademoiselle Calvez."

"Yes, Mademoiselle Calvez. She will join you."

Gisèle clutched the certificates to her chest. She would hide them in her room in case anyone else questioned her about Adeline. Until the Batiers returned, she could prove Adeline was hers.

The *Oberst* dismissed Hauptmann Milch and another officer until it was just her, standing before him alone. He tapped his pen on the desk. "The major also told me that he had one other concern. When he was examining the house, he heard something unusual down in the wine cellar."

"I went down there with him," Gisèle said. "He heard my cat."

"He mentioned the cat to me, but he was certain he heard voices as well."

"I don't know, monsieur. Parts of this house are a thousand years old. You and your men may not believe in ghosts, but some of our past residents have refused to leave. They play pranks sometimes on our guests."

"I have seen many things in my life, Madame

Rausch, but you are correct—I don't believe in ghosts."

"And I don't believe that cats can talk, so I'm not sure what to say to Major von Kluge."

"I believe we will have to consider it a misunderstanding." He glanced back at the door again. "Where is your daughter?"

"Mademoiselle Calvez is caring for her."

His gaze wandered over to the window with the broken lock. "I have a wife and three children back in Cologne. My oldest daughter gave birth to our grandson almost two years ago—he would be about your daughter's age."

Conflicting emotions flooded through her. Even though she knew this man would take her life if she was caught in her lies, confusion and something akin to compassion warred in her. It was more like sadness, not for him as much as for all the children and innocent people who were losing in this war. For the little French girl who might never know her parents and for the German grandson of this *Oberst*, the officer who would decide her fate.

Oberst Seidel dismissed her, and as she passed back through the dining hall, she saw Hauptmann Milch sitting at the table alone, pecking with two fingers on the Hermès typewriter. He was quite handsome, with his short dark hair and brown eyes, now intent on his reading. His face was clean-shaven like the rest of the men, and his

German uniform would have inspired fear in most people in France, but if one looked close enough, there was kindness etched beneath his Nazi façade.

Even as she stepped up beside him, he didn't look up. She fixed a curtain before leaning down to whisper. "Thank you."

His glance darted back toward the office and then his gaze dropped back to the typewriter. "I have done nothing," he replied, the prickliness in his voice like the thorns that protected the valley trees.

She pressed on through the main hall and down into the kitchen. Émilie was frying ham while Adeline played with blocks in her playpen. Beside her, Lisette was scooping dried acorn grounds into a pot to boil for what they called coffee—the Germans had secured crates of food but they hadn't been able to plunder any coffee beans.

She understood why the *Hauptmann* couldn't acknowledge her, but still it hurt. Perhaps, like a guardian angel, he would have to remain her benefactor in secret.

It might be difficult, but she would pretend as well that he was invisible.

Instead of taking her picnic basket to the *chapelle*, Gisèle brought a knapsack stuffed with the Germans' food, in case Michel had returned. Most of the officers were out patrolling Saint-Lô and the valley below this evening, but if one happened to stop her, she'd say she was continuing to feed the hungry in Agneaux. They could argue with her charity, as the *Oberst* had questioned her about the ghosts, but she was sticking to her original story.

No one was praying when she opened the door, but four candles continued to burn, the incense a sweet reminder of the way the Spirit moves, wafting into crevices and into the hearts of those willing to listen.

God used ordinary, often unexpected people throughout the Old Testament to rescue others—Esther and Moses and Jael, the woman who drove the tent peg through her enemy's head. Even though God could use anyone, Gisèle had never expected to find an advocate among the Germans.

Kneeling at a pew, she thanked God for using a Nazi soldier to save her life and the life of Adeline.

When she finished her prayers, she locked the entrance to the *chapelle* so no visitors would surprise her. Then she swept the sanctuary, blew out the flickering candles, and gathered the dried flowers into a pile. The aroma from the incense lingered around her as she unlocked the gate to the sacristy.

It seemed so strange to think Michel and his men were below this floor even as the women of Agneaux prayed above them. Michel and the others could hide in the tunnel, but none of them could escape God's presence, above or below the ground. The Nazis couldn't escape either. They might not care now, but one day they would be required, good or bad, to account for all they had done. Just as she would have to account for what she had done.

She slid back into the closet and opened the panel. Before she put the basket inside, she gasped.

Someone was sitting on the ledge.

The man blocked the beam from her flashlight with his hands. "Put that away, Gigi."

She collapsed against the thick coat of robes, scared and yet relieved that he hadn't been the one killed in the convoy. "Don't scare me like that, Michel."

"I needed to speak with you."

Dark whiskers peppered his smooth face. He looked thinner than she had ever seen him, and she wondered how much he'd eaten while he was gone.

"You'd best speak fast," she said as she dumped the contents of her knapsack into the waiting basket. "We have eyes and ears everywhere these days."

"Your last letter said the *boches* had taken over the château."

"Don't call them that," Gisèle whispered.

"I'm not afraid of them."

"You should be." She nudged the basket toward

him. "Your men must be quiet when they are near the house."

"Sound echoes all over down there."

"Then you must find another place to hide—"

He shook his head. "This is a meeting place for people from all over La Manche."

She reached for his hand, clutching it in hers. "They will kill you if they find you."

"I am prepared to die, but you cannot." He thumbed her cheek. "You, Gigi, must live a long life and carry the name and legacy of the Duchant family forward."

She shook her head. She didn't want to speak about Michel's dying or the family legacy. She and Michel were both going to survive this war. Michel and Lisette were to marry, and perhaps she would marry one day as well. Their children and even their grandchildren would grow up to be the best of friends.

"Have you seen Lisette?" he asked.

She nodded. "The Nazis recruited her to work with me in the château."

"They haven't—" He stopped. "She is a beautiful woman."

I squeezed his hand. "A beautiful woman who has eyes only for you."

"If something happens to me—" He stumbled on his words. "Tell her that I loved her too."

"Nothing is going to happen to you," she said, trying to reassure him.

"We won't stop fighting, Gisèle, not until the Nazis are gone."

"The officers were talking of another convoy coming through here on Wednesday."

"They are trying to fortify all the Normandy beaches against an invasion."

She prayed the Allies would invade. Soon.

"You can no longer bring us food," he said.

"But you need it—"

"If the Germans find out about this tunnel, it will jeopardize everything."

She sighed. Now she was the one who was dangerous. "How will you get food?"

"The farmers are helping us."

"Michel, I—"

A soft thud pounded on the other side of the closet, and she dropped his hand. It sounded as if someone was hitting the wall with a pillow.

He hopped up. "You must go."

She reached into the small space and hugged her brother before he slipped down into the darkness.

Quickly she replaced the panel and stepped out into the sacristy. The pounding on the *chapelle* door grew louder, someone insistent about getting inside.

Her hands trembling, she locked the gate and then threw a handful of spent candles and two bouquets of decaying flowers into her knapsack. At the back of the nave, she unlocked the door and shined her flashlight into the faces of two men: Viktor Braun and Major von Kluge.

"What are you doing?" the major demanded.

"I was praying and then cleaning out the nave."

Suspicion flooded his gaze. "In the dark?"

"We have no electricity in here," she said as she held up her light. "Only candles and lanterns and flashlights."

The major stepped into the nave. "What took you so long to answer—"

"I didn't realize it was an urgent matter," she said, desperately trying to keep her voice calm. "The villagers often knock on the door at night, wanting to pray."

She started to step outside, but the major stopped her. "We will take a look around your chapel."

"Of course," she said as he shined his flashlight toward the altar. "You may pray as well if you'd like."

His eyes were filled with indignation, but she ignored it. They reminded her of the rock by the river, immovable and cold. The aroma of the incense lingered. God's Spirit was still here, present in the midst of the evil. She prayed the men would feel the fear that came from Him, the fear of doing wrong instead of that which was right.

She waited by the door as the men tromped up the aisle. Fähnrich Braun stared for a moment at the sculpture of Christ hanging on the wall. The

Jew who had been killed by the Jewish people. But even as He hung on the cross, Jesus showed His love for both the Jews and the Gentiles.

The Nazis passed under the picture of Saint Michel and the dragon, seemingly unfazed by the power of the archangel to defeat evil, and then stopped at the sacristy. The major shook the locked gate. "Why is this locked?"

"It's a supply room." She held up her key. "Would you like me to unlock it for you?"

"Right away."

She rushed forward. Any hesitation, she feared, would alert him to the fact that she was hiding something. Inside the sacristy, the major opened the closet, and she held her breath as he combed through the robes. Then he opened the drawers in the middle of the room, rummaging through each one before he turned back to her. "What is in your bag?"

She opened it and dumped the contents onto the small table. The spent candles rolled out across the polished wood, the old flowers piling on top of them. "I always clean up when I leave," she said with a shrug.

Fähnrich Braun searched through the used supplies and when he looked up at the senior officer, she saw disappointment in his eyes.

"Let's go back to the house," the major said.

They waited for her as she relocked the gate and then the main door.

Moonlight crept over the stained-glass windows, and sadness filled her heart as she followed them past the small cemetery into the house. She had fed the Germans, but she'd balanced her work by also feeding the men who resisted them.

But Michel was right—it was too dangerous for her to continue. Until the Nazis were gone, her work feeding Michel and his men was over. Instead she would pray for Michel while she cared for Adeline.

CHAPTER 40

I checked the headlines when I got back to my room and discovered that my breakup with Austin had blitzed the national news. The media seemed preoccupied with the fact that I'd gone missing . . . and that Austin's poll numbers were slipping.

FORMER SHOO-IN FOR GOVERNOR GETS BOOT FROM FIANCÉE.

FIANCÉE OF VIRGINIA'S VALE GOES AWOL.

AUSTIN VALE FREE-FALLING IN VIRGINIA POLLS.

It seemed the monument Austin had built for himself, brick by brick, was crashing down.

My flight back to Virginia had been scheduled for Sunday morning, the day after Riley left, but I wasn't ready to return to Richmond. I called the airline and changed my flight to the following week. Then I emailed the itinerary to my parents.

A few minutes later, my cell phone rang, and I answered my mom's call.

"I just got your new flight schedule," she said.

"That was fast."

"I thought you were coming home this weekend."

"I decided to linger in the peace."

She sighed. "Austin stopped by your dad's office yesterday. He's not going to let you go easily."

"That's why I can't come home yet."

I looked out the windows at the silvery-blue ribbon of water combing through the valley. Today had been a day of questioning for me, but it had also been therapeutic.

"You should stay as long as you want, Chloe."

"I sure wish Dad would come back here with me."

"He can't—" She stopped. "The memories are too confusing for him."

"Did he tell you about Adeline?"

"He did, and I think the truth is scaring him."

I told her about Madame Calvez, about her animosity toward Mémé.

"Something horrible must have happened at the château," Mom said. "Some reason why Gisèle refused to return. It would have been impossible to live through that war unscathed."

I fiddled with the window until it opened. "I wish she would have told us."

"She wanted to remember all that was good about France," Mom said.

But now it seemed Mémé's heart yearned to find out what happened to her daughter, even if the truth wasn't good.

Riley tossed his duffel bag and suitcase into the back of the Peugeot that he'd rented in Saint-Lô. The sun was barely up, and I clung to the coffee that I'd managed to brew in the kitchen. He said he was headed over to Coutances and then driving farther down into France.

"Who are you interviewing next?" I asked.

"A Jewish officer who fought in the Wehrmacht, and then the children of four other Jewish soldiers who've passed away," he said. "When are you going home?"

"In a week or so." I hesitated. "You said that Gisèle rescued your grandfather. And that he met a Jewish soldier here at the château."

Riley nodded.

Perhaps his grandfather was a key as well to my past. Through his stories, perhaps I could figure out some of mine. "Did he write down his stories?"

"I don't believe he wrote them down, but he made a video of his stories for my family." He slammed the hatch and rounded the vehicle to stand by me. "Unfortunately, my parents have it."

"Can you get it from them?"

He grimaced. "That would mean I have to call my father."

"Is that a problem?"

Instead of answering, he climbed into the car. "If my father won't send it, I'll make you a copy when I get back to New York."

"When do you go home?" I asked.

"In a week. When I finish my other interviews." He turned the key in the ignition. "They drive on the left side here, right?"

"Only if you want to scare the pants off oncoming drivers." I tilted my head. "You do know how to drive a manual, don't you?"

"Sure I do." He glanced down at the stick shift. "It's just been a few years."

"Can't you take a train?"

He shook his head. "There is no train station where I'm going."

For a moment, I wished I could explore France with him.

"I need to return this car before I take the train back to Paris." He smiled. "If my dad will send the DVD, perhaps we can watch it before we leave."

He shut the door. The gears ground as he shifted it into first. He waved and the poor car shuddered as he steered it up the lane. It died near the top, and Riley started it again.

A few minutes later, my cell phone vibrated.

You want to fly back to New York together?

I stared down at Riley's words.

Fancy that, a man who wanted to get on an airplane with me.

Chapter 41

"Lisette!" Gisèle called as she walked through the empty corridor of the west wing.

Cold air slipped under the cracks of the closed doors, and she rubbed her arms. It had been months since she'd been on the third floor. Even though Fähnrich Braun had been reassigned back in November, she was still afraid of meeting another German alone.

When Adeline went down for her afternoon nap, Lisette volunteered to bring up linens to the north wing and clean the two bathrooms. An hour had passed, and Adeline had already awakened, ready for a walk outside before night fell. Gisèle would have taken her, but she was helping Émilie prepare for the evening meal.

Of all of them, Lisette was most comfortable among the Germans after working for almost two years at their headquarters. Since Lisette could translate, the major had sent Lucien on to Cherbourg, and when Gisèle pretended not to understand, Lisette translated for her. After months of serving the soldiers, Gisèle now spoke the basics with them anyway. Unlike Lisette, though, she maintained her distance as much as possible through the barrier of language.

In the past six months, Lisette and Adeline had developed a special bond, and Gisèle was glad that Adeline was well loved, though she still despaired that Adeline's idea of normal was to be living among the German soldiers. Some of the men liked to spoil her, while others instilled fear in her heart.

As the months passed, it seemed as if Adeline had forgotten about her parents. Adeline had begun to call her Maman and Lisette Tante. She was sad that the girl had to forget—and perhaps would never be told of—the parents who loved her. Her lies had become Adeline's reality.

While Gisèle avoided the Germans, Lisette seemed to find a sense of belonging with them and with Adeline. On long winter evenings, after dinner, Lisette told the men some of the chilling stories that Michel had told her, about those who had been murdered in the château during the revolution and about the ghosts who sought revenge. Gisèle cringed when Lisette told them about a tunnel underneath the castle that harbored dangerous trolls and how they came out at night to haunt the floors above them. The Germans laughed at her stories, and yet they kept coming back around the fireplace to listen to more.

Sometimes Gisèle wondered if the men were coming to hear Lisette's stories or if they were there to admire her beauty. Lisette had always been beautiful and she'd matured into a lovely woman, with her blond curls and shapely figure that was so unlike those of many of the hungry Frenchwomen who'd become shadows of themselves. The way Lisette flirted back with some of the soldiers made Gisèle's stomach roll, and she prayed Michel never found out how the woman he loved had toyed with them. They all had to lose a bit of themselves to satiate the enemy, she supposed, but she prayed that in their hearts, they all would remain true to God and to France.

She knocked on the bathroom door. "Lisette?"

There was no response.

Most of the men were patrolling in the valley and town, and she wondered for a moment if Hauptmann Milch was among them, though she had learned through Lisette that when he wasn't needed to type correspondence, Hauptmann Milch worked in the registration office in Saint-Lô, issuing identity cards and certificates. He avoided her, speaking only when it was of utmost necessity, but even with his brusqueness, he intrigued her. Sometimes she wondered if he was trapped like the French people who had no choice but to entertain the men they despised.

Then she heard laughter from across the hall. And a woman's voice.

A door opened, and someone stepped into the hall. Gisèle slipped back into the alcove to avoid the German. But an officer didn't walk out of the bedroom door. It was Lisette.

Usually they would leave fresh linens outside the doors, but perhaps Lisette had felt the need to make the beds. Yet that couldn't be right. She should never have gone into a room alone with one of the men.

A wave of nausea swept over her.

In the village, Gisèle had heard rumors of French-women consorting with the German soldiers in exchange for petty favors—lipstick and sugar and silk stockings—but she prayed not here in her house, with her friend.

Gisèle stepped into the corridor and Lisette whirled around. The winter light illuminated the smeared mascara under Lisette's eyes, and Gisèle wondered for the first time where her friend purchased mascara when there was none to be had in Saint-Lô. And where she found her seemingly endless supply of cigarettes.

"What are you doing?" Gisèle asked.

Lisette brushed her hands over her skirt. "I was cleaning the rooms."

"The men can care for their own rooms."

"Some of them need assistance." Lisette's hands flew to her throat, straightening the pink scarf crumpled around it. Gisèle should have felt sorrow for her friend, for the years lost and their dreams ravaged by war, but more than compassion, anger raged within her. Anger for Michel, who had remained faithful. Anger that Lisette hadn't remained strong.

If the Germans had forced themselves on her, like Braun tried with her in the cellar, her heart would have broken for Lisette, but her friend's laughter echoed in her ears. How could she give herself freely to these bastards? And then laugh with them?

"Michel is the one who loves you, not these men."

"This has nothing to do with love," Lisette replied, the passion stripped from her voice.

"Why didn't you tell me? I could have helped . . ."

"This is my secret, Gisèle. Just like you have secrets."

Gisèle hugged her arms close to her chest. "You give yourself away for nothing . . ."

Lisette's eyes narrowed and she pressed together her lips as if she teetered between anger and tears. "Don't act like a saint, Gisèle. It's not like you've taken a stand against them."

"I had no choice but to let them live here." She clenched her fists. "I don't sleep with them."

"If you think I want to do this—"

The door behind them opened, and the *Oberst* walked into the hall. He looked at Lisette with a mixture of appreciation and ridicule. The man had said he had a wife at home . . . and grandchildren. He looked much less distinguished with his untucked shirt and missing monocle. And when he tweaked Lisette's thigh.

"Stop it, Rolf," she hissed.

He ignored Gisèle, his gaze hovering on Lisette. "You'll be back tomorrow?"

"Of course."

Gisèle turned away from them both, disgusted at what was happening under her family's roof . . . and to the woman her brother loved.

CHAPTER 42

With Mémé's photo album in my arm, I trekked back up the drive to Madame Calvez's house. Riley had been gone for two days now, and in his absence, I scoured the recesses of the house, the closets and nooks, as I searched for information about Adeline. And I'd tromped through the forest, searching for any hint of the tunnel that Riley's grandfather remembered.

My search proved futile, but the woman I guessed could answer my questions was still alive, less than a mile from the château. She may not have wanted my company, but perhaps she would answer a few of my questions, if only so I'd stop bothering her.

After I knocked, Isabelle swung the door open, grinning at me.

"You lost a tooth," I said.

She grinned even wider.

I glanced behind her. "Where is your great-grandmother?"

She pointed down the short hall. "In her bedroom."

In the dimly lit hall was a photograph of three women. The oldest woman was Madame Calvez; her blond hair was bobbed and she wore a pale green pantsuit. The middle woman had long sandy brown hair and a smile that warmed the picture. Her arm was around a young girl who looked a lot like Isabelle. The girl wore a yellow ribbon in her hair and a matching bow on the wide collar of her neck.

I pointed at the girl. "Is this your mother?"

Isabelle nodded.

I tapped on the glass. "And this must be your grandmother."

"It was my grandmother—she and my grandfather died in a car accident before I was born."

"I'm sorry to hear that."

Isabelle grinned with pride. "My mother says I'm just like her."

"Where did your grandmother live?"

"Paris. My whole family lived in Paris until the government gave Grand-mère this house."

"Why would the French government give her a house?"

She shrugged as she opened the door to a small bedroom.

We found Madame Calvez in a recliner, a game show blaring music from the small television set at the foot of her bed. Isabelle turned down the volume and climbed up on the bed. Then she folded her hands in her lap like a young lady. It seemed like Isabelle was watching her great-grandmother more than Madame Calvez was watching her.

In spite of the warm air, a blanket rested over Madame Calvez's lap, and her short hair stood up around her ears. She attempted a smile when I sat on the edge of the bed. "I'm afraid I can't offer you any tea."

Leaning forward, I kissed both of her cheeks as Riley had done. "I'm not thirsty."

Madame Calvez closed her eyes for a moment and then reopened them. "The girl next door usually plays with Isabelle in the afternoons, but she took the flu."

"Are you ill?" I asked.

"No," she said. "Just old."

I held out the photo album. "I found some pictures in Gisèle's room."

Isabelle opened the cover and pointed to two women mounted on horseback. "Who's that?"

"This is my grandmother," I said. "And I believe that's your great-grandmother."

Madame Calvez leaned forward and squinted at the photo.

"It says, 'Nadine and I riding along the Vire.' I thought your first name might be Nadine."

"My name is Lisette," she replied, her voice sad. "That was Nadine Batier."

"I've never heard of Nadine."

Madame Calvez leaned back in her chair. "That's because your grandmother forgot about us all."

Shaking my head, I leapt to defend her. "I'm sure she didn't—"

Madame Calvez stopped me. "How is Gisèle?"

I took a deep breath, trying to calm myself. "Not well," I finally said. "Her mind is slipping away."

She started to say something else but stopped herself. Instead she asked, "Can you describe the pictures for me?"

With Isabelle helping me flip the pages, I told Madame Calvez about each of the photographs. Of Nadine and Gisèle sitting in the garden. Of my handsome great-uncle by his fancy roadster, and my grandmother and Michel posing by the front door after his first Communion. Of Michel looking every bit the aristocrat with his fancy riding clothes and horsewhip and hunting dogs.

"Michel was full of life," she said wistfully, and in that moment, I wondered if Madame Calvez had been in love with my great-uncle.

In her interview with Riley, she hadn't spoken of her husband or even of her daughter. If she had loved Michel, it must have broken her heart when he died.

"What do you remember most about Michel?" I asked.

Her gaze wandered to the blinds over her window. "It has been a long time."

I nodded. "My grandmother said he was fearless."

"But sometimes fear is a good thing. It keeps us alive." She paused. "There's more I would like to say, but to you, not the camera."

"I don't have a camera."

She blinked, nodding slowly. "At the beginning of the war, I thought your great-uncle Michel and I would marry, but I was never a patient woman. Four years is an eternity when you're young and you think the world is about to end."

"What happened?"

She stretched out her hand and took Isabelle's. "Could you find some cookies for our guest?"

Isabelle hopped off the bed. "The pink ones?"

"The pink ones would be just fine." Madame Calvez waited until Isabelle scrambled out of the room before she turned back to me. "When you feel powerless . . ."

I sat with her in the silence until she was ready to speak again.

"You must understand, the Nazis ruled and reigned over us. They had absolute power over everything except . . ." She swallowed, and I knew of what she spoke. "I sold my soul to the Nazis in exchange for power and a promise of protection. I thought I could save myself from them, but I discovered the hard way that the Nazis weren't very good at keeping their promises."

I closed the photo album. "After the war, were you still afraid of what they could do?"

"I wasn't afraid of what they would do to me, but I was afraid of what they would do to someone I loved."

"Who were you afraid of?" I asked quietly.

She glanced back toward the door, but Isabelle was still gone. "I was afraid of your cousin— Philippe Borde."

I'd seen that same fear in my grandmother's eyes when she spoke his name.

"What did Philippe do?"

When she shook her head, I ventured one last question. "Did you know Gisèle's daughter?"

She leaned back against the chair, her energy seemingly spent. "Gisèle didn't have a daughter."

"But what about Adeline?"

"Adeline was . . ." She closed her eyes, and a few seconds later, her chin began to bob against her neck. I had already stayed too long.

Isabelle crept back in the room, carrying three pink meringue cookies on a chipped plate. When she offered me one, I took it and nibbled on the edge. Madame Calvez's eyes were closed, and I glanced over at Isabelle who watched her as well. "Did I tell you I'm a schoolteacher?"

Isabelle shook her head, and I saw just a hint of admiration.

"And my favorite place in the whole world is, of course, the playground."

Isabelle clapped. "Mine too."

I reached out and gently squeezed Madame Calvez's hand, rousing her. "Would you mind if I took Isabelle to the park?"

She mumbled her consent before she fell back to sleep.

Isabelle skipped toward the door.

Chapter 43

Gisèle stared at the man in the front doorframe of the château, the February snow falling down behind him and his black trench coat. His fancy black *coupé* had trailed muddied tire tracks through the white carpet of snow.

Émilie usually answered the door, but after three months of working for the Germans, she obtained a pass to bicycle to her sister's home in Cahagnes and never returned. Gisèle mourned her leaving, but Émilie had taught her well. Now it was just her and Lisette, serving the Germans in silence.

"*Bonjour*," Philippe greeted her as if no other words needed to be spoken.

He had matured since she had seen him last, his face stockier and forehead balding. He looked a decade older than his thirty-two years.

He motioned toward the entryway. "May I come in?"

The familiar fear twisted in her gut again. She couldn't explain away Adeline as a friend's child now, not with the Germans occupying her house. Perhaps Philippe's visit would be short. And Adeline would remain hidden.

"Of course," she said, but she wished she could run away, like she'd done the night of the blitzkrieg. Except now, there was no place left to run.

She hadn't talked to Philippe in more than a month, but Tante Corinne wrote that Philippe had taken an important position in the Vichy government. Doing what, she never said.

Adeline toddled up to her when they stepped into the drawing room, jingling a silver bell one of the officers had given her. Her arms outstretched, Gisèle had no choice but to pick her up.

Philippe stared down at the child. "Who is this?"

"Adeline . . ." She swallowed hard. "She is my daughter."

"Your daughter?" Fire flashed in his eyes. "How old is she?"

"Two."

He glanced at the window, and she guessed he was calculating the months in his mind. It had been two and a half years since she'd seen him last. She should have said something about Adeline, during one of their brief conversations on the telephone, so he wouldn't be shocked. But with transportation so difficult now, gasoline almost impossible for a French citizen to obtain even with the coupons, she had never guessed he would show up at her door.

"Where is Lisette?" she asked, praying she wouldn't say upstairs.

"In the kitchen."

"Why don't you go play with her for a bit?"

Adeline nodded her head before she toddled toward the kitchen.

Everything had changed that afternoon Gisèle found Lisette with the *Oberst*. Lisette continued to work at the house, helping with Adeline, and she visited the servants' quarters almost every day while Adeline napped. But Gisèle and Lisette rarely spoke.

When Philippe turned back to her, the fire in his eyes was gone, replaced with a coldness as bitter as the winter air. "Is this the reason you never came to Lyon?"

"One of them."

"You should have told me you were pregnant."

"I knew you'd be angry."

His fist pressed into the back of a chaise longue. "Who is the father?"

"A man from the village. You don't know—"

His eyes blazed again. "What is his name?"

"It doesn't matter anymore."

He unbuttoned his trench coat and took it off. "I will find out."

Gisèle didn't know where Jean-Marc Rausch was, but she hoped he was far, far away. She stared at the coat on the chair. Was there another reason Philippe was here?

"I've heard you've been entertaining soldiers," he said.

"I have housed them, Philippe. Not entertained."

"Does your *amour* know?"

Irritation flamed within her. "He is my husband."

"Your husband?" His laugh crackled with sarcasm. "Of course, you must have been married to have a child."

She stepped back toward the main hall. "It's time for you to leave."

He didn't move. "You may tell people you were married, but I know the truth." He straightened the porcelain urn on the sideboard. "Where is this husband now?"

"I don't know. He was a soldier . . ."

He turned back toward her. "I don't believe you."

"You don't have to." She crossed her arms. "Why are you here?"

"I came to discuss our marriage, but I see it's no longer possible for us to marry."

Even if she wasn't pretending to be married, the

thought of marrying Philippe repulsed her. Whether or not she had a child, the idea would be revolting to him too when he realized she had been slaving in the kitchen to serve the German officers. In his mind, serving the soldiers was probably as bad as sleeping with them.

The Germans may have occupied her country, her village, but until she decided otherwise, neither Philippe nor anyone else would occupy her heart.

Major von Kluge stepped into the room, and when he saw Philippe, he lifted his palm. "*Heil* Hitler."

When her cousin returned the greeting, she cringed. Then he introduced himself. "I am Philippe Borde. Gisèle's cousin from Lyon."

Something passed between the two men, an odd look of understanding. Did the Germans already know she had a cousin living in southern France?

The major directed him toward the office. "May I have a word with you in private, Monsieur Borde?"

"Of course."

As they walked away, she heard the major say, "Your château has been most accommodating for us."

His château? The château wasn't his—

But then a terrible thought came over her. If Michel didn't return—and she disappeared as well—the château and all the Duchant property would become Philippe's. She shivered. Philippe wasn't here to check on her—at least not in a caring sort of way. He was here, she feared, to see what could be done about securing this property for himself. He knew she hadn't been married when they fled from the château that June. What if he found out that her marriage certificate read May 1940? He could have her deported for her deception.

Would her own cousin send her to a work camp? She didn't know to what extent he would go to get rid of her, and it seemed they were sending away the French people without any sort of justice. The yellow stars in Saint-Lô had been extinguished and others had disappeared as well—those who refused to hail the god Hitler. She often wondered about the children at the orphanage and the little boy who'd refused to give his name, wondered if they had been taken too. And she wondered about André and Nadine, and Nadine's parents, and her old friend Odette.

When Lisette brought Adeline back to her, Lisette nodded toward the office. "Who is here?"

"Philippe Borde."

Lisette backed away from her. "I must go."

Gisèle picked Adeline up, and the girl patted Gisèle's hair. "Sad, Maman?"

She kissed her cheek. "There is no reason to be sad when I'm with you."

Adeline looked back at the office door, and

when she stuck out her tongue, Gisèle rushed her away from the hall. "It's time for your nap."

As Adeline rested in her small bed, Gisèle sang softly like her mother had done for her years ago. When Adeline fell asleep, she stepped back into the hallway and peered down into the courtyard as Philippe drove away.

Was he here on government business as well as to inquire about the property?

Gisèle was no longer the girl who had run with Philippe during the bombing. The château was her father's home. Her brother's refuge. Her family's legacy.

One day good would defeat the evil in their midst. She didn't know when, but she clung to that hope. Philippe might expose her, but she had no regrets for what she had done.

It was too late for her to go back on her story about the marriage and there was no place for her to run. She didn't know how much longer she could hold together the pieces before everything unraveled, but like her brother, she would continue to fight. Resist.

Even when she was afraid.

CHAPTER 44

The quaint chapel had been beckoning me for days. The place where my parents and I had prayed with Mémé so long ago.

Out my bedroom window, I watched as strangers strolled down the long path from Agneaux every morning and slipped through the door. Marguerite said she unlocked the door so villagers could pray and tourists could explore the medieval treasure.

This afternoon I dressed in jeans and a T-shirt, the color of fire, before strolling across the courtyard like the locals. I wasn't alone. Madame Calvez didn't want to see me again, but Isabelle's friend was still sick, so for the fifth day in a row, Isabelle and I spent the afternoon playing at the same park where Riley had lain back in the grass and told me how God rocked his world. The quiet time, the laughter, had soothed my heart.

Isabelle made me smile, and she made me forget for a few hours all that had transpired back in Virginia. It had only been two weeks since my mom called and asked me to come to France, but it felt like a million years ago. I never could have imagined that I would be exploring the corridors of our family's château, visiting the parks with a ten-year-old, and beginning to dream about a future without Austin.

Oddly enough, I was content.

It wouldn't be long before I had to face my reality and get back on an airplane, but what I would do in Virginia now, I had no idea. There was enough money in my savings account to cushion the blow of unemployment, and my parents would let me tap into my trust fund if I drained my bank account, but I wanted to support myself. It was the Duchant in me, I supposed.

The breeze rustled the trees as Isabelle and I walked along the drive. Dozens of messages had flown back and forth between Riley and me this week. The château seemed empty without him here. Even though my own faith had been shaken, I took shelter in his and Mémé's and my parents' faith.

Tombstones were clustered together in a small yard outside the chapel. We found the graves for Vicomte and Vicomtesse Duchant—my great-grandparents—and placed wildflowers Isabelle and I had picked on top of each of them. Michel rested beside them, and I had the faintest memory of Mémé and me putting flowers on these graves before I'd left her alone to her tears.

She'd said something odd to me as we stood in front of the chapel so long ago. Something about secrets. A secret that shielded their family.

Dad thought childhood memories shouldn't be trusted, but something about this memory pricked my mind, like the thorn that had stung my finger.

I read the epitaphs on the twenty or so stones, wondering if the girl Mémé remembered might have been buried with the rest of the Duchant family, but there was no Adeline.

I pushed open the wooden door to the chapel, and Isabelle scooted around me to get inside. We were the only ones there, but the smells from time past permeated the old wood—wilted flowers and incense and dirt from the fields. The stone floor was worn smooth from years of shoes scouring it, and near the altar was a picture that captured my attention. It was a pencil drawing of a man with wings—there was a sword in one hand and the head of a dragon in the other. I suspected he was an angel, but he looked like a warrior. A sculpture of Christ's body hung on the wall, his head missing. An old gate stood open at the side.

She tugged on my hand, toward the pew. "Let's pray."

Isabelle knelt like an old pro.

Until my grandmother became bedridden, she'd attended Mass every Sunday and often during the week as well. I remembered going with her to a chapel in the months after Grandpa died. The chapel overlooked the Potomac River and I would stare down at the water. Tears had streamed down her powdered cheeks as she prayed in French, and I determined then—as a thirteen-year-old—to master the language my grandmother loved.

Isabelle folded her hands in front of her, and I

did the same, though I wasn't certain what to say. Ever since I'd begun attending church with Austin, my faith had become sterile. Riley had been so passionate about his faith, but I felt like I had lost my passion for just about everything.

I wanted it back. My passion to love kids and see the world. My desire to talk to God and not run the other way. To love again and not hide. To revel in the honesty of being able to share my story.

Isabelle prayed quietly beside me in French, and I prayed as well, that God would reveal Himself to me as He did with Riley. That He would show me what to do next.

When she finished praying, Isabelle crossed herself, and I followed suit. I didn't want to leave though. The château was full of mystery, but the chapel was different. Instead of questions, there was peace here. Answers, perhaps.

We lingered at the foot of the cross, and I knew . . .

I was at a crossroads like Riley had been. No matter what happened when I returned to the States, no matter if I never married or had children, I would have to trust God. Only He could fill those empty places left in my soul.

My peace was disturbed by the sound of gravel crunching outside. I didn't want to move, but Isabelle took my hand and urged me toward the open door.

I expected to see Pierre or Marguerite in their station wagon, or a delivery truck, but instead a black Mercedes crawled like a spider across the courtyard, searching for prey.

The door opened, and when the car's driver stepped onto the gravel, I cringed.

Austin Vale had stepped back into my world.

PART THREE

*To love another person is to see
the face of God.*

—VICTOR HUGO
LES MISÉRABLES

Chapter 45

May 1944

*B*elow the château a torrent of flames fractured dusk's fading light. Gisèle swallowed her gasp and almost dropped the bowl of mashed potatoes onto the lap of the officer in front of her. The row of paned windows in the dining hall framed the blaze, but the men were all focused on their discussion and their plates instead of on the fire raging on the hillside across from them.

The Allies were pushing hard into France, their planes becoming more daring the past few weeks as they flew farther inland with their bombs.

Had a German plane crashed near the river? Or was it a Royal Air Force plane?

The Allies, Oberst Seidel said, knew Château d'Epines was a Nazi headquarters, and he feared they would target the house. She'd heard the planes overhead at night, but the rattling of the engines didn't bring her fear. Instead they inspired her with hope. Michel had said they must do anything they could to help the Allies win this war. "Hitler has mandated that we increase the deportation of Jews," the major told his men.

"I thought the French police already sent all the Jews in Saint-Lô to work camps," Hauptmann Milch said.

"He is convinced there are more hiding here."

Gisèle would have been alarmed at their discussion had her attention not been solely focused on the fire.

As the men talked about Hitler's new mandate, she switched on the electric lights and then stepped carefully toward the windows, taking care not to gawk at the glow. The Germans in her home may not have seen the crash yet, but someone in Saint-Lô must have.

Still, if it was an Allied plane, she might be able to help the crew buy a little time.

Instead of waiting until after dinner to pull the blackout curtain across the rod, she closed them. None of the Germans even glanced up from their meal.

She stole away from the table, down into the kitchen. Adeline was asleep in the playpen, and Lisette was washing pans.

"I must run an errand," Gisèle said. "But I'll be back within the hour."

Lisette dried her hands on a towel. "It's past curfew."

"If they ask, tell them I went to lock up the *chapelle*."

"You never lock up before the nineteen hundred

hour." Lisette tossed the towel onto the counter. "They will ask questions."

She couldn't wait for another hour to go out. "Then tell them I'm unwell and have to rest in my room."

"But—" Lisette began to protest, but Gisèle was already out the door. If the crew had survived, there was no time to spare.

While the men were still eating, she retrieved a flashlight and locked her bedroom door before rushing outside and down the smoky path. The flames had subsided, and on the other side of the river, her flashlight beam rested on the blackened shell of the downed plane. At the edge of the river was a broken wing, but instead of a hooked cross painted on it, there was a star.

Her heart pounding, she clicked off her light. There was no time to waste. If the Germans hadn't seen the blaze, someone from town would surely report it to them soon.

"Is anyone there?" she shouted in English. Her mother's language.

When no one answered, she tiptoed forward until she reached the footbridge. There was no use crossing the bridge to search inside the plane— no one could have survived the impact of those flames. If they didn't parachute out, the crew would have perished.

In the moonlight she scanned the valley and hillside for any movement. If there were survivors, they would need a place to hide right away or the Germans would find them. Would they send the airmen to work camps like they did the Jews or would they execute them like they had her father and the men in the forest?

She stepped into the ribbon of trees by the river, calling out one last time. "I can take you to a safe place, but if you don't come with me now, it will be too late."

Seconds crept by, and still no one answered. Disappointed, she turned back toward the path. She'd been hoping she could help the Allies and selfishly, she had been hoping for some news of their fight. If the men weren't here, she prayed the crew had bailed out in a safe place where people would care well for them.

She had to hurry back to the house now. The Germans might not search for her in her room, but if they found her down here, they would know with certainty that she was collaborating with their enemy.

"Psstt . . ."

The whisper came from behind a hawthorn, and her heart plunged to her toes. She turned on her light, scanning the branches. "Who's there?"

A tall man limped onto the path, his forehead bloodied. Balled up in his arms was a parachute. "How do you know English?" he asked.

She swallowed. "I only know a little. My mother was from England."

He stuck out one of his hands. "My name's Eddie. From the US of A."

She studied his face in the light, the thin mustache over his lips and the bloody gash over his right eye, before extending her hand. He gave it a hearty shake.

She pulled her hand back to her side. "You have a nasty gash on your forehead."

"I'm in much better shape than *Deborah D.*"

She examined the grassy path behind him. "Where is Deborah?"

"Over there." He pointed toward the river, at the smoke still pouring from the plane. "We've flown eighteen missions together."

She wasn't sure how one was supposed to mourn the loss of an aeroplane.

A dog barked in the distance, and she shivered. "We must hurry."

"Are the Krauts near?"

She turned off the flashlight. "There are almost twenty of them. Staying on top of this hill."

He whistled.

"Stop!" she said, and her command silenced him. "Only Americans whistle like that."

He stepped back toward the trees. "My navigator injured his arm when he landed."

"Where are the rest of your men?"

He shook his head. "I don't know."

The dog barked again, closer now. Whether or not the animal was searching for them, in minutes a host of Germans—and perhaps some of her fellow French citizens—would clamor near the river to hunt for survivors. With their lanterns and flashlights, rifles and dogs, the Americans wouldn't have a chance.

Somehow she had to find a way to get them up the cliff, and then while the Germans were searching by the river, perhaps she could sneak them into the *chapelle*. She'd heard the rumors about loud Americans, but as she followed Eddie into the hawthorns and apple trees, she prayed these men knew how to be quiet as well.

A second American, a young man named Daniel, sat on a log close to the river, cradling his arm.

"Did you break it?" she asked.

He forced a smile. "Technically, a tree broke it."

Just what she needed, a smart aleck. If these men didn't take the Germans seriously now, they would soon. "We must hide your parachutes first and then I'll take you to a safe place for the night."

Not far was a wide crevice cutting through the cliff. She and Eddie stuffed the chutes into the gap and then camouflaged it with leaves and branches.

"The Germans will search all night for you," she told both men.

"Where will we hide?" Daniel asked.

She motioned him forward. "You must come with me."

The navigator hesitated.

"If you don't, they will kill you."

Daniel stood and collected his backpack, ready to follow her, and the responsibility weighed heavily on her. These Americans had decided to trust her with their lives.

If they could cross over the path before the Germans arrived, she could take the airmen west along the river, crossing under the shadow of the château before they snuck back up the forest on the other side of the house and into the *chapelle*.

But when they stepped forward, she saw a flare of lights through the smoky air, descending down the hill toward them like a swarm of bees. And then she heard Major von Kluge shouting orders.

There would be no going through the *chapelle* tonight. They had to run as fast as they could in the opposite direction.

"Hurry," she commanded.

When they heard boots hammering down the hill, Eddie and Daniel collected their backpacks and this time, they followed her quickly through the forest. She didn't know if Major von Kluge knew about this narrow path, set back from the river, but she guessed it wouldn't take his men long to find it.

Eddie lagged behind them for a few minutes, as if he needed to pay a final tribute to his plane. Then he caught up again as they hurried through the trees.

Before they moved right at the river's bend, toward the Batiers' house, she crept to the edge of the forest and scanned the bottom of the valley to her left. A pool of lights collected on the valley floor. It wouldn't be long before the Germans spread out to comb every inch of the forest and cliffs.

Would any of them wonder why she hadn't returned from the *chapelle*? Hopefully they would be too distracted by the aeroplane . . .

Still, she needed to hurry home.

It was too late to take the airmen to the locked door at the *chapelle*. For a moment, she considered trying to hide them in the Batiers' home, but the gendarmes knew about the house in the forest and if they didn't already, the Germans would find it soon. They would search all the vacant homes and the occupied ones as well until they found the crew.

There was one other place nearby that she could hide the Americans.

She prayed the cross around her neck would open the door.

CHAPTER 46

Isabelle didn't stick around for the showdown. Right after Austin stepped out of the Mercedes—and informed her that he was my fiancé—she asked if she could return home. I'd kissed her on both cheeks and sent her on her way.

If the Plaza had never happened, I'd have been flattered by his resolve to fly across the ocean to see me, like I'd felt the night he literally swept me off my feet and proposed. This time his determination wasn't romantic. It was maddening.

Now he paced in front of the château. His button-down shirt was slightly wrinkled, but he held the composure of an attorney who usually got his way. I couldn't physically remove him from the château's property—and I had a suspicion that as long as Austin wasn't threatening to hurt me, the local police wouldn't want to get involved with two Americans disputing over whether or not they remained engaged.

He leaned back and glanced up at my family's château again. "It looks like a castle."

"It is a castle!"

His gaze remained locked on the building. "How much do you think it's worth?"

I put my hands on my hips. "You flew all the way to France to ask how much the château is worth?"

"No—I came to apologize," he said, turning back to focus on me. "I still want to marry you."

"You *still* want to . . ." I said, appalled at his audacity, as if he was willing to humble himself. "I told Olivia the wedding is off."

He shook his head. "It's only been postponed."

"Austin—" I crossed my arms and asked the question I should have asked a long time ago. "Why do you want to marry me?"

He paused, his handsome eyes squinting as he seemed to search for an answer. "I need you."

"That's a lousy reason, Austin."

He seemed shocked at my retort.

"Let me help," I said. "You want me to marry you because you think I can somehow help you win this election."

"It's not just about me, Chloe. It's about us. We make a good team, a team that will last far past this election."

He was asking me to play on his team? He might have thought he was being winsome, but the blinders had been ripped from my eyes. He didn't love me. He loved the idea of having a team-mate—and a cheerleader who knew when to look the other way.

I cleared my throat. "Have you broken off things with Starla?"

He leaned back against the wall. "I will be a good husband to you, Chloe."

"Not if you're sleeping with other women."

"I will end it with her."

I thought of Isabelle, jumping from stone to stone in the park, giggling as she raced down the metal slide. What if I hadn't found out about Austin's affair? We could have been having this conversation six or seven years from now, after we had a child of our own. His infidelity would have shattered our family.

"But for how long will you end it?" I asked.

His eyes hardened for a moment and then he met my gaze again, his smile creeping back. "I won't be like my father, Chloe. Once we're married, I will be faithful to you."

I wanted to believe him, I really did, but it was impossible. Even if I forgave Austin and became his wife, his betrayal would cast a shadow over our entire marriage.

When I married, I wanted to love my husband with all my heart, knowing he would be faithful. It shouldn't have mattered—didn't matter—if my husband was the governor of Virginia. President of the United States, for that matter. I wanted to treasure the man I married, along with our children.

"I can't marry you, Austin." Why was it so hard for me to say it? "I thought I loved you, but I've discovered I don't—not as a wife should love her husband."

He didn't seem fazed by my words. "It doesn't matter, Chloe. Love is such an ambiguous word."

"But it matters to me. I want to love well in my life. I want my husband to love me." I paused. "Why didn't you ask Starla to marry you?"

"She's not from Virginia, nor is she—" He stopped. "I wanted to marry you."

"That time in the coffee shop, when you spilled my latte." I swallowed. "It wasn't really an accident, was it?"

At least he had the decency to look down at his shoes.

He should have been ashamed.

"You'd already researched me."

"Chloe—"

"You needed a wife to run for governor, and on paper you thought I would make a decent addition to your little team," I said slowly. "So you staged our meeting."

"Olivia thought you would be good for the campaign, but once I met you—"

"It was all smoke and mirrors."

My phone vibrated in my pocket and I pulled it out. There was a text from Riley.

Headed back to Saint-Lô.

When I smiled, Austin glanced at my phone. "Who is it?"

I looked up at him, the strength surfacing again. "It's time for you to leave."

Instead of getting into the car, he stepped toward the château. "I'm not leaving France without you."

Riley strutted into the formal salon an hour later, his grandfather's bomber jacket slung over his shoulder and his Moleskine journal clutched in his hand. I probably should have warned him about Austin's arrival, but I was afraid if he knew Austin had dropped in, he might bypass Saint-Lô for the airport.

The smile on Riley's face faded when he saw the man in the formal high-back chair sitting across from me.

Austin leapt up as if he was about to tackle Riley. "Who are you?"

Recognition flickered in Riley's eyes. "I'm Riley Holtz."

"Ah, the filmmaker." And with that, Austin dismissed him.

Riley tossed his jacket over the back of the couch. "And what is your name?"

He sat back in the chair. "I'm Austin Vale," he said as if he was Prince William and Riley was the pizza delivery guy waiting for a tip. Then he pointed at me. "Chloe's fiancé."

I shook my head. "We are no longer engaged, Austin."

Riley glanced at me again, and I could see the concern in his eyes. "I was expecting a package from my parents. I thought it might have arrived—"

Austin stepped up to Riley. "If you would excuse us, we were in the midst of a discussion."

Discussion wasn't quite accurate. It was more like a congressman filibustering a vote. The familiar pounding had returned to my head, and I pressed my fingers against it. Oddly enough, my head hadn't hurt after I ended the relationship with Austin, only when he showed up in France and refused to leave without me.

Clearly Austin Vale had no regard for people telling him no.

"Chloe . . ." Riley motioned toward the hallway,

his eyes vacillating between worry and angst. "Could I speak with you for a moment?"

Even though he no longer had any say as to where I went or with whom, Austin still swore under his breath when I agreed. Without a glimpse back, I slipped down into the kitchen.

Riley sat on the counter. "I thought you broke up with him."

"I did." I paced the floor in front of the fireplace. "He showed up here and somehow thought he could convince me that we should still marry."

He searched my face. "Do you still want to marry him?"

"Of course not," I said, but the concern in Riley's eyes had turned into doubt. He didn't believe me. "I'm still processing . . ."

Riley rubbed his hands together. "Will Austin love you for who you are or is his love dependent on what you will do for him?"

"It's dependent on what I do for him."

"So really Austin loves himself." Riley hopped back down from the counter. "You have to decide with certainty what you want for your future."

"I've already decided."

"Then why is Austin still here?" His dark green eyes seemed to sink into mine, and my skin flushed. In that moment, I wasn't thinking at all about the man waiting for me upstairs.

Questions knotted together in the pit of my stomach, and strength began to fill me again.

Wonder at the man in front of me. I reached for Riley's hands, like he'd done with me at the park. But this time he jumped away from me. As if I'd burned him.

I pulled back my hands, crossing them under my arms. Tears began to pool in my eyes, and I squeezed them shut, willing my emotions to flatline.

I wanted—I didn't know what I wanted except . . .

Right now, I wanted to be alone.

Riley leaned back against the counter. Quiet.

"I'm sorry . . . ," I finally said.

He shook his head. "You didn't do anything wrong."

I stepped toward the door. "I'm going to tell him to leave."

The tears were gone as I stood in front of Austin and told him once and for all that our relationship was over. There would be no wedding—not even a postponed one. And this time Austin believed me. Before I finished talking, he rushed out of the château and climbed into his car.

I stood in the dust, and for the first time since I'd left New York, I was grateful. Grateful that he'd cheated on me. Grateful that I'd been able to tell him how I felt. Grateful that he was gone from the château.

But I wasn't sure what to do about the man still left inside.

Chapter 47

The starlight made the tree limbs look like spindly gray webs painted on a black canvas. The village of beehives was silent for the night, but twigs and dried leaves crackled under the feet of the airmen. Each time the forest broadcast their presence, the Americans stopped and listened.

The hawthorns became denser along the path, and Gisèle urged them along quickly, her own heart beating at a rapid pace as she whispered prayers to her mother, begging her to petition God for guidance. She hadn't been back to the cellar since she'd found Adeline.

Eddie stopped in front of a beehive. "Where are we?"

"Near a friend's house," she whispered back.

"But—"

"You must trust me, but I must trust you as well. You can tell no one of this place."

A dog barked in the direction of town, and both men readily agreed.

Glowworms sprinkled green light in the grass, and she heard one of the men whisper, "They look like fireflies."

She hushed him and listened again for the sound

of German voices, the pulse of foreign footsteps nearby. All she heard was the rustle of leaves in the wind and the steady flow of the Vire.

The root cellar had to be close, somewhere among these hives. If only she could shine her flashlight into the trees, but with the houses in town shrouded in blackout curtains, it would be a beacon to the enemy and to the Allies alike.

So she stumbled forward in the darkness, feigning confidence in what she could not see, trusting her heavenly Father to guide her. She didn't dare tell the Americans her fears. If she couldn't find it, they would all be taken away.

There were no markings to guide her, but the moonlight glazed a silver sheen along the path. The next time she pushed back a spray of branches, she saw a rock pile in front of them.

Relief escaped her lips in a long sigh and she reached for the rope handle of the stone room, tugging the door open. It was brilliant of her ancestors to put this entrance in a cellar, hidden among the beehives. The people of Saint-Lô had probably avoided this place for centuries, and foreigners would certainly avoid the hives.

The room reeked of moldy potatoes and animal droppings, but she was more concerned by the rustling of tiny feet, shuffling into the corners.

Moving aside a stack of empty baskets, she found exactly what she'd hoped for—a small door set into the floor. She tugged on it, in case Michel had left it unlocked, but it didn't budge. As she removed the rosary from her neck, she prayed that the same key that opened the *chapelle* and the iron gate and the closet in the sacristy would open this lock as well.

She turned it slowly, unlocking the hatch, and when she lifted the door, Eddie whistled.

"Hush," she commanded again.

This time he responded with a low rumble of a laugh. "I'll apologize later."

She flipped on her flashlight and urged them quickly down the ladder, into the cavern. Along the tunnel, they stepped over pans and newspapers and passed by small rooms cluttered with bedrolls and clothing, the crevices where her ancestors and some of the townspeople hid during the French Revolution.

The next time Eddie whistled, she didn't scold him. "Who lives down here?" he asked.

"Members of the French Resistance."

"We've heard rumors about them . . ."

She stepped over another stack of papers. "I don't know that word. *Rumors.*"

"It means 'stories.' "

"Ah," she replied. "*Rumeurs.*"

He shrugged.

"The *rumeurs* are probably true."

The stench of rotting food and urine drifted through the tunnel, and her anger flared. How could her brother and the other men live like this?

It was atrocious that the gentlemen of France were forced to huddle down here in this stench like rodents. Trolls. Even as they fought for France, they were refugees in their own country. The Germans were making animals out of them all.

"How is your arm?" she asked of the man trailing behind them.

"Tolerable."

"My brother will know how to help you."

Daniel tripped, and Eddie caught him. "Is your brother down here?"

"He travels much, but he is in charge of the men who stay here."

There was pride in her voice, and she realized it was the first time she'd been able to tell someone about Michel's work. He could have hidden away in England with their grandparents, ignored the plight of his country to protect himself. For almost four years the Nazis had tried to stop him, yet he chose to continue the fight for France and for the people being persecuted in their country. So many had given up, resigned themselves to their occupants' presence, but he never quit. These Americans were fighting hard in the skies for her country, and she was immensely proud of the work her brother was doing on the ground as well.

"Perhaps your brother can help us get home," Eddie said.

"Perhaps . . ." She slowed her walk. "How long will the Allies fight?"

"Until Hitler is gone," Eddie said.

His words brought her peace. "Sometimes it feels as if the Germans will never leave."

"There are thousands upon thousands of soldiers across the Channel, waiting to fight," Eddie said. "It won't be long before the rest of our men will join your brother in fighting on French soil."

Every day she woke up afraid the Germans would find out she'd never married, that Philippe would return again and take Adeline from her, that they would uncover her brother's hiding place.

She was tired of living in fear.

The stench of human waste grew stronger, along with a cloud of cigarette smoke that hovered in the narrow tunnel, but they pressed on until the dull light in front of her merged with the edge of her beam.

"Wait here," she commanded before tiptoeing forward.

She peeked into the large room where she'd found the cigarette butts and bedding before. This time, the room was packed with men, about thirty of them, leaning against the walls or huddling around the lanterns on the floor, reading newspapers or quietly playing cards. Most of them were terribly thin, with clothes more like strands of thread dangling from their skin.

Where had they all come from? Her pittance of food wouldn't have done much to feed this many men, but it had been something to support them, to show she was resisting instead of just strengthening their enemy.

When she stepped into the room, the men quieted and they all turned to stare at her.

Michel elbowed his way through them. "Gigi, I—"

She stopped him before he began to lecture her again about coming into the tunnel. "The Nazis shot down an American plane in the valley."

His mouth dropped open before he spoke. "Were there any survivors?"

She nodded slowly. "At least two of them."

He stepped forward, his eyes wide. "Where are they?"

She cleared her throat. "In the tunnel, behind me."

In the dim light, she watched his gaze falter between frustration and curiosity and perhaps even hope. "You weren't supposed to tell anyone about this place," he said, but there was no threat in his tone, as if he was speaking out for the sake of the men waiting behind him.

"I had to hide them, Michel." She glanced at the faces of the men. "And it seems like half of Saint-Lô already knows about your tunnel."

He swept his arm out beside him. "I trust my life to any of these men."

"And you told me to trust the Americans as well."

Michel buttoned the top button on his shirt. "We were just preparing to leave for the night."

She shivered. What were they planning?

"Perhaps they can rest here until you return." She hesitated. "One man has injured his arm."

When Michel stepped into the corridor, most of the men continued whispering or playing their card games. Except one man. His gaze rested on her face, and even though his face was smudged with dirt like the others, his jawline shaded with whiskers, this man smiled at her.

When he stepped forward, her stomach somersaulted. "Do you remember me?" he asked.

She was almost afraid to speak with him but forced herself to answer. "I believe I do."

"I'm Jean-Marc," he said. "We went to primary school together."

"Rausch." She wrapped her arms across her chest. "Your name is Jean-Marc Rausch."

He smiled again, as if he were pleased that she remembered him. She was pleased as well—that he was safe, hidden in the tunnel, and that the Germans, or Philippe, couldn't interrogate him down here.

She rubbed her arms. "A lot has happened since primary school."

"What has happened to you?" he asked.

She almost told him what she had done, how she had taken his name as her own, but Michel stepped into the room, the two airmen behind him. "Daniel's arm is broken, but our doctor can set it," he said to her before he turned back to the airmen. "If we can find someone to make you *papiers d'identité*, I have a friend who can escort you down to Spain and arrange your transport back to Great Britain."

"We will need photographs to make identity papers," Gisèle said.

"We have pictures." Eddie opened his backpack. "In our emergency kits."

Gisèle took the photographs from him and Daniel. "Then I'll try and obtain papers for both of you."

Eddie hugged her and Daniel carefully shook her hand. She might never see them again, yet they were all fighting together.

Michel escorted her toward the ledge. "Where will you get the papers?" he asked.

"I have a friend . . ."

"Be careful, Gigi."

She nodded. "Are you afraid?"

In the dim light, she saw compassion in his eyes. "Of course."

"Yet you continue to fight . . ."

"Courage doesn't mean you stop being afraid." He kissed her cheeks. "It means you continue to fight, even when you're terrified."

All these years, she'd thought her brother wasn't afraid of anything.

As she climbed the steps to the *chapelle*, she tucked the men's photographs into her brassiere and brushed the leaves out of her hair, the dust off her skirt. No matter how worn she was, no matter how afraid, she would continue to fight.

"Madame Rausch!" the patrolman called out as she moved through the cemetery. "It is not safe for you to be out tonight."

Taking a deep breath, she turned to face him. "It is not safe to pray?"

He shook his head.

As he escorted her back to the château, he didn't seem to notice the smell of damp moss or perspiration on her clothes. Nor did he notice the trembling in her hands or the prayers that slipped from her lips.

It might not have been safe to pray, even in the darkness, but on nights like this, she needed to pray even more. For courage for herself, in spite of her fears. For Eddie and his navigator. For Jean-Marc and Michel. For André and Nadine. And for all those aboveground with her trying to keep the earth from cracking wide open and swallowing the people they loved.

CHAPTER 48

Riley and I trekked down the hill beside the château, to the path along the Vire, so he could record footage of the river and the valley beyond it. My headache was already gone, replaced instead with an odd giddiness, as intoxicating as the nectar-laced honeybees that danced around the hawthorn blossoms.

Riley didn't say anything else about Austin or mention our awkward exchange in the kitchen, but after he filmed the valley, he began to ramble on about a man he'd interviewed named Benjamin Tendler, a part-Jewish officer who had served in the Wehrmacht.

"Mr. Tendler knew the last name of the man who helped my grandfather with his papers. He said it was another German Jew in the Wehrmacht, a man named Josef Milch. Apparently, Milch falsified what was called an *Abnenpass* for Mr. Tendler to prove his Aryan lineage. With this document, he could stay in the military."

"I still don't understand why a Jewish man would stay in the German military,"

Riley returned his camera to his backpack. "The rest of Mr. Tendler's family was killed at Auschwitz."

"So he hid behind a German uniform?"

"How can you judge him, Chloe?" A look akin to torment flashed through Riley's eyes. "How can any of us judge?"

I instantly backed down, and we began walking again toward the town. How could I judge a man's decision to choose life over certain death, even if it meant he had to compromise what he valued? I'd hidden many times, even when the reasons for hiding weren't life-and-death.

"You're right," I said. "I can't judge him or Mr. Milch."

"Mr. Tendler said he had a picture of him and Josef someplace. He's going to try to email it to me."

"If your grandfather met Josef Milch here, perhaps my grandmother knew him as well."

Riley stopped and looked at me. "Mr. Tendler was in Saint-Lô the weeks after D-Day. He said he saw Josef here, sneaking through the night with a group of children."

"Where were the children from?" I asked.

"There was a Catholic orphanage outside of the city that had taken in Jewish children after their parents were sent to concentration camps. The Nazis raided it in the days before the Americans liberated Saint-Lô, but the children were gone."

"I wonder what happened to them."

"Mr. Tendler didn't know, but I want to get some footage of the place," he said. "I'm hoping Madame Calvez can tell us where the orphanage is."

"I'd like to go with you."

He nodded.

"Can I ask you a personal question?" he asked as we neared Madame Calvez's home.

I laughed. He'd never bothered in the past to obtain permission before asking after my personal life. "Why not?" I said. My pride had already been wrecked.

"It seems to me—" He sounded a bit nervous. "Well, what did you see in a guy like Austin?"

Instead of hiding behind my polished shield, I decided to be gut-wrenchingly real with him. "Everyone wanted Austin." I took a deep breath. "But Austin—I thought he wanted to be with me."

And with those words, I realized that Austin was not the only selfish one in the relationship. Austin wanted to marry me for what he thought I could offer him, but I too wanted to marry Austin for what he could give me. Somehow I'd mixed up my worth with Austin's love.

He turned to me. "You are valuable, Chloe. Without him."

I kept walking, no longer wanting to talk about me. "Did you leave behind a girlfriend in New York?"

He was silent for a moment. "It's been a long time since I had a serious relationship."

"Not enough women in New York for you?" I quipped, the online pictures of him looping through my mind again. He was certainly handsome enough, and confident enough, to get mobbed by a horde of single women.

"I have no desire to be in a relationship for the sake of being in one," he said. "I've made mistakes in the past, terrible ones. The next time I date a woman, I hope it's for keeps."

For some reason I blushed. Perhaps it was the intensity in his words. Or because I was still trying to figure out my upside-down emotions in the kitchen.

"One day, a man is going to try to earn your trust again, Chloe," he said. "But the only one who won't fail you is God."

A verse flooded back to me, one that Mémé used to quote for me.

Trust in the Lord with all your heart, and do not rely on your own insight. In all your ways acknowledge Him, and He will make straight your paths.

Maybe I did need to learn to trust Him completely before I trusted another man.

When Riley stopped again to film along the path, I heard laughter in the trees. Hiking a bit farther down the path, I saw Madame Calvez's house. And then I saw Isabelle on the swing, her long hair flapping in the wind as the swing pitched her toward the sky.

"Mademoiselle!" Isabelle shouted, and then switched to her English at the peak of her swing. "Miss Chloe."

I waved.

Her arms were flapping as she leaned forward and swung back toward me. "I'm flying."

She flew past me, pumping up toward the sky.

"Is that man gone?"

I shouted up to her. "Which one?"

"The mean one," she hollered as she swung past me again.

"He is."

Her swing slowed. "I didn't like him one bit."

I smiled. "I'm not particularly fond of him either."

"He said you were supposed to marry him."

"I've changed my mind."

"Good," she said. "I think you should marry Monsieur Holtz instead."

"I—"

Riley cleared his throat, and I wished I could fly with Isabelle. Far, far away.

When Isabelle saw him, she hopped off her swing and raced toward him. Kissed him on both of his cheeks. He looked as if he wanted to fly away as well.

"I will go find Grand-mère," she said, skipping toward the back door.

Riley and I stood there in an uncomfortable silence. It was strange how one minute of time—one awkward comment—put us both back on edge. I couldn't erase that moment, so I decided to make light of it. "For some odd reason, Isabelle likes you."

His smile hung crooked with his shrug. "I suppose I am irresistible."

I rolled my eyes. "Really, I think you're just plain irritating."

He laughed, and it felt so good to laugh with him.

We sat down on the patio again. "I'll wait here,"

I said. "Madame Calvez won't tell you anything if I go inside."

The back door slid open, and Isabelle hurried outside. Her brown eyes creased with worry, her smile erased.

I jumped up from my seat. "What is it?"

Her voice shook. "Something is wrong with Grand-mère."

Riley and I rushed inside.

Chapter 49

Adeline squealed when she dipped her toes into the cool lake water, and then she began twirling, both hands overhead. Gisèle spread her khaki blanket across the grassy shore and then lay down, closing her eyes as she listened to Adeline splashing in front of her and the gentle rustle of leaves overhead.

This had been her favorite spot to play in as a child, but she hadn't returned since—

She opened her eyes and looked up at the spring buds bursting from the branches, at the afternoon light that gently filtered through them and danced among the pods of green. In the past four years, she'd tried to forget that terrible night when she and Michel had found her father's body, wanting instead to remember her father when he was alive. But on days like this, her heart still ached.

Adeline splashed water toward her, and Gisèle smiled. When she was younger, she and Michel and Nadine used to jump from the dock and hold their breath under the water for as long as they could, competing to see which of them was the most tenacious. Their parents were haunted by their memories of the Great War, but the three of them weren't weighed down by the burdens of warfare. Nor were they worried one iota about their future. They had each other, a beautiful lake, and the summer sun. At the time, nothing else mattered.

The good memories of her childhood were beginning to fade. One day she would leave this château, and when she did, she wanted to remember all the laughter before their loss, before Michel joined the resistance and Nadine disappeared. Before the woman her brother loved began spending her afternoons in the servants' quarters.

Two German fighters darkened the sunlight, and she looked over to see if Adeline was frightened, but the girl only glanced up at the sky in annoyance. Then she continued playing in the shallow water. In the shattered world of her childhood, Adeline's life among the German soldiers and the aeroplanes flying were as normal as the summers that Gisèle had spent swimming in the lake.

The major had been raging for two days about the aeroplane that crashed into the valley, searching for its missing crew. But more Allied aircraft flew overhead now, both day and night, and the Germans seemed to be growing nervous.

She hadn't been able to obtain the identity papers yet, but she prayed the men in the tunnels were all safe. If she'd learned nothing else during the past four years, she had learned that life was as fleeting as dandelion seeds in a storm. In her heart, she'd begun saying good-bye to those she loved, even before they were gone.

A shout from the ridge above shattered the silence, and before Gisèle could react, a rock plummeted through the branches, hurling toward them. She lurched forward and grabbed Adeline as the boulder crashed into the lake, several meters from where Adeline had been playing. Before she could pull Adeline to shore, another rock catapulted over their heads, spraying water on both of them.

Adeline clung to Gisèle's neck, sobbing, as Gisèle scanned the ridge above them. She couldn't see anyone in the trees. Either someone was threatening them or they didn't know she and Adeline were here.

"Stop," she yelled up in French and then in German. "There's a child down here."

The woods grew still, and she sat back down on the shore and held Adeline on a towel, drying her tears along with her soaked feet. She was so tired of running and hiding and trying to protect those she loved. But when she heard the stomp of boots on the branches, she stood with Adeline clutched beside her. No matter how exhausted she was, she couldn't stop fighting, for Adeline's sake.

A solitary soldier descended the hill, and when she saw it was Hauptmann Milch, she released her tight hold on Adeline.

"Forgive me," Milch said when he stepped beside her. His German accent was strong but his voice sounded broken. "I did not know you and your daughter were here."

She looked up into his swollen eyes, and her breath caught when she realized that tears streaked his clean-shaven face. Even though she thought she had nothing left to feel, the pain in his eyes resonated in the hollows of her heart.

Adeline clapped her hands together. "*Guten Tag,* Josef."

Gisèle glanced at Adeline and then looked back up at the man in front of her. "Josef?"

He shrugged. "She asked my name . . ."

She didn't know which disturbed her more—that Adeline was learning German or that she'd begun calling the officers—their enemy—by their first names. At least this friend was the man who'd saved her life. "Why are you throwing rocks?" Gisèle asked.

He crumpled a piece of white paper in his hands.

"Something happened, and I—I didn't know what else to do."

She kissed Adeline's hair and scooted her back toward the water. "You can play again."

The pull of the water and perhaps the sight of Josef seemed to soothe Adeline's fears. When she began splashing again, Gisèle pointed the officer to her blanket. His long legs stretched across it.

"What happened?" she asked.

He tossed the paper onto the blanket. "Have you heard of the Gestapo?"

She nodded slowly.

"I just found out—" His voice cracked. "They deported my mother from Berlin."

The air seemed to deflate out of her. "But why—"

"She's not like—" He paused. "We're not like the other Germans."

She studied him again, the sadness that consumed his warm brown eyes, the boyish features that would have intrigued her if she'd met him at the university. She'd already known that Hauptmann Milch was different from the other Germans occupying her house, obsessed with fear and destruction. His secret kindnesses for her and Adeline had given her peace in the midst of the turmoil. He may not have had Nadine's dark hair and distinguished nose, but slowly she realized why the German secret police had deported his mother.

"You're Jewish," she whispered.

He nodded. "My mother was born into a Jewish family."

"What about your father?"

His gaze wandered back to the water. "When they married, my father was an officer in the German army, and my mother owned an art gallery in Berlin. Twenty years later the government began harassing the Jewish people, but instead of standing up for his wife, my father took my younger sister and brother and moved to Frankfurt."

"You were left to care for your mother."

"It wasn't a burden," he said sharply. "I wanted to care for her."

In the soft light, she didn't see a Jewish officer in a German uniform. She saw a young man who had refused to abandon his mother. A man like André, who stood by his family even when it could mean death.

"My mother is stubborn," he said. "She didn't want my help, but after the Nazis closed down her gallery, she had to rely on me until there was no place for me to work either. I tried to obtain visas from the U.S. embassy, but we were denied. They said we weren't sufficiently threatened. When the Germans began deporting the Jews who lived in the ghettos, we knew it wouldn't be long . . ."

He wiped his face with the back of his hand, and she looked toward the lake, not wanting to embarrass him.

"I was conscripted into the Wehrmacht, and I went willingly," he said, his voice weighted. "It was the only way to protect both of us."

"Does the army know your mother is Jewish?"

"The major knows, but he doesn't want to tell the others under his command. They might revolt."

"Why didn't you falsify your papers?"

"Because I thought if those in command knew who I was . . ." He picked up another rock and threw it into the water, far from where Adeline was playing. "I thought that out of respect, they wouldn't deport the mother of a *Hauptmann*."

She wrung her hands together. "They don't respect anyone."

"For the past four years, I've had to serve under a madman—" His voice broke again. "I've seen horrific things, and no matter how much I wanted to stop it, I could not."

"Because they would kill you?"

He raked his fingers through his short hair. "Because they would kill my mother."

How could she tell him that he never should have joined the German army, that he should have sacrificed his life along with his mother's? She didn't know how to respond, but no matter how much she hated the Germans, no matter how she wished the Allies would crush every Nazi in the Wehrmacht, she couldn't hate this man.

"If the war ends soon," she finally said, "there is hope that your mother will remain alive."

He nodded slowly. "That is why I must stay in the army."

And with his words, she knew he was also imploring her to understand. No one else except the major knew he was even Jewish. Defecting from the German army would mean certain death—for him and his mother. He'd trusted her with his secrets. He wanted her to understand.

"We must do what is right before God," she said. "Not before any man."

He sighed. "I no longer know what is right."

"It is right to sacrifice yourself to save another's life."

"But in order to do that, I must fight for a country—a man—who puts no value on life."

It was as if a net had dropped over all of them, trapping them together, suffocating them as they fought. Every day they had to make choices. In order to survive, she and Josef and others like them had to choose the least of the evils to do the most good.

She leaned forward, her eyes focused on the lake. "I must cook and clean and house my enemy to sustain them, even as they kill those I love and destroy my beautiful country."

"Gisèle—" When he reached for her hand, her heart leapt against her will. "I am sorry for what we have done to you."

"You haven't done anything wrong," she whispered.

"But I have—I am Jewish but I am also German."

"Josef—" She stumbled. "I'm sorry, I meant—"

He stopped her. "No one except your Adeline has called me Josef in a long time."

"I won't say it again."

"Not in the house," he said. "But out here, it is nice to hear."

She leaned forward, meeting his warm gaze so he understood. "I forgive you, Josef."

The pain eased away from his eyes. "Thank you."

Adeline's laughter brought them both back to reality, but he didn't release her hand. "What happened to her parents?"he asked.

She wanted to lie to him as she had all the others, tell him that Adeline was really her daughter. Yet as he held her hand, as he trusted her with the secrets of his past and his heart, she couldn't do it.

"The French police took them away during the roundup." She took a long breath. "I had no place to hide her but here."

Adeline picked up a rock like Josef had done and tossed it into the water. "Are both her parents Jewish?"

"Only her mother."

His hand grew tighter around hers. "I wish we could rescue them all."

She pulled her hand away and wrapped her arms around her knees. Her life was already tangled in the web; she couldn't allow her heart to be as well. "Me too." She paused. "But there is something we can do to help end this war."

"What is it?"

Turning, she reached inside her blouse and pulled out the photographs of Eddie and Daniel. His eyes grew wide when he saw them. "They need identity cards," she said.

He waved his hand. "Don't tell me anything more."

"Can you help them?"

He nodded slowly as three planes flew overhead. The shelling from antiaircraft cannons pulsed in the distance, trying to bring their enemy down.

"More aeroplanes are coming now," she said, watching the sky.

He hid the photographs in his letter. "The Allies are preparing to invade at the Pas-de-Calais."

She rubbed her bare arms. "Will they succeed?"

"I don't know," he said as he stood. "The Nazis are doing everything in their power to defend it."

"So they are worried—"

"They are always worried." He brushed off his trousers. "Major von Kluge told me to return in an hour."

Only an hour to sort through his questions. His sorrow. It was more time, perhaps, than Lucien and others had to grieve their losses, but it wasn't nearly enough.

She stood up beside him. "Thank you for helping me—for now and for the papers you made me before and for helping me in the cellar."

"In the cellar—" He looked away, and she realized that like her, he was ashamed of what happened that day. "I am sorry about that as well."

"That was not your fault." She reached for both of his hands, imploring him to look back at her. "Neither of us did anything wrong, but instead of running away—you rescued me."

He took a step away. "It is too dangerous for us to speak to each other in the house."

Dangerous—that was exactly why she wanted so badly to leave.

"When I pray at the *chapelle*," she said, "I will pray for your mother."

He kissed the top of one of her hands. "She would have liked you, Gisèle."

It wasn't until he was gone that she realized he spoke of his mother in the past tense. Perhaps in his heart, he had already said good-bye.

CHAPTER 50

Riley and I found Madame Calvez balled up on the carpet in her living room. Her arms clasped around her chest, she rocked back and forth, muttering to herself. I couldn't understand what she was saying.

Isabelle clung to my arm as I glanced up at Riley. A lot of men would have fled back out the door, but Riley didn't run. Instead he slipped onto the floor beside her. "Madame Calvez—"

She edged closer to the wall. Terrified. "Leave me alone."

"No one here is going to hurt you."

"Yes, they will," she said, her voice clear. "You lied . . ."

Riley looked at me, but I had no answers for him.

I grabbed my cell phone from my pocket. "I'll call an ambulance."

Isabelle tugged on my arm. "My mother already called an ambulance."

"Where is your mother?" I asked.

"Driving here from Paris," Isabelle whispered.

Madame Calvez's eyes surveyed the room. "You can't take me away," she cried. "Someone must care for Adeline."

My stomach clenched. Was she grieving for Adeline as well?

Riley slipped his arm over Madame Calvez's shoulder. But instead of finding comfort in his protection, she gasped and began to pummel him with her knobby fists, crying as she fought. Riley retracted his arm to protect his face against her blows, but he didn't move away.

Then, as quickly as she'd begun to hit him, Madame Calvez stopped. Her eyes flickered for a moment, and I watched as both her hands fell back to her sides, her gaze locked on the black engraving on Riley's skin. Mesmerized. He lowered his arms, and her eyes followed his tattoo.

Slowly she reached out one of her hands. For a moment, I thought she might strike him again, but her fingers gently touched his forearm. The fear in her gaze melted into compassion. "You were there."

This time Riley didn't look back at me. Instead he gently placed his hand over her fingers. "Where was I?"

She curled the sleeve on her left arm and slowly pushed it up above her elbow.

Dear God.

Etched on Madame Calvez's forearm was a series of faded numbers. The mark of the beast.

The elderly woman leaned close to Riley, whispering, one friend empathizing with another. "Birkenau," I heard her say.

He cradled her in his arms.

Chapter 51

*I*nstead of raiding Pas-de-Calais, the Allied troops stormed the northern beaches in Normandy. On the morning of June 6, German troops awakened to a swarm of aeroplanes that blackened the sky and thousands of soldiers emerging from the treacherous waters, attacking their fortresses on foot.

Major von Kluge had been raging for weeks, ever since they'd found the remains of *Deborah D.* Now, with the Allied troops fighting on French soil, he was inconsolable. Every night he berated his men over dinner as if they'd personally invited and then escorted their enemy across the English Channel.

But tonight was different. Tonight Gisèle waited outside the dining hall, a roasted chicken on her platter, as Major von Kluge ranted about the ineptness of the German military.

Shivering, she glanced up at the clock. It was already fifteen minutes past the eighteenth hour. The Germans were never late—not for their morning routine, not for patrol, certainly not for dinner. Tonight she took a bit of comfort in their lateness. The deficiency in the German army must have rattled Major von Kluge to his core.

When it appeared his tirade wouldn't end, Gisèle stepped back toward the kitchen. Lisette was sitting by the hearth in the kitchen, a cigarette in her hands. Adeline was playing on the floor with Shadow.

Lisette motioned toward the chicken. "They didn't like it?"

"Kluge was yelling at his men. Apparently the Allies are almost to Saint-Lô."

Lisette swore under her breath.

"I thought you might be pleased at the news," she said as she set down the platter.

But Lisette's face remained grave. "It's going to get ugly, Gisèle."

Gisèle glanced down at Adeline. "Why don't you and Shadow go play in the pantry?"

Adeline groaned in response, but she reached for the cat's front legs and dragged him into the pantry. Gisèle closed the door partway.

Lisette took another drag on the cigarette and then lowered her voice. "Hitler won't let his men retreat."

"How do you know?" she asked. Then wished she hadn't.

Lisette fidgeted with her scarf before meeting Gisèle's eyes again. "One of the men I know——" She paused. "He said that no matter what happens, they won't leave. As if I would be pleased with that news. They're preparing to fight, right here among the hedgerows."

"What about all the civilians?" Gisèle said, glancing over at the cracked door to the pantry. Adeline was lecturing the cat inside.

Lisette flicked ashes into the fireplace. "The civilians will be collateral."

Gisèle shuddered. "It is sick," she whispered. "They kill innocent people for no reason—"

"The Nazis are depraved and desperate." Lisette eyed the door, her hand trembling along with her cigarette. "And they hate the innocent."

"Perhaps they will have to leave the château."

Lisette's laugh sounded sour. "Only after the Allies have bombed it."

Gisèle sat down on the hearth. It had been four years since the Germans' bombs crashed down around them. They'd lived in fear of their enemies for so long; she'd never considered that the Allies might have to take their town by force as well. If the Germans refused to leave, her house would become their target.

Gisèle pointed toward the pantry. "We must protect her."

Lisette nodded.

"But where can we take her?"

"That's simple." Lisette puffed on her cigarette and the smoke drifted over her. "We can take her to your hiding place."

She stiffened, too stunned to respond at first. "What hiding place?"

"I'm not stupid, Gisèle. I know you've been

hiding Michel." Lisette closed her eyes, leaning back against the bricks. "I loved him with all my heart, but you hid him from me."

Gisèle sighed. "Michel hid himself."

"Because he didn't trust me."

Gisèle shook her head. "Because he was trying to protect you."

"It's too late now for Michel and me, but I love—we both love—Adeline. Perhaps we can hide her wherever you hid him."

Gisèle thought about Adeline's cries when she was hidden in the cellar, of her fear of dark places. She may have been three years old now, but sometimes she still cried in the dark. "They will hear her there."

The cigarette trembled in Lisette's hand again. "We can't let them hurt her."

She may have lost her friendship with Lisette, but she had no doubt of this woman's love for Adeline. "What if you take her to your apartment tonight?" Gisèle asked.

Lisette pointed her cigarette toward the ceiling. "But if I don't return—what will you say?"

"Nothing at all," she said, "unless they ask."

Lisette considered her words. "Eventually they will ask."

"Then I'll tell them the truth. We want to protect Adeline from the Allied bombs."

She heard the boots on the steps and she shut the pantry door with a solid kick. Major von Kluge stood before her, his eyes ablaze. "You are late," he barked.

Gisèle reached for the cold chicken. "I didn't want to interrupt your meeting."

"Who told you to wait?"

"I—" She stumbled on her words.

"Who?" he demanded.

She shook her head. "No one."

He slammed his palm on the kitchen table. "Why can't you people do as you're told?"

When he turned, Lisette rolled her eyes and then stepped toward the pantry. As she followed the major up the steps, Gisèle hoped the Allies would hurry to and then quickly through Saint-Lô.

CHAPTER 52

Riley insisted that he was fine, but after Madame Calvez was stabilized, the paramedic refused to leave until she'd cleaned up the scratches on Riley's face and his bloodied nose. The man I'd seen in the pictures online was gone. Transformed. I'd never forget how he had comforted Madame Calvez in the depths of her pain, her horrific memories of the concentration camp.

After the ambulance left for the hospital, Isabelle clung to my hand until her mother arrived. Then she raced into her mother's arms.

"My name is Monique," Isabelle's mother said in English before directing Isabelle to her car. "Isabelle calls you the lady of the château."

I wasn't sure if Monique meant her words to be a slight, so I chose to ignore them. "Your daughter is a delight."

Monique peeked out the window at her car. "Isabelle adores her great-grandmother, but I don't know how much longer I can send her here. These episodes are becoming more frequent."

"I can't imagine how hard it must be—"

"France wants to forget what happened to many of her people, but my grandmother will never forget. It almost seems—" She paused. "The older she gets, her memories seem more clear."

My frustration at Mémé's fading memory seemed trivial in that light. Perhaps, instead of the memories plaguing her in her last years, there was mercy in the dullness of her mind.

Monique thanked both Riley and me for our help, and as we stepped outside, I asked her, "How long was your grandmother in a concentration camp?"

"The Germans didn't send her there until after D-Day, but as the Allied forces moved closer to the camps, they kept sending their prisoners west. It was nine months before they set her free."

"Why did they send her away?" I asked.

Monique took her car keys out of her pocket. "Someone was afraid she would talk."

• • •

The silver thread of river glistened in the setting sunlight as Riley and I walked back toward the château, the silence of contemplation our third companion.

The man beside me was nothing like the man I'd been engaged to marry. Instead, his sincerity and steady confidence, and even his kindness, reminded me of my father. I wasn't trying to earn Riley's approval. I was simply enjoying his company.

He had asked me to fly home with him, but I couldn't leave yet, not until I found out what had happened to my grandmother and Madame Calvez and Adeline. Somehow they were all connected, by the thread of their stories. Like the villages on the Vire.

But how were they connected?

Madame Calvez said she was afraid of Philippe Borde. Had he sent her to a concentration camp? And after the war, why did the French government give her the home of a Jewish family?

I wished I understood where Mémé was when Madame Calvez was taken to the camp. Had she fought for her friend?

Riley said we couldn't judge, and he was right. But after seventy years, it seemed the wounds were still fresh. And somehow, Adeline seemed to be the source of both women's pain.

Mémé may not remember much now, but at one

time, she had. Was it shame that made her keep her secrets, perhaps like some of the Jewish men who'd kept their family's secrets as they served under Hitler?

"What do you think happened to Adeline?" I asked.

"I'm afraid the Nazis might have killed her," Riley said.

I nodded. It made sense. My grandmother's agony. Why she never told me about this child. She was grieving for her daughter at the end of her life.

I glanced over at him. "Are you going to the orphanage tomorrow?"

He pulled out his phone and clicked on the calendar. He stopped walking, staring down at the date.

Riley Holtz was a complicated man. Cute and charismatic when he wanted to be. Unassuming when not. And seemingly undaunted when he sat by a woman sixty years his senior, sharing her pain. Something haunted him, and while I didn't know if I'd earned the right to know what it was, I wanted to give him the gift he'd given to Madame Calvez.

"Is something wrong?" I asked.

"Tomorrow is June 24."

"Do you have another interview?"

"No. It's a . . ." He dug his hands into the pockets of his grandfather's jacket. "It's an anniversary."

But there was no celebration in his words. "The anniversary of what?" I asked quietly.

He glanced over at me, sadness etched in his eyes. "Of my daughter's . . ." His voice trailed off, but I assumed he meant his daughter's birth.

Chapter 53

*F*ootsteps drummed up and down the hallway outside Gisèle's bedroom until long past midnight. The footsteps didn't stop at her door, but their persistent pounding reminded her of the wind rattling against her windows, trying to force its way inside.

No matter how long she closed her eyes, trying to sleep, rest evaded her. Shadow rested beside her in the darkness, but it seemed so strange not having Adeline asleep in the bed below her. She was grateful Adeline was safe tonight with Lisette, but she'd grown used to having the girl in her room at night, acting as a mother.

When the war ended, Adeline would no longer be hers. Every night she prayed for the end of the war. For André and Nadine and their return home. But even though she thought her heart was numbed, it ached tonight at the thought of losing the girl who'd become her daughter.

She couldn't stay in the room for another moment, thinking about Adeline and the Germans and the bombs that could be dropped on her roof tonight. She had to go to the *chapelle* and pray.

Dressing quickly in pants and a blouse, she slid her rosary beads over her head and marched down the steps and out the front door, silently daring any of the soldiers to stop her. The stars flickering in the sky above the château reminded her of vigil candles, their steady blaze reminiscent of God's unfailing, unwavering love in spite of the storms.

There were no blackout curtains over the stained glass in the *chapelle* and the Germans forbade the glow of candlelight after dark now, so she knelt at a bench in the starlight and petitioned Mary to pray for Adeline and her parents. Then she asked Saint Michel to fight for her and Josef and her brother.

The door to the nave opened behind her, but instead of heavy boots pounding over the stone, there was only the soft pad of footsteps.

In the dim light, she recognized Josef. "What are you doing—"

"May I pray with you?"

"Of course," she said. "Where are your boots?"

"I left them beside the door."

He knelt beside her in reverence, clutching his hands to his face. Stunned, she couldn't focus again on her own prayers. She'd yet to see any of the men in her home pray.

Josef wasn't like the other men though. Since their encounter at the lake, he had done nothing to acknowledge her, and she'd tried to pretend as well that he wasn't there, but she always felt his presence. Sometimes it calmed her. Other times it confused her. But his presence never frightened her.

He reached for her hand and with his whispered prayers, he begged God for guidance. It wasn't until he released her hand that she realized she was trembling.

"Are you cold?" he asked, and the concern in his voice terrified her. He could not care about her. Nor she him.

"Why are you here?" she whispered.

He sat up on the bench. "The Allied soldiers are drawing near."

"I heard Major von Kluge—"

"Hitler is desperate for control and so are his commanders."

Her heart quickened. "Don't they control enough already?"

"Their appetite is insatiable." He paused. "Hitler has demanded we find more Jews to send to the German camps."

She rubbed her hands over her arms. The roundups in the past two years had stolen away all the Jewish people in their community. "There are none left."

"There are rumors of a Catholic orphanage outside Saint-Lô—"

She gasped.

"I'd hoped you might know of it," he said.

"What business do they have at an orphanage?"

"The major believes the nuns are hiding Jewish children among the other orphans."

She stood up in the darkness. "They cannot harm those children."

His focus remained on the sculpture of Jesus in front of them. "He is sending me and my unit out to find it tomorrow."

"But he knows about you . . ."

Josef shuffled in his seat. "The major has begun to doubt my loyalties."

She shuddered. "It is a test."

He nodded.

"But the children are not Jewish," she insisted. "At least, not all of them . . ."

"It doesn't matter what you say, Gisèle. He must send someone to the camps."

She crossed her arms. "I can't allow him to do this."

He rubbed his hands together, his gaze still on the crucifix. "Neither can I."

And then she remembered the reason he was in the German army. The woman he'd sacrificed everything for. "What will they do to your mother?"

"If my mother still lives—" His voice broke. "She would tell me to save these children."

She sat down on the bench beside him. "You are a good man, Josef Milch."

"*Nur Gott ist gut,*" he said. *Only God is good.*

They sat in silence together at the foot of the cross.

Evil might have coursed through the veins of the Nazi leader and his minions, but God was good. She might not be able to rescue everyone, but He would want her—her and Josef—to try to rescue these children from the evil.

She fingered the key in the middle of her rosary beads. Adeline was safe at Lisette's house for the night. The Germans didn't know she helped the Allied airmen. Perhaps they wouldn't find out if they hid the children in the tunnels.

But how would they travel with so many children? *For with God nothing will be impossible.*

Her mother often quoted the words from the Book of Luke when she prayed. Jesus loved the Jewish children, welcomed them to Him in the Scriptures. If nothing was impossible, she prayed He would help them protect these children.

Josef interrupted her prayers. "Major von Kluge sent me out here to find you. He wants to . . ." He paused. "He wants to interview you."

She nodded, understanding. "I won't go back to the house."

"How far away is the orphanage?"

She hesitated, knowing she must trust him and yet still afraid that Josef would deceive her. That he would tell the major her secrets in order to protect his mother.

But the Germans would find the orphanage without her. And she couldn't rescue these children without his help.

"About three kilometers on the main roads."

Eddie would have whistled, but Josef kept his eyes on the cross. "How about the back way?"

"If we take the footbridge across the river and go over the hill, it's about one kilometer."

He silently contemplated her words. "Even if we could make it there, we have no place to hide them."

She wrapped her fingers over the key again.

This was not just Michel's tunnel. It was their family's tunnel. Her tunnel. They each had a part to play in fighting this war. Michel and his men were intent on resisting the enemy, but she wanted to rescue people—the Allies and the children.

If they were caught tonight, the Nazis would send her and Josef to one of their camps—or kill them. But she'd never forgive herself if she didn't try to save the orphans.

"I have a place," she whispered. "But if you go with me, I fear there is no turning back."

He lingered for another moment, his hands clutched together as he whispered his prayers. She couldn't imagine the conflict in his soul, the unknown awaiting the mother he loved and the mandate to send defenseless children to their death.

Finally he stood up beside her, his voice strong. "I won't turn back, Gisèle."

He retrieved his boots by the door and then she locked the door to the nave.

"Come with me," she said, and she guided him through the sacristy and down into the secret spaces under her house.

"The major did hear voices," he said as they crept through the tunnel.

"Indeed."

Josef's laughter escaped his lips, and it warmed her heart. It was the first time she'd heard him laugh.

They passed quickly by the large room and then the smaller alcoves. Michel and the other men were gone, and the stench had tapered back into a more tolerable earthy smell.

"The children will be safe here, from the Germans and the bombing," he said.

She nodded. Others fought with bombs and guns to kill their enemy, but she could fight with her heart.

CHAPTER 54

I'd never heard anyone call the date of someone's birth an anniversary. But Riley didn't say anything else about his daughter, and I didn't press him.

His sorrow ballooned between us as we hiked

back toward the château. The questions in my mind unanswered. Had he somehow lost his daughter, like my grandmother lost hers? And did this mean he once had a wife or was he still married?

It shouldn't have mattered to me, but as I'd watched him tonight alongside Madame Calvez, something had shifted inside me. If I ever fell in love again, I wanted it to be with a man like this who genuinely cared about people, not just about their vote.

Riley lingered beside the door to the château, but before we said good-night, my cell phone rang and I saw my dad's number on the screen. With a quick wave, Riley headed back toward the farmhouse.

"Chloe?" my dad asked as if someone else might answer.

I confirmed that it was indeed me.

He didn't bother with pleasantries. "I just got served papers, from an attorney in Paris."

My mouth dropped open. "What?"

"Stéphane is suing for the property."

I sighed. Even though Mémé, for whatever reason, had allowed Stéphane's father to live here, Dad wanted nothing to do with the Borde family. The château had been in my family's custody for three hundred years and French inheritance laws were strict. Property like this would pass down to a nobleman's son or grandson before a distant cousin retained it. I couldn't imagine any judge siding with Stéphane, but then again, Stéphane lived in France and we were strangers in Normandy.

I heard the crisp unfolding of papers in the background. "It says that I cannot inhabit the property nor can I inherit it because I'm not a biological heir."

"Of course we're biological heirs—"

"Stéphane has new information, but I don't know what it is." The line crackled again. "He should have waited to serve these papers until after my mother is gone."

"Dad," I said slowly. "Do you remember an orphanage near the château?"

He paused. "Perhaps."

"Riley is hoping to film there tomorrow."

"What does the orphanage have to do with his documentary?"

"He's doing a story about the Jewish men who served in the German military. Riley said one of the soldiers helped rescue the children in the orphanage before the end of the war."

When my dad spoke again, I heard the brokenness in his voice. "One of my recurring dreams is about a large group of children, sneaking through the woods."

A tremor of fear mixed with sorrow sparked inside me. Perhaps one of the children was his sister.

"What happens in your dream?" I asked.

"I'm hungry and cold and terrified, frankly, until your grandmother takes my hand. And then—" He stopped.

"What is it?"

"There is a German soldier in my dream, but he doesn't scare me. He reminds me of your grandfather . . ."

"Maybe it was at the end of the war," I said, "when you were leaving."

"Perhaps, but I'll never know. My memories are like a prism, Chloe. All fragmented in the light."

Why did everything have to be so complicated?

"I'm afraid we might lose the château," my dad said. "But I'm even more afraid of what else Stéphane will dig up about the Duchants."

"We are a family," I said, "and we will love each other, no matter what happened in the past."

Chapter 55

*T*he ramparts of the old Norman forest shielded thirty orphaned children and their five chaperones as they snuck toward the river valley. When the aeroplanes rattled overhead, they would duck under the mantle of leaves, waiting until they passed.

Glowworms clung to the leaves above them and

to blades of grass at their feet, lighting their path, but Gisèle still wasn't certain how the children had managed to walk so far that night. Perhaps some of the children thought it was all a dream. It was as if they were all sleepwalking, dazed from Sister Beatrice awakening them long before dawn.

The nuns had prepared them well for a night-time evacuation. The older children dressed quickly and rolled up their bedding. Gisèle and Josef assisted the younger ones who lagged behind, and the nuns quickly prepared sacks of food to carry.

Now Sister Beatrice and two other nuns prodded their wards gently along while the older children helped those who were younger, picking them up when they stumbled. Gisèle held the hand of the boy she'd found in Saint-Lô and the hand of a girl who wasn't much older than Adeline. Josef carried the youngest child, a two-year-old boy, who'd fallen asleep on his shoulder.

Gisèle glanced over at the man beside her, towering over all of them in his uniform. The child now cuddled against his chest. At first, the children had been terrified of the German officer and initially Sister Beatrice had been furious at Gisèle for leading him to the orphanage. It hadn't taken Gisèle and Josef long to convince her of the gravity of what might happen if they didn't leave right away.

Soon Sister Beatrice was more angry that after

all these years of hiding, when the Allied forces were so close to rescuing them, the Germans were coming after her children.

A light shone at the edge of the trees, and at first Gisèle thought it was the starlight, welcoming them, but she quickly realized that it was much too bright.

"Get down," Sister Beatrice commanded, and the children sank to the ground.

Gisèle held her breath as four vehicles passed by them, waiting to hear the slamming of car doors, but only silence remained.

Josef motioned for all of them to wait as he stepped out onto the road. "Gisèle," he whispered.

Seconds later, she joined his side. The taillights of the vehicles had disappeared, and no lights glowed in the valley below, not even in Saint-Lô.

"Why are they using their headlights?" she asked. An Allied plane could see them for miles.

Josef scanned the valley in front of them. "They are in a hurry."

She shivered. When Josef didn't return to the house, had the Nazis rushed out to find the orphanage without him?

He glanced down at his watch. "They'll patrol the footpath below in a half hour."

"Should we wait?" she asked. It would take the children at least twenty minutes to get down the hill.

He put his hand on the back of the sleeping boy

in his arms. "When they find the orphanage vacant, they will comb the forest and valley until they find us."

She remembered the lights when they were searching for the airmen. The barking of the dogs. The Germans had searched for weeks for Eddie and Daniel. If they didn't get these children to the tunnel right away, they had no chance against the dragon.

"We must go," she said.

Josef whispered to Sister Beatrice, and she arranged the children and adults into small clusters. Then, with the child in his arms, Josef led the clusters quickly down the hillside. Gisèle crossed the footbridge first and ushered the children across the footpath and back into the covering of the hawthorns while Josef waited on the far side of the river until everyone was safe in the trees.

But then she heard the hammer of the boots she'd heard outside her bedroom door hours ago.

"Halt!" A man shouted, and her heart plummeted.

The German patrol had arrived.

"Who is it?" a man barked in German.

Gisèle glanced at Sister Beatrice, who was tucked back in the limbs of an apple tree. The nun didn't say a word, turning instead toward the children, outstretching her arms as if she could protect every child in her care. Gisèle clung to the rosary beads and the key around her neck as she murmured her prayers.

"It is Hauptmann Josef Milch."

They were so close to the cellar. So very close . . .

Should she join Josef? No, that would only give away the location of the rest of the children. Perhaps Josef could convince the patrol that he'd been sent on official business.

But that would be impossible. Josef still held a child in his arms.

When the man spoke again, his voice was much lower, and she strained to hear his words. "The major is looking for you."

"Benjamin?" She heard the relief in Josef's voice.

"*Ja.*"

"Von Kluge ordered me to raid the orphanage."

"I see you have followed his command." And Gisèle could imagine him looking at the child in Josef's arms. She prayed the man was a father. And that a seed of compassion remained in him.

"*Ja,*" Josef said, "but I will not send this child to the camps."

She couldn't hear Benjamin's response.

"Where are the others?" Josef asked.

"The major sent everyone else out tonight."

She shivered. Would others be awakened by German soldiers commanded to send them away?

One of the other children coughed from the trees, and the men stopped talking for a moment.

"I could not do as I was commanded," Josef whispered.

"They will search everywhere for you."

"They will not find me."

After a long pause, Benjamin spoke again. "Godspeed." She released her hold on the rosary beads, and Sister Beatrice's arms relaxed beside her.

Seconds later, Josef marched through the branches. The child had awakened, but his arms were clutched around Josef's neck.

"Why did he let us go?" Gisèle asked.

Josef held back a branch so it wouldn't cut the child. "He is a friend."

Another fleet of aeroplanes charged down from the north, and with the ground trembling under their feet, she directed the children swiftly through the thorny trees.

CHAPTER 56

Riley and I found the abandoned manor house hidden back in the forest north of Saint-Lô, hemmed in by an iron fence and canopy of trees. The sisters who worked there, Marguerite told us, had hidden Jewish children among their wards.

The front gates were open, and Riley parked his rental car inside before he dug out his camera. I took a picture of the front of the house with my phone, but I would wait to text it across the

Atlantic. If it did jog my father's memories, I wanted Mom to be near him.

The front door was locked, but there was no knob or latch on the back door, so I pushed it open. The ceiling sagged precariously over ten wooden tables and benches, convincing me not to step inside, but I stood at the doorway and took another picture.

Had the children here survived the war or had the Nazis taken them away?

I knew it took a lot of courage for my father to share his troubled dreams with me. It was humbling to forget one's childhood, especially when it was replaced with a confusing set of memories and dreams that prompted only questions. Snatches of children grouped together. Escaping in the night. The airplane ride to the States.

Another thought thundered through my mind.

Stéphane had said that my father wasn't the biological son of Gisèle Sauver. The Duchant heir.

Was it possible that my father hadn't come with his mother to help the orphans? It was plausible that he may have been one of the children needing help. Perhaps he was supposed to replace the child that Mémé lost.

If that was the case, no wonder his childhood was like a prism. Mémé, in her love for him, had invented a beautiful story about his father—the French soldier who died in the war—and a childhood growing up at the château. A story she deemed safe. She had wanted him to forget the truth and he had. Until he began to dream.

Turning, I wandered over to an old playground. With his camera on his lap, Riley was spinning slowly around on the rusty merry-go-round. He looked up at me, and I saw tears in his eyes. All the pride I'd seen in his pictures online, the cockiness that I'd once accused him of, all of it had been stripped away.

Riley wiped his tattooed arm across his face before he slowed the merry-go-round. I sat down beside him. The seconds passed in silence, the two of us watching the branches sweep across the roof of the old manor house. Somehow, in the mystery of this house, I suspected there was healing as well.

"What happened to your daughter?" I asked.

He took a deep breath. "I told you that I moved away from home before I finished high school."

I nodded.

"I wanted to act, but there was another reason I left. My girlfriend was pregnant, and I talked her into having an—" He choked on the word. "I wanted her to end her pregnancy. We were too young to have a child . . ."

I crossed my arms over my chest, not knowing what to say.

"Twelve years ago, I drove Helena to the clinic." He stood up, his eyes on the swing set. "And then I didn't even wait a week. I packed up my beater of a car and didn't just walk away from my girlfriend. I ran, all the way to New York."

I stood beside him, and he pushed a rusty bar on the merry-go-round, watching it swirl around. "My parents were furious, and I tried—I tried desperately to forget them and Helena and most of all, my lost baby. I threw myself into my own search for success, and when I failed miserably, I tried drinking and drugs and more women, as if that could somehow patch up my bleeding soul. It wasn't until my grandfather came to find me that I knew I had to stop running.

"My grandfather rescued people, but I—" His voice broke again as he pushed the rail. "I thought I'd killed my child."

My skin bristled.

"I didn't think I could forgive myself, but then—" His voice cracked. "Helena was killed in a house fire two years ago, outside Chicago. She died making sure her nine-year-old daughter wasn't trapped in her bedroom."

I shivered. "She didn't abort?"

He shook his head.

My arms slowly fell back to my sides, the wonder in his voice drawing me into his story.

"She lied to me in the clinic and then after I left, she and her family moved away. Last year, my father got a call from Helena's father. His wife had grown ill, and they couldn't care for their granddaughter anymore. My parents didn't tell me what happened, but they invited her to live with them."

I leaned back against a tree, trying to bear his burden like he had with Madame Calvez.

"Last week, when I called home to ask about my grandfather's video, my daughter answered the phone."

"What is her name?"

"Abigail." He pushed the merry-go-round again. "Her name means 'the father's joy.'"

"Oh, Riley," I pleaded. "You have to go home."

"I can't go back now. I wanted to abort her."

I tugged at his sleeve until he looked back at me. "You are no longer that man. God has given you a second chance."

He sat back down on the merry-go-round.

"Abigail needs her dad," I said. "But even more, I think you need Abigail."

Chapter 57

Gisèle tried to rub the pain out of her head. They'd been in the tunnel for more than four hours, and most of the children were asleep now on the floor. Adeline was at Lisette's apartment, but what if the Germans took Adeline from her, thinking the child was Gisèle's? Would they punish both Lisette and Adeline because Gisèle had disappeared?

She had to sneak out to Lisette's apartment and bring them both back here.

Josef studied her as he picked up two of the canteens left on the floor. "I will get water for the children and another flashlight."

Gisèle motioned him farther down the path so they could speak without any of the children hearing. The flashlight they'd found in the tunnel was still glowing, but Josef was right. The batteries wouldn't last much longer. Still, she didn't want him to leave. "They'll find you," she whispered, terrified at what the Germans would do to him.

"The children are safe," he said, his eyes upon her, tenderness in his voice. "You are safe."

"Adeline isn't safe."

"I will search for her."

How she wished she and Josef were both students at the university, five years ago. They could laugh and flirt and toast to tomorrow where neither of them had a care. The cares of today felt impossible. Overwhelming. They must find Adeline, but she did not want to lose Josef. It felt as if her heart would tear into two tattered pieces.

"Michel will return soon," she insisted. "He will help us find her."

He raked his hand through his hair, his voice sad again. "I fear your brother won't be returning."

Her pulse quickened. "Why not?"

"Major von Kluge was expecting another convoy today from Germany, but the resistance fighters blew up the tracks."

"What about Michel?"

"The train was carrying hundreds of soldiers from the front and they jumped out when the train derailed."

When he hesitated, her stomach clenched. "Josef?"

"Someone sent a wire to the major. It said that both Michel Duchant and Jean-Marc Rausch had been killed."

She clung to the side of the tunnel, the shell that had protected her brother for the past four years, gasping for breath. "Why didn't you tell me before?"

"The major wanted me to find these children, but even more, he wanted me to find you."

The realization sickened her. "He was going to hurt me."

"Your brother was found to be a leader of the resistance party and your husband was a member as well. You are guilty by association."

"Not by association, Josef. You know I am guilty, at least in their eyes."

"But innocent in the eyes of God."

She wanted to scream so loud that it would echo through the tunnel, all the way up through the wine cellar and shake the halls of the château. She wanted the men upstairs to feel her pain.

She'd known it was coming, that Michel would join their parents soon. In her heart, she'd said good-bye long ago, but with the war so close to the end, she'd hoped, desperately, that perhaps he would survive.

Josef clutched both of her hands and held them to his chest. "I will come back for you, Gisèle. For you and all of these children."

"Please find Adeline," she begged before giving him directions to Lisette's apartment. Then she slipped her rosary beads off her neck and placed the crucifix in his hand. "This is the key."

He held it to his own heart. "Indeed."

And as he left, her heart warred with itself. She knew she probably should say good-bye to him as well, but she couldn't.

Gisèle sat at the base of the cellar in the darkness, clutching the neckline of her blouse as if it was her rosary beads. Josef had been gone for hours now, much too long for checking on Adeline and filling up the canteens. Had Major von Kluge or his men found him?

She couldn't think about what might happen if they did. Her brother was gone now, and if she lost Adeline and Josef too—

She wouldn't be able to survive.

The roof of the cavern rumbled, the ground shuddering. Were the Germans bombing Saint-Lô, or was it the Allied forces who were trying to take it back from the Nazis? It didn't matter, she supposed. A bomb from the good guys or the bad guys was still a bomb. The Allies wouldn't want to kill the children like the Nazis did, but neither could they control precisely where their bombs fell. And they didn't know there were children underground near the château.

The bombing had shaken the tunnel for hours, and she feared the roof might cave in, but still they couldn't leave. As she waited, she prayed—for Josef and Adeline and for all the children in her care.

A candle flickered in the tunnel, and she looked up to see the little boy whom she'd taken to the orphanage two years ago, the one who had clung to her hand all the way down the hill last night and snuggled beside her until he fell asleep.

"What are you doing up?" she whispered.

"I don't like the bombs."

"Me neither."

He climbed into her lap.

"What is your name?" she asked as she had in that alleyway so long ago.

He leaned back against her, and this time he answered. "Michel."

"It is a good name," she said softly, wondering if that was his real name or if he'd acquired it when Lisette said he looked like Michel. "Were your parents French?"

"I don't know."

He was so young. Like Adeline, he probably wouldn't remember his parents when he grew up, but perhaps it was good that he couldn't remember. Perhaps she should pray he did forget—the bombing and the hatred, the abandonment and the fear, the hunger and the grief.

She pushed his hair back away from his eyes. "Do you know the story of Saint Michel?"

"A little."

"I used to tell it to my brother when he was younger."

"He is an angel," the boy said.

"Not just any angel. Michel is a fierce archangel, and the leader of God's army." She swallowed. "He defeated evil once already and the Scriptures say that one day Michel and his army will fight this great dragon again and defeat it for good."

"I will fight too," he told her. "Like Josef."

She prayed he would stand up against the evil in their world. "Do you want to pray with me for Josef?"

He closed his eyes. "Please help us fight," the boy prayed. "Help us not to be scared."

Then he looked back up at her.

"My brother once told me that courage doesn't mean our fears are gone. It means we continue to fight, even when we are afraid."

She might be scared as well, but she could no longer hide in this tunnel while Adeline was out there. If Josef couldn't find her, then she would have to.

The hatch rattled above them, and as they leapt to their feet, her heart rejoiced, thinking Josef had returned. But then she realized someone with an ax or another weapon was hacking away at the lock on the door. There was so little fight left in her, and yet she had to protect Michel and the other children.

She shoved him away from her. "Run!"

She would tell the Germans she was the only one down here, that she was hiding alone. She would tell them—

Michel edged back to her side. "I will fight them."

"Not now," she said, chiding herself for telling him about the archangel. "When you are older, you can fight."

But still he didn't move.

A flashlight shone down on her face, and she covered her eyes. How was she supposed to protect the children now? The Germans had killed her father. Her brother. Major von Kluge and his commander would take her life in a heartbeat if they thought she'd helped the resistance and the Jews. But like Michel—her brother and the little boy beside her—she wouldn't cower.

"Gisèle," the man above her called. She blinked in the light.

"Who is it?" she asked.

"Don't tell me that you forgot me already." The man dropped down beside her, and she could see his face, the sliver of a mustache over his upper lip. It was the pilot from the American plane. Eddie McAllister.

And he was smiling.

She dropped her arms to her sides, relief washing through her. It had been such a long time since she had seen anyone smile. "I told you not to tell anyone about this place," she said.

His grin grew a little wider. "I thought you might need a friend."

She pointed down the tunnel. "There are thirty children hiding back there. They all need a friend."

He shouted up to whoever was above him, and a group of soldiers flooded past her.

"We'll get them out."

They ran past her, and when she looked up, she saw the faint light of morning above.

She hurried up the ladder.

CHAPTER 58

The day the delivery truck arrived, Lisette Calvez was waiting by the window in the drawing room of the château, sipping a glass of red wine. "Chloe!" she called from the bed one of her grandsons had brought down when he visited from London.

I rushed down the steps from my room.

Riley had hoped the package would arrive yesterday, but it was held up at customs. Lisette and I had been watching for it all morning.

After Lisette was discharged from the hospital, I asked her to stay at the château with me. At first she had balked at the idea of living here, but Monique told her grandmother she could not continue living on her own, so she finally agreed to join me, as long as she could sleep in one of the rooms on the first floor. She'd been living with me for more than a week now. When I returned to the States, she would go back to Paris with Monique and Isabelle.

There was a story she wanted to tell me before she left, but the nurse who visited twice a day told her to stay away from stress. And the best way to avoid stress right now was to avoid talking about the past.

But Riley said Lisette and I should watch his grandfather's interview together. When I asked about stress, he thought it would bring healing instead. I figured he should know a little about healing. In the past five days, he'd texted me at least ten pictures of the most beautiful young lady smiling back at him. She had his green eyes and long honey-colored hair that she tucked back in colorful headbands.

Outside I signed for the package and clutched it close to my chest. We'd discussed having him put the interview online, password protected, but he planned to use some of the footage for his documentary. The rest of it, he said, I probably wouldn't want online either, even with a password.

I made a pot of vanilla almond tea for Lisette and me, and we sat on two upholstered chairs in the drawing room, the cups of tea between us. My heart began to race as I inserted the DVD into the laptop I'd borrowed from Pierre.

On the screen emerged a picture of the man I assumed to be Eddie McAllister, wearing a decorated hat and coat from World War II. His face was wrinkled with age, but I could see Riley in the sharpness of his eyes and, as he began to speak, the confidence in his voice. The girls must have swarmed around him in France after the war as they did Riley in New York.

At first, Eddie spoke about his early years growing up outside Detroit and about training to become a pilot for the U.S. Air Force. Then he talked about the night his plane crashed into a valley near Saint-Lô.

I leaned forward.

"My navigator and I were rescued by a lovely gal named Gisèle," he said with a smile. "She hid us—well, I promised her I wouldn't say exactly where, but she took Daniel and me to her brother and then she helped us get identity cards. Her brother Michel got us on what they called *the line,* and we were escorted by another lady all the way down to Spain, where our boys flew in to pick us up."

A voice off camera asked him what happened to the rest of his crew. "Two were shot by the Germans, but four others were hidden by farmers and eventually sent back to England too." He straightened his hat. "After D-Day, I came back to Saint-Lô. The Germans refused to leave that city, and the fighting was atrocious, but I owed it to Gisèle to help her. I had no idea what I would find there . . .

"I asked Gisèle to marry me." He laughed. "But she turned me down. It seemed she was in love with another chap, a German officer."

I stared at the screen, my head struggling to sort out his words. My grandmother, in love with a Nazi?

That wasn't right. She loved Henri Sauver.

Was this German her first husband? No, that didn't seem right either. Marguerite had said that the Germans were friendly in the beginning of the war, but my grandmother had never been in love with one . . .

She'd married Henri Sauver in 1944 after the war, but my grandfather was French. He'd resisted the Germans.

Eddie continued. "The officer was part Jewish, and he'd been the one to make us the identity papers. And I remember this little boy with us the day we went back. An orphan. He wouldn't let go of Gisèle's hand.

"The world was crashing down around her, but Gisèle refused to leave France without him. She also wanted us to find a woman named Lisette and another child, a little girl." He paused. "I can't remember the girl's name, but it was too late. They'd already been deported. It was one of my biggest regrets of the war, not being able to find them."

The voice off camera asked what happened to Gisèle. "I don't know," he said, sadness heavy in his voice. "The airplane took her to England, and I never saw her again. But I owe my life to her and Josef."

"Stop," Lisette whispered.

I turned off the DVD.

Chapter 59

※ゝ(♡)ぐ፠

Saint-Lô was on fire.

Buildings burned around Gisèle, the hedgerows flattened and charred by the bombs. Townspeople were screaming. Fleeing. The nightmare of the blitzkrieg returned, except this time the Allied forces were fighting back.

Planes blazed overhead. Gunfire echoed through

the streets. The shadows of Nazi soldiers shifted among the flames.

Gisèle took no care for herself. She had to find Lisette and Adeline and Josef. There was still time to flee in the confusion.

She wouldn't tell Lisette about Michel's death, not until they were safe in the tunnel.

The door to the apartment building had been torn from its hinges, and she rushed toward it.

"*Bonjour*, Gisèle."

She whirled around, and Philippe stepped out of the shadows.

"There are a lot of people searching for you," he said.

"I don't know why—"

"Are you looking for your daughter?" His voice was cruel. Malice wrapped around every word.

Her heart froze. "Where is she?"

"Far away." He clicked his tongue. "You shouldn't keep secrets from me."

She glanced wildly around them. Where had Adeline gone? Perhaps she could catch whoever had taken her.

But she couldn't move, couldn't run. The Nazis had taken everything from her. Everyone she loved. She'd done all she could to protect them and yet it wasn't enough. The dragon was still crushing them.

"The château is mine, Gisèle."

She felt sick. After all this, he wanted the house. "You can have it."

"Thank you." She saw the muzzle of his gun, pointed at her, and then the glint of a diamond on the end of his cuff, surrounded by black onyx and gold. She flashed back to the night she'd found her father in the tunnel. Her brother showing her what he'd found in the cave. The cuff link she'd thought a German officer left behind.

"Philippe—" She clutched the sides of her skirt. "When did you replace that?"

He lowered the gun a few centimeters. "Replace what?"

"Your cuff link."

He shook his head. "It doesn't matter."

Her resolve hardened. "You went back to the château, didn't you? The night we got stopped in Saint-Lô."

"Perhaps—"

"Did you kill my father?"

In his silence, she knew. The Germans hadn't killed her father that night. It was her cousin who'd beaten him up by the lake. And then pulled the trigger. Michel was right—Philippe would do anything to get the Duchant property.

A child cried for her mother, and Gisèle's heart clenched. She had fought as hard as she could and she had lost. She had pushed through her fears, but still she'd failed.

She heard the shuffle of feet and a little boy

stepped in front of her. Michel. He must have followed her from the tunnel. "Don't touch her," he said.

Philippe's gaze flickered down to the boy. "You seem to be collecting children, Gisèle."

She put her arm around the boy's shoulders, pulling him close to her. "He hasn't done anything wrong."

"Bravery I admire, but not stupidity."

The boy lurched forward, his fists clenched in front of him, but she held him back. She was so proud of him, standing resolute in front of her, ready to die for someone he loved.

A German soldier stepped into the smoky light. "I will take over."

Philippe's pistol shook. "She is mine," he replied in German.

Josef wrapped his fingers around her arm. "No, she is Oberst Seidel's."

She'd never heard Josef speak with such authority, as if there was no doubt that Philippe had to obey.

But Philippe refused to concede. "I will take her to the *Oberst*."

A bomb hit the prison behind her cousin, and in seconds, the centuries of stone collapsed into rubble. If Philippe didn't shoot them, it wouldn't be long before one of the soldiers or a bomb took all of them. The bombs didn't differentiate between enemies and allies.

"I said I will handle this." Josef yanked on her arm, and she lurched toward him. "You are Philippe Borde, are you not?"

Philippe's eyes narrowed. "How do you know my name?"

"Major von Kluge is searching for you." He glanced both ways before he spoke again. "He fears he might have been mistaken about the death of Michel Duchant."

Philippe dropped the gun to his side. Then he raced the other way.

Josef clasped both arms behind her back and did the same with the boy, prodding them both down the sidewalk. His two prisoners until they reached the end of town.

Then the three of them ran.

It wasn't until much later, when they reached the *chapelle*, that she saw fresh blood pooling on Josef's sleeve.

CHAPTER 60

"After the war . . ." Lisette whispered. "Gisèle never returned or tried to contact us. I didn't think she cared about what happened to Adeline. Or to me."

I reached over for Lisette's hand and we sat in silence for a moment, processing Eddie's story, which collided with both of ours.

"Hauptmann Milch was a hero," Lisette said. "Why did you tell Riley that you didn't know him?"

"There were a lot of German men named Josef." I sipped my tea. "But you knew who he was talking about in the interview."

"I figured Josef wanted to keep his story secret, like I didn't want anyone to know mine."

I let her words settle for a moment as I stared at Eddie's face, paused on the computer screen. "The orphan boy was my father, wasn't it?"

"The Germans put me on a train," Lisette said. "I don't know what happened after I left."

But I knew Stéphane was right. My father wasn't the biological child of Jean-Marc and Gisèle Rausch, nor had he helped Gisèle rescue the Jewish orphans. He was one of the orphans.

An insect landed on the table, and Lisette watched it for a moment. "In the last days of the war, the Nazis went crazy, deporting everyone they thought to be Jewish or those who they thought were harboring the Jews or members of the French Resistance. They raided the orphanage, but all the children were gone."

"Where did they go?" I asked.

She shrugged. "Perhaps your father knows."

I understood that my grandparents might have been afraid to tell people their son was a Jew after they immigrated, in case there was another war, but why had they harbored the secret for so many years after the fighting ended? They should have been proud of his heritage.

"What happened to Adeline?" I asked.

Lisette's hands trembled as she sipped her tea, the cup clattering against the saucer when she placed it down. Then she nodded slowly, as if she'd decided to trust me with the rest of her secrets. "Adeline was just a baby when Gisèle and I found her. Her mother was Jewish and her parents were deported during the war. Gisèle cared for her at the château during the war." She scooted back on her chair. "Did you know Philippe tried to marry Gisèle?"

I shook my head.

"She refused, but Philippe was deeply in debt and he needed the Duchant property to maintain his lifestyle. After he took the life of Vicomte Duchant, he determined to kill both Gisèle and her brother so the château would be his." She paused. "Have you heard of the Milice?"

Again I shook my head, feeling foolish for knowing so little about what Mémé had faced. And for being frustrated at her for not telling me what happened.

"The Milice were the French version of the Gestapo and they were a nasty bunch. Philippe joined them during the war and began to research Gisèle's story. He found out that Jean-Marc Rausch, the man she'd said she married, had been fighting in northern France on their wedding day.

He tried to deport Gisèle before the Allied troops freed Saint-Lô, but she ran away. And she left Adeline in my care."

"Mémé thought you'd been deported—"

"At the time, all I knew was that she was gone and Philippe was at my apartment. I had known him from before, back when he visited the château . . ." When she paused, I told her I understood. She didn't need to tell me more. "No one in Saint-Lô knew he was with the Milice except me. Philippe knew that the Germans would be gone soon and he feared the French would send him to prison when they found out about his role. He had me arrested, but he kept something—someone—for when I returned."

I shivered. "Adeline."

"She was collateral for my silence." She looked down at her hands. "Philippe's mother died soon after the war. He moved into the château, and I went to Paris with Adeline. For almost seventy years, I guarded his secret and he guarded mine."

I glanced out the window. "Monique's mother was Adeline."

"I changed her name back to Louise," she said. "She knew her biological parents were killed during the war, but she didn't know that her mother was Jewish. The Germans had already attacked our country twice. I wanted to protect her, in case they returned again."

"What happened to Louise?" I asked.

Lisette smiled. "She grew up in Paris and trained to be a nurse for the Red Cross. In 1966, she married a fine man. A doctor. They had five children who decided they wanted to change the world in their own way."

"You never married?"

"The only man I ever wanted to marry was killed in the war," she said. "But my friends in Paris thought I was a widow."

I reached for my cup and took a long sip of the tepid tea. "Isabelle said the government gave you the cottage."

She nodded. "The children of deported Jews began receiving compensation from the government ten years ago. By that time, Louise had passed away and I didn't want money, so I asked them for the cottage where her parents had lived before the war. No one had lived in it since 1942, and I think the local officials were pleased to have someone renovate it. I was pleased that my grandchildren and great-grandchildren could learn a bit of Louise's story."

My phone beeped and I saw a text from Riley. It was a photo, he said, that Benjamin Tendler had emailed to him. A picture of Benjamin and his friend Josef Milch.

I stared at the two men in uniform, standing in front of the hedgerows. All my life I'd been told that Henri Sauver was a French soldier, a resister of the Germans, but as I stared at the photo of the German officer next to Benjamin, there was no denying the truth. My grandfather had served Hitler in the war.

What would have happened if my grandparents' American neighbors found out that Henri had been an officer in the Wehrmacht? And that his son, my father, was a Jewish orphan?

They had to guard their secret.

I texted Riley back, asking him to wait to finish the documentary. I wasn't afraid to let the world know my father's family was Jewish, but I was horrified to tell anyone that the grandpa I loved had been a Nazi.

Chapter 61

Josef collapsed on a pew in the *chapelle*. He'd been shot in the shoulder, the blood seeping through the American bandages. As one of Eddie's friends worked on him, Gisèle wondered silently if the Americans had been the ones to shoot him as well.

"We have to take him to a hospital in London," the man said.

She knelt beside Josef, taking his hand. She couldn't lose him too.

He kissed her hand. "I'm not going to leave you."

At one time she couldn't imagine loving a German officer, but she loved Josef Milch with all of her heart. She loved him for the way he cared about the Jewish children, for the way he served under an evil man in order to protect his mother, for the way he fanned an ember of warm light for those trapped in the darkness, for risking his life to save her.

"Well, I was going to ask you to marry me," Eddie said from behind her. "But a man knows when he's been defeated."

She looked back at the American pilot through her tears. "You'll make someone a fine husband, Eddie."

He shrugged. "Maybe after this war is over."

She squeezed Josef's hand. "The Allied soldiers are taking the children to London."

Flak echoed outside the *chapelle* and she heard a bomb explode nearby. She leaned closer to Josef. "I must find Lisette and Adeline before Philippe does."

He shook his head. "They are already gone."

"But where—"

"Benjamin said they'd been taken to the trains."

Dear God. She felt as if she would be sick. "They're deporting Adeline?"

"I'm so sorry, Gisèle."

She looked toward the door. "We must get to the trains."

"It's too late."

She found Eddie's eyes again, hoping he could find Adeline and Lisette as he had Josef, but all she saw was remorse in his gaze. "The Germans still control the train station."

She shivered. "We can't leave her and Lisette."

"I have a plane ready to fly you out of here," Eddie said. "To London."

"We must find them first."

"The trains already left," Josef said.

Her heart felt as if it had shattered.

Another bomb hit nearby and she heard the terrible crash of a building caving in upon itself. Loneliness pierced the fragments of her heart.

"It's only a matter of days before we defeat the Nazis," Eddie said. "Then you can search for your friends."

"I'll search with you," Michel said beside her.

She looked back and forth between Josef and this boy who risked everything to save her. And she realized that she was no longer alone.

If Josef was right, if the trains had left, they would never be able to find either Lisette or Adeline. At least not now.

Josef rested his head back against the wooden arm of the pew. "We will find them after the war."

Gunfire ricocheted outside her beautiful *chapelle*, and she didn't want to move. All this killing, this horror, would it never stop?

Eddie held her chin in his rough hands, looking her in the eye. "You and Josef must hurry."

She pulled Michel close to her. "This boy belongs with us."

Another bomb rocked the ground, and Eddie urged all three of them out of the *chapelle*. "Go quickly."

She would pray all the way to London for Lisette and for Adeline. And the moment the fighting was over, she would find both of them.

CHAPTER 62

Dad and I spent hours searching through the boxes in his parents' attic. It seemed my grandparents had kept every piece of memorabilia they'd collected since they reached the United States, along with all of Mémé's classroom papers, bills, and sixty years' worth of the *Farmers' Almanac*. Rain streaked down the dormer windows of the attic, and my dad and I laughed and cried together as we remembered.

I thought Dad would ask Riley to stop the documentary when he found out his father was an officer in the Wehrmacht. Instead he called Riley after I flew home from France and thanked him for telling the story of Josef Milch. In Dad's eyes, Henri Sauver—his father—was a hero.

Riley's documentary about the Jewish soldiers

was scheduled to air the first of the year, and now he was trying to track down other orphaned children who had been rescued during the war.

But before he started filming his new documentary, there was another project he wanted to complete first.

My father opened a file and then he whistled. "Bingo."

I scooted over to him and saw a birth certificate for Henri Sauver. Born in Paris. August 8, 1918.

"Josef must have forged that," I said.

Instead of using Milch, he'd changed his German last name to a French one that meant "salvation."

There was a marriage license for Gisèle and Henri in the folder, and the birth certificate for Michael Sauver. It slowly occurred to me that Josef had forged my father's birth information as he had Adeline's.

I leaned back against a post. "They never adopted you."

"Perhaps not legally," he said. "But they were my parents."

"They should have made it legal . . ."

My father shook his head. "It doesn't matter now."

But it did matter, at least for their case against Stéphane. My grandfather had forged the papers for Dad's birth, perhaps to bring him to the United States with them, but châteaus in France were passed down through the bloodline of the old families. Even if Josef had the best of intentions, the French courts wouldn't side with a German officer who had taken one of their children and run away.

Josef Milch had rescued an entire orphanage of French children and raised one of the orphaned Jews as his own child. But he still should have legally adopted my dad.

"Look at this," Dad said.

I leaned over and saw the other papers in his hands. They were carbon copies of letters, inquiring after Lisette Calvez, André Batier, Nadine Batier, Charlotte Milch, Odette Laval, and Adeline Rausch. I slowly read through the responses to Henri's letters.

Lisette Calvez had returned to Paris in May 1945, one letter reported, but Odette Laval had been killed in Paris during the blitzkrieg. Nadine Batier died on a train before she reached Buchenwald, three months before André died. Charlotte Milch was killed in the gas chamber at Dachau. And according to the last letter from the French government, they had found no record of a child named Adeline Rausch.

My grandparents hadn't forgotten those they loved, the people they had left behind. They'd found out what happened to everyone except Adeline. No wonder that, in these years when memories blurred, my grandmother thought Adeline was still lost in the trees.

"Chloe!" Marissa shouted from the base of the stairs, and I hurried down to my best friend. Her hair was tied back in a knot, and the apron she wore over her jeans and T-shirt was coated with flour. She held out my cell phone and I saw two missed calls from Riley.

"Do you know what happened?" I asked.

"Of course not," she said with a laugh. "Your mom is trying to show me how to make a lemon soufflé."

As Dad and I worked, Marissa and my mother had been inspired to concoct all sorts of French desserts in Mémé's kitchen.

I called Riley back.

"Turn on your TV," he said.

"Are you certain?"

He sighed. "No."

I'd been avoiding the television all day, but with Riley on the phone, I finally braved the network news. Red and blue balloons trickled down the screen, and I saw Austin Vale on a stage with both of his parents and his sister, all their arms raised in victory. In the close-up shot, his smile almost stretched across the television screen.

Austin hadn't just charmed me. He'd charmed the entire Commonwealth of Virginia.

In that moment, I thanked God for filling the empty places inside me with contentment and peace. I was incredibly grateful to be in my grandparent's home tonight with people I loved instead of on that stage, forcing a smile alongside the new governor-elect and his dysfunctional family.

The camera panned across the front of the crowd, and I searched the screen for Vos and Wyatt. I didn't see Austin's brother or brother-in-law, but there, two rows back from the front, sat Starla Dedrick, pampered and pressed. She wasn't smiling.

"Are you okay?" Riley asked.

"I'm relieved," I said, muting the volume on the TV. "Immensely."

"No regrets," he asked, part question and part statement.

Marissa and my mother laughed in the kitchen. "Not a single one."

"I was thinking . . . ," he said.

"Thinking about what?"

"Thinking that I would like to come back to Virginia soon."

My stomach fluttered. "I'm sure Mémé would love to see you again."

"Yes, well . . ." He paused. "I want to visit her, of course, but then, I wondered if I could come down to Richmond to spend time with you, or better yet . . ."

"Yes?"

"I was thinking you might want to come up here and meet Abigail."

I sat on the bottom step. Riley's relationship with his parents was slowly mending, and it seemed

434

he'd begun to forgive himself for his selfishness in the past. He hadn't known his daughter was alive, but the guilt for encouraging his girlfriend to abort their daughter had turned into guilt for abandoning her.

Even though Abigail was too young to hear the entire story, Riley had begged her forgiveness for missing the first eleven years of her life. Their reunion had been bumpy, he said, but Abigail was slowly beginning to forgive him.

"Or we could all meet in France," he said, and I could hear his smile.

"Why are you going to France?"

"Lisette wants me to do an interview with her about Philippe Borde and the undercover work of the Milice."

"Stéphane will be furious when he finds out."

"It's Lisette's story to share," he said. "Besides, it's a good excuse for me to return to Normandy. I hear there's decent food over there."

I laughed. "Pretty good wine too."

"And a whole lot of cows."

"You should definitely go back to see the cows."

"Come to France with me," he said, his voice low.

I glanced at the television screen again, at Austin's victory smile. Instead of the lights of the television cameras, the glamour of the celebration parties to follow, my heart longed for Normandy, for the beauty and the history and the time to savor all of God's gifts, for the stories that I knew about and the stories that remained untold.

"Perhaps I will . . . ," I said.

But this time I wouldn't be running away.

This time I would be running alongside Riley and his daughter, I hoped, to the place where my heart had begun to mend.

EPILOGUE

Three Months Later

All five of Louise's children attended the memorial service for Gisèle Duchant in the Chapelle d'Agneaux, each of them telling my father how much they appreciated all she had done. Lisette read a beautiful tribute to her and so did my dad. I'd tried to read the tribute I wrote, but Riley had to step up and read it for me.

Mémé's body now rested in the small plot by the *chapelle*, beside her parents and her brother. And my father had arranged for the remains of Grandpa to be returned to France as well, so he could be put to rest beside his wife. His epitaph read:

Henri Sauver,
also known as Hauptmann Josef Milch
A man of God
And a protector of God's children

As the priest recited the Rite of Committal in front of Mémé's grave, my father clutched my hand. After my return from France last summer, I'd waited for months to tell Mémé about Adeline. With peace in her heart, I feared she would finally let go of this life for the paradise beyond.

I don't know if Mémé understood when I shared Adeline's story, but three days later, Pamela opened the window in Mémé's room and when she turned around, my grandmother was gone. It was as if she'd hitched a ride on the breeze and sailed away to those who'd been waiting for her for so long.

I imagined Josef and Adeline and Michel and my great-grandparents crowding around her, kissing her on both cheeks, showering her with their hugs. I imagined her remembering again all that happened in her life, but with joy instead of pain, for in the end she'd conquered even death.

I imagined Christ welcoming her with open arms, saying the simple but profound words.

Well done.

Along with Mémé's will, Dad had received a letter from his mother explaining much of her story in case Philippe—or his son—tried to fabricate it. No one else except Philippe had known Henri Sauver was a former Nazi officer. Just as Philippe kept Madame Calvez's secret, he kept the secret of Josef's and Michel's histories, as long as Gisèle didn't expose that he'd murdered Vicomte Duchant. And allowed him live in the château.

Philippe hadn't told Stéphane all the details of the past before he died, but he'd told his son that Michel wasn't a Duchant by birth so Stéphane could fight to retain the château.

Gisèle had clung to the good memories of her home and the *chapelle* she loved, but with the exception of honoring her brother almost twenty years ago, she never wanted to return. Still, she wanted to keep the château for her son, hoping he and his family would love France as she had once loved it.

Enclosed with her letter and will was another paper, stamped by the Commonwealth of Virginia. In 1948 Henri and Gisèle had legally adopted Michel, and—much to the dismay of Stéphane Borde—adopted children in France now received the same inheritance as biological kids. Both the United States and the French government would treat Michel Sauver as Gisèle's legal heir.

Two days ago, after Stéphane had dropped his lawsuit, Dad offered to let Lisette stay in the house year-round, but she declined; her memories inside the château were too overwhelming. This evening Monique was taking her back to Paris.

But Dad was dreaming again—this time about using the château to house other orphans, older kids in need of a home. Mémé's spirit may have been embracing those she'd lost during the war, but her legacy was alive here in Saint-Lô.

When the service was over, Abigail and Isabelle raced off to play in the park. They'd become inseparable since they had met at the airport. Both of them needed a good friend.

As Dad and I walked away from the cemetery, he slipped something into my hand. "She wanted you to have this."

I smoothed my fingers over the amber beads of Mémé's crucifix "Are you certain?"

He nodded. "Look at the cross."

I held it up and realized it was also a key.

He nudged me toward the *chapelle* door. "She said to find Cair Paravel."

The ruined castle in Narnia, before it was rebuilt.

Riley's hand enclosed mine as the two of us stepped into the *chapelle* and then through the iron gates at the side. Dust clung to the old sink and table in the sacristy and it streaked across the large closet at the side of the room.

I thought of the times my grandmother had read the Narnia books to me and how fascinated I'd been with the magical world behind the wardrobe. Oftentimes we'd create our own worlds where good always triumphed over the bad, where death had no victory.

Cair Paravel could only be found in one place within the *chapelle*.

I opened the door to the large wardrobe and the smell of mothballs flooded out. I pushed aside the robes and other vestments, and at the very back, I knelt down and searched the wall until I found a tiny keyhole on a panel. Riley shone the light from his video camera into the closet, and I used the cross to open the door.

We'd found Mémé's tunnel.

Riley's light illuminated the walls for us as we descended under the ground. They were packed with dirt, the air musty and cold. We crept forward until the passage opened into a room with old newspapers, shoes, blankets, and cigarette butts scattered like muddy snowflakes on the ground.

"It's like a time capsule," I whispered in awe.

Riley swept the room with the lens of his camera and then he zoomed in on me. "How long do you think it's been since someone was down here?"

"Probably when my grandparents hid my father and the other orphans. Seventy years ago."

I leaned down and picked up what looked like a wallet. Inside was an identity card for Michel Duchant and I stared at the look of abandonment in my uncle's eyes, the windblown hair that he hadn't bothered to comb. Behind the card was a slip of paper, folded in half, addressed to Lisette Calvez. I smiled. Perhaps my uncle had loved Lisette as much as she had loved him.

I stuck the note in my pocket to take up to Lisette.

In front of Riley and me, the tunnel had caved in, from the impact of a bomb I assumed. Where it led I might never know, but here I felt my grandmother's presence, her passion and purpose, to rescue when the enemy was determined to destroy.

I followed Riley up the steps, and when we got back into the nave, I found a broom and began to sweep the floor. When I looked up, he was watching me. "What?" I asked.

"You may not be a Duchant by blood, but you have the heart of your grandmother." He stepped closer to me, and my stomach fluttered again as it seemed to do these days whenever he drew near. He glanced over at Saint Michel and then at the stained glass glowing against the gray walls. "This would be the perfect place for a wedding, don't you think?"

I tilted my head. "Are you planning to get married?"

"Only if you'll marry me."

Riley pulled me close to him and kissed me with the tenderest of desire, as if he feared he might hurt me. And I kissed him back.

In the past months, God hadn't given me what I thought I wanted. Instead he'd given me exactly what I needed—a man who loved me and a daughter I adored, hope for the future and a peace that settled deep in my soul. And He'd blessed me with the gift of my family's story.

As Riley held me in his arms, I glanced back up one more time at Saint Michel and his defeated dragon.

Mémé's story was finished at the Château d'Epines—the château of thorns—but the Duchant family legacy, I prayed, would live on in the children of France.

AUTHOR'S NOTE

On a rainy evening in March, I wandered alone through the halls of an old mausoleum in Normandy. While visitors swarmed the white crosses above Omaha Beach, honoring the lives of courageous Americans, the German cemetery was a lonely, grim memorial to twelve thousand Nazi soldiers who'd died on French soil.

It was curious to me that the French people chose to honor their enemy with this beautiful plot, set on a hill overlooking the island of Mont Saint-Michel and the English Channel, but during my visit to France I learned something new, something the French know well. While many of the German soldiers chose to battle for the Third Reich, others were forced to fight for a madman, like those French citizens forced to make weapons for Germany and the Russian prisoners forced to build roads.

As I stood in that eerie place, reading the epitaphs of soldiers as young as sixteen, I wondered who among them had been trapped in the German army. And who were the Jewish soldiers who fought and died for Hitler, believing that by joining the Wehrmacht they could protect them-selves or someone they loved?

Until I began researching this novel, I had no

idea that so many men of Jewish descent were in the Wehrmacht. No one knows the exact number—many of these men probably took this secret to their grave—but Bryan Mark Rigg in *Hitler's Jewish Soldiers* estimates that 150,000 Mischlinge fought during World War II. He interviewed a number of these men in recent years. Some of their stories were courageous, others cowardly, but all of their stories fascinated me.

The past slowly may be forgiven in France, but it will not be forgotten. What Hitler and his fellow Nazis did to the people of France was evil. Seventy-six thousand Jews were deported from France during World War II, eight thousand of those children. Only 3 percent of those "sent east" returned home. Horrific . . .

While visiting France, I heard stories about the Germans who occupied France for four years and I heard the stories of the resilient French people who chose to resist them. Thousands of men and women, conflicted in their hearts, stood against evil and sacrificed their lives so others could live. Some were shot. Others sent to concentration camps. Many of them refused to talk about their service even after the war.

This novel is loosely based on the life of one such heroine—a noblewoman named Genevieve Marie Josephe de Saint Pern Menke. Genevieve was raised in a medieval château outside Saint-Lô called Château d'Agneaux. The tunnels under the de Saint Pern home are no longer accessible, but the stories of her heroism are being passed down through generations of Menkes.

As a young woman, Genevieve rescued Allied airmen and volunteered for the French Red Cross as a driver and medic. She was awarded two Croix de Guerre medals for bravery in war—the first one for courageously telling a German officer that "an honorable man would not kill innocent people" and then successfully negotiating the release of the villagers in Germolles from execution by firing squad.

Genevieve married an American officer and moved to the United States after the war though she returned often to France. She passed away in 2010, but her legacy of courage and kindness continues on through her children and grandchildren. I hope this glimpse into her story and the stories of so many other heroic men and women during World War II inspires you as much as it has inspired me.

ACKNOWLEDGMENTS

Thank you to the entire Menke family for gifting me with Genevieve's remarkable story. To Kellee Menke Hernandez, who first told me about her beloved grandmother, and her parents, Doug and Ann Menke, who graciously answered my many questions, shared their favorite memories of Genevieve, and critiqued my rough manuscripts—I am so grateful for all of you. To both Darwin and Emmanuelle Menke for their hospitality—I loved spending time with your family, overlooking the lights of Paris. To Liz Menke for helping me navigate the French language, and to Anthony (Tony) "Yany" Menke, the oldest of the five Menke boys, for sharing the memories of his mother as well as educating me on the landed aristocracy in France. And a huge thank you to Herman Menke, an American lieutenant who fell in love with a French noblewoman seventy years ago and moved from Washington State to France with her in their twilight years. Herman asked me to portray the marvelous things his wife did in this novel, and I hope I have given her the honor she greatly deserves.

Thank you to my agent, Natasha Kern, for her enthusiasm for this story, and to my wonderful editor, Beth Adams, for all her wisdom in helping me build it. To my dear friend and sister Ann Menke, who invited me to spend an unforgettable week at her family's *manoir* and shared her love of Normandy with me. To my other "sistas"—Orlena Ballard and Mary Kay Taylor—who ventured to France with us and ended up stranded in a spring blizzard. Thank you for your flexibility and laughter, and for rescuing me when I got trapped behind the barbed wire on the Norman coast . . . Apparently "*sortie de secours*" does not mean "exit to the beach."

To my new French friends who shared their heroic stories with humility: Serge and Marie Charlotte Letourneur, the daughter and son-in-law of leaders in the French Resistance, thank you for welcoming us into your home and sharing both your stories and the pieces of an Allied parachute found after D-Day—I will treasure our day together. Jean ("Bobby") Veuillye for sharing your love for America with us and your childhood memories of the war. And Monique Lopez, who welcomed Darwin, Ann, and me with a warm heart and a kiss on each cheek. She remembered well the German occupation, but those memories were too painful for her to share.

To Martha DeLong for sending me her father's stories about fighting in France. George Edick passed away while I wrote this novel, but his legacy lives on . . .

To six amazing ladies who journey with me

through every manuscript—Michele Heath, Nicole Miller, Leslie Gould, Dawn Shipman, Kimberly Felton, and Kelly Chang. I can't tell you how much I appreciate each one of you! To Julie White, my longtime friend and elementary schoolteacher extraordinaire—thank you so much for sharing with me the many reasons you love teaching. To Lyn Beroth and Paul and Sheila Herbert for their gracious help with the authenticity of European birth and marriage certificates. To Sean and Adam at the Hillside House for the peaceful retreat and for spoiling me as I worked on this book.

Thank you to my family and friends for their consistent prayers and support, and my dad, Jim Beroth, who flew out to Portland to help care for my girls while I was in France. And thank you to my husband, Jon, for his love and encouragement, and our sweet daughters—Karlyn and Kinzel— for cheering me on. I am so blessed by each one of you.

He will wipe every tear from their eyes, and there will be no more death or sorrow or crying or pain. All these things are gone forever.

—REVELATION 21:4

Thank you most of all to our Savior, Jesus Christ, for His promise that one day all things evil will be destroyed.

ADDITIONAL COPYRIGHT INFORMATION

CHÂTEAU OF SECRETS
Melanie Dobson

INTRODUCTION

Gisèle is a young noblewoman whose world changes abruptly when German invaders bomb her hometown of Saint-Lô. Her beautiful home, the Château d'Epines, becomes the local headquarters for German officers. What no one else knows but her is that underneath the château are winding tunnels where her brother and fellow French Resistance fighters hide. Secrets abound within her heart, the walls of the château, and the snaking tunnels underneath.

Gisèle's granddaughter, Chloe, lives a life far removed from the times of war that her grandmother endured. After calling off her engagement to a prominent political candidate, Chloe agrees to participate in a documentary featuring her family history and the château in Normandy. She is surprised to learn that the documentary filmmaker, Riley, is interested in uncovering the story of Jews who served in Hitler's army. How would that relate to her family? And she is even more shocked to learn that there are tunnels under the Château d'Epines that saved lives.

As Chloe follows Riley on the documentary

journey, she discovers secrets held by both her grandmother and the château that encompass profound depths of love, loyalty, and sacrifice entwining their generations.

TOPICS AND QUESTIONS FOR DISCUSSION

1. The idea of secrets is introduced early in the novel. Gisèle considers the following question: "When did a secret cross over the gray wasteland between protecting one you loved and destroying him" (page 10)? In what ways did Gisèle's secrets protect the ones she loved? In what ways did Gisèle's secrets harm or cost the ones she loved, such as Lisette or even herself? How have you seen a secret destroy?

2. Initially, Chloe is engaged to marry Austin. Chloe acknowledges that she has lost herself in this relationship though, "Somewhere along the line, I'd forgotten exactly who I was, silhouetted by those with greater dreams than my own" (page 92). How do Chloe's romantic choices and consequences compare and contrast to Gisèle's, both in her refusal of Philippe and in her love for Josef? How does each woman's choice affect her identity?

3. The events surrounding Gisèle's young adult life differ drastically from those that surround

Chloe's. Different generations experience diverging degrees of luxuries, experiences, hardships, and upbringings that define their thresholds of "norm" and pain. How do you think someone from Gisèle's generation views those of today's generation? How have you judged someone in an older generation? What have they faced that you have not?

4. In an eloquent comment on World War II, Gisèle says, "Hatred, it seemed, was a powerful unifier of even the greatest enemies. Hatred for the Nazis had also unified those resisting them" (page 133). Love is also a powerful unifier, seen in Josef's desire to protect his mother and those who sacrificed their lives to protect Adeline. Describe how you have experienced the unifying power of both hatred and love.

5. After witnessing members of the resistance being shot to death, Gisèle thinks twice about being able to fight the Germans. "She might not be able to fight the dragon, but she prayed she could rescue this boy" (page 151). How do you see Gisèle continue to "fight the dragon" against the Germans even after she thinks this to herself? Describe an experience in your life that despite its trauma, you continued fighting the dragons.

6. When the Germans come to live at the Château d'Epines, Gisèle asks herself, "Should she stand

for all that was good and refuse them, even if it cost her her life? Or should she . . . compromise her morals to save her life—and the lives of those in her care" (page 220)? What decision would you have made if you were in her shoes? Why? Describe an experience in your life when you felt judged by others for making a decision that seemed the lesser of two evils.

7. In Chapter 30, Chloe tells her dad about finding Gisèle's marriage certificate and Adeline's birth certificate. How do you think this made him feel? Describe a time when you learned a secret that impacted or involved others. How did it make you feel?

8. Gisèle wrestles with the biblical command to "Love your enemies and pray for those who persecute you" (page 232). When was she supposed to love her enemy and when was she supposed to resist? And somehow, in the great mystery of faith, was it possible for her to do both? Do you think Gisèle did both? Explain. Do you think it is possible to do both in the Christian faith? Have you ever received love from a perceived enemy or prayed for an enemy? Describe the situation.

9. Riley tells Chloe, "It tells a lot about a person when you find out what or who they're willing to

die for" (page 200). In light of this statement, how would you describe and characterize Josef? Do you think Josef or Gisèle went too far to protect those they loved? How do you personally draw the line between protecting, serving, or loving others against sacrificing too much of yourself?

10. Riley's grandfather tells him that "we never know what we truly believe until we are standing in a trench, surrounded by the enemy" (page 295). Identify the "trenches" in Chloe's story that facilitate her discovery of who she truly is and what she believes. Were these events challenging, painful, or untroubled events? How have the "trenches" in your own life shaped you?

11. Philippe's debt drove him to make horrific decisions in order to obtain the château. How does his self-centered behavior contrast to the selfless actions of Gisèle's brother Michel? Secondly, consider and discuss the effects of their choices on the generations that follow. Describe an area in your life where you are influenced by a family member's prior decision(s).

12. Josef is a rescuer in numerous ways. At what cost to himself did he become the unlikely hero and of whom? Describe how you would feel to know that a soldier of one nation begins fighting

with and *for* the perceived enemy. How do you see this occurring today?

13. Imagine Gisèle and Lisette being able to see each other later in their lives prior to Gisèle's memory loss. What do you think the women would share with each other? What do you think each woman would feel toward the other?

14. Consider the novel being told from the *Oberst's* perspective, a man defending and sacrificing for his country, beliefs, and family. How do you judge and compare his level of sacrifice?

ENHANCE YOUR BOOK CLUB

1. Two of Gisèle's favorite quotes were the following: "You've never lived until you've almost died" by Guy de Maupassant and "I have learnt that all men live not by care for themselves but by love" by Leo Tolstoy (page 171). Discuss which of these quotes speaks the most to you. Why? Decide as a group a way everyone can lovingly serve someone this week, be it with time, money, or skills.

2. Outline your family tree to the extent that you can. Which two people in your family lineage inspire you the most? Why? What mysteries

remain in your family tree, if any? If there are gaps in knowledge, seek out the information.

3. The main characters in *Château of Secrets* make weighty decisions, often at great expense. "They all had to lose a bit of themselves to satiate the enemy . . . but that she prayed that in their hearts, they all would remain true to God and to France" (page 313). Discuss how you relate to this in the spheres of your vocation, relationships, finances, or time. What "enemy" do you feel like you must satiate for a greater purpose? Make one change if you believe you have sacrificed too much in a particular area and ask the group for accountability.

4. Write a letter of thanks to a U.S. soldier or veteran. If you do not know one, visit the websites "Letters to Home," "A Million Thanks," or "Operation Gratitude" to participate in sending words or small gift packages to a soldier, veteran, or wounded warrior.

5. Document your own personal story, either in its entirety or segments. Your story is a piece of history and significant to loved ones. Share a portion of it with the group.

A CONVERSATION WITH
MELANIE DOBSON

1. How did you first come to know of the story of Genevieve Marie Josephe de Saint Pern Menke on whom this story is loosely based? How do her children and grandchildren describe her?

After Genevieve passed away in 2010, her granddaughter shared Genevieve's stories of courage and faith with me. I was captivated by Genevieve's bravery in standing up against the Nazis when they could easily have killed her, and by the stories of her hiding the French Resistance underneath the family's château while the Germans occupied it. The Menke family partnered with me as I wrote this novel, and Ann Menke, Genevieve's daughter-in-law, graciously invited me to their family's *manoir* and former château in Normandy. Genevieve left a beautiful legacy as an elegant, courageous, feisty Norman woman who was strong in character and devout in her faith. Her husband, children, and grandchildren adored her, and I hope readers are inspired by her story as well.

2. Do you always visit the places where your books are set? Why is it helpful? What did you love most about your trip for this book?

I always visit the main setting of my books to discover what makes the place unique. The Internet is fantastic for accumulating general details about a location, but good sensory description—the local sights, smells, sounds—breathe life into a novel. And once I can see the setting in my mind's eye, I no longer get stuck on the details. My brain is freed to focus on the story.

I enjoyed everything about my trip to France—eating the crusty bread and local cheese, biking through the villages, staying in a medieval château with three dear friends. Also, I loved spending time with Genevieve's family and visiting with new friends in Normandy who welcomed us into their homes.

3. This novel is steeped in the historical detail of World War II and the Battle of Saint-Lô. What was your research process like?

Before I started writing *Château of Secrets*, I read through a stack of resources about the war as well as a number of interviews with Jewish men who fought in the German army. To help me visualize the details, I obtained photographs of the Battle of Saint-Lô along with film footage of Frenchmen resisting the Germans. My time in Normandy was the most important step in the research process. I learned a tremendous amount by exploring the Utah Beach D-Day Museum, strolling through Saint-Lô, and visiting with men and women who shared their memories of the occupation and the war.

4. Many of the main characters in this novel make great sacrifices for freedom, be it tangible or emotional. What does freedom mean to you?

Years ago a friend asked what I valued most in life, and my quick response was *freedom*. In hindsight, what I really meant was independence—the selfish freedom to do what I wanted, whenever I wanted. Much has happened since I answered that question, and the freedom I value now is more internal—freedom from anxiety and bitterness and fear. Instead of striving for things that deplete me or allowing my thoughts to whirl with anger and frustration, I try to focus on what God has called me to do and rely on Him for provision, direction, and peace. I don't always succeed at letting go, but this renewed faith in Christ has given me great freedom on the inside.

5. What would you describe as the main theme(s) in *Château of Secrets*?

The heart of this novel is about sacrifice—what happens to those willing to risk their life to rescue others and what happens to those who betray innocent people in an attempt to save themselves.

Some of the characters lost their life in this story while others found healing in their later years. In the Book of John, Jesus said these beautiful words, "Love each other in the same way I have loved you. There is no greater love than to lay down one's life for one's friends."

6. What do you want readers to experience or take away from this novel?

Château of Secrets is about seemingly ordinary people who stood against evil, often working in secret as they fought against the Nazis and protected innocent people marked for death. As I wrote this story, I was reminded that we have many opportunities today to stand against evil and protect those who are suffering. We may not be risking our life, but it is always extraordinary to sacrifice finances, time, and even our pride to help someone in need.

7. With which character do you relate the most? Why?

I'd like to say that I relate to Gisèle's heroic choices to rescue Adeline and other orphaned children, but since I've never been in her situation, I can't honestly say what I would do. I do identify deeply with the mixed emotions of many of the characters—Gisèle's faith and fear, Chloe's anger and relief, Michel's optimism in spite of the circumstances, the conflict in Josef's heart over his terrible dilemma, and both Lisette and Riley in their regrets and ultimately redemption.

8. Michel tells Gisèle "Courage doesn't mean you stop being afraid . . . It means you continue to fight, even when you're terrified" (page 359). How do you personally strive to live this out?

Fear is the personal dragon that I fight daily. Sometimes it's fear of failure or the unknown. Sometimes it's fear for my children or my husband. Sometimes it's seemingly ridiculous things that keep me up at night.

Last year my family spent Christmas serving orphans in Uganda. I was afraid of countless things before and during that trip, but I knew we were supposed to go in spite of my fears and the experience changed our lives. God, in his faithfulness, continues to help me fight against this dragon, and I'm incredibly grateful that He never leaves nor forsakes us.

9. How does your degree and background in journalism influence your writing of fiction?

I pursued a career in journalism because I love to learn. Writing was and still is a fun outlet for me to dig deep as I research both historical events and contemporary people and places. I approach the writing of each new book as a journalist, delving into the time period and details of the events and location first. After a few weeks of research, my characters and plot begin to emerge from the factual accounts of the past.

10. A line from your website highlights your gift as a writer: "My issue is not about finding time to write. It's about finding time to live around my writing." With a passion for writing, what are the things that can stifle your creativity? What or who inspires and energizes you again?

Faux busyness stifles my creativity. Often when I'm on deadline, I'll lose myself to all sorts of seemingly urgent tasks like vacuuming the house or cleaning out the garage. In order to eliminate distraction, I like to escape to a coffee shop with a steady buzz of noise or a quiet hotel where I can immerse myself in my imaginary world. As a family, we also try to keep the Sabbath each week. After a day of rest, I'm rejuvenated and ready to write first thing Monday morning.

11. What will you be working on next?

I've just started a novel about a forty-five-year-old woman named Heather who returns to England to prepare her childhood home for sale. As she and her daughter work together, Heather discovers that her parents hid a terrible secret from her and their village when she was a girl. In spite of the risks to her heart and her future,

Heather decides to pursue the truth about what happened in the beautiful gardens behind her family's cottage and in the gardens of the castle next door.

12. When you are not writing, what do you do for fun?

I love exploring new places, hiking in the mountains, playing Settlers of Catan with friends, line dancing, working in my garden, taking yoga classes, reading novels with surprise endings, and most of all, laughing with my family while we dance, hike, or explore together.

Center Point Large Print
600 Brooks Road / PO Box 1
Thorndike ME 04986-0001 USA

(207) 568-3717

US & Canada:
1 800 929-9108
www.centerpointlargeprint.com